The Bubble and Beyond. Fictitious Capital, Deb

Michael Hudson

The Bubble and Beyond

Fictitious Capital, Debt Deflation and the Global Crisis

Michael Hudson

ISLET

Dresden

2012

www.michael-hudson.com
www.islet-verlag.de

Hudson, Michael, 1939–
The Bubble and Beyond.
Fictitious Capital, Debt Deflation and Global Crisis
Michael Hudson

ISBN 13: 978-3-9814842-0-5

TABLE OF CONTENTS

ACKNOWLEDGEMENTS

I am grateful to Steve Keen, Henry Liu, Dirk Bezemer and Yves Smith for the discussions we have had over the years in clarifying the chapters and basic argument put forth in this book and to my Modern Monetary Theory colleagues Randy Wray, Stephanie Kelton and Marshall Auerbach at the University of Missouri (Kansas City).

For over ten years my Gang8 colleagues Geoffrey Gardiner, Gunnar Tomasson and Arno Daastol (for many years my webmaster) have joined in an ongoing critique of how orthodox schools retain the Ricardian tradition of describing how economies would work without free credit creation and debt. That is of course why these schools (like Ricardo himself) have received backing from the financial sector, which seeks to make its product—debt—invisible to economists, politicians and the general public.

In addition to setting this book in type, Cornelia Wunsch has been a part of this project from the beginning, and has provided the most important editorial guidance and encouragement. David Kelley, my fellow advisor to Congressman Dennis Kucinich, has egged me on to focus my argument more clearly.

Starting in 2005, Lewis Lapham gave me a popular forum for my ideas in *Harpers*, for which Nigel Holmes provided the illustrations for the "The New Road to Serfdom." He also drew the charts for compound interest in Chapter 2. Alex Cockburn at *CounterPunch* and Michel Chossudovsky at *Global Research* provided me with popular electronic forums for my reporting of current events. Yves Smith at *Naked Capitalism* and Stephanie Kelton at UMKC's *New Economic Perspectives* have published my articles and provided discussants that have shaped some of these chapters.

In New York the late Bob Fitch, Bertell Ollman, Xulin Dong and Sabri Oncu have read and given me instructive feedback on most of the chapters in this book. My colleagues Jeff Sommers (along with Dirk Bezemer noted above) have co-written articles with me on the neoliberal disaster in Latvia.

In Japan, Bill Totten has provided much help, and in the Basque Country, Joseba Felix-Tobar has integrated my theories with my UMKC colleagues. Pacifica Network broadcasters Bonnie Faulkner, Amy Goodman and Suzi Weissman have conducted interviews that have led me to state my ideas more forcefully. Likewise at i-tulip, Eric Janszen has been a good source of back-and-forth discussion over the years.

Karl Fitzgerald at Prosper Australia in Melbourne has served as my webmaster for michael-hudson.com for the past few years. Lynn Yost has been an indefatigable friend and editor, while Keith Wilde has been proofreading my articles for many years.

In Germany, Frank Schirrmacher and Nils Minkmar at the *Frankfurt Allgemeine Zeitung* have pushed me to discuss the political implications of my financial analysis, while Martin Bartels and my colleagues at the Boeckler Stiftung meetings in Berlin have helped spur me to define my theories more clearly. Most recently, Rob Johnson has invited me to present my summary paper (Chapter 20 in the present volume) at the April 2012 meetings in Berlin of the Institute for New Economic Thinking (INET).

I could not have completed this book without the tender care and nurturing given by my wife Grace, who has fought valiantly to keep me distraction free.

PREFACE

This treatise on economic theory traces how industrial capitalism has turned into finance capitalism. It claims that the finance, insurance and real estate (FIRE) sector has created a kind of "balance sheet wealth" not by new tangible investment and employment, but financially in the form of debt leveraging and rent-extraction. Such *rentier* gains are an overhead that is overpowering the economy's ability to pay. As a result, the present state of the economy is one of austerity rather than the expanding markets envisioned in earlier epochs. Much like in a radioactive decay process, we are passing through the short-lived and unstable phases of a Bubble Economy and casino capitalism that now threaten to settle into leaden austerity and debt deflation.

This situation confronts society with a choice: either to write down debts to a level that can be paid (or indeed, to write them off with a Clean Slate), or to permit creditors to foreclose, concentrating property in their own hands (including whatever assets are in the public domain to be privatized) and imposing a combination of financial and fiscal austerity on the population. This scenario will produce a shrinking debt-ridden and tax-ridden economy.

The latter is the path that the Western nations are pursuing today. It is the opposite path from that which classical economists advocated and which Progressive Era writers expected. Their optimistic focus on technological potential was thwarted by the political stratagems of the vested *rentier* interests fighting back against the classical idea of free markets and economic reforms to free industrial capitalism from the legacy of medieval and even ancient privileges and essentially corrosive, anti-social behavior.

This is not a natural or inevitable form of evolution. It is a detour from the kind of economy and indeed free market that classical economists sought to create. With roots in the 13th-century Schoolmen discussing Just Price, the labor theory of value was refined as a tool to isolate economic rent as that element of price that had no counterpart in actual or necessary costs of production. Banking charges, monopoly rent and land rent were the three types of economic rent analyzed in this long classical tradition. These *rentier* charges were seen as unnecessary and exploitative special privileges carried over from the military conquests that shaped medieval Europe. A free market was defined as one free of such overhead.

This classical view of free markets as being free of an unearned "free lunch" was embodied in the Progressive Era's financial and tax reforms. But the *rentiers* have fought back. The financial sector seeks to justify today's deep-ening indebtedness on the ground that it "creates wealth" by debt leveraging. The banks' product is debt overhead, after all. The problem is that this leaves debt deflation in its wake as debtors try to pay by reducing their consumption and investment. A shrinking economy falls further into arrears in a debt spiral.

The question today is whether a new wave of reform will restore and indeed complete the vision of classical political economy that seemed to be shaping evolution a century ago on the eve of World War I, or whether the epoch of industrial capitalism will be rolled back toward a neofeudal reaction defending *rentier* interests. What is up for grabs is how society will resolve the legacy of debts that can't be paid. Will it let the financial sector foreclose, and even force governments to privatize the public domain under distress condi-tions? Or will it write down debts to what can be paid without polarizing wealth and income, without dismantling government and privatizing the public domain, and without turning tax policy over to financial lobbyists pretending to be objective technocrats?

To provide a perspective on the financial sector's rise to dominance over the industrial economy, Part I reviews how classical economists developed the tools to measure how banks and money managers have come to play role that land-lords did in Physiocratic and Ricardian theory: as beneficiaries of feudal priv-ileges that oblige society to pay them for access to credit as well as land. As land ownership has been democratized, new buyers obtain credit to purchase homes and office buildings by pledging the rental income to bankers. About 80 percent of bank loans in the United States, Britain and other English-speaking countries are real estate mortgages, making land the major bank collateral. The result is that mortgage bankers receive the rents formerly taken by a hered-itary aristocracy in post-feudal Europe and the colonies it conquered.

Part I. *Fictitious Capital and Economic Fictions*

The first chapter in this volume, "Two Traditions of Financial Doctrine," describes the long line of analysis that has recognized that there are many ways to structure financial markets—productive rather than parasitic ways. It was presented in August 2000 in Narvik, Norway at Eric Reinert's "The Other Canon" foundation. In keeping with the group's advocacy of protective tariffs to promote high value-added industries characterized by increasing returns, this paper describes the tradition of steering banking systems to finance indus-trial capital formation with productive credit. Germany and France put in place industrial banking systems in conjunction with government protection of heavy industry (largely armaments, to be sure) and social reforms such as pen-sion systems, public health and national transport systems.

I was unable to convince the attendees at the Norwegian meeting to include the financial dimension of industrial reform in their canon, so this paper is published here for the first time. I had no greater success in getting commercial publishers to accept the history of banking and finance that I was writing. As one editor explained to me, warning that the financial bubble would collapse was like trying to sell a book about how everyone would have bad sex after the age of forty.

Academically, I ran into the fact that the long tradition distinguishing between productive and unproductive credit and indeed the role of debt has been excluded from the economics curriculum. The anti-classical school has replaced Progressive Era financial analysis with a happy-face view in which finance only adds to economic activity by providing credit, never corrodes it with debt—as if one party's credit were not another's debt!

These market structures and broad economic patterns that classical political economists placed at the center of their analysis are treated as "exogenous" by today's academic mainstream. Monetarist teachings omit the study of how nations have shaped banking practice to finance growth. Free trade doctrine and a pro-financial ideology of deregulation go together: "free markets" for predatory behavior and unearned income. Today's mainstream Washington Consensus accordingly advocates free trade and minimal public regulation or taxation. These policies are capped by privatization and a "flat tax" on employment, while un-taxing real estate, property and high income brackets.

The older path—by which today's successful lead nations caught up with others and then achieved dominance—pursued active protectionist industrial and agricultural policy and state intervention. This tradition advocates government subsidy of investment in infrastructure, education, research and development, progressive taxation of income and of *rentier* returns (land rent, financial returns and monopoly gains), and a financial system that encourages tangible capital formation.

Critics of free trade and financial deregulation have defined the proper aim of national policy to be active regulation and tax policy to shape markets so as to maximize capital formation, in ways that raise productivity and living standards. This is achieved by public investment in basic infrastructure, tariffs and subsidies to promote capital formation, education, research and development, capped by steering the banking system towards productive credit creation to finance industrial capital formation.

By rejecting the classical distinction between productive and unproductive labor and credit, today's national income accounts classify *rentier* gains as "earnings" on a par with wages and profits, adding to national product rather than simply being transfer payments. This approach treats all wealth as being earned as part of the production process, not extracted from the economy in the form of a free lunch ("economic rent") by *rentiers*.

Pro- and anti-government approaches both lead to central planning, but in different sets of hands. Economists writing in the tradition from European mercantilism through 19th-century American, German and French protectionism to Progressive Era reformers, Social Democratic parties and the New Deal shared a broad approach to **public** planning. In practice, every market is planned and organized by some parties or others, ever since the Neolithic rhythms of agricultural planting and harvesting. The euphemism "free market" means **central planning by the banks and high finance** — by Wall Street, the City of London, Frankfurt, the Paris Bourse and centers further eastward. Their plan involves un-taxing *rentier* income and wealth, headed by land-price gains (the "unearned increment") and financial deregulation. This shifts the allocation of capital and policy planning out of the hands of government into those of the banking sector.

This financialization of the economy (and indeed, of the political system) is more centralized than public planning by elected officials. And whereas government planning tends to be long-term, financial planning under neoliberalized conditions is hit-and-run. Whereas government planning is supposed to promote capital formation and full employment, today's financial planning makes returns by stripping assets, inflating asset-prices (the Bubble Economy) and minimizing the return to labor relative to *rentier* returns.

The second chapter, "Mathematics at the Root of the Crisis," reviews how economists through the ages have been aware that interest-bearing debt grows by purely mathematical principles independent of the economy's course and ability to pay. Contrary to textbook free-market theory, interest rates are not based on the expenses of creditors or linked to the production of real output. Interest is a transfer payment, much like a tax — a charge without a corresponding cost of production, paying for the privilege of creating bank credit electronically in today's world. It is predatory rather than productive, adding to price without reflecting intrinsic cost-value. It is a form of economic rent — although not one that Ricardo discussed when he limited the concept to landlords rather than to the banking sector or monopolies.

The third chapter, "How Economic Theory Came to Ignore the Role of Debt," shows how Ricardo untracked the analysis of debt's effects by treating the economy as if it operated on barter. It may seem surprising that his labor theory of cost-value (and the role of rent reflecting the excess of prices and income over such costs) followed a tradition that was applied to banking since the Canon Law of the 13th century. But his objective was to claim that debt and finance do not really matter. As the leading bank theorist of his day—and in effect the Parliamentary lobby for Britain's banking class—Ricardo logically should have been the last person to treat the economy as if it operated on barter, without credit or debt. After all, the preceding century had a rich discussion of how Britain's public debt was burdening the economy with taxes to carry its interest charges. Ricardo disagreed, and argued that paying debts or other capital transfers can never cause an economic crisis. It was landlords receiving groundrent that threatened to bring industrial capitalism to a halt, not bankers extracting interest.

For more than a century mainstream economic models have treated money simply as a veil, and credit as oiling the wheels of commerce. This ignores the burdensome effects of financialization, which become invisible (that is, "exogenous"). More money or credit are presumed to affect price relations as "counters" symmetrically across the economy, but do not change the distribution of wealth and income or create a debt burden. The reality is that credit and debt intrude into the economy, altering asset prices (the valuation of real estate, stocks and bonds) relative to wages and current prices. New credit bids them up; paying back debts—with interest—drains money from the economy as a whole. Yet the national income and product accounts treat banking on a par with industry, as part of the productive sector. Interest is treated as payment for providing a service (credit creation)—part of the economy's surplus (the financial sector's "earnings,") not a charge against it.

Despite the problems of interest expanding into the productive economy, Marx expected banking to become subordinate to the needs of industry on the way to becoming socialized in time. The fourth chapter, "The Industrialization of Finance and the Financialization of Industry," describes his hope that industrial capitalism would mobilize the financial sector to serve its needs. But instead of achieving a symbiosis with industry, as seemed to be the wave of the future in the form of German and Central European industrial banking, finance has followed Anglo-American banking practice and found its major market in the rent-extracting activities of real estate and monopolies.

The ensuing debt problems are not recognized in today's depiction of how economies operate. The fifth chapter, "The Use and Abuse of Mathematical Economics," describes how the academic mainstream has embraced unrealistic models simply because more complex scope and realistic methodology cannot produce the neatly determined equilibrium solutions—highly favorable to *rentier* interests—that have so trivialized post-classical economics over the past century.

Chapter 6 closes Part I by summarizing the changing view of the character of economic crises caused by *rentiers*, from Ricardo and Marx to today's Bubble Economy culminating in uncollectible debts, junk mortgages and bad gambles in Wall Street's financial casino. The banking sector's demand for government bailouts is turning the financial problem into a fiscal problem so serious that it threatens to sink economies in something worse than a merely cyclical downturn. A Lost Generation subjected to debt deflation is more descriptive than the trivializing term Great Recession. If it were merely a cycle, there would be a more or less natural recovery. But that is being blocked as economies are forced to choose between saving the banks and high-income investors from suffering a loss (by keeping the debt overhead on the books and taking bad debts onto government balance sheets) or writing down the debts so as to pave the way for recovery.

Western economies stand at a critical turning point. What blocks them from freeing themselves from their debt overhead is a political problem: The credit that has bid up asset prices was created largely on the base of wealth owned by the richest 1% — and they have gained control of ostensibly democratic governments. Between 1979 and 2004 the 1% raised their share of the returns to wealth in the United States — interest, dividends, rents and capital gains — from 38 percent of the national total to 58 percent. Little of this wealth was created industrially by building factories to employ labor to produce goods and services to sell at a markup. Investors sought "total returns" mainly in the form of capital gains, not current income. The government encourages this by taxing capital gains at only a fraction of the rate levied on wages and profits. So the vast overgrowth of financial overhead is largely autonomous from "real" economic growth. The result is that much as environmental pollution causes global warming, new credit has been extended to bid up real estate and other asset prices, "heating up" the bubble economy.

For Marxists there is a certain irony in this. The financial crisis that plagues today's world does not stem primarily from the "real" economy. Little of the credit that has bid up prices for real estate, stocks and bonds came from savings generated from productive investment employing or exploiting labor (except to loot its pension funds). It was created largely electronically, on computer keyboards. The banking system has been decoupled from the real economy. The financial sector's independent and self-referential expansion path is independent of the "real" economy's surplus, or its ability to support this overhead. Financial returns are made in extractive ways, as a subtrahend *from* the surplus created by labor and tangible capital, rather than funding capital accumulation. Productivity is raised by working labor harder and exploiting it more, not by technology.

Hegel was right: the owl of wisdom flies at night. Only at the end of an epoch can its dynamics be seen for what they are and where they have been leading. Most people only want to think about a financial crash after it has happened. Only then does a pressing reason arise to realize that the economy does not need to be structured in this way, and that the time has come to contemplate alternatives.

Part II. *From Inflated Debts to Debt Deflation*

Part II juxtaposes the Financial, Insurance and Real Estate (FIRE) Sector to the "Real" Economy. It focuses on the analysis of debt deflation in today's world—the rising debt overhead and speculative dynamics that have led to today's "postindustrial" crash. Asset-price inflation leads to increasingly fictitious financial claims. They are fictitious because they are uncollectible without pushing the economy into widespread foreclosures and privatization that transfers property and infrastructure into the financial sector's hands. This is what the European Central Bank is now orchestrating in Ireland, Greece and Italy, following neoliberal policies in Iceland and Latvia.

Chapters 7 and 8 describe the symbiosis between banking and real estate that is unique to the 20th century. In contrast to Ricardo's expectation that banking would retain its early focus on international commerce—and hence, on industrial capital formation to provide foreign markets with British exports in exchange for raw materials—banking has found real estate to be the key, along with its traditional market in creating monopolies and trusts. Some 80 percent of bank loans in the United States and Britain are mortgages, and consequently they account for 70 percent of the economy's interest payments.

This has reversed the major thrust of classical economic reform seeking to tax land rent, "de-privatizing" it from the old landed aristocracies. As recently as the Progressive Era at the turn of the 20th century, the most immediate threat seemed to be that economies would pay a rising share of income to these absentee landlords (and monopolists) as economic rent. Land prices would rise because the growing population would raise the man/land ratio (with little new land area being supplied), and because of rising prosperity in general. This would enable landowners and infrastructure monopolists (especially the railroads) to concentrate society's rising wealth in their own hands, enjoying the "unearned increment" of rising land prices. Although site values, status and prestige reflected not just the land itself but public infrastructure investment in roads and public transportation, the proximity to schools and to cultural or commercial centers, private owners fought attempts to tax this "free lunch" as the basis of modern fiscal systems.

But acquiring property required a bank loan. This meant that a property's value depends on how much a bank will lend prospective buyers. Chapter 7, "Property is worth whatever a bank will lend against it," explains how real estate has been financialized. The great price run-up accordingly reflected not simply the "real" factors discussed by economists focusing on an economy as it would exist without banking and finance (which of course does not describe any real modern economy!), but the terms on which banks lend: the interest rate at which property rents are capitalized into bank loans; the amortization rate (how long it takes to pay off a mortgage); the down payment, and most recently, the degree of criminalization and fraud as "liars' loans" gave a spurt to housing prices in the United States. By 2007 one needed to take into account the portfolio of tricks that banks use to assign high value to properties without much regard to their actual market price or the ability of borrowers to repay the loan out of their income.

Because real estate is the largest asset category in modern private sectors, some 80 percent of "capital gains" actually take the form of rising land prices. Chapter 8, "The Real Estate Bubble at the Core of Today's Debt-leveraged Economy," charts banking's symbiosis with real estate. Most of the rise in wealth for most families has stemmed from the debt-leveraged price of their homes. The same is true for commercial real estate, and for financial investments throughout the economy. Financialization has created an enormous rise in the value of assets on nations' balance sheets. But it also has created an enormous rise in debts—which remain in place when asset prices crash, causing Negative Equity.

The tax system encourages this debt pyramiding. Interest and depreciation absorb most of the cash flow, leaving no income tax due for most of the post-1945 period. Most important, capital gains are taxed at a much lower rate than are current earnings. Investors do not have to pay any capital gains tax at all as long as they invest their gains in the purchase of new property.

This tax favoritism to real estate—and behind it, to bankers as mortgage lenders—has spurred a shift of U.S. investment away from industry toward speculation, mainly in real estate but also the stock and bond markets. Today's financialized economies carry their debt burden by borrowing against capital gains to pay the interest and taxes falling due.

Since the 1980s corporate raiders have adopted the real estate speculator's motto, "Rent is for paying interest." They promise their financial backers and junk-bond holders that corporate cash flow is for paying interest. To the extent that banking and high finance have interfaced with industry since the 1980s, it has been largely to "financialize" companies—by funding corporate raiders to buy out stockholders and introduce short-term management practices. Chapter 9, "Junk-Bonding Industry," describes how today's debt-driven financial system is both inflationary and deflationary. It is inflationary in a novel way: Credit produces capital gains by supplying increasingly easy low-interest financing for borrowers to spend on bidding up property and stock market prices. Companies forego tangible investment in order to increase their share prices by buying back their stock and even borrowing to pay higher dividends.

The media welcomed this asset-price inflation as constituting a new form of wealth creation – as long as asset prices rather than wages or consumer prices are being inflated. But credit is debt, and debt needs to be paid— absorbing income that otherwise would be spent on goods and services. The result is debt deflation.

The tax laws encourage debt leveraging by permitting interest on takeover loans and related speculation to be tax deductible. The stock market has become a vehicle for replacing equity with debt. This is the opposite trend from what Saint-Simon and subsequent 19th-century theorists of industrial banking sought to promote. Money is made not by what Marx described as making money (M) to hire labor to produce commodities (C) to sell at a markup (M′) but by avoiding the production process altogether by M–M′, making money "work."

But money doesn't work in the sense that labor or tangible capital expends effort to produce commodities. Credit is debt, and debt extracts interest. Financial salesmen who promise investors, "Make your money work for you" actually mean that society should work for the creditors—and that means for the banks that create credit.

The effect is to turn the economic surplus into a flow of interest payments, diverting revenue from tangible capital investment. As the economy's reproductive powers are dried up, the financialization process is kept going by easing credit terms and lending—not to produce more goods and services, but to bid up prices for the real estate, stocks and bonds being pledged as collateral for larger and larger loans.

Giving tax deductibility to this indebtedness aggravates the federal budget deficit, forcing a shift of taxes onto consumers and producers. This has given financializers an excuse to propose privatizing Social Security to send public retirement contributions into the stock market, via wage set-asides turned over to money managers. Chapter 10, "Privatizing Social Security to Rescue Wall Street," describes how such proposals reflect those of Pension Fund Capitalism in the 1950s. The financial myth was that pension funds would finance capital investment and employment to fuel a steady upgrade. If the world worked in the way these happy-face models suggest, we all would be living lives of leisure now—not working harder and longer just to break even. Turning retirement savings over to financial managers has made the saving process part of finance capitalism, not industrial capitalism. After the dot.com bubble crashed in 2000, the incoming George W. Bush administration sought to channel Social Security set-asides into the stock market to create a new wave of capital gains.

The key to understanding the financial sector's strategy is that its activities and revenue do not constitute a part of economic growth, but a subtrahend, paid **out of** the economic surplus. At first the influx of credit (other parties' debts) inflates asset prices (but not necessarily commodity prices or wages), but ends in debt deflation. Chapter 11, "Saving, Asset-Price Inflation, and Debt Deflation," describes my analysis of debt deflation as the major cause of crises. The exponential growth of debt service absorbs the economic surplus, diverting spending away from the purchase of goods and services. This undercuts the economy, leading savings to be invested increasingly in interest-bearing loans rather than in tangible capital formation. Since the 2007 crash, the National Income and Product Accounts report paying down debts as "saving" (the negation of a debt is positive "saving"). *This debt repayment now plays the role that hoarding and non-spending played in Keynesian economics in the 1930s.*

The purpose of this financialization is described in Chapter 12, "Saving our Way into Poverty." Corporate industry, real estate and the economy at large is viewed as a vehicle to securitize cash flow or surplus revenue to pay out as interest and dividends—and most of all, to generate "capital gains." From the bank marketing director's vantage point, the aim is to capitalize all income flows into debt service. For the first time in history, large numbers of people—and government managers—have come to believe that the way to get rich is by running into debt, not staying out of it.

The motivation for taking on debt is to buy assets or claims rising in price. Over the past half-century the aim of financial investment has been less to earn profits on tangible capital investment than to generate "capital" gains (most of which take the form of debt-leveraged land prices, not industrial capital). Annual price gains for property, stocks and bonds far outstrip the reported real estate rents, corporate profits and disposable personal income after paying for essential non-discretionary spending, headed by FIRE-sector charges.

Part III. *The Global Crisis*

Inasmuch as interest is a cost of production and enters into the cost of living, financialized economies become more high-cost and hence uncompetitive. Yet the dynamic of globalization in today's world is predominantly financial. The explanation is the ability of U.S. banks to create "free" credit, now that the dollar has been unlinked from gold — combined with the consequent and simultaneous de-linking of the international financial system and central bank reserves from the constraint that previously existed from time immemorial.

Chapter 13, "Trade and Payments in a Financialized Economy," explains how debt leveraging raised the price of housing, while financializing pension funding and Social Security was diverting so much revenue away from commodity markets that debt-leveraged economies were unable to compete internationally.

Chapters 14 through 16 explain how the United States is in the leading position to create credit and debt without limit or constraint, enabling its banking and financial system to become the main source of the global financial bubble. Since the gold standard ended in 1971 as a result of U.S. military spending in Vietnam and other countries, the main sources of dollars pouring into the world's central banks are U.S. overseas military spending and financial takeover investment. Chapter 14, "How U.S. Quantitative Easing fractures the global economy," explains how this makes the global central bank monetary base essentially confrontational in nature. Financial aggression today achieves what military conquest did in times past.

The result can only be to impoverish economies. Chapter 15, "America's Monetary Imperialism: Dollar Debt Reserves without Constraint," explains how central banks have little option but to recycle their inflow of dollars back into loans to the U.S. Government. The result is that rather than causing a crisis and forcing the Federal Reserve to raise interest rates (as other central banks were obliged to do prior to 1971), the U.S. balance-of-payments deficit serves to finance the Treasury's domestic budget deficit. Since the Treasury-bill standard has replaced the gold exchange standard, a U.S. payments deficit enables the government to lower interest rates rather than raise them. The United States has ended up as the only economy able to set a monetary policy exclusively with domestic gains in mind — mainly the subsidy of bank lending and capital gains to sustain its bubble economy.

Foreign countries have long found this system unfair. For one thing, it makes U.S. foreign military spending the foundation of global monetary reserves. Chapter 16, "The 'Dollar Glut' Finances America's Global Military Build-up," describes this phenomenon. Chapter 17, "De-dollarizing the Global Economy," describes the moves to create a more symmetrical and equitable alternative led by the BRICs.

Chapter 18, "Incorporating the *Rentier* Sectors into a Financial Model," explains my model of debt deflation, based on viewing the FIRE sectors as overhead, living off the economy rather than contributing to its surplus.

Part IV. *The Need for a Clean Slate*

Chapter 19, "From Democracy to Oligarchy" analyzes the political consequences of my financial analysis. It traces the various stages through which finance capitalism has become increasingly unstable, culminating in the Bubble Economy's collapse into Negative Equity and polarization between creditors and debtors. To enforce austerity, the financial sector needs to subvert democracy as in the United States, or replace it with outright centralized oligarchy as in Greece, Italy and other countries ruled by "technocrats" on behalf of the creditors.

The concluding Chapter 20, "Scenarios for Recovery," summarizes the basic theme of this book: Financialized economies face chronic depression if they do not write down the debt overhead they have run up. I review the range of policies needed to write down the debts and restructure the financial system so that a Bubble Economy is not restored.

The political problem that blocks nations from scaling down debts is the fact that the financial sector has gained control of economic policy and planning. Its managers are willing to plunge economies into depression and a shrinking spiral of debt deflation rather than relinquish their creditor claims.

A long-standing tactic to block reform is to promote economic theories saying that no reform is necessary. This pits the 1% against the 99%—and gives them a vested interest in promoting junk economics. When they say that "There is No Alternative," they mean to achieve this by ensuring that there is no discussion of alternatives. That is why the history of economic thought has been dropped from the economics curriculum, and an anti-government, dumbed-down individualistic travesty put in its place.

SOURCES

Early drafts of the key chapters in this book have been published over the past decade so as to get my main points into circulation in a timely fashion, and to receive feedback for how best to present ideas (which seemed to many like premature financial pessimism at the time) on why and how the worldwide Bubble Economy had to collapse. The result is something like a Dickens serial published out of order, with the most important new points first so as to institutionalize my basic approach.

An early version of Chapter 1, "Two Traditions of Financial Doctrine," was delivered in Narvik, Norway in August 2000 organized by Erik Reinert to mark the founding of his foundation, "The Other Canon."

An early version of Chapter 2, "The Magic of Compound Interest," was published as "The Mathematical Economics of Compound Interest: A Four-Thousand Year Overview," *Journal of Economic Studies* 27 (2000):344–363, and revised more recently in the *Post-Autistic Economic Review*.

An earlier version of Chapter 3 was published on "How economic theory came to ignore the role of debt" was published in the real-world economics review, issue no. 57, http://www.paecon.net/PAEReview/issue57/Hudson57.pdf

Chapter 4, "Marx on the Industrialization of Finance Capital—and the Financialization of Industry," was published earlier as "Marx to Goldman Sachs: The Fictions of Fictitious Capital, and the Financialization of Industry," *Critique* 53 (Vol. 38 /3: August 2010), pp. 419–444.

An early version of Chapter 5, "The Use and Abuse of Mathematical Economics," was presented at a 1997 meeting of the German Historical School in Heilbronn and published in the *Journal of Economic Studies* 27 (2000): 292–315, and an updated version was later published in the *real-world economics review* 55 (December 2010), pp. 2–22.

Chapter 7, "A Property is Worth what a Bank Will Lend," originally was published as "The New Road to Serfdom: An illustrated guide to the coming real estate collapse," *Harpers*, vol. 312 (no. 1872, May 2006): 39–46, and "Tax the Land," *Harpers*, vol. 317, (no. 1902, November 2008): 40–42.

Chapter 8, on "Real Estate at the Core of Today's Debt Leveraged Economy," was presented to the 2006 Boeckler Foundation conference in Berlin devoted to heterodox post-Keynesian economics, and then published it in the inaugural issue of the Chinese journal published by the School of Marxist Studies in Beijing as "The Transition from Industrial Capitalism to a Financialized Bubble Economy," *World Review of Political Economy* 1/1 (Spring 2010), pp. 81–111.

Chapter 10, "Privatizing Social Security to Fuel Asset-Price Inflation," originally was published as "The $3.7 trillion Pyramid: Why Social Security Won't Be Enough to Save Wall Street," *Harpers*, vol. 310 (no. 1859, April 2005), pp. 35–40.

I presented Chapter 11, "Saving, Asset-Price Inflation, and Debt Deflation," at a meeting of heterodox economists at the University of Missouri (Kansas City), which is the core of Minskyan and other non-mainstream analysis. It is published in L. Randall Wray and Matthew Forstater, eds., *Money, Financial Instability and Stabilization Policy* (Edward Elgar, 2006), pp. 104–124. I am grateful to Edward Elgar for permitting me to reprint it here.

Chapter 13, "Trade and Payments in a Financialized Economy" was first published as "Trends that can't go on forever, won't: financial bubbles, trade and exchange rates," in Eckhard Hein, Torsten Niechoj, Peter Spahn and Achim Truger (eds.), *Finance-led Capitalism?* (Marburg: Metropolis-Verlag, 2008), pp. 249–272.

Chapter 14, "U.S. 'quantitative easing' is fracturing the global economy," *real-world economics review* 55, (December 2010), pp. 8294.

Chapter 15, "America's Monetary Imperialism," *Global Dialogue* 5 (2003):73–81.

Chapter 16, "The 'Dollar Glut' Finances America's Global Military Build-up," in *Global Research* (March 29, 2009). De-Dollarization

Chapter 17, on De-Dollarization. My expanded *Financial Times* articles on the emergence of the BRICs, *International Economy*, *i-tulip*.

Chapter 18 summarizes my model of financialization. I presented a preliminary analysis at the Boeckler Foundation meetings in Berlin in October 2011.

Chapter 20 was presented at the Institute for New Economic Thinking (INET) conference in Berlin on April 13, 2012.

I am grateful to Nigel Holmes for providing the original illustrations for compound interest in Chapter 2, and for the *Harpers* article "The New Road to Serfdom."

Introduction

TODAY'S FINANCIAL CRISIS AND THE CRISIS IN ECONOMIC THEORY

"Did nobody see this coming?" asked Queen Elizabeth after the September 2008 financial meltdown spread from Wall Street to the City of London and on to the Paris Bourse, Frankfurt and Tokyo. Many people saw that the dancing would end, of course.[1] But Wall Street salaries and bonuses reflect one's quarterly performance, so nobody was going to call a halt. A person only needs to make a fortune once in a lifetime, after all, and this was it—the years leading up to 2008. As long as the dancing was speeding up in a frenzy like Ravel's *Bolero*, standing on the sidelines would have meant losing status by letting rival money managers report better returns. Short-term returns, to be sure, but the financial sector lives in the short run. Whatever one could grab was a free gift out of the bailouts that governments gave after September 2008 on the pretense (or naïve hope) that saving the banks would save the economy as it careened toward collapse. Most bankers were more realistic. They took the money and ran, seeing that the game in fact is over.

More optimistic economists and "public servants" follow Treasury Secretary Tim Geithner and Federal Reserve Chairman Ben Bernanke in believing that the economy can be saved by squeezing out enough personal and corporate income to keep the debts afloat—as if it can pay without shrinking (or even *while* shrinking). Governments are giving bonds and central bank credit to save banks and bondholders—the wealthiest 1%. The losses and negative equity are to be shifted onto the public balance sheet, making "taxpayers" bear the burden—the 99%.

What needs to be asked is why there is no recovery despite governments giving the banks so much money. When the Federal Reserve provided a torrent of bank reserves at 0.25 percent interest with its Quantitative Easing policy in summer 2011, why didn't this low interest rate succeed in inducing new invest-

---

[1] Dirk Bezemer, "Why some economists could see the crisis coming," *Financial Times*, September 7, 2009. For a roster of financial Cassandras see Alphaville, *Financial Times*, July 13, 2009: "Who saw it coming and the primacy of accounting," posted by Tracy Alloway.

ment and reviving real estate prices as promised? Why are property markets still shrinking as the Great Recession succumbs to Debt Deflation?

If these anomalies cannot be explained, then the current neoliberal logic is part of the problem. Obstructing discussion of alternatives, it insists that there is no need for large debt write-downs to cure today's financial malaise, except perhaps a few pragmatic "haircuts." Economies are supposed to stabilize automatically, not be driven out of balance by predatory lending. The solution is to let austerity work to squeeze out ("free") enough income to enable debts to be carried and for government budgets to balance — by cutting spending if sufficient revenue is not forthcoming.

How Financial "Solutions" Make the Debt and Fiscal Problems Worse

Much as junk science ignores environmental pollution and denies global warming, junk economics denies that what is stifling today's recovery is debt pollution. Any "solution" based on keeping the unpayably high debt overhead in place must cause debt deflation and economic shrinkage. Austerity increases default rates, plunging the economy (and hence, banks) into negative equity and reducing tax revenue as economies try to squeeze out enough more debt service to prevent defaults. Arrears mount up at compound interest, causing a wave of foreclosures that must end in a cascade of bankruptcies, and further declines in property prices — causing even larger public deficits, more debt arrears and foreclosures. This leads to anti-austerity riots by debtors while creditors press for privatization selloffs under distress conditions.

When one finds wrongheaded policies continued for decades on end (today's financial orthodoxy is the same that endorsed many decades of destructive IMF austerity "stabilization" programs), there always is a special interest benefiting. Neoliberalism supports the interest of banks seeking to extract debt service against alternatives to rescue the real economy from over-indebtedness. "There Is No Alternative" (TINA), said Margaret Thatcher. More giveaways to the financial sector are urged to "restore confidence," defined as renewed borrowing to bid asset prices back to their former Bubble levels.

Something has to give. The coming few generations will struggle over whether it will be the "real" production and consumption economy or the financial sector's claims *on* it.

The financial sector is leading in this battle, and hopes to make its gains irreversible. Banks hold a trump card by threatening to plunge the economy into crisis if they do not get their way, reversing the past eight-century trend toward more humanitarian pro-debtor laws.

The creditors' winning streak has proceeded so far since 1980 that it may take a half-century at least to reverse their power grab, because the task is much harder now than it was a hundred years ago. The flowering of classical economics into the Progressive Era familiarized public discourse sufficiently to almost resolve the *rentier* problem by the eve of World War I. But the *rentiers* fought back, insisting that debt cannot cause a serious problem (as if all credit were productive!), and mounting an attack on the idea that governments can play a positive economic role as regulators of finance or its major customers (real estate and monopolies), or as a rival public-option investor in infrastructure. Predatory monopolists and political insiders have sought to monopolize the public domain, using a financial squeeze to force governments to accept their self-serving "solution"—one that makes matters worse.

The problem with their business plan is that bank profits and speculative gains are extracted from the economy, not additions to real output. Indeed, with interest rates ranging up to 29 percent for credit cards and distress levels for European government debtors, where is there room for growth in a recovery in economies growing by only about 1 percent annually? The 99% are getting poorer and deeper in debt, while the 1% is getting richer. This polarization is the opposite of the more progressive distribution of income and wealth that was occurring throughout the 20th century prior to 1980.

Politicians follow economists (and their major campaign contributors) in being in a state of denial. Rather than acknowledging that the economy is insolvent, they greet each new upward zigzag of statistics as a sign of recovery. But the financial sector, which now (2012) accounts for 40 percent of U.S. corporate profits, is requisitioning most growth on behalf of the top 1%. Congress's 2008 Troubled Asset Relief Program (TARP) and much larger Federal Reserve and Treasury bailouts saved the super-rich financial elite while leaving the rest of the economy deeply in debt to the 1% of taxpayers. They took 93 percent of U.S. income growth in 2010. And of **this** growth, 37 percent "went to just the top 0.01 percent, a teaspoon-size collection of about 15,000 households with average incomes of $23.8 million."[2]

Many observers express surprise that financial and fiscal austerity is stifling rather than helping recovery for the 99%. But what is happening is simply a replay of the IMF "conditionalities" imposed on hapless Third World debtors from the 1960s onward, which added the term "IMF riot" to the English

---

[2] Steven Rattner, "The Rich Get Even Richer," *New York Times op-ed.*, March 26, 2012, based on data from Thomas Piketty and Emmanuel Saez, "The Evolution of Top Incomes: A Historical and International Perspective," http://elsa.berkeley.edu/~saez/piketty-saezAEAPP06.pdf

language. Voters are told that the way to recover is to bleed the body politick, not nourish markets with public infrastructure and social spending. A false alarm is sounded that government budget deficits will increase consumer prices—with no discussion of how private-sector credit *deflates* economies. The problem is that credit is debt—and paying debt service to bankers and bondholders (and various grades of loan sharks) leaves less income available to spend on goods and services. So debt deflation is today's major problem, not inflation.

> The problem is that credit is debt and paying debt service to bankers and bondholders (and various grades of loan sharks) leaves less income available to spend on goods and services.
> So debt deflation is today's major problem, not inflation.

A New Diagnosis of Today's Economic Crisis

Policies to deal with debt problems have a long pedigree. Long before Christian and Islamic denunciations of usury, and even before the Jewish Jubilee year of debt forgiveness that Jesus sought to revive, Sumerian and Babylonian Clean Slates freed debtors from bondage and prevented land and wealth being concentrated in the hands of foreclosing creditors. Starting some time before the first royal proclamations are documented c. 2450 BC in Sumer, the Near Eastern takeoff kept the debt overhead within the economy's ability to pay for thousands of years.

The Industrial Revolution recognized the problem of savings and debts mounting up at compound interest. With an almost religious fervor Saint-Simon and his followers in 19th-century France advocated that banks shift their lending away from interest-bearing loans to equity-based investment, taking their returns as a share in profits rather than a stipulated interest charge. Marx described the periodic business crashes of his day as a result of interest-bearing debt building up. To elaborate his analysis, he collected the most noteworthy warnings of how the mathematics of compound interest grew inexorably to exceed the economy's ability to pay (see Chapter 2).

Most reformers have a faith that economic rationality will overcome blind alleys and failures to realize potential. They expect that their reforms will be adopted because global competition will favor economies that make them. Retaining a faith that the material forces of history would lead banking to finance industrial capital formation, Marx was an optimist when it came to the long run. After all, finance ultimately has to make its money off the "real" economy. Interest can only be paid out of economic growth, or else it shrinks markets and creditor claims collapse (see Chapter 4).

The question is whether finance will promote economic growth and rising living standards, or create unproductive credit and use government to enforce creditor claims by imposing austerity reducing large swaths of the world population to debt peonage. The longer we look back in time, the more clearly we find this issue defined. During World War I, for example, British economists debated whether German industrial banking, based on equity financing and long-term relationship with clients, was superior to the more hit-and-run Anglo-Dutch-American merchant banking that had evolved out of trade financing (see Chapter 1). After the Allies defeated Germany, banking in most countries took the Anglo-American path. The stock market has remained a game for insiders rife with fraud. Banking has focused on real estate mortgages and takeover loans for properties and companies already in place.

In the 1920s, John Maynard Keynes warned that the tangle of Inter-Ally arms debts and German reparations would collapse the international financial system as a result of trying to pay foreign exchange far beyond its ability to do so. He distinguished the "transfer problem" – trying to pay debts denominated

> The question is whether finance will promote economic growth and rising living standards, or create unproductive credit and use government to enforce creditor claims by imposing austerity reducing large swaths of the world population to debt peonage.

in foreign currency — from the domestic "budgetary problem" of financing government deficits in local currency monetized by the central bank.[3] Today's German fear that central bank credit creation is dangerously hyper-inflationary fails to recognize that all hyperinflations have resulted from balance-of-payments deficits collapsing exchange rates, thereby raising import prices and hence domestic prices. Never in history has hyperinflation resulted from governments monetizing domestic spending.

Debt had receded as a central problem by the time World War II ended. There were few civilian products to buy during war, so families emerged in 1945 with substantial liquidity and little debt. They wanted houses and appliances, automobiles and refrigerators, and the proliferation of products offered by the new technology. Credit was needed to finance this postwar takeoff, and it was natural for bankers to make their money financing new consumer spending and real estate.

> **G**erman fear that central bank credit creation is dangerously hyper-inflationary fails to recognize that all hyperinflations have resulted from balance-of-payments deficits. Never in history has hyperinflation resulted from governments monetizing *domestic* spending.

Loans were made carefully until the 1980's. A 30 percent down payment typically was required to get a mortgage, which was to be amortized over thirty years — almost an entire working life. By 2008 banks were giving out zero-down-payment mortgages with no amortization, "interest only" loans — at exploding interest rates after three years. Until the 1980's, most bank guidelines called for housing costs not to absorb more than a quarter of the debtor's income. Today the ratio is over fourty percent. A property's price is whatever banks were willing to lend, so these constraints prevented the price of housing

---

[3] I summarize his views in *Trade, Development and Foreign Debt: A History of Theories of Polarization v. Convergence in the World Economy* (2nd ed. ISLET 2010), Chapter 16, pp. 313–336.

from rising much above the cost of renting. Banks capitalized rental values at the going rate of interest, which rose steadily for thirty-five years, from 1945 to 1980. The rising rate lowered the multiple by which rental income could be capitalized into bank loans (see Chapter 7). So the great explosion in housing prices—and hence, living costs—has occurred since 1980.

The path toward more reckless lending was led by the "monetarist" Chicago School. This seems ironic at first sight, because they follow the Austrians in drawing a picture of the economy as if it operates on barter. Prices are considered only a "veil," and so money also is only a set of "counters," not a financial system of credit and debt. Instead of relating credit to the dynamics of debt, they focused narrowly on the correlation between the money supply (variously measured) and commodity prices—but not asset prices! Yet most money is spent in the capital markets by "investing" in real estate, stocks and bonds, not paid for goods and services. Heavily endowed by the financial sector, monetarism's "learned ignorance"—or as Thorstein Veblen expressed it, an educated incapacity to understand economic problems—has become mainstream and gained control of the major refereed journals, where they have imposed a tunnel vision where the role of debt is concerned.

How Debt Service Affects the Cost of Living, Doing Business, and the Balance of Payments

Taking much the same line that Britain's Bullionists voiced after the Napoleonic Wars ended in 1815, Milton Friedman's followers followed the logic of David Ricardo in downplaying the idea that debt or international payments transfers could pose serious problems. Ricardo's labor theory of value had no room for this debt overhead. It was as if economies operated debt-free and on barter (see Chapter 3). This "ignore debt" approach reflected his interest as a bond broker and role as Parliamentary spokesman—today we would say lobbyist—for the banking class in countering the widespread opposition to public debt.

In Book V of *The Wealth of Nations*, Adam Smith had described how each new borrowing to finance Britain's seemingly endless wars with France was funded by a specific tax to pay its interest charge. Malachy Postlethwayt and others explained how this rising debt overhead (and the taxes to carry it) threatened to price British producers out of world markets by increasing the cost of labor and hence of doing business.

When asked in Parliament about the effect of "capital transfers" such as military subsidies or debt payments to foreign creditors (the Dutch were heavy investors in Britain's Crown Corporations), Ricardo insisted that all such payments set in motion self-equilibrating adjustments that returned the payments outflow back to the country where they originated. There could be no balance-of-payments or foreign debt crisis.

The same logic implicitly applies to domestic debt: Payments to bankers are spent back into the economy. As modern discussions trivialize the idea, "we owe the debt to ourselves," so consequently it doesn't matter that, on balance, the 99% owe debt to the 1%.

The assumption that *rentiers* spend their income in the domestic economy is an old story. Malthus said that landlords buy coaches and fine clothes, and hire coachmen and other servants. This led Keynes to credit him with empha-sizing the role of demand in the circular flow of income. But financiers recycle most of their receipt of debt service into new loans, which extract yet more interest. Their consumption spending is mainly on luxury real estate, fine arts trophies and jewelry. When the supply of safe investments is exhausted, they lower their standards and lend more to less credit-worthy borrowers—and turn to buy whatever trophies remain available.

> **I**nterest is treated as "profit" earned by producing the bankers' product: the debt taken on by borrowers. Treating the banks' privilege of debt creation as tangible industrial investment conflates money and credit as a "factor of production," so that interest, penalties and fees appear as part of the production process, not external to it.

Reminiscent of Baudelaire's quip, "The devil wins at the point where the world believes that he doesn't exist," finance capital prefers to drop the debt overhead from sight. Post-Ricardian analysis of how income was distributed among labor (wages), landowners (groundrent) and industrial or commercial capital (profits) did not take account of the payment of interest to bankers (Ricardo's own class!). Interest is treated as "profit" earned by producing the bankers' product: the debt taken on by borrowers. Treating the banks' privi-lege of debt creation as tangible industrial investment conflates money and credit as a "factor of production," so that interest, penalties and fees appear as part of the production process, not external to it. But if credit creation and its financial charges are a result of monopoly privilege extraneous to production (in contrast to the cost of industrial plant and equipment ultimately reducible to labor) then the National Income and Product Accounts (NIPA) are an exercise in double counting.

The NIPA do not include asset-price gains, that is, "capital" gains, most of which reflect rising prices for land, stocks and bonds, and the capitalized value of monopoly privileges. Friedman credited the Canadian-American astronomer and economist Simon Newcomb for first formulating the Quantity Theory of Money in algebraic terms. But his own monetarism stripped away the dimension of debt that Newcomb had stressed in discussing America's Civil War financing. A nation fights war with its men, weapons and other current goods and services, Newcomb wrote. Financing wars on a pay-as-you-go basis, out of taxes as Adam Smith urged, falls on current taxpayers (at that time, mainly the wealthy), not future taxpayers obliged to pay bondholders. However, running up government debt created a *future* transfer of payments from Western U.S. taxpayers to Eastern bondholders, whose grandchildren would receive payments of interest and principal.[4] Public borrowing thus forces the government to tax the future economy to pay debt service to a financial class. This tax adds to the break-even cost of doing business.

The United States avoided this by printing Greenbacks to monetize the Civil War's budget deficits. That is what central banks were founded to do (except for today's European Central Bank). This was no more inflationary than private credit being spent into the economy.

The focus of most 19th-century discussion was on public debt, but the same logic applies to the private sector. Debt financing imposes interest and kindred financing charges that increase the break-even price that must be covered. Employees also must earn enough to cover financial charges on their credit-card debt, education loans and other bank loans, as well as on the mortgage debt that inflates housing prices. As financial charges rise to absorb more corporate cash flow, real estate rents and wages, debt-burdened economies find themselves priced out of world markets. International trade competition now reflects financial, insurance and real estate (FIRE) charges more than the price of bread and other basic commodities (see Chapter 13).

The analysis of debt along these lines helps explain why economies polarize as creditors in the top 1% of the economic pyramid receive debt service as financial tribute from the bottom 99%. It also explains why the solutions being proposed by policy makers to keep the debt overhead (and hence, payments to

---

[4] I discuss Newcomb's life and writings in *America's Protectionist Takeoff, 1815–1914: The Neglected American School of Political Economy* (ISLET, 2010).

the financial sector) on the books are so dysfunctional. And the fact that today's academic curriculum excludes this line of analysis helps explain why so many observers announce their surprise when economies buckle under the debt overhead.

Central banks are trying to re-inflate property prices back to their former Bubble levels in hope of helping banks escape from negative equity. The idea is to lower interest rates and provide looser credit to help the economy "borrow its way out of debt." When this doesn't work, as in Ireland (where property prices have fallen by two-thirds), the government takes bad bank loans directly onto the public balance sheet. This public debt requires taxes to pay interest to creditors providing the bailout money to sustain the financial system as is.

> As financial charges rise to absorb more corporate cash flow, real estate rents and wages, debt-burdened economies find themselves priced out of world markets. International trade competition now reflects financial, insurance and real estate (FIRE) charges more than the price of bread and other basic commodities.

Without the ability to simply monetize new debt (for instance, in "cash for trash" swaps as in the United States), carrying charges on this debt must be paid out of higher taxes. This imposes fiscal austerity on top of financial austerity. The internal contradiction here is that squeezing out more revenue to pay bondholders shrinks the economy, and hence its ability to pay taxes and debt service. The crisis deepens as national budgets and bank balance sheets fall further into deficit.

Such seeming backfiring (which "nobody could have foreseen") is not accidental. It serves the financial sector by rationalizing government bailouts for the 1% at the expense of the 99%. Earlier writers warned that such policies raise costs by burdening the economy with more regressive taxation. But to the financiers making fortunes at public expense, it pays to dull popular understanding of how financial systems inflate the debt overhead. The resulting blind spot reduces protest against government policy makers who sacrifice the "real" production and consumption economy to financial predators.

The Financial Threat to Democracy

This book describes why the situation must worsen until society deals with its debt overhead in the way that every successful economy has done: by writing down debts to the ability to pay. In administrative practice this usually means writing them off altogether—along with the savings that indebt the economy on the "oligarchic" asset side of the balance sheet.

The traditional path of least resistance has been to wipe out savings and debts together in a convulsion of bankruptcy. The 1929 and 1931 crashes led to the 1931 moratorium on German reparations and Inter-Ally debts. The Mexican and subsequent Latin American insolvencies led to the Brady Plan sovereign debt write-downs in the 1980s. But by far the most important example was the 1948 Allied Currency Reform in Germany. It annulled domestic debts (on the ground that most were owed to former Nazi creditors) except those owed by employers to employees as part of their normal pay-check obligations, and basic working bank balances. By rendering Germany debt-free and hence without the cost of carrying it's a financial overhead, this led to the nation's Economic Miracle.

As part of dismantling the Nazi economy's web of savings and debts, however, the Allies imposed Anglo-American commercial bank practice to replace Germany's industrial *ordo* banking rooted in the Bismarck era. And in time the European Central Bank (ECB) was formed under rules that impose a financial straitjacket on government monetary and fiscal policy. Financial planning is relinquished to bankers, whose tunnel vision is leading to a continent-wide austerity. Indeed, the emerging post-2008 financial oligarchy has used the sovereign debt crisis as an opportunity to attack democracy. Instead of managing the Euro to promote economic growth and raise living standards, economies are drained to make bankers and bondholders whole. Economies are being impoverished to pay domestic and foreign bankers and financial gamblers. Keeping debts on the books means keeping their interest payments and penalties, capped by pressure on governments to privatize assets that remain in the public domain. Much like the theology of "saving appearances" in the convoluted but unrealistic mathematics of medieval astronomy, what is saved is the idea that the debt overhead can be paid without stifling the economy's production and spending power. The 21st century thus threatens to roll back the 20th century's gains, by artificially nurturing the financial overgrowth rather than pruning it down to size. And it is being done to serve today's authoritarian financial theology.

The Greek word *hubris* meant overgrowth, as in that of bushes or other vegetation. In humans it connotes overweening pride, with the classic connotation of injuring others. "Pride goes before destruction, a haughty spirit before

a fall," says the Bible (Proverbs, 16:18). But in today's world hubristic greed
seeks to postpone the fall—by shifting financial injury onto the economy.

Hyman Minsky explained how the business cycle is basically a financial
cycle, characterized by increasingly risky bank credit. Lending standards are
loosened as debt service grows so large that borrowers no longer are able to
amortize their loans, and ultimately not even to pay the interest. At this point
(which Minsky called the Ponzi phase of the credit cycle) banks postpone
default by lending their customers the money to pay whatever amounts are
falling due. The effect is to add the interest onto the debt principal. The process
continues until banks or their regulators realize that the loan balances are
largely fictitious, exceeding the debtors' ability to pay.

Since 2008, governments have kept this debt overgrowth in place even at
the cost of plunging economies into austerity. They are creating new public
debt and swapping it for toxic financial waste to bail out banks for loans gone
bad. The pretense is that without taking these losses onto the public balance
sheet, the financial system would "freeze up." But most banks still have enough
assets to reimburse insured "plain vanilla" depositors and maintain basic
credit-clearing functions. So there is no intrinsic need for governments to save
bank stockholders and most risk-taking counter-parties from loss. What is being
saved is the system's "fat," not the bone.

> **F**inancialized globalization seeks to widen the web of debt throughout the world, achieving what formerly was won by military force.

A large contributor to this problem is the decision to make interest payments tax deductible. The policy gives a tax advantage for investors to acquire
asset ownership by borrowing rather than by direct purchase. It reflects an
epoch when credit was an intrinsic cost of commercial trade. But most bank
credit now is extended to buy real estate or take over companies, not to finance
the production, sale and shipping of products. The main objects of bank credit
are property, mineral wealth and monopoly privileges (now headed by privatized infrastructure), not new tangible capital formation.

What has contributed most seriously to making rent-seeking privileges the
major object of bank credit creation instead of new production and capital
formation is the anti-classical policy of slashing taxes on land rent and natural
resource rent, as well as on asset-price gains ("capital" gains in asset prices)

and short-term financial speculation ("carried interest"). The resulting economic polarization has created special interests that raise the national cost structure by steering the economy more deeply into debt. Household and business budgets are squeezed while government social programs are cut back. Industry and labor bear the loss as austerity reduces spending, even as debts to the financial sector increase its gains and enable the wealthy to acquire (privatize or "grabitize") more property at distress prices.

The financial sector's hijacking of public policy is crowding out the spending needed to pull economies out of their downturn. The Eurozone has taken the extreme position of rejecting a central bank doing what the Bank of England, Federal Reserve and other central banks were created to do: monetize government deficits. Instead of helping to pull the economy out of depression, the ECB demands that debt-strapped governments add a tax burden to the debt overhead, so as to limit the budget deficit while creating a hemorrhage of bank subsidies. The fiscal burden is shifted on to the overall economy while finance is un-taxed. And to top matters, the ECB finally did create money after this policy led to government insolvency in 2011. It did so not to rescue the economies of Ireland, Greece or Italy, but to create a public bailout facility to refinance the bad debts held by German, French and other banks.

So the world finds itself drawn into a new form of economic warfare. Waged by finance against industry as well as labor, it also is against government — at least, democratic government, which is turned into a vehicle to extract revenue and sell off assets to pay a creditor oligarchy. The trick is to convince voters to support a policy that shrinks the economy and throws government budgets into deficit, adding a fiscal crisis on top of the debt crisis — which the financial sector sees as an opportunity to turn nations into a grab bag for assets and further control.

The effect is to make financialized economies higher-cost and hence less competitive — and less able to pull themselves out of depression by exporting more. Competitive advantage shifts to less debt-ridden economies, especially those whose real estate is less debt leveraged and public infrastructure provides basic services at cost or at subsidized rates. Politically, this means economies whose financial sectors have not gained enough power to capture the state, its central bank and regulatory agencies — or the academic economics curriculum, for that matter.

But financialized globalization seeks to widen the web of debt throughout the world, achieving what formerly was won by military force. In the name of "wealth creation" the financial sector has euphemized and transformed political ideology to such a degree that most countries are applauding the most predatory grab of the public domain (government enterprises, land and mineral rights) since the Enclosure Movements of the 16th through 18th century in England, and earlier military conquests of the New World and most of Europe.

What is not recognized is that the effect of financializing an economy is much the same as levying tribute following armed conquest. Property ownership is transferred, on terms that block governments from taxing revenue that is "expensed" as interest or escapes through tax-avoidance transactions with offshore banking centers. Sell-offs of public monopolies such as roads and other infrastructure are turned into opportunities for rent extraction. This turns the economy into a set of tollbooths as user-fees raised on labor, industry and other non-financial "real" activity. Revenue is "freed" of anti-monopoly rules and price regulation, and even from taxation as property taxes are cut to leave more revenue "free" to be paid as debt service.

> The effect of financializing an economy is much the same as levying tribute following armed conquest.

The Progressive Era did not envision that campaign financing would make politics part of the "market economy" by enabling the FIRE sector to buy political support for its debt leveraging. Government was supposed to regulate high finance, not cater to it. But the financial sector's influence has become dominant by appropriating the central bank, Treasury and other agencies capable of remunerating it (or blocking public attempts to tax or regulate it). These financialized arms of government are filling the vacuum created by limiting the government's social welfare role. Rather than investing in infrastructure, central bank money creation and borrowing are limited to bailouts, subsidies and tax cuts for banks and their major customers.

These developments threaten the United States and Europe with losing their democracy. What remains of Progressive Era agencies and programs are being shrunk by starving them of tax revenue. In the words of Grover Norquist, the parts of government not under FIRE-sector control should be shrunk to a small enough size to be put in a bathtub and drowned. Government's post-democratic role is to use public taxing and debt-creating authority to remunerate the financial sector, while privatizing property and what remains of the Commons.

Financial lobbyists seek to tie the hands of government and disable its ability to regulate banks and their major clients, and above all to create its own money and to tax what the classical economists called unearned income (economic rent) and financial gains. Attempts to tax property and asset-price gains are resisted, especially attempts to provide (or maintain) public options such as supplying banking services as basic infrastructure (as in the old Post Office banks). Internationally, bankers demand that governments pay creditors by privatizing whatever assets can be sold. Buyers borrow the purchase price from the banks, expensing their revenue as tax-deductible interest payments. These privatization policies together cause a fiscal squeeze that forces governments even further into dependency on bankers and bondholders.

A perverse financialized kind of circular flow has been created. Income formerly paid as taxes and public user fees ends up being paid to privatizers, who pass it on to their financial backers as interest. Part of this revenue is used to buy political support to free it from taxation, including lobbying to purchase political favors from lawmakers in today's pay-to-play system — and to deter regulation of predatory lending or prosecution of fraud. Tax favoritism for debt leveraging raises the economy's price structure — not as a result of "more money chasing goods," but because privatized monopolies impose "tollbooth" charges for services that governments formerly provided free of cost (as in roads), at subsidized rates (postal service) or at minimum cost. Prices for privatized monopolies include interest charges, financial fees and dividends, high executive salaries and public relations costs to advocacy groups to plead their case to the people that all this is more efficient than public ownership.

> **T**ax favoritism for debt leveraging raises the economy's price structure, not as a result of "more money chasing goods," but because privatized monopolies impose "tollbooth" charges for services that governments formerly provided free of cost (as in roads), at subsidized rates (postal service) or at minimum cost.

What is deemed "efficient" is to shift planning out of public hands to those of bankers. Yet public policy aims (or is supposed to aim) at raising output, employment, capital formation and living standards. Financialized planning is short-term, and aims to capitalize the economic surplus into debt service at the going rate of interest. The business plan of finance capital is to expand interest and amortization charges to the point where they absorb all disposable consumer income over and above essentials, all business cash flow and real estate rent over and above break-even costs, and government revenue over basic police and other necessary functions.

And then the economy collapses! How else can matters end when debt obligations grow exponentially as interest charges mount up? Debts grow at compound interest, swollen by penalties on arrears. Unpaid bills are added onto the debt balance, until foreclosure time arrives, transferring property to creditors under distress conditions. Vulture funds clean up.

The dynamic has happened before, most notoriously in the Roman Empire after 133 BC when creditors used violence against the Gracchi and other reformers. Violence and corruption are essential tactics to impoverish the economy while creating more billionaires at public expense. The $13 trillion in Bush-Obama bailout giveaways after September 2008 endowed a power elite that threatens to rule the rest of the 21st century if no reforms occur along the lines advocated by classical political economy, the Progressive Era, New Deal and, most recently, Modern Monetary Theory (MMT).

Economic reformers a century ago found it necessary to create a new academic discipline, "sociology," to avoid the narrow-mindedness that Bertell Ollman calls "market mystification."[5] But economists theorizing along sociological lines are now classified as "institutionalists" and relegated to the basement of the social sciences. Mainstream textbooks leave out the role of gunboats, fraud and unearned income. They describe a hypothetical world characterized by diminishing marginal utility (no mention of greed or wealth addiction) and diminishing returns (while productivity soars in the real world). Managers are held to need more salaries to "induce" them to create wealth — that is, corporate profits, by cutting salaries for their employees to "lower labor costs." Every increase in employment is supposed to raise wages ("the demand for labor"), thereby making economies less competitive (rather than raising their productivity as a result of better schooling, diets and so forth).

Treating markets merely as clearing mechanisms to balance quantities supplied and quantities demanded, applying grade-school mathematics to find a

---

[5] As Ollman (*p.c.*) has expressed his criticism to me, the problem is that economists think of markets "simply as a venue for TRANSACTIONS. The key is, what is being transacted? If it is goods, how are they produced and how is their price determined, how is credit or payment arranged, and on what terms. The RESULT of how the overall system operates appears in "the market." But that's not where you start. That's like starting with Union Square for the farmers' market in New York. It focuses on an individual buyer and seller — not on wholesalers, transportation, fees charged out of revenues, or farm inputs, taxes, etc." See "Market Mystification in Capitalist and Market Socialist Societies," in Bertell Ollman ed., *Market Socialism: The Debate Among Socialists* (Routledge 1998).

hypothetical equilibrium point, distracts attention from how "wealth creation" is achieved by insider dealing, tax favoritism and outright fraud as the financial sector disables public agencies in an increasingly polarized economy. We can best understand the Thatcherism and Reaganomics of the 1980s by looking at their dress rehearsal: the U.S.-sponsored military regime in Chile after 1973. The Chicago Boys realized that in order to create a "free market" controlled by their constituency, the bankers, it is necessary to control the press and educational system to neutralize opposition. Operation Condor pressed this social engineering to the point of exiling or killing those who disagreed with the Chicago program. Their guiding principle was the same as that of Stalin: "No person, no problem." That is what TINA meant in practice: "No alternative ideas, no problem." Labor union leaders and journalists, professors and politicians were murdered throughout Latin America and even in the United States for opposing the financial oligarchy's power grab and the economic theory to rationalize this usurpation. Wealth was concentrated in the hands of rentiers most willing to indulge in violence and what the Russians have called "grabitization."

So we are brought back to the role of gunboats and force, political lobbying to buy politicians, mass media promising that the path to get rich most easily is to take on as much debt as possible, and an academic curriculum saying that this is more efficient than public investment or operating a less highly debt-leveraged economy. It is as if the real world's power grab by the financial oligarchy does not properly belong in scientific analysis. Failure of academic models to acknowledge it produces an ideology that falsifies the way the world really works.

What is needed to save democracy from turning into oligarchy is to recognize how predatory this financial strategy has become, and how far today's lending has diverged from productive credit. This classical distinction has been dropped—indeed, expurgated—from the academic curriculum. Debt crises such as the West is now experiencing are treated as if they are "exogenous" or an anomaly, not the policy result of financial conquest.

This political (and academic) capitulation to finance capital leads one to question the Progressive Era's faith that the material imperatives of industrial development will steer social evolution upward. Industrial capital was expected to seek profits by expanding investment. Banks were supposed to be the brains, allocating credit where economic gains were highest—gains that would enrich society as a whole.

But the opposite is occurring—not an economy of abundance but one of austerity and debt peonage. Socialists who stand on the sidelines repeating the rhetoric of class war between industry and labor (a conflict that never has disappeared, to be sure) miss the threat to labor *and* industry posed by banks joining with *rentiers* from the real estate and insurance sectors and monopolies. This makes criticism of financial malstructuring neither left nor right wing. It spans the political spectrum, because the entire economy is threatened by the austerity that results from financial dynamics operating unchecked—and ultimately bankrupts the banking sector itself.

Part I

FICTITIOUS CAPITAL AND ECONOMIC FICTIONS

"Did nobody see this coming? Why did nobody notice it?"

> Queen Elizabeth II,
> in a visit to the London School of
> Economics on November 4, 2008.

"Now let me state at the outset what role the Department plays and does not play in addressing these challenges [record fraud in investment banking and securities].

The Department of Justice investigates and prosecutes federal crimes.... As a general matter we do not have the expertise nor is it part of our mission to opine on the systemic causes of the financial crisis. Rather the Justice Department's resources are focused on investigating and prosecuting crime....

Our efforts to fight economic crime are a vital component of our broader strategy, a strategy that seeks to foster confidence in our financial system, integrity in our markets, and prosperity for the American people."

> U.S. Attorney General Eric Holder,
> testifying in January 14, 2010 to the
> Financial Crisis Inquiry Commission
> (FCIC),
> cited by UMKC Prof. Bill Black,
> "The High Price of Ignorance"
> <http://www.nakedcapitalism.com
> /2011/11/bill-black-the-high-price-of-
> ignorance.html>, November 7, 2011.

1

TWO TRADITIONS OF FINANCIAL DOCTRINE

Today's leading nations have achieved their global advantage as a result of a strategy based on industrial and agricultural innovation employing well educated, highly paid, high-productivity labor. A tradition whose roots extend back to before the Industrial Revolution has advocated public infrastructure investment, subsidies to key industries, and encouragement to skilled immigrants, as well as protectionist economic policy. This tradition also called for national control of banking and financial systems to steer money and credit creation to promote tangible capital formation as a precondition for achieving international competitiveness and indeed, leadership.

When setting out to re-couple banking and credit to tangible capital formation today, it is not necessary to re-invent the analytic wheel. The logic was clarified even before the nineteenth century's blossoming of heavy industry. French economists from John Law through Colbert advocated economic planning financed by an industrial banking system. After the Napoleonic reforms, the Saint-Simonians inspired a virtual industrial religion. Their ideals underlay the Credit Mobilier, founded in 1852, and shaped Marx's ideas of how banking needed to be transformed to finance industrial capitalism.

In its financial dimension the "Other Canon" tradition recognizes that credit is not inflationary if it is used to employ new labor productively. But tight money and economic austerity deter capital investment, research and development. This leads to currency collapse aand rising prices to the extent that it depresses production. Banking policies need to steer credit along lines that encourage industrial and human capital formation in order to encourage a prosperity in which money and credit—and investment—increase output more than product prices or asset prices.

The guiding idea is that loans should finance direct investment in productive enterprise, not enable borrowers merely to bid up real estate and stock market prices by using credit for speculation, corporate raiding, takeovers and management buyouts. Without drawing a distinction between productive and unproductive lending along these lines, the price consequences of increasing money and credit cannot be gauged. In this respect the tradition of industrial financial systems recognizes the linkages that exist between industrial policy, tax strategy and national monetary and banking systems. By relating credit increases not merely to prices but to new hiring, purchasing power and output, it designates the proper role for banks, insurance companies and stock markets as being to mobilize savings and credit to upgrade technology, social infrastructure, employment and productivity.

Domestic control of banking and insurance therefore is needed not only to steer credit most efficiently to maximize capital formation and production while raising living standards, but also to help avoid financial dependency on the leading credit-creating nations. In addition, to save economies from having to pay even more domestic currency as foreign-debt service when the exchange rate declines (as a result of balance-of-payments outflows to foreign creditors as a result of credit dependency, and to foreign food and industrial exporters as a result of import dependency), the financial reform movement advises that loans should be extended in local currency rather than dollarized. The exchange rate also needs to be protected from financial inflows pushing it up and making home manufactures more expensive in world markets.

This pro-industrial financial doctrine has spanned the political spectrum from right to left, religious to secular. The broad approach of Sir James Steuart and Rev. Josiah Tucker in 18th-century Britain was applied after the Napoleonic Wars by anti-Bullionists led by Henry Thornton and Thomas Tooke. In the United States, Alexander Hamilton's 1791 *Report on Manufactures* emphasized the need for a national bank to finance industry (although early attempts along these lines engaged largely in land deals). From Henry Clay and Calvin Colton through subsequent protectionists, a new national bank charter became a major plank of Whig and then Republican party platforms. After the 1907 financial panic a National Monetary Commission was created and urged America to emulate the large German investment banks. As matters turned out, however, the Federal Reserve System was created in 1914 under a Democratic administration that favored decentralization and British-type merchant banking. In academia, Thorstein Veblen contrasted financial engineering to industrial engineering, and emphasized the pecuniary economy's financial dimensions and its links to land speculation. His institutionalist approach was elaborated by John Commons, while Harold Moulton pioneered the study of financial macroeconomics at the Brookings Institution.

Industrial banking principles were most firmly grounded in the Reichsbank and other large German banks, while the German Historical School and "State Socialists" (academic "Socialists of the Chair") emphasized the financial dimension of large-scale industrial development. Rudolf Hilferding's *Finance Capital* (1910) elaborated Marx's approach to reflect twentieth-century conditions, and was followed by socialists such as Vladimir Woytinsky as the world economy succumbed to the Great Depression. In Britain, John Hobson and H.S. Foxwell wrote along similar lines, and in the 1920s, John Maynard Keynes analyzed the debt burden imposed by lending and financial specula-tion. Joseph Schumpeter, and later his student Hyman Minsky, theorized about how to finance industrial innovation and capital formation in contrast to the existing tendency business upawingsto culminate in "Ponzi schemes" and stock market bubbles as their final phase.

As a logical counterpart to distinguishing between productive and unpro-ductive labor and spending (*i.e.*, investment vs. consumption), classical econo-mists contrasted productive from unproductive debt. The term "productive" meant productive of profit, which was considered to be necessary to induce capital to be invested in any given undertaking rather than elsewhere. Produc-tive labor or spending accordingly was employed to produce or trade goods for sale at a price covering the capitalist's wage outlay and capital expenditures and yield normal profit. By contrast, money spent hiring servants or doctors, lawyers and other professionals for consumption purposes was viewed as eco-nomic overhead ("unproductive consumption"), as were employees in not-for-profit sectors (religious officials, government bureaucrats and so forth).

Along parallel financial lines, productive loans provided resources for bor-rowers to employ to earn enough profit to repay the debt with its stipulated interest. The merchant borrowed money to conduct his trade, and the indus-trial capitalist might borrow to build factories and plant, machinery and other means of production to create goods sold at a profit. Adam Smith estimated the natural rate of profit to be twice the interest rate, so that the gross profit would be divided evenly between the creditor as a silent partner and the entre-preneur.

By contrast, consumer borrowing represented an unproductive form of debt. Its interest charges had to be paid out of the income the debtors earned elsewhere or, ultimately, by their selling off assets to pay the creditor. Govern-ment debt likewise was unproductive, at least to the extent that its proceeds were used to wage wars that destroyed property rather than created capital out of the profits made from the loan. Government borrowing to defray social welfare costs also represents what the classical economists would have called unproductive borrowing.

Some forms of credit and public spending thus are more desirable than others. Helping speculators bid up the price of real estate already built, and of equities in companies already in existence, merely funds and an overgrowth of debt as borrowers seek to ride the wave of asset-price inflation.

It is primarily in the United States and Britain that opponents of financial regulation have denied any need to channel credit systems along "productive" lines. Indeed, they deny that credit and foreign "capital transfers" (military spending or private capital flight) can creat an imbalance, thanks to self-stabilizing equilibrium tendencies. A common thread along this line runs from Ricardo and his contemporary Bullionists to today's monetarists. In the 1920s, Jacques Rueff in France and the Swedish-U.S. economist Bertil Ohlin denied that the debt service imposed by German reparations could cause serious financial disruption. A similar approach led to Frederick Hayek, Milton Friedman and subsequent Chicago School opponents of government activism, as well as to the IMF's austerity programs that squeeze out short-term surpluses to finance foreign-debt service and capital flight rather than tangible capital formation.[1] This approach does not recognize debt service as causing problems for the exchange rate or deflating output levels, or that regulatory actions may encourage credit to be allocated along "productive" lines. Just the opposite, such actions are held only to be destabilizing.

When currencies come under pressure as a result of capital flight, monetarists advocate raising interest rates so as to borrow enough money to stabilize exchange rates. This policy is endorsed even at the cost of depressing the economy. Raising interest rates increases the cost of debt-financed capital investment, thereby slowing its growth. Meanwhile, austerity keeps prices low (and hence, the purchasing power of debt service high). As the domestic market shrinks and over-capacity emerges, lending money or investing abroad becomes more remunerative than investing it in new factories, plant and equipment at home.

The Industrial Revolution found itself confronted with banking systems designed to fund national war debts, not investment in factories, machinery and innovation. In continental Europe, protective tariffs and government investment in transport and other public utilities went hand in hand with industrial banking. By contrast, British and U.S. merchant banking looked at collateral rather than at the means of production that could be newly created with credit.

Ultimately at issue was whether financial systems should fund capital formation or real estate and stock market bubbles. Today's deregulatory ortho-

---

[1] I contrast the narrow monetarist approach taken by Ricardo and other Bullionists to that of the Anti-Bullionists in Ch. 14 of my *Trade, Development and Foreign Debt. How Trade and Development Concentrate Economic Power in the Hands of Dominant Nations* (2nd, rev. and ext, ed.) [Dresden: ISLET 2009], esp. p. 280; those of Rueff and Ohlin vs. Keynes and Moulton in Ch. 16; and the IMF's pro-creditor doctrines of financial austerity in Chs. 17 and 18.

doxy does not distinguish corporate takeover funding or land speculation from tangible capital investment. And yet despite the rising importance of capital gains in total investment returns monetarist orthodoxy views money almost solely in reference to commodity prices rather than correlating it with asset prices—or, for that matter, with the debt overhead.

Already in the 18th century, political economists explained why monetary policy should avoid deflation. Populations needed adequate purchasing power to buy the goods and services the economy was potentially able to produce. In 1767, in the process of countering David Hume's early version of the quantity theory of money, Steuart denounced austerity policies of the sort that the IMF imposes on debtor countries today. Economists who deplore today's decoupling of financial markets from industrial capital formation thus can find a long pedigree of what Schumpeter called filiations in the writings of Law, Tucker and Steuart, the anti-Bullionists and Saint-Simonians. These writers analyzed the adverse impact of monetary deflation in their discussions of the role of money and credit in setting labor and industry to work, increasing output, and attracting capital and immigrants (especially skilled labor) from other countries.

What is remarkable is that the pedigree of plans to harness banking systems to finance industrial capital formation remains untaught today. The economic curriculum has been captured by a monetarist orthodoxy that excludes an analysis of the problems caused by monetary austerity, high interest rates, and the debt overhead that is aggravated by decoupling bank lending and stock markets from the financing of tangible investment.

The Political Arithmeticians and Their View on Financing Industry

Inasmuch as nations without gold or silver mines were obliged to run trade surpluses to pay for their imports of monetary bullion, monetary theory was linked inherently to trade theory. At issue was what policies were best suited to drawing in money from abroad so as to set the wheels of commerce and industry in motion.

Thomas Mun, Charles Davenant, Steuart and other writers whom Smith called mercantilists went far beyond the idea of merely mercantile "marketplace" analysis. The term they often used to describe themselves was Political Arithmetic. They used economic statistics and quantifiable relationships to demonstrate that more money and credit were likely to finance increased production under the conditions existing in the 18th century. This increased output absorbed the growth in spending power, so that prices did not need be inflated when money flowed in to pay for a rising volume of exports.

One of the most important common denominators of Political Arithmeticians seeking to build up national industry was the perception that the power to earn gold was more important than the supply of gold itself. Britain and the Netherlands (Spain's former colony) had watched Spain and Portugal dissipate the gold they had taken from the New World. Although they were themselves least endowed with mines or other natural resources, they had put in place an active industry that had drawn the world's wealth to their shores. This view had become popular by the time Governor Keith of Massachusetts expressed it in 1738:

> ... although *Spain*, by possessing the Mines of *Mexico* and *Peru*, may be said to be richer in that respect than any other Nation; ... and tho' it may furnish the *Spaniards* with all the Product of other Mens Labour, which the most exquisite Luxury can desire, in the main it destroys Industry, by encouraging Sloth and Indolence, which inevitably must introduce both a Neglect and Contempt of the Arts and Sciences; whereas an industrious Commonwealth, who keeps her subjects employed in Manufactures, and Foreign Trade, by continually furnishing *Spain* with such Things as there is a constant Demand for, to supply that People's Conveniency, and feed their Pleasures, must needs in Return command as great a share of *Spanish* Bullion as they want; so that in fact the Spanish Riches consist in digging up Gold and silver out of the Earth for other People, whose superior Skill and Industry, in applying it to its proper Use, absolutely determines the Value of that Kind of Wealth; which, if it be not kept in continual Motion and employed in Trade, never fails to enervate the Owners ...[2]

In much the same vein Tucker explained that it made a great difference whether Britain earned bullion from broadly based industry employing a large proportion of the population, or whether this money came merely from commerce or piracy without industry, as Spain and Portugal had looted their colonies.[3] An anonymous pamphlet writer observed in 1782 that the effect of monetary inflows depended on "how that wealth was acquired, whether by force or labour, by foreign conquest or internal industry." In just the opposite way from the mechanisms assumed by today's IMF austerity programs for debtor economies, he explained:

---

[2] William Keith, *History of the British Plantations in America* (London 1738: 34 f.)
[3] Josiah Tucker, *Four Tracts on Political and Commercial Subjects* [1774] (2nd ed. Gloucester 1776: 21–26).

Each addition to the quantity of productive stock will create new demands for labour, and add new spurs to industry and ingenuity. The annual produce of the nation and the course of its power will be thus rapidly increased.[4]

Only if this money were merely "acquired by foreign conquests, and paid in tribute to the public treasury" would its effects be similar to those suggested by Hume. The balance of trade and price relationships thus depended mainly on a nation's political and social institutions.

Economists writing in this tradition saw that the consequences of a monetary inflow depended on the extent to which it was used to employ labor. These writers did not assume an automatically fully employed economy. Hence, monetary inflows could have the effect on spurring output, not merely working to raise prices. Already in 1650, William Potter wrote that: "An encrease of money cannot possibly occasion an encrease in the price of commodities," because it would raise output proportionally.[5]

By the same token, a shrinking money supply would not necessary lower prices in the same ratio. To the extent that tight money caused unemployment, it would lower output, leaving fewer goods and services available to absorb the economy's purchasing power. This would raise prices even as production fell, as Law pointed out in 1705:

Most People think scarcity of Money is only the Consequence of a Balance due [that is, a trade deficit]; but 'tis the Cause as well as the consequence, and the effectual way to bring the Balance to our side, is to add to the Money.[6]

Plentiful money and a domestic credit system erected on this base was a precondition for putting labor to work and inducing capital investment.

Hume himself noted in his 1752 essay "Of Money":

In every kingdom, into which money begins to flow in greater abundance than formerly, everything takes a new face; labour and industry gain life; the merchant becomes more enterprising, the manufacturer more diligent and skilful, and even the farmer follows his plough with greater alacrity and attention.[7]

---

[4] Anon., *Political Observations on the Population of Countries* (London 1782: 19–23).

[5] Potter, *The Key to Wealth* (1650: 10), quoted in Douglas Vickers, *Studies in the Theory of Money: 1690–1776* (Philadelphia 1959: 21).

[6] Law, *Money and Trade Considered, with a Proposal for Supplying the nation with Money* (Edinburgh 1705: 115f.)

[7] Hume, *Political Discourses*, in E. Rotwein, ed., *David Hume: Writings on Economics* (Madison, Wis.: 1970: 34f.)

A growing supply of money and income thus worked to increase employment and output before prices increased. As Vickers summarizes Hume's views:

> What we should call an elasticity of supply is postulated … The inflation initially is a profit inflation, rather than a price inflation. Rises in turnovers and profits are realized, rather than rises in prices. Changes occur in the 'manners and customs of the people.'[8]

Steuart devoted Chapter 28 of his *Principles of Political Oeconomy* to criticizing the limitations of what has been called the price-specie flow adjustment mechanism as postulated by Hume: the idea that an increase in the money supply will raise prices proportionally, discouraging exports while making imports more attractive, until the trade balance returns to equilibrium. For economies suffering serious trade deficits, a monetary drain and falling prices were likely to be buffeted by the waves of financial crisis depressing their production levels below the break-even point, throwing them into bankruptcy. Producers could not operate at a loss for long in the face of falling prices and still remain in business, nor could employment be maintained when wages fell below subsistence levels. "If a certain number of inhabitants be employed in a necessary branch of consumption, there must be a certain demand preserved for it," Steuart pointed out. Rather than recovering its former balance, the balance of trade and payments might stabilize at a lower level of employment, population and economic activity.

Tucker, Steuart and their contemporaries were well aware of the fact that workers, especially skilled labor, followed the international flow of money and prosperity. Hume's friend James Oswald wrote to him in 1749 that although a monetary inflow and its associated

> quick demand, in the first instance, tends to raise the rate of wages, yet, as it is corrected by the attraction of new inhabitants, it only produces permanently that good effect, while the want of it in poor countries destroys the manufacture themselves, and sends out the manufactures.[9]

Hume's essay "Of the Balance of Trade" acknowledged that "a diminution of specie" is "in time commonly attended with the transport of people and industry." For nations running a trade and related balance-of-payments surplus, wrote Steuart,

---

[8] *Op. cit.*: 228.
[9] Oswald to Hume, October 10, 1749 (in *ibid.*: 195 and 77).

no sooner will demand come from abroad, for a greater quantity of manufactures than formerly, than such demand will have the effect of gradually multiplying the inhabitants up to the proportion of the surplus above mentioned, provided the statesman be all along careful to employ these additional numbers, which an useful multiplication must produce, in supplying the additional demand.[10]

As long as employment, investment and productivity kept pace with rising monetary stocks and wages, there need be no increase in the general price level, and hence no falling off of exports. Steuart accordingly concluded that "the riches of a country [*i.e.*, its money supply] has no determined influence upon prices" that could be stated with certainty, "a fact which Mr. Hume has attended … on one occasion, although he has lost sight of it on several others."[11] Or, as Schumpeter has put this thought in more recent times, "any satisfactory theory of the money supply implies a theory of the economic process in its entirety."[12]

The reason why modern academic orthodoxy has shunted aside the ideas of Law, Tucker, Steuart and their like-minded contemporaries is reflected in Hayek's denigrating observation that "The suggestive and interesting, but essentially wrongheaded chapters on money in James Steuart's *Political Oeconomy* had no very wide influence."[13] Yet in their day they were felt so widely that when Smith brought his *Wealth of Nations* to the same Scottish publisher that had printed Steuart's work, he avoided using the title, "*Principles of Political Economy*," to which classical economic treatises for the next century by Ricardo, John Stuart Mill and their contemporaries would return. Smith adopted the tactic that subsequent neo-liberal orthodoxy would use with regard to the classical, protectionist,socialist and other economists who sought to speer banking and financial systems to fund tangible capital formation rather than just "make money from money": simply ignore them, and write a censorial history of economic thought as if they did not exist: If the eye offend thee, pluck it out.

For more than two centuries monetarist writers have focused on the relation between money and prices alone, taking for granted the existing level of employment and production. Under the assumption of practically full employment, the effect of monetary inflows can only be to push up prices. Treating

---

[10] *Principles*, I.: 268.
[11] *Principles*, I: 405.
[12] Schumpeter, *History of Economic Analysis* (New York 1954: 286.)
[13] Hayek, introduction to the 1939 reprint of Henry Thornton, *Enquiry into the Nature and Effect of the Paper credit of Great Britain* (London 1802). Hayek does not explain how Steuart's ideas were wrong.

prices as the only variable, the monetarist approach assumes as given what the Other Canon views as the topic of major interest: the role to be played by public policy and social institutions. What was most interesting, the anti-monetarists pointed out, was how monetary inflows and credit could set underemployed labor and undercapitalized industry in motion.

This is the approach that Britain, the United States, Germany and France adopted as policy in their most successful formative centuries. Yet monetarist historians (most notoriously Jacob Viner) have written this tradition out of their surveys of economic thought. Today's students are taught Hume's partial version of the quantity theory of money without reference to the qualifications stressed by Tucker, Oswald and Steuart. They are not taught that in the Bullion Debate, and again in the 1920s debate over German reparations and debt-servicing capacity, monetarist theories of the balance of payments were the losing side analytically. The deflationary monetary policies promoted by financial interests have been imposed throughout the 20th century, but led to widespread depression and crisis in the 1930s, and again since the 1960s for debtor countries subjected to the International Monetary Fund's austerity programs.

This monetarist doctrine reflects a methodology that has become today's orthodox "market fundamentalism," or politically in Chile and Russia, as "market authoritarianism." And, to cap matters, the Chicago School has interwoven free-trade theory with a pro-creditor "hard money" advocacy of privatization and "dollarization" for trade-dependent debtor economies.

By contrast, a common denominator may be traced through protectionist, socialist and other doctrines of government planning in aiming to modernize industry, agriculture and labor skills. Especially when voiced by economists in nations seeking to "catch up," such writers have tended to be pro-debtor in the sense that they would subordinate debt claims to the objective of maximizing society's productive powers over time. The basic approach has been advocated in the 20th century most notably by Keynes and the American New Deal macro-economists and institutionalists.

Nowhere are institutional structures given more emphasis than in the financial sphere. As Tucker, Steuart and other early writers noted, money and banking are highly embedded in legal and political structures. For this reason most advocates of this approach exemplify what the German writer Georg Friedrich Knapp called the *State Theory of Money* in 1906. This approach also called chartalism or cartalism) views money as a government creation, inasmuch as governments imbue credit-money with value by accepting it in payment for taxes or other public fees. In addition, bank reserves rest ultimately on holdings of government securities, and deposits are guaranteed by the state.

Creditary doctrines are inherently historical in character, inasmuch as financial systems are products of fiscal and legal institutions. Before reviewing specific doctrines of how best to structure an economy's financial institutions, I therefore will first review the role of government in shaping financial systems, juxtaposing the broad institutionalist vantage point to the monetarist "Chicago" view.

How Central Banks Turn Public Debt into Credit-Money

Finance was one of the last dimensions to be incorporated into modern theories of economic development. Even among economists who recognized the degree to which growth in production and employment needed credit, there was little discussion prior to the 19th century of how to mobilize banking systems specifically to finance industrialization. What ultimately was needed was to distinguish productive lending for tangible capital investment from parasitic lending that aimed at making money merely by "zero-sum" means such as building up an interest-yielding debt overhead willy-nilly.

The essence of any credit system is its ability to provide monetary means of payment beyond the accumulation of gold and silver bullion. Promises of future payment — IOUs — circulate as credit-money. As a practical matter, to be sure, bank notes and bank checks are backed not only by the bank's own loan portfolio, but by collateral pledged in the form of marketable assets. Mortgage loans are secured by the real property whose purchase is being financed, while merchants pledge their goods in shipment to secure the bank (along with its depositors and recipients of its bank notes and checks) against the risk of non-payment.

The great challenge for financial systems has been to extend credit to fund new means of production, out of whose revenue the loan can be repaid. Such lending represents the most productive form of credit, but has been the last to develop historically. Collateral-based lending came first, and remains the foundation for credit provided to most private-sector borrowers. Even today, bankers are fearful of extending loans against means of repayment not yet in existence. Their notorious conservatism leads them to prefer lending against collateral they can seize to pay the loan balance in case of default. The tendency thus is to look backward at what already has been produced, not forward at what may be achieved by a productive use of credit.

Industrial banking required a system of paper credit as a precondition, and this is where central banks come into the picture. However, they were not created in the first instance to supply credit for industrialization. Their initial objective was to finance government deficits, mainly war spending. In a nutshell, public credit was developed as an alternative to borrowing from the international bankers of the day, *e.g.*, Italian banking families in late feudal Europe, and Dutch and other foreign investors in later centuries.

In retrospect it seems inevitable that credit-money based on uncollateralized promises to pay out of future revenue would be based in the first instance on government tax revenue. Rulers levied new taxes to pay each new loan, or at least to carry its interest charges. These borrowings were not productive, as their proceeds were not used to build up the economy's productive powers and hence its ability to pay. Just the opposite: War loans almost invariably were burdensome, for their proceeds were used to wage territorial wars that destroyed rather than creating property. No early loans were made to finance public capital formation, except for what incidentally happened to be associated with military armaments.

In addition to the power to levy taxes, governments have the unique ability to print promissory notes as currency (or to coin money) and to create a demand for it by declaring it legal tender as a means of paying taxes, other public fees or charges, and all debts generally. This imbues government debt-money with a tax-payment value, which in turn determines its general purchasing power over goods and services. Gradually it came to be recognized that this paper currency—in essence a readily assignable form of government debt—could be used in place of gold and silver coinage, that is, commodity-money. Nations did not need to run trade and payments surpluses to ensure sufficient coinage to sustain employment and investment if they managed their public debt and fiscal system adroitly to create a credit superstructure.

It is not the purpose of this survey to write a capsule summary of economic history, except to trace the evolution of banking and financial theory as it relates to the mobilization of savings or creation of credit to promote economic development. Industrial credit doctrines emerged only in the nineteenth century, many centuries after European merchant banking was catalyzed by the Crusades and the vast influx of gold that followed the looting of Constantinople in 1215, and the even greater influxes following the colonization of the New World.

From time immemorial religion and war have been the crucibles from which monetary systems have emerged. The monetary metals were given sanction as religious contributions, while temples oversaw the weights and measures in which the means of payment were denominated, and served as safe-keeping havens for savings at the civic level as early as Mesopotamian times. Wars forced realms into debt, from lowly peasant cultivators up to rulers, topped in time by Europe's feudal monarchs and modern governments. From these war debts have stemmed the proliferation of taxes to carry their interest charges—

and hence, postwar deflation. At least ancient Mesopotamian rulers chose the less destructive alternative of clean slates to wipe away the rural debt overhead.

Two medieval Church orders, the Templars and Hospitallers, developed far-flung systems to help knights transfer their money from one place to another along the Crusade routes and, over the longer term, pilgrimage routes from one shrine to the next. Travelers could draw on accounts established on an embryonic form of the modern credit card, on the basis of credit to be paid off later, after their return back home. Or, the Templars were able to receive payments in one of their local branches and to pay out an equivalent amount in another land, charging an agio fee for this money-changing and transfer. Even larger were the donations of property to these orders, in return for which the donors usually asked for the equivalent rental value for their lands as long as they remained alive. Much as lending had helped break down the traditional communal sanctions against alienating land in ancient Mesopotamia, so the process recurred in medieval Europe, especially as the lands being turned over were for a sanctified Christian purpose. Making the land transferable opened the floodgates to what in time became a widespread forfeiture of land to creditors.

It was fairly easy to elaborate the Crusades' banking services to provide trade credit as a specific application of international money transfers. As the purpose of loans became more secular, private families (starting with those most closely linked to the Church) elaborated such banking to provide trade credit and, as a byproduct of lending to rulers, war loans as well. Mercantile credit financed the shipment of goods from one place to another, pledging the credit guarantees of wealthy banking families behind export sales and orders.

Mercantile IOUs were as yet far from becoming a currency used by the population at large. Their use was restricted to the commercial sphere and the even larger flow of royal payments to Rome. From the thirteenth through fifteenth centuries, royal finances dovetailed into Church finances via the transfer of Peter's Pence and other contributions. It was largely to systematize this flow of religious tribute that merchant bankers helped organize European trade in wool and textiles. England paid an equivalent value of the money owed to Rome in wool, which the bankers sent to Flanders and other weaving centers to be woven into finished textiles.

Kings were the largest customers for loans, for the simple reason that they were the most able to raise the funds to repay them. Down to the time of Napoleon the monarchs of Britain and France borrowed vast sums to wage territorial wars. To finance this almost constant warfare they levied a widening array of taxes, whose proceeds were pledged to their creditors. The typical procedure was to levy a new tax to carry the interest costs of each new loan.

A proliferation of taxes ensued, reflecting the rising expenses of warfare and its capital-intensive warships, canons, and the cost of hiring mercenaries. But as the wars interrupted trade flows, the ability to pay usually was reduced, and bankers often came to regret their loans. This risk element came to a head with Edward III's French campaigns.

By the late 17th century, England and France had approached the limits of their ability to borrow and tax. A supplementary source of revenue was found by creating monopolies as Crown Corporations and selling them to private buyers. England's government sold the East India Company a trade monopoly in 1600, followed by other mercantile monopolies, against which Adam Smith protested as their earnings were squeezed out in the form of higher prices charged to British consumers. After the 1688 "Glorious Revolution," England replaced its Stuart dynasty with a more liberal "reform" regime. In need of money, it looked at its assets and means of raising new credit in ways that would not involve yet heavier taxes or consumer prices.

The solution was to create the first modern central bank: the Bank of England, which in 1694 was sold the monopoly of issuing bank notes, whose value the government underwrote by agreeing to accept them in payment of taxes. The Bank's Charter forbade goldsmiths from issuing notes of their own, as the Bank took over this practice. For this privilege the government was paid £1.2 million, or rather, was loaned this amount by the Bank's founders. The Bank issued paper currency backed by reserves consisting of the original £1.2 million that had been invested in royal debt.

By the 19th century a central principle of the Other Financial Canon had become familiar: The essence of money no longer consisted only of gold and silver bullion as an asset to be bartered for other goods or services. Public debt-notes could be spent as currency, at least for paying taxes, and by extension for other transactions of equal worth. The value of this money did not stem so much from its purchasing power over goods and services as from the degree to which governments monetized their debts and the way they levied taxes. The descriptive theory explaining these phenomena came to be called the State Theory of Money, as noted above. It views modern money is an embodiment of public debt—just as international monetary reserves take the form of U.S. Treasury debt held by the world's central banks.

This character of money does not bear directly on the present paper's central topic of how to link the financial system to the dynamics of capital investment and technological modernization. However, it provides a necessary institutional background to recognize that money and credit are something more than merely "counters" by which trade and exchange are contracted.

"Money" is the embodiment of public and private debt. This balance-sheet aspect of modern financial systems forms the essence of creditary analysis.

To be sure, industrial modernization was not the objective of state credit-money in its formative centuries. Governments spent tax proceeds and borrowed money to wage wars, not to sponsor technological innovation, except for relatively modest subsidies to promote science and technology, largely with a military application in mind. But for the most part, capital investment and modernization were left to the private sector.

> **M**oney and credit are something more than merely 'counters' by which trade and exchange are contracted. 'Money' is the embodiment of public and private debt. This balance-sheet aspect of modern financial systems forms the essence of creditary analysis.

It was a task in which the banking and financial system found little interest in playing. From early antiquity, handicraft workshops had been financed by the large public institutions (most characteristically by the temples and palaces of Mesopotamia) or by the households of chieftains or other wealthy individuals — but never on credit. Searching through antiquity's records, the classical historian Moses Finley found not a single "productive" loan for direct investment, only trade credit and usurious distress lending.

No industrial credit had yet developed at the time Adam Smith wrote *The Wealth of Nations*, although by 1762 the Duke of Bridgewater had run up what was then an astronomical debt to finance his canal-building activities. But Smith's Scottish contemporary James Watt could have told him that organizing a factory to manufacture steam engines was so much more costly than pin making as to require outside financing. Neither Watt nor other inventors were able to borrow from banks the early funds needed to introduce their inventions, but had to rely on their own families and circle of friends. However, as technology played little role in Smith's analysis, neither did its financial requirements, as shown by his words of advice:

> What a bank can with propriety advance to a merchant or undertaker of any kind, is not either the whole capital with which he trades, or even any considerable part of that capital; but that part of it only, which he would otherwise be obliged to keep by him unemployed, and in ready money for answering occasional demands.[14]

In other words, financing was provided for moving goods already produced to market, but little more.

Banking institutions were mercantile, able to finance sales of goods already produced (through bills of exchange) but not their manufacture, as this could not be done simply by discounting bills for immediate payment. Bankers only were familiar with procedures to evaluate the borrowing capacity of enterprises whose assets could be fully collateralized and rapidly liquidated, or which could pledge a known and easily foreseeable income, as was the case with real property. The automobile had to wait over half a century to obtain financing.[15] As the financial historian George Edwards has summarized:

> The investment banking houses had little to do with the financing of corporations or with industrial undertakings. The great investment houses bitterly opposed the numerous corporate issues which were floated in 1924 and 1825.... The investment houses for a long time refused to take part even in the financing of the British railways.[16]

Not liking competition, bankers opposed the extension of credit beyond the narrow commodity-money base they alone possessed. This threatened to deny manufacturing the funding needed to finance the Industrial Revolution's capital investment. Manufacturers turned increasingly to the stock and bond market, and adopted the practice already established and legitimized by governments in issuing long-term notes rather than relying on short-term bank loans. (In recent decades the same phenomenon has occurred in the United States, as large corporations now issue their paper directly rather than going through the banks for credit.)

This narrow focus of bankers merely on what they could take as interest rather than on what their funding might create led American advocates of industrialization to oppose their activities outright, as they were more likely to be predators than helpers. The first major American economist, Daniel Raymond expressed his belief that

---

[14] Vol. I, Book II, ii

[15] David Beasley, *The Supppression of the Automobile: Skullduggery at the Crossroads* (New York, Greenwood Press, 1988).

[16] Georg Edwards, *The Evolution of Finance Capitalism* (London 1938):16f.

Every money corporation is prima facie injurious to national wealth, and ought to be looked upon by those who have no money with jealousy and suspicion. They are, and ought to be considered, as artificial engines of power, contrived by the rich for the purpose of increasing their already too great ascendancy and calculated to destroy that natural equality among men which God has ordained and which government has no right to lend its power in destroying. The tendency of such institutions is to cause a more unequal division of property and a greater inequality among men than would otherwise take place.[17]

The Canadian-American astronomer and monetary theorist Simon Newcomb observed that money in itself could not produce goods and services, but it was needed to employ labor and pay for needed economic inputs. In his *Critical Examination of our Financial Policy during the Southern Rebellion* (1865), he wrote: "The military power of a nation is measured by the amount of industry which it can divert into the channels of war," that is, by the size of its economic surplus in the form of military hardware and support of soldiers. "The question now is, Does money increase the amount of skill and labor which can be thus turned into the channels of war?" Newcomb's answer was no. However, the issue of fiat money could enable governments to pay for military service and technology, diverting output (and the labor to produce it) to government use by displacing civilian spending on food, clothing and other necessities.[18]

If money is debt, then it involves at least a contingent payment from debtors to creditors, starting with the debtor governments who issue money and bonds. Newcomb saw that the major problem caused by financing wars by bond issues rather than by levying taxes on a pay-as-you-go basis lay in the fiscal strains conveyed to posterity. A bond issue could not really transfer the war's cost onto future generations. That was just a figure of speech. In an analysis that might equally well be applied to today's Social Security debate, he explained:

> The generation that wages the war must be the one to shed its blood, feed its armies, and cast the shot and shell which its armies are to use. Food, clothing, shot and shell are the real expenses of war. In running to debt for these articles, we do indeed bequeath to posterity the work of raising the money to pay for them. But posterity not only raises the

---

[17] *Thoughts on Political Economy* (Baltimore 1820): 429.
[18] Simon Newcomb, *A Critical Examination of our Financial Policy during the Southern Rebellion* (New York 1865): 37–44. I summarize his ideas in *America's Protectionst Takeoff 1815–1914. The Neglected American School of Political Economy* (ISLET 2010): 215–225.

> money, but also receives the pay, so that we may as logically say that posterity gets paid for the war as to say that it pays for it.[19]

This observation contains the balance-sheet kernel of creditary economics: One party's savings represent another's debt, just as one party's tax payment ends up in the pockets of some beneficiary of government spending. This means that the consequences of any given public debt and tax policy depend on who owes whom. Newcomb accurately predicted that the policy of financing wars by loans would cause "an antagonism of interests between the East and the West" based on the fact that these geographic sections "may have entirely different pecuniary interests."[20] The Civil War led to taxes being collected from America's Western states to pay the Eastern bondholders who held some 80 percent of the war bonds. The West responded by advocating inflationary policies to relieve itself of the debt burden, not only of government bonds but of the mortgages entered into during the inflationary Civil War episode. And as Newcomb had forecast, the East sought deflationary monetary policies, much as today's U.S. creditors have done vis-à-vis third debtor countries obliged to pay their debts in the manner that the Western states had done after America's Civil War, by exporting raw-materials and—even more drastically—by selling off their raw materials patrimony and other natural endowments in what is, in essence, a forfeiture of these assets to global creditors.

Newcomb observed that as an alternative to taxation or issuing war bonds, the government paid for war material—and troops—by printing greenbacks.[21] These were essentially debt notes. Indeed, Newcomb observed that a public debt of any proportion could be discharged overnight simply by printing the words "legal-tender" on each bond and circulating the paper as money, although he disapproved of so drastic a policy.

Henry Carey, the most influential American economist of the day, argued against a speedy return to specie payments on the ground that this would entail monetary deflation that would injure the nation's industrialists, who tended to be net debtors. He found the major flaw in Newcomb's reasoning to lie in the assumption of what today is called the neutrality of money. If the backing of money was the government's ability to levy taxes and regulate the money supply—and hence the pace of inflation or deflation—then monetary analysis had to proceed beyond general price indices to analyze what Newcomb himself had begun to analyze: the problem of which classes and geographic sec-

---

[19] Newcomb, *ibid.*: 37–44. I summarize his ideas in *America's Protectionist Takeoff: 1815–1914* (ISLET 2010): 215–225.

[20] *Ibid.*: 66 ff.

[21] *Ibid.*: 114.

tions paid taxes, and who received their proceeds (that is, who the bondholders were). The policy conclusions for evaluating monetary deflation or inflation depended on the identity of the creditors and debtors in terms of their geographic and industrial profile.[22]

In the process of developing his monetary and public debt analysis, Newcomb developed a mathematical statement of the Quantity Theory of money. The basic set of relationships had been stated in plain English by Hume and his generation, but not in mathematical symbols, which our own epoch treats as the criterion for truly scientific formulation. This already had been done by Wilhelm Roscher in 1854, although in German, hardly a language recognized by Anglo-American historians of economic thought. What is especially noteworthy is that Newcomb was much more careful than subsequent theorists to specify how limited was the sphere of money being analyzed. Represented by the symbol V, standing for the Volume of money, it consisted only of "industrial circulation," which he defined as the market output of goods and services, excluding financial transactions. Newcomb was careful to explain that this monetary equation applied only when

> we exclude from the monetary flow all such transfers as loaning money, or depositing it in a bank, because these are not balanced by reverse transfers of wealth or services.[23]

Of course, such capital transactions represent the major demand for money in all modern economies. Each day the equivalent value of an entire year's national income or gross national product passes through the New York Clearing House and its counterparts in London, Paris, Frankfurt and Tokyo. These facts make the quantity theory not so relevant, as most money is spent on bonds, stocks, real estate and their interest and dividend payments, as well as for taxes and other public charges.

The value of national debt-money reflects the taxing power of governments and the currency's purchasing power over property, goods and services. What gives this money its value is the government's acceptance of it in payment of taxes and other public fees, not from its commodity backing in bullion.

---

[22] Newcomb discussed Carey's economic views in his review article on "Carey's Principles of Social Science," *North American Review* 103 (1866): 573–580.

[23] Newcomb, *Principles of Political Economy* (New York 1885): 347, 322, 339, 344, 390–94. His version of the modern quantity theory, $MV=PO$ (or PT) was $K \times P = V \times R$, where K represented the industrial circulation (the output of goods and services, today signified by O for output or T for transactions), P the price level, V the volume of money (M for money in today's formulation), and R the rapidity of circulation (today called V for velocity).

The combination of fiscal policy and bank regulation determines the volume of credit and how savings are recycled, overshadowing labor costs in determining international trade competition. Taxes, interest and rent are not "factor costs," for they are not paid to factors of production for direct inputs. They are rather in the character of overhead. As such, they are best thought of as transfer payments.

The Role of Financial Reform in the Economic Optimism of the Nineteenth Century

It was French and German theorists who pioneered the theory of credit that was needed to finance the Industrial Revolution. In France, the Saint-Simonians described the need to create an industrial credit system aimed at funding means of production rather than military destruction. In Germany, Bismarck's "state socialism" found its financial expression in the Reichsbank and other great industrial banks, whose long-term financing formed part of the "holy trinity" of banking, industry and government planning. The common denominator among the various new theorists was an emphasis on the institutional character of money, and on its dual balance-sheet character as an embodied debt as well as an asset to its holder.

There are two ways that a loan can be repaid. If its proceeds are invested to produce a profit, the lender can receive interest out of the venture's proceeds. Otherwise, the borrower must reduce his own consumption or sell off his assets to pay the debt charges. The great question confronting the heavy-industrial epoch on the eve of the 19th century and its Steam Revolution was whether the financial system would stifle or serve the spread of industrial technology and productivity.

The idealistic spirit of early industrial and banking reform shines through the 19th century. The Saint-Simonian reformers attracted supporters ranging from socialists to investment bankers, winning government backing for their policies under France's Third Empire. Outside of France, Saint-Simon's influence extended to socialists such as Karl Marx, John Stuart Mill and Christian Socialists in many countries, as well as industrialists in Germany and protectionists in the United States and England. The common denominator of this broad political spectrum was the recognition that an efficient banking system was needed to finance industrialization, on which a strong national state and military power depended. At issue was what kind of market the economy would have, for this would determine how it would use its resources and wealth, as mediated by the financial system.

Despite the fact that Britain was the home of the Industrial Revolution, it was French and Germans who moved banking theory into the industrial stage in their drive to help their nations catch up. It was their countries' relative backwardness that led their policy makers to step back and view matters from a broad perspective rather than merely continuing existing pre-industrial practices. By contrast, English and Dutch merchant banking had been so successful that these countries were easily able to maintain their established practices. Merchant bankers were experienced in lending against collateral and discounting sales orders, while the Bank of England's directors became adept at maintaining the value of sterling by raising interest rates to attract short-term funding when needed. But neither group had much to say about how to supply industrial credit.

By the 1820s, in the aftermath of the dislocations caused by resumption of normal trade relations after the Treaty of Ghent ended the Napoleonic Wars in 1815, it was becoming clear that banking and credit structures were determining which economies would end up in control of the Industrial Revolution's immense gains of productive powers and wealth. The French had a particular reason to focus on financial reform. They had lost their war with England largely through Napoleon's inability to master the techniques of transferring payments internationally to support French troops and allies. The nation's financial system had not evolved much since the pre-Revolutionary ancien regime. The ground for a sophisticated analysis had been prepared by Physiocracy under Francoise Quesnay and his *Tableau Economique*, a progenitor of national income accounting and planning. But what really was needed were actual banking institutions to extend long-term industrial credit to economies whose major financial activity hitherto had been usury and lending to the government. To modernize the nation's finances, the doctrines of Saint-Simon and his followers provided the guiding philosophy that found institutional expression in 1852 with the Crédit Mobilier.

Today's "free" market advocates are undiscriminating supporters of the financial sector's domination of the economy, without regard for how savings and credit are invested. Their "value free" economics claims that it would be wrong to define one way of making money as being better or more socially beneficial than any other way. Attempts to prevent investors from maximizing returns, regardless of how these are achieved, would make markets inefficient, they, so the ideal of "market socialism"—shaping or "tweaking" markets to behave in certain desired ways by subsidies and tax policy—is a chimera.

Today's orthodox canon repeats this mantra again and again, to the point where it has drowned out all discussion of how to distinguish between productive and unproductive forms of credit, investment and employment. Governments are told that they should not endorse any particular mode of recycling savings or extending credit as opposed to any other mode, but should let bankers and financiers make money wherever they find opportunities most remunerative.

Spreading this pro-creditor value-free doctrine via the world's finance ministries and central banks, Chicago School monetarists speak of free markets as liberating wealth from public regulation and oversight. Yet the 19th-century market reformers were quite different. To them, the aim of freer markets was to replace privilege with merit, and also to replace the debt burden by mobilizing money-capital to invest in upgrading industry, technology and what today is called human capital. The proper role of government was to coordinate productive bank lending while checking the tendency of "passive" wealth to take parasitic forms. This is why French socialists and early Marxists stood in the forefront of market reformers, although the "market" they had in mind was different from that endorsed today by market evangelists.

The Saint-Simonian movement illustrates how much more far-reaching the industrial reformismers sought to abolish economic inequities and market "imperfections" as compared to today's neoliberal market advocates. Like many well-born aristocrats throughout history, the Count Claude-Henri de Saint-Simon (1760–1825) came to attack inherited privilege as tending to turn wealth into a passive, parasitic rentier burden on society. Heirs sought to live in the easiest way, off rent and interest rather than actively investing their inheritance. Saint-Simon's 1819 satire *Parabole*, published when he was nearly sixty years old, depicted the governing classes living off their unearned inheritance rather than earning their fortunes through personal merit and ability.

Two years later he published *Du Système Industriel*. This attracted numerous followers, of whom the most effective were Prosper Enfantin (1796–1864) and Saint-Amand Bazard (1791–1832), who really created the Saint-Simonian school after their master's death in 1825. Their ideas were summarized in *Doctrine de Saint-Simon, Exposition, Premiere année (1828–29)*. Bazard was a follower of the politician-general Lafayette, under whom Saint-Simon had served in the American War of Independence.

The Saint-Simonians became the intellectual heirs of Lafayette's circle seeking to replace the pre-Revolution society based on status and privilege with one based on merit. "Almost every one who is well known of the generation which dates from 1830 belonged more or less to the school of Saint-Simon," observed Charles Gide in his biographical article on Saint-Simon for *Palgrave's Dictionary of Political Economy*. Saint-Simon's followers included the social theorist Auguste Comte, the economist Michel Chevalier, the socialist Pierre Leroux, the engineer Lesseps—whose plans for canals elaborated ideas initiated by Saint-Simon—and the brothers Emile and Isaac Pereire, who founded the Crédit Mobilier.

In a public letter to the Chamber of Deputies in 1830, Enfantin and Bazard summarized their doctrine that the economic system should reward merit rather than inherited privilege. "The followers of Saint-Simon believe in the natural inequality of men, and look on this inequality as the basis of association, as the indispensable condition of social order. All they desire is the abolition of every privilege of birth without exception, and as a consequence the destruction of the greatest of all these privileges, the power of bequest, the effect of which is to leave to chance the apportionment of social advantages, and to condemn the largest class in number to vice, ignorance, and poverty. They desire that all instruments of labour, land, and capital, which now form, subdivided, the inheritances of private owners, should be united in one social fund, and that this fund should be operated on principles of association and by a hierarchy, so that each one will have his task according to his capacity, and wealth according to his work."

It was in industry that talent was deemed best able to show its abilities. But talent needed money to back it, and this is where a reformed financial system was needed. Each city was to be headed by a mayor acting as *chef-industriel* (head of industry), in charge of who would receive what means of production and income. These industrial chiefs would be appointed by yet higher economic "priests," who would hold theocratic power over society. In this doctrine lay the seeds of a rather cultish socialism as well as centralized government *dirigisme*.

In any economy most wealth and assets are inherited, mainly in the form of real estate, bonds and stocks yielding rent, interest and dividends. Saint-Simonian reformers claimed that these tributary claims on society's income and output did not perform an active, productive function. They were a form of overhead, a legacy of the dead hand of the past stemming from the Norman military conquest of France in feudal times, the hereditary nobility that the French Revolution had overthrown politically, but not yet economically. It would be the task of 19th-century doctrines of social progress, capped by the social welfare legislation that coped with the Great Depression in the 1930s, to tax such wealth and use the proceeds for public purposes.

It would seem at first glance that this desire to replace inherited wealth and position with a meritocracy would be shared by today's market reformers, yet they have not pressed their reforms in this direction. Just the opposite. At their urging, taxes have been reduced since 1980 (and indeed, since World War II), above all on real estate and finance capital. (Outright abolition of the wealth tax was a central plank in the Republican 2000 U.S. presidential election campaign.) As seen from a 19th-century perspective, today's "trickle-down" mode of progress and reform (one hesitates to call it modern) would be deemed anti-

progressive by un-taxing inherited wealth, landed property and other sources
of unearned income.

Early advocates of industrialization sought to bring governments out of
the feudal era by shifting their role from that of supporting an idle aristocracy
to coordinating reforms in the ways society employed and accumulated wealth.
In this respect today's canon of orthodoxy has inverted the "original" free
market canon by advocating the downsizing of government by cutting taxes,
above all those which fall on wealth (such as the estate tax) and on the financial sector rather than on labor.

Most important, today's postindustrial orthodoxy sees little value in upgrading manufacturing. What it welcomes as a "new" era — the "service economy" — is beginning to look like a relapse into real estate concentration in the
context of a growing debt overhead, vesting new hereditary interests as wealth
is concentrated in the hands of financial families and institutions. Appropriation of property, or, at least its income, by means of loans and credit has
replaced the feudal epoch's "primitive accumulation" by military seizure. This
is the opposite of what 19th-century industrial optimists hoped to bring about.

The financial innovations advocated by the Saint-Simonians were more
far-reaching than the principles advocated by today's market reformers. Paramount among their financial reforms was the desire to ensure that lending
would be productive, not usurious as in past epochs. They criticized existing
patterns of lending and financial investment for indebting the rest of society
without putting in place new means of production to enable this debt to be
paid off. To rectify matters the Saint-Simonians urged that government coordinate industrial planning.

Every economy is planned by someone or other. The question is who is to
do the planning? Today's world is run by financial planners working for investment banks, commercial banks and institutional investors, with macroeconomic policy handled by central banks and Treasury Departments,over whose
appointees Wall Street and other financial centers wield veto power. The chief
executive officers of major corporations are concerned mainly with financial
strategy, not industrial engineering, labor relations or sales. So running a corporation has become essentially a financial task. The objective is to raise the
company's stock price by such strategies as using earnings to buy one's own
equity, planning corporate takeovers and raids ("mergers and acquisitions"),
arranging debt pyramiding with creditors, and orchestrating intra-conglom-
erate pricing on a global scale so as to take profits in international tax havens.
Such planning in today's environment is more likely to downsize operations
and scale back research and development than to expand production and
employment.

These financial objectives are not what optimists had in mind, in an epoch when the Industrial Revolution still seemed to hold enough promise to attract idealists to analyze its potential. Saint-Simon, early socialists and the large German banks that flowered in the Bismarck era held that finance was needed to play a central role by funding technological innovation. The essence of the state-sponsored planning they endorsed was that its time frame was long-term. By contrast, the short run effectively has become the long term for today's market fundamentalists. Research and development are downsized so as to leave more income to pay dividends and interest, while the debt burden is made heavier by deflationary pro-creditor policies that keep economic expansion on a short-term leash.

The Saint-Simonians saw the Industrial Revolution as introducing a new type of "economic man" in the form of the industrial capitalist ("*travailleur*"). In contrast to the Schumpeterian entrepreneur, he was more in the character of a financial engineer seeing where credit could best be applied. He alsowas more than just the "projector" of John Law's day, in seeing the field of credit as being direct industrial investment, not merely speculative or mercantile gains. But it was bankers who were glorified above all as the future organizers and promoters of industrialism. According to the compilation *Religion saint-simonienne, Economie politique et Politique* (Paris: 1831: 98), "the banks perform the role of capitalists in their transactions with those travailleurs, to whom they loan money," enabling these "industrious people" to obtain financing for their enterprise (*ibid.*: 45; significantly, Marx quotes these passages in Capital III: 714). Charles Pecqueur's *Theorie Nouvelle d'Economie Sociale et Politique* (Paris 1842: 434) urged that production be ruled by what the Saint-Simonians called the *Systeme general des banques*.

It was left to Emile Pereire (1800–1875) to begin putting such a system in place. A leading Saint-Simonian in the 1830s, he built France's first railway line (running from Paris to St. Germain), and later developed other routes. He contributed a number of essays to the Saint-Simonian *Revue Encyclopedique*, collected in his 1832 *Considérations sur les Finances de la France et des États Unis*. In 1852 he formed the Société Génerale du Crédit Mobilier as a joint-stock bank with his younger brother Isaac (1806–1880), who explained the institution's financial philosophy in *Le Rôle de la Banque de France et l'Organisation du Crédit en France* (1864) and *La Politique Financière* (1879). Their guiding principle was to supplant the usurers of past epochs by providing low-cost long-term credit that would enable industrialists to buy machinery and expand production. In particular they sought to replace the banking families who hitherto had monopolized French finance.

In discussing the pro-finance view's pedigree it would not be fair to neglect its early blind spots. The major problem with any attempt to shape markets from above is insider dealing. All successful economies are "mixed economies," with public oversight and market incentives co-existing. Without proper checks and balances one gets "crony capitalism" or its Soviet-style bureaucratic coun- terparts. Nowhere is this need for mutual checks and balances more clear than in the fate of Crédit Mobilier, whose close connections with the government of Napoleon III prompted it to indulge in fatal speculation that drove it bank- rupt in 1867, and into liquidation in 1871.

The reasons for the bank's failure are instructive of the inherent tension between the two financial philosophies discussed in this paper. Rather than extend loans directly to its customers, the Crédit Mobilier invested in stocks and bonds issued by these companies. "The institution was in effect a gigantic holding company engaged in financing and managing industrial enterprises," notes one financial historian.[24] "The securities of the controlled companies were used as assets on which the Crédit Mobilier issued its own securities, to be sold to the public. For a number of years the Bank was highly successful, and performed notable service in promoting railroads and public utilities." It had close relations with Louis Napoleon as Emperor.

Its underlying logic was to provide long-term equity capital and bond financing rather than short-term debt. The idea was that external financing would give industry freedom from the short-term constraints imposed by con- servative banking practice in the past. But this freer supply of credit proved to be the bank's undoing, precisely because equity is more responsive to the debtor's earning power than is a straight debt, whose interest and amortization payments are fixed. When business conditions turned down under the Crédit Mobilier's arrangements, it suffered as creditor along with its debtors. The ide- alism of this harmony of interests was intended to keep the debt burden in check. But it led to the bank's collapse, as it could not in turn make its depos- itors or creditors share in its own losses. This was especially the case as the Crédit Mobilier became essentially a pyramid scheme, borrowing at a low rate of interest and investing in securities whose returns were expected to be higher. When the economy was thriving, this worked, but over the course of every business upswing a time comes when this is no longer the case. In France, this happened in 1866.

Subsequent financial scandals plagued the large international capital invest- ments of the nineteenth century, headed by the Suez and Panama Canals (both of which had been early Saint-Simonian projects), America's railway land give-

---

[24] George W. Edwards, *The Evolution of Finance Capitalism* (1938): 51.

aways to the robber barons, and their subsequent stock and bond waterings that gave high finance a bad name generally. The moral is that as aggregations of finance capital and the ability to extend credit grow larger, more concentrated and more closely linked to government and favored industrial customers, the banking system tends to become parasitic and even corrupt.

If the bank managers do not succumb to such temptations from inside the system, parasites attack from outside. So large a supply of institutional savings was mounting up in America in the 1980s that Drexel Burnham's crew of corporate raiders seemed a godsend when they began to issue high-interest junk bonds to finance their clients' corporate raids and takeovers. When the dust settled, this exercise had left debt-burdened and even bankrupt companies in their wake, bankrupted much of the Savings and Loan Industry and the Federal S&L Deposit Insurance Corporation (FSLIC) at a cost of some $300 billion. Simultaneously in Japan, "convoy banking" provided another example of insider dealing to finance a real estate bubble. An unparalleled share of bank loans went to speculators, schemers and criminals. The bursting of the Asian Bubble in 1998 revealed financial systems were lacking proper checks and balances — and lacking a better alternative use of savings.

Today's market orthodoxy has inverted the 18th- and 19th-century reformers' spirit, by endorsing financial gain-seeking indiscriminately, even when credit is channeled into parasitic rather than productive lines. No doubt a 19th-century industrial optimist would be surprised at the extent to which the objective of today's financial institutions is not to fund industry, but to load it down with debt; not to finance public investment, but to dismantle and privatize it. These distortions in today's monetarist policies have stripped away the dimension of moral authority with which the Saint-Simonians, socialists, German bank theorists and other advocates of industrial progress sought to achieve, in contrast to what to today has become the mainstream.

Marx's Optimistic Views on Industrial Finance Capitalism

Engels attributed Marx's hopes with regard to the prospects of industrial banking to the ideas of Saint-Simon adding that Marx spoke "only with admiration" of his "genius and encyclopedic brain."[25] Marx believed that Saint-Simonians such as Charles Fourier and Auguste Comte were being romantically utopian in their hope to reconcile capital and labor rather than basing their system on the class conflict. This political disagreement led him to speak sarcastically of Saint-Simon's "world-redeeming credit-phantasies,"

---

[25] *Capital*, vol. III (Chicago 1909): 710, fn 116.

yet he in fact shared Saint-Simon's financial optimism. This optimism is revealed most explicitly in his assertion that the banking and credit system "signifies no more and no less than the subordination of interest-bearing capital to the conditions and requirements of the capitalist mode of production."[26]

In describing the virtue of credit as being to free society from the need to rely on usurers' hoards, Marx expressed the leading principle of nineteenth-century industrial bank reform. What made industrial bank credit different "from usurer's capital" was "the totally changed character of the borrower ... He receives credit in his capacity as a potential capitalist."

Marx believed that banking institutions would take their shape from the mode of production. Industrial capitalism's irresistible dynamic material force would transform lending practices so as to finance production on an expanding scale, thereby going far beyond the old-fashioned usury and even beyond the Anglo-American merchant-banking philosophy. In his 1861–63 drafts for what would become the later volumes of *Capital*, Marx called the banking system "the most artificial and the most developed product turned out by the capitalist mode of production."[27] And in his statement that, "On the whole, interest-bearing capital under the modern credit-system is adapted to the conditions of the capitalist mode of production," he seemed to be describing something that already had become a *fait accompli*. The parasitic usury of former epochs was being transformed into productive lending to finance the expansion of industry.

In this belief, to be sure, Marx stated criteria for the characteristics of a productive financial system with remarkable clarity for his time. His analysis shows that already in his day the anti-inflationary obsession of monetarist politics had become apparent. Instead of promoting the thriving market needed to expand industrial capital investment, he warned, creditors demanded legislative policies to protect the economic value of their loans by imposing a deflationary austerity. If successful, he warned, this policy would stifle industrial capital's need for expanding markets. "The value of commodities is therefore sacrificed, for the purpose of safeguarding the phantastic and independent existence of this value in money," he wrote in a passage that anticipated the arguments of Keynes in the 1930s. "As money-value it is secured only so long as money itself is secure. For the sake of a few millions of money many millions of commodities must therefore be sacrificed,"[28] along with employment and investment.

It should be noted that when Marx drafted his financial ideas, German banking had not yet really taken off. The raw material he had at hand was primarily the Saint-Simonian theorizing in France, and British banking practice.

---

[26] *Ibid.*: 704 f.
[27] *Capital*, vol. III: 712)

Financial distortions such as stock waterings and overcapitalization as a general policy by financial robber barons lay in the future. Marx thus focused on what he hoped would become a logical industrial banking policy. Subsequent Marxists, of course, wrote in an epoch in which finance capitalism was taking on a life of its own, increasingly parasitic on the industrial core. But in the 1860s it appeared that industry would shape financial evolution, not the other way around.

Yet Marx also recognized that usury existed as an ancient practice independent of the mode of production, and growing by its own dynamics of compound interest. Usurer's capital "does not confront the laborer as industrial capital," but "merely impoverishes this mode of production, paralyzes the productive forces instead of developing them," and prevents the social productivity of labor from developing. "Usury centralises money wealth … It does not alter the mode of production, but attaches itself as a parasite and makes it miserable. It sucks its blood, kills its nerve, and compels reproduction to proceed under even more disheartening conditions."[29] But usury did not change the mode of production; it merely transferred the ownership of assets over to usurers, making life harder for the laborer.

Nonetheless, Marx believed that any conflict of interest between financial and industrial capital would be settled in favor of the latter. "This violent fight against usury, this demand for the subordination of the interest-bearing under the industrial capital," he elaborated,

> is but the herald of the organic creations that establish these prerequisites of capitalist production in the modern banking system, which on the one hand robs usurer's capital of its monopoly by concentrating all fallow money reserves and throwing them on the money-market, and on the other hand limits the monopoly of the precious metals themselves by creating credit-money.[30]

Marx acknowledged the old reliance on usurers for credit would survive for "such persons or classes … as do not borrow in the sense corresponding to the capitalist mode of production."[31] But the great financial achievement of industrial capitalism was (or would be) to create a superior outlet for lending at interest than the consumer usury and war lending that characterized pre-industrial banking. Productive lending would provide credit on the basis of evaluating the borrower's ability to repay the creditors by investing the proceeds productively, not merely to pledge (and in due course, forfeit) the

---

28 *Ibid.*: 607.
29 *Ibid.*: 699 f.
30 *Ibid.*: 707.
31 *Ibid.*: 704 f..

collateral. The credit system, properly institutionalized, thus truly would become society's means of planning the future.

To be sure, it would have to be a future whose economic growth would be able to keep up with the compound interest rate, as banks would keep on reinvesting their loan repayment proceeds in new lending to bring more and more capital into being. That was the essence of industrial capitalism's expansive force, and Marx believed that its surplus-producing powers would be up to the task. The "hard-money" system that represented the legacy of usury-capital — a system essentially synonymous with today's monetarism — no longer would be able to block society from achieving its technological potential once banking system came into being. Industrial capitalism would catalyze an industrial banking system to provide itself with productive, low-interest credit.

Germany's Linkage between Banking, Heavy Industry and Government under Bismarck

Nearly all historically minded economists shared this optimistic view of finance capital's subordinate role. The German Historical School pointed to the fact that interest rates tended to fall steadily with the progress of civilization; at least, rates had been falling since medieval times. Credit laws were becoming more humanitarian, and the debtors prisons described so graphically by Charles Dickens were being phased out throughout Europe, while more lenient bankruptcy laws were freeing individuals to start afresh with clean slates. Public debts in Europe and North America were on their way to being paid off during the remarkable war-free century 1815–1914. Savers and investors were seeking out heavy transport, industry, mining and real estate to fund, mainly through the bond market. The consensus among economists was that the debt burden would be self-amortizing. Debt problems were curing themselves, by being co-opted into a socially productive credit system.

Industrial banking policies reached their highest expression in Germany, where the Reichsbank and large private banks developed close linkages with the government and heavy industry. Developing cross-holdings in the stocks of their major customers, these banks undertook much of the planning needed to guide long-term strategic development. The ensuing debate concerned how governments could best use financial policy to promote industrialization.

Although Britain had taken the lead in the Industrial Revolution, banking had played little role in funding it. British and Dutch merchant banking extended short-term loans on the basis of collateral such as bills for merchandise shipped ("receivables") and inventories, but did not undertake much long-term lending to finance investment in factories or other direct investment. As noted above, James Watt and other innovators were obliged to raise investment money from their families and friends rather than from banks.

Even today most corporate direct investment is financed out of internally generated earnings, not bank loans. Apart from mortgage lending and auto financing, most bank credit is short-term. As matters have turned out, emperors of finance subdued captains of industry. What is striking is how unlikely the prospect of a corrosive and unproductive debt overhead appeared a century ago.

Germany's banking philosophy followed largely from the country's relative poverty and backwardness as compared to England. Whereas British banks continued to focus on mercantile financing rather than industrial financing, German banks played a leading role in planning their economy's industrialization. The British economy had grown so large and specialized that its banks performed specialized functions. But the German banks from the outset engaged in a broad range of activities ("mixed banking"). Edwards observes that they

> stressed investment operations and were formed not so much for receiving deposits and granting loans but rather for supplying the investment requirements of industry. The main reason for the development of mixed banking was the lack of capital which forced industry to turn to the banks for assistance.[32]

The basic profile of Germany's supply and demand for funds was unique for the time. "A considerable proportion of the funds of the German banks came not from the deposits of customers but from the capital subscribed by the proprietors themselves. In this respect the German banks differed from the British banks which derived the greater part of their funds from the depositors." This feature prompted German banks to resist the excesses found in American finance of the period, as they only emitted bonds and stocks "to the actual cash value of the property of the corporation being financed."

U.S. financial manipulators, by contrast, engaged in "stock waterings" that "overfunded" companies by bond issues and borrowings far beyond their needs or capacity to carry. The difference was pocketed by the directors of these corporations—a practice that led much American industry to stay clear of banking and financiers out of self-protection. It was this practice that led Marx to criticize the idea that this problem was inherently economic rather than one of personal abuse and the absence of proper checks and balances.

> Those who say that there is merely a lack of means of payment, have either the owners of bona fide securities alone in view, or they are fools

---

[32] Edwards, *op. cit.*: 68.

who believe that it is the duty and power of banks to transform all bankrupt swindlers into solvent and solid capitalists by means of pieces of
paper.[33]

German practice steered remarkably clear of this problem. And in Austria,
the Credit Anstalt für Handel und Gewerbe became a much more successful
"step-daughter" of France's Credit Mobilier than the parent had been. In
France, however, economic policy had changed sharply after the Franco-
Prussian War (1871). An anti-Semitic reaction arose to the Jewish banking
families that had dominated French finance, and in 1878 royalist leaders
founded the Union Generale to "Christianize" banking.

> The Bank organized a group of business enterprises, and used the
> simple financial device of applying its funds to purchase its own stock
> and that of its controlled companies. The consequent rise in the price
> of these securities then enabled the Bank to increase the capitalization
> of its companies, and the new funds were again used to purchase the
> outstanding securities.[34]

This increased the Bank's shares from 1,000 in 1881 to over 3,000 in 1882, but
they then collapsed to 450 in just a few weeks. But the idea of financial
manipulation for its own sake, decoupled from tangible wealth creation, had
been established in principle and carries on until this day. It was a principle
against which advocates of the Other Financial Canon would warn repeatedly
in decades to come.

When war broke out in 1914, Germany's rapid victories over France and
Belgium seemed to reflect the superior efficiency of its financial system. To
some observers the Great War appeared as a struggle between rival forms of
financial organization to decide not only who would rule Europe, but also
whether the continent would have laissez faire or a more state socialist economic system. In 1915, shortly after fighting broke out, the German Christian
Socialist priest-politician Friedrich Naumann summarized the continental
banking philosophy in Mitteleuropa. In England, Prof. H. S. Foxwell drew on
Naumann's arguments in two essays entitled "The Nature of the Industrial
Struggle," and "The Financing of Industry and Trade."[35]

Foxwell quoted with approval Naumann's contention that the old individualistic capitalism, of what he calls the English type, is giving way to the new,
more impersonal, group form; to the discipline, scientific capitalism he claims
as German.

---

[33] *Capital* III: 606.
[34] Edwards 1938: 85.
[35] *Economic Journal* 27 (September and December 1917), pp. 323–27 and 502–15.

This conclusion followed from Naumann's claim that: "Into everything today there enters less of the lucky spirit of discovery than of patient, educated industry. To put it otherwise, we believe in combined work." Germany recognized more than any other nation that industrial technology needed long-term financing and government support. In the emerging tripartite integration of industry, banking and government, Foxwell concluded, financing was "undoubtedly the main cause of the success of modern German enterprise."[36] The nation's bank staffs already included industrial experts who were forging industrial policy into a science. Bankers and government planners were becoming engineers under the new industrial philosophy of how governments should shape credit markets. In America, Thorstein Veblen voiced much the same theory in *The Engineers and the Price System*.

The political connections of German bankers gave them a voice in formulating international diplomacy, making "mixed banking ... the principal instrument in the extension of her foreign trade and political power." But rather than recognizing the natural confluence of high finance, heavy industry and interventionist government policy, English common law opposed monopolies and other forms of combination as constituting restraints on trade, while Britain's medieval guilds had evolved into labor unions that had embarked on a class war against industrial employers. Germany's historical form of organization was the professional guild developed at the hands of masters, leading to industrial cartels.

Foxwell's articles implied a strategy of capital working with governments to undertake military and diplomatic initiatives promoting commercial expansion. The economic struggle for existence favored growing industrial and financial scale, increasingly associated with government support. The proper task of national banking systems was to finance this symbiosis, for the laws of economic history were leading toward political centralization, national planning and the large-scale financing of heavy industry.

The short-term outlook of English merchant bankers ill suited them for this task. They based their loan decisions on what they could liquidate in the event of loan default, not on the new production and income their lending might create over the longer run. Instead of taking risks, they extended credit mainly against collateral available for seizure: inventories of unsold goods, money due on bills for goods sold to customers but not yet paid for, and real estate.

British bankers paid out most of their earnings as dividends rather than investing in the shares of the companies that their loans supposedly were building up. This short time horizon forced borrowers to remain liquid rather than giving them the leeway to pursue long-term strategies. Foxwell warned

---

[36] *Ibid.*: 514.

that British manufacturers of steel, automotives, capital equipment and other heavy industry were becoming obsolescent largely because the nation's bankers failed to perceive the need to extend long-term credit and promote equity investment to expand industrial production. By contrast, German banks paid out dividends (and expected such dividends from their clients) at only half the rate of British banks, choosing to retain earnings as capital reserves and invest them largely in the stocks of their industrial clients. Viewing these companies as allies rather than merely as customers from whom to make as large a profit as quickly as possible, German bank officials sat on their boards and extended loans to foreign governments on condition that these clients be named the chief suppliers in major public investments.

To sum up, although Britain was the home of the Industrial Revolution, little manufacturing had beenwas financed by bank credit in its early stages. Most industrial innovators were obliged to raise money privately. Britain took an early lead in stock market promotion by forming Crown corporations such as the East India Company, the Bank of England and the South Sea Company. And despite the collapse of the South Sea Bubble in 1720, the run-up of share prices in these monopolies from 1715 to 1720 established London's stock market as a popular investment vehicle for the Dutch and other foreigners as well as for British investors. But industrial firms were not major stock issuers. The stock market was dominated by railroads, canals and large public utilities.

Britain's stockbrokers were no more up to the task of financing industrial innovation than were its banks, having an equally short-term frame of reference. After earning their commissions on one issue, they moved on to the next without much concern for what happened to the investors who had bought the earlier securities. "As soon as he has contrived to get his issue quoted at a premium and his underwriters have unloaded at a profit," complained Foxwell, "his enterprise ceases. 'To him,' as the *Times* says, 'a successful flotation is of more importance than a sound venture.'"[37]

Much the same was true in the United States. Rejecting the methodical German approach, the Anglo-American spirit found its epitome in Thomas Edison, whose method of invention was hit-and-miss, coupled with a high degree of litigousness to obtain patent and monopoly rights. America's merchant heroes were individualistic traders and political insiders who often operated on the edge of society's laws to gain their fortunes by stock-market manipulation, railroad politicking for land giveaways, and insurance companies, mining and natural resource extraction.

---

[37] *Ibid*: 502.

Neither British nor American banks were technological planners for the future. Their job was to maximize their own short-run advantage, not to create a better and more productive society. Most banks favored large real estate borrowers, along with railroads and public utilities whose income streams easily could be forecast. Manufacturing only obtained significant bank and stock market credit once companies had grown fairly large. By the 1920s Britain's joint-stock banks were broadly criticized for their failure to finance domestic industry, and for favoring international clients rather than domestic ones.[38]

The Symbiosis between the Financial, Insurance and Real Estate (FIRE) Sectors

As the Industrial Revolution gained momentum, economists anticipated that banking and finance would be absorbed into the industrial system. The attention of economic theorists still remains focused on industrial technology and innovation, and the population shift from agriculture to urban industry. Textbooks (and lobbying exercises) depict bankers as extending credit to enable industrialists to build new factories and employ workers to produce more goods. Loans do not become problematic, but can be paid out of profits generated by the capital investment they finance. This appealing story is used to plead for special tax treatment for financial institutions on the ground that their credit creation adds to economic welfare. Interest is deemed as tax-exempt expenditure, even when corporate raiders use predatory credit.

Yet the symbiosis that has emerged over the past century has been primarily between the financial, insurance and real estate sectors. The great bulk of assets in modern economies — and hence, collateral for bank loans — has been real estate. Some 70 percent of commercial bank lending in the United States and England takes the form of mortgage credit. The estimated market value of real estate exceeds the depreciated value of all the plant and equipment in the entire United States. Loan officers know that the bulk of growth in their bank's loan portfolio will consist of mortgage loans. The more rapidly such credit is created, the more funds are channeled into new mortgage financing to bid up the price of real property, making such lending appear self-justifying, at least in the short and intermediate run.

---

[38] Lloyd George called them "the stronghold of reaction." See Thomas Johnston, *The Financiers and the Nation* (London 1934: 138). Ernest Bevin, G. D. H. Cole and other members of the British Labour Party criticized banks in *The Crisis* (London 1931). See also G. D. H. Cole, *The Socialisation of Banking* (London 1931), and John Wilmot, *Labour's Way to Control Banking and Finance* (London 1935). The Labour Party's proposed solution was to nationalize the Bank of England, and in 1933 recommended the socialization of the joint-stock banks as well. Keynes was sympathetic in his article on "A New Economic Policy for England," *Economic Forum*, Winter 1932–33: 29–37.

Of the properties financed, land (the value of the site) typically represents about half the total, and all of the capital gain when the property is sold. And the great bulk of depreciation (capital consumption allowances) is reported in the real estate sector. This is because when an industrial machine wears out, it usually must be scrapped in order to keep up with the pace of technological advance. But buildings can be depreciated over and over again, thereby shielding their owners from income-tax liability (especially inasmuch as their interest charges are tax deductible). The upshot is that the tax system (especially in the United States) is much more favorable to real estate than to industry. It is easier to borrow against real property, and the total returns (after-tax earnings plus capital gains) are higher.

The financial industry has fought to support special tax breaks for real estate, recognizing that the money that is freed from the tax collector will be available to pay interest. Political contributions and lobbying efforts by real estate owners are followed by those of the financial sector, overshadowing those of manufacturing. Yet in lobbying for cuts in capital gains taxes, both the real estate and financial industries (backed by the insurance industry) present these gains as accruing to industry as a result of innovation, as if this typified modern capitalism. The reality is that most capital gains continue to accrue to real estate. It is only since about 1996 that, for the first time, stock-market gains are beginning to overshadow the growth in real estate gains in the U.S. national balance sheet. The effect is equally corrosive and the reasons for this development are set out in chapter 8 below.

Why don't economists call a spade a spade and come right out and start their analytic description of modern economies with a profile of where most wealth is accumulated, and the fact that it consists more of land-price gains than growth in manufacturing enterprise? The explanation is to be found in the fact that real estate is by no means as romantic as industry. Most people admire innovators and creators, but resent landlords—and usually also bankers and insurance companies as well, for being more parasitic than creative. There is a general awareness of the obvious fact that the growth in mortgage lending does not add to the supply of land, whose site value is created by public infrastructure investment and the general level of prosperity. In any case, the great bulk of property loans are for land and buildings already in place. The growth of real estate lending thus provides borrowers with credit to compete against each other to buy as many properties as they can, bidding up land prices in the process. The upshot is a bubble, not an industrial boom.

Financial spokesmen argue that this kind of asset-based lending is , inasmuch as it provides real estate owners with properties that enable them to pay the interest charges and still (they hope) come out with a capital gain in the end.

To help spur this large credit market, the financial lobby has joined hands with the real estate lobby in the United States to gain special tax breaks for real estate.

Bankers know that whatever the tax collector does not take will be left available to pay interest to lenders. Developers bid against each other with regard to the size of the mortgage they will pay the lender, and hence the volume of mortgage debt service they will pay their banker out of rent. This bidding normally continues up to the point where all the available net rental income over costs is paid in the form of interest.

Mortgage lending commonly provides from 80 to 100 percent of the property's purchase price (or even more as seen in the bubble Economy's years leading up to the September 2008 crash). This is a highly leveraged rate — it has a high debt/equity ratio. This kind of mortgage debt pyramiding provided the model for junk-bond financing used by corporate raiders in the 1980s, and for the flood of public assets being privatized in Britain, continental Europe and Third World countries. The distinguishing feature of such purchases of real estate, corporations or public entities already in place is that new loans are attached without creating new tangible investment. Instead of new tangible capital formation there is more typically a downsizing and carve-up as revenue is used to pay interest and amortization up to the maximum extent available over and above operating costs.

The fact is "post-industrial" practice made this dynamic quite different from that which optimists envisioned at the outset of the Industrial Revolution. Instead of mobilizing savings to fund new means of production, today's banking system merely is loading the economy's assets down with debt. What seems to be occurring is functionally akin to the pre-industrial mode of lending. The difference is that pre-industrial usury was dominated by individual family lenders, but the new post-industrial debt system is occurring on a large, corporate scale. It has merged with industry primarily to the extent that the financial sector has gained control of the economy's manufacturing companies, treating them like real estate to squeeze out as large a rentier income as possible and then sell the companies off for a capital gain.

Asset-Price Inflation, Financial Bubbles and the Blind Spots of Monetarist Orthodoxy

In his preliminary discussion of the quantity theory of money, Simon Newcomb pointed out that most money in modern economies is spent on assets, not goods and services. Yet monetarism looks only at the linkage between money and commodity prices and wage rates, leaving asset prices out of account. The only linkage appears to occur in the impact of monetary tightness on interest rates: Higher (or lower) rates reduce (or raise) the value of bonds, stocks and real estate.

Today's orthodoxy has so expurgated the analysis of capital asset-price gains that one looks in vain through today's economic statistics for a meaningful time series of the economy's largest category of assets: real estate, of which the largest component is the land or site value. In the United States, the balance sheets published by the Federal Reserve System are the result of political lobbying that vastly undervalues land. The reason presumably is because land-price ("capital") gains represent a "free ride" that is difficult to justify in terms of the personal enterprise and innovation that underlies most textbook model-building. An illusion is created that assets are the result of manmade invest-ment, not provided freely by nature and imbued with value by society at large.

This distorted view has not helped economics become more empirically grounded. Rather, it has driven it to favor expository forms that use higher math without reference to actual statistics. This absence of an empirical check increases the likelihood of losing sight of the reality one is supposed to be describing. But of course, if the aim of economic theory is to lobby for partic-ular interests as opposed to those of the economy at large, reality is not exactly the prime desideratum in the first place.

Analyzing the genealogy of financial bubbles thus has been left mainly to socialist, protectionist and other proponents of subordinating banking systems to finance tangible capital formation. Rather than viewing business cycles as occurring smoothly as a result of the automatic stabilizers postulated by the orthodox theory of Wesley Mitchell and the National Bureau of Economic Research, Hyman Minsky traces how productive lending at the start of the upswing gives way to bank loans that become increasingly risky. The final phase is "Ponzi" lending, in which the bank loan cannot be paid out of oper-ating revenue, but is borrowed from the bank. In effect, the interest falling due is simply added on to the loan balance, presumably to be paid out of the cap-ital gain that the borrower may (or may not) reap. This approach recognizes that today's wealth-seeking has come to focus on capital gains, not profits. In-deed, the real estate industry has not reported profits to the income-tax collector since World War II. Savings and credit are not being invested in new tangible capital formation, but are channeled to increase prices for assets in place.

Monetary pro-finance theory depicts interest charges as being paid out of profits (real estate rental cash flow. But for sectors seeking "total returns" mainly in the form of asset-price gains, the only way to keep the volume of bank loans solvent is for the financial bubble to keep on expanding. Under Ponzi-phase lending, the debtor is obliged to pay interest by selling (or at worst, forfeiting) the asset to pay off the loan, or must obtain the money elsewhere. Such sales end the run-up in property values, threatening to bring the system crashing down as a price-ratchet downward places the system in jeopardy—and with it, the economy's volume of savings that have been recycled into such loans. Their market value falls below the level needed to cover existing savings deposits. This is what happened with the U.S. S&L crisis in the late 1980s. Bailing out the savers obliges the government either to increase its borrowing, or to raise taxes on non-savers (mainly labor).

The Japanese economy entered this phase in 1990 with the bursting of its real estate and stock market bubble. In view of the similarity between bubble economies operating in the Ponzi phase, it is reasonable to ask whether Japan may represent the economic future of today's highly indebted economies in Europe and North America. To answer this question, it is necessary to measure debt-servicing capacity, and also the way in which new bank credit increases asset prices.

This is a line of investigation to which monetarist orthodoxy has paid little attention. It averts its eyes from the structural problems to which economies succomb as a result of foreign and domestic debt, and the shift of credit from productive to unproductive lending (including speculative loans extended in the hope that capital gains will continue to accrue to rescue borrowers and lenders alike). In past decades such crises were treated as anomalous; only the upswing was the norm. But today the entire world seems to be moving simultaneously into a debt-burdened state.

This may leave the monetarist orthodoxy irrelevant, as its advocates deny in principle that chronic and structural financial malstructuring may occur. Yet today's financial engineering (or what the Japanese called *zaitech*) is a form of malstructuring to the extent that it severs the banking and credit system from tangible capital formation.

By 2000, the U.S. and other leading economies have entered a Ponzi stage that has lasted remarkably long. Market prices for stocks, bonds and real estate have soared even as real wages have drifted downward and the economy's largest firms have downsized their U.S. operations. In past business cycles, wages have recovered and consumer prices have risen. But today's price gains have been contained almost entirely within the economy's asset markets. This has caused an economic polarization between wealth-holders and income earners that is almost unprecedented in modern times. It is becoming the distinguishing feature of what is being welcomed as a new post-industrial economy. Yet this economy finds remarkably little recognition in orthodox monetarist analysis.

The Role of Monetarist Doctrine in the Privatization of Public Infrastructure

A dam Smith criticized the royalist governments of his day for indulging in
vainglorious territorial wars that burdened the economy with debt. He
just as harshly criticized governments for financing these debts by creating and
selling off ("privatizing") monopoly privileges. The East India Company and
other Crown corporations burdened consumers by charging extortionate
prices. Seeking profits in this way (in what today would be called a zero-sum
game) weighed down the nation's cost structure.

The sanctioning of such public monopolies was hardly an example of industrial planning. It stemmed from Britain's need to dispose of the enormous debts
run up in the course of its almost constant wars with France in Europe, North
America and India. These wars were seen to be economically corrosive not
only as a result of the direct costs in terms of manpower and material, but
also the postwar legacy of public debts that loaded down the economy with
taxes to carry their interest charges. Britain's policy of exchanging these bonds
by creating monopoly privileges—which were sold off for payment in the form
of these war bonds—creating vested mercantile interests at odds with the rest
of the economy and its industrial competitiveness. This was the essence of
Smith's opposition to mercantilism. He was so pessimistic as to the ability and
willingness of governments to act positively that he denounced the most industrially minded political economists as well, focussing more on tax policy.

Two centuries ago "the funding system" was held widely to be the hand-
maiden of belligerent policies. Adam Smith pointed out that populations
would balk if they were taxed to finance wars on a pay-as-you-go basis, but
were less sensitive to the costs of war when governments resorted to borrowing.
This perception led him to oppose public debts, as one of the surest financial
and fiscal reforms to promote peace.

Industrial banking theory and Modern Monetary Theory (MMT) likewise
seek to free labor and capital from the burden of public debt and the taxes
levied to carry it. Toward this end, a fiscal dimension of financial reform has
dealt with tax policy. From antiquity through feudal times, governments
financed their budgets from rental revenues generated by assets in the public
domain: the land and subsoil mineral rights, forests and fisheries. More
recently, public utilities representing natural monopolies (roads, railroads and
airlines, telephone, radio and television systems using the electromagnetic spectrum, power and water systems, etc.) were created in the first instance to provide economies with low-cost essential inputs. Users typically were charged for
these services at the government's supply price, often at subsidized rates.

Privatization promises to manage these services more efficiently, while removing the operating costs of public agencies from the government budget. In the process, however, it removes their revenue and turns it over to institutional investors as interest and dividends. Public services formerly provided at the government's supply price or at subsidized rates (or even free) will be priced at a uniform rate set high enough to cover profit payouts, interest and other financial charges, as well as substantial raises for the chief executives.

Foreign creditors and owners of these privatized enterprises (along with wealthy domestic investors) remit their interest and dividends abroad, breaking the circular flow of spending within the home economy. The effect is to dollarize what formerly were public services denominated in domestic currency. Local price structures are subordinated to those of the globally dominant economies whose governments are most active in shaping world markets.

A major rationale for privatization has been to undertake the investment needed to keep up with global technology. But public telecommunications and transport systems or other utilities may be managed at least as economically as privately owned ones. There is no intrinsic reason why private and public ownership should pursue different management policies. The differences stem from political rather than economic constraints. Upgrading equipment and providing new services requires funding which in principle can be repaid out of the user-fees charged or costs saved. But today's neoliberal orthodoxy seeks to deprive governments of the right to borrow or create the money needed to expand and modernize.

"Latecomer" nations such as Germany and much of continental Europe in the 19th century, Latin America and Asia undertook government investment in public utilities and rent-yielding oil and mineral resources. Yet so great an opposition grew to government spending in general, and public debt in particular, that the major public enterprises faced budgetary constraints that blocked them from borrowing to modernize at the rate needed to keep competitive with those of other countries. Telephone, television and radio systems, power and water companies, bus companies, railroads and airlines, as well as nationalized industries such as steel in Britain and other countries were starved for capital as a result of an indiscriminate categorizing of all government borrowing as unproductive and hence potentially inflationary. Revenues for government enterprises were consolidated into the overall budget so that they could not be used to meet their own investment needs or those of other public agencies.

This constraint has created an unnecessary behavioral dichotomy between private and public ownership. There is no inherent reason why public utilities and other infrastructure, minerals and land should not generate the same returns for government as for private owners. Most savings from privatization result from shifting to non-union labor and cutting services to low-volume users. Public managers could follow these policies that if given authorization to do so, but there is still a popular desire for governments to stick to traditional social values. So strong is the ideological schizophrenia that it is considered unrealistic to expect voters to endorse public agencies to do what privatizers are expected do. It has been deemed necessary to relinquish the potential cost savings inherent in public ownership in order to let private managers (often the same individuals who ran these enterprises in the public sector) make "economic" decisions, that is, ones too unpopular to be applied by officials who are accountable to voters. Socially minded politics and an increasingly asocial economics thus have developed two different ideologies.

Privatizing the revenue generated by public enterprises or natural resource rents in the public domain involves both a fiscal and a financial sacrifice. Relinquishing these revenues obliges governments to make up the difference by taxing labor and tangible non-financial capital. Owners of the resources and enterprises being privatized will tend to leverage their cash flow as collateral to borrow money to buy yet more such assets. Their hope is that stock-market prices for the privatized enterprises will rise by more than the interest charges they must pay. Owners and managers who take their returns in the form of capital gains pay lower taxes than investors who earn profits by direct investment. Also, the borrowings that private managers make to leverage their own equity investment converts erstwhile taxable earnings into non-taxable income. This aggravates the fiscal deficit while diverting savings away from funding new tangible investment. A debt-ridden bubble economy oriented toward capital gains and asset price inflation replaces the old industrial economy.

Denying the distinction between productive and unproductive debt, today's neoliberals rationalize all private-sector debt as producing an economic benefit, assumed to be equal to the value of the interest charge. Except for government debt, any given type of credit is deemed as productive as any other form. Public debt alone is considered unproductive in the sense of being inflationary, as if it has no counterpart in output. This ideology reflects an anti-government social philosophy that endorses and extremist "market fundamentalism" and economic austerity whose "value-free" deregulatory policies have paved the way for financial systems to inflate stock market and real estate bubbles as readily as to fund tangible capital formation.

Selling public infrastructure and key industrial and banking sectors to pay foreign debts (or simply to lower income and wealth taxes) leads to future payment outflows that further lower the rate at which a country's labor and exports exchange for those of creditor nations with more assertive market regulation.

Summary: How Industry-Oriented Banking Philosophy Differs from Today's Monetarism

Money is not merely a veil, a set of counters passively reflecting economic activity in prices and wage levels that rise or fall in keeping with changes in the money supply. It was recognized clearly enough in the 19th century that money and credit may put industry and labor in motion before prices begin to rise. Wages may increase, but productivity may rise even more, keeping prices stable. Monetary deflation not only lowers prices by reducing demand, it leads to unemployment and makes the burden of debt-service heavier. Instead of lowering prices and making exports more competitive over the intermediate and long runs, reduced output makes the deflationary or debt-burdened country even more dependent on foreign suppliers. A falling exchange rate may initiate the kind of self-feeding decline that results from IMF austerity programs. This basic pattern is not a new phenomenon. It was warned against already in the 17th and 18th centuries.

Given the experience and theoretical advances that had been achieved by the end of the 19th century, one may ask why serious economists would advocate such destructive policies today. One part of the explanation is to be found in their political assumption that the economic system's primary objective should be to stabilize the value of debt — that is, claims on the economy for interest and amortization — rather than permitting the economic value of these claims to be eroded by rising wages or commodity prices. This value judgment juxtaposes creditor interests to the rest of the economy.

Creditor nations have shown a desire to make debtor countries dependent on them, carrying their debts by producing exports of a type that do not compete with creditor-nation industries. These exports consist primarily of raw materials and low-wage products produced by a labor force that does not require higher education for high-technology production. The upshot is that to the extent that debtor countries grow, most of their surplus is transferred as interest payments. Their key assets are attached by the growing debt overhead, or into remitted as dividends as debtors agree to sell off their natural resources and public monopolies to raise the money to try and reduce their foreign debt burden. Yet the remission of interest, earnings and dividends causes the cumulative balance-of-payments deficit and its associated foreign debt to grow exponentially over time, beyond the ability to be paid.

A crisis erupts at the point where there is general recognition that the volume of debts has grown too large to be paid, that is, to be paid without transferring ownership and political control to the creditor nations. This forces a policy choice between whether to repay the debt at the cost of losing domestic self-dependence, or letting the debts go. Wealthy nations often write off their debts at this point, but debtor countries are constrained from doing this by the threat of international sanctions — and also by their ideological reliance on the economic and financial doctrines accepted by the creditor nations. There is not yet widespread recognition of the extent to which these economic doctrines are self-serving, least of all in the Finance Ministries and central banks of debtor countries where economic policy-making is concentrated.

The problem of international debt poses the question of just what kind of monetary and credit base is most liberating by fostering new investment and employment. Already by the 18th century, today's creditor nations sought to break free of financial dependency on other nations, and to keep the interest payments in their own domestic economies by supplementing gold and silver commodity-money with paper debt money and bank credit. In the leading nations, this money rested on the foundation of government debt via central banking systems whose reserves were invested in this debt, that is, lent to governments. This is the system started by the Bank of England in 1694.

Early economists recognized that there are numerous categories of using money: not only to buy goods and services, but also to pay debt service and taxes, and an even larger use: to buy stocks and bonds or financial assets and real estate. Early formulators of the Quantity Theory of Money had a broader scope than today's monetarism in recognizing the limited scope of theories that related money and credit only to commodity prices, not to bond, stock and real estate prices.

Industrial banking reform criticizes this approach on two grounds. First, it points out that most money is spent on financial assets and other assets (as well as debt service and fiscal transactions, which may be viewed as a debt to the state). Second, it recognizes that many prices are beyond the ability of domestic monetary policy to influence. For instance, international oil prices are set by the global market, independent of any country's monetary policy, except possibly that of the United States by virtue of its large size.

A financial-fiscal reform approach realizes the linkage between savings and debt: Except for savings invested in equity (common stock) and hard assets, most are lent out, and hence find their counterparts in debtor obligations to the saver-creditors. Furthermore, most of the interest on such savings is reinvested ("recycled") in yet new lending. The effect is for the mass of savings/debts to grow autonomously and exponentially, under its own steam, without regard for the economy's ability to pay. This is what makes debt crises inevitable.

The process is self-feeding, so that the financial system polarizes the economy. The larger the debt overhead grows to overshadow the "real" economy, the more its flow of interest and amortization tends to be channeled into unproductive lines. The rising ratio of interest to national income deflates the domestic market for goods and services, making direct investment less profitable.

Looking through history, one must conclude that financial systems do not automatically evolve and mutate to optimize society's technological potential. Today's credit institutions are developing in ways that threaten to be incompatible with maximizing industrial potential, by diverting savings and credit away from financing productive enterprise to corrosive or, at best, zero-sum activities that benefit particular debtors. Politicians find that their campaign contributions may be maximized by cutting taxes for the wealthiest brackets, and then financing the ensuing fiscal deficit by borrowing the money back from them. Instead of funding new means of production, "bubble" credit is being extended to real estate speculators, corporate raiders and others to bid up the price of real estate and corporate stock or other assets already in place. Such credit may seem productive at first glance, in the sense that asset-price inflation may enable the borrowers to repay the loan with interest. But this is achieved at the price of increasing the economy's debt overhead, raising its fixed costs accordingly

If industry has not broken with the Chicago School's financial philosophy to advocate some modern version of the ideas voiced already by Saint-Simonians writers, it is largely because the goals of today's industrial corporations have become increasingly financial in character. Financial strategists rather than industrial engineers now run most manufacturing companies. Wall Street controls "Main Street," not the other way around as was expected by early observers of the Industrial Revolution. It is the essence of today's "postindustrial" economy that finance capitalism has absorbed industrial capitalism and subordinated its drive for profits via new tangible capital investment, employment, research and development with a drive to obtain financial gains. The picture revealed by today's national income and product accounts and balance-sheet analysis shows that "capital gains" now consist largely of bubble gains from rising stock, bond and real estate prices, not rising flows of earnings.

Corporate industry has been taken over so thoroughly by the financial sector that there is little industrial voice left as such. Wall Street does not reflect the drives of industrial capital, but rather those of finance-capital. Contra

Marx, these two drives have diverged rather than converged. Just as in the late 17th century the goldsmiths (as proto-monetarists) fought against the Bank of England, so monetarist policies are now stifling industrial potential and raising the specter of the industrial epoch sinking back into the ancient usury problem.

Industrial capital may claim to share a certain harmony of interests with labor, including hopes for a prosperous home market, and for labor productivity brought about by higher educational and living standards. Industry as well as labor face a common enemy in the form of finance capital and the austerity programs it favors. Globalism of the Washington Consensus and Chicago School variety threatens to load existing assets down with debt, absorbing profits and stifling new employment.

> The economic tragedy of our time is the decoupling of banking, the stock market and the rest of the financial sector from the funding of new capital formation.

Since 1971, when America withdrew from the London Gold Pool and thereby severed the traditional linkage between debt-money and gold, economies have dealt with their debt problem by trying to inflate their way out of debt. But credit is debt, so this means "borrowing one's way out of debt." That is the internal contradiction of today's financialized economy. The inflation tends to be concentrated in the financial and real estate markets, in the form of asset-price inflation even in the face of wage deflation and commodity-price inflation. Increasingly, financial and real estate investors — the economy's "savers" — seek returns in the form of capital gains (asset price inflation) rather than current income. Interest rates may fall as the core economies (those in control of their own financial systems and money supply) are flooded with liquidity, while dependent economies (especially dollarized economies outside of the United States, such as Russia) are deflated and made even more dependent on raw materials exports. The withdrawal of revenue to pay foreign investors deflates economies, reducing their ability to create their own credit systems to inflate their way out of debt, as this debt is dollarized and hence immune from domestic monetary policy. In this way financial control is concentrated in the creditor nations and lost by the debtor countries.

Monetarist orthodoxy does not discuss or even acknowledge this financial polarization. This leaves academic economists discussing a hypothetical parallel universe. So one can understand why many political economists late in the 19th century began to prefer to call their discipline sociology or even anthropology.

The problem ultimately is methodological and philosophical, concerning the proper scope of economic thought. The economic tragedy of our time is the decoupling of banking, the stock market and the rest of the financial sector from the funding of new capital formation. This phenomenon only can be analyzed by distinguishing between wealth and overhead. And any such distinction rests ultimately on a concept (or set of concepts) dividing the economy's employment, investment and lending into categories of "productive" and "unproductive," or "earned" or "unearned" income.

This was the essence of classical political economy. For over a century, the neoclassical (that is, anti-classical) counter-revolution has insisted that all economic activity is productive. This philosophical approach understandibly is preferred by the most unproductive sectors, and by recipients of what the classical economists called unearned income (or "economic rent"), wishing to claim that their wealth and revenue is as justifiably earned as all other forms.

That was not the view of the Saint-Simonians, who pointed to the extent to which wealth was inherited rather than created by its owners. It was not the view of Adam Smith, who described landlords as loving to reap where they had not sown. It was not the view of Ricardo and subsequent rent theorists who showed that rent was a "free ride," an element of price that found no counterpart in costs defrayed by the rent recipient.

If industry has not broken from the Chicago School's financial philosophy, it is because the goals of today's industrial corporations have become increasingly financial in character. Manufacturing companies are now being run by financial rather than industrial engineers. Wall Street controls "Main Street," not the other way around. It is the essence of today's "postindustrial" economy that finance capitalism has absorbed industrial capitalism and subordinated its drives for profits with a drive to obtain financial returns, including capital gains (that is, asset-price gains) from channeling credit into securities and real estate markets. Thus, contra Marx, the dynamics of finance capital have diverted from those of industrial capital to the point of stifling industrial potential and raising the specter of plunging the industrial epoch back into the ancient usury problem that nineteenth-century observers believed was becoming a thing of the past.

Looking through history, one must conclude that financial systems do not automatically adjust and mutate to optimize society's technological potential. Today's credit institutions are developing in ways that threaten to be incompatible with maximizing industrial potential, but to divert savings and credit away from financing productive enterprise to corrosive or, at best, zero-sum gambling activities that benefit particular corporate raiders, aggressive companies or real estate operators who pledge earnings and rents to their bankers, hoping to ride the wave of asset-price inflation. Instead of funding new means of production whose revenues are able to repay the loan with interest, "bubble" credit is extended to these borrowers to bid up the price of corporate stock, real estate and other assets already in place.

If asset price inflation were real wealth creation, we would all be prosperous by now, not falling into negative equity as economies succomb to debt deflation.

Chart 1: Financial Strategies — Predatory versus Productive

Monetarist Orthodoxy	Pro-Industrial Finance
Sympathies lie with creditors.	Sympathetic to debtors, especially industry and consumers.
Primary concern with maintaining the value of debt.	Primary focus on increasing output and employment.
Willing to impose economic austerity to squeeze out debt service.	Puts the goals of employment and investment above that of repaying debts.
Assumes that all debts can be paid by sufficiently deflationary monetary policy	The ability to pay is limited to the net surplus.
Denies that chronic structural problems exist.	Acquiesces in inflation to erode the debt overhead high interest rates or outright cancellation of debts that cannot be paid
High interest rates and tight money keep down prices and stabilize the exchange rate.	Interest rates are a cost, and hence raise prices.
Views money narrowly as affecting only prices for goods and services. Ignores assets and wealth.	Recognizes that deflation impairs the ability to pay, and makes economies more dependent, thus widening their trade deficits.
The financial sector should not be regulated, and should make money in any way it chooses.	Most money is spent on financial speculation, real estate, securities and loan payments, not goods.
All credit is productive. If a debt was not productive, it would not be borrowed.	Credit should serve as a means of financing enterprise, not usury and unproductive activities.
Credit lowers costs by financing "competition."	Contrasts productive and unproductive lending, and finds a tendency towards the latter in business expansions. Unproductive debt is an overhead whose financing charges add to the economy's cost structure.
Considers government debt entirely parasitic.	Endorses public borrowing for direct investment.
Public enterprises should be privatized to pay off public debts.	Opposes forced sales of public assets to pay bad debts. Such debts should be cancelled.
Defines money narrowly as cash and bank deposits (assets), opposes government self-financing through debt-money.	Views money in terms of debt, and hence the flow of funds; defines "money" as the entire credit/asset supply available to be collateralized and discounted.
Emphasizes central bank control of the money supply. Wants to discourage informal credit outside of the large financial institutions.	The central bank can only control the discount rate (in Britain) or Federal Funds rate (in U.S.) for overnight bank reserves.
Seeks to untax "capital," especially FIRE sector; shifts taxes to labor (incl. sales taxes).	Would tax *rentier* income and remove tax deductibility for raiding & debt pyramiding
Claims that, money was invented by individuals to lower transaction costs as compared to barter.	Money was developed in the public institutions and used for internal accounting, then as a means of denominating debt and later, taxes.

Prices are determined by supply and demand.	Early prices and interest rates were administered.
When governments got into the act, problems arose.	Problems arose as lending was privatized and became usurious.
Constraints on interest rates and prices never work.	These administered rates were remarkably stable.
Entirely private "market" economies are best.	The most successful economies are mixed.

2

THE MAGIC OF COMPOUND INTEREST:
MATHEMATICS AT THE ROOT OF THE CRISIS

Money is saved and reinvested in the expectation that it can grow without end. But are enough debtors able to pay to enable savings to keep on growing on an economy-wide scale? Ever since interest began to be recorded in ancient Mesopotamia, the defining financial character of economies has been the tendency for debts to multiply so rapidly that large numbers of debtors have had to settle their obligations by selling or forfeiting their property. Throughout most of recorded history such asset transfers are so widespread as to transform the distribution of land and other wealth.

Perception of the problems caused by debts/savings growing at compound interest on an economy-wide scale is obscured if one takes merely an individualistic approach. From the vantage point of bankers and other lenders, all that seem to matter are the computer printouts of the debts owed to them, the yield on each obligation and the dates on which payments are scheduled to fall due. Each loan is paid off in one way or another, after all. Retirees and some other savers live off their interest and dividends, but banks and insurance companies, pension and retirement funds, mutual funds and trusts seek to "keep their money working for them," plowing their receipts of debt service back into new loans and investments there is little analysis of how their customers are to pay these debts, much less how the economy can carry its debt overhead. And there is an assumption that debts are taken on voluntarily, not mounting up as arrears or borrowed out of necessity—or simply out of the need to obtain home ownership, an eduation or pay foremergenies.

As the process is essentially an exponential function, the dynamics of interest-bearing debt can be understood only through mathematics. The laws governing the growth of debt were at the core of religious doctrines of the ancient Near East, of Judaism, early Christianity and Islam. Matters hardly could have been otherwise in light of the role played by rural usury in the expropriation of families from their land, reducing them to bondage to their creditors.

Economic models that neglect the self-multiplying character of debt will miss the source of today's most pressing financial problem: the tendency of debts to grow more rapidly than the economy's ability to carry them. Formulae describing the growth of savings put out at interest—the mirror image of what debtors owe—date back some four thousand years.

One can see why the long-term dynamics expounded by Ricardo and Malthus led economics to be called the Dismal Science. It was dismal because it described economies sinking into a state of entropy as population growth pressed against the limits of land and capital under conditions of diminishing returns—the idea that each additional unit of labor produces less output. There was little anticipation that labor output per man-hour would soar in agriculture and mining as much as in industry.[1]

The Dismal Science shows no such pessimism when it comes to debts mounting up at interest. The mathematical principles of how societies run more deeply into debt are the same as those that describe the exponential buildup of savings, but they seem to have eluded notice. I believe that the reason is that a realistic logic implies a need for public intervention to challenge creditor claims. Debts are viewed from the vantage point of creditors to whom savings are owed, but not in terms of the economy's ability to pay. Such one-sided theorizing avoids confronting the price that societies must pay as they strive to carry an increasingly top-heavy financial overhead, owing sums that seem to be soaring off toward infinity.

What the Babylonians Recognized but Modern Economists Overlook

Four thousand years ago mathematics played a major role in training Sumerian and Babylonian scribes. Most were employed in palace and temple bookkeeping, and their schoolbook exercises emphasized manpower allocation problems such as calculating how many men were needed to produce a given amount of bricks or dig canals of a given size. Model exercises also dealt with the expected growth of herds and the doubling times of money lent out at interest.

When the prime commercial lending rate of U.S. banks peaked at 20 percent in 1980 it touched what had been the normal commercial rate for silver from Sumer c. 2500 BC through the Neo-Babylonian epoch in the first millennium. By the time Alexander the Great conquered the Near East in 331 BC the rate had remained remarkably stable at the equivalent of 20 percent for more than two thousand years. It was not set with any particular reference to profit levels or other means to pay, but simply was a matter of mathematical convenience, reflecting the Mesopotamian way of computing fractions by division into 60ths. A bushel of barley was divided into 60 "quarts," and a *mina-*

---

[1] This is done because only the assumption of damping functions can provide determinate a priori mathematical solutions to economic exercises—as if it were mathematics that makes economics a science, not the realism of its assumptions. I survey the unrealistic use of mathematics by economists in chapter 5 below.

weight of roughly one pound was composed of 60 shekels. Paying interest at the rate of $^1/_{60}$ each month added up to $^{12}/_{60}$ per year, or 20 percent in decimal notation. A mina lent out at this rate would produce 60 shekels in five years, doubling the original principal.

A model Babylonian scribal exercise from circa 2000 BC asks the student to calculate how long it will take for a mina of silver to double at the normal rate of one shekel per mina per month.[2] The answer is five years at simple interest—the common time period for backers to lend money to traders. Assyrian loan contracts from about 1900 BC called for investors to advance two minas of gold, getting back four minas in five years.

The same idea is expressed in an Egyptian proverb: "If wealth is placed where it bears interest, it comes back to you redoubled."[3] Another popular image compared making a loan to having a baby. The word for "interest" in every ancient language meant a newborn, either a goat-kid (máš) in Sumerian, or a young calf—*tokos* in Greek or *foenus* in Latin. The "kid" or "calf" paid as interest was born of silver or gold, not from borrowed cattle as some modernist economists once believed, missing the metaphor at work.[4] Rather, the reproduction of numbers was viewed in sexual terms. What was born was the "baby" fraction of the principal, $^1/_{60}$. Only when these accruals of interest had grown to be as large as their parent, after the fifth year, were they deemed "adult" enough begin having new interest "babies" on their own, for everyone knows that only adults can reproduce themselves. Thus, compounding began only after the principal had reproduced itself—"matured"—by the time 60 months had passed.

How long could the process go on at these rates? A relevant scribal problem asks how long it will take for one mina to become 64, that is, 2^6. The solution involves calculating powers of 2 ($2^2 = 4$; $2^3 = 8$ and so forth).[5] A *mina* multiplies fourfold in 10 years, eightfold in 15 years, sixteenfold in 20 years, and 64 times in 30 years. The 30-year period consisted of six five-year doubling periods.

---

[2] The example comes from a Berlin cuneiform text VAT 8528. Karen Rhea Nemet-Nejat, *Cuneiform Mathematical Texts as a Reflection of Everyday Life in Mesopotamia* (New Haven 1993, AOS Series Vol. 75) provides a bibliography. Most of these exercises are schoolbook problems, not statistics resulting from real-life examples, but precisely for this reason their principles illustrate the relationships being expounded.

[3] Miriam Lichtheim, *Ancient Egyptian Literature*, II: 135.

[4] I discuss the sexual mathematical imagery of antiquity's words for interest in "How Interest Rates Were Set, 2500 BC–1000 AD: *Máš*, *tokos* and *fœnus* as metaphors for interest accruals," *Journal of the Economic and Social History of the Orient* 43 (Spring 2000): 132–161.

[5] This arithmetic exercise comes from VAT 8525. It is discussed by Hildegard Lewy, "Marginal Notes on a Recent Volume of Babylonian Mathematical Texts," *Journal of the American Oriental Society* 67 (1947): 308 and Nemet-Nejat, *op. cit.*: 59f.

It will be noted that these Babylonian examples are composed from the vantage point of lenders and investors, not the debtor. Once the debt is repaid, the transaction is over as far as the borrower is concerned. The money is not simply left to accumulate. Investors who wanted to keep their money multiplying had to draw up new loan contracts. This meant taking their gain (assuming that the venture was successful) and finding a new borrower or trade venture. With the passage of time it must have become harder to find enough ventures to absorb the savings that were mounting up.

Successful traders and merchants normally were able to pay such rates out of their business gains. If the ship was robbed by pirates or sunk, or if the caravan was robbed, the lending laws of the epoch said that the merchant did not have to pay his backer. Commercial lenders shared in the risk of the merchants. But the volume of trade could not keep on multiplying exponentially. Interest accumulated in the hands of lenders more rapidly than they could find commercial opportunities.

Creditors found their major non-commercial market to be rural usury, and this is where the most serious problems occurred, especially when crops failed or military hostilities interrupted the harvest. Agricultural interest rates were more extortionate in this sector, typically 33 1/3 percent, reflecting the normal sharecropping rate of a third of the crop. Interest rates of 50 or even 100 percent might be charged, often for only short periods as creditors (mainly palace officials) demanded whatever they could get from cultivators in distress or in arrears in what they owed in fees to palace collectors.

Matters were further aggravated by the fact that unlike the case with mercantile loans, cultivators bore most of the risk in rural lending. The loan usually took the form of prepayment against the crop, on which the palace's share was estimated as if normally high yields would materialize. But the crop often turned out to be less, squeezing the cultivator, whose crop shortfall became a debt. Sharecroppers or others unable to break even or pay their stipulated rents or fees to the palace under these adverse conditions were forced to borrow out of need, and once they ran into debt it was hard to extricate themselves.

As rural loans were made primarily to enable cultivators to pay taxes or get by hard times, not to buy property or finance investment of their own. Inevitably, rural usury led to the forfeiture of land and crop rights. The way to obtain property was by lending against it, not by borrowing money to buy it.

At the interest rate of 33 1/3 percent, Babylonian agricultural debts doubled in three years. A frequent practice was for debtors to pay interest by pledging their family members as bondservants to work for their creditors. § 117 of Hammurapi's laws (c. 1750 BC) stipulated that such bondservants be freed after three years, apparently recognizing that at this point the creditor had received labor services equal in value to the original debt. The law stipulated at this point the loan should be deemed to have been paid and the pledge should be liberated to rejoin her (or his) family. The implication is that doubling the debt principal represented a moral and practical limit.

At no time in history has output grown at sustained rates approaching the 33 ¹/₃ percent rate of interest charged for agricultural loans, or even the 20 percent commercial rate. When the loan proceeds were used to pay tax arrears or for consumption, interest charges ate into the cultivator's modest resources, obliging him to raise sums beyond his ability to produce and thus enabling creditors to obtain the debtor's family members as bondservants, followed by the land itself. This threatened to expropriate the citizen army members traditionally free cultivators on the land.

Sterile Money and Insatiable Usury

Greek records point to the charging of interest in the Aegean around 750 BC, probably being introduced by Syrian ("Phoenician") traders.[6] Following Egyptian decimalized practice, Greek interest rates typically were set at 10 percent. This made the doubling time for loans ten years. But although this was only half the Mesopotamian rate, it did not save cultivators from running into such serious problems that debt revolts occurred. Sparta's "Lycurgan" reforms went so far as to ban the use of precious metals as money and made the land inalienable, and hence safe from forfeiture for debt arrears.

By the 7th century the oligarchies in Corinth and other cities were overthrown and driven into exile by popular leaders ("tyrants") who cancelled the debts of their supporters and redistributed the land of the exiled families. One of the last cities to experience a debtors' revolt was Athens, where Solon lay the foundations for economic democracy by banning debt bondage in 594 BC. But Greek cities subsequently drew the line, and some even obliged their administrators to pledge not to cancel the population's debts.

By the 3rd century, BC, Sparta's formerly egalitarian economy was polarizing between large landowners and families who had lost their property through debt foreclosure. Some families had become wealthy and lent to those

---

[6] I suggest a scenario for how this diffusion is likely to have occurred in "Did the Phoenicians Introduce the Idea of Interest to Greece and Italy—And if So, When?" in Gunter Köpcke, ed., *Greece Between East and West: 10ᵗʰ–8ᵗʰ Centuries BC* (Berlin: 1992): 128–143. For a defense of the still controversial idea that the charging of interest began in Mesopotamia's temples and palaces, see "Reconstructing the Origins of Interest-Bearing Debt and the Logic of Clean Slates," in Michael Hudson and Marc Van De Mieroop, eds., *Debt and Economic Renewal in the Ancient Near East* (CDL Press: Bethesda, Md., 2002).

in need, with the loans collateralized by their lands. This disenfranchised much of Sparta's citizen-army. Toward the end of the century, kings Agis and Cleomenes tried to save matters by cancelling the population's debts, but by this time the power of vested interests had grown strong enough to exile both rulers. Cleomenes was murdered, and Sparta's final reformer, Nabis, was overthrown by neighboring oligarchic cities, calling on Rome for aid.

The Etruscans, Romans and other Italians seem to have adopted the practice of charging interest on debt from Greek and Near Eastern traders around 750 BC. Probably reflecting the division of the year into twelve months, they used the duodecimal system of fractions based on dozens. The Roman pound was divided into twelve troy ounces, and the legal rate of interest was set at $1/12$ ($8\frac{1}{3}$ percent). This was the lowest major rate in antiquity, but it nonetheless proved to be beyond the ability of cultivators to pay, especially when they were called away from their land to fight in the almost constant warfare of the period.

As civilization's center moved west from the Near East to Greece and then to Italy, the decline in interest rates resulted from the mathematical system of fractional weights and measures rather than from declining productivity or profit rates. Despite this decline (and hence the longer time it took for a debt to double), the debt burden became increasingly serious as the early practice of royal debt cancellations became a thing of the past. Livy, Diodorus and Plutarch described how Rome's creditor oligarchy shifted taxes onto the less prosperous classes, pushing them into bankruptcy and ultimately destroying the money economy itself, bringing on a Dark Age that reverted to local subsistence production in which the Christian Church emerged to ban usury outright.

The point of intersection between usury and the living organic economy occurs when money-loans must be paid out of the reproduction of crops and herds, or other output and revenue. Although the money that creditors lend out is not itself productive, borrowers need it to pay for the resources they need to be productive, including the expense of providing for their families in emergency conditions.

Aristotle's *Politics* (I.10 at 1256, c. 330 BC) pointed out how inappropriate was the metaphor of debts reproducing themselves, because silver was sterile: "The taking of interest is contrary to nature, because money by nature cannot produce anything and is intended only to serve the purpose of exchange," that is, as a means of payment. In contrast to the reproductive power of animals, money's appropriate function was to be a means to facilitate trade, not to intrude into property relations. One might say that the "real" economy was organic; the money economy and its debt relations were inorganic and purely mathematical. This is why the expansion path of interest-bearing debt diverged from that of the underlying economy. Rural usurers broke up society's natural balance—and in the process its military foundation—by charging exorbitant interest rates, ending up with the impoverished debtor's property.

The idea that money was sterile explains the frequent literary depiction of usurers as old homosexuals, incapable of reproducing themselves. When Livy (VIII.28) wrote his history of Rome, he probably knew only the bare fact that in 326 BC the Papirian law abolished the right of creditors to keep their debtors literally in bonds. In the melodramatic Stoic fashion of his day, he drew on an established archetype to compose a dramatic scenario for the events leading up to Rome's debt revolt. He portrayed the Roman crowd rioting to protest a lustful usurer, Lucius Papirius, who had abused a boy left in his charge as a debt pledge, "regarding the boy's youthful bloom as added interest on his loan." When the boy rejected the creditor's advances, Lucius

> ordered him to be stripped and beaten. Mangled by the blows, the boy rushed into the street and complained loudly of the usurer's lust and brutality. A vast crowd gathered, inflamed with pity for his youth and outrage for the wrong, and considering too the conditions under which they and their children were living, and they ran into the Forum and from there in a compact body to the senate house. Forced by this sudden outbreak, the consuls convened a meeting of the senate, and as the members entered the senate house the crowd exhibited the lacerated back of the youth and flung themselves at the feet of the senators. The strong bond of credit was on that day overthrown through the mad excesses of one individual. The consuls were instructed by the senate to lay before the people a proposal 'that no man be kept shackled or in the stocks, except such as, having been guilty of some crime, were waiting to pay the penalty; and that the goods but not the person of the debtor should be the security for money lent.'

Personified as sterility, usury appeared as antithetical to the normal social reproductive process. The moral of Livy's story was that rather than creating families, creditors broke them up by seizing their members as pledges, as well as foreclosing on their subsistence lands. On the broadest plane of analysis money cannot really reproduce itself; only the tangible, living economy can do that. The point of intersection between usury and the living organic economy occurs when money-loans must be paid out of the reproduction of crops and herds, or other output and revenue. Although the money that creditors lend out is not itself productive, borrowers need it to pay for the resources they need to be productive, including the expense of providing for their families in emergency conditions.

The poverty caused by usury at the bottom of the economic scale found its counterpart in splendor at the top, for although money itself was sterile, it enabled usurers to draw society's wealth into their own hands. Yet as they turned life into a scramble for metal, they were as mean with themselves as they were with others. Some usurers spent lavishly to gain approval, but more often they acted miserly and did not even spend money on themselves, sacrificing their own worldly enjoyment to an insatiable, increasingly compulsive property acquisition for its own sake. Wealth addiction became the natural counterpart to the exponential growth of debt.

Greek dramatists portrayed the limitless greed for money as a disease of the psyche. In Aristophanes' last play, *Ploutos* (388 BC), the character Karion remarks that a person may become over-satiated with food—bread, sweets, cakes, figs and barley—but no one ever has enough wealth. His friend Chremelos agrees:

> Give a man a sum of thirteen talents,
> and all the more he hungers for sixteen.
> Give him sixteen, and he must needs have forty,
> or life's not worth living, so he says. (lines 189–193)

As the French classicist Jean-Pierre Vernant paraphrases this thought:

> Ultimately, wealth has no object but itself. Created to satisfy the needs of life, as a mere means of subsistence, it becomes its own end, a universal, insatiable, boundless craving that nothing will ever be able to assuage. At the root of wealth one therefore discovers a corrupted disposition, a perverse will, a *pleonexia*—the desire to have more than others, more than one's share, to have everything. In Greek eyes, *ploutos* (wealth) was bound up with a kind of disaster,[7]

above all with hubristic behavior whose defining characteristic was not just the egoism of wealth but the injury its holders did to their victims, most characteristically through usury.

---

[7] Jean-Pierre Vernant, *Origins of Greek Thought* (Ithaca, New York 1982): 82.

Self-enrichment through usury made money in an asocial way, one that was compulsive rather than warm, self-referential and metallic rather than interactive in an organic way. "Woe to you who add house to house and join field to field till no space is left and you live alone in the land," declaimed the prophet Isaiah. Since Mesopotamian times the way to acquire property (and labor) most quickly was through usury and foreclosure, but creditors would live alone once they had cleared the land of everyone by foreclosing on their subsistence holdings. Usury became the economics of autism, a narcissistic social-personality defect that low-surplus communities could not afford and indeed took pains to prevent from developing among their own members.

The Exponential Doubling and Redoubling of Debt

For thousands of years religion paid more attention to the problems caused by the exponential growth of debt than do modern economists. Under Babylonia's "divine kingship," rulers were expected to "restore order" by canceling rural debts, liberating bondservants and redistributing lands that had been forfeited to creditors or sold under duress. This practice was echoed in Judaism's Jubilee Year (Leviticus 25), while throughout Greece a more secular cry arose for cancellation of the debts and redistribution of the land. Early Christianity denounced usury, as did the Koran and medieval Canon Law.

Martin Luther depicted the growing mass of usurious claims on the poor and the rest of society as the "great huge monster … who lays waste all … Cacus," who "would eat up the world in a few years." The monster was epitomized as a usurer scheming "to amass wealth and get rich, to be lazy and idle and live in luxury on the labor of others." Once Cacus got hold of a man and imbued him with the insatiable desire for money-wealth, the victim became in turn a villain, a "usurer and money-glutton" who "would have the whole world perish of hunger and thirst, misery and want, so far as in him lies, so that he may have all to himself, and every one may receive from him as from a God, and be his serf for ever.… For Cacus means the villain that is a pious usurer, and steals, robs, eats everything."[8]

---

[8] The passage occurs in Luther's 1540 Wittenberg pamphlet, *An die Pfarrherren wider den Wucher zu predigen* ["That the priests should preach against usery"]. Although Marx footnoted this passage in *Capital* (Vol. I, London 1887: 604 and Vol. III, ch. xxiv: 463 f.), it is missing from Vol. 45 of Luther's works (Fortress Press, 1962) dealing ostensibly with his economic writings. That so important a denunciation of interest would be omitted attests to the cognitive dissonance with which denunciations of interest strike modern secular and religious minds. Yet from the Bronze Age onward, such denunciations have been in the forefront of all religions in societies where interest has been charged to needy debtors.

John Napier's 1614 *Mirifici Logarithmorum Canonis descriptio* juxtaposed exponential number series to their simple arithmetic expansion. Ninety pages of tables were added to 57 pages of explanatory text that introduced the word "logarithm," literally "the number of the ratios" (from Greek *arithmos*, "number," and *logos*, "word, logic, ratio"). The technique greatly simplified calculations involving exponential functions, including those of interest-bearing debt as well as navigational and astronomical problems. Napier's second book on logarithms, the *Robdologia* (1617), illustrated the exponential principle by means of a chess-board on which each square doubled the number assigned to the preceding one. A subsequent economic writer cast this principle into the form of a Persian proverb telling of a Shah who wished to reward the inventor of chess, a subject, and asked what he would like. The man asked "as his only reward that the Shah would give him a single grain of corn, which was to be put on the first square of the chess-board, and to be doubled on each successive square; which, to the surprise of the king, produced an amount larger than the treasures of his whole kingdom could buy."[9]

A poetic application of this mathematical idea appears at the outset of Shakespeare's *A Winter's Tale*, published a few years before Napier. The metaphor of "a cipher … standing in a rich place" indicates the logarithmic exponential by which a debt multiplied as it mounted up unpaid at compound interest.[10] The passage has caused speculation on how and when Shakespeare might have known Napier or his circle, but the most striking point is how many dramatists and novelists have paid more attention to debt than do modern economists. The novels of Dickens, Balzac and their contemporaries as well as early British drama are filled with debt imagery, reflecting the role it played in nearly everyone's life.

---

[9] Quoted in Michael Flürscheim, *A Clue to the Economic Labyrinth* (Perth and London 1902): 330 ff.

[10] Expressing gratitude for the nine months of hospitality he has received, the character Polyxenes uses the florid metaphor of a burdensome debt that can never be repaid. The idea is that to take the time to thank his host properly would consume yet more time, using up yet more hospitality for which yet more thanks would be due in a never-ending series. (In this passage the words "without a burden" mean without debt.)

> Nine changes of the watery star [the moon] hath been
> The shepherd's note since we have left our throne
> Without a burden: time as long again
> Would be fill'd up, my brother, with our thanks;
> And yet we should for perpetuity,
> Go hence in debt: and therefore like a cipher,
> yet standing in rich place, I multiply
> With one we-thank-you many thousands more that go before it.

Doubling Numbers:
"The Miracle of Compound Interest"

64TH SQUARE
the pile of pennies is
4.5 trillion miles high
(and is worth
$9.2 sextillion)

43RD SQUARE
2.2 million miles
($4.4 trillion)

Neptune
2.7 million
miles away

40TH SQUARE
271,147 miles
($550 billion)
Moon
238,000
miles away

PENNIES ON A
CHESSBOARD
The miracle
of compound
interest—what
happens when
you double
numbers

25TH SQUARE
8.2 miles
($16.8 million)
Everest
5.5 miles
high

20TH SQUARE
1,360 feet
($524,288)
Empire State
Building
1,250 feet

10TH SQUARE
16 inches high
($5.12)

8TH SQUARE
the pile of pennies
is 4 inches high
(and is worth
$1.28)

EACH SQUARE IS DOUBLE THE ONE BEFORE

48TH SQUARE
$140.7 trillion
69 million miles high

32ND SQUARE
$2.2 billion
1,059 miles high

16TH SQUARE
$327.68
85 feet high

1ST SQUARE
one penny
1/32 inch thick

© 2012 Nigel Holmes

Although political economy became a popular genre, it dealt only periph-
erally with debt relations without really integrating them into its core. However,
one of Adam Smith's contemporaries, the Anglican minister and actuarial
mathematician Richard Price, graphically explained the seeming magic of how
debts multiplied exponentially. His 1772 *Appeal to the Public on the Subject of the
National Debt* described how

> Money bearing compound interest increases at first slowly. But, the rate
> of increase being continually accelerated, it becomes in some time so
> rapid, as to mock all the powers of the imagination. One penny, put out
> at our Saviour's birth at 5% compound interest, would, before this time,
> have increased to a greater sum than would be obtained in a 150 mil-
> lions of Earths, all solid gold. But if put out to simple interest, it would,
> in the same time, have amounted to no more than 7 shillings 4½d.[11]

In his *Observations on Reversionary Payments*, first published in 1769 and running
through six editions by 1803, Price elaborated how the rate of multiplication
would be even higher at 6 percent:

> A shilling put out at 6% compound interest at our Saviour's birth would
> … have increased to a greater sum than the whole solar system could
> hold, supposing it a sphere equal in diameter to the diameter of Saturn's
> orbit.[12]

Rather naïvely, Price suggested that Britain's government make use of this
exponential principle to pay off the public debt by creating a sinking fund that
itself would grow at compound interest. The idea had been proposed a half
century earlier by Nathaniel Gould, a director of the Bank of England. Parliament would set aside one million pounds sterling to invest at interest in a
sinking fund, where it would build up the principal by reinvesting the dividends
annually. The idea is familiar today when people reinvest their stock market
gains. In a surprisingly short period of time, Price promised, the fund would
grow large enough to enable the government to extricate itself from its entire
debt—by establishing financial claims on the rest of the economy! "A state
need never, therefore, be under any difficulties, for, with the smallest savings, it
may, in as little time as its interest can require, pay off the largest debts."[13]

What Price had discovered was how the exponential growth of money
invested at interest multiplies the principal by plowing back the dividends into

---

[11] Richard Price, *Appeal to the Public on the Subject of the National Debt* (London, 1772): 19.
[12] Richard Price, *Observations on Reversionary Payments* (London, 1769): xiii, fn. a.
[13] *Ibid.*

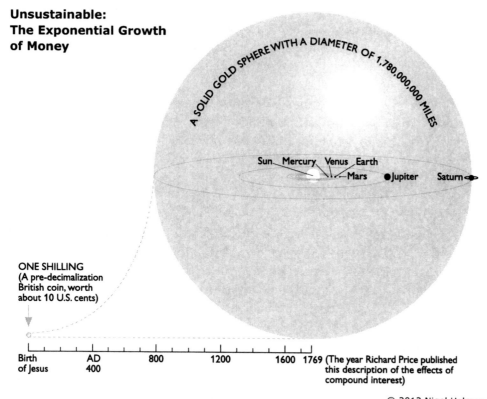

**Unsustainable:
The Exponential Growth
of Money**

A SOLID GOLD SPHERE WITH A DIAMETER OF 1,780,000,000 MILES

Sun Mercury Venus Earth
—Mars ●Jupiter Saturn

ONE SHILLING
(A pre-decimalization
British coin, worth
about 10 U.S. cents)

| Birth of Jesus | AD 400 | 800 | 1200 | 1600 | 1769 (The year Richard Price published this description of the effects of compound interest) |

new saving. It is the explanation for how savings snowball in the hands of bankers, bondholders and other savers who keep on reinvesting their dividends. At its root is the principle taught to Babylonian scribes four thousand years ago, when the compound interest phenomenon was just getting underway on a large scale.

Today, interest is compounded annually, quarterly and even daily by banks, and it is done automatically rather than obliging savers to go out and find new credit-worthy borrowers. The major difference is that in Babylonia compounding began only after five years had passed, and at the expiration of each loan or investment the creditor had to draw up a new loan document. This meant finding a new borrower whose enterprise seemed likely to generate the money to pay the doubled sum available to be lent out. Price's proposed compound-interest fund was expected to keep on accruing *ad infinitum*, on the assumption that there always would be enough opportunities to find remunerative projects.

Economic history provides a corrective sense of proportion by showing that in the two thousand years since the birth of Christ the European economy has grown at a compound annual rate of 0.2 percent, far less than the level at which interest rates have stood in recent times. The proceeds of much of this growth have had to be allocated to pay debt service, absorbing the revenue that otherwise would be available for direct investment and enhancement of living standards. This shrinks the "organic" or "real" economy's ability to produce a surplus to pay creditors, invest and increase consumption. Economies, like individuals, ultimately may be bankrupted by their inability to pay compounding interest charges on a mathematical or "inorganic" financial expansion path that has no limit.

Something has to give. The political fight in nearly every economy for thousands of years has been over whose interests must be sacrificed in the face of the incompatibility between financial and economic expansion paths. Until quite recently, creditors have lost, for the simple reason that never in history has any economy been able to turn a penny—or any other sum—into a surplus large enough to pay creditors a solid sphere of gold reaching out to Saturn's orbit. This is the point that modern economists and futurists fail to appreciate. No doubt many people saved pennies back in Roman times, and indeed, hundreds of talents of silver and gold were lent out at high rates of interest. Yet nobody had accumulated a vast volume of gold nearly as large as the earth itself, or even as large as a city block. The volume of gold in the world today could fit into a single large fortress.[14]

The inference is that what savers hope to obtain in interest cannot materialize in practice. Financial claims run ahead of the economy's ability to produce and pay. Expectations that interest payments can keep on mounting up are "fictitious," as Marx and other 19th-century critics put it. When indebted economies and their governments cannot pay, bankers and investors call in their loans and foreclose, causing the kind of crises that distinguish modern business cycles and, in the past, always have wiped out savings along with the bad debts.

---

[14] Consolidated Goldfields of South Africa used to emphasize in its annual reports that all the gold produced in the world to date, including antiquity, could fit into a cube just 15 meters on each side. Official global gold holdings as of March 2001 amounted to 28,560 metric tonnes. Each tonne contains 32,151 troy ounces. At the price of $257.70 per ounce, this worked out to some $8.285.313 per tone, or $236.6 billion for the world's central banks taken together. They are estimated to hold just 12 percent of the world's total gold stocks, making the global total in private and government hands worth an estimated $1.9 trillion. This is only a small proportion of global debt.

The reality is that the accrual of savings (that is, debts) is constrained by the economy's ability to carry these debts. Recognizing that no society's productive powers could long support interest-bearing debt growing at compound rates, Marx poked fun at Price's calculations:

> The good Mr. Price was simply dazzled by the enormous quantities resulting from geometrical progression of numbers…. he regards capital as a self-acting thing, without any regard to the conditions of reproduction of labour, as a mere self-increasing number, subject to the growth formula
> Surplus = Capital $(1 + \text{interest rate})^n$ [15]

No wonder Adam Smith found that no nation in history had paid off its public debt, and that Britain's tax revenues had become "a fund for paying, not the capital, but the interest only, of the money which had been borrowed …" As for the political idea of a sinking fund, Smith pointed out that it

Owing to the recycling of interest receipts into new lending, what grows geometrically are savings (*i.e.*, debts on the liabilities side of the balance sheet) …

is a subsidiary fund always at hand to be mortgaged in aid of any other doubtful fund, upon which money is proposed to be raised in any exigency of the state.[16]

To ambitious monarchs or parliamentary leaders, the fund would be an irresistible temptation as governments simply would turn around and re-borrow an equivalent sum for whatever was set aside to pay off the debt, or indeed whatever was needed to finance yet new wars.

In 1798, a generation after Price put forth his argument for a sinking fund, the Rev. Thomas Robert Malthus drew the contrast between geometric and

---

[15] Karl Marx, *Grundrisse notebooks* (1973): 842 f., incorporated into *Capital* III: xxiv).
[16] Adam Smith, *Wealth of Nations*, Bk. V.

arithmetic rates of growth in the way that most economic students recognize today. Picking up his fellow minister's imagery, Malthus asserted that populations tended to grow "geometrically" unless checked by natural forces such as famine, disease or war, while the means of subsistence—the populations of animals and plants consumed by humans—could grow only "arithmetically" at a simple rate of interest. It followed that social programs to provide more money for the poor would be self-defeating, because they would have more children ("multiply their numbers"), pressing against the limits of subsistence and forcing their living standards back down to minimum survival levels.[17]

The financial proposals that made readers familiar with Malthus's contrast are all but forgotten today. Few economists remember that the mathematics of compound vs. simple interest was first applied to the rates at which savings and debts double and redouble. Malthus' idea that fertility rates would rise to reflect higher income levels has not materialized, but the financial principle described by Price remains apt: Owing to the recycling of interest receipts into new lending, what grows geometrically are savings (*i.e.*, debts on the liabilities side of the balance sheet), not population.

Private individuals soon tried to make use of the compound interest principle. Peter Thelluson, a wealthy Swiss merchant and banker who had settled in London around 1750, set up a trust fund that was to accumulate and reinvest its income for a hundred years and then be divided among his descendants. His £600,000 estate was estimated to yield £4500 per year at 7½ percent interest, producing a final value of £19,000,000, over thirty times the original bequest.

Thelluson's will was contested in litigation that lasted 62 years, from his death in 1797 to 1859. Under William Pitt the government calculated that at compound interest—even as low as 4 percent—the trust would grow so enormous as to own the entire public debt by the time a century had elapsed. This prompted legislation known as Thelluson's Act to be passed in 1800, limiting such trusts to just twenty-one years' duration. By the time all the lawyers were paid, "the property was found to be so much encroached on by legal expenses that the actual sum inherited was not much beyond the amount originally bequeathed by the testator."[18]

---

[17] The demographic reality is that fertility rates taper off as incomes rise. Over time, breakthroughs in agricultural and mining technology have increased productivity in these sectors more rapidly than has occurred in manufacturing, so that food and other consumption goods have grown faster rather than more slowly than population.

[18] *Palgrave's Dictionary of Political Economy*, citing the Annual Register (1797) and *Chambers' Encyclopaedia* vols. 8 and 10.

But the savings of the living have continued to mount up. The banker Geoffrey Gardiner observes that in the late 1970s,

> the burgeoning oil revenues of the producers were further gilded by the addition of high interest earnings. At their highest British interest rates had the effect of doubling the cash deposits of the oil-producers in only five years, or 16.3 times in twenty years! ... The wisdom of an earlier age, which had led to the passing of 'Thelluson's Act' to discourage the establishment of funds which compounded interest indefinitely, had been forgotten.[19]

This is essentially the principle voiced by Francis Bacon in his famous essay on usury:

> Usury bringeth the treasure of a realm into few hands, for the usurer, being at certainties, and the other at uncertainties, in the end of the game most of the money will be in the box, and a State ever flourisheth where wealth is more equally spread.[20]

It was echoed in 1840 by the French socialist Proudhon's axiom that the financial "power of Accumulation is infinite, [yet] is exercised only over finite quantities." "If men, living in equality, should grant to one of their number the exclusive right of property; and this sole proprietor should lend one hundred francs to the human race at compound interest, payable to his descendants twenty-four generations hence,—at the end of 600 years this sum of one hundred francs, at five per cent., would amount to 107,854,010,777,600 francs; two thousand six hundred and ninety-six times the capital of France (supposing her capital to be 40,000,000,000, or more than twenty times the value of the terrestrial globe!"[21] Hopes to increase human welfare through higher economic productivity would be stifled, Proudhon warned (in good Saint Simonian fashion), if the self-expanding power of interest-bearing claims were not checked by policies to replace debt with equity investment.

Socialist Analyses of the Dynamics of Compound Interest

The instability that is caused as the exponential growth of interest-bearing claims overwhelm economies has been analyzed mainly by socialists and by rather crankish writers at the right wing of the political spectrum. It seems

---

[20] Geoffrey Gardiner, *Towards True Monetarism* (London 1993): 135.
[19] Francis Bacon, *On Usury*, Essays (1625).
[21] P. J. Proudhon, *What is Property*, First Memoir, Eighth Proposition (New York, n.d.: 215).

that only reformers out of the mainstream have been willing to cast doubt on the viability of savings loaned out without constraint, for it challenges the sanctity of debt. What ultimately is at stake is whether debt convulsions are inevitable, and whether the debts in fact can be paid.

We are speaking of nothing less than the feasibility of economic redemption. To recognize that debts and savings grow independently of the capacity to pay is to throw into question the assumption that savings invested in loans can be redeemed. Most economists have shied away from suggestions that

> **D**ebt deflation occurs when purchasing power is removed from the spending stream of labor and business by siphoning debt service (interest and amortization) from their incomes, and using government tax revenues to pay bondholders rather than to spend it on public spending or infrastructure investment, education, health and other social welfare.

unlike merely cyclical self-correcting wavelets, financial crises tend to grow worse until insolvencies wipe out savings that have been badly invested. There is a preference for praising the saving/debt process, although people are beginning to question whether governments should go so far as to bail out savers at the top of the economic pyramid.

Bankruptcy has long been the financial consequence of savings being recycled into real estate, stock market holdings and bonds that lose their value. A century ago crashes would have wiped out both sides of the balance sheet, bad financial claims and liabilities together. But today's defaults threaten the ability of banks to pay their depositors, and of insurance companies to pay their policy holders, on a scale that is without precedent. There is a growing reluctance to write off bad loans, even at the cost of keeping debt- and savings-ridden economies insolvent. The most recent example is Japan, whose savings were placed in speculative real estate and stock market loans in the Bubble Years of the 1980s. To write off these bad loans would involve writing off the savings that are their balance-sheet accounting counterparts. The price Japan has paid for not coming to terms with the fact that these debts have lost their backing has been to remain mired in depression since the early 1990s, with over 60 percent of its tax revenues devoted to debt service (as of 2000).

The financial dynamics unfolding today were foreseen a century ago. Marx called money lent out at interest a "void form of capital,"[22] and described high finance as based on "imaginary" or "fictitious" capital. It was fictitious because it consisted not of the means of production but of bonds, mortgages, bank loans and other financial claims **on** the means of production. It was fictitious because in the end its demands for payment could not be met. Attempts to service the rising debt burden deflated the market for commodities, causing gluts that led to crises in which businesses scrambled for money and the banks themselves were caught short and failed. Interest charges ate into profits, deterring investment in plant and equipment by diverting revenue to economically empty financial operations. A growing wedge of disposable personal and business income was absorbed by debt service, leaving less to be spent on goods and services. In these respects financial capital was antithetical to tangible physical capital.

Marx described productive capital investment by the formula M–C–M′, signifying money (M) invested to produce commodities (C) that would sell for yet more money (M′). But the growth of "usury capital"—mortgage lending, personal loans, credit card debt, trade finance, government bond financing for war deficits—all this consisted of the disembodied M–M′, making money simply from money itself in a sterile operation. Yet despite this sterility, finance capital achieved dominance over tangible industrial capital in the foreclosures that followed in the wake of crashes. Transfers of property from debtors to creditors were inevitable as the growth of financial claims surpassed the ability of productive power and earnings to keep pace.

Debt deflation occurs when purchasing power is removed from the spending stream of labor and business by siphoning debt service (interest and amortization) from their incomes, and using government tax revenues to pay bondholders rather than to spend it on public spending or infrastructure investment, education, health and other social welfare. As the domestic market shrinks, labor and business have less ability to repay their debtors. In this deteriorating situation people tend to save even more (if they can), to protect themselves against their prospective loss of income or loss of a job, much as Japan's consumers saved more as their economy fell into depression in the 1990s. Their

---

[22] In Volume III of *Capital* (ch. xxx) and Volume III of *Theories of Surplus Value* (both published posthumously from notes made in the early 1850s; Chicago 1909): 461.

fears became a self-fulfilling prophecy as the economy slowed further, causing even more real estate and business loans to go bad.

Yet, as chapter 4 below describes in greater detail, having analyzed finance capital's tendency to grow exponentially, Marx did not incorporate this idea into his long-term system. Having provided a compendium of historical citations recognizing the self-expanding character of money-capital multiplying at compound interest, he announced that finance capital would be subordinated to the dynamics of industrial capital rather than growing to dominate it. "In the course of its evolution, industrial capital must therefore subjugate these forms and transform them into derived or special functions of itself." With an optimistically Darwinian Victorian ring he wrote that the destiny of industrial capitalism was to mobilize finance capital to fund its economic expansion, rendering usury an obsolete vestige of the "ancient" mode of production. "Where capitalist production has developed all its manifold forms and has become the dominant mode of production," Marx concluded his draft notes for *Theories of Surplus Value*, "interest-bearing capital is dominated by industrial capital, and commercial capital becomes merely a form of industrial capital, derived from the circulation process."[23] The financial problem would take care of itself as industrial capitalism mobilized savings more productively than ever before had been the case.

European and North American public debts did indeed seem to be on their way to being paid off during the relatively war-free century 1815–1914. As savings were mobilized to fund heavy transport, industry, construction and mining, the economy's debt burden actually seemed likely to be self-amortizing by being linked to industrial capital formation. As the *Technocracy Study Course* published by Technocracy, Inc.—one of the movements of the 1920s and '30s that retained emphasis on the importance of compound interest—put matters:

> The physical expansion of industry was, in a period from the Civil War to the World War, a straight compound interest rate of growth at about 7 per cent per annum. During that period, the debt structure was also extending at a similar rate of increment. Since the World War ... the rate of physical expansion has been declining, and physical production has been progressively leveling off. Thus, for the period prior to the World War there was a close correspondence between the rate of growth of the debt structure, and of the physical industrial structure. Since the World War, while the physical structure has been leveling off

---

[23] Karl Marx, *Theories of Surplus Value* (Chicago 1971), III: 468.

in its growth, the debt structure, not being subject to the laws of physics and chemistry, has continued to expand until now the total long- and short-term debts are only slightly less than the entire wealth, or monetary value of all the physical equipment. *As time progresses this discrepancy between the rate of growth of the physical equipment and that of debt must become greater, instead of less.* The implications of this will be interesting to consider.[24]

The Technocracy Inc. movement based its financial views on "the Compound Interest Property of Debt," according to which "debt is expected to generate more debt, or to increase at a certain increment of itself per annum," around five percent over the long term. But like Marx, having drawn attention to this dynamic, the Technocrats dropped matters there, without formulating a positive policy recommendation.

> # T
> ## he principle which asserts that a dollar will grow into two dollars in a number of years, and keep on multiplying until it represents all of the wealth on earth ...
> J. W. Bennett (1898)

Other economic reformers managed to ignore financial problems altogether. Yet the statistics compiled by Thorold Rogers in *Six Centuries of Work and Wages* (1885: 539 ff.) indicated that English labor had lived as well on the eve of the discovery of America in the mid-15th century as in the late 19th-century factory towns.[25] The surplus was accruing to the owners of wealth. Reflecting the political success of Marxian socialism as compared to the sectarianism of other movements, there was a growing denunciation of industrial capitalists rather than financiers or landlords.

---

[25] Technocracy, Inc., *Technocracy Study Course* (New York 1934): 136 f. (italics in original).
[24] Thorold Rogers in *Six Centuries of Work and Wages* (London 1885): 539 ff.

Flürscheim and Bennett Put Compound Interest at the Center of Their Economic Analysis

A number of obscure financial writers in the 1890s found the most serious threat to prosperity to be the growth of interest-bearing debt. The problem on which they foundered was what to do about it. Banning interest outright appealed only to a few religious fundamentalists. Some reformers called for government banking, whose earnings would finance public spending while keeping the credit monopoly out of private hands.

Another proposal that has attracted lasting (if cultish) attention was to steadily reduce the value of money and financial claims by imposing a monetary stamp duty that would offset the interest yielded by such investments. This financial tax would have the advantage of freeing the rest of the economy—labor and capital—from taxation. Thanks to Keynes, the best remembered advocate of this policy is the Swiss-German Silvio Gesell. His money tax was inspired by Henry George's land tax. Together, he pointed out, the money and land tax would mobilize all the economy's *rentier* income to support the community rather than an exploitative class.

Gesell was influenced by the German-American Michael Flürscheim, who had been Henry George's major European collaborator. His *Clue to the Economic Labyrinth* was published in Australia by Marx's British publisher, Swan Sonnenschein. Other critiques of interest bearing debt—most notably, J. W. Bennett's *A Breed of Barren Metal* (1895) and John Brown's *Parasitic Wealth* (1898)—were printed by Marx's U. S. publisher, Charles H. Kerr. Bennett and Brown agreed with land reformers that the economy's surplus was being siphoned off in the form of *rentier* income, but pointed out that most land rent ended up being taken by creditors in the form of interest, which also absorbed a rising share of industrial and monopoly profit.

Along with the fight over deflationary gold policies (in opposition to the free coinage of silver), the debt problem propelled monetary issues to the forefront of economic reform for the next two decades. A spate of books were inspired by the financial panic of July 1893 that led banks and commercial houses to suspend payment, throwing millions of American workers into the streets as factories were closed. The deflationary aftermath saw mortgage charges bankrupt farmers as the government rolled back prices to the point where the price of gold had stood prior to the Civil War inflation. Prices for crops and other goods fell, but debts were fixed in value, making it harder for them to pay.

Bennett described a *rentier* caste drawing the world's wealth into its hands as the inventive powers of industry were outrun by the inexorable mathematics of compound interest, "the principle which asserts that a dollar will grow into two dollars in a number of years, and keep on multiplying until it represents all of the wealth on earth."[26] The most serious economic problem facing America, he explained, was that

> under the laws of interest and rent the capitalists of the country ... each year receive an amount of wealth so large that they are able to save from it a sum greater than the yearly net increase of the wealth of the nation.[27]

Bennett emphasized that the problem with saving was not merely that money saved was not spent on current goods and services, but that it was lent out at interest. Economies became more unstable as "interest-bearing wealth increases in a ratio which is ever growing more and more rapid,"[28] leaving few assets unattached by debt. John Brown (1898: 81f.) explained how rapidly this process occurred:

> At ten per cent the principal is doubled every seven years, so that in less than a century the interest is 16,384 times the principal, and after that the principal increases at such a stupendous rate that the figures soon become unmanageable. At five percent the principal doubles every fourteen years, just half as rapidly as at ten per cent. Interest accumulates in a geometric ratio, while savings increase arithmetically. Thus if $10 is saved up, say every seven years, in 140 years the principal will amount to $200. If, however, ten dollars is put into a bank at ten per cent interest every seven years, at the end of 140 years the principal will have become over twenty millions of dollars![29]

Here, he concluded, "is the subtle principle which makes wealth parasitic in the body of industry—the potent influence which takes from the weak and gives to the strong; which makes the rich richer and the poor poorer; which builds palaces for the idle and hovels for the diligent."[30]

These dynamics explained the financial crises that plagued economies "whose financial systems are founded on rent and interest-taking." Creditors called in their loans when they saw how risky business conditions had become as a result of the growth of debt, producing scallop-shaped upswings followed by abrupt crashes—"a trade depression every ten years or oftener and panics

---

[26] J. W. Bennett, *A Breed of Barren Metal* (Chicago 1895): 87.
[27] *Ibid.*: 151.
[28] *Ibid.*: 49.
[29] John Brown, *Parasitic Wealth* (Chicago 1898): 81f.
[30] *Ibid.*

every twenty years," Bennett explained, as "there are not available assets to meet [creditor] demands and at the same time keep business moving."[31]

The mathematics of compound interest also explained "the extremely rapid accumulation of wealth in the hands of a comparatively few non-producers," as well as "the abject poverty of a large percentage of the producing masses."[32] Interest charges were responsible for "the failure of improved machinery to better the conditions of the producing masses in a degree at all commensurate with the increased producing power which it has given to the laborer," Bennett elaborated. "The financial group becomes rich more rapidly than the nation at large; and national increase in wealth may not mean prosperity of the producing masses."[33] Countering Frederick Bastiat's banal claim that everyone was paid according to the economic service performed, he pointed out that non-producers received "much the largest salaries," for "one's income is often in inverse ratio to the service which he does his fellow men."[34]

Much as had occurred in Rome and other civilizations that succumbed to usury, the accrual of financial fortunes—or more to the point, their failure to find their counterpart in new tangible capital investment—threatened to undermine the American economy

> … and lead to its decay and final destruction.
>
> There is not enough wealth produced to meet all of these obligations. Either the current expenses of production cannot be paid or the fixed charges of rent and interest cannot be met. If current expenses are not paid, manufacturing plants deteriorate, fixed capital is encroached upon, wages are reduced and laborers thrown out of employment. Current obligations are not met. The business man finally becomes bankrupt, or the wage-workers become bankrupts and outcasts depending on charity for support. If interest is not paid, then the wealth hypothecated for the loan is appropriated by the lender, and the borrower, failing to meet his obligations, becomes a bankrupt.[35]

Rather than seeing finance in an inherently symbiotic relationship with tangible activity, Bennett and Brown hoped that economies might operate without charging interest. But how could businesses get by without credit? Could credit be advanced without interest being charged? If not, how could

---

[31] J. W. Bennett (1895): 93.
[32] Ibid.: 80.
[33] Ibid.: 102
[34] Ibid.: 111.
[35] Ibid.: 85.

short-term credit be prevented from mounting up to unmanageable proportions over time as loans were rolled over rather than repaid, or simply had
their interest accruals added on to the debt balance? "If interest-taking is
right," argued Bennett, then "compound interest-taking is right.... And what
makes matters worse, it is not one dollar that is assumed to have the power of
indefinitely increasing, but several billions of dollars."[36]

In the long run economies would have to succumb, while polarizing along
the way:

> A syndicate of less than one hundred American capitalists, if allowed
> to collect interest on their capital at a low rate and re-invest for 150
> years or less, would at the end of that time own the earth and all real
> and personal property thereon. This is a simple mathematical proposi-
> tion, capable of exact demonstration, and any one who doubts the truth
> of this statement may set all doubts at rest by computing compound
> interest on one and one-half billions of dollars for one hundred and
> fifty years, at five per cent per annum.[37]

These financial critics went beyond orthodox economists by showing that
interest-bearing debt grew by its own mathematical laws. But they were unable
to propose a way in which the expansion paths of physical production and
interest-bearing claims might co-exist so that debts and the ability to pay grew
at similar rates. The idea of an interest-free system—or the need for debt
cancellations—was too radical for most people to contemplate. It was more
popular to advocate general strikes or outright revolution to seize the means of
production and expropriate the proprietors—or at least to tax them—than to
set about designing a financial system that somehow might avoid credit crises.

If these financial critics writers are forgotten today, it is because most
reformers focused on more immediate problems such as ameliorating the
oppressive conditions of factory life and urban poverty, legislating standards for
public health and safety in the workplace, and breaking up or regulating the
emerging trusts and monopolies. Little popular momentum to restructure the
financial system could arise until a more acceptable alternative could be found
than banning interest (Bennett and Brown) or depreciating money's value
(Gesell and the subsequent Social Credit movement).

One of the most thoroughgoing expositions of the problems caused by
compound interest was by the advocate of land and debt reform, Michael
Flürscheim:

---

[36] *Ibid.*: 47f.
[37] *Ibid.*

It is true that the employer is the sponge which sucks up the profit, the greater value (Mehrwerth, as Marx calls it) of labor's product, but only to yield it to the rent and interest lords, as well as to the middlemen, who together press it out of him as quick as he gets it, barely leaving him on the average the hard earnings of his own work, and, what is worse, taking the power from him of increasing production to its full potentiality."[38]

Contrasting finance to physical capital, he called on labor and industry to attack "the real enemy," the financial interests that who ended up with most industrial profit in the form of debt charges, as well as most of the rent collected by landlords—profits and rents squeezed out of labor and consumers.

The above brief summary shows that already a century ago some writers were able to describe dynamics that seem quite modern today, yet have struck monetarist economists as anomalous rather than inherent problems. Financial claims for payment, Flürscheim explained, constituted the bulk of the world's capital, not factories and other industrial means of production:

When an orator or writer has to reply to a socialist's attack upon capital as the oppressor of labor, he points to what orthodox economy calls capital, and speaks of our wonderful progress due to our improved means of production and distribution, whereas his antagonist thinks of Government bonds, of land monopoly, of mining rights, of all kinds of tribute claims selling at Exchange for certain amounts, and not at all falling under the orthodox definition of capital, though representing that capital which people principally have in view when they use the term.[39]

The reality was that finance capital stood at odds with—and subdued—industrial capital and other physical capital. The problem lay not in the personal character of bondholders and bankers, but in the impersonal mathematics of compound interest that led savings to build up in ways that indebted society's economic assets. "All exertions, all improvements in the methods and tools of labor, the strictest economy, the severest self-denial, are powerless to compete with the rapidity of self-increase possessed by capital placed at compound interest, and they cannot keep up with its demands."

To illustrate the dynamic at work, Flürscheim composed an allegory in which the Spirit of Invention was pitted against the Demon of Interest and his offspring, Compound Interest, in a battle to see whose powers were stronger. The Spirit of Invention had an army of tools and machines, water power, air

---

[39] Michael Flürscheim, *Clue to the Economic Labyrinth* (Perth and London 1902):116.
[38] *Ibid.*:347.

and wind power, fire and steam power to drive machinery. But Flürscheim asked whether its minions really would bring about a golden era, or whether this power could be conquered by finance capital and made to serve it by producing an economic surplus for its own use, as financial tribute, rather than serving mankind in the form of higher living standards.[40]

The strategy of Compound Interest followed what Napier had described centuries earlier, in 1617. The moral was that no matter how greatly technology might increase humanity's productive powers, the revenue it produced would be overtaken by the growth of debt multiplying at compound interest. Strictly speaking, it is savings that compound, not debts themselves. Each debt is settled on an individual basis in one way or another, but creditors recycle their interest and amortization into new interest-bearing loans. The only problem for savers is to find enough debtors to take on new obligations. "What is compound interest?" Flürscheim asked. "Is it anything else than the fresh investment of earnings of capital?" The major source of loanable funds is repayments on existing loans, re-lent to finance yet new debts. Individual loans are repaid, but there is no diminution in the volume of savings. Rather, interest receipts swell the volume of savings.

J. P. Morgan and John D. Rockefeller are reported to have called the principle of compound interest the Eighth Wonder of the World. Flürscheim described Napoleon as having voiced a similar idea upon being shown an interest table and remarking: "The deadly facts herein lead me to wonder that this monster Interest has not devoured the whole human race."

Flürscheim commented: "It would have done so long ago if bankruptcy and revolution had not been counter-poisons." And that is just the point, of course. Something must give when the mathematics of interest-bearing debt overwhelms the economy's ability to pay. For awhile the growing debt burden may be met by selling off or forfeiting property to creditors, but an active public policy response is needed to save the economy's land and natural resources, mines and public monopolies, physical capital and other productive assets from being lost to creditors.

Political responses to this problem are aggravated by the fact that the largest and most powerful creditors often are foreigners. Finance capital is much more cosmopolitan than land and industrial capital, and more mobile even than labor. The mathematics of savings/debt leads not only to domestic antagonism, but shapes global diplomacy by pitting international creditors against debtor economies. In this ultimate showdown global finance is arrayed against national

---

[40] *Ibid.*: 327–333.

government autonomy. This is the key to understanding international relations from the papal Italian bankers of the 14th century in debtor countries such as England through today's IMF, World Bank and WTO maneuverings.

In the early decades of the 20th century such problems still seemed distant, despite Britain's role as the world's banker. Even the 1907 financial crash, which hit the United States hardest, did not create a crisis in economic theory. The financial problem appeared to be technical and monetary in character, solvable by providing yet more credit (and hence, increasing the volume of debt) so as to expand the money supply beyond the tight limits imposed by

Market mechanisms are able only to enforce a state of financial chaos, giving the appearance of being rational only in the sense that each element of this chaos can be assigned a price. There is no *a priori* mathematical solution that can explain the outcome. When trends intersect, the economy's crash point must be determined politically.

gold supplies ("specie"). A lender of last resort, the Federal Reserve System, was created in 1914. What really saved the day was the use of debt—government bonds and commercial bills-of-payment—as reserves for the banking system's credit creation.

For a century of peace, rising infrastructure investment had buoyed the savings/debt expansion by expanding productivity and raising incomes throughout the world. But World War I was about to break out, and its demands for destructive rather than productive investment ushered in a new line of financial theorizing, starting with the Inter-Ally debts and German reparations that were the Great War's financial legacy. It was these debts that would pose the Transfer Problem (the limits of how much could be paid from one national currency to another, "hard" currency), bringing on the Great Depression and in short order World War II.

The "Magic of Compound Interest"

The mathematics of compound interest dictate that debt service on the economy's rising ratio of savings and debts to income will tend to grow to the point where debt service absorbs an amount equal to the entire available economic surplus. Unless growth in savings—that is, the economy's debt overhead—finds its counterpart in a parallel growth in the ability to pay, more income must be squeezed out to pay interest on the rising volume of debt.

Germany after World War I is an example. It was able to pay reparations and other foreign debts only by borrowing new money. The "cure" for its debt problem thus turned out to be yet more debt, even as the economy's productive enterprises were stripped to pay creditors. Such "do it with mirrors" exercises can only succeed temporarily, because their underlying principle is that of a chain letter. By absorbing revenue that is needed to finance tangible direct investment, payment of debt service makes it increasingly difficult for economies to carry their debts.

Market mechanisms are able only to enforce a state of financial chaos, giving the appearance of being rational only in the sense that each element of this chaos can be assigned a price. There is no *a priori* mathematical solution that can explain the outcome. When trends intersect, the economy's crash point must be determined politically.

The solution will be shaped by the fact that financial power tends to transform itself into political power, and also into legal and even cultural power as it seeks to shape the electorate's perceptions in ways that serve its own objectives. On the most abstract level, society's shape is being transformed by the principle of compound interest working out its power politically, fiscally and in the intellectual plane of academic economics. In this respect finance has an intrinsic personality and an implicit evolutionary strategy, even if this worldview is not fully conscious.

It is not a pleasant view and that is why so many people avert their eyes. Banks and large institutional investors are coming to welcome crises as affording a grab-bag of new opportunities, now that they have mobilized government support for their initiatives.

The result is a new kind of class war, with new—financial—modes of exploitation. Today's global dynamics can be viewed as a struggle for domination (if not outright survival) between an alien financial dynamic that has been introduced into the world's industrial core, muvh like a new species introduced to an island environment with no natural checks. In this respect the proliferation of debt/savings is much like the mathematics of ecological pollution. We might think of it as debt/savings pollution swamping the economic environment while stifling "real" (that is, non-financial) growth.

In his book *Consilience*, Edward O. Wilson points out how impossible it is for the world's financial savings to grow at compound interest *ad infinitum*.[41] To demonstrate how rapidly the limit may be approached, he cites "the arithmetical riddle of the lily pond. A lily pod is placed in a pond. Each day thereafter the pod and then all its descendants double. On the thirtieth day the pond is covered completely by lily pods, which can grow no more." He then asks, "On which day was the pond half full and half empty? The twenty-ninth day."

By the time people feel obliged to argue over whether the financial glass is half empty or half full, we are on the brink of a financial crisis in which something must give—usually labor's income and savings. Exponential growth is not sudden. It may be slow, but it is inexorable. It also is unnatural, for the natural shape of economic phenomena is an S-curve, not an upward exponential sweep toward infinity.

Whether or not the predatory behavior of financial institutions causes a political crisis depends on how aware the population is with regard to what is happening. It is the task of financial lobbies, and the politicians and academic economists they support, to distract the population to other concerns. And it is the task of junk economics to promote the myth that economies tend naturally to return to equilibrium and equity when left alone, not to polarize in ways that favor *rentiers* and enable them to take over government, education, the popular press and cultural norms generally.

The financial sector's planners themselves recognize that the global economy is now living in this immediately pre-crash "last day." That is why they are taking the bailout money and run. If the crisis still seems distant to the rest of society, it is because people still think in terms of the entropic equilibrium mathematics that most economic model-builders employ rather than thinking exponentially.

The Inability of Financial Checks to Keep the Exponential Growth of Debts (and Savings) in Line with the Ability to Pay out of Economic Growth

Thelluson's Act of 1800 represented an attempt to provide a "moral and legal check" on the rate of reproduction of interest-bearing savings, to borrow a term from Malthusian population theory. Malthus himself had borrowed Price's imagery of how compound interest led to the exponential growth of debt, so it is fitting that financial dynamics should find demographic paral-

---

[41] Edward O. Wilson, *Consilience* (New York 1998): 313.

lels. After all, Malthus warned, it was the principle of compounding that spurred populations to multiply more rapidly than food production. This idea was implicit in the passage of Thelluson's Act, but few economists picked up on it.

Malthus held (wrongly) that fertility rates would increase and families would have more children if their incomes rose or the Poor Laws provided them with more means of subsistence. The actual tendency is for fertility rates to decline as incomes rise over time. Economists seemed on stronger ground in theorizing that supply pressures on food, raw materials and labor raise costs during the course of the business cycle, eroding the profits and cash flow out of which debts can be paid. Companies nonetheless must pay their debts, even as interest charges absorb their (shrinking) profits. Their losses create risky conditions in which a desperate demand for credit arises just to raise the money to pay bills. Interest rates increase as profits and incomes fall.

A point is reached where the financial bubble bursts, bringing the volume of debt back in line with the ability to pay. Such defaults and bankruptcies are the financial equivalent of the Malthusian checks of starvation and mortality. Much as the pace at which populations grow is determined by fertility relative to death rates, so the rate at which savings (and their mirror image, the economy-wide volume of debt) double and redouble is determined by the rate of interest subject to the financial check of bankruptcy. Interest rates alone thus do not determine the overall growth of savings, just as fertility rates alone do not determine the overall rate of demographic growth.

The checks cited by Malthus—war, pestilence, famine and starvation, as well as the moral check of abstinence—find their counterpart in the financial dynamics of savings and debts. Poverty is associated with high mortality rates as large proportions of children die in poor societies. High fertility rates occur as families compensate by having many children—but not by enough to increase the overall population. Likewise in the financial sphere, where the risks of default and bankruptcy are high, interest rates rise. As Adam Smith noted, the rate of interest often is highest in countries going fastest to ruin. But savings are wiped out by poverty and by the financial counterpart to emigration, in the form of capital flight. The flow of savings and of populations is from poor to rich countries.

Warfare has been a great spur to the growth of public debt, but it also has been accompanied by inflations that have wiped out much of the debt burden, as well as peoples' savings. (To be sure, postwar deflations have reversed this process.) Corporate takeovers, the financial equivalent of raiding and looting, also have increased the volume of debt, at high interest rates in the form of junk bonds. On the other hand, such credit likewise has suffered high default rates.

Malthus criticized the Poor Laws for encouraging the growth of population by giving the poor enough income to survive, marry and have children. The equivalent financial subsidy takes the form of government bailouts for banks and savers. This sustains the growth of savings—financial claims on the economy—by preventing the wipeouts that normally bring debts back in line with the economy's capacity to pay. Wealthy savers and financial institutions become public wards, much as the welfare systems of past centuries subsidized the poor. Modern critics have called such guarantees Moral Hazard, and urged governments to stop the practice, which is just the opposite of a Moral Check to the growth of savings and debt.

One form of voluntary restraint might take the form of fiscal and regulatory policies that encourage equity rather than debt financing, or that require interest payments to be made out of after-tax rather than pre-tax income. Similar moral checks include the religious sanctions against interest-taking found in Islam. But today's fiscal policies encourage debt financing rather than equity investment, while the usury laws that held down interest rates in past centuries have been abandoned. Today's governments act to forestall tight labor markets by raising interest rates, with the intention of deterring new investment and hiring, so as to hold wages down by maintaining a margin of unemployment. This increases the power of finance over labor.

Central bank policies that raise interest rates to slow new direct investment and hiring make economies even less able to carry their debt burden. In this respect the buildup of savings and encouragement of debt financing encourages a buildup of financial returns rather than tangible capital investment. Thus is antithetical to the goal of promoting high wages and rising labor productivity. The rate of interest is permitted to govern the doubling times of savings without the moral, political and religious checks that have rolled back the growth of financial overhead throughout history. there is only one ultimate solution: Debts that cannot be paid, won't be. The open question is, will this tear economies apart as the financial sector fights against this fate?

3

How Economic Theory Came to Ignore the Role of Debt

Starting from David Ricardo in 1817, the historian of economic thought searches in vain through the theorizing of mainstream economists for an acknowledgement of how debt charges

    (1) add a non-production cost to prices,
    (2) deflate markets by diverting purchasing power that otherwise would be spent on goods and services, and thereby
    (3) discourage capital investment and employment, and hence
    (4) put downward pressure on wages.

What needs to be explained is why government, academia, industry and labor have not taken the lead in analyzing these phenomena that remain all but forgotten — indeed, carefully ignored — by the mainstream economics curriculum.

I suppose one would not expect the tobacco industry to promote studies of the unhealthy consequences of smoking, any more than the oil and automobile industries would encourage research into environmental pollution or the linkage between carbon dioxide emissions and global warming. So it should come as little surprise that the adverse effects of debt are sidestepped by advocates of the idea that bankers rather than government planners should allocate the economy's resources and manage its development. Claiming that good public planning and effective regulation of credit markets is impossible, monetarists are silent with regard to how financial interests shape the economy to favor their own product: debt, growing at an exponential rate.

Governments throughout the world now leave monetary policy to the Central Bank and Treasury, whose administrators are drawn from the ranks of bankers or their academic factotums or outright lobbyists. Naturally enough, they seek to shape financial policy in their own interests. Backed by the Chicago School's advocacy of financial austerity, these doctrinaire financial planners oppose full-employment policies and rising living standards, not only as being inflationary but as consuming the economic surplus that is owed to creditors. The fear regarding inflation is that rising wages will increase prices, reducing the volume of labor and output that a given flow of debt service is able to command. The even more destructive fear is that rising wages will eat into the economic surplus that today's financial doctrine believes should be capitalized at the going rate of interest and financialized, that is, pledged for debt service.

Inasmuch as monetary policy is made by the central bank rather than by the Department of Labor, governments choose to squeeze out more debt service even at the expense of employment and direct investment. The public domain is sold (on newly created credit, which the government could have created itself) off to pay bondholders, even as governments cut taxes that deepen budget deficits — which then are financed by running up yet more debt. Most of this new debt is bought by the financial sector (including international institutions) with money from the tax cuts they receive from governments that are ever more beholden to them. The policy is capped by shifting the fiscal burden onto labor, by un-taxing finance, real estate and other interest-paying sectors.

The more economically powerful the FIRE sector becomes, the more it is able to translate this power into political influence. The most direct way has been for its members and industry lobbies to become major campaign contributors, especially in the United States, which dominates the IMF and World Bank to set the rules of globalization and debt proliferation in today's world. Influence over the government bureaucracies provides a mantel of prestige in the world's leading business schools, which are endowed largely by FIRE-sector institutions, as are the most influential policy think tanks. This academic lobbying steers students, corporate managers and policy makers to see the world from a financial vantage point.

Existing rules and practices are taken for granted as "givens" rather than asking whether economies benefit or suffer as a whole from a rising proportion of income being paid to carry the debt overhead (including mortgage debt for housing being bid up by the supply of such credit). Finance and banking courses teach how managers can obtain interest and asset-price gains by creating credit or using other peoples' savings, not how an economy may best steer savings and credit to achieve the best long-term development.

One would expect views on debt and credit creation to be determined by whether one is a creditor or a debtor, an investor, government bureaucrat or economic planner writing from the vantage point of labor or industry. But despite the variety of interest groups affected by debt and financial structures, one point of view has emerged almost uniquely, as if it were scientific truth rather than the financial sector's own self-interested spin. The discussion of finance and debt has been limited to monetarists with an anti-government ax to grind and vested interests to defend, and above all to promote financial deregulation.

This monetarist perspective has become more pronounced as industrial firms have been turned into essentially financial entities since the 1980s. Their objective is less and less to produce goods and services, except as a way to generate revenue that can be pledged as interest to obtain more credit from bankers and bond investors. These borrowings can be used to take over companies ("mergers and acquisitions"), to defend against such raids by loading themselves down with debt (taking "poison pills"), or to indulge in "wealth creation" by buying back their own shares on the stock exchange or simply to payout as dividendsrather than undertaking new direct investment. IBM has spent about $10 billion annually for several years to support its stock price in this way. As these kinds of financial maneuvering take precedence over industrial engineering, the idea of "wealth creation" has come to refer to raising the price of stocks and bonds that represent claims **on** wealth ("indirect investment") rather than direct investment in capital spending, research and development to increase production.

Labor no longer voices an independent perspective on such issues. Early reformers shared the impression that money and finance simply mirror economic activity rather than acting as an independent and autonomous force. Even Marx believed that the financial system would naturally evolve in a way that reflected the needs of industrial capital formation.

Today's popular press writes as if stock and bond prices and interest rates, reflect the economy's business conditions rather than influencing them. There is little recognition of financial dynamics intruding into the "real" economy in ways that are antithetical to nationwide prosperity. Yet it is well known that central bank officials claim that full employment and new investment may be inflationary and hence bad for the stock and bond markets. This is why governments raise interest rates to dampen the rise in employment and wages. This policy holds back the advance of living standards and markets for consumer goods, reducing new investment and putting downward pressure on wages and commodity prices. As tax revenue falls, government debt increases. Businesses and consumers also are driven more deeply into debt. Ultimately, the monetarist world view thus is self-destructive. Yet it is widely applauded at each step along the way.

If today's economy were the first in history to be distorted and depressed by such strains, economists would have some excuse for not being prepared to analyze how the debt burden increases the cost of doing business and diverts income to pay interest to creditors. What is remarkable is how much more clearly the dynamics of debt were recognized some centuries ago, before financial lobbying gained momentum. Already in Adam Smith's day it was a common perception that public debts had to be funded by tax levies, impairing the economy's competitive position by raising the price of living and doing business.

Before Ricardo: How National Debts Were Seen to Impair Economic Competitiveness

An important predecessor of Adam Smith, the merchant Mathew Decker, emigrated from Holland to settle in London in 1702. In the preface to his influential *Essay on the Causes of the Decline of the Foreign Trade*, published in 1744, he attributed the deterioration in Britain's international competitiveness to the taxes levied to carry the interest charges on its public debt. These taxes threatened to price its exports out of world markets by imposing a "prodigious artificial Value ... upon our Goods to the hindrance of their Sale abroad." Taxes on food and other essentials pushed up the subsistence wage level that employers had to pay, and hence the prices they had to charge as compared to those of less debt-ridden nations.

The tax problem thus was essentially a debt problem, which in turn reflected royal military ambitions. Eight centuries of warfare with France had pushed Britain deeply into debt. Interest on the government's bonds was paid by levying excise taxes that increased prices. The cost of doing business was raised further by the high prices charged by the trading monopolies such as the East India Company (of which Decker himself had been a director) that the government created and sold to private investors for payment in its own bonds.

The system of funding wars by running into debt rather than on a pay-as-you-go basis was called Dutch Financing because, as Adam Smith explained,[1] "the Dutch, as well as several other foreign nations, [have] a very considerable share of our public funds." In fact, they held more than half of these securities, including shares in major Crown corporations such as the East India Company and Bank of England, on which Britain paid a steady flow of interest and dividends that absorbed much of its trade surplus. "As Foreigners possess a Share of our national Funds," Smith wrote (anticipating the complaint of global debtors ever since), "they render the Public in a Manner tributary to them, and may in Time occasion the Transport of our People, and our Industry."

The economic popularizer Malachy Postlethwayt estimated that Seven Years War (1757–63) cost Britain £82 million. In the year the conflict broke out, his pamphlet on *Great-Britain's True System* explained how the taxes levied to service the public debt had increased the nation's cost structure:

> the Sum-Total of these Taxes is at least 31 per Cent. of the annual Expense of the whole People of England. Now, where is the Nation with which we can enter into a Competition of Commerce on equal Terms? And what Matter is the 1 or 2 per Cent. Advantage we boast over some of our Rivals in the interest of Money, towards restoring the Equality between them and us?[2]

---

[1] Adam Smith, *The Wealth of Nations*, vol. V, iii; Cannan ed.: 452.
[2] Malachy Postlethwayt, *Great-Britain's True System* (London 1757): 165.

The economy's financial problem was whether to lend its savings to the government (almost exclusively to finance wars) or invest them in industry and commerce. "The more the Nation runs into Debt," Postlethwayt warned, "the more Money will be locked up in the Funds, and the less will there be employed in Trade."[3] Taxing the population to pay interest to public creditors would drain money that otherwise could be used to fund private investment. "Before such Debt took Place, every body possessed their whole Gains," he added "If the present public Debt instead of being encreased, was paid off, the Profits of the Manufacturers, Tradesmen and Merchants, &c. would be all their own," doubling their rate of profit. "This would be equal in every Respect to a Bounty to that Amount on all our Productions and Fabricks: with that Advantage we should be able to undersell our Neighbours; Our People would of Course multiply; Our Poor would find ample Employment; even the aged and infirm might then earn enough to live upon; new Arts and new Manufactures would be introduced, and the old ones brought to greater Perfection."[4]

Inasmuch as paper credit was convertible into bullion, the outflow of capital and dividends reduced the monetary base for Britain's credit superstructure. This threatened to leave the nation with no wherewithal to employ labor, and hence little domestic market for its own products. Like many of his contemporaries, Postlethwayt decried the remittance of debt service to Dutch investors on the ground that the outflow of bullion led to a monetary stringency, resulting in less production and higher prices.[5] This is just what modern third world debtors have suffered for the past half-century under IMF austerity programs in order to pay their foreign-currency debts.

Even if all the debt were held at home, Postlethwayt warned, "it would not upon that account be less pernicious." Taxpayers would pay the bondholders, who tended to spend their revenue unproductively. Even worse:

> Funding and Jobbing too often … introduces Combination and Fraud in all Sorts of Traffic. It hath changed honest Commerce into bubbling; our Traders into Projectors; Industry into Tricking; and Applause is earned when the Pillory is deserved."[6]

He then described what modern analysts call the crowding-out phenomenon:

> The national Debts first drew out of private Hands, most of the Money which should, and otherwise would have been lent out to our skilful and industrious Merchants and Tradesmen: this made it difficult for such to borrow any Money upon personal Security, and this Difficulty

---

[3] *Ibid.*: 20f.
[5] *Ibid.*: 53.
[4] *Ibid.*: 52f.
[6] *Ibid.*: 21.

soon made it unsafe to lend any upon such Security; which of Course destroyed all private Credit; thereby greatly injured our Commerce in general ... "[7]

These complaints seem so modern that one may ask why Postlethwayt has been so neglected all these years. He might have been speaking of today's Latin American and Asian debtors in concluding that Britain's wars and standing armies

> hath overwhelmed the Nation with Debts and Burthens, under which it is at present almost ready to sink; and it hath not only hindered those Debts from being paid off, but will daily contribute to enhance them; for while there is more to be got by Jobbing, than by dischargeing our Debts, all Arts will be used to encrease the new Debts, not to redeem the Old.[8]

The protests by Smith and Decker against the sale of public monopolies likewise anticipated today's complaints that the monopoly profits, dividend payouts and interest payments by the former public utilities that Britain sold off to cope with its national debt problems in the 1980s and '90s have increased the costs that consumers and industry must pay.

The great systematizer of mercantilist principles, James Steuart, pointed to to the international problems posed by Britain's public debt:

> if we suppose governments to go on increasing, every year, the sum of their debts upon perpetual annuities, and appropriating, in proportion, every branch of revenue for the payment of them; the consequence will be, in the first place, to transport, in favour of the creditors, the whole income of the state, of which government will retain the administration.[9]

In view of what has happened to today's debt-wracked economies, such warnings as those of Steuart were prescient. Britain's government was threatened with the prospect of being turned into a mere collection agent for overseas bondholders and a rising financial interest at home.

If public borrowing forced up interest rates and diverted money away from productive investment, agricultural and industrial productivity could not keep pace with the growth in debt-service charges. The implication was that wars eroded rather than built British international power, because the decisive levers

---

[7] *Ibid.*: 69.
[8] *Ibid.*: 22 f.
[9] James Steuart, *Principles of Political Œconomy* (London 1767): II, 349 ff.

in Anglo-French rivalry lay beyond the military battlefield, above all in the financial sphere. Higher debts and taxes threatened to increase Britain's production costs and export prices, impairing its balance of trade regardless of the nation's military victories. Bullion would flow out and industry would stagnate, leaving Britain without the monetary sinews needed ultimately to defend itself against nations growing economically stronger.

Adam Smith's Views on the Debt Issue

Smith's protest against government profligacy and taxation was essentially an argument against war debts. He saw that new wars could be financed only by running further into debt, as populations were unwilling to support them when they had to pay taxes to defray their costs directly on a pay-as-you-go basis and thus felt the full economic burden immediately. The landed gentry, whose members formed the cavalry and officer corps, supported wars out of patriotism but opposed the proliferation of public debts whose interest charges were defrayed by taxes that fell ultimately on their own property. When the barons had opposed royal taxation in medieval times, rulers avoided the tax constraint by borrowing from Italian bankers and other lenders.

By the 18th century, governments had turned to more anonymous Dutch and domestic investors. This created a vested interest of bondholders. They portrayed their lending in as patriotic and economically productive a light as they could, claiming to provide capital to the nation. However, Smith wrote: "The opinion that the national debt is an additional capital is altogether erroneous."[10] Debt was the opposite of an engine of development. A nation's real wealth lay in its productive powers, not its money or the buildup of financial securities, which were only the shadowy image of real wealth. In fact, Smith explained, the policy of funding wars by bond issues diverted money that taxpayers could use more productively for direct investment. Taxes to pay debt service were

> defrayed by the annual destruction of some capital which had before existed in the country; by the perversion of some portion of the annual produce which had before been destined for the maintenance of productive labour, towards that of unproductive labour.[11]

Smith thus joined Decker, Postlethwayt and other critics of the Funding System in observing that public debts forced up taxes to pay interest charges—money that otherwise would be "employed in maintaining productive labour."

---

[10] Adam Smith, *The Wealth of Nations*, Vol. V, iii; Cannan ed., 460 ff.)
[11] *Ibid.*

Whereas industrial and commercial borrowers invested the proceeds to acquire capital whose earnings served to pay off the debt, governments borrowed to wage wars. A deteriorating economic spiral ensued as the taxes needed to carry these debts threatened to "diminish or destroy the landlord's ability to improve his land, and induce the owner of capital to remove it from the country."[12]

By the time Smith published *The Wealth of Nations* there seemed to be little likelihood of Britain paying down her national debt. Tax revenues had become "a fund for paying, not the capital, but the interest only, of the money which had been borrowed ..." He warned that at some point the burden of war debts would drive the belligerent nation bankrupt: "Bankruptcy is always the end of great accumulation of debt."[13]

Public bondholders felt little obligation to promote long-term investment for the nations to whose governments they lent money. Although "a creditor of the public has no doubt a general interest in the prosperity of the agriculture, manufactures, and commerce of the country, he has no interest in the good condition of any particular portion of land, or in the good management of any particular portion of capital stock." All that creditors really cared about was the government's power to levy taxes to raise the revenue to pay their debts. When the debt and tax burden had impoverished a country, they could remove their capital to other lands to repeat the process, as has happened again and again.

In sum, the ability of Britain's government to wage war rested on its power to run up debt, which in turn rested on the power to tax. The struggle to free the economy from taxes involved freeing it from public debt, and this required constraints on royal ambitions. Tax charges were not direct production costs, but were the price to be paid for military self-indulgence financed by bonds and other borrowings or the sale of the public domain and monopolies. Such taxes and sell-offs threatened to grow as military technology was becoming more capital-intensive for shipbuilding and cannon, and as the field of conflict with France stretched to America.

In this perception lay the seeds of the economic individualism of Adam Smith and many of his Whig contemporaries. If Britain were to secure a commercial advantage, it would have to reduce the taxes that had been imposed to carry its war debts. This entailed loosening the Old Colonial System so that economic competition would replace military and political coercion.

---

[12] *Ibid.*: 464 f.
[13] *Ibid.*: 450 f.

How Ricardo's Value Theory Ignored the Impact of Debt and Interest Charges

The debt discussion peaked at a time before most modern readers imagine that economic theory began. It was the bond broker Ricardo who ended the discussion rather than moving it forward. His labor theory value focused on the direct costs of production, measured in labor time. Credit and interest charges did not appear in his model. Workers earned the subsistence wage, and capital was valued in terms of the labor needed to produce it. Land was provided freely by nature, and its natural fertility (and hence, economic rent) was not a cost of production. As for the taxes to which Ricardo referred in his 1817 *Principles of Political Economic and Taxation*, they were the tariffs levied on agricultural products, not taxes levied to pay bondholders. Yet as the economic historian Leland Jenks has observed, Britain's government paid out some three-fourths of its tax revenue as dividends to bondholders in the typical year 1783. "Nine million pounds were paid to rentiers when the entire annual turnover of British foreign trade did not exceed thirty-five millions."[14]

By 1798, in the wake of the American and French Revolutions, William Pitt's financial policy of borrowing rather than running government on a tax-as-you-go basis imposed interest charges so heavy that, in Jenks' words,

> the nation was mortgaged to a new class of society, the *rentiers*, the fund-holders, for an annual sum of thirty million pounds, three times the public revenue before the revolutionary wars. The bulk of this sum was being collected in customs, excise and stamp duties, and constituted an engine by which wealth was transferred from a large consuming public to the much smaller number who owned consols,[15]

that is, government bonds with no fixed maturity, paying interest only—forever.

Prices for gold and other commodities had drifted upward after the paper pound's convertibility into gold was suspended in 1798. This set the stage for postwar depression after the Napoleonic Wars ended in 1814 and the Bank of England decided to restore the convertibility of sterling currency into gold at the low prewar price level. Debtors had to repay their obligations in money that was becoming more expensive, giving bankers and bondholders a free ride. Seeking to avoid blame, they nominated Ricardo for a safe seat in Parliament to represent their interests.

He set about to convince voters (still made up mainly of property holders) that the nation's economic problems were not caused by debt deflation, but by the Corn Laws, as Britain's agricultural tariffs were called. These high tariffs

---

[14] Leland H. Jenks, *The Migration of British Capital to 1875* (New York 1927): 14ff.
[15] *Ibid.*

supported high domestic prices for agriculture on the logic that high food prices would support rental earnings that could be invested to increase output. Over time this would enable Britain to replace imports with higher domestic production levels. But Ricardo argued that higher prices merely would give protected industries a free lunch, above all in the form of land rent, assuming no investment of this revenue to enhance productivity. His value theory provided a way to measure this unearned income, the element of price that had no counterpart in cost outlays except for the least efficient, highest cost (zero-rent) producers.

Given the subsistence conditions of the day, wages reflected food prices. These in turn reflected agricultural productivity. As Britain's population growth forced resort to poorer soils to produce the crops needed to feed it, producers on the most fertile land enjoyed a widening margin of market price in excess of their own low costs. The marginal supply price was determined by production costs on the least fertile soils, as long as protective tariffs blocked consumers from buying from lower-cost suppliers abroad.

Ricardo portrayed this agricultural cost differential — economic rent — as the paradigmatic form of unearned income, leaving interest charges out of his discussion. Economic rent was an element of price that had no corresponding cost of production for well-situated producers. The best way to minimize it, he explained, was for Britain to open its markets to foreign producers, so that low-yield high-cost soils would not need to be brought into cultivation. In exchange, foreigners would be asked to open their own markets to British manufactures. Each nation would produce what it was "best" at producing.

This tradeoff became the new objective of British diplomacy, whose market-oriented strategy replaced the Old Colonial System's coercive prohibitions against colonial manufacturing. Underlying this new policy was the perception that if Britain were to undersell its potential rivals to become the workshop of the world, it needed to minimize the money wages it paid its labor. The work force could be fed least expensively by importing grain rather than supplying it with high-cost domestic production. From 1817 through the repeal of the Corn Laws in 1846 the great political struggle in Britain therefore was between the free-trade Manchester School and the protectionist landed interest. In the United States, Germany and other countries the fight was between industrial protectionists and agricultural free traders who hoped to exchange their raw materials for relatively cheap British manufactures.

Ricardo was the first major economist to be a financier since John Law, who had managed France's Mississippi Bubble a century earlier, in the 1710s. At first glance it seems ironic that a bond broker should have developed classical trade theory in a way that viewed exchange essentially as barter rather than analyzing of how public and private-sector debt levels influenced production costs. Of all people who should have been aware of the financial elements of costing, it would seem that a bond broker would have had a comparative advantage in incorporating such considerations into his trade theory. Yet one looks in vain for a discussion of how debts and the taxes to carry them affected prices and international pricing.

Today, global competitiveness in automotives, steel-making and other capital-intensive industries turns less on wage rates than on variations in the cost of financing investment—interest rates and debt/equity ratios, taxes, subsidies and land or rent charges. Yet such financial considerations do not appear as elements of production cost in Ricardo's value theory, nor do they appear in today's Chicago School monetarism that stands in line with Ricardian doctrine. By focusing on labor-time proportions, Ricardo implied that non-labor expenses such as interest did not really matter.

As for taxes, they mattered to the extent that import tariffs forced up the price of labor's food and other necessities, but there was no memory of the long analytic tradition that attributed taxes to the Funding System's interest payments on the public debt. Hence, the policy conclusion of Ricardo's comparative labor-time approach to international trade theory was not that nations should avoid going into debt, but that they should abolish their tariffs to lower prices. There was no discussion of how the terms of trade shift against debtor countries, throwing their labor into competition with that in the creditor nations.

This limited and biased approach took bond brokers and bankers off the hook from accusations that their debt charges impaired the nation's well being. Furthermore, Ricardo's advocacy of free trade and its consequent focus on specialization of production among countries in itself promised to create a growing commercial lending market and an even larger bond market to finance transport infrastructure such as railroads, canals and shipbuilding.

No prior economist had claimed that public and private debt levels did not affect competitiveness. Yet this is what Ricardo's trade and value theory implied by not acknowledging any impact of debt service on international competitiveness, despite the fact that the drain of bullion to pay foreign creditors required monetary stringency. In these respects he was like an individual viewing the world around him, but not seeing himself in the picture. He denied that paying foreign debts had any serious economic impact, depicting them as being self-financing by an automatic monetary adjustment process. This makes his theory well suited to rationalize the kind of deflationary austerity measures that are imposed today on hapless debtor countries and provides the conceptual foundation for modern IMF and World Bank austerity doctrines.

Inasmuch as money and credit are forms of debt, one would think that monetarists working for central banks, finance ministries and business schools would analyze the debt burden and its interest charges, but they chose to follow Ricardo's shift of emphasis away from discussing its impact. Yet so powerful was his labor theory of value—powerful largely because of its abstraction, not its economic realism—that it led subsequent generations to speculate about how economies might function if debt and other non-labor costs had no effect on national competitiveness, living standards and the polarization of incomes and wealth.

Europe's 1815–1914 century of relative peace reduced the need for war financing, alleviating concerns about the public debt. The soaring productive powers of labor, capital and land enabled economies to carry higher levels of debt, financed readily by the growth of savings. The financial interests threw their weight behind industry. Opposing the landed aristocracy's Corn Laws, economic theory focused on price competitiveness as determined by labor productivity (without relating this to wage levels),using food prices as a proxy for wage levels. Credit was depicted as financing capital formation, headed by public spending on railroads, canals and other internal improvements in Britain and overseas.

Landholders had not yet become a major market for lenders. Except for insiders, personal and mortgage debts were viewed more as emergency measures than as a catalyst to get rich quickly. For all but a few financial operators the practice of debt pyramiding—borrowing money to buy properties rising in price—would have to await the modern era of asset-price inflation. There was little hint that financiers and real estate interests would join to form a *rentier* bloc. Nobody anticipated the degree to which urban real estate would develop into the banking system's major loan market, in which developers, speculators, absentee owners and homeowners would pay most of the land's net rental revenue to mortgage lenders.

From the Critique of Economic Rent to the Critique of Property Rights of Rentiers

Ricardo was the first major economist to portray protectionist landlords as having interests at odds with those of society at large. However, he believed that the rent problem—economic free rides—could be solved and British industrialization put on a firm footing by embracing free trade. His doctrines supported the flowering of trade credit and international investment, which were making quantum leaps forward in his day.

The opposition of Ricardian value and rent theory to Britain's vested interests, the landed aristocracy surviving from Britain's feudal past, made his approach appear progressive. Adam Smith had remarked that landlords liked to reap where they had not sown, he also described their objective as being to promote prosperity inasmuch as they were the major beneficiaries of a thriving economy and growing population. Ricardo agreed that they were its major beneficiaries, but accused them of gaining passively via a free ride—economic rent. He believed that economic rent was caused by factors inherent in nature (*e.g.*, fertility differentials), and that nothing could alter "the original and inde-structible powers of the soil" responsible for the natural superiority of some lands to others. When Malthus argued that landowners would invest their rental income in the land to improve its yields so as to earn more revenue, Ricardo replied that even if landlords did this, it would not overcome the dif-ferentials in soil fertility responsible for causing economic rent. Overall produc-tivity might rise if fertilizer or machinery were applied to the soil, but the yield *proportions* would remain unchanged!

As resentment against the public debt and creditors waned, hostility toward landlords peaked. Yet although Ricardo accused protectionism of increasing rents, he did not challenge the property rights of landlords to receive them. He shifted the economic policy debate away from the interest problem to that of rent, but did not question the property rights of landed rentiers any more than those of financial *rentiers*. It was the philosophic radical John Stuart Mill, son of the Richardian economic journalist and popularizer James Mill, who made a more far-reaching argument against the right of landlords to receive rent that once had accrued to the public domain. For J.S. Mill such rent was the ultimate free ride. He believed that rents (most of which were collected from inherited lands) should be returned to the public domain as the tax base, as it had been in feudal times.

This brought into question property rights as such, an inquiry that was pursued with the greatest intensity in France, and soon would be questioned even more radically by the Marxists. It was first in France, in the wake of the French Revolution's overthrow of the monarchy and feudal aristocracy, that a more radical challenge to property would be made, including a challenge to the interest collected by the banking families that had emerged to create a new, post-feudal power.

Banking Theory and Industrialization

Although British banks were all in favor of the flourishing trade that pro-industrial policies promised to bring about as Britain became the work-shop of the world, they played little role in developing an industrial credit market. What they had done for centuries was to provide short-term trade credit, discount bills of exchange and transfer international payments. Such lending promised to grow as a result of the global specialization of production that Ricardo's free-trade policies aimed to promote, but that was the extent of matters. Railroads, canals and other infrastructure used the stock and bond markets rather than banks for their long-term funding. Even so, Britain's securities markets did not provide its industry with long-term credit to anywhere near the degree achieved by the financial systems developed in continental Europe.

The economic dislocations in all countries after 1815 made it clear that banking and financial structures would determine which nations would ride the crest of the Industrial Revolution. Stepping back to take a broad view of what their nations needed to catch up, it was French and German policy makers that moved banking theory into the industrial age (as discussed in the preceding chapter).

If economies were to avoid systemic financial crisis, they would have to either carry the burden of financial claims accruing at compound interest, or periodically annul such claims. Most observers assumed that industry's productive forces somehow would be up to the task. Captains of industry were expected to steer the ship of state while industrial engineers would do the planning. Rather than watering stocks to load down enterprises with "fictitious capital" and ruining the world's colonial regions as they had done in Egypt and Persia, financiers would coordinate global industrialization. Financial systems would adjust to the underlying "real" economy, becoming a subordinate and derivative layer. Wealth creation would take the form of building up society's means of production and employment, not merely inflate stock market prices ("paper wealth").

The Post-Classical Reaction Analyzes Interest without Examining Money, Credit or Debt

Classical economic analysis was inherently political by virtue of dealing with society's most basic dynamics. It sought to free economies from the legacy of feudalism, above all a landed aristocracy. To promote these reforms the labor theory of value served to isolate economic rent as constituting unearned income, an element of pricing that represented a free lunch rather than a cost involving productive effort. To the extent that rent and interest were not bona fide production costs, they were brought under fire as appropriate sources of taxation or outright nationalization of the *rentier* claims and property rights that produced them.

These policy conclusions made it inevitable that an individualistic and anti-government reaction would arise against the reformist spirit of J. S. Mill as a halfway house to the revolutionary conclusions of Marx. The aim was nothing less than to change the topic.

The first big shots were fired in 1871, by Anton Menger in Austria and Stanley Jevons in Britain. Looking at the economy from a psychological vantage point that placed consumers rather than employers and businesses at the center, the Austrian individualists and British utilitarians based their perspective on individuals choosing what products to buy and whether to consume them in the present or defer their gratification to the future, in exchange for an interest payment.

The logical method was that of *ceteris paribus*, assuming that "all other things remaining equal." This approach made it possible to avoid thinking about the financial dynamics that were shaping the 19th and early 20th centuries. The psychological theory discussed interest rates as reflecting the degree of impatience to consume goods in the present rather than in the future, without reference to the magnitude of debt that resulted.

For starters, William Nassau Senior's "abstinence" theory represented interest as payment for a sacrifice on the part of savers, a "return" to reward them for the "disutility" or "service" of not consuming their income on the spot but deferring their gratification. Everything appeared to be a matter of choice, not contractual necessity or economic need. Financial fortunes were created by the impatience of the poor. Left out of this picture were military conquest, enclosure of the public domain, and inheritance of these grabs.

The monetary implication was that money was something saved to be lent out. No reference was made to how bank credit was created, or to the forfeiture of property that ensued when things went wrong. Yet the world's economies were being shaped by "things going wrong," not according to the neat textbook models.

If credit can be created at will, there is no need for abstinence. Banks are corporate institutions, and have no psychology to consume, but accumulate profits without any diminishing psychic utility. A financially realistic theory would focus on the banking system's credit creation and on the fact that governments are their major borrowers. Treasury bonds dominate financial markets and form the banking system's reserves. It is for purely political reasons that governments borrow from banks and *rentiers* — owing most to the wealthiest ranks of the population — rather than taxing wealth more heavily or simply monetizing public debts.

No gunboats appeared to enforce a creditor-oriented international diplomacy in this individualistic theorizing, nor were railway stock and bond waterings recognized. There was no coercion of debtors, and no unearned free lunch for *rentiers* and stock jobbers. Such considerations went beyond the measuring rod of utilitarian psychology, having disappeared into the miasma of *ceteris paribus*.

Adam Smith estimated that businessmen operating with borrowed funds would pay half their profits to their backers as interest. The interest rate thus would be half the rate of profit prior to interest charges. A century later the Austrian economist Eugen von Böhm-Bawerk reversed the causality, making profit rates depend on the rate of interest. He pointed out that businessmen would not tie up their money in a venture unless they could make more by investing in time-taking "roundabout" production techniques than they could make simply by lending out their money. On this basis the primary return to industrial and finance capital alike was interest. Profit reflected the time needed to plan and put in place complex capital investments, factoring in the time process by discounting investments at the rate of interest.

In the 1930s the Chicago economist Frank Knight explained that business profits represented the risk premium over and above the basic interest rate offered by risk-free bonds. Interest thus was made primary. Profit was treated as secondary, not as the system's key dynamic as had been the case in classical political economy. There was no thought of asset stripping, or of today's practice of corporate raiders coming in and slashing projects with long-term payouts, stopping research and development to take the money and run. The modern phenomenon of "financialization" makes no appearance in the abstract individualistic approach.

Theories of consumer preference for current over future consumption and other psychological reflections or profit-rate considerations do not require a discussion of the financial system, its volume of debt and the impact of its carrying charges on economic activity. There is no analysis of the phenomenon of compound interest, by which money breeds money.

To avoid "over-complicating" their analysis by taking into account the real-life phenomena of inflation and deflation, the polarization of wealth, and the ways in which debt service affects market demand and commodity prices, post-classical economists discussed production and consumption as if people lived in a debt-free barter economy. As Keynes described this new orthodoxy:

> Most treatises on the principles of economies are concerned mainly, if not entirely, with a real-exchange economy; and—which is more peculiar—the same thing is largely true of most treatises on the theory of money.[16]

---

[16] "A Monetary Theory of Production" (1933), in *The Collected Writings of John Maynard Keynes* 13: *The General Theory and After* (London 1973): 409f. Along these lines Keynes criticized Alfred Marshall for stating explicitly in his 1890 *Principles of Economics* (pp. 61 f.) "that he is dealing with relative exchange values. The proposition that the prices of a ton of lead and a ton of tin are £15 and £90 means no more to him in this context than that

Money was treated not as a political institution (*e.g.* to enable governments to pay their debts, or by governments giving value to money by accepting it as tax) but as a commodity whose value was determined by supply and demand. This assumed that money was a fixed volume that could easily be defined. Credit made little appearance.

Keynes warned that it would be dangerous for economists "to adapt the hypothetical conclusions of a real wage economics to the real world of monetary economics." The kind of thinking that underlay "real-exchange economics ... has led in practice to many erroneous conclusions and policies" as a result of "the simplifications introduced.... We are not told what conditions have to be fulfilled if money is to be neutral."[17]

If money were not neutral, neither was the debt burden. Yet Milton Friedman theorized that

> Holders of foreign currencies [such as U.S. dollars] want to exchange them for the currency of a particular country in order to purchase commodities produced in that country, or to purchase securities or other capital assets in that country, *or to pay interest on or repay debt to that country*, or to make gifts to citizens of that country, or simply to hold for one of these uses or for sale ... Other things the same, the more expensive a given currency, that is, the higher the exchange rate, the less of that currency will in general be demanded for each of these purposes.[18]

The implication is that countries will "choose" to pay less on their foreign debts as the dollars in which these debts are denominated become more expensive. But in reality they have no choice. Countries that try to pay less as the debt burden becomes more expensive to service are held in default and confronted with international sanctions, trade barriers and a loss of foreign markets. It is much the same when debtors have to pay their debts as domestic prices and

---

the value of a ton of tin in terms of lead is six tons ... 'We may throughout this volume,' he explains, 'neglect possible changes in the general purchasing power of money. Thus the price of anything will be taken as representative of its exchange value relative to things in general' [Keynes's italics].... In short, though money is present and is made use of for convenience, it may be considered to cancel out for the purposes of most of the general conclusions of the Principles."

If money is ignored, then so are savings, debts and their carrying charges. The role of money as a medium in which to pay debts is missed entirely, as is the monetization of debt in the form of free credit creation.

[17] *Ibid.*

[18] Milton Friedman, "The Case for Flexible Exchange Rates," *Essays in Political Economics* (Chicago 1953), repr. in Caves and Johnson, eds., *Readings in International Economics* (Homewood, Ill. 1968): 415 (italics added).

incomes fall. The debt burden becomes heavier. Price and income deflation thus not only shifts the proportions around, the basic structure and distribution of wealth is altered as a result of inexorable debt obligations.

Few economists ventured to specify the highly unrealistic conditions that would have to be met in order for monetary and credit disturbances, debt service and asset prices to be neutral. With sardonic humor Keynes observed:

> The conditions required for the 'neutrality' of money, in the sense in which this is assumed in .... Marshall's *Principles of Economics*, are, I suspect, precisely the same as those which will insure that crises do not occur. If this is true, the real-exchange economics, on which most of us have been brought up and with the conclusions of which our minds are deeply impregnated ... is a singularly blunt weapon for dealing with the problem of booms and depressions. For it has assumed away the very matter under investigation.[19]

John H. Williams, Harvard professor and advisor to the New York Federal Reserve Bank on the balance of payments observed:

> About the practical usefulness of theory, I have often felt like the man who stammered and finally learned to say, 'Peter Piper picked a peck of pickled peppers,' but found it hard to work into conversation.[20]

Such criticisms could be levied with even greater force against economists who ignore the role of debt and the revenue that needs to be diverted to pay debt service.

Economists who recognized that payment of debt service was not a part of the "real" economy but a subtrahend proposed that it be excluded from national income and product accounts altogether. Alfred C. Pigou reasoned in *The Economics of Welfare* that these accounts should exclude income

> received by native creditors of the State in interest on loans that have been employed 'unproductively,' *i.e.*, in such a way that they do not, as loans to buy railways would do, themselves 'produce' money with which to pay the interest on them. This means that the income received as interest on War loan—or the income paid to the State to provide this interest—ought to be excluded.[21]

---

[19] Keynes, *op. cit.*

[20] John H. Williams, "The Theory of International Trade Reconsidered" (1929), repr. in *Postwar Monetary Plans and Other Essays*, 3rd ed. (New York: 1947): 134f.

[21] Alfred C. Pigou, *The Economics of Welfare* (London 1920).

One wonders what Pigou might have said about the American practice of railroad directors issuing bonds to themselves gratuitously with no real *quid pro quo* —"watering the stock."

Excluding debt service from national income and produce accounts (NIPA) meant that its deflationary impact on incomes and prices—that is, the diversion of revenue from the production and consumption processes to pay debt service—could not be measured. Price adjustments are factored in by a GDP "price deflator" but the degree to which paying debt service interfers with the circulation of revenue between producers and consumers is lost—the phenomenon of debt deflation.

The limited analytic scope suggested by Pigou's definition of economic welfare would be logical if the aim of economic accounts were only to trace the growth of output and consumption. But measuring debt deflation—the degree to which debt service absorbs the economy's revenue—requires a calculation of all interest payments. To the extent that *rentiers* spend their interest receipts on consumer goods and capital investment, such spending would appear in the national production and consumption statistics. But this is a relatively small phenomenon—although it is the narrow point on which neoclassical utilitarian treatments of interest base themselves. To understand the dynamics of booms and depressions, debt pyramiding and economic polarization between creditors and debtors, it is necessary to include the effects of interest being plowed back into new lending, and thereby take into account the financial system as a whole. Yet this is not what Keynes himself did in discussing the rate of interest, saving and investment without integrating debt service into his income theory.

How Keynes Discussed Saving and Investment without Considering Debt Deflation

K eynes distinguished himself in the 1920s by defining the limits that existed to debt-servicing capacity, above all with regard to the Inter-Ally debts and German reparations stemming from World War I.[22] By 1931 he was pointing out that

> the burden of monetary indebtedness in the world is already so heavy that any material addition would render it intolerable.… In Germany it is the weight of reparation payments fixed in terms of money … In the United States the main problem would be, I suppose, the mortgages of the farmer and loans on real estate generally.[23]

---

[22] "An Economic Analysis of Unemployment" (1931, repr. 1973): 343–373.
[23] *Ibid.*

Keynes criticized deflationary monetary proposals as threatening to derange the financial superstructure of "national debts, war debts, obligations between the creditor and debtor nations, farm mortgages [and] real estate mortgages," throwing the banking system into jeopardy and causing "widespread bankruptcy, default, and repudiation of bonds."

But by 1936 he was concerned mainly with the shortfall in consumption resulting from people's propensity to save. Pointing out that new investment and hiring would not occur without stronger markets, his *General Theory of Employment, Interest and Money* described the solution to lie in getting people and governments to spend more. The countercyclical government hiring that he advocated would lead to budget deficits, which would have to be financed by debt. Yet the role of debt and its carrying charges was ignored in Keynesian macroeconomics. This loose end became a blind spot that has led to the most confusion among his followers.

Already in 1902, John Hobson's *Imperialism* warned that growing debt levels would lead to underconsumption. Creditors would collect money at home and search for new fields abroad to lend at relatively high rates, to less debt-ridden economies most in need of public infrastructure and other capital investment. This dynamic, Hobson believed, was the taproot of a new form of imperialism, one that had become financial rather than military in character.

Keynes took exception to Hobson's underconsumptionist views. As late as 1931 he viewed the problem of recovery as one of lowering interest rates to make direct investment more remunerative than buying bonds.[24] Writing to Hobson, he expressed the hope that lower interest rates also would solve the problem of debt deflation, but admitted that public spending might be needed to fill the gap created by the diversion of revenue to service debts. Hobson's point "that 'money savings may continue to grow faster than they can be profitably invested' would only be the case in the event of the rate of interest failing to fall fast enough," Keynes believed. But if it fell to zero (as happened in Japan in the late 1990s and in the United States under the Federal Reserve's Quantitative Easing program supplying reserves at 0.25 percent interest), the only solution would be "more spending and less saving." Hobson reiterated that the rate of interest was only of limited efficacy. "In certain situations of boom or slump its action seems very slight and unreliable.[25]

---

[24] 1973: 356f.
[25] Letters to Hobson dated Oct. 2 and 14, 1931, in Keynes, *Collected Writings*, vol. 13 (1973): 330–336.

Keynes came to accept this position by the time he published the *General Theory* five years later. His description of the liquidity trap helped swing the political pendulum back toward government activism, using deficit financing to pump enough income into the economy to replace the purchasing power that debt service absorbed and saving withdrew from the private sector's spending stream. In time, Keynesian liberalism would call for government spending to employ labor that would spend its income on goods, whose sale would provide profits for industrial investors. "The system is not self-adjusting," he wrote in 1933, "and, without purposive direction, it is incapable of translating our actual poverty into our potential plenty."[26] Expenditures that pushed the U.S. Government budget $1 billion into deficit in 1931, he told an American audience, "are just as good in their immediate effects ... as would be an equal expenditure on capital works; the only difference—and an important one enough—is that in the former case we have nothing to show for it afterwards."[27] The same was true of war spending, of course.

Keynes understood the financial sector as clearly as any economist of his day, yet he wrote in a way that diverted attention from the deflationary character of debt. Blaming high interest rates for inducing savers to buy financial securities that not find a counterpart in new direct investment, he went so far as to call for "euthanasia of the *rentier*." He criticized Say's Law, that production creates its own demand by paying employeesand capital-goods producers who, inturn, spent their income on byinf what was produced. But he did not make clear what proportion of saving resulted from paying debt service; that is, he did not distinguish loan repayments from fresh discretionary saving. National income statistics today count paying off a debt as "saving," because it is a negation of a negation (debt). And increasingly, saving takes the form of compulsory payments to creditors (see chapter 11 below).

Having spent years emphasizing that debt payments are not a matter of discretion but reflect contractual obligations, Keynes dropped this idea in his *General Theory*. Much confusion has resulted from the Saving = Investment equation, as if all saving took the form of tangible direct investment in factories, machinery, construction and other means of production. His use of the word "hoarding" had connotations of money kept in a mattress, but its more prevalent forms were "indirect" investment in securities and debt pay-downs. This role of debt and debt-service was not noted clearly by his followers in Britain, the United States or other countries.

---

[26] *Collected Writings* (1973): 491.
[27] *Ibid.*: 356 ff.

In a 1934 article Keynes noted that anyone who rejected the idea that economies adjusted automatically to any external disturbance—in particular to debt problems—was labeled a crank. He placed himself in their ranks, and his *General Theory* acknowledged the writings of the Swiss-German economist Silvio Gesell as representative of this approach. On the other hand, he noted:

> The strength of the self-adjusting school depends on its having behind it almost the whole body of organised economic thinking and doctrine of the last hundred years. This is a formidable power.... It has vast prestige and a more far-reaching influence than is obvious. For it lies behind the education and the habitual modes of thought, not only of economists, but of bankers and businessmen and civil servants and politicians of all parties."[28]

Keynes acknowledged that he still had one foot in the orthodox tradition. In the end, all he could do was blame economists for not having developed "a satisfactory theory of the rate of interest" to serve as the regulator of saving, investment and employment. But how could this be done, without tracing the effect of interest rates on the doubling times of debts, the economy's ability to pay, and the consequences of forfeiture under distress conditions?

Debt and Interest Rates Are Autonomous from the "Real" Production and Consumption Economy

K eynes was not the first economist pointing to savings as not being an unalloyed benefit. Marx had described how the "new aristocracy of finance, a new sort of parasites in the shape of promoters, speculators and merely nominal directors ... demands ... precisely that others shall save for him."[29] The saving in this case takes the form of debt repayment with interest, much as British money lenders advertise that buying a home helps buyers save by building up equity via their mortgage payments each month. The liquid "savings" in the form of debt payment accrue to the lenders, not the debtors. But it was mainly fringe groups that warned of the collision course between the debt overhead and the "real" economy's production and consumption trends.

From the Austrians through Fisher and Keynes, economists sought to deduce the rate of interest on the basis of consumer utility and capital productivity. Their dream of integrating the determination of interest rates into price and value theory was something like trying to untangle the Book of Revelation.

---

[28] "Poverty in Plenty: Is the Economic System Self-Adjusting?" *The Listener*, Nov. 21, 1934 (Keynes, *ibid.*: 488).

[29] *Capital* III: 519f.

Their search to discover a neat mathematical solution, determinable in advance, culminated in Keynes's attempts to formulate a "monetary theory of production" incorporating interest rates and money. Unfortunately, he was mixing apples and oranges. The source of confusion lay in the assumption that money and credit have a tangible, real cost of production that can be factored into a general, integrated theory of production, investment and employment.

In reality no such unified field theory is possible, because finance is autonomous from the production-and consumption "real" economy. The government's central bank administers interest rates and commercial banks may make reckess of fraudulent loans.

At first glance it might seem that a "real" cost of interest might be imputed by calculating and pro-rating the administrative and overhead costs incurred by banks and other creditors, taking into account their loss ratios to assign appropriate risk premiums. But an analysis of their income and expense accounts shows how tautological such a measure would be. Salaries and bonuses, dividends and reserve funds or new projects (including mergers and acquisitions) reflect whatever revenue creditors obtain. Such pseudo-costs are after-the-fact, not foreseeable in advance in the sense that labor, materials and capital-goods costs are foreseeable.

The reality is that bank credit today has no cost of production beyond a modest administrative overhead. Interest rates have no determinate foundation in the "real" economy's production and consumption functions, although they intrude into that system's circular flow by siphoning off debt service, late fees—and public bailouts when the financial system becomes too "decoupled" from the "real" economy. Such financial charges cannot be assigned to labor or other "real" costs of production. The administered prices for interest and underwriting fees are akin to economic rent, out of which the financial sector's bloated salaries and bonuses are paid. Utilitarian economics does not apply to looting.

The credit system's dynamics are based on the flow of funds and terms of debt repayment. This system is no more intrinsically linked to the economics of production and consumption than is the weather. Where the financial and "real" spheres intersect, they do so in the way that comets intersect with the planetary system—sometimes with devastating collisions that abruptly alter trajectories. To extend the analogy to include compound interest, one should imagine the havoc that would be wreaked by comets whose mass was growing by x percent in real terms each year, relative to the constant mass of the planets. The chance of crashes increases exponentially under such conditions, and their consequences become larger.

Mathematical sophistication is of little help when applied to what is assumed to be a debt-free economy. Without analyzing the degree to which wages, profits, rents and taxes are burdened by interest payments to creditors, economic theory will be unable to provide meaningful forecasts or policy recommendations. It was on this ground that Keynes chided economists for reasoning as if the world operated on a barter basis. They used *ceteris paribus* methodology to prevent monetary "distortions" from interfering with their analysis of wages, profits and rents, neglecting to add financial reality back into the picture they were drawing. The study of banking and credit was shunted aside into a sub-discipline, to be analyzed in isolation from "real exchange" problems. This missed the point that finance ultimately is more real than barter exchange, as money is the objective of businesses and consumers alike. And this characterization of a "real" economy and "real" index-deflated prices created the most distorted picture of how economies function (and, sometimes, collapse).

Finance and interest cannot be derived from production and consumption functions, but their impact **on** these functions can be traced, just as the impact of weather can be traced after the fact, but not explained as a product of economic conditions. A credit-based theory of pricing would start with the perception that debt service represents a rising share of the cost of producing and distributing goods and services. Today, the major factors determining international cost differentials are variations in the costing of capital—not only the rate of interest but also debt/equity ratios, loan maturities, depreciation and tax schedules. These are not production costs but are imposed from outside the real-cost system.

Matters are aggravated by the fact that goods and services are sold in markets where debt service absorbs a rising share of the revenue of labor, business, real estate and government. This causes debt deflation, reducing the economy's ability to buy products, while rising debt service adds to production costs. No meaningful analysis of demand (or of the degree to which Say's Law applies) can be drawn up without taking into account the volume of debt service.

Ignoring the role of debt leaves it free to devastate the economic system. Beaudelaire famously remarked that the devil would defeat humanity at the point where he was able to convince it that he did not really exist. Financial interests have promoted the idea that money and credit are merely a veil, passively reflecting economic life as "counters" rather than being determined by financial institutions actively steering and planning economies. The study of debt and its effects have all but disappeared from the curriculum. In an academic version of Gresham's Law, the financial sector's approach to the debt problem has driven other perspectives out of the intellectual marketplace.

Policy-makers take the financial and banking system for granted rather than discussing what kind of a system best would serve society's long-term development and best cope with debts that grow too large to be paid without fatally polarizing economies between creditors and debtors.

Posing the debt-repayment problem leads naturally into the analysis of what public responses are most appropriate. This line of analysis is anathema to the vested financial interests, and finds little support in academic economic departments (many of which depend increasingly on FIRE-sector endowments and subsidy).

It trivializes the debt problem to treat it merely as one of finding an appropriately low rate of interest to equilibrate financial supply and demand, consumer preference and profit opportunities, as if there were some (low) rate of interest that will enable loans to be paid out of the productive investment of their proceeds or out of consumer incomes without default. The rality is that most loans are not invested in tangible capital formation that increase the borrower's revenue and hence debt-paying capacity. And even if they were, the problem lies in the inexorable mathematics of compound interest. What needs to be examined is how to cope with the fact that interest accrues according to a autonomous mathematical principle with the inherent tendency of debts to multiply in excess of the economy's ability to pay. Negative equity on an economy-wide basis is the consequence of the prior miraculous "wealth creation." At this point the financial problem becomes political.

4

THE INDUSTRIALIZATION OF FINANCE AND THE FINANCIALIZATION OF INDUSTRY

In his draft notes on "Interest-Bearing Capital and Commercial Capital in Relation to Industrial Capital" for what became Vol. III of *Capital* and Part III of *Theories of Surplus Value*, Marx wrote optimistically about how industrial capitalism would modernize banking and financial systems. Its historical task, he believed, was to rescue society from usurious money lending and asset stripping, replacing the age-old parasitic tendencies of banking by steering credit to finance productive investment.

The commercial and interest-bearing forms of capital are older than industrial capital, but ... [i]n the course of its evolution, industrial capital must therefore subjugate these forms and transform them into derived or special functions of itself. It encounters these older forms in the epoch of its formation and development. It encounters them as antecedents ... not as forms of its own life-process. ... Where capitalist production has developed all its manifold forms and has become the dominant mode of production, interest-bearing capital is dominated by industrial capital, and commercial capital becomes merely a form of industrial capital, derived from the circulation process.[1]

From antiquity through medieval times, investment was self-financed—and hence was undertaken mainly by large public institutions (temples and palaces) and by the well to do. It was the great achievement of industrial capitalism to mobilize credit to finance production, subordinating hitherto usurious interest-bearing capital to "the conditions and requirements of the capitalist mode of production."[2] "What distinguishes the interest-bearing capital, so far as it is an essential element of the capitalist mode of production, from usurer's capital," Marx wrote, is "the altered conditions under which it operates, and consequently the totally changed character of the borrower ..."[3]

---

[1] *Theories of Surplus Value*, Part III (Moscow: Foreign Languages Publishing House, 1971): 468.

[2] *Capital*, Vol. III (Chicago: Charles H. Kerr, 1909): 710. All subsequent quotations from *Capital* are from this edition, unless specifically noted (as in footnotes 15 and 36).

[3] *Ibid.*: 705.

Marx expected the Industrial Revolution's upsweep to be strong enough to replace this system with one of productive credit, yet he certainly had no blind spot for financial parasitism.[4] Money-lending long preceded industrial capital and was external to it, he explained, existing in a symbiosis much like that between a parasite and its host. "Both usury and commerce exploit the various modes of production," he wrote. "They do not create it, but attack it from the outside."[5] In contrast to industrial capital (tangible means of production), bank loans, stocks and bonds are legal claims *on* wealth. These financial claims do not create the surplus directly, but are like sponges absorbing the income and property of debtors—and expropriate this property when debtors (including governments) cannot pay. "Usury centralises money wealth," Marx elaborated. "It does not alter the mode of production, but attaches itself to it as a parasite and makes it miserable. It sucks its blood, kills its nerve, and compels reproduction to proceed under even more disheartening conditions. ... usurer's capital does not confront the laborer as industrial capital," but "impoverishes this mode of production, paralyzes the productive forces instead of developing them."[6]

Engels noted that Marx would have emphasized how finance remained largely predatory had he lived to see France's Second Empire and its "world-redeeming credit-phantasies" explode in "a swindle of a magnitude never witnessed before."[7] But more than any other writer of his century, Marx described how periodic financial crises were caused by the tendency of debts to grow exponentially, without regard for growth in productive powers. His notes provide a compendium of writers who explained how impossible it was in practice to realize the purely mathematical "magic of compound interest"–interest-bearing debts in the form of bonds, mortgages and commercial paper growing independently of the economy's ability to pay.[8]

This self-expanding growth of financial claims, Marx wrote, consists of "imaginary" and "fictitious" capital inasmuch as it cannot be realized over time. When fictitious financial gains are obliged to confront the impossibility of paying off the exponential growth in debt claims—that is, when scheduled debt service exceeds the ability to pay—breaks in the chain of payments cause crises. "The greater portion of the banking capital is, therefore, purely fictitious

---

[4] See for instance *ibid.*: 700: "In place of the old exploiters, whose exploitation was more or less patriarchal because it was largely a means of political power, steps a hard money-mad parvenu."

[5] *Ibid.*: 716.

[6] *Ibid.*: 699 f.

[7] *Ibid.*: 711 fn. 116.

[8] It is only in the English-language translations of Marx's *Theories of Surplus Value* III (1971): 296 f., 527–37) for instance, that one can find Martin Luther's denunciation of usurers, not in Luther's *Works* published by Fortress.

and consists of certificates of indebtedness (bills of exchange), government securities (which represent spent capital), and stocks (claims on future yields of production)."[9] A point arrives at which bankers and investors recognize that no society's productive powers can long support the growth of interest-bearing debt at compound rates. Seeing that the pretense must end, they call in their loans and foreclose on the property of debtors, forcing the sale of property under crisis conditions as the financial system collapses in a convulsion of bankruptcy.

To illustrate the inexorable force of usury capital unchecked, Marx poked fun at Richard Price's calculations about the magical power of compound interest, noting that a penny saved at the birth of Jesus at 5% would have amounted by Price's day to a solid sphere of gold extending from the sun out to the planet Jupiter.[10] "The good Price was simply dazzled by the enormous quantities resulting from geometrical progression of numbers. ... he regards capital as a self-acting thing, without any regard to the conditions of reproduction of labour, as a mere self-increasing number," subject to the growth formula Surplus = Capital $(1 + \text{interest rate})^n$, with n representing the number of years money is left to accrue interest. The exponential all-devouring usury "assimilates all the surplus value with the exception of the share claimed by the state."[11] That at least was the hope of the financial class: to capitalize the entire surplus into debt service. "Under the form of interest the whole of the surplus over the necessary means of subsistence (the amount of what becomes wages later on) of the producers may here be devoured by usury (this assumes later the form of profit and ground rent)."

Although high finance obviously has been shaped by the Industrial Revolution's legacy of corporate finance, institutional investment such as pension fund saving as part of the industrial wage contract, mutual funds, and globalization along "financialized" lines, financial managers have taken over industrial companies to create what Hyman Minsky has called "money manager capitalism."[12] The last few decades have seen the banking and financial sector

---

[9] *Capital* III: 552.

[10] In his *Grundrisse* notebooks (1973: 842 f.) incorporated into *Capital* III (ch. xxiv): 463.

[11] *Capital* III: 699.

[12] "Capitalism in the United States is now in a new stage, money manager capitalism, in which the proximate owners of a vast proportion of financial instruments are mutual and pension funds. The total return on the portfolio is the only criteria used for judging the performance of the managers of these funds, which translates into an emphasis upon the bottom line in the management of business organizations." Hyman P. Minsky, "Uncertainty and the Institutional Structure of Capitalist Economies," *Working Paper* no. 155, Jerome Levy Economics Institute, April 1996, cited in L. Randall Wray, "The rise and fall of money manager capitalism: a Minskian approach," *Cambridge Journal of Economics* 33 (2009): 807–828, and also in Wray, "Minsky's Money Manager Capitalismand the Global Financial Crisis," 2010, http://www.levyinstitute.org/pubs/conf_april10/19th_Minsky_PPTs/19th_Minsky_Wray.pdf.

evolve beyond what Marx or any other 19th-century writer imagined. Corporate raiding, financial fraud, credit default swaps and other derivatives have led to de-industrialization and enormous taxpayer bailouts. And in the political sphere, finance has become the great defender of deregulating monopolies and "freeing" land rent and asset-price gains from taxation, translating its economic power and campaign contributions into the political power to capture control of public financial regulation. The question that needs to be raised today is therefore which dynamic will emerge dominant: that of industrial capital as Marx expected, or finance capital?

Marx's Optimism that Industrial Capital Would Subordinate Finance Capital

Despite Marx's explanation of how parasitic finance capital was in its manifestation as "usury capital," he believed that its role as economic organizer would pave the way for a socialist organization of the economic surplus. Industrial capital would subordinate finance capital to serve its needs. No observer of his day was so pessimistic as to expect finance capitalism to overpower and dismantle industrial capitalism, engulfing economies in parasitic credit such as the world is seeing today. Believing that every mode of production was shaped by the technological, political and social needs of economies to advance, Marx expected banking and high finance to become subordinate to these dynamics, with governments accommodating forward planning and long-term investment, not asset-stripping. "There is no doubt," he wrote, "that the credit system will serve as a powerful lever during the transition from the capitalist mode of production to the production by means of associated labor; but only as one element in connection with other great organic revolutions of the mode of production itself."[13] Governments for their part would become socialist, not be taken over by the financial sector's lobbyists and proxies.

Discussing the 1857 financial crisis, Marx showed how unthinkable anything like the 2008–09 Bush-Obama bailout of financial speculators appeared in his day. "The entire artificial system of forced expansion of the reproduction process cannot, of course, be remedied by having some bank, like the Bank of England, give to all the swindlers the deficient capital by means of its paper and having it buy up all the depreciated commodities at their old nominal values."[14] Marx wrote this *reductio ad absurdum* not dreaming that it would come true in autumn 2008 as the U.S. Treasury paid off all of A.I.G.'s gambles and other counterparty "casino capitalist" losses at taxpayer expense, followed by the Federal Reserve buying junk mortgage packages at par.

---

[13] *Capital* III (Chicago, 1905): 713.
[14] *Capital* III (Moscow: Foreign Languages Publishing House, 1958): 479.

Marx expected economies to act in their long-term interest to increase the means of production and avoid over-exploitation, under-consumption and debt deflation. Yet throughout his notes for what became *Capital* and *Theories of Surplus Value*, he described how finance capital took on a life of its own. Industrial capital makes profits by spending money to employ labor to produce commodities to sell at a markup, a process he summarized by the formula M–C–M′. Money (M) is invested to produce commodities (C) that sell for yet more money (M′). But usury capital seeks to make money in "sterile" ways, characterized by the disembodied (M–M′). Growing independently from tangible production, financial claims for payment represent a financial overhead that eats into industrial profit and cash flow. Today's financial engineering aims not at industrial engineering to increase output or cut the costs of production, but at the disembodied M–M′—making money from money itself in a sterile "zero-sum" transfer payment.

As matters have turned out, the expansion of finance capital has taken the form mainly of what Marx called "usury capital": mortgage lending, personal and credit card loans, government bond financing for war deficits, and debt-leveraged gambling. The development of such credit has added new terms to modern language: "financialization," debt leveraging (or "gearing" as they say in Britain), corporate raiding, "shareholder activists," junk bonds, government bailouts and "socialization of risk,"—as well as the "junk economics" that rationalizes debt-leveraged asset-price inflation as "wealth creation" Alan Greenspan-style.

Fictitious Capital

Bankers and other creditors produce interest-bearing debt. That is their commodity as it "appear[s] in the eyes of the banker," Marx wrote. Little labor is involved. Calling money lent out at interest an "imaginary" or "void form of capital,"[15] Marx characterized high finance as based on "fictitious" claims for payment in the first place because it consists not of the means of production, but of bonds, mortgages, bank loans and other claims *on* the means of production. Instead of consisting of the tangible means of production on the asset side of the balance sheet, financial securities and bank loans are claims *on* output, appearing on the liabilities side. So instead of creating value, bank credit absorbs value produced outside of the *rentier* FIRE sector. "The capital of the national debt appears as a minus, and interest-bearing capital generally is the mother of all crazy forms…"[16] What is "insane," he explained,

---

[15] *Capital* III: 461.
[16] *Ibid.*: 547.

is that "instead of explaining the self-expansion of capital out of labor-power, the matter is reversed and the productivity of labor-power itself is this mystic thing, interest-bearing capital."[17]

Financialized wealth represents the capitalization of income flows. If a borrower earns 50 pounds sterling a year, and the interest rate is 5 percent, this earning power is deemed to be "worth" Y/I, that is, income (Y) discounted at the going rate of interest (i): 1000 pounds. A lower interest rate will increase the capitalization rate—the amount of debt that a given flow of income can carry. "The forming of a fictitious capital is called capitalising. Every periodically repeated income is capitalised by calculating it on the average rate of interest, as an income which would be realised by a capital at this rate of interest." Thus, Marx concluded: "If the rate of interest falls from 5 to 2½ percent, then the same security will represent a capital of 2000 pounds sterling. Its value is always but its capitalised income, that is, its income calculated on a fictitious capital of so many pounds sterling at the prevailing rate of interest."

Finance capital is fictitious in the second place because its demands for payment cannot be met as economy-wide savings and debts mount up exponentially. The "magic of compound interest" diverts income away from being spent on goods or services, capital equipment or taxes. "In all countries of capitalist production," Marx wrote, the "accumulation of money-capital signifies to a large extent nothing else but an accumulation of such claims on production, an accumulation of the market-price, the illusory capital-value, of these claims." Banks and investors hold these "certificates of indebtedness (bills of exchange), government securities (which represent spent capital), and stocks (claims on future yields of production)" whose face value is "purely fictitious."[18] This means that the interest payments that savers hope to receive cannot be paid in practice, because they are based on fiction—junk economics and junk accounting, which are the logical complements to fictitious capital.

Finance capital sees any flow of revenue as economic prey—industrial profit, tax revenue, and disposable personal income over and above basic needs. The result is not unlike the "primitive accumulation" by armed conquest—land rent paid initially to warrior aristocracies. And much as the tribute

---

[17] *Ibid.*: 548.

[18] *Ibid.*: 551 f. (Ch. xxix: The Composition of Banking Capital). The term fictitious capital passed into general circulation. In the United States it meant capitalized unearned income ("economic rent," income without cost-value, mainly in the forms of groundrent and monopoly rent as well as financial extraction of revenue). Henry George picked it up in *The Condition of Labor* (1891), referring to the "fictitious capital that is really capitalized monopoly" (in *The Land Question and Related Writings*, New York, Robert Schalkenbach Foundation, 1982): 201 f.). Book 3, Chapter 4 of George's *Progress and Poverty* (1879) is titled, "Of Spurious Capital And Of Profits Often Mistaken For Interest."

taken by the military victors is limited only by the defeated population's ability to produce an economic surplus, so the accrual of interest on savings and bank loans is constrained only by the ability of borrowers to pay the mounting interest charges on these debts.

The problem is that the financial system, like military victors from Assyria and Rome in antiquity down to those of today, destroys the host economy's ability to pay.

The Falling Rate of Profit as Distinct from Financial Crises

Focusing on profit as reflecting the industrial exploitation of wage labor, many students of Marxism have read only Vol. I of *Capital*. Many make an unwarranted leap from his analysis of wage labor to assume that he was an underconsumptionist. The capitalist's desire to pay employees as little as possible (so as to maximize the margin they would make by selling their products at a higher price) is taken as a proxy for the financial dynamics causing crises, discussed in Vol. III of *Capital*.

Marx's analysis did note the problem of labor's inability to buy what it produces. "Contradiction in the capitalist mode of production," he wrote: "the labourers as buyers of commodities are important for the market. But as sellers of their own commodity — labour-power — capitalist society tends to keep them down to the minimum price."[19] To avoid a glut on the market, workers must buy what they produce (along with industrialists buying machinery and other inputs). Henry Ford quipped that he paid his workers the then-high wage of $5 per day so that they would have enough to buy the cars they produced. But most employers oppose higher wages, paying as little as possible and thus drying up the market for their products.

This was the major form of class warfare in Marx's day, but it was not the cause of financial crises, which Marx saw as being caused by internal contradictions on the part of finance capital itself. Interest charges on rising debt levels absorb business and personal income, leaving less available to spend on goods and services. Economies shrink and profits fall, deterring new investment in plant and equipment. Financial "paper wealth" thus becomes increasingly antithetical to industrial capital, to the extent that it takes the predatory form of usury-capital — or its kindred outgrowth, financial speculation — rather than funding tangible capital formation.

In developing his model to analyze the flows of income and output among labor, capital and the rest of the economy, Marx's starting point was the first great example of national income accounting: Francois Quesnay's *Tableau*

---

[19] *Capital* II (Moscow: Foreign Languages Publishing House, 1957): 532.

Économique (1758) describing the circulation of payments and output in France's agricultural sector, labor, industry and the government. As a surgeon to the king, Quesnay saw this circulation of income as analogous to that of blood within the human body. However, his *Tableau* neglected the need to replenish stock—the seed and other output that needed to be set aside to plant the next season's crop. Marx noted that much as rural cultivators needed to defray the cost of replenishing their seed-corn, industrialists needed to recover the cost of their capital investment in plant, equipment and kindred outlays, in addition to receiving profits.

This recovery of capital outlays is called depreciation and amortization. Marx expected it to rise relative to profits, in order to reimburse investment in capital equipment (and by logical extension, research and development). This is what he meant by the falling rate of profit. Just as bondholders recover their original capital principal (a return *of* financial capital) quite apart from the interest, so capitalists must recover the cost of their original investment.

Marx expected technology to become more capital-intensive in order to be more productive. His "falling rate of profit" referred to the rising depreciation return of capital to reflect this recovery of costs. Plant and equipment needed to be renewed as a result of wearing out or becoming technologically obsolete and hence needing to be scrapped even when it remains physically operative. As Joseph Schumpeter emphasized in his post-Marxist theory of innovation, technological progress obliges industrialists either to modernize or be undersold by rivals.

This rising capital-intensiveness is not a cause of crises. As Marx argued in Book II of *Theories of Surplus Value* against Ricardo's views on the introduction of machinery, it creates a demand for more capital spending and hence employs more labor, averting an underconsumption crisis. However, financial crises still occur (Marx pointed to eleven-year intervals in his day) as a result of the interest-bearing savings of the wealthy lent out to government, business and (mainly since Marx's day) real estate and individuals, erupting when debtors are unable to pay this self-expanding financial overhead of "anti-wealth."

No concept has confused students of Marxism more than this seemingly straightforward idea.[20] At issue is the shifting composition of cash flow: earn-

---

[20] It often surprises both ends of the political spectrum to learn that it was Marx who firmly established depreciation as an element of value theory. As Terence McCarthy wrote in his initial English language translation of Marx's *Theories of Surplus Value* (which he translated under the title of *A History of Economic Doctrines* (New York: Langland Press 1952): xv): "As a logical consequence of his examination of Physiocracy, Marx was led to a study of the Economic Theory of Depreciation. So complete is his analysis of this aspect of income formation that, if *Capital* has been called the bible of the working class, the

ings before interest, depreciation and amortization (ebitda). To the extent that depreciation and amortization rise (or as industry becomes more highly debt leveraged), less profit is reported to the tax authorities and recorded in the National Income and Product Accounts. Marxists who attribute a crisis of capitalism to declines in reported rates of profit overlook the fact that the real estate, mining and insurance sectors wring their hands all the way to the bank with tax-deductible cash flow counted as "depreciation."

How Real Estate, Mining and Debt-Leveraged Business Exemplify a Pseudo-Falling Rate of Profit

The largest sector in today's economies remains real estate. Land is the single largest asset, and buildings report most depreciation. To be sure, this is a travesty of economic reality inasmuch as it reflects a distorted set of tax laws that permit absentee investors to depreciate buildings again and again, as if they wear out and lose value through lack of upkeep (despite landlords being legally required to maintain rental properties intact), or by obsolescence (even as construction standards cheapen). These depreciation writeoffs occur at rising prices each time a property is sold at a capital gain (most of which reflects the land's rising site value).

This pretense — along with the tax deductibility of interest — has enabled real estate investors to declare virtually no taxable income for more than a half century since World War II. It is as if a bond- or stock-holder could avoid paying income tax on interest and dividends by getting a tax credit as if the bond or stock were becoming worthless—and for each new buyer to repeat this charge-off, as if the asset loses value with each sale even as its market price rises! To cap matters, "capital gains" (some 80 percent of which typically occur in the real estate sector) are taxed at only a fraction of the rate levied on "earned" income (wages and profits), and are not taxed if they are spent on buying yet more property.

These tax dodges benefit property owners — and behind them, bankers, because whatever the tax collector refrains from taking is "free" to be paid as interest for yet larger mortgage loans. This makes financial interests the ultimate beneficiaries of distorted tax accounting. Such tax favoritism for the FIRE sector is fictitious tax avoidance, capitalized into "capital" gains. This obvi-

---

History might well be called the bible of the Society of Cost Accountants. ... Over the whole society, failure to provide adequate depreciation reserves is, Marx implies, to negate economic progress and to begin consumption of that portion of the value of the product which Marx believes belongs neither to the laborers in industry, nor to their employers, but to the economy itself, as something which must be 'restored' to it if the economic process is to continue."

ously is not what Marx meant by the falling rate of profit. In his day there was no income tax to inspire such "junk accounting." The aim of permitting buildings to be depreciated again and again is not to reflect economic reality but to save real estate investors from having to declare taxable earnings ("profit"). And thanks to the notorious depletion allowance, the oil and mining sectors likewise operated free of income taxation for many decades. Insurance and financial companies are permitted to treat the buildup of liquid reserves as an "expense" against hypothetical losses. The function of these giveaways is to shift the fiscal burden off land and minerals, oil and gas, real estate and debt-leveraged industry.

When an ostensibly empirical statistical map (or the economic theory behind it) diverges from reality, and a tax policy diverges from broad social objectives, one invariably finds a special interest at work subsidizing it. In this case the culprit is high finance as untaxed property revenue is free to be capitalized into larger debts. And as it has regressed to what Marx described as usury capital, it has allied itself with real estate and rent-extracting monopolies. Instead of nationalizing them or taxing their economic rent and "capital" gains, today's tax system favors *rentiers*.

The Financial and Industrial Antipathy to Post-Feudal Rent-Seekers

The financial sector's alliance with manufacturing rather than real estate in David Ricardo's day is rooted in medieval European banking as it emerged at the time of the Crusades. Christian sanctions against usury were broken down by a combination of the prestige of the major creditors—Church orders, followed by bankers tied to the papacy—and that of their leading borrowers: kings, to pay Peter's Pence and other tribute to Rome, and increasingly to wage war.

As creditors, the Templars and Hospitallers pioneered the transfer of funds across Europe. Next to royal borrowing the major market for credit was foreign trade, which flowered with the revival of economic activity fueled largely by the gold and silver looted from Byzantium in 1204. This business prompted the Churchmen to define a fair price for bankers to charge for the international transfer of funds—*agio*. This became the major loophole in which money lending could occur, most notoriously in a fictitious "international" arrangement via the "dry exchange." These financial practices—war lending to kings for spending abroad, and money changing as commercial activity revived—made banking cosmopolitan in outlook.

The Napoleonic Wars (1798–1815) impeded trade, and hence its import and export financing. France's naval blockade had the effect of a protective tariff wall. Britain's landlords increased crop production, albeit at a rising cost.

Conversely, other countries built up their own manufacturing. Resumption of foreign trade after the Treaty of Ghent restored peace in 1815 caused economic crises for these newly vested interests. Imports threatened to undercut the prices that British landlords received, reducing their land rents, prompting them to press for agricultural tariffs — the Corn Laws. Meanwhile, British manufactures undersold foreign production, prompting American and French industrialists to press for tariff protection. Britain, the United States, France and Germany thus experienced a fight between free traders and protectionists.

Having grown wealthy during Britain's rise as a manufacturing power, its bankers looked forward to a resumption of trade financing, with Britain serving as "workshop of the world"—and banker to it. David Ricardo, the leading advocate for Britain's bankers, lobbied for free trade and an international specialization of production, not national self-reliance. The resulting tariff fight culminated in 1846 with repeal of the Corn Laws. Unless Britain imported low-priced crops, Ricardo argued, rising domestic food prices as a result of diminishing returns on Britain's limited soil area would prevent British industry from exporting competitively — and hence, would not be able to expand trade financing from British banks.[21]

Debt appeared nowhere in Ricardo's labor theory of value. He was silent when it came to the original analysis of cost value — the medieval Churchmen's concept of Just Price with regard to *agio* charges. Adam Smith, Malachy Postlethwayt and other writers had focused on the extent to which the taxes levied to pay interest on the national debt increased the cost of living. James Steuart had pointed to the exchange rate problems caused by sending money abroad for debt service (mainly to the Dutch) or military spending and subsidies. Ricardo would have none of this. He insisted before Parliament that banking never could cause an economic problem! "Capital transfers" from military spending, debt service and international investment would be automatically self-financing.

This was the genesis of today's "free market" deregulatory theory. Ignoring the debt dimension, Ricardo became the doctrinal ancestor of Milton Friedman's Chicago School of monetarists. The difference is that whereas they insist that there is no such thing as a free lunch, he defined economic rent as unearned income. "Ricardian socialists" extended the concept of economic rent to a full-fledged attack on landlordism. The Ricardian journalist James

---

[21] I discuss Ricardo's views and the more advanced response of his contemporaries in *Trade, Development and Foreign Debt: How Trade and Development Concentrate Economic Power in the Hands of Dominant Nations* (2nd ed. ISLET 2010 [available on Amazon.com]; orig. pub. London: Pluto Press, 1992).

Mill advocated Britain's "original" Domesday Book principle that groundrent should be the tax base. His son, John Stuart Mill, became a leading advocate of nationalizing the economic rent that landlords made "in their sleep" and the "unearned increment" of rising land prices.

The drive to break the power of landed aristocracies in Britain, France and other countries became the major political fight from the century spanning 1815 and World War I. It was basically a class struggle between capital and landowners. The demand "that rent should be handed over to the state to serve in place of taxes," Marx explained, "is a frank expression of the hatred the industrial capitalist bears towards the landed proprietor, who seems to him a useless thing, an excrescence upon the general body of bourgeois production."[22] By taxing the land's rental income and that of subsoil minerals provided freely by nature, industry could free itself from the sales and excise taxes that raised the cost of living and doing business.

Since the 13th century the labor theory of value had been refined as a tool to isolate the elements of "empty" pricing that had no counterpart cost of production. Rent and interest were a vestiges of medieval privilege from which industrial capitalism sought to purify itself. Its idea of free markets was to liberate society from the overhead of groundrent, monopoly rent and interest, bringing land and finance into the public domain—"socialize" them by transforming banking and finance capital to serve the needs of industrial capitalism.

Marx expected industrial capitalism to pave the way for socialism by freeing Europe (and in time, its colonies and the continents of Asia, Africa and Latin America) from the carry-over of land rent imposed originally by military force, and from financial usury capital. The tacit assumption was that industrial financial systems would play as progressive a role in these regions as they were expected to do in the core. The *Communist Manifesto* credited the bourgeois economics of land taxers and kindred reformers in France and Britain with seeking to move society beyond the feudal mode of production. However, it criticized Europe's revolutions of 1848 for stopping short of helping labor. The fight to tax the land's rent—as the Physiocrats had sought to do with their Single Tax (*L'Impôt Unique*) and as Mill, Cherbuliez, Hilditch, Proudhon and other reformers advocated—was basically a fight by industry (and its financial backers) to minimize the cost of feeding labor, not to raise wages and living standards or improve working conditions. Most reformers left private property

---

[22] *The Poverty of Philosophy* [1847] (Moscow, n.d.): 155. *Theories of Surplus Value* III: 396–98 quoted Antoine Cherbuliez, *Richesse ou pauvrete* (Paris: 1841): 128, whose title and content seems to have inspired Henry George's *Progress and Poverty* (1879): "Rent thus would replace all state revenues. Finally industry, liberated, released from all fetters, would take an unprecedented leap forward …"

in place, limiting their aims to freeing markets from the rake-off of economic rent by landlords and monopoly privileges, and only secondarily from the interest charged by bankers and usurers.

Marxists accordingly criticized "utopian" socialists and anti-socialist individualists such as Henry George for dealing only with the land issue or naïve monetary reforms without addressing labor's fight to improve its working conditions and ultimately to free itself from private property in the means of production. Arguing against followers of George, Louis Untermann noted that in Germany, Ferdinand Lassalle found in Ricardian economics an implicitly socialist program, but "never indulged in any illusions as to the efficacy of that Single Tax idea for the emancipation of the working class."[23] This required a government that would play an active role promoting labor's interests vis-à-vis industrial capital, not only through regulatory reforms but by outright state ownership of the means of production under working-class control.

The Argument over How Productive an Industrial Role High Finance Would Play

The 1815–1914 century was relatively free of war. America's Civil War was the most devastating. But instead of borrowing from bankers, the North issued its own greenback currency. This success prompted bankers throughout the world to redouble their propaganda for "hard money," as if bank credit was inherently sounder than public money creation. Subsequent development does not support this claim.

The Franco-Prussian War saddled France with a reparations debt that it was able to finance without causing any great disturbance. Economists attributed the decline of interest rates over time to the world becoming more secure. Public spending was increasingly for infrastructure to support industrial progress. There was heavy arms spending, to be sure, especially on navies, but it aimed largely to build up industry in a three-way alliance between industry, government and high finance. Governments and the large banks were emerging as national planners via their allocation of credit and public spending.

The most productive industrial financing practice emerging on the European continent, especially in Germany where banking developed the closest linkages with the government and heavy industry. The relative absence of large fortunes made a virtue of necessity. Germany's lag in industrial development obliged its banks and government agencies to take a long-term view based on building up strength over time. Rather than following British and Dutch banks by making straight interest-bearing loans against collateral already in place,

---

[23] *Socialism Vs. Single Tax. A Verbatim Report of a Debate held at Twelfth Street, Turner Hall, Chicago, December 20th, 1905* (Chicago: Charles H. Kerr & Co. [1907]):4f.

the Reichsbank and other large banks engaged in a broad range of activities ("mixed banking"), including equity cross-holdings with their major customers. (After World War II, Japan's cash-starved economy and widespread destruction likewise led its banks to establish close debt-equity relationships with their customers in order to provide sufficient liquidity to build for the future.)

Germany's rapid victories over France and Belgium after war broke out in 1914 were widely viewed as reflecting the superior efficiency of its banking system. To some observers the Great War appeared as a struggle between rival forms of financial organization, to decide not only who would rule Europe but also whether the continent would have laissez faire or a more state-socialist economy. In 1915, shortly after fighting broke out, the German Christian Socialist priest-politician Friedrich Naumann summarized the continental banking philosophy in *Mitteleuropa*. In England, Herbert Foxwell drew on Naumann's arguments in two essays published in the *Economic Journal* in September and December 1917,[24] quoting with approval Naumann's contention that "the old individualistic capitalism, of what he calls the English type, is giving way to the new, more impersonal, group form; to the discipline, scientific capitalism he claims as German." In the emerging tripartite integration of industry, banking and government, finance was "undoubtedly the main cause of the success of modern German enterprise."

What is striking is how unlikely the prospect of corrosive and unproductive debt appeared a century ago. To be sure, Turkey and Egypt were ruined by foreign debt, and massive fraud and insider dealing occurred in ambitious projects such as the Panama and Suez Canals. But the logic of far-reaching financial reform was formulated with evangelical fervor, most notably in France. Count Claude-Henri de Saint-Simon's *Du Système Industriel* (1821) inspired an ideology based on the perception that successful industrialization would require a shift away from interest-bearing debt to equity funding. Banks would be organized much like mutual funds.

Glorifying bankers as the future organizers of industry, the Saint-Simonians saw the Industrial Revolution as introducing the capitalist *travailleur,* a financial engineer judging where credit could best be applied.[25] Prominent Saint-Simonians included the social theorist Auguste Comte, the economist

---

[24] H. S. Foxwell, "The Nature of the Industrial Struggle," *Economic Journal* 27 (1917): 323–27, and "The Financing of Industry and Trade," *ibid.*: 502–15).

[25] *Capital* III: 714, quoting *Religion saint-simonienne, Economie politique et Politique* (Paris: 1831: 98 and 45). Marx cites the 1831 compilation *Religion saint-simonienne* describing banks as enabling "industrious people" to obtain financing for their enterprise, and Charles Pecqueur, *Theorie Nouvelle d'Economie Sociale et Politique* (Paris 1842: 434) urging that production be ruled by what the Saint-Simonians called the *Systeme general des banques.*

Michel Chevalier, the socialist Pierre Leroux, and the engineer Ferdinand Lesseps whose plans for canals elaborated ideas initiated by Saint-Simon. Outside of France their influence extended to Marx, John Stuart Mill and Christian Socialists in many countries. "Marx spoke only with admiration of the genius and encyclopedic brain of Saint-Simon," noted Engels.[26]

In 1852, Emile Pereire and his younger brother Isaac formed the *Société Générale du Crédit Mobilier* as a joint-stock bank. Their aim was to provide low-cost long-term equity financing for industrialists to expand production, replacing the Rothschilds and other banking families who had monopolized French finance by. However, as government insiders got into the game they corrupted the institution. The Austrian *Credit Anstalt für Handel und Gewerbe* became a more successful application of *Credit Mobilier* principles.

Banking in the English-speaking countries remained more in the character of what Marx described as usury capital. British and Dutch practice had long used debt leverage to establish royal monopolies, *e.g.*, as when the Bank of England's monopoly of money issue was obtained in exchange for payment in government bonds. (U.S. bankers do much the same to today's debtor countries, threatening them with financial crisis if they do not relinquish financial control of the public domain to global banks.)

Based on capitalizing existing income streams as collateral, Anglo-Dutch banking seemed obliged either to modernize along more industrial lines or make its economies financially obsolete. Foxwell warned that British steel, automotives, capital equipment and other heavy industry was in danger of becoming obsolescent largely because the nation's bankers failed to understand the need to extend long-term credit and promote equity investment to expand industrial production.

The problem had its roots in the conditions in which British banking took shape. At the time Adam Smith wrote *The Wealth of Nations*, neither his Scottish contemporary James Watt nor other inventors were able to obtain bank loans to introduce their discoveries. They had to rely on their own families and friends, as industrial credit had not yet developed. Banks issued bills of exchange to finance the shipment of goods once these were produced, but not their manufacture. Procedures were in place to discount bills for immediate payment, and to evaluate the borrowing capacity of enterprises whose assets could be quickly liquidated, or well attested income streams that could be cap-

---

[26] *Capital* III: 711 fn. 116. Saint-Simon's weakness, according to Marx, was that of many land taxers, namely, his failure to see the antagonism between the bourgeoisie and the proletariat. He blamed this on the Fourierist desire to reconcile capital and labor, which Marx believed to be impossible.

italized to carry bank loans, as in the case with real property. The preferred collateral was real estate, along with railroads and public utilities with a stable
income stream.

The Duke of Bridgewater ran up immense personal debts to finance his
canals by 1762, to be sure, but these were secured by mortgages against his
property. But early innovations such as the automobile had to wait over half a
century to obtain financing. "The investment banking houses had little to do
with the financing of corporations or with industrial undertakings. The great
investment houses bitterly opposed the numerous corporate issues which were
floated in 1824 and 1825," summarizes one financial historian. "The investment houses for a long time refused to take part even in the financing of the
British railways."[27]

British bankers were prone to insist that companies they controlled pay out
most of their earnings as dividends and remain highly liquid rather than providing enough financial leeway for them to pursue a long-term investment
strategy. By contrast, the major German banks paid out dividends at only half
the rate of British banks, retaining their earnings as a capital reserve invested
largely in the stock of their industrial clients. Treating their borrowers as allies
rather than merely trying to make a profit as quickly as possible, they expected
their customers to invest their profits in expanding production rather than
paying them out as dividends.

Britain's bond and stockbrokers were no more up to the task of financing
industrial innovation than were its banks. The fact that manufacturing companies could obtain significant funding only after they had grown fairly large
prompted broad criticism of Britain's joint-stock banks by the 1920s for their
failure to finance industry and their favoritism toward international rather than
domestic clients.[28] Much as American "activist shareholders" do today after
earning their commissions on an issue, they moved on to the next project
without much concern for what happened to the investors who had bought
the earlier securities. "As soon as he has contrived to get his issue quoted at a

---

[27] George W. Edwards, *The Evolution of Finance Capitalism* (1938): 16f.

[28] Lloyd George called them "the stronghold of reaction" (see Thomas Johnston, *The
Financiers and the Nation* [London 1934: 138]). Ernest Bevin, G. D. H. Cole and other
members of the British Labour Party criticized banks in *The Crisis* (London 1931). See
also Cole, *The Socialisation of Banking* (London 1931), and John Wilmot, *Labour's Way to
Control Banking and Finance* (London 1935). The Labour Party's proposed solution was to
nationalize the Bank of England, and in 1933 to recommend socializing the joint stock
banks as well. Keynes was sympathetic in "A New Economic Policy for England,"
Economic Forum, Winter 1932–33: 29–37.

premium and his underwriters have unloaded at a profit," complained Foxwell in 1917, "his enterprise ceases. 'To him,' as the Times says, 'a successful flotation is of more importance than a sound venture.'"[29]

Defeat of Germany and the Central Powers in 1917 paved the way for Anglo-Dutch banking principles to become ascendant. Wall Street from the outset had followed the practice of hit-and-run stock manipulations and short-term financial extraction of the sort that Marx and other Progressive Era writers believed was becoming a thing of the past. U.S. railroad barons and financial manipulators were notorious for issuing "watered stock" to themselves, "overfunding" companies with bond borrowings beyond their needs or capacity to carry. The directors of these corporations pocketed the difference—a practice that led much American industry to stay clear of banking and Wall Street out of self-protection.

Neither economists nor futurists anticipated that economic practices might regress. The working assumption is that a positive evolution would occur to more productive forms. But the banking practices of finance capitalism have regressed toward short-term predatory lending. Reversing an eight-century trend, financial laws have become more creditor-oriented. The tax system also has become regressive, reversing the Progressive Era's financial-fiscal program by un-taxing property and wealth, shifting the fiscal burden onto labor and industry.

The Symbiosis of Finance Capital with Real Estate and Monopolies Rather than Industry

Marx expected industrial capital to use its rising power over governments to nationalize land and use its rent as the basic fiscal revenue. But it has been the banks that have obtained the lion's share of land rent, capitalizing it into interest-bearing loans to new buyers.

Landed aristocracies no longer dominate the political system, yet fiscal favoritism for real estate has never been stronger, precisely because property ownership has been democratized—on credit. Real estate accounts for some 70 percent of bank lending in Britain and the United States, making it by far the major market for bank loans, not industry and commerce as anticipated a century ago. This explains why the financial sector now stands behind real estate interests as their major lobbyist for property tax cuts. Mortgage interest now absorbs most of the land's "free" rental value, which is capitalized into debt overhead rather than serving as the tax base.

---

[29] *Ibid.*

Voters have come to believe that their interest lies in lowering property taxes, not raising them. Homes are the major asset for most households, and real estate remains the economy's largest asset. Land is still its largest component—and some 80 percent of "capital" gains in the U.S. economy are land-price gains Site values are increased by public investment in streets, water and sewer facilities and transportation hubs, in school systems, by zoning restrictions, by the general level of prosperity, and most of all, by whatever bankers will lend.

Six variables are at work: (1) lower interest rates for capitalizing land rent into mortgage loans, (2) lower down payments, (3) slower rates of amortization (that is, giving borrowers longer to pay off the mortgage), (4) "easier" credit terms, *i.e.*, looser standards for "liar's loans" and kindred, the more credit can be extended to bid up real estate prices. Meanwhile, banks recycle their interest income into new loans—and also into campaign contributions to politicians who pledge to (5) lower property taxes, leaving more rental income to be paid to banks as interest to carry yet larger mortgage loans. Debt leveraging inflates property prices, creating (6) hopes for capital gains, prompting buyers to take on even more debt in the speculative hope that rising asset prices will more than cover the added interest, which is paid out of capital gains, not out of current income.[30]

Recent years are the first time in history that homeowners and indeed, entire economies have imagined that the way to get rich was to run deeper into debt, not to pay it down. Home ownership is the defining criterion for belonging to the middle class. Some two-thirds of the British and U.S. populations now own their own homes, and upward of 90 percent in Scandinavia. This diffusion of property ownership has enabled the propertied and financial interests to mobilize popular opposition to taxes on commercial and rental real estate as well as homes. (California's Proposition 13 is the most notorious case in such demagogy.)

Government moves to check *rentier* interests are depicted as "the road to serfdom." Yet untaxing property and finance obliges governments to make up these tax cuts by raising taxes that fall on consumers and non-FIRE-sector business. This shrinks the economy, lowering its ability to pay the rent needed to pay the bankers on their mortgage loans. So we are brought back to the problem of debt deflation and the capitalization of interest charges into higher prices.

An income profile for the typical U.S. wage earner shows the degree to which the cost of living now reflects FIRE sector costs more than prices for

---

[30] I chart these variables in Michael Hudson, "The New Road to Serfdom: An illustrated guide to the coming real estate collapse," *Harpers*, Vol. 312 (No. 1872), May 2006:39–46.

commodities produced by labor. Some 40 percent of blue-collar wage income in the United States typically is spent on housing. (Recent attempts by the Federal Deposit Insurance Corp. to reduce the proportion absorbed by mortgages to 32 percent have encountered strong bank opposition.) Another 15 percent or so is earmarked to pay other debts: student loans to get the education required for middle class employment, auto loans to drive to work (from the urban sprawl promoted by tax shifts favoring real estate "developers"), credit card debt, personal loans and retail credit. FICA paycheck withholding ostensibly for Social Security and Medicare (a euphemism for the tax shift off the higher income brackets) absorbs 11 percent of payroll costs, and income and sales taxes borne by labor add another 10 to 15 percent.

This leaves only a third of wage income available to spend on food and clothing, transportation, health care and other basic needs. This has transformed the character of global competition, yet it is cognitive dissonance as far as academic theories of international trade and investment are concerned. Economics theorizing remains shaped by Ricardo's success at diverting attention away from the debt and financial overhead as a main economic problem.

This is not how matters were supposed to turn out for Progressive Era reforms of industrial capitalism. The fight to minimize *rentier* rake-offs in the form of economic rent from land, commercial monopolies, banking and kindred rent-seeking "tollbooth" privileges has failed. It has failed largely because of the symbiosis between the financial sector and the rent-seekers that have become its major customers as access to bank credit has been democratized.

On the broadest social level, the ostensible "free market" lobbying effort sponsored by banks to shift the property tax onto labor and industry has become a campaign against government itself. The aim is to shift planning—along with public enterprises and their revenue—out of the hands of public agencies to those of Wall Street in the United States, the City of London, the Paris Bourse, Frankfurt, Hong Kong, Tokyo and other financial centers.

The problem is that the vantage point of financial planners is more short-term than that of government. And being short-term, it is extractive, not productive.

Finance Capital's Raid on Industry

Marx defined "primitive accumulation" as the seizure of land and other communally held assets by raiders and the subsequent extraction of tribute or rent. Today's financial analogue occurs when banks create credit freely and supply it to corporate raiders for leveraged buyouts or to buy the public domain being privatized. Just as the motto of real estate investors is "rent is for paying interest," that of corporate raiders is "profit is for paying interest." Takeover specialists and their investment bankers pore over balance sheets to find undervalued real estate and other assets, and to see how much cash flow is being invested in long-term research and development, depreciation and modernization that can be diverted to pay out as tax-deductible interest.

Whatever is paid out as income taxes and dividends likewise can be turned into tax-deductible interest payments. The plan is to capitalize the target's cash flow (ebitda) into payments to the bankers and bondholders who advance the credit to buy out existing shareholders (or government agencies). For industrial firms such leveraged buyouts (LBOs) are called "taking a company private," because its stock ownership is no longer publicly available.

Permitting interest to absorb the revenue hitherto paid out as taxes and (after-tax) dividends to stockholders is diametrically opposite to replacing debt with equity funding as Saint-Simon and subsequent reformers hoped to bring about. The logical end—and the dream of bank marketing departments—is for all cash flow—earnings before interest, taxes, depreciation and amortization—is to be paid out as interest, leaving nothing over for taxes, capital renewal and modernization to raise labor productivity and living standards. All land rent, corporate profit, tax revenue and personal income over and basic spending is to be pledged to banks and bondholders as interest.

Under such conditions fortunes are made most readily not by industrial capital formation but by indebting industry, real estate, labor and governments, siphoning off the economic surplus in interest, other financial fees, bonuses, and "capital" gains. Populations willingly go into debt as it appears that gains can be made most easily by buying real estate and other assets on credit—as long as asset prices rise at a pace higher than the rate of interest.

Today's financial investors aim at "total returns," defined as earnings plus capital gains—with increasing emphasis on the latter gains in real estate, stocks and bonds. Industrial companies increasingly are "financialized" to produce such gains for investors, not to increase tangible capital formation. The "bubble" or Ponzi phase of the financial cycle aims to create the financial equivalent of a perpetual motion machine, sustaining an exponential debt growth by creating enough new credit to inflate real estate, stock and bond prices at a rate that (at least for a while) enables debtors to cover the interest falling due.[31] As a recent popular phrase puts it, financial collapse is staved off by the indebted economy trying to "borrow its way out of debt."

---

[31] Hyman P. Minsky accordingly called this the Ponzi phase of the financial cycle in "The Financial Instability Hypothesis," Levy Institute *Working Paper* No. 74, May 1992, and *Stabilizing an Unstable Economy* (New York: McGraw-Hill Professional, 1986).

This asset-stripping dynamic, which Marx characterized as usury capital, is antithetical to that of industrial capital. Based on the liabilities side of the balance sheet, financial securities take the form of anti-wealth—legalized claims **on** the means of production and income earned productively. The underlying dynamic is fictitious, because it cannot remain viable for long. It sustains interest payments by stripping assets, leaving the economy with less ability to produce a surplus out of which to pay creditors. And indeed, the financial sector destroys life on a scale similar to military conquest. Birth rates fall, life spans shorten and emigration soars as economies polarize.

This is the "free market" alternative to Progressive Era and socialist reforms. It typifies the IMF austerity plans that epitomize centralized planning on behalf of the global financial sector. Yet pro-financial ideologues depict public ownership, regulation and taxation as the road to serfdom, as if the alternative endorsed by Frederick Hayek, Ayn Rand and Alan Greenspan were not a road to debt peonage. And the endgame of this dynamic is a financial crash, wiping out savings that have been lent out beyond the indebted economy's ability to pay.

> **I**f economies tend naturally to act in their self-interest, how did the financial sector gain such extractive power to raid and dismantle industry and shed its tax burden?

It is at this point that the financial sector wields its political power to demand public bailouts in a vain attempt to save the preserve the financial system's ability to keep on expanding at compound interest. Much as environmental polluters seek to shift the cleanup costs onto the public sector, so the financial sector demands cleanup of its debt pollution at taxpayer expense. The fact that this is now being done in the context of ostensibly democratic politics throws a leading assumption of political economy into doubt. If economies tend naturally to act in their self-interest, how did the financial sector gain such extractive power to raid and dismantle industry and shed its tax burden?

If Darwinian models of self-betterment are to explain the past century's development, they must show how creditors have translated their financial power into political power in the face of democratic Parliamentary and Congressional reform. How has planning become centralized in the hands of Wall

Street and its global counterparts, not in the hands of government and industry as imagined almost universally a century ago? And why has Social Democratic, Labour and academic criticism become so silent in the face of this economic Counter-Enlightenment?

The answer is, by deception and covert ideological manipulation via "junk economics." Financial lobbyists know what smart parasites know: The strategy is to take over the host's brain, to make it believe that the free luncher is part of its own body. The FIRE sector is treated as part of the economy, not as draining the host's nourishment. The host even goes so far as to protect the free rider, as in the 2008–09 bailouts of Wall Street and British banks at "taxpayer expense."

When such growth culminates in financial wreckage, banks demand public bailouts. They claim that this is necessary to enable them to resume lending. But they will not lend more against property already so deeply indebted that it remains in negative equity. Hoping to turn the crisis into an opportunity for further financial incursions into the industrial economy, bank lobbyists propose that governments help indebted homeowners and real estate investors avoid default by cutting property taxes yet further—shifting the fiscal burden yet more onto labor and non-financial business. Tax cuts on wealth are promoted as if they will be invested rather than used to pay the financial sector more interest or be gambled on currencies and exchange rates, interest rates, stock and bond prices, credit default swaps and kindred derivatives.

Economic evolution does not necessarily follow the path of greatest efficiency. The oligarchic, creditor-oriented Roman Empire collapsed into the Dark Age, after all. Financially destructive policies may overwhelm technological potential. Bubble-type prosperity is based on debt-leveraged asset-price gains at the expense of the economy at large. Rising housing prices raise the cost of living, while rising stock and bond prices increase the cost of buying a retirement income—leaving pension funds unable to make good on their promises.

Pension-Fund Capitalism and Other Financial Modes of Exploiting Labor

Finance capital's modes of exploiting labor go far beyond that of industrial capital employing it to sell its products at a profit, and even beyond simple usurious lending to labor (above all for housing). Most innovative has been the appropriation of labor's savings via pension funds and mutual funds. In the 1950s, General Motors and other large companies offered to contribute to funds to pay pensions in exchange for slower growth in wages. This policy (which

Peter Drucker patronizingly called "pension-fund socialism")[32] turned over wage set-asides to professional money managers to buy stocks and junk bonds to make financial gains—but not in a manner that necessarily promotes industrial capitalism. Money would grow through the proverbial "magic of compound interest," making money purely from money (M–M').

The dream is to manage labor's savings on a commission basis, steering it to inflate stock and bond prices. And indeed, pension-fund savings did fuel a stock market run-up from the 1960s onward. In the process, they provided corporate raiders and other financial managers with funds to use against labor—and against industrial capital itself. Pension fund managers played a large role in the junk bonding of industry in the 1980s. And finding themselves graded on their performance every three months, fund managers back raiders who seek to gain by downsizing and outsourcing labor. They typically find their fortune (and even job survival) to lie in using pension savings not in ways that increase employment, improve working conditions or invest in productive capital formation, but in making gains purely by financial means—corporate looting that strips assets to pay dividends and increase short-term stock prices, or simply to pay off creditors.

Meanwhile, the largest sellers of stocks have been managers and venture capitalists "cashing out" by selling into a market fueled mainly by labor's wage set-asides. Pension funds thus turn out to play a key role in enabling finance capitalists to realize their gains—only to be their fate to be left holding an empty bag in the end. Selling off stocks to pay retirees creates an outflow of funds from the stock market that reverses the initial price run-up.

"Money manager" capitalism aims to financialize Social Security and Medicare along similar lines, sending a new tsunami of public funds into the stock market to produce capital gains.[33] A dress rehearsal for this plan was staged in Chile after its 1973 military coup. The Chicago Boys who advised the junta called it "labor capitalism," a cynical Orwellian term that Margaret Thatcher adopted for her program of privatizing Britain's public utilities. (The "labor" here represents the exploited party, not the beneficiary.) A slice of its wages is withheld and turned over to the employer's financial affiliate (the *banco*

---

[32] Peter Drucker, *The Unseen Revolution: How Pension Fund Socialism Came to America* (New York: Harper & Row, 1976). See also Drucker's *Post-Capitalist Society* (New York: Harper Business, 1993): 77: "Pension fund capitalism is fundamentally as different from any earlier form of capitalism as it is from anything any socialist ever envisage as a socialist economy."

[33] I trace this campaign in "The $4.7 trillion Pyramid: Why Social Security Won't Be Enough to Save Wall Street," *Harpers* 310 (No. 1859, April 2005): 35–40.

for the Chilean *grupos*). When a high enough pension reserve is accumulated, the employer transfers it to the *banco* or kindred affiliate in an offshore banking center, leaving the industrial employer a bankrupt shell.

The actuarial fiction is that corporate, state and local pension funds (and Social Security) invested financially can grow exponentially by enough to pay for retirement and health care. This goal cannot be met in practice, because the "real" economy is unable to grow at a rate required to support the growth in debt service. Widespread awareness of this fact has led to the corporate ploy of threatening bankruptcy if unions do not agree to replace defined-benefit pensions with defined-contribution programs in which all that employees know is how much is docked from their paycheck, not what they will end up with. General Motors went bankrupt as a result of its inability to fund the pensions guaranteed by their defined-benefit plans.

Financial claims rise exponentially, beyond the economy's ability to pay. Bubble economies try to postpone the inevitable crash by inflating prices for real estate, stocks and bonds by enough to enable debtors to take out higher loans against the property they pledge as collateral. Governments balance their budgets by privatizing public enterprises, selling "tollbooth" privileges on credit to buyers who bid up their prices by debt leveraging. Financial underwriters reap commissions and insiders making a killing as sales prices for stocks are underpriced to guarantee first-day price jumps. (Mrs. Thatcher perfected this ploy, making unprecedented fortunes for early players and underwriters in the privatization game.)

A crash occurs at the point where this disparity is widely recognized. To bankers, the antidote is to lend enough new credit to re-inflate prices real estate and other assets, enabling new buyers to borrow the credit to buy property from defaulters. Rather than scaling back the U.S. economy's over-indebtedness, for instance, the Treasury and Federal Reserve have bailed out the banks to save them from taking a loss on debt write-downs.[34] The dream is to keep the compound interest scheme expanding *ad infinitum*. But the pretense that fictitious finance-capital claims can be paid must be dropped at the point where financial managers desert the sinking financial ship. Their last act before the bubble bursts is the time-honored practice of taking the money and running— paying themselves as large bonuses and salaries as corporate treasuries (and public bailouts) allow.

---

[34] Since September 2008 the U.S. Federal Reserve has engaged in "cash for trash" swaps, accepting junk mortgages at their nominal "mark to model" values. The Treasury has printed bonds for their these swaps, and taken Fannie Mae and Freddy Mac onto its own balance sheet, giving public guarantees that "taxpayers" will make good on all losses.

Conclusion

Finance capitalism has become a network of exponentially growing interest-bearing claims wrapped around the production economy. The internal contradiction is that its dynamic leads to debt deflation and asset stripping. The economy is turned into a Ponzi scheme by recycling debt service to make new loans to inflate property prices by enough to justify yet new lending. But a limit is imposed by the shrinking ability of surplus income to cover the debt service falling due. That is what the mathematics of compound interest are all about. Borrowing to make speculative gains from asset-price inflation does not involve tangible investment in the means of production. It is based simply on M–M′, not M–C–M′. The debt overhead grows exponentially as banks and other creditors recycle their receipt of debt service into new (and riskier) loans, not productive credit.

Half a century of IMF austerity programs has demonstrated how destructive this usurious policy is, by limiting the economy's ability to create a surplus. Yet economies throughout the world now base their pension planning, medical insurance, state and local finances on a faith in compound interest, without seeing the inner contradiction that debt deflation shrinks the domestic market and blocks economies from developing.

What is irrational in this policy is the impossibility of achieving compound interest in a "real" economy whose productivity is being eroded by the expanding financial overhead raking off a rising share. Meanwhile, a fiscal sleight-of-hand has taken Social Security and Medicare out of the general budget and treated them as "user fees" rather than entitlements. This makes blue-collar wage earners pay a much higher tax rate than the FIRE sector and the upper income brackets. FICA paycheck withholding has become a forced "saving in advance," ostensibly to be invested for future "entitlement" spending but in practice lent to the Treasury to enable it to cut taxes on the higher brackets. Instead of financing Social Security and Medicare out of progressive taxes levied on the highest income brackets — mainly the FIRE sector — the dream of privatizing these entitlement programs is to turn this tax surplus over to financial managers to bid up stock and bond prices, much as pension-fund capitalism did from the 1960s onward.

A century ago most economic futurists imagined that labor would earn higher wages and spend them on rising living standards. But for the past generation, labor has used its income simply to carry a higher debt burden. Income over and above basic needs has been "capitalized" into debt service on bank loans used to finance debt-leveraged housing, and to pay for education (originally expected to be paid out of the property tax) and other basic needs.

Although debtors' prisons are a thing of the past, a financial characteristic of our time is the "post-industrial" obligation to work a lifetime to pay off such debts. Meanwhile, the FIRE sector now accounts for 40 percent of U.S. business profit, despite the tax-accounting fictions cited earlier.

Financial lobbyists have led a regressive about-face toward an economic Counter-Enlightenment. Reversing an eight-century tendency to favor debtors, the bankruptcy laws have been rewritten along creditor-oriented lines by banks, credit-card companies and other financial institutions, and put into the hands of politicians in what best may be called a financialized democracy—or as the ancients called it, oligarchy. Shifting the tax burden onto labor while using government revenue and new debt creation to bail out the banking sector has polarized the U.S. economy to the most extreme degree since statistics began to be collected.

The Progressive Era expected planning to pass into the hands of government, not those of a financial sector at odds with industrial capital formation and economic growth. Nearly everyone a century ago expected infrastructure to be developed in the public domain, in the form of public utilities whose services would be provided freely or at least at subsidized rates in order to lower the price of living and doing business. Instead, public enterprises since about 1980 have been privatized—on credit—and turned into tollbooth privileges to extract economic rent. Bankers capitalize these opportunities, which are sold on credit. Little is left for the tax collector after charging off interest, depreciation and amortization, managerial salaries and stock options. The resulting tax squeeze impoverishes economies, obliging governments either to cut back their spending or shift the fiscal burden onto labor and non-financialized industry.

The resulting financial dynamic is more like what Marx described as usury-capital than industrial banking. In the spirit of the Saint-Simonians he believed industrial capitalism to direct credit into productive capital formation, he expected that financial planning would pave the way for a socialist reorganization of society. Instead, it is paving the road to neoserfdom. Financial operators are using credit as a weapon to strip corporate assets on behalf of bankers and bondholders. Employees can afford homes and other property (and indeed, entire corporations) only by borrowing the purchase price—on terms that involve a lifetime of debt peonage, and indeed (in most countries) bearing personal liability for negative equity when housing prices plunge below mortgage levels. Government planning has become subordinate to the dictates of unelected central bankers and the International Monetary Fund imposing austerity programs rather than funding capital formation and rising living standards.

Having analyzed finance capital's tendency to grow exponentially, Marx nonetheless believed that it would be subordinated to the dynamics of industrial capital. With an optimistic Darwinian ring he shared the tendency of his contemporaries to underestimate the ways in which the vested interests would fight back to preserve their privileges even in the face of democratic political reform. He expected industrial capitalism to mobilize finance capital to fund its expansion and indeed its evolution into socialism, plowing profits and financial returns into more capital formation. It was the task of socialism to see more of this surplus spent on raising wages and living standards while improving the working conditions—and spent by government to freely provide an expanding range of basic needs, or at the very least at subsidized prices. Infrastructure spending and rising living standards thus would become the ultimate beneficiaries of capital formation, not landowners, monopolists or predatory finance.

This is not how matters have worked out. More of the economic surplus is being siphoned off as land rent and interest. Yet many of Marx's followers conflate his analysis of industrial capital with the financial dynamic of "usurer's capital." The latter is not part of the industrial economy but grows autonomously by "purely mathematical" means, running ahead of the economy's ability to produce a surplus large enough to pay the exponentially soaring financial overhead.[35] And in contrast to his analysis of industrial capital, Marx explained why the financial overgrowth—recycling savings into new loans rather than investing them productively in tangible capital—cannot be sustained:

The credit system, which has its focus in the so-called national banks and the big money-lenders and usurers surrounding them, constitutes enormous centralisation, and gives to this class of parasites the fabulous power, not only to periodically despoil industrial capitalists, but to interfere in actual in a most dangerous manner—and this gang knows nothing about production and has nothing to do with it.[36]

Society therefore faces a choice between (1) saving the economy, by writing down debts to the ability to carry without stripping the economy; and (2) saving the financial sector, trying to preserve the fiction that debts growing at compound interest can be paid. For pensions and other public programs, for example, this means a choice between (1) paying them on a pay-as-you-go basis, out of the "real" economic surplus; and (2) the fictitious assumption that funds can earn annual returns of 8 percent or more to provide for labor's retirement by asset-price inflation fueled by debt leveraging and purely financial maneuvering (M–M′).

---

[35] *Capital* III (Moscow: Foreign Languages Publishing House, 1958): 700
[36] *Ibid.*: 532.

If economic evolution is to reflect the inner logic and requirements of society's technological capabilities, then finance capital must be subordinated to serve the economy, not to be permitted to master and stifle it. That is what John Maynard Keynes meant by what he gently called "euthanasia of the *rentier*." In practice it means that governments must prevent property rents and other returns to privilege from being capitalized into bank loans.

To save society, its victims must see that asset-price inflation fueled by debt leveraging makes them poorer, not richer, and that financialization is the destroyer and exploiter of industrial capital as well as of labor. The objective of classical political economy was to bring prices in line with socially necessary costs of production. This was to be achieved in large part by taxing away economic rent in order to prevent it from being capitalized into loans to new buyers. Buying rent-extracting opportunities on credit increases prices for basic needs, turning society into a "tollbooth economy." It also forces governments to compensate by raising taxes on labor and tangible capital.

Many Social Democratic and Labour parties have jumped on the bandwagon of finance capital, not recognizing the need to rescue industrial capitalism from dependence on neofeudal finance capital before the older conflict between labor and industrial capital over wage levels and working conditions can be resumed. That is what happens when one reads only Volume I of *Capital*, neglecting the discussion of fictitious capital in Volumes II and III and *Theories of Surplus Value*.

5

The Use and Abuse of Mathematical Economics

> There are more things in heaven and earth, Horatio,
> than are dreamt of in your philosophy.
> (Hamlet, Act I, scene v)

"Whoever enters here must know mathematics." That was the motto of Plato's Academy. Emphasizing the Pythagorean proportions of musical temperament and the calendrical regularities of the sun, moon and planets, classical philosophy used these key ratios of nature as an analogue for shaping order in society's basic proportions. The population's optimum size, the city's geometric shape and its division into equal "tribal" fractions for voting and fighting in the army were mathematically idealized. But there was little quantitative analysis of economic relations, and certainly no thought that unregulated market forces would assure social harmony. There was no statistical measurement of the debts that wracked the Greek and Roman economies, or of overall output, its distribution and value.

We now have such measures, but can we say that mathematics provides the key to understanding the major economic problems of our time? More specifically, has the marginalist and monetarist application of mathematics become so nearsighted as to lose sight of the economy's structural problems?

The education of modern economists consists largely of higher mathematics, which are used more in an abstract metaphysical way than one that aims at empirically measuring society's underlying trends. It is now over a century since John Shield Nicholson remarked that "The traditional method of English political economy was more recently attacked, or rather warped," by pushing

> the hypothetical or deductive side … to an extreme by the adoption of mathematical devices…. less able mathematicians have had less restraint and less insight; they have mistaken form for substance, and the expansion of a series of hypotheses for the linking together of a series of facts. This appears to me to be especially true of the mathematical theory of utility. I venture to think that a large part of it will have to be abandoned. It savors too much of the domestic hearth and the desert island.[1]

---

[1] John Shield Nicholson, *Principles of Political Economy* (London 1893): 122.

If today's economics has become less relevant to the social problems that formed the subject matter of classical political economy a century ago, its scope has narrowed in large part because of the technocratic role played by mathematics. This paper asks whether this has been an inherent and inevitable development. Has the narrowing of scope of economics since the anti-classical reaction of the 1870s — the so-called neoclassical revolution of William Stanley Jevons, Carl Menger, and later of Alfred Marshall and his followers, culminating in today's Chicago School — been inherent in the mathematization of economics? Or, does it follow from the particular way in which mathematics has been applied?

What is the proper role for mathematics to play? Is there such a thing as bad mathematical economics? What kinds of problems do its formulations tend to exclude?

Mathematical Economics as Tunnel Vision

A clue to the modern role of mathematical model-building is provided by the degree to which higher mathematics was deemed unnecessary by 18th-century moral philosophy and the political economy that emerged out of it. To be sure, the labor theory of value was formulated in quantitative terms from William Petty through Ricardo and Marx. Britain's political arithmeticians used statistics, as did the German cameralists. The quantification of magnitudes gives concrete empirical expression to one's logic. But statistical calculations of price indices or various formulae for measuring labor and capital costs are a far cry from model-building.

What has become the distinguishing feature of mathematical economics is its formulation of problems abstractly in terms of just a few selected functions, excluding all categories that cannot be expressed in its bare equations. Key dimensions of economic life have been neglected that need not logically have been omitted, such as land pricing. Despite the emphasis that Ricardo gave to rent theory, the land nationalization debate stimulated by John Stuart Mill, Herbert Spencer and Henry George, and the central role that Thorstein Veblen assigned to urban land in Absentee Ownership, land-price gains have been ignored by today's price theory. Macroeconomic analysis likewise excludes asset-price gains ("capital gains") from its definition of economic returns.

A significant role of mathematization has been to impose this narrowness on economic analysis. By focusing on how individuals spend their income on consumption goods, or defray such consumption by saving at an interest rate that allegedly reflects their "time preference" schedules, marginalist mathematics diverts the economist's eye away from the methods used to acquire and build up wealth.

The big picture—society's long-term transformation—is excluded from analysis on the ground that its dynamics cannot be sufficiently mathematized. Reiss has located the appropriate quotation from William Roscher:

> some scientists (attempted to) fit laws of economics in algebraic formulae ... But, of course, the advantage of the mathematical mode of expression vanishes the more, the more complex the facts to which they are applied become.... In every description of the life of a nation the algebraic formulae would become so complicated that they render a continuation of work impossible.[2]

To be sure, there are ways to reason mathematically with regard to national economic development, and even to changes in the economic system. Brooks and Henry Adams suggested applying the idea of phase change that had been developed by the American mathematician Willard Gibbs.[3] But this suggestion fell on deaf ears. The concern of modern mathematical economists is not with social evolution and changing the status quo, but with analyzing the workings of marginal phenomena within the existing status quo.

The earliest expounders of economic relationships in terms of abstract mathematical functions were virtually ignored in their own day primarily because political economy had not yet narrowed into individualistic consumerism or technocratic business planning. It remained an extension of moral philosophy and public policy-making. The technical problems with which the early mathematical economists dealt, such as psychological utility and price formation based on supply and demand, were still far from being deemed to be the highest concern. The marginalists would make a true breakaway by viewing the consumer rather than the producer/employer as the focal point of the economic system, and discussing the economy more from the vantage point of individual psychology than from that of national industrial and financial transformation.

The early mathematical economists concerned themselves with narrower topics such as price formation, business cost accounting and railroad planning. Gossen's mathematical formulation of utility theory was not widely noticed precisely because he focused on problems hitherto considered too mundane to be deemed an essential part of political economy's core. Likewise, von Mangoldt's editor Kleinwaechter disparaged his mathematical illustration of the

---

[2] William Roscher, *Grundlagen*: 67 f. as quoted by J. Reiss, "Mathematics in Economics: Schmoller, Meyer and Jevons," *Journal of Economic Studies* 27 (2000): 477–91.

[3] Henry Adams, *The Degradation of the Democratic Dogma* (New York, 1919), introduction by Brooks Adams. For a discussion of the application of exponential growth to the movement of history, especially the economic applications of energy, see William H. Jordy, *Henry Adams: Scientific Historian* (New Haven: Yale University Press, 1953).

principles of price formation as "redundant ballast" in view of the fact that no statistical quantification was applicable. He expunged von Mangoldt's graphic examples altogether.

As for Wilhelm Launhardt's railway economics, it was considered too technical to be classified as political economy proper. His analysis did not deal with how railroads reduced transport costs, thereby benefiting the locational value of farmland, residential and commercial property along the trackway, making fortunes for real estate speculators. As any urban planner knows, this "external" effect of railways on land prices is so large as to overwhelm the narrow direct economies involved.

Early applications of mathematical notation and graphs to economic problems thus were ignored largely because they were deemed to be more in the character of engineering or merely technical business analysis than full-fledged political economy. The most essential concerns of political economy and German Nationaloekonomie were not amenable to streamlining in mathematical form. And indeed, while today's mathematical economics serves technocrats and financial strategists, it imposes a nearsighted perspective that distracts attention from what formerly was most important, in order to focus on what is merely marginal. In this sense economics has been overly distilled into the microeconomics of price theory, along with a rough macroeconomic income and output statement.

This is not to say that the building blocks of classical political economy could not be expressed quantitatively. The concept of rent served as a measure of unearned revenue by defining it as the excess of price over cost-value. Diminishing returns (or for the American protectionists, increasing returns) could be formulated mathematically, as could the productivity advantages of high-wage labor. What could not be treated with the mathematics then at hand was the political resolution of long-term structural strains. No chaos theory yet existed to deal with broad quantum leaps that occurred as political and institutional changes were introduced from outside the economic system. And as far as the dynamics of history were concerned, no mathematical formula could express the broad range of complexities that literary exposition could provide.

What made political economy the queen of the social sciences in the 19th century was its focus on the transformation of nations. It dealt with the policies most appropriate for their long-term social evolution — their legal and institutional structure, technology and financial organization. At issue was how economic institutions should be improved. The *ceteris paribus* methodology of marginalism did not deal with such broad contextual issues. It presupposed that the social structure remained constant, and then implied that no change was needed, as economies would respond to disturbances automatically by settling at a new equilibrium. Such an approach does not have much appeal to social reformers, environmentalists, political regulators or historians dealing with the structural aspects of economic development.

Marxism emerged as the preeminent alternative to the emerging marginalist economics largely because it was almost the sole survivor of classical political economy. In addition to retaining the classical breadth of scope and the idea of stages of development, Marx used irony and the idea of inner contradictions as a logical method of interpreting economic history. This was not a method that could well be expressed mathematically. Although Marx used arithmetic examples to illustrate the rates of profit and surplus value for enterprises employing differing proportions of labor and capital, this was not a mathematical model of the economy. The Communist Manifesto hardly could be expressed in mathematical formulae, and no Marxist tried to express dialectical materialism mathematically.

It has taken a hundred years to drive out what formed the most vital concerns of classical political economy: the shape of social evolution, the strains it tends to develop and the indicated responses by the state. As long as these concerns remained paramount, there would be little reason to celebrate the first users of mathematical functions as having made a great breakthrough. Their "discovery" would have to await the time in which economics narrowed its scope and dropped its concerns with long-term transformation.

The role of political economy in the 19th century was precisely to indicate the most appropriate policies for self-direction. That is what made it political economy. But as economics became increasingly technocratic, it dropped the political dimension. And as it has narrowed and come to take the institutional and political environment for granted, the mathematical formulation of economic functions has come to be used as the criterion for acceptable theorizing. The role of mathematics in fact has been to exclude problems that are more than marginal. A basic condition for regression analysis to be applied, for instance, is a constant social and political environment.

In this way mathematical economics has become the ultimate vehicle to make the policy trivialization of economics politically acceptable, establishing status quo economics as a pseudo-science by virtue of using mathematical symbolism. As Wolfgang Drechsler has quipped, mathematics has helped enthrone irrelevance as methodology. The key aspect of the mathematization of economics has been its logical necessity of stripping away what the new economic orthodoxy sought to exclude from the classical curriculum: the socially sensitive study of wealth, how it is acquired, and how its distribution (indeed, its polarization) affects social development.

The Semantics of Mathematical Equilibrium Theory

If mathematics is deemed to be the new language of economics, it is a language with a thought structure whose semantics, syntax and vocabulary shape its user's perceptions. There are many ways in which to think, and many forms in which mathematical ideas may be expressed. Equilibrium theory, for example, may specify the conditions in which an economy's public and private-sector debts may be paid. But what happens when not all these debts can be paid? Formulating economic problems in the language of linear programming has the advantage of enabling one to reason in terms of linear inequality, *e.g.*, to think of the economy's debt overhead as being greater than, equal to, or less than its capacity to pay.

An array of mathematical modes of expression thus is available to the economist. Equilibrium-based entropy theory views the economy as a thermodynamic system characterized by what systems analysts call negative feedback. Chaos theories are able to cope with the phenomena of increasing returns and compound interest, which are best analyzed in terms of positive feedback and intersecting trends. Points of intersection imply that something has to give and the solution must come politically from outside the economic system as such.

What determines which kind of mathematical language will be used? At first glance it may seem that if much of today's mathematical economics has become irrelevant, it is because of a fairly innocent reason: it has become a kind of art for art's sake, prone to self-indulgent game theory. But almost every economic game serves to support an economic policy.

Broadly speaking, policies fall into two categories: laissez faire or interventionist public regulation. Each set of advocates has its own preferred mode of mathematical treatment, choosing the approach that best bolsters their own conclusions. In this respect one can say that mathematics has become part of the public relations apparatus of policy-makers.

The mathematics of socialism, public regulation and protectionism view the institutional environment as a variable rather than as a given. Active state policy is justified to cope with the inherent instability and economic polarization associated with unregulated trade and financial markets. By contrast, opponents of regulation select a type of equilibrium mathematics that take the institutional environment for granted and exclude chronic instability systems from the definition of economic science, on the ground that they do not have a singular mathematical solution. Only marginal problems are held to be amenable to scientific treatment, not quandaries or other situations calling for major state intervention.

Marginalist mathematics imply that economic problems may be solved merely by small shifts in a rather narrow set of variables. This approach uses the mathematics of entropy and general equilibrium theory to foster the impression, for instance, that any economy can pay almost all its debts, simply by diverting more income from debtors to creditors. This is depicted as being possible without limit. Insolvency appears as an anomaly, not as an inevitability as in exponential growth models.

Looking over the countries in which such theorizing has been applied, one cannot help seeing that the first concern is one of political philosophy, namely, to demonstrate that the economy does not require public regulation to intervene from outside the economic system. This monetarist theory has guided Russian economic reform (and its quick bankruptcy) under Yeltsin and his oligarchy, as well as Chile's privatization (and early bankruptcy) under Gen. Pinochet, and the austerity programs (and subsequent bankruptcies and national resource selloffs) imposed by the IMF on third world debtor countries. Yet the reason for such failures is not reflected in the models. Empirically speaking, monetarist theory has become part of the economic problem, not part of the solution.

The Subjectivity of Statistical Categories

Early statistics dealt with public finances, debt and the economy's tax-paying capacity. The focus was on the ruler's fiscal ability to tax the economy and to finance deficits (mainly in times of war) through public debt. From this primary concern rulers developed an interested in how to make their economies richer, so that they could generate more public revenue. This study was called Political Arithmetic. To the extent that laissez faire policies were advocated, it was as an economic plan to encourage economic growth and hence to enhance the ruler's power to tax.

Classical political economy developed largely out of the anti-royalist political ideology of the French Physiocrats and Adam Smith opposing government regulations and taxation. The emerging individualistic discipline came to define the statistical categories that shaped peoples' quantitative perception of economic phenomena.

Accounting formats require a theoretical conceptual apparatus. Categories must be defined before actual statistics can be collected. Any set of categories is itself a conceptual structure of the parts that make up the overall picture. Empirical statistics thus reflect theoretical accounting categories, for better or worse. To mathematize economic models using obsolete or dysfunctional concepts hardly can be said to be scientific, if we define science as the understanding of how the world actually works.

It is difficult to see where economies are generating wealth without dividing their activities into the classical categories of productive vs. unproductive, i.e., wealth-creating labor vs. economic overhead. Unfortunately, few economists remember the great debate over this issue that lasted for over a century.

A case in point is the GNP accounting format developed by Simon Kuznets. Its elements are neither inherent nor entirely objective. All activities are held to be productive, rather than some (such as crime prevention, medical treatment, environmental cleanup costs and warfare) being in the character of economic overhead. The production and sale of cigarettes is counted as output, and the medical treatment of smokers as yet more national product. Crime prevention is counted, but criminal earnings are not reflected in the national income statistics.

On the other hand, the national income and product accounts do not reflect the major way in which the largest sectors — real estate, mining, fuels, forestry, and even banking and finance — take their economic returns, namely, as capital gains. These sectors appear to be operating without earning any taxable profit, and their capital gains are not traced. The accumulation of real estate fortunes and stock-market gains have become the way in which wealthy people, and money managers and homeowners have built up their wealth. But this distinguishing financial phenomenon of the present decade — asset-price inflation — is lost from view by formats that treat capital gains as "external" to their model of how the economy works.

Today's national-income concept of saving gives the appearance that at the end of 1998 the domestic U.S. saving rate was a negative two percent of national income. Yet savings are being built up at an unprecedented rate. The low statistical rate of savings simply reflects the high degree to which new savings find their counterpart in debt, including loans to real estate and stock market speculators seeking the afore-mentioned capital gains, rather than being invested directly in the form of new tangible capital.

Meanwhile, a rising proportion of liquid savings is coming from the world's criminals and kleptocrats. Yet national income statistics neglect the economic role played by crime, fraud and other illegal activities, despite their important economic role in generating many of society's major new fortunes. Only what is socially approved seems to be counted among society's shaping dynamics. In the 1930s, when Roy Ovid Hall tried to include smuggling and other illicit activities in his balance of payments reports for the U.S. Department of Commerce, he was told sanctimoniously to desist from such behavior.

What is not seen probably will not be taxed. In the United States, real estate and financial interests have actively discouraged collection of meaningful statistics on land-price gains. Congressmen and government bureaucrats have sought to rationalize the real estate gains of their major constituents and campaign contributors. Federal Reserve flow-of-funds statistics attributed so much of the price rise to the inflation of construction costs that in 1994 the value of all corporately-owned land in the United States appeared to be a negative $4 billion! The actual land value of U.S. real estate, by comparison, was over $9 trillion at the time, as I estimate on the basis of the Census Bureau reports.

These seemingly objective official statistics only distract attention from the reasons why so large a proportion of the economy's savings is being diverted away from new direct investment into real estate and stock market speculation. The party that suffers most is the government tax collector and of course, the majority of taxpayers onto whose shoulders the tax burden is being shifted). In this respect, the aim of statistics has been inverted from their original function of informing the state how much can be taxed, to concealing taxable gains from users of modern national income statistics.

Problems, Dilemmas and Quandaries

Students are taught that economics is about making choices between scarce resources, but when resources really become scarce, economists tend to call it a crisis. Every such problem is stated in such a way as to imply a ready solution. Only marginal problems are recognized, not real dilemmas or quandaries. The idea of "scarcity" is just a "little bit" of scarcity—nothing that a slightly higher price won't cure (for output) or a bit lower wage (for employment problems).

Most economic models postulate that unemployment, for instance, can be solved by appropriate adjustments. "Trickle-down" theories of prosperity accordingly call for reductions in wage levels, while Keynesian theories call for or increased public spending to spur demand. Both approaches view savings as financing investment, which is assumed to take the form of tangible capital formation rather than a stock market or real estate bubble.

The important thing is that no structural problems are recognized, that is, no problems that cannot be solved by marginal quantitative adjustments in incomes, prices and wage levels, the money supply and the interest rate. It is in this respect that the mathematics of laissez faire monetarism are microeconomic, depicting the economy narrowly rather than broadly through the long-distance lens of historical development. The analysis may be valid as far as it goes, but it doesn't go very far, as it formulates problems marginally rather than with an eye for structural reform. Looking for small adjustments, such economics misses the degree to which the economy is losing its flexibility and is structurally rigidifying.

For public relations purposes, policy advocates present their "solutions" in a way that appears to make everyone better off. At least somebody's income is depicted as gaining, as if this automatically makes each inhabitant better off for living in a richer society (richer for whom?). Every solution seems to be a free lunch for the economy at large. What are not recognized are situations in which economies collapse because critical break-even conditions cannot be met. When this occurs, economies face dilemmas or, even worse, quandaries.

A dilemma is a situation in which whatever path or "horn" one chooses, it involves pain and the sacrifice of well-being. Somebody or some social value must lose out. Obstacles present themselves on every side, and if the economy avoids being impaled on one horn, it will fall on the other.

It should be noted that falling on one's face is a state of equilibrium. Death is indeed the ultimate state of equilibrium. So is national austerity and its transfer of property from debtors to creditors, and from domestic governments to foreign institutional investors. But marginalist and monetarist equilibrium economics employ a mathematics that does not recognize the possibility of serious dilemmas developing, or of economies falling into quandaries whose financial and economic constraints prevent technological "real" potential from being realized. The preferred method of mathematical economics is general equilibrium analysis in an environment in which only small marginal disturbances are envisioned, not major structural problems or legal changes in the economic environment.

Economies fall into a quandary when the preconditions for a real solution are lacking. Debtors default on their payments, real estate prices fall, and asset prices for bonds and stocks also fall. Banks are unable to cover their deposit liabilities as the market value of their loan portfolios falls. The government is called on to bail them out by issuing bonds, and to pay the interest charges either by raising taxes or cutting back spending programs. The budget is balanced by selling public enterprises to foreign investors, whose remission of profits and dividends creates a balance-of-payments exchange drain that lowers the currency's exchange rate.

The situation becomes worse as the government borrows from the IMF and is forced to enact an anti-Keynesian austerity program. IMF riots break out, the government falls and a dictatorship oriented to serve global financial institutions is installed, friendly to the capital flight which strips the economy of its resources all the faster. Money-capital flees abroad and skilled labor emigrates as the economy shrinks, with no technological cause indicated in the policy models being applied.

Marginal analysis avoids dealing with such quandaries, and the quantum leaps necessary to escape. It selects a rather narrow set of phenomena (labor and materials costs, the interest rate, income and the pattern of demand) to produce models that show how economies might settle at an equilibrium point if left free from outside political interference. What is missed is the degree to which the world economy is being pushed further and further out of balance.

Mathematical Economics as a Distraction from Economic Reality

Is it sufficient atonement that so many economists upon retirement merely give an apology acknowledging that, yes, perhaps their economics have all really been just a waste of time? Upon leaving office, each new president of the American Economic Association gives the expected speech showing that he knows full well it is all just a game, and chastises his colleagues for not being more realistic. But do they not have some obligation to set things right? Or is the problem that they cannot see what has to be done?

Although academic economists hardly have shown themselves to be in favor of free markets in their own life, seeking the insulation of tenured positions and sinecures, they know well where their own money comes from. It comes from their ability to endorse creditor-oriented "free-market" policies and condemn government regulation. This premise has led their mathematical models to focus on how individuals can make money in our pecuniary society, but not how public entities can be better run.

The more libertarian the theory, the more authoritarian the economic pedagogy tends to be, precisely because its reasoning rests on specious foundations. In Pinochet's Chile, Chicago economists showed their intellectual intolerance of a free market in economic ideas by closing the economics and social science departments of all universities save for the Catholic University in which they ruled unchallenged. Consensus was established not through reason, but by removing from the scene all who disagreed with their extremist policies.

Over the past generation, courses in mathematical economics have displaced the traditional courses in economic history and the history of economic thought that might have familiarized students with alternatives to today's monetarist orthodoxy. Equilibrium theorizing has expunged a broad understanding of how economies work, and even the long dynamics of economic history, especially where the dynamics of debt are concerned.

The failure of mathematical economics to analyze our epoch's financial strains suggests that its aim has not really been to explain the world as much as to censor perceptions that imply that the financial status quo is unstable and hence must be regulated. Such findings are not congenial to monetarists in their capacity as the political lobby for the financial sector. By ignoring the problems caused by the growing debt overhead, monetarist orthodoxy has removed economic planning from the democratic political process and placed it in the hands of financial technocrats. The effect has been to create a new (and highly centralized) elitist planning in the world's finance ministries and central banks.

This poses the question of whether the most important phenomena and dynamics are being mathematized. Do today's general equilibrium, monetarist and national income and product models correlate the appropriate phenomena, or do they omit key dynamics?

To contemporary economists, mathematics has become the badge of scientific method. But is the use of mathematics scientific ipso facto? To what extent may it be methodologically abused?

Many economists are trained in calculus and higher mathematics without feeling much need to test their theories quantitatively. They tend to use mathematics less as an empirical measuring tool than as an expository language, or simply as a decoration to give a seemingly scientific veneer to their policy prescriptions. Mathematics rarely is used to analyze statistically the financial tendencies working to polarize wealth and income, or how economies change their shape as they grow.

This shape is distorted by the inherent tendency for financial claims—bonds, bank loans and other financial securities—to grow more rapidly than the economy's ability to carry them, much less to pay them off. The volume of such claims tends to grow by purely mathematical principles of self-expansion independently from underlying economic trends in wealth and income, and hence from the ability of debtors to pay. Savers/creditors load tangible capital assets and real estate down with debts that in many cases are not repayable except by transferring ownership to creditors. This transfer changes the economy's structural and, in due course, political shape.

But today's monetarist models foster an illusion that economies can carry any given volume of debt without having to change their structure, e.g., their pattern of wealth ownership. Self-equilibrating shifts in incomes and prices are assumed to enable a debt overhead of any given size to be paid. This approach reduces the debt problem to one of the degree to which taxes must be raised to carry the national debt, and to which businesses and consumers must cut back their investment and consumption to service their own debts and to pay these taxes. The task of economic regulation is reduced to one merely of setting an appropriate interest rate to reflect profit rates and consumer time-preference patterns. An array of measures is selected from the overall credit supply (or what is the same thing, debt securities) to represent "money," which then is correlated with changes in goods and service prices, but not with prices for capital assets—bonds, stocks and real estate.

Such economic models all but ignore rent-seeking exploitation and the proverbial free lunch, yet real-world economics is all about obtaining a free lunch. That is why one seeks to become a political insider, after all. Yet such considerations are deemed to transcend the narrow boundaries of economics. These boundaries seem to have been narrowed precisely so as to limit the recognized "problems" only that limited part of economic life that can be mathematized, and indeed, mathematized without involving any changes in the social environment.

The resulting logical constructs of modern mathematical economics were not created without some degree of protest. Already a generation ago F.J.Dyson complained that "Mathematical intuition is more often conservative than revolutionary, more often hampering than liberating." Citing Ernst Mach's observation that "The power of mathematics rests on its evasion of all unnecessary thought and on its wonderful saving of mental operations," he worried that too much real-world complexity might be discarded.[4]

Certainly the mathematical "badge of science" has distracted attention from the tendency for economies to veer out of balance.[5] The problem is that to achieve a single determinate, stable solution to any given problem (always posed as a "disturbance" to a pre-existing balance), general equilibrium theorists are driven to assume diminishing returns and diminishing marginal utility in order to "close the system." Such an approach is not a passive tool in the sense of an X-ray machine revealing the essential skeleton of reality. It is more a distorting mirror, in the sense that it formulates problems in a way that makes them appear amenable to being solved with a single determinate solution.

This singular solution is achieved by postulating a production function based on falling productivity as more labor is applied to capital and land. As for consumption, each added unit is assumed to give less and less satisfaction, so that more revenue is saved as economies become wealthier. This means a falling marginal utility of income: The more one earns, the less one feels a need to earn more. This is fortunate, because most models also assume diminishing returns to capital, which is assumed to be invested at falling profit rates as unemployment declines. Income and wealth thus are portrayed as tapering off, not as soaring and polarizing until a financial collapse point, ecological limit or other kind of crisis is reached. It should be noted that the above variables all but ignore the economy's growing debt overhead relative to its assets, and the associated flow of interest.

A particular kind of mathematical methodology thus has come to determine what is selected for study, recognizing only problems that have a single determinate mathematical solution reached by or what systems analysts call negative feedback. By contrast, a positive feedback model would depict an economic polarization that has an indeterminate number of possible resolutions as conflicting trends will intersect, forcing something to give. At such points the economic problem becomes essentially political. This is how the real world operates, but to analyze it would drive economists into an unstable universe in

---

[4] Freeman J. Dyson, "Mathematics in the Physical Sciences," *Scientific American* 211/3 (Sept. 1964): 132f.

[5] I discuss this problem in *Trade, Development and Foreign Debt: How Trade and Development Concentrate Economic Power in the Hands of Dominant Nations* (ISLET 2009, 2nd ed., revised and expanded).

which the future is up for grabs. Such a body of study is deemed unscientific (or at least, uneconomic) precisely because it cannot be mathematized without becoming political.

The Hypothetical "Parallel Universe" Approach to Economics

Marx defined political economy's task as being "to lay bare the economic laws of motion of modern society."[6] By contrast, equilibrium theory describes how market relations might settle at a stable resting point if only the world were something other than it is. An economic universe is envisioned that is not in political motion and that is not polarizing. This hypothetical world is characterized by automatic self-adjusting mechanisms, so that active government policies appear unnecessary. It is a world free of the financial dynamics of debt growing at compound rates of interest.

One must suspect a political reason for the aversion felt by economic model-builders to the real world's financial dynamics. To acknowledge their tendency to create structural problems would imply just what it did in Sumerian and Babylonian times: The desired economic balance must be restored by fiat, that is, from outside the economic system. Neglect of the debt overhead therefore is a prerequisite for economic models to generate laissez faire conclusions. A "what if" universe is postulated — the kind of world that might exist if finance capital were not a problem. After all, what is not quantified is less likely to be perceived and regulated.

Economies are supposed to be able to pay their debts simply by saving more. The working assumption is that saving is invested productively, not in creating yet new debts. Sufficient saving and investment thus are assumed to enable any society's growth in debt to proceed ad infinitum, as creditors are assumed to invest their earnings to further expand output and raise living standards. Any increase in saving is deemed to be good, regardless of whether it is invested productively or parasitically, physically or financially. Yet such saving in reality consists not only of direct investment in tangible capital formation. It also takes the form of stock market investment and real estate speculation in the ownership of assets already in existence, merely bidding up their price.

What is neglected is today's most characteristic pattern of lending: the investment of savings in the form of financial claims on wealth — bonds, mortgages and bank loans. Channeling savings in this way enlarges the volume of financial claims attached to existing productive assets in an exponentially expanding process. This debt overhead extracts interest charges which are recycled into yet new loans rather than financing new means of production to help economies "grow their way out of debt."

---

[6] *Capital*, I: 14.

In recent decades such debt claims have grown more rapidly than tangible investment in factories and farms, buildings and homes, transport and power facilities, communications and other infrastructure. Economies have been obliged to pay their debts by cutting back new research, development and new physical reinvestment. This is the essence of IMF austerity plans, in which the currency is "stabilized" by further international borrowing on terms that destabilize the economy at large.

Cutbacks in long-term investment also are the product of corporate raids financed by high-interest junk bonds. The debts created by businesses, consumers and national economies cutting back their long-term direct investment leaves these entities even less able to carry their mounting debt burden. They are forced to live even more in the short run. Interest rates rise as debt-strapped economies become riskier, for as Adam Smith observed, "interest rates usually are highest in countries going fastest to ruin."[7] And as interest rates rise, yet more money is shifted away from direct investment into lending at interest, until the system is torn apart from within. Capital flees abroad, the currency falls and unemployment rises.

No doubt a point must come at which the burden grows so large that it shakes the public out of its hope that matters somehow will return to normal. In the end the global economy must be obliged to do what Adam Smith said every debtor government historically was obliged to do: let its debts go. Now that global debts are becoming dollarized, however, it is less possible for a national economies simply to inflate their way out of debt so as to make what Smith called a "pretended payment." The only options are default or outright repudiation. But it has become academic fashion to imagine alternative "virtual realities" in which no such debt problems exist.

This turns economics into something akin to science fiction. The literary critic Colin Wilson has observed that in evaluating such fiction, the proper question to be asked is, what if the world were really like this? What does such speculation teach us?

Let us ask that question of today's monetarist fantasies. Fearing government regulation to be corrosive, monetarism warns that governments should not act to shape the economic environment. In particular they should not seek to regulate financial markets, for that would kill the goose that lays the golden eggs.

But is this Planet Earth, or a hypothetical world in which the charging of interest either was never invented, or was banned long ago? Such theorizing may be useful as an exercise in "alternative history" as it might have evolved in some parallel universe. But monetarist mathematics are not those of earthly reality. The economist's idea of science itself appears otherworldly. Not being

---

[7] Adam Smith, *Wealth of Nations*: 213.

amenable to a singular determinate mathematical solution, the problem of analyzing the incompatibility between the growth in debt claims and the economy's ability to pay is deemed unscientific. In this respect the way in which modern economists use mathematics diverges from what a scientific empirical economics would be.

The main criterion for success in modern economics is its ability to maintain internal consistency in the assumptions being made. As in science fiction, the trick is to convince readers to suspend their disbelief in these assumptions. The audience is asked to take seriously problems posed in terms of a universe in which money is spent on the production of current goods and services or saved, but not lent out to create a debt problem. Students are asked to believe that debts will not tend to grow beyond the means to pay, and that any disturbance in the economic balance will be met by automatic stabilizing responses rather than requiring action from outside the market economy. In sum, to believe that the growth in debt overhead is not a serious problem, it is necessary to suspend our natural disbelief in the fiction that shifting the money supply can steer interest rates to a precise level that will keep the economy's debt and credit, new saving and direct investment in balance.

Economics versus the Natural Sciences: The Methodology of "As If"

What is even more remarkable is the idea that economic assumptions need not have any relationship to reality at all. This attitude is largely responsible for having turned economics into a mock-science, and explains its rather odd use of mathematics. Typical of the modern attitude is the textbook *Microeconomics* by William Vickery, long-time chairman of Columbia University's economics department, 1992–93 president of the American Economic Association and winner of the 1997 Nobel Economics Prize. Prof. Vickery informs his students that "pure theory" need be nothing more than a string of tautologies:

> Economic theory proper, indeed, is nothing more than a system of logical relations between certain sets of assumptions and the conclusions derived from them. The propositions of economic theory are derived by logical reasoning from these assumptions in exactly the same way as the theorems of geometry are derived from the axioms upon which the system is built.
>
> The validity of a theory proper does not depend on the correspondence or lack of it between the assumptions of the theory or its conclusions and observations in the real world. A theory as an internally consistent system is valid if the conclusions follow logically from its

premises, and the fact that neither the premises nor the conclusions correspond to reality may show that the theory is not very useful, but does not invalidate it. In any pure theory, all propositions are essentially tautological, in the sense that the results are implicit in the assumptions made.[8]

This disdain for empirical validity is not found in the physical sciences. Ptolemaic astronomers were able to mathematize models of a solar system revolving around the earth rather than the sun. The phlogiston theory of combustion was logical and even internally consistent, as is astrology, former queen of the medieval sciences. But these theories no longer are taught, because they were seen to be built on erroneous assumptions. Why strive to be logically consistent if one's working hypotheses and axioms are misleading in the first place?

> "In any pure theory, all propositions are essentially tautological, in the sense that the results are implicit in the assumptions made."
>
> Nobel Prize winner William Vickery

Lacking empirical testing and measurement, economics narrows into a mock-science of abstract assumptions without much regard as to whether its axioms are historically grounded. The self-congratulatory language used by economists euphemizes the resulting contrast between economics and science. "Pure" theorists are depicted as drawing "heroic" generalities, that is, banal simplicities presented in a mathematical mode called "elegant" rather than simply air-headed. To the extent that the discipline uses mathematics, the spirit is closer to numerology than to the natural sciences. Indeed, astrology also is highly technical and mathematical, and like economics it deals with forecasting. But its respectability has not lasted. Is this to be the destiny of today's economic orthodoxy? At first glance the sophistical tendency would appear to find an antecedent in John Stuart Mill's 1844 essay "On the Definition of Political Economy; and on the Method of Investigation Proper to it":

---

[8] William Vickery, *Microeconomics* (New York 1964):5 (italics added).

In the definition which we have attempted to frame of the science of
Political Economy, we have characterized it as essentially an abstract
science, and its method as the method *a priori*.... Political Economy,
therefore, reasons from assumed premises—from premises which might
be totally without foundation in fact, and which are not pretended to be
universally in accordance with it. The conclusions of Political Economy,
consequently, like those of geometry, are only true, as the common
phrase is, in the abstract; that is, they are only true under certain sup-
positions, in which none but general causes—causes common to the
whole class of cases under consideration—are taken into account.[9]

Mill's objective here was to isolate the principles appropriate to each dimension of social science, so as to avoid the confusion that resulted from inter-
mixing them. Recognizing that people and societies were multidimensional,
his logical method sought to segregate the various dimensions of social existence layer by layer, so as to deal separately with the economic pursuit of
wealth, the political policy arena, and the respective subject matters of the
other social sciences then emerging. This was not logic for its own sake, but for
the sake of a systematic analysis proceeding step by step.

However, post-classical equilibrium economists have pursued logical consistency as an objective in itself. Disembodied from reference to how the real
world operates, logic has been turned into a game. Rather than forecasting
how the world will respond to the strains now building up, economists project
existing trends in a political and social environment that is assumed to be
unchanging. When this becomes a condition of the mathematical analysis itself,
the idea of economics merely as "logical consistency" plays a much less logical
role than it did in Mill's day.

The problems inherent in this approach are typified by Nobel Prizewinner
Paul Samuelson's conclusion of his famous article on "The Gains from Trade":
"In pointing out the consequences of a set of abstract assumptions, one need
not be committed unduly as to the relation between reality and these assumptions."[10] This attitude did not deter him from drawing policy conclusions
affecting the material world in which real people live. He defended his Factor-
Price Equalization Theorem (which states that under a regime of free trade,
wages and profits will tend to equalize throughout the global economy) by
claiming simply that:

---

[9] John Stuart Mill, "On the Definition of Political Economy; and on the Method of Investigation Proper to it" in *Essays on Some Unsettled Questions in Political Economy* (London
1844): V.46.

[10] Paul Samuelson, "The Gains from Trade," *Canadian Journal of Economics and Political Science* 5:(1939):205: reprinted in *Papers*, 1966 II: 782 [781–971].

Our problem is ... a purely logical one. Is 'If H, then inevitably C' a correct statement? The issue is not whether C (factor-price equalization) will actually hold; nor even whether H (the hypothesis) is a valid empirical generalization. It is whether C can fail to be true when H is assumed to be true. Being a logical question, it admits of only one answer, either the theorem is true or false.[11]

Contrasting this theorem with the real-world tendency of international incomes and wages to polarize rather than equalize, Gerald Meier observes: "It need not ... come with any surprise that factor returns have been so different ... when in short, the restrictive conditions of the theorem have been so clearly violated in reality."[12] But is it not sophistical to speak of reality violating a theory? Theory violates reality, not the other way around.

If one must be logical, why not start with realistic rather than merely hypothetical assumptions? The answer, I am afraid, is that realistic assumptions do not lead to the policy conclusions pre-selected by economic ideologues. This would explain why Samuelson-type trade theories continue to treat the international economy as a thermodynamic system to be analyzed by entropy theory, whereas the real-life world economy is an expanding system in which labor migrates and capital flows from low-income "cold" economies to high-income "hot" ones.

Wrong-headedness rarely is accidental; there usually is a self-interested policy motive. In his essay on "How Scientific are the Social Sciences?" Gunnar Myrdal observes: "Facts do not organize themselves into systematic knowledge, except from a point of view. This point of view amounts to a theory." He emphasizes that "contrary to widely held opinions, not only the practical conclusions form a scientific analysis, but this analysis itself depends necessarily on value premises."[13]

What modern economics lacks is an epistemological dimension, the capacity for self-reflection so as to perceive the extent to which economic theorizing tends to be shaped by narrow self-interest. There is a bankers'-eye view of the world, as well as the perspective of financial manipulators, industrialists and so forth. It was the strength of Marxism to deal with economic theorizing critically on this level. Perceiving class biases, Marx viewed economic theory critically as apologetics for advocates of one policy or the other, a

---

[11] Paul Samuelson, "International Factor-Price Equilibrium Once Again," *Economic Journal* 59 (1949): 182 [181–197]; reprinted in *Papers*, 1966 II: 869–885.

[12] Gerald Meier, *The International Economics of Development; Theory and Policy* (New York 1968): 227.

[13] Gunnar Myrdal, "How Scientific are the Social Sciences?" see *An International Economy: Problems and Prospects* (New York 1956): 336.

rhetorical system pleading for special interests. The 19th-century American protectionists likewise pointed to international biases between lead nations and latecomers regarding free trade theorizing. Today, a self-centered monetarist world view serves the global financial interests that have emerged to dominate the "real" economy. To understand its blind spots, an awareness of the self-serving motivations underlying Chicago School monetarism is necessary.

We are entitled to ask whose interests are served when economists claim that their assumptions need have no connection with reality, yet then proceed to make policy recommendations. Why do so many economics departments teach the assumptions of, say, the Heckscher-Ohlin-Samuelson theory of international equilibrium rather than starting from more realistic assumptions capable of explaining the real world's financial and economic polarization?

The products of low-wage economies exchange for those of better-paid labor for a number of reasons. Productivity differences have long been cited, but another factor also is at work: chronic depreciation of the currencies of low-wage countries as a result of the capital transfers they make in a vain attempt to service their foreign debts. In the end these debts will prove unpayable as they mount up at interest beyond the economic means to pay. The austerity programs used by the IMF and other creditor institutions are defended by models that conceal this mathematical inevitability. By depriving debtor economies of capital, educational programs and other basic infrastructure, austerity makes it harder for indebted countries to catch up. Matters are aggravated further by privatization programs that serve in effect as voluntary and self-imposed forfeitures of public assets to foreign and domestic creditors.

Creating a statistical profile of financial relationships is impaired by the fact that when wealthy individuals operate out of offshore banking centers, they appear nominally as "foreigners" in their own countries. Yet economists have constructed models in which such offshore havens, foreign debt, land values, and the composition of savings and debt appear as statistical black holes. Such omissions help these models serve as fairy tales to rationalize today's untenable status quo. Everyone is depicted as ending up in a stable and even equitable equilibrium.

A striking analogy of the impossibility of the world's financial savings continuing to grow at compound interest ad infinitum is pointed out by Edward O. Wilson, citing

> ... the arithmetical riddle of the lily pond. A lily pod is placed in a pond. Each day thereafter the pod and then all its descendants double. On the thirtieth day the pond is covered completely by lily pods, which can grow no more.

He then asks, "On which day was the pond half full and half empty? The twenty-ninth day."[14]

By the time people feel obliged to argue over whether the economic glass is half empty or half full, we are on the brink of the Last Days. To financial optimists, it may be pointed out that growth in the economy's savings is simultaneously growth of its debt overhead. As debts grow, less and less saving is recycled into tangible direct investment. This may be good news for stock market and real estate speculators as savings are used to inflate the stock market and real estate bubble. But in the end the economy shrinks precisely because this "faux wealth" serves as a distraction, drawing savings away from direct investment in tangible capital formation.

What is lacking in the models preferred by vested interests is the use of mathematics to project the point at which trends intersect. At these crisis points economic forces do not have an inherently economic "solution," for the response must be political, by forcing a policy conclusion to be made.

A relevant mathematical economics would include an analysis of how wealth is turned into political power by campaign contributions, ownership of the popular press and media, and the subsidy of education and culture. These public relations for the vested interests promote "solutions" to crises that increasingly favor these interests as the economy polarizes. The analysis of such phenomena is dismissed by general equilibrium theorizing that assumes a constant and unchanging political environment. Changes in laws are deemed to be exogenous to the subject matter of economics proper. The word "exogenous" is heard so often these days (along with "externalities") that one wonders just what is left in economics proper. At issue for a more relevant empirical economics are the dynamics of social history, political institutions and the environment, not just the mechanics of supply and demand.

Governments tend to become the debtors of last resort. The culmination of this process is found in modern financial bailouts of private-sector ("socializing the losses" to savers). So we are brought back to Adam Smith's maxim that no government has ever repaid its debts. This is why nobody's savings have mounted up to become the equivalent of a solid sphere of gold extending from the sun out beyond the orbit of Saturn. The 12th-century accumulation of wealth of the Knights Templar was seized by Philip the Fair, who dissipated it in warfare. The wealth of the large Italian banking families subsequently was lost in loans to Britain's kings, who dissipated the proceeds in waging their perpetual wars with France. Most early debts were wiped out by wars, and by their inflationary aftermath in more recent times. Other fortunes were lost

---

[14] Edward O. Wilson, *Consilience* (New York 1998): 313.

through confiscation, and bad judgment such as often is found with risky foreign investment. Some fortunes were dissipated by one's heirs or turned into
land acquisition and other prestige asset ownership.

The relevant point for the social historian is that financial fortunes cannot
continue to accumulate in the aggregate, precisely because the mathematics of
compound interest are economically untenable. Throughout history it has
become increasingly difficult to keep such fortunes viable. Money has been
plowed back into increasingly risky new loans in ways that may impoverish
and polarize the surrounding society to the extent that they find no counterpart in new tangible investment enhancing the economy's means to pay.

The moral of all this is that there are different kinds of mathematical economics. What the Cornell philosopher E. A. Burtt referred to as the metaphysical
foundation of modern physical science has become a politically tinged meta-
physics in the hands of monetarists and neoclassical economists. Just how far
their non-quantitative spirit diverges from the origins of economics is reflected
in the closing words of David Hume's *Enquiry Concerning Human Understanding*:

> When we run over libraries, persuaded of these principles, what havoc
> must we make? If we take in our hand any volume; of divinity or school
> metaphysics, for instance; let us ask, *Does it contain any abstract reasoning
> concerning quantity or number?* No. *Does it contain any experimental reasoning
> concerning matter of fact and existence?* No. Commit it then to the flames:
> for it can contain nothing but sophistry and illusion.[15]

Mathematizing the Economy's Monetary and Financial Dimension

Not all trends proceed at the same rate. At some point certain major trends
must intersect, and something must give. This is the definition of a crisis—
literally a crossing or intersection of trends where the political structure must
accommodate itself to promote one trend or the other.

The example with which most people are familiar was made famous by
Malthus, who argued that population growth tended mathematically to grow
in excess of the economy's ability to supply food. The result, he concluded,
must be starvation, wars or other "natural checks," or else a voluntary limit to
population growth. Since the late 1960s the Club of Rome has warned that
modern resource-consuming trends are unsustainable in light of the world's
more limited growth in the supply of fuels and minerals, fresh water and air.

What these warnings achieved was to bring to peoples' attention the fact
that whereas most mathematical economics has focused on foreseeable, nar-

---

[15] David Hume, *Enquiry Concerning Human Understanding* (1748): 132 (section xii, part iii).

rowly determined consequences, over time the indirect "external" economies of commercial behavior tend to be larger than these direct economies. But they also have tended to evade mathematical and statistical treatment.[16]

The limits-to-growth warnings proved to be premature a generation ago, but one cannot say the same thing for the growth of debts/savings at compound interest year after year. Any statistician plotting the growth of an economy's debt quickly finds that existing trends are not sustainable. The growth of debt has become the major cause of economic downturns, austerity and financial polarization, creating financial crashes and, in severe cases, social crises.

Debt may be viewed as financial pollution, entailing major cleanup costs. Public policy is needed to cope with the incompatibility between the inability of consumers, businesses and governments to pay their stipulated debt service except by transferring an intolerable proportion of their assets to creditors. These transfers are done through bankruptcy proceedings, the liquidation of corporate or personal assets under distress conditions and (in the case of government debts) privatization selloffs.

The indicated solution is to limit the proliferation of debt by borrowing less, for instance, and to channel savings more into equities and tangible investment than into debt-claims on economic output. If present trends continue, it will be necessary to write off debts when they become too overgrown. This entails writing off the savings that have been invested in debt-securities — and this has now become the major political problem of our epoch. Yet monetarists — the very people who claim to specialize in financial science — see this crisis as an anomaly rather than a natural consequence of pursuing Chicago School policies. They urge economies to submit to financial austerity by sanctifying debts rather than saving themselves and their labor force at the expense of debt and savings trends.

An enormous volume of statistical research has been produced to analyze money and prices, and their links to interest rates and hence to the prices of bonds and other financial assets. When examining such research one should bear in mind that monetarism focuses on only part of the credit supply: bank deposits and "high-powered money" in the form of reserves invested in government debt. In reality the economy's entire range of securities and other

---

[16] As early as 1849, Daniel Lee attempted to quantify the environmental depletion suffered by raw-materials exporters in his agricultural supplement to the U.S. Patent Office report. This "external" effect of foreign trade became an essential component of E. Peshine Smith's 1853 *Manual of Political Economy* (see Hudson 1975 [2010] for a discussion). Carey's Law of Association postulated that economies grow more productive at the intensive margin as they become more dense. But free traders have ignored these broad consequences, and used rhetorical invective censorially to dismiss them as "externalities."

assets is available to be monetized or, more literally, creditized. The potential credit supply consists of the volume of marketable securities and debts outstanding (which their holders can collateralize as the basis for yet more credit) plus equity in "real" assets, that is, the portion of tangible asset values to which debts have not yet been attached.

Most money and credit is spent on transactions in financial securities, not on "real" goods and services. Each day the equivalent of almost an entire year's U.S. national income passes through the New York Clearing House to buy stocks, bonds, mortgages and other bank loans. It thus is misleading to correlate the money supply only to transactions in current goods and services ("national product"). Such correlation analysis is not necessarily causal in any event. It is all too easy to mistake cause for effect. It therefore would be misleading to leave out of account the pricing of financial assets (bonds, stocks, and marketable debt securities such as mortgages, packaged consumer loans and so forth) and of the tangible assets (land and buildings, factories and equipment) on which this credit is spent. Nonetheless, these asset transactions seem to have disappeared from statistical sight as the focal point of monetarist analysis has shifted away from wealth and assets to consumer spending. For instance, despite the fact that the major asset for most families (at least in America and Britain) is the home in which they live, no adequate statistical time series for land and buildings is collected or published. In many cases one is obliged to estimate real estate values by looking at the growth of mortgage credit as a minimal proxy.

The very idea of what constitutes money remains in a state of confusion. To describe it simply as a set of counters neglects the fact that bank deposits and savings do not take the form of money as an abstract asset in itself, like gold or silver bullion. Rather, currency and bank money are debt/credit instruments. One person's saving usually finds its counterpart in other peoples' debts. If an individual or company deposits money in a bank or savings and loan association, a large portion of the deposit will be lent out as mortgage credit. Or, a saver may put money in a money market fund that channels its inflows into government bonds and corporate IOUs. The definition of "money" thus needs to be grounded in the overall superstructure of credit and debt.

An expanding superstructure of financial claims for payment grows and attaches itself to the economy's income and assets. These claims find their counterpart in liabilities on the opposite side of the financial system's balance sheet (*e.g.*, the debts owed by the banks to their depositors, by insurance companies to their policy-holders, and so forth). They are securitized by the issue of bonds, mortgages and other IOUs. They represent the savings of people and the institutions through which people hold their savings, including pension fund contributions, Social Security, bank loan portfolios, insurance company reserves, and so forth. All these savings/debts must be paid out of future revenue.

Financial securities are not simply a mirror image of "real" economic activity, the "other" side of the balance sheet of assets and debts. They are a claim for payment that may be equal to, less than or greater than the economy's ability pay. When it comes to deciding what must give, the economy or its financial superstructure, the latter turns out to be more powerful—and hence, more "real"—than the economy's tangible flows of output and income. Entire economies are being crucified on the altar of debt and subjected to austerity and its foregone economic development. On this basis financial institutions have become the major economic planners of our epoch, usurping the former role of governments. Yet monetarists profess to oppose such centralized planning. What they evidently oppose is planning by elected officials with a broader set of social concerns than those of monetarist technocrats.

At the microeconomic financial level it seems wise to maximize one's return on equity by indulging in debt pyramiding. But for the economy as a whole these savings/debts accumulates rapidly. Wealthier economies tend to become the most highly indebted precisely because they have the most savings. Interest and amortization payments to savers tend to increase beyond the economy's overall ability to pay as debt service absorbs more and more personal disposable income and corporate cash flow. This constrains personal and business spending, creating the phenomenon of debt deflation. Yet no mathematical models depicting this process has been deemed acceptable by today's monetarist orthodoxy.

If there is any planning to be done with regard to the banking and financial system, the central issue of mathematical economics as applied to the financial sector should focus on how economies should cope with the tendency for debts to mount up until a crisis erupts? Monetarist models deny that any practical debt limit exists. Economies are supposed to "solve" their debt problem simply by succumbing to austerity, which is presented as the solution to the problem rather than a sign of having entered the financially moribund stage.

Perception of the debt-overhead problem is concealed by the characteristic feature of today's finance capitalism: an asset-price inflation of property markets, that is, rising land and stock market prices. This asset-price inflation goes hand in hand with debt deflation of the "real" goods-and-service producing economy. The failure to model this dichotomized economy is not the fault of mathematical economics as such, but reflects the constrained reasoning at the hands of the monetarist school that has monopolized economics departments in the world's universities.

Monetarist models serve largely to distract popular attention from the extent to which more wealth is being generated more by the asset-price inflation — than by building new factories to employ more people. What has happened is that the classical distinction between productive and unproductive credit has been replaced by an ostensibly value-free theory claiming that money earned in one way is just as economically worth while as money earned in any other way. This is supposed to be the case regardless of its consequences for employment, national prosperity or other effects held to be extraneous to purely financial concerns.

"Hard" facts tend to be the preoccupation of technocratic economics, whose predictions focus on the short run, that is, on marginal changes rather than structural transformations. But economic truth involves a much broader evaluation of society and even culture, as economic theory itself may be viewed as an exercise in cultural history. To the extent that "free market" monetarist economics has now become the world's de facto form of global planning, it threatens to bring about a poorer and more unfree world. If its models and their euphemisms do not make it clear just why this is the case, the reason is a politically motivated blind spot. Monetarist planning subjects the world to austerity to pay debts to a creditor class absorbing a growing proportion of the world's wealth, leading to economic polarization.

It is a world succumbing to economic collapse, heating up financially, ecologically and geographically to a critical mass. It also is heating up militarily as local provinces seek to secede from governments that are being turned into collection agents for global lenders. Yugoslavia is the most notorious recent example.

Trying to sell today's road to financial serfdom is much like trying to sell cigarettes. Popular fears of coughing, lung cancer, and other adverse effects are countered by advertising promises that cigarettes actually freshen the breath and are associated with vigorous outdoor life as epitomized by the Marlboro Man. Scientists are hired to provide a confusing flood of statistical analysis to dispute claims about smoking being causally associated with ill health, pretending that it is all just a coincidence. Neither the personal victims of smoking nor the public health agencies that must defray many of their medical costs are able to pierce the veil of such professionalized confusion.

In a similar way economists have been mobilized to serve creditor interests. Many of these hired guns act as public relations lobbies for global financial interests, often by joining think tanks that serve as advertising agencies to promote these interests. Their assigned task is to depict austerity as laying a sound foundation for future growth rather than promoting a self-feeding collapse. As poverty intensifies, governments are urged to bail out the economy's savers at taxpayer expense, cutting back wages even while shifting the tax burden from property onto labor. When the promised prosperity fails to materialize, the austerity lobby argues that the problem is simply that monetarist policies have not been followed intensively enough to "work their magic." But like most magic, the purported "magic of the marketplace" is merely a trick performed by model-builders so deftly that most peoples' eyes cannot quite follow what is happening.

As Erik S. Reinert has asked, if mathematical economics as practiced by the monetarists should face a product liability suit, what would be the appropriate judgment? If today's Chicago School orthodoxy were to be tested by reality, it would flunk the test. Jobs have been downsized. Lives have been shortened and the quality of life has declined as Chicago graduates and their clones have monopolized the staffs of national Finance Ministries, Treasury departments, central banks and the leading international financial institutions, using their positions to censor alternative economic analysis.

The crisis created between the economy's growth in debt and its ability to pay should be the starting point of mathematical economics.

6

THE FINANCIAL CHARACTER OF TODAY'S CRISIS AND WHY ECONOMISTS AVOID CONFRONTING IT

E conomists are the last people one should ask to explain today's crisis. Although they say their discipline is about how to allocate scarce resources among competing ends, they refer only to small marginal movements within the existing set of institutional relationships, tax laws and loopholes, political alignments—and peoples' gullibility. There is no free lunch, unearned income or exploitation in this textbook world, and hence no need for government regulation or economic reform. "Free market" advocates seem always to be shocked, shocked to hear that there is insider dealing, fraud and deception going on. Gambling, perhaps, but only to hedge against risk and stabilize markets, never to crash them.

This paradigm excludes reality as an anomaly. The recent Bubble Economy should have rendered its logic obsolete by showing it to depict a fictitious parallel universe that never really existed. If its post-classical tunnel vision survives, there must be strong vested interests supporting its happy-face ideology and benefiting from today's economic mess.

Rent-seekers and their bankers claim that if governments agree to step aside and stop regulating and taxing, economies will settle naturally at a stable and fair equilibrium. Automatic stabilizers will maintain full employment to run economies optimally, while price and income adjustments ensure that everyone's income and wealth reflects their productive contribution to economic growth. This is why they call it a crisis when resources or money get scarce and debts cannot be paid—and blame it on disturbances from outside the economy. Presumably an accident that won't happen again, not a systemic problem.

The refusal to recognize unproductive grabbing of unjustified income is subsidized by powerful interests that benefit by deterring economic reform, opposing public regulation and blocking progressive taxation of predatory income skimmed off without adding to production or the economic surplus but carved out of it. This revenue—which classical writers called economic rent— is extracted from business cash flow and appropriates the productivity gains that were supposed to raise living standards. At least that was the promise back in 1945 when World War II ended and productivity breakthroughs began to soar.

This rosy pro-*rentier* view of how a "free market" operates opens the gates for the frauds, insider dealing and unproductive predatory finance that are assumed not to exist. It is as if economies are not polarizing between creditors and debtors, culminating in foreclosure time and financial austerity. If the world really worked in the way that opponents of public regulation tell the story, there would be no need for fiscal and financial reform. But the reality is that economies polarize and shrink when they are stripped of the checks and balances put in place by the classical economists and Progressive Era reformers.

That is the problem the world faces today. It is the result of the financial sector loading down economies with loans without any idea of just how debtors are to pay out of their normal earnings. Banks and other creditors use their receipt of interest and fees to make yet more loans that further increase the debt overhead.

What has confused populations in recent years is that this debt creation appears to "create wealth" when credit is lent in a way that inflates prices for real estate, stocks and bonds. Asset-price inflation is what fueled the post-1980 stock market takeover boom, the dot.com bubble, and the enormous 30-year bond market rally from 1980 to 2011. Interest rates fell almost steadily as the Federal Reserve flooded the U.S. banking system with credit, raising the prices of existing bonds and increasing the multiplier by which banks could capitalize a given flow of real estate rent or business income into a loan. Property and financial securities are worth whatever banks will lend to new buyers or corporate raiders — and credit standards were lowered steadily, capped by the 2001–08 real estate bubble.

Until 2008, prices for housing or rewards for staging a corporate raid rose faster than carrying charges on the debt, so balance sheets reported rising net worth. But these were only "paper gains"—balance sheet net worth, not real wealth. Tangible capital investment slowed, and wages and disposable personal income were flat, or even falling if one takes into account FICA wage withholding and other taxes, rising debt service and housing costs. Many families were able to maintain their living standards only by borrowing. The idea was that once they got onto the "home ownership on credit" treadmill, they could simply take out home equity loans against the rising price of their property, treating it like the proverbial piggy bank. This is the kind of wealth creation that Federal Reserve Chairman Alan Greenspan celebrated. The secret of perpetual motion seemed to have been discovered, at least in the financial universe if not in the physical world. It was a godsend to bank loan offices, whose product is debt, after all.

Just as a Bubble Economy is financial and usually reflects the failure of public checks and balances to protect the economy from debt creation growing faster than the ability to pay, so most crises are resolved by public giveaways to the banks and other *rentier* interests, as if the alternative to the resulting asset grab and polarization of wealth would be economic collapse. Creditors buy up real estate, infrastructure and debt-strapped companies on the cheap.

The underlying debt dynamic is masked by the fact that crises typically are triggered by fraud or embezzlement. Blame for the crash of September 2008, for example, has focused on junk mortgage loans to NINJA borrowers (with No Income, No Job and no Assets) and fictitious property valuations given unwarranted credit ratings. But these are only the outcroppings of the basic imbalance between the debt overhead and the ability to pay.

Mainstream economics shies from dealing with this tendency for debt service to absorb more and more of the economic surplus. Instead of treating the financial sector as acting in extractive and outright parasitic ways as it becomes autonomous from production, bank-friendly economists depict it as part of the "real" economy. National income statistics recognize the symbiosis of finance with insurance and real estate (FIRE) by grouping them together, but treat their interest, fees and rents as earnings for providing real services.

Economic models stop short of acknowledging how "free markets" are shaped by high finance using part of its gains to capture governments and their regulatory agencies, starting with the central bank and the criminal justice system so as to neutralize their checks and balances against predatory finance. Wall Street backs politicians, public relations "think tanks" and business schools that provide a logic (or at least a cover story) for shifting taxes off interest and rent onto labor and industry. When this ends up shrinking the economy and causing debt defaults, financial lobbyists demand that the central bank and Treasury issue new public debt to bail out banks, brokerage houses and hedge funds for loans gone bad.

In his 1987–2006 tenure as Federal Reserve Chairman, Mr. Greenspan promoted debt leveraging as the paradigmatic form of "wealth creation." The "wealth" in this case is balance-sheet net worth, inflated by easier lending terms extended to a widening range of borrowers at rising risk. Bank balance sheets become increasingly fictitious, and when reality raises its ugly head and the debt bubble bursts, asset prices plunge—but the debts remain in place, bringing foreclosures that transfer property from debtors to creditors. Even government assets are privatized, creating yet a new category of lending for banks to finance on credit.

This financial turmoil makes little appearance in mainstream economic models. The monetarist Chicago School reflects a view popular since David Ricardo's day, describing the economy as operating on barter beneath "the veil of money," without debt problems. What passes for macroeconomics these days takes national aggregates without layering them into the top 1 or 10 percent vis-à-vis the bottom 99 or 90 percent. The private sector is described homogeneously as "households," without segregating the McMansions and lordly estates from the pueblos and middle class row houses. Wealth acquired by "capital gains" on credit—mostly on real estate, corporate raids and in the hedge fund casinos—are deemed as socially positive as wealth acquired by investing in tangible capital to employ labor to produce goods and necessary services.

It is as if finance capitalism is part of industrial capitalism, not as having given way to casino capitalism quickly collapsing into a negative equity economy leading to debt peonage. Instead of bailing out the "real" production and consumption economy (the "bottom 99%") by writing down debts to reflect the ability to pay, governments are acting as debt enforcers. Claiming to support "price stability," they insist that this can be maintained only by keeping unemployment high. So even as credit-inflated asset prices soar for real estate, stocks and bonds, the prices on which monetarists and central bankers focus are consumer prices and wages. Debt deflation is permitted in the Bubble Economy's wake, but not rising wages or social spending.

The economic theory used to justify this policy is a highly selective portrayal ("model") of how society works. Depicting interest and rent as "earnings" on a par with profits on tangible capital investment gives the impression that the FIRE sector produces a surplus instead of being what France's Physiocrats called sterile, or even worse: a deadweight eating parasitically into the economy. As bank loans turn land rent, monopoly privileges and infrastructure access fees into a flow of interest payments, they use some of this revenue to throw their lobbying power behind these rent extractors. The idea is to advocate lower taxes on *rentier* revenue so as to leave more available to pay interest. Land rent, monopoly privileges and patent rights are capitalized into bank loans, becoming the backing for today's financial sector and the economy's savings.

This creates a symbiosis among the economy's rent-yielding sectors. Some 80 percent of bank loans are real estate mortgages, and the balance of loans are to buy financial securities already issued or to take over companies, or consumer loans to be paid out of revenue earned in the normal course of employment, not by investing the bank credit productively. Even in the case of U.S. student loans (whose volume now exceeds that of credit card debt), this lending has not enabled many students to earn enough return on their education to pay their creditors. As debt deflation shrinks the economy, there are few employment opportunities for new graduates. Lacking jobs, they are obliged to live at home with their parents. Arrears on their student debts mount up, immune from the prospect of being wiped out in bankruptcy proceedings. The government has guaranteed these high-profit loans to the banks, yet the loans cannot be paid without polarizing the economy between creditors and debtors.

Vested interests defend tax favoritism and public guarantees backing this *rentier* behavior and sponsor a self-serving economics denying that debts need to be written down to reflect the ability of debtors to pay. This approach rejects the classical contrast between cost-value (what is technologically and socially necessary to produce a good or service) and economic rent ("unearned" income, including capital gains). Rejecting the distinction between earned and unearned income and wealth, the value of financial securities and other assets is assumed to capitalize revenue streams reflecting real effort and enterprise.

Also rejected is the idea that reform can make economies more efficient by minimizing unearned income and unproductive credit. Post-classical (that is, pro-*rentier*) models reason as if the economy is imprinted with the existing political and institutional structures, somewhat like patterns on a balloon. It can be inflated by credit creation or deflated by debt service, but keeps its basic proportions. Keynesian fine tuning aims at injecting enough purchasing power to maintain full employment, and the Fed sets an interest rate intended to supply just the right amount of credit—without changing the economy's institutional structure, tax system or political relationships. It is as if prices for goods and services, real estate, stocks and bonds are affected symmetrically and proportionally across the board. Under this assumption, any change is deemed to be "exogenous." So economic reform is not a topic in this discussion. There is no recognition of a free lunch or special privilege polarizing the distribution of income and wealth, to say nothing of being regulated or even fully taxed. Just the opposite: Public regulation, taxation and public investment are accused of being distortions, and indeed the road to serfdom. From the vantage point of the free lunchers, the past eight centuries of reforms appear as a distortion. Only their own extraction of income is deemed to be distortion-free.

This attitude explains why new public debt is issued (as in the Federal Reserve's post-2008 "cash for trash" swaps and taking Fannie Mae and Freddie Mac onto the government's balance sheet) to bail out bankers and speculators from having to take a loss, but the "real" economy is not being rescued. A bad-debt crisis is inevitable, because no exponential growth of credit can be sustained for long. Politicians rationalize bailouts by claiming that they are selecting priorities—and that economy's payments system will collapse if debts are written off. But keeping them on the books enables creditors at the top of the pyramid to steadily increase their share of wealth and income. Retail banking could have been rescued while folding up Citibank and Bank of America. But the financial sector seeks to convince politicians to accept the tunnel vision that Margaret Thatcher summarized in her intellectually and socially deadening slogan: "There is no alternative" (TINA). More blatantly, the bankers waive their final weapon: the threat to plunge the economy into chaos if they don't get their way.

This tunnel vision—and the debt overhead it has facilitated—is the economic tragedy of our time. It is tragic not only because the financial system bases its operations on extractive rather than productive lending, but because this is so unnecessary. It doesn't have to be this way! There is an alternative. That in fact is what classical political economy was all about.

The financial problem ultimately is rooted in fiscal policy. This makes it political. If classical political economy had succeeded in its reform program of taxing the land's site value (created not by the landowner's own efforts but by local transportation and other infrastructure investment and the level of general prosperity), this revenue would not have been available to be capitalized into bank loans and paid out as interest. This would have held down debt-leveraged housing prices, while saving governments from having to tax labor and productive business.

This was the logic underlying the classical program to make economies more fair and equitable as well as more competitive by minimizing their cost structure. Taxing economic rent and regulating monopoly pricing was seen as the alternative to taxing productive labor and tangible capital. Progressive Era economists hoped to invest this revenue in infrastructure. If governments had kept basic infrastructure in the public domain, prices for its services would not reflect the privatizers' interest charges and other financial fees for loans taken

> This tunnel vision—and the debt overhead it has facilitated—is the economic tragedy of our time. It is tragic not only because the financial system bases its operations on extractive rather than productive lending, but because this is so unnecessary.

out to buy it, or the exorbitant salaries and bonuses that have accompanied the sale of these assets on credit. The public option would provide essential services (transportation, communications, etc.) at cost or on a subsidized basis, or as freely as roads and sidewalks. The aim was to minimize the cost of living and doing business. This is the logic by which a public option for banking and regulations against casino-capitalist gambling, collateralized debt swaps and extortionate gouging by credit card companies would have helped avert today's polarization between *rentiers* and the productive economy.

But post-classical economic models neglect the distinction between necessary production costs and unnecessary "watered" costs. Income distribution is discussed without taking into account capital gains from real estate and stock market bubbles. There is almost no recognition that for real estate, finance and globalized investment today, the name of the game is capital gains, fueled by asset-price inflation. Wealthy individuals try not to earn (or at least to declare) taxable income, thanks to the fact that interest is tax deductible while capital gains and *rentier* revenue are replete with special loopholes and taxed at much lower rates than "earned income" in the form of wages and normal business profits.

This tax favoritism for debt financing as opposed to equity investment leads the debt overhead to reach a critical mass. The only way to avoid a crash is to lend debtors the credit to pay interest and even the amortization falling due. This is what U.S. banks did when they wrote "negative interest" mortgages that simply added the interest onto the debt balance, until it reached 125 percent or some other specified proportion of the original principal. The effect was an exponentially growing debt curve—the "magic of compound interest," society's paradigmatic free lunch. It can be sustained only by lending larger and larger amounts against collateral that is rising in price. An equivalent effect is achieved by channeling credit into the purchase of assets to raise their price at a high enough exponential rate to cover the accrual of interest, so that banks can rewrite their loans at the collateral's higher, debt-inflated price.

Lower interest rates enable a given stream of revenue to be capitalized into a larger loan principal. Under Mr. Greenspan's stewardship, the Federal Reserve supplied enough credit by 2008 to drive down interest rates to as low as they seemed likely to go. (To be sure, long-term rates were driven down even further by 2011 as banks tried to revive the plunging housing market.) Lower amortization rates also reduced carrying charges. Many mortgage debts were made perpetual, covering only the interest payments instead of being self-amortizing. Finally, banks were able to make larger loans by requiring lower down payments. Whereas 30 percent equity was normal prior to the 1990s, banks were making 100 percent loans by the early 2000s—indeed, even 105 percent loans to enable borrowers to pay fees to the mortgage originators and title insurers who were Wall Street's partners in crime.

The reality is that perpetual motion no more can be created in economies than in physical nature. As asset-price inflation raises the price of buying a retirement income (because higher stock and bond prices reduce the dividend and interest yield), pension funds cannot support retirees at the typically 8 per cent rate assumed for annual returns (compounded annually to pay enormous sums out of "capital" gains. Reality imposes itself on "mark-to-model" calculations that are stock in trade of the GIGO (garbage in, garbage out) toolkit used by financial fraudsters.

By 2006 an estimated one-sixth of new U.S. homebuyers were speculators. Rents fell as these buyers sought tenants to carry as much of the mortgage as possible while waiting for prices to rise by enough to pay off the bank loan with interest and still leave the hoped-for capital gain. The fantasy was to pay off their debts out of these gains, not out of operating revenue. The plan was to buy property whose carrying charges that cover the debt service—as long as the rate of price gain remained higher than the rate of interest. But the economy was not expanding and rents did not keep pace as debt deflation diverted spending away from goods and services. When rents fell, buyers had to make up the shortfall from other revenue or by drawing down their own savings—or by borrowing yet more from the banks. Seeing the economy growing top-heavy with debt, wise investors cashed out. Prices stopped rising. Foreclosure time arrived.

Treating money and credit simply as a veil misses this drive for asset-price gains to obtain balance-sheet wealth by debt leveraging. The "value-free" neoliberal approach assumes that competition will keep prices in line with technologically necessary production costs, but does not take account of rent seeking on credit. It must fail as a business plan in the end, because adding financial costs to family and business budgets increases break-even prices beyond necessary cost-value. This enables other economies to undersell debt-ridden ones.

Yet fortunes are still made most easily today by obtaining financial claims on existing wealth, not by increasing production. To the extent that free lunches are obtained this way, they are a quid without quo—revenue without a corresponding real cost of production. Yet the recent Bubble Economy has not deterred the textbook assumption that economies will "return" to equilibrium and fair income distribution when disturbed. Why then are there so many riots?

Throughout most of history the largest fortunes have been carved out of the public domain or achieved by insider dealings. A historically based reality-based economics thus should focus on the military conquests that created Europe's landed aristocracy, land grants in its colonies, the real estate give-aways to America's 19th-century railroad barons, and the recent financial give-aways to recipients of the $ 13 trillion in post-2008 U.S. financial bailouts that have endowed a power elite to rule the 21st century.

Ricardo's Theory of Economic Rent Leading to a Crisis of British Industry

The leading theories of crisis were formulated as warnings of what would happen if economies failed to reform themselves by freeing markets from the special financial and property privileges inherited from Europe's feudal epoch—landlordship, banking and the monopolies that medieval Europe bequeathed to industrial capitalism. Northern conquerors carved landlordship out of territories they defeated levying groundrent and monopoly rent as the primordial forms of tribute. In due course Italian bankers emerged out of Church orders to lend kingdoms the funds to pay tribute to Rome, and then to wage wars.

Prior to 1815, Britain's landed interest and industrial capital both feared the overgrowth of debt owed to bondholders, especially to the Dutch who owned much government debt and stock in the Crown monopolies. But as normal trade resumed after the Napoleonic Wars ended, industry and banking formed an alliance of against the landed interest. In 1846 they succeeded in repealing Britain its protectionist Corn Laws, negotiating free trade to make Britain the "workshop of the world"—and also the world's banker, making profits by financing foreign trade, mainly foreign raw materials for British manufactures.

The 19th century saw two major lines of theorizing about of how industrial capitalism would experience a crisis. The first was David Ricardo's warning against landlords seeking protectionist trade policy to promote national self-sufficiency in food production—at rising prices and hence land rents. Assuming that diminishing returns would push up food prices at the margin of cultivation. Unless the rising cost of producing food at home was checked by importing lower-priced crops from abroad, the landlords' rising receipt of groundrent would absorb the entire surplus. Industrialists would have to pay labor a higher wage to cover the cost of higher-priced food, ending capital profitability and thus stifling further progress.

This logic was based on technological nonsense. It assumed diminishing returns in agriculture—just as the revolution in soil chemistry (the use of fertilizers, pesticides), new seed varieties and mechanized farm production powered a century of remarkable productivity gains. Ricardo's pessimistic approach denied that fertilizers or capital improvements could change the "original and indestructible powers of the soil" in the form of natural fertility.

This focus on diminishing returns distracted attention from earlier worries about financial crisis stemming from public debts imposing heavy carrying charges paid by a proliferation of excise taxes. At the time Ricardo wrote his *Principles of Political Economy and Taxation* in 1817, three-quarters of British government's budget was spent on debt service, mainly as a result of its centuries of warfare with France. His labor theory of value (and its logical complement, his definition of economic rent as the margin of market price over actual costs of production ultimately reducible to the cost of labor) treated income and wealth in "real" terms, reducible to labor time and wages. It was as if economies operated on a barter basis, with money and credit (and hence, debt) being only a veil. There was no monetary and financial dimension, no debt service eating into income, no "capital transfer" problem of paying foreign debts.

As Britain's Parliamentary spokesman for its banking industry (today we would say lobbyist), Ricardo based his price theory on Malthus's ideas of population growth forcing resort to poorer soils, increasing the cost of producing food. Rising crop prices would provide a windfall gain—economic rent—for landlords on the better lands cultivated first. The increase in land rents would grind industrial capitalism to a halt, at least in Britain, as long as it relied on domestic agriculture to feed its work force. Rising prices for subsistence would price the economy's manufacturers out of world markets and shift industrial power to less densely populated countries with better soils and hence (so Ricardo assumed) lower prices.

Adam Smith's *Wealth of Nations* had denounced the policy of shifting the fiscal burden onto labor and industry by a proliferation of sales taxes and other excise taxes. Ricardo used his labor theory of cost-value (including the labor embodied in making capital goods) and market price (reflecting the excess of economic rent over and above the cost of production on well situated land) to oppose tariff protection for agriculture. British industry could retain its global dominance by abolishing the protectionist Corn Laws (introduced in 1798 during the Napoleonic Wars with France) so as to buy food in the cheapest markets it could find—mainly in North America. Free trade in grain would enable industrialists to feed their labor force as inexpensively as foreign manufacturers could. Given Britain's industrial head start, it could remain the workshop of the world.

After the revolutions of 1848 drew the middle classes and labor back industrial and finance capital in the drive for democratic political reform, the consensus ideology of the Industrial Revolution was to free economies from the legacy of special privilege and hereditary favoritism. It was left to John Stuart Mill and subsequent "Ricardian socialists" to advocate taxing land rent. That became the great political fight in Britain from 1848 to World War I, high-lighted by the Budget Crisis of 1909–11. It required electoral reform and an extension of the franchise to reduce the landed interest's control over Parlia-ment. Reformers throughout Europe and America sought to re-establish banking, basic infrastructure and land ownership (or at least the land's rent) in the public domain. Evolution seemed to favor nations that invested the eco-nomic surplus in tangible public and private capital formation rather than unproductively to extract land rent and monopoly rent with borrowed credit at interest.

The American School's Technological Optimism as an Alternative to Ricardian Pessimism

Britain's free trade negotiations after 1846 offered other countries tariff-free access to its agricultural markets if they would give British industry access to their own domestic markets. This revived the tariff debate in the United States. Henry Clay had coined the term "American System" in the 1840s for the Whig program of protective tariffs, internal improvements and a national bank. Henry Carey and his followers such as E. Peshine Smith soon pointed out that thanks to the progress of science and technology, increasing returns characterized agriculture as well as industry and transportation. By the 1850s a distinctly American School of political economy developed with regard to how increasing returns would transform economies, above all as a result of rising energy usage per worker.

To obtain such productivity gains, they argued, U.S. manufacturers needed to be protected from Britain's industrial head start. This logic was embodied in the Republican Party's founding program in 1853, and guided U.S. devel-opment after it won the 1860 presidential election behind Abraham Lincoln. Smith went into the State Department with his long-time Rochester, New York law partner, William Seward. In the 1870s, Seward arranged for Smith to go to Japan as advisor to the Mikado to guide that nation's protectionist industri-alization.

By the end of the 19th century the American School developed in a number of directions. In contrast to theorizing that assumed wages to be able to fall without reducing labor productivity, the Economy of High Wages theory held that better paid labor was more productive labor as a result of being better fed, better clothed and above all, better educated. All this cost money, but it enabled high-wage economic such as the United States to undersell low-wage economies.

The economic problem was expected to be more sociological than one of scarcity. Simon Patten, the first economics professor at the major early business school, the Wharton School at the University of Pennsylvania, described a high productivity Economy of Abundance in which the temptation to over-consume would challenge the traditional morality of stalwart altruism inherited from subsistence societies.

Many of Patten's students became sociologists or social workers. His student Rexford Tugwell became a member of Franklin Roosevelt's Brains Trust and was appointed governor of Puerto Rico, later teaching at the University of Chicago as an institutionalist in the days before Chicago went hard-line monetarist. But despite the American School's influence on U.S. economic policy for a century, protectionists and institutionalist ideas have been stripped from mainstream histories of economic thought. A censorial post-classical economics shifted the focus, traumatized by how Marx and other reformers mobilized classical economics to counter the *rentier* sector's special privileges and continue the restructuring process initiated by France's Physiocrats.

Marxian Socialism

Writing within the tradition of classical value theory but from the vantage point of labor, Marx viewed the essential crisis under capitalism as political. Capitalism would avoid stagnation by evolving into socialism. The transition would save it from underconsumption and economic polarization resulting from financial and industrial capital impoverishing labor.

Whereas Ricardo saw profits declining as a result of a rising share of income going to landlords, Marx saw profits falling as a proportion of the industrialist's cash flow as what today is called depreciation and amortization increased—the return of capital, as well as the return to capital (profit). As production became more capital-intensive in its drive to raise productivity, capital/output ratios and capital investment per worker would increase. This meant that industrialists would have to recapture the original cost of their capital investment, in addition to making a profit. And like Adam Smith, Marx assumed a 50:50 share of debt and equity in his numerical examples. Assuming a steady interest rate, it followed that as production became more capital-intensive, financial charges would rise. But the political force of industrial capitalism would modernize finance and industrialize it, he optimistically believed.

Given the progress of science over the past few centuries, it is only natural that most technological views of the future are optimistic. Rising productivity has been a long-term trend, even in food production and mining. Despite the Ricardian assumption of diminishing returns that still characterizes textbook models, and despite Club of Rome limits-to-growth campaigning and peak-oil warnings, crises have stemmed not from the production sector but from the financial sector—and behind it, from the concentration of wealth in the hands of *rentiers*, monopolists and privatizers that have carved special privileges and property rights out of the public domain.

Like the American protectionists, Marx was a technological optimist. Describing agriculture as becoming industrialized, lowering food prices by raising productivity, he saw technological innovation as constantly lowering costs, making much industrial capital obsolete before it physically wore out. To the extent that the pace of technological innovation gained momentum, obsolescent high-cost capital would have to be written off and replaced even though the physical lifetime of the machinery was not yet worn out. This rising productivity was unlikely to cause a chronic over-production crisis under capitalism, he wrote, because more labor would be employed in the capital goods sector as production became more capital-intensive.

Marx's followers have focused on the relationship between industrial capital and labor, and on the internal contradictions of capitalism that Josef Schumpeter later elaborated as "creative destruction" within the capitalist class as innovators invested to undersell competitors by lowering production costs. But Marx also re-introduced the pre-Ricardian emphasis on finance and debt. In his draft notes for Volume III of *Capital* and Book III of *Theories of Surplus Value* he discussed how the purely mathematical growth of finance capital at exponential rates caused financial imbalance—the "magic of compound interest." The excessive autonomous buildup of finance capital formed the core of his theory of the business cycle. But these cyclical mini-crises were not the existential theory that Ricardo forecast in what Marx characterized as the Armageddon of industrial capitalism. He optimistically expected finance to become industrialized, on its way ultimately to becoming socialized.

Yet despite the fact that Ricardo's technological assumptions of diminishing returns was so wrongheaded and anachronistic even in its own day—not to mention his special-interest pleading for the banking industry—subsequent mainstream economics remains focused on his ideas rather than pursuing the more realistic development of classical political economy at the hands of Marx or those of the American School of technology theorists, institutionalists and Progressive Era social reformers. The explanation lies in the fact that

Ricardo's pleading for the financial sector appeals to the major backers of today's academic economics. Realistic analysis showing the problems of financial overhead and extractive rent-seeking is precisely what led to its rejection, in accordance with the time-honored criterion for acceptability by vested *rentier* interests: "If the eye offends thee, pluck it out."

Post-classical Theorizing Defends the rentiers *as Productive, in Proportion to Their Wealth*

In criticizing the strictly Ricardian views of the American anti-socialist journalist Henry George, Marx wrote that industrial capital always had a visceral hatred of landlords. The historical task of industrial capitalism, after all, was to purify society of the carry-over from feudalism's landed aristocracy — not only its land ownership and groundrent but also its control of the upper house of legislatures, by which it managed to block reform in many countries. In Britain the political struggle came to a head in 1909–10, when the House of Commons sought to pass a revenue bill based on a land tax. A constitutional crisis ensued, resulting in a ruling that the House of Lords never again could block a House of Commons revenue bill.

But by the time World War I broke out in 1914 the momentum for taxing landed property had passed. Finance capital was in the ascendant. And whereas in Ricardo's day it had thrown its political support behind manufacturing industry — seeing international trade as the major private-sector market for banking, as it had been since the 13th century — by the 20th century urban real estate was becoming much more valuable important than agricultural land. Britain's wealthiest individuals were still the post-feudal families holding groundrent on Kensington and other high-value London neighborhoods, but home ownership and commercial real estate was well on its way to becoming democratized — on credit. Given the high price of real estate relative to income, it could be bought only by borrowing from the banks. Some 80 percent of bank lending in most English-speaking countries now takes the form of real estate mortgages. This has led the banking and financial sector to reverse its earlier attack on the landlord class — above all the post-Ricardian thrust of John Stuart Mill and other "Ricardian socialists" to fully tax groundrent or nationalize the land outright.

Today's ultimate recipients of land rent are not the hereditary owners as was the landlord class in Ricardo's day; they are the banks. No 19th-century economic writer expected this. From Britain to the United States, the great political fight was to socialize land rent either by taxing it or by nationalizing it. The thrust of classical value and price theory was to distinguish between earned income (wages and profits on industrial capital investment) and unearned income: economic rent, paradigmatically by landlords but also, by logical extension, monopoly rent, interest and other returns to privilege. The most important privilege today is the banking system's privilege of creating credit.

After the Great War's aftermath derailed the path of development toward which the Progressive Era seemed to have been leading. The vested financial and property interests mounted an ideological counter-attack, and a major arena was economic theory. The new theory's political aim — its value system, price theory, monetary theory and the tax policy this theorizing implied — reflected the shift in alliances between finance capital, real estate and industry. Instead of continuing to oppose the landed interest, the 20th century's democratization of property ownership — on credit — led to a symbiosis of finance, insurance and real estate (FIRE). To the extent that finance interfaces with industry, it has been to financialize industrial companies, not to industrialize the financial system as seemed to be occurring in the late 19th century from Germany and Central Europe to Japan. And to the extent that finance interfaces with government, it is first of all to finance the public construction of capital infrastructure, and then to force its sell-off — at prices far below the original cost — to buyers on credit, permitting them to factor in a proliferation of financial charges into the access fees they extract from the population. The result is the opposite direction of evolution from which 19th-century economic Darwinians expected. Instead of lowering a nation's cost structure to make it more internationally competitive, financialization increases prices across the board.

As noted above, the definition of "free markets" has been turned upside down. Instead of freeing markets from rent-seeking, taxing groundrent and keeping major infrastructure monopolies in the public domain, economies were deregulated to "free" finance to load industry and government with debts, turning profits and disposable personal income into interest charges. Taxes have been shifted off real estate and finance onto labor and industry, while the post-1980 New Enclosure movement has increasingly privatized the public domain. And to cap matters, under the slogan of "free markets" as the antithesis to "the Road to Serfdom" (defined for all practical purposes as public regulation of the FIRE sector) planning has been centralized in the financial centers, from Wall Street to the City of London, the Paris Bourse and Frankfurt.

It thus seems ironic that governments have become the major sponsors of private finance capital. Lenin was the most astute in applying Marx's theory of finance capital to the eruption of the Great War, in Imperialism. At the time he wrote it in 1916, it was natural to focus on private finance capital. But what the war did was create an entirely new dynamic (or "synthesis," as Marxists would say): inter-governmental debt, headed by the U.S. demands for Inter-Ally arms debts that led the Allies to demand German reparations to cover their payments of debt service to the United States. Wall Street organized a triangular flow of U.S. purchases of German state and local bonds, providing the Reichsbank with dollars to pay the Allies to pay the United States. And after World War II, the International Monetary Fund, World Bank and most recently the European Central Bank have acted as executive committees on behalf of international finance (mainly Wall Street, thanks to the Washington Consensus that dominates these creditor institutions). The result is an international imposition of financial and fiscal austerity on debtor countries, starting with Third World countries in the 1960s and culminating in the asset stripping of Iceland and Greece today (2011).

The financial sector's attempt to turn the economic surplus into debt claims threatens to leave economies in poverty by collateralizing wealth to pay interest rather than invest in tangible capital formation, rising living standards or environmental preservation. And the vested interests threaten to plunge economies into crisis if governments move to check their interest by reviving the Progressive Era's policy to check the power unearned wealth, finance and monopolies.

That is the essence of today's global crisis. Yet the financial and other *rentier* interests are capturing the public debate, mass media and academic economics. Inverting classical economics, they have re-defined "free markets" in a way diametrically opposed to what was meant a century ago. Instead of meaning markets free of economic rent, interest and monopoly power, the term now means markets free for predatory finance and kindred *rentiers* to dismantle public regulation and free themselves from taxation. Such an economy "frees" the new financial oligarchy to reverse democracy, stifle growth and stop living standards from rising.

The resulting dominance of the financial sector over industrial capital, real estate and commerce (and increasingly over family budgets) threatens to absorb the economic surplus today, bringing on precisely the form of economic Armageddon that Ricardo forecast landlords would create in the absence of free trade in grain, and which Mill, Henry George and other critics of landlord said would create economic crisis of the public sector failed to collect the land rent created by no effort of capital investment of landlords themselves.

The world economy is being thrown into a financial crisis based largely on mortgage debt so large that it not only absorbs all the land rent, but requires payment from wages and salaries as well as industrial profits. Ricardo's barter-based, bank-free and debt-free economic theory did not recognize this kind of financial crisis. And all economic logic of the 19th and early 20th century assumed the rule of law. But today, junk mortgage lending and outright fraud are proliferating on an unprecedented scale, beyond the ability of the courts or criminal prosecutors to cope with. And in contrast to the effect of 19th-century Parliamentary and Congressional reform in promoting democracy politically, governments throughout the world are becoming subordinated not to the landed aristocracy this time around, but to financial *rentiers*. It is they to whom John Maynard Keynes referred in 1936 in his gentle term "euthanasia of the *rentier*," by which he meant a rationalization of the financial system.

Instead of such rationalization occurring, the *rentiers* have fought back, joining in an alliance of finance capital with real estate to create the symbiotic FIRE sector. The national income and product accounts often are unable to distinguish financial from real estate earnings in today's epoch of vertical integration between banks, real estate brokers and appraisers. By 2008, Wall Street investment bankers were packaging junk mortgages into loans, and "casino capitalist" institutions placed bets on how long it would take for this "toxic waste" to explode, bringing down the economy in a convulsion of bankruptcy.

So in retrospect, the 19th century's warnings of how the crisis of capitalism would unfold turned out to be too optimistic. They did not anticipate how the *rentier* interests would mount a counter-attack to block governments from industrializing (to say nothing of socializing) banking and insurance systems. The "independence of the central bank" is applauded as the "hallmark of democracy" rather than seeing it as a victory for the new financial oligarchy. The financial system has disabled the U.S. legal system by buying the right to name the heads of Congressional committees dealing with banking, and backing the political campaigns of judges committed to applying the law in the interests of their financial supporters.

Summary of Part I

Whereas Ricardo's view of class war was between industrial capital and the landed aristocracy, Marx's shifted the focus to industrial capital vis-à-vis labor — assuming that industrial capital was well on its way to winning its war against the landed aristocracy. And as for finance capital, Marx assumed that it would become subordinate to industrial capital.

But the seeming servant has become the master. Instead of banking becoming industrialized as seemed to be happening at least in central European banking prior to World War I, industry has been financialized. The shift gained momentum in the 1980s, as central banks first in the United States and then in Western Europe and Japan became free of the foreign exchange and gold bullion convertibility constraints that had existed prior to 1971. Corporate raiders now raise credit to take over industry, paying out cash flow as interest and dividends instead of investing in fixed capital formation or longer-term research and development.

Only a reduction in debt and higher wages can spur real recovery. But this is blocked by austerity policies that impose debt deflation. The solution needed for today's broad economic downturn is easier bankruptcy, especially for educational loans, and for mortgages to be brought in line with today's lower market prices and affordability. But when the financial sector gains control of policy, its prime objective is to protect creditors from taking major losses on loans gone bad and gambles against bettors unable to pay (*e.g*, Lehman Bros. and A.I.G. after September 2008). Something has to give — and the financial sector has achieved sufficient power to sacrifice general prosperity in order to squeeze out debt service. So new capital investment and hiring shrink, and economies fall into depression — leading to yet more bankruptcies and foreclosures in the private sector, and privatization sell-offs by debt-strapped governments.

The Role of Governments in Sponsoring Financial Exploitation

Saving used to mean putting money away out of earnings to be able to spend. But today, "saving" in the national income statistics takes the form mainly of paying down debts taken on in times past. Current earnings are not available for spending; they are earmarked to pay the banks for credit cards, to pay the mortgage, to pay student loans, auto loans, retail store credit. The era of free choice is over — the choice being offered is, "Your money or your life."

The term "debt deflation" was popularized by Irving Fisher writing in the Great Depression of the 1930s. Markets collapsed under the weight of Inter-Ally debts and German reparations stemming from World War I, and speculative credit as the U.S. Federal Reserve flooded financial markets to enable American banks and investors to lend Germany the money to pay reparations to the Allies to pay their debts to the United States. Lenin had written that wars were inevitable because finance capitalists in leading creditor nations would be unable to reach market-sharing agreements as to how to carve up the world amongst themselves and their leading industrial, mining and other clients. But what turned out to be most intransigent were U.S. Government claims on the Allied Powers for payment for arms supplied prior to U.S. entry into the Great War. Keynes blamed this claim on the Allied governments turning on Germany to pay them the money being demanded by the U.S. Government.

The amount demanded exceeded the reasonable amount that could be paid, making breakdown inevitable, first in 1929 and then finally in 1931 when standstill agreements were reached among the governments. It was too late to save Western economies from the Great Depression that recovered only as a result of the new public spending peaking in World War II.

After 1945 the international economy was reorganized along creditor-oriented lines sponsored by the United States as major global creditor, with nearly 80 percent of the world's monetary gold stock. But starting with the Korean War, military spending pushed the U.S. balance of payments into deficit in the 1960s, forcing the dollar off gold in August 1971. August seems to have become the traditional time of international crisis, from the guns of August 1914 to closing the London Gold Pool in 1971 to the financial crisis of August 2011 that saw gold jump once again in response to a flight out of financial debt claims.)

The Eurozone is re-creating a similar inter-governmental debt tangle today against its own members. This time the aim is not to pay for military war as in the 1920s, but to wage a 21st-century mode of financial warfare by creditors against debtor economies. First Ireland and Greece and then Italy, Spain and Portugal were directed to bail out their insolvent banking systems by imposing austerity and letting the banks "earn their way out of debt" by creating credit to lend to private buyers of the land and public domain that debt-burdened governments were to sell off. So instead of the Ricardian socialism directed against landlords and monopolists or Marxian socialism aimed at raising living standards and rationalizing industrial organization, the world is threatened with a lapse back into neofeudal *rentier* power.

This financial aggression is similar to military asset grabs. Just as in overt warfare, creditors seek the land and other real estate, public infrastructure and other assets from debtors in Ireland and Greece, and now Portugal, Italy and Spain as well. In place of tribute as such, they demand debt service. And the way to achieve this is by creating crisis, using their control of the payments and credit system as leverage to stifle economies that do not obey their demands. This is why today's global financial system is in crisis once again, largely because of inter-governmental debt overwhelming private-sector capital movements, and because of international financial institutions (headed by the multinational but U.S.-dominated International Monetary Fund and World Bank, the European Central Bank and the U.S. Federal Reserve system) seeking to impose austerity and heavy taxation for what has metamorphosed from military warfare to financial warfare — in this case, against debtor economies.

Part II

INFLATED DEBT AND DEBT DEFLATION

"I was never able to explain to the American people in a way in which they understood it why these rescues were for them and for their benefit, not for Wall Street."

> Henry M. Paulson Jr., the former Treasury secretary, to the Financial Crisis Inquiry Commission in May 2010.
> Quoted in Gretchen Morgenson, "The Rescue That Missed Main Street," *The New York Times*, August 27, 2011.

7

A Property Is Worth Whatever a Bank Will Lend

Never before have so many Americans gone so deeply into debt so willingly. Housing prices have swollen to the point that we have taken to calling a mortgage—by far the largest debt most of us will ever incur—an "investment." Sure, the thinking goes, $100000 borrowed today will cost more than $200000 to pay back over the next thirty years, but land, which they are not making any more of, will appreciate even faster. In the odd logic of the real estate bubble, debt has come to equal wealth.

And not only wealth but freedom—an even stranger paradox. After all, debt throughout most of history has been little more than a slight variation on slavery. Debtors were medieval peons or Indians bonded to Spanish plantations or the sharecropping children of slaves in the postbellum South. Few Americans today would volunteer for such an arrangement, and therefore would-be lords and barons have been forced to develop more sophisticated enticements.

The solution they found is brilliant, and although it is complex, it can be reduced to a single word: rent. Not the rent that apartment dwellers pay the landlord but economic rent, which is the profit one earns simply by owning something. Economic rent can take the form of licensing fees for the radio spectrum, interest on a savings account, dividends from a stock, or the capital gain from selling a home or vacant lot. The distinguishing characteristic of economic rent is that earning it requires no effort whatsoever. Indeed, the regular rent tenants pay landlords becomes economic rent only after subtracting whatever amount the landlord actually spent to keep the place standing.

Most members of the rentier class are very rich. One might like to join that class. And so our paradox (seemingly) is resolved. With the real estate boom, the great mass of Americans can take on colossal debt today and realize colossal capital gains—and the concomitant *rentier* life of leisure—tomorrow. If you have the wherewithal to fill out a mortgage application, then you need never work again. What could be more inviting—or, for that matter, more egalitarian? That is the pitch, anyway. The reality is that, although home ownership may be a wise choice for many people, this particular real estate bubble has been carefully engineered to lure home buyers into circumstances detrimental to their own best interests. The bait is easy money. The trap is a modern equivalent to peonage, a lifetime spent working to pay off debt on an asset of rapidly dwindling value.

Most everyone involved in the real estate bubble thus far has made at least a few dollars. But that is about to change. The bubble will burst, and when it does, the people who thought they would be living the easy life of a landlord will soon find that what they really signed up for was the hard servitude of debt serfdom.

The new road to serfdom begins with a loan. Since 2003, mortgages have made up more than half of the total bank loans in America—more than $300 billion in 2005 alone. Without that growing demand, banks would have seen almost no net loan growth in recent years.

Why is the demand for mortgage debt so high? There are several reasons, but all of them have to do with the fact that banks encourage people to think of mortgage debt in terms of how much they can afford to pay in a given month—how far they can stretch their pay checks—rather than in terms of the total amount of the loan. A given monthly payment can carry radically different amounts of debt, depending on the rate of interest and how long those payments last. The purchasing power of a $1,000 monthly payment, for instance, nearly triples as the debt lingers and the interest rate declines.

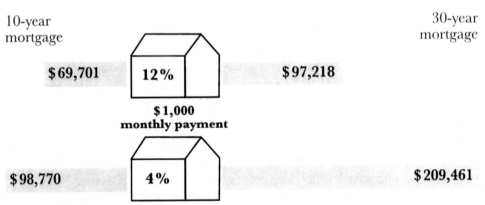

Fig. 1: A monthly $1,000 payment can carry different levels of debt

As it happens, banks are increasingly unhurried about repayment. Nearly half the people buying their first homes last year were allowed to do so with no money down, and many of them took out so-called interest-only loans, for which payment of the actual debt—amortization—was delayed by several years. A few even took on "negative amortization" loans, which dispense entirely with payments on the principal and require only partial payment of the interest itself: the extra interest owed is simply added to the total debt, which can grow indefinitely. The Federal Reserve, meanwhile, has been pushing interest rates down for more than two decades.

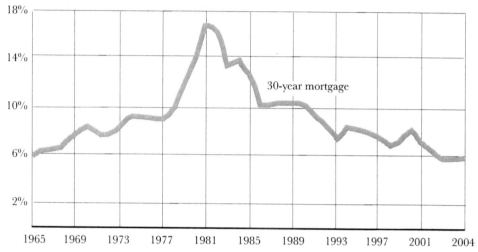

Fig. 2: Interest rates have been falling since 1981

The IRS has helped create demand for debt as well by allowing tax breaks —the well-known home-mortgage deduction, for instance—that can transform a loan into an attractive tax shelter. Indeed, commercial real estate investors hide most of their economic rent in "depreciation" write-offs for their buildings, even as those buildings gain market value. The pretense is that buildings wear out or become obsolete just like any other industrial investment. The reality is that buildings can be depreciated again and again, even as the property's market value increases.

Local and state governments have done their share too, by shifting the tax burden from property to labor and consumption, in the form of income and sales taxes. Since 1929, the proportion of tax burden has almost completel reversed itself.

In recent years, though, the biggest incentive to home ownership has not been owning a home per se, or even avoiding taxes, but rather the eternal hope of getting ahead. If the price of a $200,000 house shoots up 15 percent in a given year, the owner will realize a $30,000 capital gain. Many such owners are spending tomorrow's capital gain today by taking out home-equity loans. For families whose real wages are stagnant or falling, borrowing against higher property prices seems almost like taking money from a bank account that has earned dividends. In a study last year, Alan Greenspan and James Kennedy found that new home-equity loans added $200 billion to the U.S. economy in 2004 alone.

It is also worth noting that capital gains—economic rent "earned" without any actual labor or industrial investment—are increasingly untaxed.

All of these factors have combined to lure record numbers of buyers into the real estate market, and home prices are climbing accordingly. The median price of a home has more than doubled in the last decade, from $109,000 in 1995 to a peak of more than $206,000 in 2005. That growth far outpaces the consumer price index, and yet housing affordability—the measure of those month-to-month housing costs—has remained about the same.

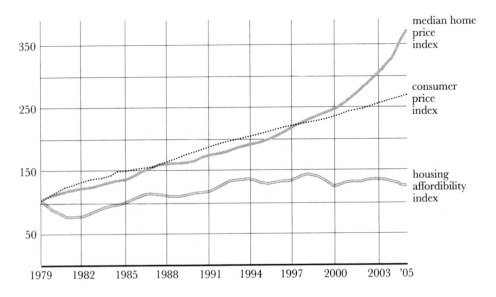

Fig. 3: Housing prices have far outpaced consumer prices even as monthly payment remain affordable

That sounds like good news. But those rising prices also mean that more people owe more money to banks than at any other time in history. And that's not just in terms of dollar—$11.8 trillion in outstanding mortgages—but also as a proportion of the national economy. This debt is now on track to surpass the size of America's entire gross domestic product by the end of the decade.

Even that huge debt might not seem so bad, what with those huge capital gains beckoning from out there in the future. But the boom, alas, cannot last forever. And when the growth ceases, the market will collapse. Understanding why, though, requires a quick detour into economic theory. We often think of "the economy" as no more than a closed loop between producers and consumers. Employers hire workers, the workers create goods and services, the employers pay them, and the workers use that money to buy the goods and services they created.

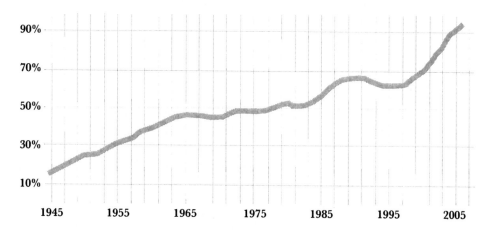

Fig. 4: Mortgage debt is rising as a proportion of GDP

As we have seen, though, the government also plays a significant role in the economy. Tax hikes drain cash from the circular flow of payments between producers and consumers, slowing down overheated economies. Deficit spending pumps more income into that flow, helping pull stalled economies out of recession. This is the classical policy model associated with John Maynard Keynes.

A third actor also influences the nation's fortune. Economists call it the FIRE sector, short for finance, insurance, and real estate. These industries are so symbiotic that the Commerce Department reports their earnings as a composite. (Banks require mortgage holders to insure their properties even as the banks reach out to absorb insurance companies. Meanwhile, real estate companies are organizing themselves as stock companies in the form of real estate investment trusts, or REITs—which in turn are underwritten by investment bankers.) The main product of these industries is credit. The FIRE sector pumps credit into the economy even as it withdraws interest and other charges.

The FIRE sector has two significant advantages over the production/consumption and government sectors. The first is that interest wealth grows exponentially. That means that as interest compounds over time, the debt doubles and then doubles again. Theeighteenth-century philosopher Richard Price identified this miracle of compound interest and observed, somewhat ruefully, that had he been able to go back to the day Jesus was born and save a single penny—at 5 percent interest,compounded annually—he would have earned himself a solid gold sphere 150 million times bigger than Earth.

The FIRE sector's other advantage is that interest payments can quickly be recycled into more debt. The more interest paid, the more banks lend. And those new loans in turn can further drive up demand for real estate—thereby allowing homeowners to take out even more loans in anticipation of future capital gains. Some call this perpetual-motion machine a "post-industrial economy," but it might more accurately be called a rentier economy. The dream is that the FIRE sector will expand to embrace the fortune of every American—that we need not work or produce anything, or, for that matter, invest in new technology or infrastructure for the nation. We certainly need not pay taxes. We need only participate in the boom itself. The miracle of compound interest will allow every one of us to be a rentier, feasting on interest, dividends, and capital gains.

In reality, alas, we can't all be rentiers. Just as, in Voltaire's phrase, the rich require an abundant supply of the poor, so too does the rentier class require an abundant supply of debtors. There is no other way. In fact, the vast majority of Americans have seen their share of the rental pie decrease over the last two decades, even as the real estate pie as a whole has expanded. Everyone got a little richer, but rich people got much, much richer.

We will be hard-pressed to maintain even this semi-blissful state. Like any living organism, real economies don't grow exponentially, or even in a straight line. They taper off into an S-curve, the victim of their own successes. When business is good, the demand for labor, raw materials, and credit increases, which leads to large jumps in wages, prices, and interest rates, which in turn act to depress the economy. That is where the miracle of compound interest founders. Although many people did save money at interest two thousand years ago, nobody has yet obtained even a single Earth-volume of gold. The reason is that when a business cycle turns down, debtors cannot pay, and so their debts are wiped out in a wave of bankruptcy along with all the savings invested in these bad loans.

Japan learned this lesson in the Nineties. As the price of land went up, banks lent more money than people could afford to pay interest on. Eventually, no one could afford to buy any more land, demand fell off, and prices dropped accordingly. But the debt remained in place. People owed billions of Yen on homes worth half that—homes they could not sell. Many commercial owners simply went into foreclosure, leaving the banks not only with "non-performing loans" that were in fact dead losses but also with houses no one wanted—or could afford—to buy. And that lack of incoming interest also meant that banks had no more reserves to lend, which furthered the downward spiral. Britain's similarly debt-burdened economy inspired a dry witticism: "Sorry you lost your job. I hope you made a killing on your house."

We have already reached our own peak. As of last fall, even Alan Green-span had detected "signs of froth" in the housing market. Home prices had "risen to unsustainable levels" in some places, he said, and would have exceeded the reach of many Americans long ago if not for "the dramatic increase in the prevalence of interest-only loans" and "other, more exotic forms of adjustable-rate mortgages" that "enable marginally qualified, highly leveraged borrowers to purchase homes at inflated prices." If the trend continues, homeowners and banks alike "could be exposed to signifi- cant losses." Interest rates, meanwhile, have begun to creep up.

So: America holds record mortgage debt in a declining housing market. Even that at first might seem okay — we can just weather the storm in our nice new houses. And in fact things will be okay for homeowners who bought long ago and have seen the price of their homes double and then double again. But for more recent homebuyers, who bought at the top and who now face decades of payments on houses that soon will be worth less than they paid for them, serious trouble is brewing. And they are not an insignificant bunch.

The problem for recent homebuyers is not just that prices are falling; it's that prices are falling even as the buyers' total mort- gage remains the same or even increases. Eventually the price of the house will fall below what homeowners owe, a state that economists call negative equity. Homeowners with nega- tive equity are trapped. They can't sell — the declining market price won't cover what they owe the bank — but they still have to make those (often growing) monthly payments. Their only "choice" is to cut back spending in other areas or lose the house — and everything they paid for it — in foreclosure.

Free markets are based on choice. But more and more homeowners are discovering that what they got for their money is fewer and fewerchoices. A real estate boom that began with the promise of "economic freedom" almost certainly will end with a growing number of workerslocked in to a lifetime of debt service that absorbs every spare penny. Indeed, a study by The Conference Board found that the proportion of households with any discretionary income whatsoever had already declined between 1997and 2002, from 53 percent to 52 percent. Rising interest rates, rising fuel costs,and declining wages will only tighten the squeeze on debtors. But homeowners are not the only ones who will pay. The overall economy likely will shrink as well. That $200 billion that flowed into the "real"economy in 2004 is already spent, with no future capital gains in the works to fuel more such easy money. Rising debt-service payments will further divert income from new con- sumer spending. Taken together, these factors will further shrink the "real" economy, drive down those already declining real wages, and push our debt- ridden economy into Japan-style stagnation or worse. Then only the debt itself will remain, a bitter monument to our love of easy freedom.

How Untaxing Land Rent Raises Housing Prices

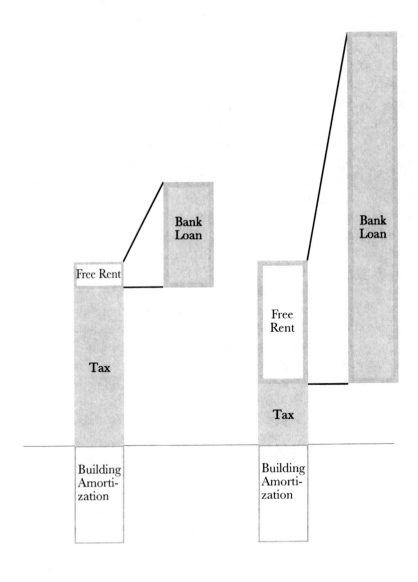

8

THE REAL ESTATE BUBBLE AT THE CORE OF TODAY'S DEBT-LEVERAGED ECONOMY

From St. Simon's followers in France to Marx and other reformers prior to World War I, nearly all financial observers expected banking to become the economy's industrial planning agency, alongside government. But contrary to their expectation that banking would become industrialized, the opposite has occurred: Industry has been financialized. Companies are being turned from means of production into vehicles to extract interest, generate banking fees and register stock market gains for the banking and financial sector.

Capital formation today is financed mainly out of retained business earnings. The stock market also was supposed to supply investment funding, but since the 1980s it has been turned into a vehicle for corporate raiding. By permitting interest to be tax-deductible and taxing capital gains at low rates (and often not at all), the tax code favors replacing equity with debt. The effect is to make asset-price inflation the quickest mode of "wealth creation"—buying real estate, monopolies and financial securities on credit, and hoping to emerge with a "capital" gain.

This is true above all for real estate, which remains the largest asset in every economy and hence the banking sector's largest customer. Some 70 percent of bank loans in the United States, Britain and Australia are real estate mortgages. This paramount role of land and buildings as recipients of credit creation has created what national income accountants call the FIRE sector—an acronym for finance, insurance and real estate.

This symbiotic sector is political as well as economic. Translating its economic power into political control, bankers support real estate owners in lobbying to roll back property taxes, slash income taxes on higher wealth brackets and dismantle public bank regulation. This policy is guided by the realization that whatever revenue the tax collector relinquishes will be "free" to be capitalized into mortgages and other loans, and paid as interest—to be recycled into new loans to bid up property prices further, justifying yet further new lending.

From antiquity down through medieval times, land provided the main source of taxes. But starting with the Revolt of the Barons in England in 1258–65, its owners used their control of Parliament to shift the fiscal burden onto the rest of the economy. The thrust of classical economic reform was to make land once again the basic source of public revenue. Seeking to free labor and capital from the burden of rent and interest, Progressive Era reformers sought to fully tax the land's rent or nationalize it outright.

It is natural for land prices to increase over time as a result of infrastructure spending, the general level of prosperity, and property tax cuts. Governments invest in transportation, public schools and other infrastructure (water and sewer services, gas and electricity) and give rezoning permits providing valuable development privileges. All this raises the rental value of sites as populations grow and become more prosperous. But what turns out to be mainly responsible for the rising price of land today is mortgage credit. A property today is worth as much as banks will lend against it. As the volume of credit has grown exponentially, banks have lowered their credit standards to the point where most rental value (or its equivalent value to homeowners) is paid out as interest.

New homebuyers are obliged to take on a lifetime of debt to obtain housing as property prices have soared. The irony is that this "democratization" of housing is called the bulwark of the middle class rather than debt peonage. As real estate bubbles burst and leave debts in their place, owners with negative equity (mortgages in excess of plunging market prices) are unable to sell, frozen into their homes, the result is not unlike medieval serfs tied to their land. Today's post-industrial society is coming more and more to look like a regression to debt peonage.

Until recently, buying property was much like buying a bond. In fact, the original meaning of rente (a French word) was an interest-bearing government bond, later extended to include land receiving a regular periodic payment. Land was priced at "so many years purchase" of its rent. A property's worth was calculated by discounting its flow of rental income (or equivalent value, for homeowners) at the going rate of interest: Price = rent/interest. A lower interest rate in the denominator gave a higher multiple. A $10,000 annual income can be capitalized into a $2 million price at 5 percent interest (20 years purchase) or $2.5 million at 4 percent, but only $1 million at a high interest rate of 10 percent (10 years purchase).[1]

---

[1] William Petty, *Treatise of Taxes and Contributions* (London 1662): 26: "Having found the Rent or value of the usus fructus per annum, the question is, how many years purchase ... is the Fee simple naturally worth?" Marx (*History of Economic Theories*, tr. Terence McCarthy [New York: 1952]: 5) notes that Petty deduces the rate of interest from rent "as the general form of surplus value."

What additionally is factored in today is the expected price rise (*i.e.*, Price = (rent + ΔP)/interest). Buyers acquire property on credit, planning to pay off their debt by refinancing their mortgages (or "cashing out") as asset prices are inflated. Hyman Minsky described this phenomenon as culminating in the Ponzi stage of the financial cycle: Debts are carried simply by adding the interest onto the principal, creating a rising upsweep of indebtedness—"the miracle of compound interest."[2]

A Bubble Economy is based on debt leveraging in search of "capital" gains. Inasmuch as real estate is the economy's largest sector and land its largest component, these gains are headed by rising site value. The annual rise in land prices has far outstripped growth in national income since the late 1960s, becoming the driving force in today's financialized mode of "wealth creation."

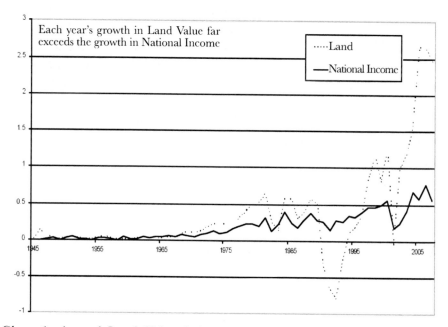

Chart 1: Annual Land-Value Gains Compared to Growth in National Income

Under Alan Greenspan's chairmanship of the Federal Reserve Board (1988–2006), the government sought to enable debtors to carry their obligations by borrowing the interest against the rising market price of their property. Current income plays a declining role as property buyers aim at maximizing "total returns," defined as income plus capital gains—especially

---

[2] Hyman P. Minsky, *The Financial Instability Hypothesis*, Working Paper No. 74, May 1992 (The Jerome Levy Economics Institute of Bard College). Prepared for *Handbook of Radical Political Economy*, ed. Philip Arestis and Malcolm Sawyer (Edward Elgar: Aldershot, 1993).

the latter. The policy to keep the financial bubble expanding is asset-price inflation sufficient to keep increasing real estate prices by enough to enable debtors
to refinance their mortgages and other loans. Applying the maxim that "Rent
is for paying interest," real estate investors are willing to pledge the net rental
income to mortgage bankers in order to get a chance to make a capital gain.
Asset-price gains become the key, not saving out of earnings or direct investment and enterprise. As the Federal Reserve's 2004 *Survey of Consumer Finances*
noted: "Changes in the values of assets such as stock, real estate, and businesses are a key determinant of changes in families' net worth."[3]

This creates a symbiosis between finance, insurance and real estate—the
FIRE sector at the core of the Bubble Economy. Its basic dynamic is a feedback
between bank credit and asset prices. The more credit and the easier the terms
on which it is available—the lower the interest rate, the lower the amortization rate, and the lower the down payment required—the larger the loan can
be made. And as debt leveraging increases, it is easier to go into debt to ride
the wave of asset-price inflation than to earn profits by investing in industry.
Why invest money in an industrial factory or other company that takes years
to organize production and mount a marketing program to develop sales on
which to make a profit that is taxed at 30 percent, when you can buy land and
simply sit back and make capital gains that exceed profit rates and are taxed
at only half as much?

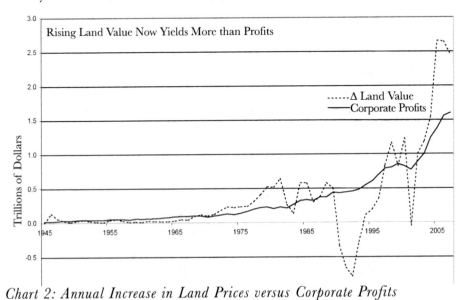

Chart 2: Annual Increase in Land Prices versus Corporate Profits

---

[3] "Recent Changes in U.S. Family Finances: Evidence from the 2001 and 2004 Survey of
Consumer Finances," *Federal Reserve Bulletin*, 2006: A1–A38.

Yet the national income and product accounts (NIPA) do not count capital gains. These occasionally are surveyed by the Internal Revenue Service's Statistics on Income, but the only regular estimate of such gains is the Federal Reserve's flow-of-funds statistic for land prices. The Fed estimates that price for the nation's raw land rose by $2.5 trillion for 2007 (I find $3.5 to $4 trillion to be more realistic, for reasons discussed below). At over 20 percent of U.S. national income, this land-price gain was four times than the amount by which national income grew, and two-thirds more than total U.S. corporate profit (much of which itself derived from mortgage financing and brokerage). So today's "postindustrial" economy turns out to be mainly about real estate. If it is a "service economy," the services in question are mainly those of the FIRE sector.

From Asset-Price Inflation to Debt Deflation

Inflated asset prices have made fortunes for investors, and also for many homeowners who saw the market value of their homes rise by more than they were able to earn in a year. Financial promoters hawked a dream that people could maintain their life styles and get rich by capital gains rather than by what they could earn and save. Families who found that their wages and salaries were not enough to make ends meet were tempted to sustain their living standards by taking out home-equity loans. Banks appeared to have created a postindustrial mode of wealth creation by issuing enough credit to keep bidding up property prices—and to keep the boom going by lending yet more against collateral rising in value. Not to play this game was to be left behind as the affordability of housing rose further and further beyond the means of most families to pay without cutting back their expenditure elsewhere.

The problem with such bubbles is that once underway, asset-price inflation becomes the only way to sustain the debt burden. Debt-financed speculation must accelerate or else end in a wave of bankruptcy. The problem is that carrying charges on this debt divert income away from being spent on consumption and investment. Using debt leverage to bid up property prices loads the economy down with interest and amortization commitments to pay creditors. Prospective buyers must devote more and more of their working life to pay off the debts needed to buy a home, automobile, education or health care. That is the essence of debt deflation.

The policy of lowering property taxes has subsidized speculation, by enabling more income to be paid as interest. The banks gain, capitalizing the proceeds of property tax cuts into yet larger loans. This raises the carrying costs of real estate (and business) financed on credit, while forcing taxes to be levied elsewhere to stabilize public revenue. If public spending is not cut back in response to foregone tax receipts, the shortfall must be made up by borrowing, by taxing non-property income at a higher rate, or by selling off the public domain.

This is not how matters were supposed to work out. The Progressive Era a century ago advocated that taxes should fall mainly on rent and other property returns. The aim was to free economies from rent and interest, so that prices would only reflect necessary costs of production—wages and profits for labor and capital. But governments have pursued the opposite fiscal philosophy since World War I, and especially since 1980. They have lowered property taxes and refrained from imposing a resource-rent tax on minerals, fuels or the broadcasting spectrum. They also have deregulated monopoly prices rather than kept them in line with production costs, and cut capital-gains taxes to just half the rate levied on wages and profits.

On the logic that capital gains built up net worth just as saving did America's original 1913 tax code treated them as regular income. As Treasury Secretary Andrew Mellon explained:

> The fairness of taxing more lightly income from wages, salaries or from investments is beyond question. In the first case, the income is uncertain and limited in duration; sickness or death destroys it and old age diminishes it; in the other, the source of income continues; the income may be disposed of during a man's life and it descends to his heirs.
>
> Surely we can afford to make a distinction between the people whose only capital is their mental and physical energy and the people whose income is derived from investments.[4]

This logic is applicable to today's Bubble Economy. After a real estate bubble bursts, "total returns" no longer drive balance sheets. What Alan Greenspan lauded as "wealth creation" in the form of rising property prices has the opposite effect from tangible capital investment. Instead of lowering production costs, seeking gains from debt leveraging builds interest charges into the cost of living and doing business. This slows economic growth, by diverting income to pay creditors instead of to spend on production and consumption.

The Symbiosis of Finance and Real Estate

Ever since the United States enacted its first modern income tax in 1913 the financial sector has thrown its weight behind real estate and sought to shift the burden off property. This is quite a turnabout from David Ricardo's day, when finance backed repeal of Britain's high agricultural tariffs and land

---

[4] Andrew Mellon, *Taxation: The People's Business* (New York 1924): 63.

rents. At that time it seemed that industry and foreign trade would become the largest market for banks. But as matters have turned out, real estate has achieved this position.

The financialization of real estate is a distinctly 20th-century phenomenon, going hand in hand with the democratization of property ownership. Long after the end of feudalism, landlords remained the wealthiest and most liquid class. But the 19th and 20th centuries saw banks finance the spread of home ownership. In the early decades of the 19th century, residential mortgage lending was left mainly to local savings banks. Many of banks were set up to help immigrants or workingmen save up small change each week, as reflected in the names for some of the largest New York savings banks: Seamans, Emigrant, the Bowery and Dime Savings Banks. But banking since World War I has focused on real estate mortgage lending as property throughout the world has become increasingly democratized, American-style.

By the 1930s, savings and loan associations (S & Ls) were formed to aim at middle-class depositors and homebuyers. After the return to peace after 1945 the construction boom and suburbanization created a thriving mortgage market. Since the 1980s, most savings banks and S & Ls have been converted into commercial banks.

As this has occurred, interest payments have expanded to absorb most of the rental value of commercial properties and owner-occupied housing. And as property became more widely owned and democratized, it was fairly easy for the largest investors—and mortgage bankers—to stir up popular opposition to real estate taxation. But homeowners are not much better off. What formerly was paid to the tax collector is now paid to bankers as interest.

This is the opposite of what the classical economists recommended. Nobody a century ago expected land rent to be paid out as mortgage interest to such a high degree—or that heavily mortgaged real estate would become the backing for the banking system. Banks were supposed to finance industrial capital formation, not create credit merely to bid up prices for land sites supplied by nature, rent-extracting monopoly and property rights and to buy companies already in place.

Debt expansion for such purposes may seem self-justifying as long as asset prices are rising steadily. This price run-up is euphemized as "wealth creation" by focusing on the inflation of financial and property prices, even as disposable personal income and living and working conditions are eroded. The problem is that rising price/rent multiples and price/earnings ratios for debt-financed properties, stocks and bonds oblige wage earners to go deeper into debt, devoting more years of their working life to pay for housing and to buy income-yielding stocks and bonds for their retirement. Homeowners thus do not gain by this higher market "equilibrium" price for housing. Higher prices simply mean more debt overhead.

A simple example should make the problem clear. Suppose Mary Smith owns home free and clear of any debt that had cost her $100,000 to buy. Suppose Jane Doe later buys the same exact home, but the price has risen to $250,000. To buy it, Jane needs to take out a $100,000 mortgage. Who is in a better financial position? On paper, Jane has a $50,000 equity advantage ($150,000, as compared to Mary's $100,000). But she only owns 60 percent of the home's value, and must pay her bank $600 a month — payments that Mary does not have to make.

Prior to the real estate bubble Mary's house has $100,000 equity with low taxes and no interest charges. By the time Jane buys the house, she must go into debt to outbid other potential buyers. The land area hasn't increased (nature is not making any more), and buildings slowly depreciate, but the debt overhead rises, leaving less income available for consumption or saving.

Mortgage credit inflates property prices (for a while), but is such "paper wealth" worth the carrying charge? Families a century ago dreamed of owning their home free and clear. They stayed out of debt to avoid worrying about losing the homestead. But these days the only way for many families to get a home is to borrow enough to pay prices set by buyers willing to pay the entire rental value to the bank for interest on the loan needed to buy it, in the hope of selling out later for a capital gain. In the above example, for instance, matters are aggravated if Jane tries to make ends meet by borrowing against the higher market price of her home. When real estate prices fall back, her debts and their carrying charges will remain in place, threatening to leave her with negative equity. This is the condition into which a quarter of U.S. real estate was estimated to have fallen by autumn 2009.

Investors are tempted to believe they are better off as long as asset prices rise faster than debt, improving their balance sheet. But by absorbing rents, business profits and disposable personal income, the debt overhead entails future clean-up costs. The credit that bid up prices to "create wealth" during the Bubble Economy's run-up leaves "debt pollution" in its wake after asset prices collapse. Living standards, business investment and new construction must be cut back to pay the bill for pumping up asset prices that have receded. Higher real estate and other asset prices provide no more economic benefit than do higher consumer prices. One party's income or gain is another party's expense.

Real estate bubbles are a symptom of debt creation, shaped and sponsored by governments cutting property taxes and thus leaving more revenue to be pledged to bankers as debt service. Modern debt peonage obliges families to take on a lifetime of debt to gain access to housing, an education and health care. The class war takes on a decidedly financial dimension, as Alan Greenspan explained to Congress: Rising mortgage debt has made employees afraid to go on strike or even to complain about working conditions. Employees become more docile in a world where they are only one paycheck or so away from homelessness or, what threatens to become almost the same thing, missing a mortgage payment. This is the point at which they find themselves hooked on debt dependency.

What has been lost along the way is the economy's traditional set of proportions. From 1945 to 2000, for example, the total value of U.S. real estate remained in a fairly stable proportion to national income (about 250 percent). The dot.com bubble of the 1990s inflated stock market prices, but real estate resumed its dominant role as the Federal Reserve flooded financial markets with credit after the market downturn of 2000. Fueled by rising debt ratios, real estate prices soared to the unprecedented levels of 325 percent of national income.

Debt pyramiding was encouraged by looser terms for bank lending—low, zero or even negative down payments, while unprecedented fraud by mortgage brokers and local banks exaggerated the income and hence debt-carrying power of homebuyers, making soaring mortgage loans appear to be affordable. However, adjustable-rate mortgages (ARMs) guaranteed that loans affordable at low "teaser" rates of interest would become unaffordable when their carrying charges re-set at higher rates, forcing homebuyers into the "Ponzi" stage of having to borrow the interest. Defaults that initially were thought to be a known risk turned out to be an inevitability.

The Magnitude of Real Estate Revenue, and Its Increasing Payout as Interest

The National Income and Product Accounts (NIPA) depict the entire economy as if every activity were organized as a business—even owner-occupied housing. The word "rent" appears in only one line (Table 2.1, line 12). It is not a rent that actually is paid, but an imputed "as if" estimate of what homeowners would pay if they rented out their dwellings to themselves. This typically amounts to only 1 or 2 percent of national income.

Commercial and residential property income is reported as "real estate earnings," corporate and non-corporate. Most property investment is organized as partnerships, so most rental revenue accrues to non-corporate real estate. So closely intertwined are the real estate and financial sectors that for many years the NIPA were unable to separate their earnings.

Owners pay some of these earnings in taxes, but pass on most to their bankers. The relevant cash-flow concept is ebitda: earnings before interest, taxes, depreciation and amortization. This can be compiled by adding real estate earnings (non-corporate and corporate, Tables 6.12 and 6.17), interest (Table 6.15) taxes paid at the state and local level (Table 3.3) plus federal taxes, capped by the most remarkable category in which ebitda is buried: depreciation (Tables 6.13 and 6.22 respectively for non-corporate and corporate real estate depreciation).

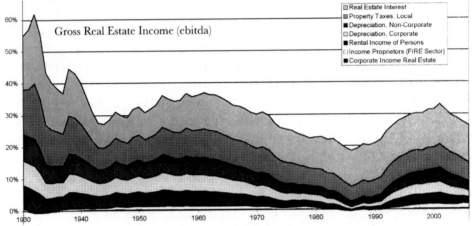

Chart 3: Real estate ebitda as a percentage of national income, 1930–2007

Real estate ebitda (including the rental value of owner-occupied homes) topped 60 percent of national income when the U.S. economy entered the Great Depression in the 1930s. This ratio fell by half by the time World War II ended, to just 28 percent, reflecting the shrinkage in personal income available after defraying other living costs.

Homeowners' "rental equivalent" and commercial cash flow rose from 1945 until 1960 as the postwar economy grew wealthier and more income was available to spend on homes and office space, whose location traditionally has been the major factor defining social status. But for the next twenty years the rest of the economy grew more rapidly than real estate. That sector's cash flow fell back under 25 percent of national income through the mid-1980s — until the watershed 1981 tax subsidy reversed matters. Real estate ebitda accelerated sharply after 1985, recovering to nearly a third of national income by 2000.

As noted above, classical writers expected land prices to rise as population increased and economies grew more prosperous and urbanized. The intention was to tax real estate's rising rental value, but two tax breaks have prevented this from happening. First is the tax deductibility of interest charges, which have absorbed most real estate cash flow since 1945. Nobody anticipated that so much interest would be paid out as to leave scarcely any income to be reported to the tax authorities. A second tax pretense permits landlords to over-depreciate buildings as if they are losing book value even while their market price is rising. The result is that despite the real estate boom, property pays an ever-shrinking share of local and federal taxes.

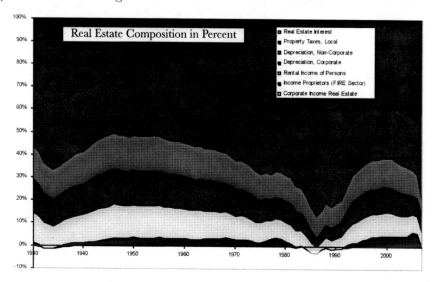

Chart 4: Composition of Real Estate Ebitda, 1930–2007

Shifting State and Local Taxes off Property onto Consumers

The well-known phrase of real estate agents to explain pricing—location, location and location—refers mainly to the proximity of transportation and good schools, which the United States historically has financed by taxing property. Localities could recapture the cost of this infrastructure spending by taxing the market value it adds to real estate sites. Instead, tax favoritism for real estate obliges federal, state and local budgets to look elsewhere for financing—mainly to tax sales and consumer income, and to borrow from the wealthy who have been un-taxed. The result is that property owners enjoy rising prices substantially in excess of what they pay in taxes.

Prior to the 1930s property taxes accounted for about two-thirds of state and local government receipts. But the Great Depression obliged localities to look to sales taxes as property values shrank—and to income taxes in recent decades. Despite the postwar rise in property prices, states and localities have shifted taxes off property owners onto wage earners and consumers almost steadily, so that property taxes now make up only about 20 percent of state and local revenues (Chart 8). This is less than a third of their proportion ninety years ago.

Real estate downturns prompt property owners to campaign for their taxes to be reduced to save them from defaulting on their mortgages. Today's "negative equity" squeeze on mortgage debtors no doubt will increase political pressure for further tax shifts off property, avidly supported by bank lobbyists. The rhetoric is anti-government, but it mainly benefits bankers and large commercial owners.

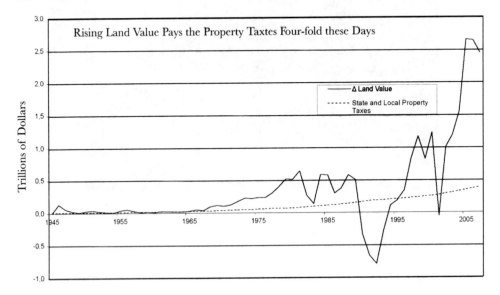

Chart 5: Annual Rise in Land Prices, Compared to Property Taxes

The national tax shift off real estate has been even more regressive than the local tax shift. Finance and real estate have obtained "small print" tax breaks so enormous that only a modest proportion of their gains — which represents most of the economy's wealth — is counted as taxable income. Lobbyists have persuaded lawmakers to define taxable income in ways that leave property owners with no earnings to declare after deducting interest and a basically fictitious bookkeeping charge for depreciation. Landlords are allowed to pretend that their property is losing money as buildings are "used up." This tax ruling promotes a Bubble Economy by making it most economic for investors to put as little of their own money down as possible, using debt to a maximum degree. It also encourages investors to sell their property every few years, after depreciating their buildings so that new buyers can start depreciating them all over again.

This fiscal favoritism for property is a major factor polarizing wealth ownership in the United States. The effect is to wage a war on the middle class, despite the political values and seeming self-interest of most Americans in a more progressive tax system.

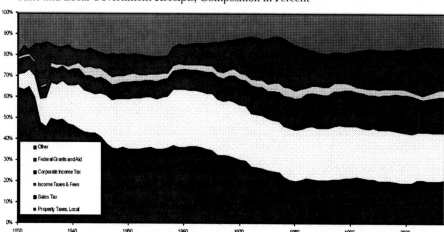

State and Local Government Receipts, Composition in Percent

Chart 6: Property Taxes, as a Percent of Overall State and Local Revenues, 1930–2007.

Over-Depreciation of Buildings

It took until the mid-19th century for economists to recognize depreciation as an element of value. Surprising as it may seem, it was Marx who first established it as a necessary charge in pricing commodities. In his critique of the French Physiocrats, he pointed out that when Francois Quesnay produced his national income account for France, the *Tableau Économique*, in 1759, he overlooked the need to replenish seed, inventory and capital stock.[5] In addition to covering their basic expenses, buying tools and raw materials and paying rent and taxes, cultivators need to set aside seed grain plant the next season's crop. This seed is not available to be sold.

Just as bondholders get paid back their principal as well as interest, investors are permitted to recoup their original capital outlay without it being taxed as income. The recoupment period is spread over the expected lifetime of machinery, patent rights or other assets. Failure to acknowledge the need for

---

[5] The Wall Street analyst Terence McCarthy observed that Marx's analysis of the Economic Theory of Depreciation was so complete that, "if *Capital* has been called the bible of the working class, the *History* [he is referring to *Theories of Surplus Value*] might well be called the bible of the Society of Cost Accountants.... Over the whole society, failure to provide adequate depreciation reserves is, Marx implies, to negate economic progress and to begin consumption of that portion of the value of the product which Marx believes belongs neither to the laborers in industry, nor to their employers, but to the economy itself, as something which must be 'restored' to it if the economic process is to continue." Marx, (New York 1952: xv). This was the first English language translation of Marx's *Theories of Surplus Value*.

this replacement out of sales revenue would give an overly optimistic picture of how well the economy is operating. Not to renew seed and capital investment would result in asset stripping—paying out revenue without maintaining a viable capital stock.

Economists recognize that depreciation results as much from technological obsolescence as from physical wearing out. Technology is continually improving, raising productivity and cutting costs. Rivals' innovation forces factories to modernize or be priced out of the market, sometimes obliging machinery to be sold as scrap metal before it actually wears out. But most depreciation statistically occurs where one might least expect it—in real estate.

This seems strange, because landlords rarely let their buildings wear out. They typically spend 5 to 10 percent of their rental income on maintenance and repairs, and periodically replace their plumbing and heating systems, electric wiring and windows. Buildings constructed prior to World War II— already a few lifetimes in the Internal Revenue Service's depreciation schedule sell at a premium because they tend to occupy prime locations and are better built than their modern counterparts. Contractors have cut construction standards each decade, replacing 4-by-4 beams and copper plumbing with cheaper materials such as 2-by-4s and plastic, and making walls of aluminum siding tacked onto soft insulation.

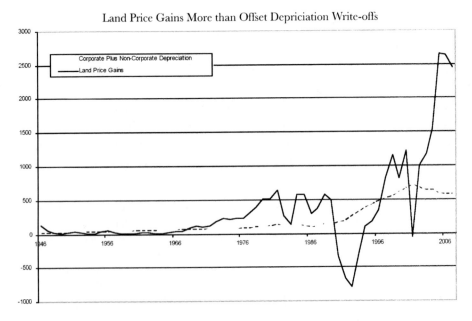

Chart 7: Land-Price Gains Compared to Depreciation Write-offs

The fact that most buildings are kept in good repair has led many countries not to permit landlords to depreciate them. It would be logical for landlords to depreciate their buildings only if they "bled" them by letting them run down. This would violate many commercial leases and is even against the law in many cities for residential buildings. But that has not prevented lobbyists in the United States from turning the depreciation allowance into a stratagem to shelter rental income from taxation. Instead of depreciating in the way that industrial capital does, real estate accrues capital gains as land prices tend to rise far in excess of the rate at which buildings "wear out." Most properties are sold and resold, wish new landlords able to start depreciating buildings anew with each sale—at the higher sales price.

Land is not depreciable. Being supplied by nature, it has no cost of production. It is not used up in the process of yielding a revenue, nor does it become technologically obsolete. Yet most property assessors pro-rate each sales price so that the value of buildings appears to rise proportionally to the overall gain. After buildings have been depreciated once, they can be resold and depreciation write-offs can start all over again, without limit, at so high a rate as to offset a large portion of the new landlord's erstwhile taxable income.

This poses a logical problem: How can buildings gain in assessed valuation if they are supposed to be depreciating? Indeed, how can the economy's most sustained capital gain—that of real estate—reasonably be depicted as operating at a loss for years on end?

The explanation is to be found in the ability of lobbyists to find lawmakers willing to distort the tax code's small print in a way that makes owning real estate much like owning an oil well in the heady days of the oil-depletion allowance. No profit appears in this "Hollywood accounting." From the 1954 tax act through its sequels in 1972, 1979 and the Economic Recovery Tax Act of 1981, the depreciation treatment became increasingly generous to real estate investors. The 1981 tax code assumed a short 15-year lifetime for buildings—and let property owners write off the assessed value of their buildings at twice this rate by using a convoluted "double declining balance" method. Owners could deduct twice the permitted $1/15$ of the purchase price of a building in the first year (that is, 14 percent as a "non-cash" expense), as if it would last just $7\frac{1}{2}$ years. The accounting schedule stretched out the remaining depreciation period by one year in each successive year—to 16 years in year two, 17 years in year three, and so forth. This meant that in the second year the owner could write off twice $1/16$ (or another $12\frac{1}{2}$ percent) on the remaining balance, and recover 55 percent of the building's valuation in just five years.

The 1986 tax reform stretched out the depreciation rate on residential buildings to $27\frac{1}{2}$ years (and nonresidential buildings to $31\frac{1}{2}$ years), but grandfathered in new buildings if they had obtained a certificate of occupancy for rental. The resulting depreciation write-offs for the real estate sector as a whole were large enough to leave no net taxable income to declare during the 1989–92 downturn. This pretense enabled investors to keep on earning rental income free of taxation, as if nothing "really" was being earned. Economic fiction became a fiscal reality, even to the point of being confirmed by seemingly empirical national accounting data.[6]

When one finds a statistical distortion at work, a special interest is almost sure to be involved. Misrepresentation and a false empiricism becomes a highly professionalized part of the economics of deception. The result is junk statistics. Unlike investment in machinery, property tends to rise in price, thanks to the land's rising site value. The deception that buildings are depreciating results in a fictitiously high ratio of ostensible building valuation to land. Precisely because the land site ostensibly cannot be depreciated, the tax privilege of depreciating buildings provides a motive for maximizing their valuation.

Despite the reported net $5.1 billion pretax loss, $5.9 billion after-tax loss and $1.2 billion negative cash flow in 1990, real estate corporations paid $3.9 billion in dividends and were the largest source of interest for banks, maintaining the almost steady rise during the postwar period. Yet the NIPA show it often not to be earning any income and paying almost no income tax.

The effect is to encourage commercial property to change owners every few years, keeping it in perpetual motion to minimize its tax liability. Owners typically sell property when a building has been largely depreciated, and the new landlord can start depreciating it anew. In this way a building that already has been depreciated by its former owner achieves a new life. Like cats, a building seemingly has nine lives and can be written off again and again, turning real estate and its depreciation allowance into the economy's largest tax shelter. This explains why a sector that seems chronically to be losing money enjoys soaring investment and dividend payouts. While real estate investors pretend that their property is losing value as their buildings wear out, the site's locational value rises to more than compensate. Replacement-cost accounting likewise assumes a higher value for buildings, and hence a higher write-off each time a new buyer plays the game.

---

[6] This phenomenon has far-reaching implications for the so-called declining rate of profit. Marx attributed this to the rising organic composition of capital—and hence, an increasing rate of capital consumption (depreciation) relative to profit. However, his point of reference was industrial capital, not real estate. The latter's dominant economic role requires that it be segregated from the industrial economy's statistics. Otherwise, the rate of return on capital investment would be considerably understated.

From 1981 through 1995 real estate investment trusts (REITs) and other corporate real estate the depreciation write-off was so large as to produce fictitious accounting losses for tax purposes, despite their rising cash flow and dividend payouts. By buying real estate, investors acquired so large a tax deduction that they often have been able to use it as a charge against other sources of income.

Most commercial investment is organized as partnerships to obtain the financial benefits of incorporation while taking "book losses" as credits against the personal income of property investors. Like corporate real estate, these partnerships enjoyed freedom from income taxation during the second half of the 1980s, although the explosive take-off in rents rendered more income taxable over the two decades stretching from the mid-1980s through 2005 (Chart 8). Property prices soared as buyers earned income in excess of carrying charges and come out with a capital gain — and a tax write-off to boot.

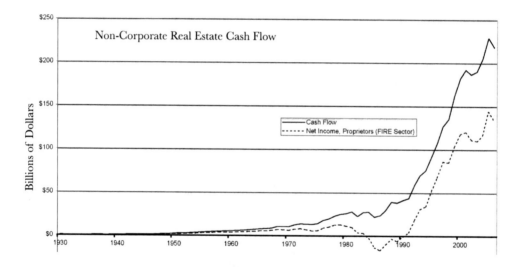

Chart 8: Non-Corporate Real Estate Cash Flow

Homeowners are not able to make this depreciation pretense, only absentee owners. But even without being able to take a depreciation write-off against their wages and salaries, they have ridden the wave of asset-price inflation to build up their net worth. Applauded as ushering in an era of postindustrial prosperity, tax-subsidized debt pyramiding became a new mode of wealth creation — a seemingly permanent capital-gains economy.

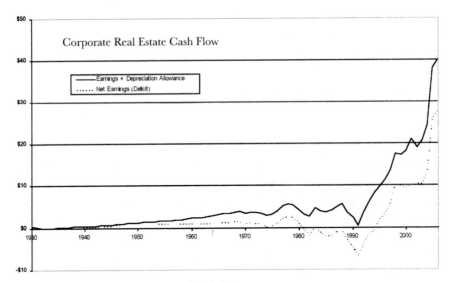

Chart 9: Corporate Real Estate Cash Flow

How the Fed's Appraisal Philosophy Attributes Land Values to Buildings

A ssessors in most U.S. cities estimate land at 40 to 60 percent of real estate value, tending toward the higher ratio. Federal Reserve statistics also show that land represents the largest element of real estate's market price, despite the fact that their methodology substantially undervalues land relative to buildings. Fed statisticians treat land as a residual left over after valuing buildings at their reproduction cost, including capital gains that reflect rising construction costs.

The problem with this land-residual methodology is that it leaves an unrealistically low residual for land—so low that earlier Federal Reserve estimates produced a negative $4 billion number for corporately owned land in 1994. The Fed has since reorganized its categories to moderate this irrationally low calculation, but continues to defend its methodology.[7]

Treating land sites as a residual (after over-estimating the value of buildings at replacement cost) makes land prices appear more volatile than overall real estate. The seeming fallback after 1990 in the land's residual value as a proportion of national income (Chart 13) is largely a statistical illusion as the pace of construction-price inflation increased the Federal Reserve's calculation for the replacement cost of buildings, leaving less residual for land, where the real market value lies. The steep rise in land valuation from 1995 to 2007 reflects the reduction of interest rates engineered by the Federal Reserve flooding the economy with liquidity to promote "wealth creation."

---

[7] The Board of Governors of the Federal Reserve System publishes "Balance Sheets for the US Economy" and has published papers defending the land-residual method. It is criticized in Ronald Banks, ed., *Costing the Earth* (London: Shepheard & Walwyn, 1989).

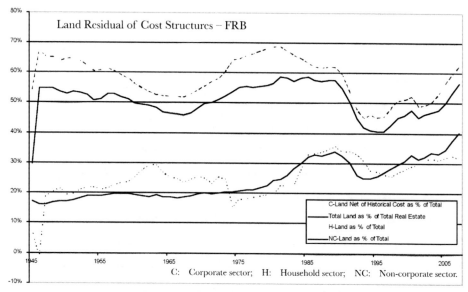

Chart 10: Land Residual Cost of Structures. (Source: FRB, Flow of Funds)

The inflation of land prices has been the driving force in real estate's dominant role in the U.S. economy. The Fed helped inflate real estate prices by lowering interest rates (enabling bankers to capitalize rental income at a higher multiple) and flooding the banking system with enough credit to enable prospective buyers to bid up prices. Fed Chairman Greenspan lauded the "wealth effect" for raising consumption levels on the way up, especially as homeowners took out home equity loans to sustain their living standards, while refraining from regulating lending to keep it honest.

It should be clear from the foregoing analysis that real estate is doing much better than appears at first statistical glance. Buildings are not really deteriorating, thanks to their ongoing repair and maintenance. Although the NIPA depict real estate as operating at a loss, investors actually are getting rich through asset-price inflation creating capital gains.

So this poses an important policy question: Is it socially useful to increase real estate prices by providing tax breaks for running up mortgage debt and for absentee building owners? This might be argued if the reason why property owners are going deeper and deeper into debt is that rising construction costs increase the cost of buildings and other capital improvements. But if higher prices (and hence, larger mortgage loans necessary to buy real estate) simply reflect higher prices for land sites that have no cost of production, then to actively support property prices merely makes new buyers pay more — and specifically, pay more debt service to mortgage bankers. Higher land prices simply increase the cost of providing homes, office buildings and industrial plant. Taxing the land's rising rental value would not reduce its supply (nor would taxing the rising reproduction cost of buildings already in place lead to their removal from the market) but taxing the construction of new buildings would do so.

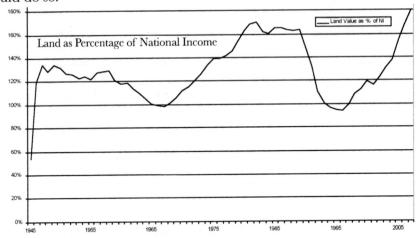

Chart 11: Land-Residual Valuation, as Percentage of National Income

The more real estate growth consists of investing in capital improvements, the more it can be argued that rising property prices elicit more investment in the form of construction activity. But this argument cannot be made if what is being bid up is simply the land's access price. Higher site prices do not induce more land to be supplied, because it is provided freely by nature. The only way to increase site values is to provide more transportation access. It has long been argued that the public sector should recover the cost of this infrastructure by taxing the increase in rental and site values along the route.

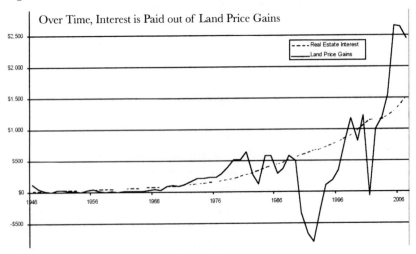

Chart 12: Land-Price Gains Compared to Mortgage Interest.

Tax Favoritism for Capital Gains

When owners sell their real estate, they are supposed to report the recovery of past depreciation write-offs as a capital gain — the sales price minus the depreciated book value. But capital gains are taxed at a much lower rate than "earned" income — if at all! The tax code permits investors to avoid paying a tax at the point of sale if they build up of wealth by reinvesting their sales proceeds to buy new property of equal or greater cost.

The hypocrisy behind this tax logic is revealed by the Federal Reserve's own statistical treatment that estimates building values as rising. Using a construction price index that assigns an annual cost increase to buildings, the Fed subtracts their hypothetical replacement cost from its overall property valuation based on Census Department figures. The residual is assigned to the land. The faster building costs rise, the slower land sites seem to appreciate — sometimes not much at all.

Missing the logic that guides Bubble Economy investors and homeowners, the NIPA do not take account of soaring land prices or other asset-price gains. Like the tax filings on which they are based, these national accounts look much more pessimistic than how investors view matters. They report merely that real estate often goes many years on end without earning an income.

Investors are just as happy to see these gains left out of the public accounts, because there is less pressure to tax them, in contrast to the late 19th century when the classical reformers focused attention on them. The less political pressure is brought to bear to tax or even take note of capital gains, the larger loans borrowers will take on, making mortgage lenders the ultimate beneficiaries of the fiscal giveaway.

Owners argue that they deserve to have their investment "keep up with inflation" — the rising cost of a new building to replace the one they are selling (after having sheltered its income by depreciating it). The Fed's logic serves to justify this claim — and hence, the land-price gains that John Stuart Mill described as a passive, unearned increment that should be taxed away. But if the driving forces behind rising real estate prices are credit, public transport spending and other infrastructure — and the overall level of prosperity — why are landlords allowed to write off their cost as if their investment is being eaten away?

No other part of the economy is inflation-indexed. Wage earners do not receive higher paychecks to reflect inflation. Landlords can avoid paying an income tax on their cash flow while industrial companies and their employees are obliged to save out of the income left after paying taxes. Real estate investors thus are given a tax break based on a concept of economic fairness that they alone are permitted to enjoy in claiming merely to be "breaking even" with inflation as construction costs rise — while at the same time pretending that depreciation is consuming their capital. This helps explain why most people no longer try to save by putting earnings in the bank.

Most families — and businesses — now seek to build up their net worth mainly via capital gains, buying homes and other assets whose price is expected to rise. Subsequent personal saving takes the form of paying down debts taken on to buy property.

	Maximum Capital Gains Tax Rate (%)		Top Marginal Income Tax Rate	
	Individuals	Corporations	Individuals	Corporations
1942–43	25%	25%	88%	40%
1944–45	25	25	94	40
1946–50	25	25	91	38
1951	25	25	87.2	50.8
1952–53	26	26	88	52
1954	26	26	87	52
1955–63	25	25	87	52
1964	25	25	77	50
1965–67	25	25	70	48
1968–69	25	27.5	70	48
1970	29.5	28	70	48
1971	32.5	30	70	48
1972–78 (Oct)	35	30	70	48
Nov. 1978–June '81	28	28	70	46
June 1981–86	20	28	50	46
1987	28	34	38.5	40
1988–89	33	34	33	34
1990–92	28	34	31	34
1993–95	28	35	39.6	35

Source: Joint Committee on Taxation (1995), "Tax Treatment of Capital Gains and Losses," JCS–4–95, February 13, 1995, and Office of the Secretary of the Treasury, Office of Tax Analysis (1985), "Report to Congress on the Capital Gains Tax Reductions of 1978."

Chart 13: Comparison of Capital-Gains Tax Rate with Normal Income-Tax Rates, 1942–1995

Paying out Real Estate Rental Income as Interest

Reflecting real estate's status is the U.S. economy's largest asset, by far the most interest in the is paid on mortgage debt (Charts 14, 15 and 16). Rising property prices oblige new buyers turn over most of its rental cash flow or value to mortgage lenders. As long as the Bubble Economy creates land-price ("capital") gains by enough to cover the interest payments, real estate owners are willing to pay out current income as debt service. But this arrangement cannot last, because adding the interest onto the debt balance year after year entails more and more charges.

As interest rates rose after 1945 to their high of about 15 percent in 1980, the volume of interest payments increased from just 1 percent of national income to 12 percent in the mid-1980s. As mortgage interest rates receded, the ratio of interest payments to national income fell below 8 percent in 2001, but then resumed its upward trend as new debt markets were developed, headed by subprime lending and the derivatives trade. Falling interest rates since 2000 offset the rising debt burden as the Federal Reserve flooded the U.S. economy with credit, but carrying charges now threaten to skyrocket if interest rates rise back to "normal" levels.

> Giving homeowners and property inves-tors a tax subsidy, while maintaining the rule of thumb that mortgage pay-ments should equal 25 percent of personal income, merely replaces the cost of tax pay-ment with an interest payment to bankers.

The composition of interest on the economy-wide level has remained basi-cally stable. By far most interest is paid on mortgage debt, whose growth is subsidized by making interest payments tax deductible. The higher the degree of subsidy, the more debt can be afforded. And conversely, ending tax deductibility would reduce the amount of debt that a homebuyer can afford to take on. This would lower the equilibrium price that could be afforded. What seems at first glance to be an economic benefit to homebuyers—making their interest payments tax deductible—thus turns out to be largely illusory. The subsidy ends up being passed on to the banks.

Giving homeowners and property investors a tax subsidy, while maintaining the rule of thumb that mortgage payments should equal 25 percent or some such ratio of personal income, merely replaces the cost of tax payment with an interest payment to bankers.

Adam Smith suggested as a rule of thumb that interest rates tend to be about half the profit rate. For a commercial or industrial enterprise financed entirely on credit, interest would absorb half the gross profit. But since the 1980s the ratio has risen as debt leveraging has spread throughout the economy. "Share-holder activists" (the euphemism for corporate raiders) are financializing industry along much the same lines as real estate with its high debt/equity leveraging, turning profits and cash flow into interest via buyouts leveraged with high-interest "junk" bonds.

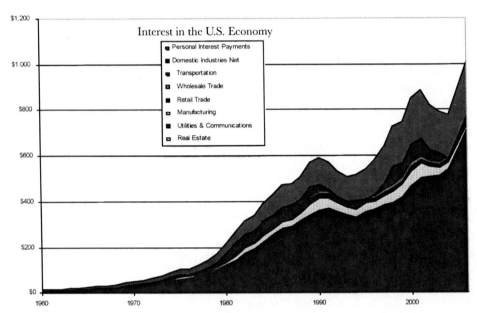

Chart 14: Interest in the U.S. Economy

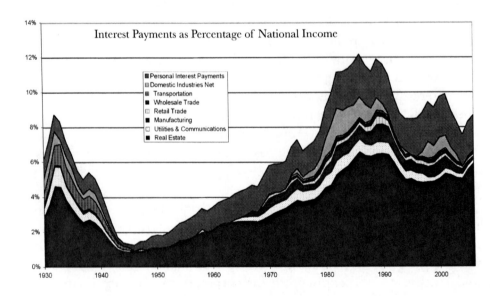

Chart 15: Interest Payments as a Percentage of U.S. National Income

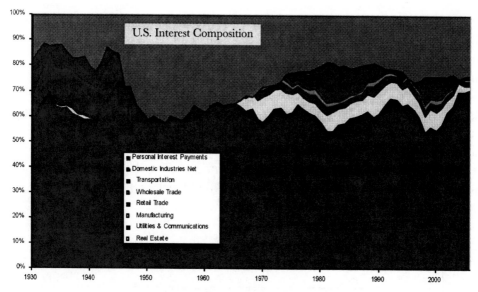

Chart 16: U.S. Interest: Percentage Composition

For commercial investors the choice of whether to buy a rent-yielding property on credit to use one's own money is a business decision shaped by prospects for after-tax returns. Debt financing is not a necessary operating cost but a business choice by investors to buy property with loans instead of using their own money. The government alters the investment equation by making such payments tax-deductible as if they were a necessary cost of doing business. The effect is that interest payments expand to absorb the revenue hitherto paid out as taxes, and the tendency is to absorb whatever is un-taxed. Making interest tax-deductible encourages debt pyramiding. This in turn leads to political pressure for tax cuts when investors suffer the inevitable debt squeeze as the economy shrinks in response to debt deflation.

From Asset-Price Inflation to Debt Peonage

Today, banks and other mortgage holders have become the major parties in U.S. real estate. Overall U.S. homeowners' equity has fallen from 70 to under 50 percent of property values as the United States shifts from an ownership to a debtor economy.

In contrast to industrial capitalism, financialization squeezes out an economic surplus not by employing labor to produce commodities for sale at a markup but by getting labor and industry into debt. It extracts a financial surplus in the form of interest, not profits on production and sales. And finance capitalism uses this surplus to extend yet new interest-bearing loans, not to invest in tangible capital formation. When income is insufficient to pay bondholders, financial managers extract revenue by carving up and selling off assets. Such zero-sum (or even negative-sum) transfer payments do not promote growth but polarize the distribution of wealth in ways that dry up the domestic market for consumer goods and investment goods.

Financialization also acquires wealth from governments by appropriating the public domain or monopoly rights in settlement of debt. In the United States the railroad barons became land barons with a stroke of the privatiza-tion pen—along with the emerging mining and timber oligarchy. By this time real estate, mining and forestry were becoming part of the FIRE sector, dom-inated by finance. In America this meant Wall Street; in England, the City of London.

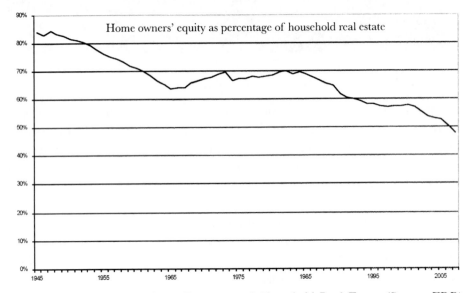

Chart 17: Homeowners' Equity as Percentage of Household Real Estate (Source: FRB)

It often is overlooked that inequality of wealth far exceeds that of income. This is because the wealthiest 10 percent of families prefer to take their returns not as income but in the form of the much less highly taxed capital gains. And while the population's bottom 90 percent hope to catch up by going into debt to buy homes and other property, the insatiable growth in debt needed to keep a real estate and finance bubble expanding imposes financial charges that polarize wealth ownership. These debt charges grow so heavy that debtors are able to pay only by borrowing the interest. They do this increasingly by pledging real estate or other assets whose prices are being inflated by a combination of cen-tral bank policy and Treasury tax concessions. The problem is that in addi-tion to going further into debt, the policy of un-taxing property and financial wealth forces labor and tangible industrial capital to pick up the fiscal slack.

Governments have become the property bubble's ultimate enablers. Ostensibly created simply to give liquidity to mortgages (which traditionally were held by the banks that originated them), the semi-public Federal Home Administration (FHA), Federal National Mortgage Association (FNMA) and Freddie Mac became the largest buyers, packagers and ultimate guarantors of U.S. mortgages, buying them up as fast as banks and mortgage brokers could issue them—some two-thirds of all U.S. home mortgages. These government-sponsored agencies then sold bonds backed by these mortgage holdings to institutional buyers who trusted that the government would stand behind them regardless of how poor the underlying quality of mortgages were. This was analogous to the Federal S & L Insurance Corp. (FSLIC) bailing out risk-taking institutional depositors in S & Ls two decades earlier, in the 1980s. FNMA and Freddie Mac bonds amounted to $5.3 trillion, as much as the entire publicly held U.S. Government debt.

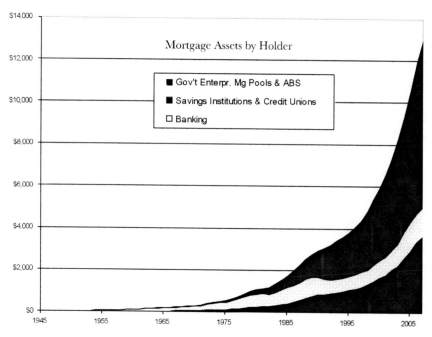

Chart 18: FNMA and Freddie Mac have become the largest Mortgage Holders

Accounting fraud by FNMA managers helped create a false sense of confidence by buyers unfamiliar with how crooked the U.S. financial sector was becoming as deregulation let banks run wild. When the collateral value backing their mortgage-backed securities plunged, the FHA, FNMA and Freddie Mac duly reported losses and called for public bailouts—of themselves and their institutional clients, not for defaulting homeowners. But by

July 2008 it was reported that under "fair value" accounting rules the mortgages failed to cover obligations by over $5 billion, share prices for the two semi-public agencies had fallen by 90 percent from 2007 to 2008. A Wall Street Journal editorial commented that: "The double irony amid the current credit crunch is that our politicians have been promoting Fannie and Freddie as mortgage saviors even as their risk of insolvency has grown. Chuck Schumer, Chris Dodd and many others have encouraged the duo to take on even greater mortgage risk as the housing slump has unfolded. They're the arsonists posing as firemen while putting more dry tinder around the blaze."[8] Rather than letting bad debts go under, Congress set about trying to re-inflate the home mortgage market so as to enable homeowners suffering negative equity to raise the money to pay their debts—debts owed almost entirely to large institutional investors and ultimately to the population's wealthiest 10 percent.

Real Estate in a Debt-Leveraged Economy

The fact that land-price gains have long overshadowed real estate cash flow (ebitda) has made property investors willing to pledge their rental income to bankers as interest. Rather than seeking current income (or for homeowners, rental value) the aim is to ride the wave of asset-price inflation. So the fact that overall real estate net cash flow (ebitda) is about a third of national income, this was by no means the whole story. In terms of total returns—cash flow plus asset-price gains—real estate generated an amount that rose as high as half of reported U.S. national income in 2005. That year's $2.5 trillion in higher land prices amounted to about 20 percent of reported national income, while real estate cash flow (ebitda) added even more ($3 trillion). And this still leaves another trillion dollars or so for the Fed's calculation of capital gains for buildings' "replacement cost" which actually should be treated as site value.

Conclusion: The Larger the Tax Giveaway, the More the Mortgage Debt Grows

Tax favoritism for real estate, corporate raiders and ultimately for their creditors has freed income to be pledged to carry more debt. Mortgage lenders consider that a "virtuous circle" is created when the right to deduct interest paid on debt leveraging "frees" income to be pledged for larger bank loans. But this credit has been used to fuel asset-price inflation, raising the entry price of home ownership and the cost of buying corporate stocks and bonds to yield a retirement income. But it does not increase production and output. Families

---

[8] James Politi and Ben White, "Freddie and Fannie in turmoil," *Financial Times*, July 11, 2008, and "The Price of Fannie Mae," *Wall Street Journal* editorial, July 10, 2008.

get off the rent treadmill only to get onto the debt treadmill. Rental income hitherto paid as taxes is now paid as interest on credit extended to new buyers, while taxes on consumer income and sales also rise.

The idea is that shifting taxes off property and finance promotes a "free market." What it actually does is favor the debt-leveraged buying and selling of real estate, stocks and bonds, distorting markets in ways that de-industrialize the economy.

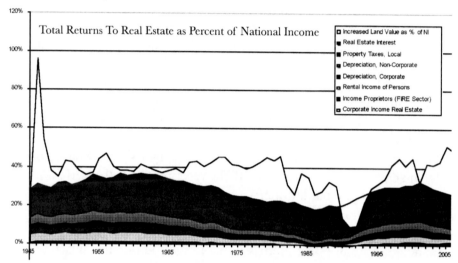

Chart 19: Adding Land-Price Gains to National Income Provides a Measure of Total Return

This is the tragedy of our financial system today. Credit creation, saving and investment are not being mobilized to increase new direct investment or raise living standards, but to bid up prices for real estate and other assets already in place, and for financial securities (stocks and bonds) already issued. The effect is to load down the economy with debt without putting in place the means to pay it off, except by further and even more rapid asset-price inflation—and sale or forfeiture of property from debtors to creditors.

This kind of economic distortion is largely the result of relinquishing planning and the structuring of markets to large banks and other financial institutions. In the name of "free markets" the economics profession has celebrated the shift of planning and tax policy to the financial sector, whose lobbyists have rewritten the tax code and sponsored deregulation of the checks and balances put in place in the Progressive Era a century ago.

At that time it seemed that banking and finance would be industrialized, while landed wealth and monopolies would become more socialized and their "free lunch" (economic rent) fully taxed. Rather than real estate prices rising as we are seeing today, this "free lunch" (what John Stuart Mill called the "unearned increment") would provide the basic source of public finance, including the financing of public infrastructure.

The classical policy of basing tax policy on the land's rising rental value was intended to have two positive effects. First, it would free labor and industry from the tax burden as this was shifted back onto property. Second, paying this rental value to the government would make it unavailable to pledge to mortgage lenders as interest and capitalized into larger bank loans to bid up real estate prices. This would prevent rent-extraction from becoming the objective of new credit, absorbed as interest by the banks.

But the vested interests have fought back. Financial lobbyists have extracted fiscal favors for real estate and pressed for deregulation of monopolies as the major source of interest and collateral for bank loans and bonds. The largest gains of all are made by privatizing enterprises from the public domain, most notably in the post-Soviet kleptocracies but also from debt-strapped Western governments.

This is a travesty of the "free markets" that lobbyists for the banks and the wealthy in general claim to advocate. If the revenue currently used for interest and depreciation were paid property taxes, this would free an equivalent sum from having to be raised in the form of income and sales taxes. This was the classical idea of free markets.

Financial and real estate lobbyists encourage the popular misconception that higher property taxes squeeze homeowners and wage earners. The reality is that taxing the land's rental value would reduce interest charges by an amount equal to the tax. Real estate prices would become more affordable as the interest now paid to banks to support a high debt overhead would go to lowering the income- and sales-tax burden. This would reduce the cost of production and living proportionally, by about 16 percent of national income.

Prices and rents for housing and office space are set by the market place. Interest and taxes are paid out of this rental value. This means that homeowners and renters would pay the same amount as they now do, but the public sector would recapture the expense of building transportation and other basic infrastructure out of the higher rental value this spending creates. The tax system would be based on user fees for property, falling on owners in a way that collects the rising value of their property resulting from the rent of location, enhanced by public transportation and other infrastructure, and from the general level of prosperity, for which landlords are not responsible but merely are the passive beneficiaries under current practice.

In sum, fiscal policy would aim at recapturing the land's site value created by public infrastructure spending, schooling and the general level of prosperity.

The economy's debt pyramid would be much lower as savings take the form of equity investment once again, rather than a minority position in a debt pyramiding operation. Slower growth of debt, housing and office prices, and lower taxes on income and sales would make the economy more competitive internationally.

But as matters stand, a Bubble Economy weakens the national fiscal position as well as burdening industry and the nation's competitive position. International equilibrium can be maintained only if all other economies are financialized in a symmetrical fashion — a proliferation of the debt burden that in fact has become a distinguishing characteristic of today's globalization.

9

Junk-Bonding Industry

Fiction: Banks and stock markets finance capital formation to help companies grow and expand.

Reality: The stock market has become a vehicle for leveraged buyouts and corporate takeovers to load companies down with debt. This diverts profits away from being used for new investment while raising break-even costs, making financialized companies (and economies) less competitive.

The mythology of our time depicts the stock market as financing industry by providing equity capital—buying shares in companies, in contrast to interest-bearing bonds and bank loans. But companies have long been financing most capital investment out of retained earnings. Banks play little role in financing new plant and equipment, research and development. To top matters, the investment bankers who underwrite new stock issues and the hedge funds offering to buy out existing stockholders at a price gain seek to profiteer at the expense of industry more than help it. Underwriters, leading money managers and a new brand of corporate raider euphemized as "activist shareholders" take the lion's share of gains that occur after setting a low Initial Public Offering (IPO) price and then holding on for the jump that normally follows almost immediately. Companies normally receive only part of the market's valuation of their stock after a month, week or even the day of its issue.

The fact that this practice has been going on for over a century and has become worse rather than better shows that it is not an innocent pricing error by investment bankers who are supposed to know a reasonable price for a company. It is systematic deception by Wall Street, the City of London and other finance-capital centers. Governments play along with this exploitative financial fiction for their own reasons—headed by their support for the financial sector rather than industry.

It is hardly an innocent coincidence, for example, that the fraction of corporate value received by new stock issuers in Britain's major public utilities was lowest in Mrs. Thatcher's privatizations of the 1980s. Her Conservative Party advisors underpriced shares of British Telephone—and later those of the railroads and other companies formerly in the public domain—to give the customers of these firms a chance to benefit as capitalists-in-miniature, making quick first-day or first-week gains. But they lost out as prices were jacked up and service standards declined. Privatized bus companies sold off their centrally located terminals for their real estate value and cut back money-losing service. For the railroads, ticket prices soared, more trains crashed and passengers were jammed as London's real estate bubble of the 1980s and '90s forced people to live far away from their jobs in order to afford housing, which absorbed a rising share of their paychecks.

The policy was characterized as "Sorry you've lost your job. We hope you made enough money cashing out on your home or in the stock market to make up for it." The idea was for the victims of this process—the bottom 99%—to make enough one-time gains from carving up and inflating the economy to mute their opposition to the widening polarization between creditors and debtors, that is, between the financialized sector and the rest of the economy.

The stock market became an arena in the new financial warfare as it was turned into a vehicle for takeovers, mergers and acquisitions based on replacing equity with debt leveraging. Federal Reserve statistics show that more U.S. stocks have been retired since 1980 than issued. Despite the flurry of Initial Public Offerings (IPOs) during the high-tech dot.com bubble, the net flow of funds has been out of the stock market, not into it. The stocks that have been retired have been replaced with debt—"junk bonds," other bonds, mortgages and bank loans.

Credit to corporations is created to buy assets already in place or to ship goods and services already sold and waiting for payment, not to invest in new plant and equipment or employ labor to produce more. Meanwhile, corporate raiders and management buyout teams now purchase entire companies on credit. The post-1980 mushrooming of such credit was catalyzed by high-interest "junk" bonds, but as the Federal Reserve flooded the economy with credit, banks were able to ease loan standards and lower interest rates each year. Takeover credit became much more accessible. Raiders were able to obtain increasingly low-cost financing to buy out companies with returns on equity of 9 percent or more. The wealth of the population's richest 1% soared so rapidly as progressive taxes were slashed.

The logical culmination of this process is for the entire economy to be bought out by financial managers, or at least come under their control. The problem for society is that the aims of financiers are quite different from those that textbooks describe as being the aims of industrial entrepreneurs: namely, to invest in factories, plant and equipment and hire labor to apply new technology to produce more output at lower cost, creating the promised economy of abundance. Taking over companies with borrowed credit seeking to make quick gains on

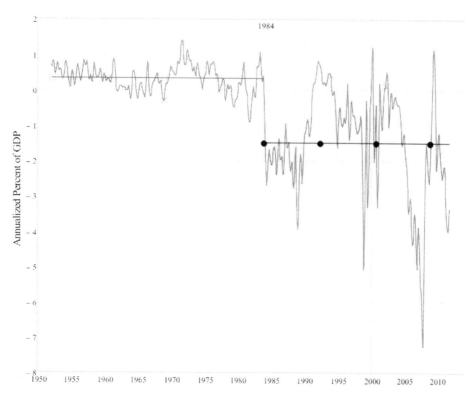

Fig. 1: Federal Reserve flow of funds: Net stock-market disinvestment, 1980–2010.

their stock prices—or to take the companies private, break them up, seize their pension funds, cut services, work labor more intensively or outsource employment and downsize, and then to re-float the "streamlined" carcass— has become so pervasive that well-run companies fear being targeted. Their defense is to take "poison pills" by borrowing to buy up their own stock, making it more costly to raiders—while leaving themselves with less debt leeway for prospective raiders to capitalize into takeover loans. The idea is to use up their debt servicing capacity in advance, indebting themselves so heavily that no raider could hope to saddle them with enough more debt to pay for a takeover.

For most companies these days, buybacks create capital gains for stock-holders—gains that are taxed at a much lower rate than dividend payouts. They also increase the value of the stock options that corporate managers give themselves—options whose value often exceeds their salary. But these debt-leveraged buyouts, buybacks and stock manipulation leave less revenue to invest in expanding business. So financial "gain-seeking becomes decoupled from tangible capital formation as managers spend earnings to push up the price of their stock by buybacks rather than by investing to generate more earnings.

Corporate Takeovers Replace Equity with Debt

Fiction: Bank loans and bond issues finance productive capital investment, creating profits that borrowers use to pay off their loans.

Reality: Banks extend most credit against property already in place. Most corporate bond issues since the 1980s have been to finance takeovers. This inflates asset prices, but does not finance tangible capital formation. Interest must be paid out of income streams already in place — or by cutting back capital spending and squeezing more out of employees or their pension funds.

The underlying fiction is that debt leveraging can "create wealth." What makes the indebting of industry so ironic is that it is being done via the stock market, which was founded to provide equity capital as an alternative to debt. This original role has now been reversed.

At first glance one might imagine that the 1992–2001 stock market boom might have led companies to take advantage of rising price/earnings ratios and replace bonds with stock. But the tax code favors debt financing rather than equity. Corporate dividends are paid out of after-tax profit, while interest is a pre-tax charge. At the 50 percent corporate income-tax rates still typical in the 1980s, companies could pay out twice as much in pretax interest as they could pay in after-tax dividends. The asymmetrical tax treatment has been a major incentive in turning the stock market into a vehicle for buying companies by loading them down with debt — at the tax collector's expense.

The pretense for making interest on bank loans and bonds tax-deductible is that it is considered to be a necessary cost of doing business. But takeovers are not part of the production and consumption economy. This market distortion prompts investors to shift away from equity financing to debt financing. As interest rates were receding from the 20 percent rate they reached in 1980, pension funds and other institutional investors sought higher rates of return — by lending to corporate raiders seeking to take over companies. Drexel Burnham took the lead in popularizing high-interest bonds. They were called "junk" because they increased the debt/equity ratio of companies far beyond traditional banking norms. So even as the stock market boomed with takeover offers, companies did not use this to reduce their debt overhead. Debt ratios soared.

Companies became more financially fragile. Stock dividends can be cut back when earnings decline, but interest must be paid regardless of how much the company earns. If a company cannot pay, it is declared insolvent and turned over to its creditors, wiping out stockholders. This became the fate of many companies skating on the increasingly thin financial ice — becoming more fragile because of tax favoritism for debt financing.

The reasons for this favoritism toward creditors is not technological, and did not spur capital investment. Banks, pension funds and other institutional investors lend to raiders and corporate empire-builders simply to buy up stock. The strategy of "financial engineering" is to make capital gains by downsizing and breaking up companies, or to bid up their stock prices rather than investing in more capital or hiring more employees.

Stock buybacks dispose of the surplus cash that acts like a red flag attracting raiders. Companies that operate in the old-fashioned way of building up capital investment and cash reserves find that their liquid assets and un-mortgaged property attract predators. So the spread of corporate debt becomes contagious, because it obliges companies to defend themselves by depleting their working capital and going so deeply into debt that few assets or earnings remain to be pledged to creditors.

The Adverse Effect of Debt-Financed Raids on Long-Term Corporate Investment

Fiction: Debt leveraging increases returns on equity as funds can be borrowed at a lower interest rate than companies expect to earn, enabling companies to pay off their debts.

Reality: Issuing high-interest "junk" bonds to buy out stockholders and "take companies private" raises the proportion of cash flow absorbed by interest, leaving less for new direct investment. So capital formation and employment slow, reducing economic growth.

The problem is that this kind of defense emulates the very policies that raiders threaten. Supporting a stock's price by buying it up or paying out more in dividends often involves dismantling a company's long-term investment plans and running up enormous debts. The company may make ends meet by cutting costs and employment drastically. This is what CBS did in 1987 when the "white knight" Larry Tisch fired employees and sold off $2.65 billion of CBS subsidiaries.

Tisch emerged from the new generation of corporate raiders who refined the practice of issuing bonds to buy out stockholders and their companies. In the spirit of the real estate principle that "rent is for paying interest," they organized takeover funds, arranged bank loans and issued bonds similar to mortgages. These were not productive debts to finance new capital investment. Rather than generating more profits, these new loans simply replaced equity.

Their interest charges had to be paid out of existing earnings—and by stripping assets.

All this was applauded by politicians on the right and left alike. In the spring of 1985, Senator Jesse Helms and other rightwing politicians backed Ted Turner's attempt to take over CBS. Their main objective was to change the station's liberal programming. Turner had founded the innovative Cable News Network (CNN), but lacked the resources to take over CBS. The only way he could do so was to offer $5 billion in high-interest bonds—the equivalent of $150 a share at a time when CBS stock was selling at a fraction of this price.

Wall Street was unimpressed. It thought he could deliver more right wing programming but not the dollars he promised. His basic business approach already had caused his Atlanta Braves baseball team to flop. Baseball players take years of professional training to reach the major leagues. Farm systems are run at a loss to provide this preparation, much like corporate R&D. Seeking to avoid such costly investment, Turner cut back on scouting ("research") and minor league development, and simply hired free-agent players from other teams. This meant selecting players past their prime and often injury-prone. The result was a money-losing last-place team. In 1990 he finally appointed a general manager who turned the team's fortunes around by developing one of baseball's best scouting and minor league systems. But this was after his CBS experience.

One of CBS's major stockholders was Larry Tisch, holding 5 percent of CBS stock. Soon after being elected to its board of directors, he announced his intention to save the company. Riding in like the proverbial white knight, he mobilized his family's holdings in Loews to buy 24.9 percent of its stock by September. This kept CBS in ostensibly friendly hands inasmuch as Tisch already was a board member.

Having made his money by diversifying his Loews theater chain into hotels and insurance, He was known for cutting payrolls and other costs. The first thing he did at CBS was to reduce its staff and begin negotiating to sell off assets, starting with its magazines for $650 million, and CBS Records to Sony for $2 billion. There were rumors that he might even sell the company's New York "Black Rock" headquarters and lease it back, raising cash but increasing the annual (tax deductible) rental outlay.

By the end of 1987 these policies had doubled Tisch's original $951 million investment in CBS. The company's total worth rose to about $7 billion, and it was in a cash-rich position—a bonanza for its stockholders, the largest of whom was Tisch himself. But in the process of "saving" CBS he just what its officers and employees had feared Turner would do: sell off its properties and lay off workers. The white knight became almost indistinguishable from the raider.

Stock Buybacks to Increase Share Prices

Increasingly, corporate buybacks reflect management's desire to raise the stock price as an aim in itself, not merely to deter takeovers. In addition to serving the interests of shareholders in the short run, buybacks enable managers to exercise their stock options at a higher price. The drawback is that they divert revenue away from being invested to expand the company's long-term business.

During the 1990s, IBM routinely spent $10 billion of its earnings each year to buy its own stock. The company also borrowed. In effect, it was borrowing to bid up its stock price, not to expand research and development. In 1980, for instance, it contracted out its software technology for personal computers to Microsoft, and subsequently let other producers develop leadership positions for chips and associated hardware. Other companies did the same thing. By 2005 even staid General Electric announced in that it would sell its Swiss Reinsurance Company for $6.8 billion and use the proceeds to buy its own stock and raise its dividend payout.[1]

In 2004 the S&P 500 companies spent $197 billion on buying their own shares to support their price. The pace accelerated to over $100 billion a quarter by March, 2006, by which time these buybacks were running at a rate large enough to "cover this year's Medicare budget." Standard and Poor calculated that

> 268 of the companies in the S&P 500 bought back shares in the first quarter, with nearly 110 of them cutting their diluted shares outstanding by at least 4% from a year earlier. ... Exxon Mobil Corp., Microsoft Corp. and Time Warner Inc. were the biggest buyers of their own shares during the first quarter, spending $14.37 billion combined, according to S&P.

As the *Wall Street Journal* report concluded:

> A company that aggressively buys its own shares on the market can give investors a skewed picture of its earnings growth. When a company reduces its shares outstanding, it will report higher earnings per share,

---

[1] "Cash-Rich Firms Urged to Spend," Wall Street Journal, November 21, 2005. The article quotes hedge-fund manager Jeff Matthews as noting that "investors' demands for stock buybacks and the like are prompting some companies to do the wrong thing. . . . hedge-fund managers like himself are paid based on their portfolios' annual performance. So they tend to be short-sighted when they see a company with lots of cash and a languishing share price. 'I don't think it has as much to do with what's in the long-term interest of the company as in the long-term interest of the hedge funds,' he says."

even if its total earnings don't grow by a penny, simply because those profits are spread across fewer shares. Exxon Mobil's net income rose 6.9% in the first quarter, but that turned into a 12.3% earnings-per-share increase after share buybacks, according to S&P.[2]

Paying Greenmail to Deter Financial Raids

Raiders may negotiate "greenmail" payments to end their takeover threat. The target company agrees to buy the raider's stock at a price that gives him a nice profit on top what became a customary 0.375 percent ($^3/_8$ of a percent) commitment fee to the go-go investors who backed the greenmailer, the banking house that committed itself to underwrite the takeover, and the legal costs incurred in the cross-suits between the prospective raider's company and its target.

The attempted takeover of Phillips Petroleum by T. Boone Pickens and Carl Icahn illustrates the standard ploy. Icahn produced a financial plan to sell off $3.7 billion of Phillips' assets to pay for the takeover, leaving Phillips with about $11 billion in debt compared to only $800 million in common stock. This would have produced nearly a 14:1 debt/equity ratio, compared to the average 1:1 ratio for the oil industry as a whole. Debt-servicing charges would have added to Phillips' production costs, making it less competitive within the oil industry—and too cash-poor to sustain the exploration and development needed for long-term growth.

This is why Phillips and other companies fought hard against such raids. They did not want to dismantle their production and investment position simply to let bondholders strip their assets and income stream. So Phillips negotiated a settlement that left it independent, while Pickens made $90 million and Icahn over $50 million on the increased value of their stockholdings. Drexel Burnham Lambert got $1 million for letting Icahn use its name.

Biographies have been written about leading raiders such as Carl Icahn, T. Boone Pickens, Carl Lindner, Michael Milken and Ivan Boesky, Henry Kravis and their colleagues, along with stories about their takeover targets: Nabisco's $22 billion leveraged buyout, Beatrice Foods, Revlon, Goodrich,

---

[2] "Big Companies Put Record Sums Into Buybacks. Repurchases Aim to Bolster Shares but They Also Signal Hesitancy to Invest in Growth," The Wall Street Journal, June 12, 2006. Cisco Systems "approved the repurchase of an additional $5 billion of its own stock, on top of a $35 billion repurchase plan it announced five years ago. The week before, Tribune Co. announced a $2 billion buyback, to be financed by debt, in a decision that sparked controversy on the company's board, with representatives of the Chandler family, one of the company's biggest shareholders, objecting to the massive outlay."

Wierton Steel and the various airline buyouts and bankruptcies.[3] Books could just as well have been written about companies that resisted takeovers by taking "poison pills" whose effects were nearly as bad as what the raiders would have done.

But personal and even corporate biographies run the risk of missing the forest for the trees. The junk-bond phenomenon is more than just an adventure story about some Wall Street raiders leveraging debt on a vaster scale than their real-estate counterparts. At stake is the fate of Americans who do not get rich from this financialization of industry. For instance, when the Leucadia takeover group bought out the National Intergroup conglomerate, no purchaser could be found for its Weirton Steel division. As a last resort Leucadia sold the plant to its employees. Rather than see it closed down, they cut their own wages and promised to pay for the steel plant with high-interest bonds. This turned the labor force into something akin to indentured servants working off the debts with which Leucadia saddled the plant.

This kind of debt-financed raiding increased the cost for Weirton to produce each ton of steel, and for Phillips to produce each barrel of oil. The additional unit cost may be computed by dividing debt service by physical output before and after the takeover attempt. On an economy-wide level, higher interest charges have become a major factor pricing U.S. goods out of world markets. So claims that leveraged buyouts and other debt pyramiding is part of the "free market" economy on its way to a Darwinian survival of the fittest refers only to asset markets and balance-sheet wealth (and indeed, wealth at the top of the economic pyramid, achieved by indebting the bottom 99%), not to "markets" leading to more competitive pricing.

Stock Market Strategies to Obtain Capital Gains Rather than Profits and Dividend Yields

Fiction: Stocks are worth more because earnings are growing.

Reality: Stock prices reflect the flow of funds steered into (or out of) the market by tax laws, pension and retirement funding, and Federal Reserve credit bubbling to lower interest rates and hence raise the "capitalization rate" of a given after-tax revenue stream.

Financial bubbles inflate stock market prices for reasons that have little to do with "real" wealth creation. By pushing down interest rates after 1981, for

---

[3] For the $22 billion Nabisco takeover as the high point of excess from the 1980s see Bryan Burrough and John Hellyar, Barbarians at the Gate (1990). Drexel-Burnham's escapades and the prosecution that bankrupted Drexel and sent Michael Milken and Ivan Boesky to jail insider dealing are highlighted in Connie Bruck's The Predator's Ball (1988).

example, the Federal Reserve increased the "capitalization rate" of existing income streams. Borrowing terms became easier. But while debt-leveraged capital gains the market price of companies (and real estate) raised balance sheet net worth, this is done at the expense of earnings. Higher interest charges were built into a company's break-even costs. So what rose was not net income or tangible wealth, but the ratio of stock prices to earnings—and of course, the value of stock options given to upper management.

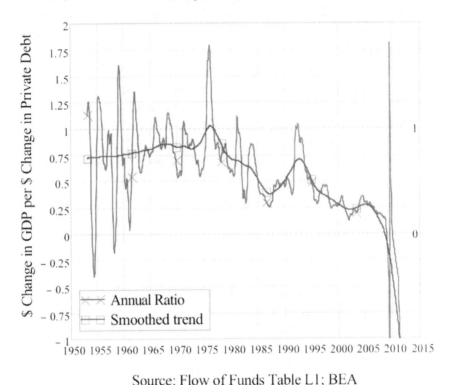

Source: Flow of Funds Table L1; BEA

Fig. 2: Falling rate of GDP growth per increase in debt

Until the 1980s, making capital gains on stocks tended not to involve actually taking over a company. Brokerage houses and investors looked for companies with undervalued assets, especially real estate bought long ago when prices were lower. Many auto supply stores, dairy distribution companies and other small companies had storage operations or retail outlets in neighborhoods where property prices were soaring. These companies also tended to have stable but not rapidly growing sales, which the stock market capitalized at low price/earnings ratios. Outside buyers could take over such companies, close them down and turn a $10 million sales-distribution business into a $20 million real estate deal by selling the property to developers. Or, a brokerage firm could buy the stock, provide its analysis to clients and watch them bid up the price—and then sell its holdings to make a trading profit.

Rising share prices in the stock market do not provide much benefit for the companies that initially issued them, unless firms issue new equity as well. By the 1960s the most noteworthy stock-market action consisted of corporate mergers. Aggressive conglomerates would offer to buy companies at a price higher than their stock was trading for. A 25 percent premium usually was sufficient inducement for shareholders to accept the offer. So if a company's stock was trading at $20 a share, an ambitious buyer might offer $25 a share. Brokerage firms and their clients pored over balance sheets looking for prospective takeover targets.

Growth companies with high price/earnings ratios sought to merge with slower growing firms by exchanging their high-priced stock for the relatively low-priced stock of these firms. This is what AOL did when it merged with Time Warner. Although Ted Turner's company had much larger assets and earnings, the stock market valued these at a lower price/earnings ratio, enabling AOL to swallow it much like a crocodile biting off a prey much larger than itself. The hope was that the newly merged company's stock price would enjoy a high price/earnings ratio. But the plan backfired as the bloom evaporated from AOL. The stock plunged to near the old Time Warner price/earnings ratio, making it one of the worst merger deals in history.

Apart from undervalued real estate, dominant market positions and intellectual property rights, the main bait for mergers was cash on hand—bank accounts, well funded pension plans, and low debt ratios. A new breed of financial manager accumulated cash simply by paying bills more slowly, and cutting costs by squeezing out more work—holding output steady in the face of attrition for the work force, and outsourcing employment to non-union labor. All this was considered to be the essence of sophisticated management practice.

Unprecedented amounts of credit became available to finance corporate buyouts. Instead of merely doubling one's money by buying a company for $10 million in one's own cash and selling it for $20 million, a ten-fold return—1,000 percent—could be made by borrowing $9 million of the purchase price, turning a debt-leveraged $1 million equity investment into a $10 million capital gain. The ideal was not to put in any of one's own money at all, but to finance the takeover entirely on credit. The return on this zero equity (that is, 100 percent debt pyramiding) was mathematically infinite. Going into debt became the way to get a free lunch. But it was not free for the companies being taken over, or for their employees or for the economy at large.

A new class of corporate raiders emerged in the 1980s. Their idea was to buy a company and cut costs—but not by raising productivity through capital investment and new technology. It was more like new landlords bleeding a hitherto well-maintained building and cutting the staff (or shifting to non-unionized labor), while increasing earnings by raising prices (much like raising rents). Corporate raiders looked for bankers to put up the money, just as real estate developers had long done. The bankers for their part saw these ambitious individuals as providing a major new growth market for loans. What made this harmony of interests work was the free ride that the government provided by letting corporations deduct interest payments from their reported income. The tax subsidy promoted the practice of loading industry down with debt, with the consequence that firms pay about twice as much of their income as interest as they could pay in after-tax dividends.

What made "junk" bonds—and mergers and acquisition in general—risky for the economy at large was that their proceeds were not used to increase productivity or overall earning power. The funding simply was used to bid up stock prices. At best, the strategy was to buy a company, "streamline" its management, run it more "efficiently" in the short run to squeeze out more earnings. Raiders might take a company private—that is, off the stock market—and turn it into a privately owned company, streamlining it and often selling off the parts at a capital gain. The aim was to cash out by selling the company back on the stock market.

At first, target companies tried to protect themselves by bringing RICO claims against raiders—a law initially designed to prosecute the Mafia. But the higher courts ruled that what raiders and their junk-bond backers were doing was legal. The trials of Michael Milken and his client Ivan Boesky did not focus on corporate raiding and indebting as such, but on the insider dealing that was the key to the takeover deals negotiated by Drexel Burnham Lambert. Before making a takeover announcement, the perpetrators would buy stock options for the companies they targeted. Options could be bought at a low price, and on credit. Suppose a raider planned to offer $30 a share for a company whose stock was selling at only $20. For perhaps only $1 he could buy an option to buy the shares at $20—and then watch his offer drive them up toward $30.

The legal problem was that under Franklin Roosevelt's New Deal reforms that followed the stock market crash of 1929, prospective buyers are legally required to give markets "full knowledge." This transparency principle is the premise on which free-market economics is supposed to work. Milken's "Drexel gang" violated it.

The Economy-Wide Effect of Financializing Industry

S ome prominent financial leaders arrayed themselves against raiders loading industry down with junk bonds and depleting capital reserves via stock buybacks. Henry Kaufman resigned from the Salomon Brothers board of directors (and later from the firm itself) to protest its underwriting of debt-for-equity swaps. Felix Rohatyn of Lazard Frères also warned of the risk of burdening balance sheets with high interest obligations. The corporate lawyer Martin Lipton wrote a public letter to Senator Proxmire defending companies against raiders:

> These takeovers move assets into hands that profit by cutting off ... research and development and capital improvements and instead divert those revenues to paying the debt incurred to acquire the assets. One can analogize the situation to a farmer who does not rotate his crops, does not periodically let his land lie fallow, does not fertilize his land and does not protect his land by planting cover and creating wind breaks. In the early years he will maximize his return from the land. It is a very profitable short-term use. But inevitably it leads to a dust bowl and economic disaster. ... Day after day the takeover entrepreneurs are maximizing their returns at the expense of future generations that will not benefit from the research and development and capital investments that takeover entrepreneurs are forcing businesses to forego.[4]

Takeovers raid the social functions of capital, not just the company (whose shareholders may make a nice capital gain by selling their stock to raiders). These social costs do not show up on corporate balance sheets. Economists call them "external diseconomies"—consequences borne by society at large, as when debt-financed speculation leaves companies too cash-strapped to undertake new productivity-raising investment. Projects with long lead times are the first to be cut back, because they making companies ripe for takeover by a raider coming in to increase short-term earnings by reducing R & D and bleeding the company much in the way that landlords improve their cash flow by failing to keep up their rental properties.

   Communities suffer when jobs are lost as raiders improve short-term earnings by cutting back on employment. Workers who formerly paid taxes now collect unemployment insurance. Meanwhile, the shift to pay interest rather than paying out earnings as dividends aggravates the federal budget deficit, creating pressure to increase taxes on the economy's non-financial sectors. The past thirty years' experience with junk bonds and corporate raiding, seeking the

---

[4] *American Lawyer*, May 1986.

best short-term management to raise stock prices — on credit — has burdened industry and the economy at large with financial overhead charges. Yet the economics profession followed bank lobbyists in advising that economies perform best over the long run by living in the short run, moving from one short-term spurt to the next. "Liquidity" Is the preferred euphemism for interest-bearing credit.

Typical of the applause for debt leveraging was President Ronald Reagan's 1985 *Economic Report of the President*. Noting that "contests for corporate control are part of a larger merger and acquisition process that plays an important role in the economy's adjustment to changing market circumstances," it endorsed debt-financed buyouts on the ground that whatever generates the highest return is the most efficient use of resources, concluding that "there is no economic basis for regulations that would further restrict the … process."

This ideology of financial deregulation has promoted the junk bonding of industry, and ultimately a crash as the economy has been de-industrialized. Living in the short run, financial operators jumping from one company to another, loading each one down with debt in order to increase returns on equity. And this has been applauded. By 2006 the *Financial Times* wrote that: "With pressure on institutional investors to deliver short-term gains, corporate hell-raisers — once vilified as 'vultures' and 'speculators' — have become champions of better governance."[5]

"Creating wealth" by debt pyramiding is encouraged by the tax system's failure to distinguish between productive investment and speculation. Capital gains obtained by raiding a company or manipulating its stock are taxed at only half the rate as income earned by building a factory to increase output and jobs. And adding insult to injury, debt leveraging is subsidized by making interest payments tax deductible — aggravating the fiscal squeeze.

Nothing about this debt subsidy is a natural or inherent in markets. As Keynes pointed out in the 1930s, capital markets function best when governments adjust the rules to serve longer-term growth objectives. An obvious first step toward improving industry would be a tax structure that favors equity capital rather than debt, and holding stocks on a longer-term basis.

The Inevitability of Debt Default

Already before the bankruptcy of high-risk S&Ls in the 1980s, observers warned about the bankruptcy danger for companies whose earnings could not cover their high interest charges, and those that had indebted

---

[5] "Raiders rolling back the years," *Financial Times*, August 16, 2006.

themselves with poison pills to defend against financial takeovers. Securities and Exchange Commission Chairman John Shad warned that "even a mild recession" might force some companies into default on their junk bonds. "The more leveraged takeovers and buyouts today," he concluded, "the more bankruptcies tomorrow,"[6] leaving lawyers and accountants to carve up the hapless target companies to pay their creditors.

But the SEC has little authority to overrule the issue of junk bonds. It was not designed to protect the economy by setting rules for financing or taxing to promote long-term investment and financial viability. Its role is only to protect stockholders by pressing for full financial disclosure and other technical market functions such as limiting insider dealing and collecting accurate statistics for stock and bond investors.

Deposit insurance agencies — the FDIC and the Federal Savings and Loan Insurance Corp. (FSLIC) — likewise were unable to block junk-bond investments by banks and S&Ls. Defaults soon led to insolvency for savings institutions that held such bonds. Columbia S&L in Beverly Hills had nearly half (some $2 billion) of its depositors' funds in junk bonds. Its insolvency helped empty out FSLIC, which had permitted S&Ls to deviate far from their original purpose of financing homebuilding. The low price of Columbia's stock already by 1986 reflected the view of most investors that the S&L had jeopardized its long-term solvency by seeking high yields. Financial deregulation let these institutions invest in junk bonds for no better reason than to pay depositors a few percentage points more for a temporary period of time — at the cost of ending up losing their principal. The process occurred quite rapidly.

The financial problem is symbiotic with today's fiscal policy of taxing business earnings higher than capital gains on stock and bond speculation. This pro-financial tax philosophy is the diametric opposite of what classical economists advocated. It steers savings and new credit creation into loans, building up debt. By encouraging debt-leveraged buyouts, the tax-deductibility of interest has turned securities markets into vehicles for pension funds and other institutional traders to find the quickest returns by acting as short-term speculators rather than long-term investors.

Diverting Stock-Market Gains from Companies to Investment Bankers

Silicon Valley's dot.com and Internet leaders became multi-millionaires and sometimes even billionaires when their companies were floated on the stock market in the 1990s. They have become poster boys for the claim that

---

[6] Wall Street Journal, December 12, 1987.

Wall Street rewards innovation. Yet they received only a portion of the money raised by the Initial Public Offerings (IPOs) of stocks in their companies on the day they went public and over the next few trading days. Their venture capitalists took the lion's share as sleeping partners, along with the investment bankers who marketed these stocks.

First-day price jumps of 100 to 400 percent were normal for IPOs in the information sector, sometimes more than seven-fold. The higher the jump, the more successful the flotation was deemed to be — successful in attracting investment bank clients to the next underwriting. The earliest buyers got the quickest and largest gains. The companies got only the initial offering price — less underwriting commissions typically 7 percent — higher than the 6 percent commission charged by real estate brokers. In addition to this rake-off, the bankers who underwrote these offerings got much of the price run-up for their own trading account.

These gains made the interest of Wall Street inherently opposed to that of companies going public, which received far less than their stock proved to be worth after only a few hours of trading. Many small buyers who jumped onto the bandwagon lost their shirts after the bubble burst in 2001. The process is best described in the prosecutions mounted in 2002–04 by New York State Attorney General Eliot Spitzer, who fined Wall Street's leading firms over $1.5 billion for engineering price jumps in an illegal way. Still, their gains far outweighed the penalties negotiated with law enforcement agencies.

The felony case against Frank P. Quattrone is illustrative. Employed as a stock analyst by Credit Suisse First Boston to tout high-tech shares, he was convicted on May 3, 2004, for destroying evidence in the government's investigation of his firm's wrongdoing. Prosecutors showed that what passed for research was a con job, for which his firm paid a fine of $100 million — without admitting criminal wrongdoing (thus avoiding a raft of civil lawsuits by its victims).

The Linux flotation provides an object lesson for the kind of insider dealing that became rife. When Credit Suisse brought the company (then called VA Linux) public in December 1999, it pretended that Linux's prospective earning power justified an initial offering price of $30. But by the end of first day the stock had changed hands numerous times as it soared to $320. It then fell back to close at $239.25, more than seven and a half times what it had sold for in the morning. This price exceeded what Linux would be selling for by the end of 1999 — still remarkably high, considering that its shares would plunge to just 54 cents by 2002 and then would settle in the $2 range, about 1 percent of the first day's peak price.

Who benefited the most? At the head of the pack were the underwriters, followed by the favored pension funds and other institutions who got first crack at the shares and flipped them to new buyers by mid-day. Then came the venture capitalists that helped fund Linux. In the final position were the "content providers" who actually created the company's technology. They didn't receive anything like the $239 their stock ended up selling for in the first day. They didn't even get all that much of the $30 a share at which the stock was issued, after Credit Suisse First Boston took its commission and the venture capitalists got their share.

The venture capitalist's role is to find innovative individuals and start up a company for about $10 million, retaining control over how it is spent. They draw up a partnership agreement replete with small print spelling out how many shares of common and preferred stock they will get, and what proportion of the money they will receive when the company goes public—with management fees for themselves (usually about 2.5 per cent). As one reporter has described,

> preferred equity gains leverage when a company is sold for close to its original valuation, or a small multiple. The funding deal can be structured so that a venture capital fund with 20 per cent preferred equity stake takes up to 40 per cent of the sale proceeds, plus a dividend, and "double dips" by claiming 40 per cent of the remaining capital gain. A technology entrepreneur who has a 30 per cent equity stake may end up with less than 5 per cent of the proceeds.[7]

The bulk of the money raised accrues to the venture capital partners and their investment bankers. Retail investors are shut out of the most lucrative action. To protect their interest and stop "crony finance-capitalism," Congress passed the Oxley-Sarbanes Act in 2002. The idea was to put all customers on the same footing. It was a good idea as far as it went, but its reforms and those that followed Mr. Spitzer's prosecutions were mainly administrative. A more structural solution was needed to refocus stock ownership on the longer term rather than quick in-and-out trading.

One reform under discussion is to require initial buyers (including institutional investors) to hold stock for a reasonable period of time, at least a month. This is still short-term as capital markets go. Another suggestion is a stock-transfer "Tobin" tax. This would absorb a high margin of speculative gains traded on highly debt-leveraged terms. The average high-tech stock trades so rapidly that it now is normal for an amount equal to a company's entire stock

---

[7] John Gapper, "Google's auction exposes intermediaries' phoney war," Financial Times, May 5, 2004.

issue to turn over every day. This increasingly frenetic stock trading is Wall Street's most profitable activity. And most of this trading is on credit, enabling banks to charge interest on financing this speculation. Now supplemented increasingly by complex computerized derivatives, it is gambling on probability curves, decoupled from tangible capital investment.

Google Attempts to Avoid Short-Term Financial Constraints

R ealizing that it would take a long time for more far-reaching reforms to be enacted, the Internet search company Google sidestepped at least the most obvious traps. It began preparations in 1999 when it sold 10-percent partnerships to Sequoia Capital and Kleiner Perkins Caufield & Byers for $12.5 million each. The holdings of these two venture capital firms ended up being valued at about $40 billion, for a 1,600-fold return on their investment. As for the investment bankers, Google limited their commission to just 3 percent, less than half the usual 7 percent rake-off. And to avoid the usual rapacious underpricing of its shares, it hired Morgan Stanley and Credit Suisse First Boston to hold a "Dutch auction." Prospective buyers were invited to submit their bids, and a price would be set to clear the market. The idea was to exclude speculators by giving all buyers an equal opportunity to buy shares at the moment of issue.

Google's founders Larry Page and Sergey Brin spelled out their critique of this process in a letter they included with the "Owners Manual" for their stock offering in 2004. Contrary to Wall Street tradition, they explained that they would not make quarterly earnings estimates, because their focus was on the long run rather than the short term:

> In our opinion, outside pressures too often tempt companies to sacrifice long-term opportunities to meet quarterly market expectations. Sometimes this pressure has caused companies to manipulate financial results in order to "make their quarter." In Warren Buffett's words, "We won't 'smooth' quarterly or annual results: If earnings figures are lumpy when they reach headquarters, they will be lumpy when they reach you."

To make sure that stock market investors would not have an opportunity to oppose this strategy, publicly traded shares would have only a tenth of the voting power of those kept by the company's founders. As they explained:

> If opportunities arise that might cause us to sacrifice short-term results but are in the best long-term interest of our shareholders, we will take those opportunities. ...

Although we may discuss long-term trends in our business, we do not plan to give earnings guidance in the traditional sense. We are not able to predict our business within a narrow range for each quarter. We recognize that our duty is to advance our shareholders' interests, and we believe that artificially creating short-term target numbers serves our shareholders poorly. We would prefer not to be asked to make such predictions, and if asked we will respectfully decline. A management team distracted by a series of short-term targets is as pointless as a dieter stepping on a scale every half hour. ...

We will not shy away from high-risk, high-reward projects because of short-term earnings pressure.[8]

Logical as this approach seemed to be, Wall Street did not approve. "Let's hope this doesn't become a precedent," one banker remarked. A hedge fund manager told the *New York Times* that he thought

shareholders should punish Google for its failure to give new investors the same rights as its founders. Once a company goes public, its founders must understand and accept that they are responsible to public shareholders and are no longer fully in control.[9]

This was the mentality that Google sought to avoid. Its stock was issued at a price of $100 by Dutch auction on August 19, 2004, and then doubled by October and tripled by the following June—just what the company also had tried to avoid. But at least the price run-up seemed motivated by a better understanding of the company's long-term earning power, not by the kind of insider deals to favored customers that had inspired Google to avoid the typical Wall Street ways.

Underwriting Rip-Offs to Deprive the Public and Private Sectors of Realistic Asset Value

G oogle learned what to avoid by watching how underwriters handled most stock issues. The most egregious examples occurred outside of the United States, above all for privatizations of public enterprises. Shares in these companies were underpriced as a political ploy to promote privatization, starting

---

[8] "Excerpts from 'Owner's Manual' Included With Offering," *The New York Times*, April 30, 2004.

[9] "Google Says To Investors: Don't Think of Flipping," and "An Egalitarian Auction? Bankers Are Not Amused," *The New York Times*, April 30, 2004. See also Frank Norris, "Google May Have Pre-empted Regulators on Public Offerings," *The New York Times*, May 4, 2004.

with British Telephone in 1982. The guiding idea of Mrs. Thatcher's Conservative Party was to make these stock issues a "steal" for employees and customers of these firms, as well as for investors in general to make quick windfall gains.

For starters, British stock underwriters received a quite unnecessary windfall. The government made no attempt to negotiate lower issue fees than the 7 percent monopoly rate that underwriters were used to charging small and untested companies for new issues without clear earnings prospects. The public enterprises being sold off already had an established earnings stream, so little research was needed. Two percent or at most 3 percent would have been enough to obtain the underwriting services needed to sell the stock, given the enormous size of the issue. But providing a free lunch at public expense became the essence of the new finance capitalism.

The post-1980 rise of finance capital can be attributed in large part to its ability to privatization of public and private-sector capital on credit. Britain's government could have received five or six times as much as it did by offering only about 20 percent of British Telephone initially in order to establish a logical—and much higher—market price, and then selling the balance of the company. Instead, it underpriced the entire company's value to stock market investors and underwriters. The magnitude of this and similar giveaways is so large as to be transformative, because the largest capital investment in most economies prior to the financial conquest of the 1980s was infrastructure in the public domain. By focusing on "capital formation" as being a private-sector phenomenon, economics textbooks—and financial "free market" lobbyists—distract attention from the privatization giveaways that have been a major factor in enabling the economy's wealthiest 1% to sharply increase their share of wealth and income.

The process was capped by the privatized infrastructure monopolies to raise access prices ("rent extraction") and transform industrial economies into rentier tollbooth economies. This transformation was achieved in part by the financial sector using its rich takings to mount an attack on government price regulation (making the spurious claim that "free markets" were ones that permit monopoly gouging), untaxing property rents and capital gains (on the claim that "free markets" needed a flat tax falling on labor, not on finance or real estate), and using the power of advertising and subsidy to drown out the concept of free markets that had been developing in the last few centuries of Western civilization. This was the essence of Thatcherism. And in America, Ronald Reagan's team applauded it as the wave of the future. The barbarians were at the gates.

One might expect that this experience would dissuade underwriters from claiming that they give investors and corporate clients a fair idea of the value and prospective dividend stream for the shares being issued. But privatization stocks were not priced to take into account the fact that earnings would rise as private management was freed from the behavioral constraints that public companies had to follow. Yet it was precisely to break "free" of such regulation that public companies were being privatized by the Thatcherites! So it was mainly investment bankers and underwriters, stockbrokers and money managers that made money from their rake-off fees, administrative overhead charges and short-term trading gains. These financial operators depict themselves as key intermediaries mobilizing peoples' hard-earned savings to fund innovations that propel the economy forward. Yet what Wall Street and the City of London has been selling is debt leveraging, downsizing and outsourcing, privatization and de-unionization — culminating in austerity planning and what is best characterized as a race to the bottom. The economy shrinks, and many small savers are left holding an empty bag with a mountain of debt attached to it. It was not how economic futurists a century ago expected the era of progress and abundance to develop.

The main talent that underwriters and money managers really need to succeed is greed, and this is something that cannot be taught in school. Its spirit is extractive and parasitic, not productive. Its route to success is not to make profit in the classical way, by capital investment to produce goods and services. Bankers and financial managers prefer the easier route of making money by transferring property into their own hands, and "extracting rent" by siphoning off real estate and stock market gains fueled by debt-leveraged asset-price inflation, and monopoly rents from key technologies such as Microsoft or "intellectual property" such as Walt Disney.

Some Almost-Successful Takeover Attempts of 2005

Fiction: Corporate takeovers streamline inefficient management by cutting the fat.

Reality: Financial predators cut bone and muscle as they reduce investment programs with long lead-times. They increase returns by paying bills more slowly and running companies deeper into debt—to raise stock prices, not production.

Companies traditionally increased their dividends by investing in tangible capital to earn more profits, or cutting costs and/or raising prices for their products. But by 2005 an aggressive new source of financing developed. The idea was to mortgage corporate real estate and pay out the loan proceeds as dividends. This promised to make money in a purely financial way, by stripping assets to increase stock prices. Rather than investing in new capital to expand the business, raiders aim is to acquire assets already in place and sell them for a price gain, or even borrow against them to bid up stock prices. Earnings would be fully paid out instead of being invested in tangible capital formation. Financial managers would take the money and run, leaving indebted corporate shells in place of solvent companies.

Raiders (now euphemized as "activist shareholders") need buy only 5 or 6 percent of a company's stock or round up hedge funds and other speculators in order to mount a proxy fight and pressure companies to raise dividend payouts and share buybacks. Their tactic is to pledge corporate assets for debt service, using the stock market as a vehicle to replace equity with debt. Whatever assets were not already collateralized, especially cash or pension funds, became a red flag similar to the curse that plagues countries with rich oil deposits—a target tempting predators to buy a company's stock on credit. *Financial Times* columnist John Gapper described how dangerous sizeable corporate cash holdings could be:

> Companies have made themselves vulnerable to activist hedge funds by playing safe in the past three years. After the scare of the collapses of Enron and WorldCom, they paid down debt and amassed cash in case they suffered a similar crisis. Now, according to Standard & Poor's, US companies hold $1,300bn of cash and liquid assets—more than 10 per cent of all balance sheet assets.[10]

Next to liquid cash assets, corporate raiders concentrated on real estate. Among the hottest targets are food chain stores with property in prime locations that accounted for a high proportion of their net worth. Hedge funds take short-term loans to buy land-rich companies, and repay this bridge financing by mortgaging the property. Retail stores in particular own prime real estate locations, especially the large British grocery chains—and in the United States, the major restaurant chains.

Liquidating Corporate Assets

Fiction: The stock market raises long-term equity capital as an alternative to debt.

Reality: The stock market is becoming a vehicle for corporate raiders to untrack long-term investment planning by indebting companies to the hilt, cashing out, and running.

---

[10] John Gapper, "Hedge fund agitators deserve to be heard," *Financial Times*, November 17, 2005.

Hedge fund managers pressed predatory finance to new limits in November 2005. Carl Icahn, one of the most notorious raiders from the 1980s, bought over 3 percent of Time Warner stock, and other hedge funds controlling a similar amount joined him to stage the largest proxy fight in U.S. corporate history. Lazard also set a precedent by acting as his advisor—the first time a staid Wall Street investment bank joined in attacking a blue-chip company, its traditional client base. Its 343-page report by Bruce Wasserstein urging Time Warner to bid up its stock price by raising its annual buybacks from $5 billion to $20 billion. He also suggested that the company break itself into four parts and sell them off to pay quick dividends to stockholders.

Around the same time, William Ackman's Pershing Square Capital hedge fund bought options on 4.9 percent of McDonald's. McDonald's was land-rich, owning more than a third of the land underneath its 13,500 restaurants in the United States and 30,000 worldwide. This un-mortgaged property was bankable, providing a borrowing opportunity that made the company a takeover target in the closing months of 2005. Mr. Ackman rounded up Vornado Realty Trust to buy another 1.2 percent, and a few other funds joined in to mount a proxy contest for control of the company. Among them was Whitney Tilson's hedge fund T2 Partners. Tilson, earlier had urged Wal-Mart to buy back its stock and "take advantage of the low interest-rate environment and take on debt, allowing it to both expand and buy back shares."[11] The raiders thus shared a similar mentality and game plan.

This was the second fast-food company that Mr. Ackman had attacked. Earlier he had cornered 9.3 percent of Wendy's stock, enough to force it to spin off its Horton's coffee-shop division and pay out the proceeds as dividends. His plan for McDonalds was even bolder: The company would sell two-thirds of its restaurants for $3.3 billion, and raise $9 to $15 billion more by mortgaging its real estate to the hilt, using the proceeds to buy back its shares. It would spin off its wholly owned restaurants into a distinct property company (McOpCo), which would lease them back to McDonald's, while selling 20 percent of its shares to raise a further $1.3 billion.

Mr. Ackman forecast that these policies would enable McDonald's to triple its dividend from 67 cents to $2 per share, raising its stock price by about 10 percent (around $2 to $4 per share), despite the fact that it would reduce the company's net worth by paying out the value of its assets.[12] For Mr. Ackman's plan to work, buyers of McDonald's shares would focus on its short-term dividend yield, not on the company's long-run prospects as it became more financially fragile.

---

[11] "Cash-Rich Firms Urged to Spend," Wall Street Journal, November 21, 2005.
[12] "Investor urges McDonald's to sell off restaurants," Financial Times, November 14, 2005.

McDonald's officers explained that the plan would discourage prospective new franchise purchasers, who naturally would fear that the proposed real-estate affiliate would charge high rents. That is what landlords tend to do, after all. So making money as a landlord would reduce the viability of the fast-food operation. And on purely financial grounds the debt leverage proposal would strip the company's assets and leave it deeply indebted. Chief financial officer Matthew Paull characterized Mr. Ackman's plan as "financial engineering."[13] But as the *Wall Street Journal* observed: "In the hedge-fund world, 'financial engineering' isn't a pejorative."

It was not as if McDonald's needed rescuing. Since 2002 it had raised its dividends by 185 percent, tripling its share price at a time when most stock market averages were drifting downward. In any event, none of the hedge-fund proposals involved restaurant management as such. Their aim was pure asset stripping—borrowing against property not yet pledged as collateral, and paying out the loan proceeds to shareholders to produce a price jump—brief, but sufficient to enable the hedge funds to dump their shares for a quick killing.

The tragic consequence, for the economy at large as well as the companies being raided, is that after the financial dust had settled, the company would be left deep in debt. As the above-cited *Wall Street Journal* report summed up the threat: "Even the very best management teams aren't safe in today's free-for-all corporate environment." In the new financial perspective, "Holding so much [cash] is inefficient: companies reduce their return on equity by having too little debt. That makes the smaller ones targets for private equity funds."

As matters turned out by February 2006, Mr. Icahn and Mr. Ackman failed in their takeover attempts. Mr. Ackman did succeed in debt-leveraging his hedge fund's holdings of McDonald shares, and cleaned up when the stock jumped by 11 percent by January 2006. But at least McDonald's remained in one piece. So did Time Warner, where Mr. Icahn was unable to convince most shareholders that he could significantly improve its stock performance. Its shares remained stuck around $18, far from the $26 level he claimed his policies would produce. Lazard, which had negotiated a fee of $5 million for every $1 increase in Time Warner's share price, also lost.[14] Still, the attack forced the company to quadruple its share buybacks from $5 billion to $20 billion annually, and slash operating expenses by $1 billion. This prompted Fitch Ratings to downgrade the company's bonds a notch, from BBB+ to BBB.

---

[13] Alan Murray, "Attack on McDonald's Heralds a New Order," *Wall Street Journal*, November 23, 2005.

[14] "Icahn Plan For a Split Gets a Push," *The New York Times*, February 8, 2006.

Taken together, these two episodes show how little today's post-modern hit-and-run finance has to do with actual capital formation. It turns upside-down the original idea of creating joint-stock corporations. They were expected to transform financial organization by creating large companies that would finance their expansion by raising permanent funding in the form of equity capital rather than debt. The advantage of equity was supposed to be that companies could pay their backers out of profits. If they make losses or their profits fall, they can cut back dividends accordingly. So equity reduces the risk of bankruptcy, making shareholders partners with the active manager-owners. But if companies do not pay the scheduled interest charges owed to creditors, they come under creditor control and stockholders may be wiped out.

The short time frame of financial managers thus loses the advantage of long-term, flexible equity funding. Stock markets are subjecting companies to short-term management seeking gains by trading stocks and downsizing — that is, in ways that are largely decoupled from providing new financing for corporate investment. Today's financial management philosophy — reinforced by the tax code and deregulation of corporate oversight — calls for cutting back R&D, downsizing the labor force, raiding pension-fund reserves and degrading defined-benefit plans into defined-contribution schemes. These policies are imposing a debt overhead on industrial capitalism as finance capital takes over industry, real estate and monopolies.

Junk Statistics

Fiction: Corporate land has almost no market value.
Reality: Land accounts for most growth in corporate property value.

In view of real estate's importance in determining corporate net worth — and hence, borrowing power, as the McDonald's episode illustrates — one might expect Federal Reserve statistics on America's balance sheet to provide a fair valuation of corporate land. But its economists treat the market value of real estate as consisting mainly of buildings, not land sites. Starting with a market appraisal based on Census Department estimates for overall property prices, Fed statisticians then estimate the original cost of buildings and multiply this number by the Commerce Department's index of construction costs to calculate their replacement cost. Whatever statistical residual remains between this estimate and current market value is attributed to land. The pretense is that buildings gain value simply as a result of price inflation increasing their replacement costs. Yet their owners are depreciating them — claiming that they are "recouping their capital," even as their market price is being inflated by while inflation or easier credit, public infrastructure spending and general prosperity. These are not recognized as having any effect—presumably because it is harder to justify such "free lunch" gains for landowners. When they do sell their depreciated properties, they do not even have to pay low capital gains taxes if they reinvest their money in buying yet more property. So the tax system subsidizes a free-lunch *rentier* economy.

The seemingly empirical statistical nonsense that this methodology produces is illustrated by the fact that in some years this "land residual method" has left no land value at all! The Fed's replacement-cost index for buildings rose so far in excess of actual market prices that by 1994 it reported the market value for U.S. corporately owned land as being a *negative* $4 billion. The implication was that America's corporations, as a whole, would have been willing to pay anyone $4 billion just to take all the negatively valued land they owned off their hands. The land's apparently negligible statistical valuation was "crowded out" by the replacement-cost index.

When systematic on-going error is continued for generation after generation, there invariably is a special interest involved. In the case of land valuation, this interest goes back to the classical debates of the 18th and 19th centuries, above all the attempt by the Physiocrats, Adam Smith, John Stuart Mill, Henry George and the Progressive Era to tax land rent as society's major form of unearned income and wealth. The idea was that taxing land rent would save it from being pledged to the banks as interest, and thereby would keep down housing prices (which are set at however much banks will lend). A land tax also would free governments from having to burden labor and industrial capital, thereby keeping their supply price low (as taxes, like interest, raise the price of production via the cost of living and doing business).

But since World War I the *rentiers* have fought back to shift taxes off themselves onto labor, consumers and even industry. Empowered by the symbiosis between finance, insurance and real estate (FIRE), rent extractors have fought to keep their free lunch out of the hands of government precisely because it is free, and easy to obtain. As J. S. Mill explained, land rent and rising prices for land are a gain that landlords make "in their sleep." And since his day the democratization of property ownership on credit has enabled landlords to sell out—with banks providing the mortgage loans to buyers who bid against each other to see who will pay the largest proportion of the land rent to the banks in exchange for the loan to acquire the property. Not only homeowners do this, but corporations seeking to turn around and sell the land at a higher price.

If the Fed's estimates were realistic and corporate property value resides in its buildings, little gain could be made in tearing down properties to gentrify or rebuild. But prices for commercial and industrial sites have been soaring in prime locations such as New York's midtown, downtown Tribeca neighborhood and even the Lower East Side and darkest Brooklyn, as well as in Chicago's Loop and on the South Side's gentrified neighborhoods in which Barack Obama played so active a role on behalf of the Pritzker and Crown families. So the Fed's economists had enough good sense to be properly embarrassed by their unrealistic land valuations, and stopped breaking out corporate land value separately in their balance-sheet estimates since their 1994 report. This behavior of the Fed shows the degree to which seemingly empirical economic and financial data are still being subjected to ideological distortions lingering over from the 19th century's tax reform debate seeking to tax land rather than labor and manmade capital investment. It is testimony to the ability of rentier interests—indeed, the FIRE sector acting in concert—to conceal the degree to which wealth is not earned by labor or enterprise as modern popular morality holds should be the case.

The absurdity of the Fed's low land-price statistic is shown by the avidity with which speculators search for companies with undervalued or "undermortgaged" land—sites that official statistics hold to be nearly worthless. The more reasonable procedure is that which inspired Mr. Ackman and other corporate raiders—to start with land prices and assign the residual value to buildings. If the Federal Reserve's balance-sheet statistics were realistic, stock market raiders would not be able to make quick gains in the way that Mr. Ackman's hedge fund tried to extract from them McDonald's—"capital gains" that actually reflect the property's growing site value that could be liquefied by mortgaging it.

"Like a Plague of Locusts": Stock Ownership without Responsibility

Fiction: The stock market sets share prices responsibly to reflect long-term growth prospects.

Reality: Companies are valued in terms of their short-run liquidation value.

Making money financially is not the same thing as earning income by industrial investment. Providing easy tax-deductible credit for corporate raiders and hedge funds has turned high finance into a hit-and-run game by making a company's breakup value more important than how much it can produce and earn over the longer term. It seems not to matter that companies are left highly indebted with little cushion against economic downturns. The bubble mentality views a liquidity cushion or unpledged net worth as a free asset not "making money."

For many years corporate raiders have looked for companies that carry assets at less than their current market value. Such companies can be bought at a discount and their real estate, licensing rights or other assets sold off for a capital gain. The government has subsidized such takeovers by lowering taxes on capital gains below those on earning profits, wages and salaries. This encourages financial speculation and the indebting of corporate industry rather than new capital investment.

Much of the problem could be cured by stopping the practice of permitting interest to be counted as a tax-deductible cost of doing business. This distortion encourages raiding and "value extraction" by loading companies down with debt. What determines a firm's worth under today's conditions is how much it—or an outside bidder—can borrow against its liquidation value. In today's Orwellian financial vocabulary, "wealth creation" is based on asset stripping, not tangible capital formation. This prompted Franz Müntefering, former chairman of Germany's Social Democratic Party, to tell his fellow politicians at a conference in April 2005: "Some financial investors don't waste any thoughts on the people whose jobs they destroy." Hedge funds and buyout firms harmed the national interest by draining companies of their wealth and shrinking the economy's employment prospects. "They remain anonymous, have no face, fall like a plague of locusts over our companies, devour everything, then fly on to the next one."

Most money now is made not by making goods and services but by buying and selling assets, from real estate, stocks and bonds to entire companies, and using financial engineering to leverage this trading on credit. The financial sector describes wealth as increasing as long as asset prices rise. But the "wealth" in question consists of financial securities and claims, not the "real" production-and-consumption economy. It is created seemingly out of nothing—out of the financial system's ability to create debt and attach it to properties. This engineers higher asset prices by using debt to pyramid one's own minimal equity—freely created credit that has no cost of production.

Some companies are shunning the stock market altogether. When Koch Industries, for instance, reached an agreement to take Georgia Pacific private, the logic in avoiding the stock market was similar to that of Mr. Müntefering. As Georgia-Pacific's chairman and chief executive A.D. 'Pete' Correll explained, "private ownership will allow the company to make investments that might well have been eschewed by public shareholders." Whereas shareholder "activists" wanted the company to pay out its revenue instead of reinvesting it, "Georgia-Pacific may now be able to put more money into its commodity building-supply businesses."[15]

---

[15] "Koch Industries Agrees to Buy Georgia-Pacific," The Wall Street Journal, November 14, 2005.

For hundreds of years, family firms have gone public to obtain capital needed to expand. But since 1980 this historical trend has been reversed. As ownership has diffused, it became divorced from day-to-day corporate management. Companies are retiring their stock and going private. They are using their earnings not to invest in expanding their scale of operations, but to buy up their own stock, either to support its market price (thus making it more expensive to potential raiders) or to retire it and leave the company the personal property of its new owner. Companies are stripping themselves down to retain only those divisions with the highest and shortest-term payouts.

The prosecution of Frank Quattrone showed that Wall Street earnings estimates were as little concerned with reality as were the junk mortgage packages in the lead-up to 2008 or the happy-face estimates of Greek sovereign debt before 2011. These examples should suffice to controvert the assumption that market efficiency is assured by "full knowledge."

Fiction: Bank loans finance productive capital investment, creating enough profit to enable borrowers to pay off their loans.

Reality: Banks extend most credit to buyers of property already in place, enabling corporate raiders and real estate speculators to pay interest as their loans inflate asset prices.

This price rise enables debtors to pay interest charges by taking out larger loans. But as bonds have been issued more to finance corporate takeovers than new capital investment since the 1980s, the effect has been to shrink the industrial economy's ability to carry the growing debt overhead.

Today's debt-driven financial system is both inflationary and deflationary. It is inflationary in a novel way: Credit produces capital gains by supplying easy, increasingly low-interest financing for borrowers to spend on bidding up property and stock market prices. Companies forego tangible investment in order to increase their share prices by paying higher dividends or buying back their stock. The media welcomed this asset-price inflation as constituting a new form of wealth creation — as long as asset prices rather than wages or consumer prices are being inflated. But credit is debt, and debt needs to be paid — absorbing income that otherwise would be spent on goods and services. The result is debt deflation.

The underlying problem, as Aristotle noted long ago, is that money as such is sterile. Brokers may advertise "Let your money work for you," but money doesn't really work. People work. Money seeks to obtain the surplus they produce. And when the creditor's gain is the debtor's loss, making money financially is a zero-sum game for the economy as a whole. "Making money from money" means using credit to leverage asset purchases in search of capital gains. The process has little linkage with increasing production or living standards. Labor may be worked more intensively to squeeze out enough revenue to carry the rising debt burden. But this is exploitation in a non-productive form. Employees are indebted more deeply, and a sense of desperation replaces the hoped-for leisure economy.

Part of finance capital's problem is its high liquidity, seemingly a virtue as compared to fixed industrial capital. Hitherto staid institutions are turning their portfolios over at a dizzying rate as they jump like fleas on and off of quick zigzags in stock market values. The hope is simply to outperform the Dow Jones Industrial Average (and other fund managers) on a monthly basis. The long-term position of companies whose stocks are being traded so frenetically is a secondary consideration, because stocks are sold before the long run ever arrives.

> Today's debt-driven financial system is both inflationary and deflationary. It is inflationary in a novel way: Credit produces capital gains by supplying easy, increasingly low-interest financing for borrowers to spend on bidding up property and stock market prices.

Financializing Industry Abroad

Financial parasitism is becoming worldwide as the trend toward neoliberal (that is, pro-financial) ideology makes it more difficult for nations to regulate their financial markets and protect their industry from debt. The *Financial Times* recently reported:

> Private equity groups operating in Europe are loading the companies they buy with record levels of debt, new data show. In particular, the so-called 'leveraged ratio'—or the ratio of debt to core earnings—has risen sharply, suggesting that some companies could struggle to repay debt if their performance deteriorated suddenly. … One measure of this trend is the ratio between a company's debt and its core earnings—earnings before interest, tax, depreciation and amortization—seen in the debt markets. In March, companies raising finance that had a rating below investment grade had debt that was 5.73 times

ebitda, according to S & P's Leveraged Commentary Data. This is the highest figure since the leveraged loan market started to be tracked in Europe in the late 1990s."[16]

The phenomenon is global, not confined to the United States. The strategy of financialization is not only to appropriate the public domain via privatization, but to take companies traded on the stock exchange "private," that is, for individuals to form hedge funds to raise the funding to buy them out on credit. The British retailer Debenhams, for instance, was bought in this way. The new owners sold off its stores for cash, which they paid out to their backers, and then agreed to lease them back. "The enfeebled company was then sold back to the stock market. ... This is not pro- but anti-wealth-creation. ... private equity has been able to carry short-termism to new extremes. This is said to raise productivity and performance." However, Will Hutton argued: "The chief reason British business remains at the bottom of the international league tables for innovation, research and development, and productivity growth is because of too much takeover and too much private equity. Innovation lowers short-term profits."[17] This financial devouring of wealth is achieved by the ability of banking interests to lobby for a perverse set of tax incentives "that favour takeover [and] need to be removed." But both the Conservatives and Labour Parties have accepted the logic that debt-leveraged asset-price inflation is "wealth creation."

> **B**ut credit is debt, and debt needs to be paid—absorbing income that otherwise would be spent on goods and services. The result is debt deflation.

Similar global pressure is at work in Japan. "Growing corporate terror of takeover is spurring companies to use excess cash to pay higher dividends. This cuts cash reserves, making companies less attractive as targets. It also

---

[16] Gillian Tett, Louisa Mitchell and Peter Smith, "Private equity acquisitions loaded with debt," *Financial Times*: May 25, 2006. Ebitda is an acronym for earnings before interest, taxes, depreciation and amortization.

[17] Will Hutton, "Private equity is casting a plutocratic shadow over British business," *The Guardian*, February 23, 2007.

pleases existing shareholders," increasingly foreigners.[18] But these payouts are made by sacrificing long-run investment.

Summary

Fiction: Productivity gains lower production prices over time.
Reality: Interest charges on debt pyramiding raise the cost of doing business by so much as to offset productivity gains, diverting revenue away from new investment and consumption.

The nation's highest-paid individuals work on Wall Street, where they devote an enormous amount of effort and even innovation to make money financially. Unfortunately, they are part of a system that has become dysfunctional for the economy at large. Financial gain seeking has been decoupled from long-term capital investment, and now undercuts it by being predatory.

Textbook formulae describing stock market behavior neglect the associated fiscal distortions that lead financial managers to load industry down with debt, and treat as "exogenous" the behavior of lobbyists backing politicians committed to shifting the tax burden onto labor and industry. There is little hint of how self-defeating the recent structural changes in the economy's financial and tax policies have been in polarizing property and wealth distribution and the incidence of debt.

Profits and capital gains are described as resulting from farsighted investors taking risks. But rather than being far seeing, the financial time frame is short-term. Speculators have survived by shifting the risk onto society ("taxpayers"), most notoriously in the post-2008 bailouts. As Cadbury-Schweppes chairman John Sunderland recently decried the situation in a speech to Britain's Investor Relations Society: "The pressure on the sell side has, in my view, made analysts very focused on the near-term … research tends to be more sensational, and on roadshows there is increasing pressure to put us in front of hedge funds rather than traditional long funds."[19]

By 2006, hedge funds were accounting for nearly half the trading flows on the London and New York stock exchanges, although they only owned a small percentage of equity in these two markets. Their aggressive trading has played a major role in subordinating the industrial economy to financial management.

---

[18] "Japanese payout hunters face gamble on cultural change," *Financial Times*, March 30, 2006.
[19] Stefan Stern, "The short-term shareholders changing the face of capitalism," *Financial Times*, March 28, 2006.

"Mark Goyder, who runs the UK-based think tank 'Tomorrow's Company,' believes that … where 'shareholder value' may once have referred to the long-term creation of wealth, today's short-term financial investor demands action that can influence the share price even on a daily basis. Add in the misguided belief, known as 'agency theory,' that management's remuneration has to be closely tied to share prices, and you have a recipe for very short-term thinking."[20]

Misguided beliefs are not accidental. The natural tendency is to see matters realistically. Wrong-headed economics requires a blizzard of rhetoric to distract attention from the extractive character of today's financial markets. Euphemisms replace functional description, and the financial sector's first task is to deny in principle the idea of an economic free lunch. All debt is deemed "productive," that is, financing investment in the means to pay it off with the stipulated interest charge. Every sector of the economy is assumed to help every other sector grow, so that all income is earned productively as finance helps industry. The "proof" is simply to correlate the growth of rates of finance and the industrial sector. But one could just as well correlate these two time series with global warming, rising costs for health insurance or any other variable. The idea of causality has been left behind by today's post-modern mathematical fads.

This ideological set of blinders ("guidelines") has inspired academics committed to rationalizing the *status quo* to turn the word "risk" into a euphemism for almost any kind of free lunch. For investment bankers and corporate raiders, the main risk is that regulators may close the loopholes that make speculative "risk-taking" un-risky, while shifting the actual risk onto industrial companies and their employees—whose available revenue is shrunk by rising charges for debt service—and ultimately onto taxpayers via central bank and Treasury bailouts.

Financial lobbyists treat our financial situation and increasingly regressive tax structure as being natural and hence inevitable—and therefore not subject to change by earthly reformers. Their public-relations campaign promotes the idea that unregulated (and un-taxed) financial markets are all for the best, as if driven by an Invisible Hand. And they are not referring to the invisible hand of insider dealing (*e.g.*, that Eliot Spitzer's prosecutions revealed).

The preceding pages have described how the first myth in this economic fiction story is that the stock market raises money to provide companies with equity capital to build factories and employ more people. The reality is that investment bankers and speculators obtain most of the price established by

---

[20] *Ibid.*

the end of the first day's trading of new public offerings. For companies already established, the stock market has become a vehicle for raiders to buy out stock-holders and burden companies with debt, forcing companies to spend their earnings on buying their own stock to support its price.

The traditional industrial objective of corporate officers was to build up their company's net worth—the value of its plant and equipment, inventories, real estate and other investments over and above its debts. But since the 1980s, stock-market wealth creation has gone together with debt pyramiding. As long as financial managers find it easier to make money by stripping assets than by undertaking new direct investment, the debt burden will make economies more fragile. Only asset-price inflation kept the market value of assets high enough to cover the rising volume of corporate debt mounting up more rapidly than the value of stocks, the book value of assets or sales over the past decade.

The question is, how long can this continue? Which expansion path ultimately will end up higher: that of debt, or that of the assets bought on credit?

The answer from every historical epoch is that financial dynamics end up more powerful. And by deterring new capital formation, they often work in the opposite direction from technology. The resulting debt crisis disproves the assumption that people—or entire economies—recognize their self-interest. Yet this is the axiom on which free-market economics is based.

As noted earlier, the simplest cure would be to remove the tax-deductibility of interest charges. It is one thing for investors to buy real estate, stocks, bonds or other assets and make a gain; it is another thing to borrow freshly-created credit to do this, subsidized by taxpayers. (The subsidy ends up being used to pay the banks that create the credit.) As an Australian critic James Cumes recently observed: "In 1997, non-financial [U.S.] corporations paid $218.1 billion in dividends from $337.7 billion in after-tax profits. In 2002, they paid dividends of $285.8 billion out of sharply lower profits of $197.0 billion. In other words, they financed a substantial and growing part of their dividends by drawing on their cash reserves or borrowing. In past, more normal times, the distribution was about half and half—half after-tax profits went to dividends, half were undistributed. ... Dividend payments have been rising to an all-time high as a share of national income, while profits, by the same measure, have fallen to an all-time low. Excessive and what would once have been regarded as highly imprudent dividend payments are now used to prop up overvalued stock prices."[21]

---

[21] Note on Gang8 e-mail list, June 2006.

Fiction: Income that is un-taxed will be invested productively to help the economy grow.

Reality: Income that is un-taxed will be pledged to pay more interest to banks and bondholders— and this bank credit will bid up the price of the real estate and corporate revenue that is being untaxed.

All this has profound implications for tax policy. Since the U.S. income tax was first enacted on the eve of World War I—with capital gains being taxed at the same rate as other income—business has waged a constant struggle to get un-taxed, by shifting the burden onto labor and consumers. The argument is that lower taxes will leave more income to be reinvested, to earn more profits by hiring more labor to produce more goods and services to raise living standards.

The world now has learned that this is nonsense. The reality is that the real estate motto, "Rent is for paying interest," has become the corporate motto as well: "Corporate earnings are for paying creditors," in exchange for loans to buy companies or at least to bid up their share prices. The tradeoff is not over whether companies either will pay taxes or invest. It is between companies paying taxes to the government or interest to their banks and bondholders. Most business tax reductions have ended up being paid as debt service, thereby expanding the debt burden that business must carry, instead of reducing cor-porate costs and making industry more competitive. The effect is to divert more credit and savings to the financial sector, increasing the debt that finan-cially leveraged companies must pay, and the resulting tax shift that the economy's labor and consumers must pick up.

What makes the downsizing of employment by today's financial managers so ironic is the avid support by pension funds as well as by mutual-fund small investors for takeovers, share buybacks and the general indebting of industry. Fund managers ostensibly representing the interest of retirees and labor have bought into the junk-economics myth that it pays to maximize the short-term performance of their stock portfolio, without regard for how this may impair long-term industrial investment and employment. Fund managers are told that to forego the drive for capital gains is a failure to use the financial portfolio to its "best" use. There has been almost no European-style attempt to use em-ployee or consumer stock ownership to steer corporate policy in the interests of the labor force on whose behalf these stocks and bonds are held.

"In the beginning" and throughout all antiquity, industrial capital was self-financed. There was no productive lending to invest in workshops or other means of production, but only to finance trade in goods already produced. In the Bronze Age (before 1200 BC) most manmade capital was owned by the large economic institutions of the epoch: the temples and palaces of the ancient Near East. In classical Greece and Rome the civil governments or temples owned the mines, mints and basic infrastructure, and this continued to be the case up through the Renaissance. There was no public debt or debts owed by the temples or to the large estates on which the division of labor took place. Land as well as workshops and high-cost investments were owned outright. These assets might be leased out to private managers, but remained in the public domain — and debt-free.

The most productive banking was to finance foreign trade, as well as transferring funds geographically. Consumer usury was universally denounced, but lending to kings — mainly for war-making — legitimized domestic money lending. Still, finance refrained from participating in or funding the major innovations of the Industrial Revolution. James Watt could not get bank credit, nor could Henry Ford. The major innovators borrowed against their real estate, and from their families and friends for start-up capital.

Public investment in canals and other basic infrastructure was self-financed. At a local level, this was done largely by taxing property owners. Only after these capital investments became going concerns would banks be willing to lend against their property, sales and income stream already in place, not to create new means of production.

Almost without economic theorists or even historians noticing, the basic form of competition today is no longer primarily among industrial entrepreneurs to lower prices and undersell their competitors, as Joseph Schumpeter described "creative destruction" via technological advance. The competition today is among financial raiders to acquire industrial companies and turn their assets into debts, to be paid out to the raiders and the banks and bondholders who back them.

The drive for lower costs today is not one of technological advances in productivity as was expected a century ago. It is a drive to lower costs by lower wages, lower taxes — and lower financing costs under a distorted tax system by replacing "high cost" (but low break-even) equity capital with ostensibly "low-cost" tax-deductible debt financing that raises break-even costs.

Every new economic system emerges from its predecessors. Finance capitalism emerged from the Industrial Revolution's industrial capitalism. But finance capital almost always has been antithetical to industrial capital formation, as well as to the much larger capital investment by the public sector in creating basic infrastructure such as roads and other transportation, ports and air fields, water and sewer systems, public utilities. These are being privatized and financialized today, and formerly public services provided at cost or freely are being replaced by tollbooths.

This is what has been happening to industrial firms taken over by financial managers since the 1980s. Instead of productive tangible capital investment in the means of production, finance capital produces debt to attach to existing assets in the public and private sector alike. It used part of the proceeds to buy control of government, above all by purchasing control of the electoral process and the mass media. The result was not only direct financial parasitism on the industrial economy, but cultural and intellectual parasitism to depict all this as being progressive and even part of natural evolution toward globalization—financial-style.

Tax favoritism for debt service treats even takeover debts as an inherent and normal cost of doing business. Yet the resulting financial dynamic is de-industrializing the United States, Britain and other economies that are "going financial." Returns are paid to bond and stock holders rather than being recycled into tangible capital formation. These payments are "crowding out" the commitments that these companies earlier took to defer labor's wages by paying pensions later on.

Labor leaders negotiated lower wages in exchange for future retirement payments. In exchange for reduced wage demands, employers agreed to set aside a portion of their higher cash flow and invest it in a pension fund, thereby giving workers a stake in their employers. So labor acted with foresight, preferring to take its return later in life. But financial lobbyists now assert that corporations are being made uncompetitive and even forced into bankruptcy by labor demands for unpayable high-cost pensions and health care.

The employers thus are breaking their word—or more to the point, new financial managers have taken over and claim that these promises made by past executives must be downsized. Raiders and other managers are paying out pension fund assets to backers, along with a rising share of profits and cash flow. The effect is to leave companies sufficiently broke that their managers claim that a *force majeur* emergency prevents them from paying. Labor unions are given the choice either to scale down their claims or have the company declare bankruptcy.

The effect of debt leveraging collateralizing all available assets is to leave companies in a high-cost position. Even healthy corporations have felt obliged to take on debt as a "poison pill" to deter financial raiders from taking them over and borrowing against their assets to pay themselves, leaving debt-ridden carcasses in their wake. Bankruptcy is a means of wiping out financial obligations to employees in order to pay large institutional creditors—while shifting their pension-fund and healthcare obligations onto the government pension-insurance agency.

The hypocrisy of the financial takeover movement is exemplified by New York (that is, Wall Street) Sen. Chuck Schumer. His Orwellian-titled Shareholder Bill of Rights Act of 2009 aimed ostensibly "to prioritize the long-term health of firms and their shareholders" as if these aims were identical. But as a group of corporate lawyers observed, the specific provisions of the proposed act would give shareholders the ability to carve up companies with debt, not heal them:

Excessive stockholder power is precisely what caused the short-term fixation that led to the current financial crisis. As stockholder power increased over the last twenty years, our stock markets also became increasingly institutionalized. The real investors are mostly professional money managers who are focused on the short term.

It is these shareholders who pushed companies to generate returns at levels that were not sustainable. They also made sure high returns were tied to management compensation. The pressure to produce unrealistic profit fueled increased risk-taking. And as the government relaxed checks on excessive risk-taking (or, at a minimum, didn't respond with increased prudential regulation), stockholder demands for ever higher returns grew still further. It was a vicious cycle.

> ... Institutions should discontinue the practice of compensating fund managers based on quarterly performance. And corporations should follow the lead of General Electric by discontinuing the practice of issuing quarterly earnings guidance.[22]

The problem is that bank credit has played an increasingly intrusive rather than productive role in recent centuries. To cap matters, it has become outright parasitic in organizing today's leveraged buyouts (LBOs), creating computerized credit default swaps, arranging tax-avoidance money laundering, and lobbying for tax subsidy for debt financing—to be paid by imposing austerity on the economy at large. At the end of this road lies bankruptcy for companies, wipe-out of their pension plans (beyond the ability of the Pension Benefit Guarantee Corp. to pick up the pieces, given its reticence to levy risk premiums proportional to risk), and finally bank insolvency as debt deflation shrinks the economy and forces borrowers to default. At that point the banks demand public bailouts at taxpayer expense, shifting bad private-sector debts onto the public balance sheet. So entire economies are crippled even more. The bankers' last act is to take what bailout money they can and run. This is

---

[22] Martin Lipton, Jay W. Lorsch and Theodore N. Mirvis, "Schumer's Shareholder Bill Misses the Mark," *Wall Street Journal*, May 12, 2009.

what they did in QE II in summer 2011, reportedly sending the entire $800 billion in new Federal Reserve credit abroad in foreign-currency interest rate arbitrage.

The "internal contradiction" in financialization is that while it "extracts value" from companies for the raiders, the debt that it creates raises the break-even cost of production. So debt-leveraging an industrial company has a similar effect to taxing it more, or raising wage levels: unless it has monopoly power, it is priced out of the market.

> The internal contradiction in financialization is that while it extracts "value" from companies for the raiders, the debt that this creates raises the break-even cost of production. So debt-leveraging an industrial company has a similar effect to taxing it more, or raising wage levels: unless it has monopoly power, it is priced out of the market.

There is only one way left to continue: to globalize the financialization process, spreading the tactic to other countries so that everyone's cost of production rises as industrial firms across the world are loaded down with debt to enrich a financial overclass. This is what is occurring today. But it is a dangerous tactic. Other countries may resist. And by promoting equity rather than debt financing, these economies will out-compete the more debt-ridden, financialized economies. Without a mutual financial suicide pact at this point, the tendency toward global free trade will be blocked.

10

PRIVATIZING SOCIAL SECURITY TO RESCUE WALL STREET

From the time he took office in 2001, a major economic initiative of George W. Bush was to privatiye Social Security, formerly the "third rail" of American politics. This was a difficult sell after the dot.com bubble crashed, demonstrating that the stock market could plunge as well as soar—and also showing that Wall Street's money managers were not society's most honest citizens. But egged on by Alan Greenspan at the Federal Reserve and Wall Street campaign contributors, the new president's drive pushed toward a peak in 2005.

Given that the maneuver was both stupid and unnecessary, one must ask why the pretense over the past decade that Social Security is a clear and present danger. Indeed,why has President Obama picked up his predecessor's drive to steer FICA wage withholding into the stock and bond market with even more urgency? Why is it a problem at all, given that the program's alleged deficiencies, if there are any, will not manifest themselves until at least 2018. This is not quite the same as worrying about the sun's eventual collapse into a black hole, but for most politicians a problem that lies thirteen years in the future is nearly the same thing. Clearly all is not what it seems.

Bush himself offered two reasons for his radical boldness. The first—that Social Security is "in crisis"—is easily dismissed. Government actuaries, backed by economists from across the political spectrum, insist there is no funding problem. The Social Security Administration will take in more money than it pays out for the next thirteen years (as of 2005, when this article was first published). It has built up a reserve of $1.8 trillion in interest-bearing Treasury bonds for the years after that; and any later shortfall can be covered easily by even a partial rollback of the Bush tax cuts for the rich.

Bush's second argument sounded more promising. If the American people would follow his plan, he said, they too could grow rich.[1]

---

[1] Bush's opponents noted a possible third reason, which is that he hoped to roll back the New Deal in favor of smaller government. No doubt Bush disliked the New Deal, but it is hard to envision taxing employees to send funds into the stock market as a small-government alternative. A federally mandated transfer of funds—whether it is from taxpayer pockets to Treasury bills, as with Social Security, or from taxpayer pockets to the stock market, as under Bush's proposed changes—is still a federally mandated transfer of funds.

The way the system works now, the government withholds 13.2 percent of your paycheck, up to $120,000 in annual income. In return, it promises to provide a monthly payment—a pension—from the time subscribers turn sixty-two until the time they die. The Bush and Obama administrations' alternative remains somewhat nebulous, but what is clear in all the variations presented thus far, employees and employers will be able to put some of the wage withholding into the stock market, in the form of "personal savings accounts."

The Only Way for the Stock Market to Grow Is to Steer More Pension Savings into It

Vice President Dick Cheney described the benefits of these personal savings accounts in January. His example was a young woman who put away $1,000 every year for forty years. The Social Security Administration currently puts her money into Treasury bills, which at present return about 2 percent, so in forty years that investment would have returned about $61,000. Not too bad. "But if she invested the money in the stock market," Cheney said, "earning even its lowest historical rate of return, she would earn more than double that amount—$160,000. If the individual earned the average historical stock market rate of return, she would have more than $225,000—or nearly four times the amount to be expected from Social Security."[2]

That's a lot of math. Cheney's main point was that an upbeat assessment of the stock market—about 7.5 percent annually over forty years, by his reckoning—would easily exceed the 2 percent offered by Treasury bills. There is no arguing that $225,000 is more than $61,000.

On the other hand, it is not as if you get a lump sum from the Social Security Administration when you retire. The woman Cheney cited could have ended up taking in much more than $61,000 if she lived long enough, but the average annual payment to retirees today is about $11,000. Or she could die on her sixty-second birthday. Like any other investment—or any other form of insurance, for that matter—Social Security is somewhat of a gamble. But then so is the stock market. By Cheney's estimation, however, today's stock market is a much better bet. "Over time," he concluded, "the securities markets are the best, safest way to build substantial personal savings."

---

[2] Any relationship between the solvency of Social Security and the prospect of these personal accounts is purely rhetorical. Just before Bush's 2005 State of the Union address a reporter asked a "senior administration official" at a background briefing whether it was accurate to say that personal savings accounts themselves would have "no effect whatsoever on the solvency issue." The surprisingly candid response was, yes—"that's a fair inference." Toward the end of his tenure in 2008, Bush admitted that Social Security holdingswere only an accounting book entry on the Treasury, not actually real.

That is the argument, anyway. The stock market is the main chance in America, and Bush and Obama want to let all of us in on the action. The one sure mark of a con, though, is the promise of free money. In fact, the *only* way the stock market is going to grow is if we the people put a lot more of our money into it. What Bush and Obama seek to manufacture is a new stock market boom—or, more accurately, a bubble—bankrolled by the last safe pile of cash in America today. Their plan is a Ponzi scheme, in which Social Security itself is playing the role of the last sucker to join the game before it goes the waz of the real estate bubble.

Retirement savings are by far the most important source of money on Wall Street. The Federal Reserve Board reports that private and public retirement accounts, not including Social Security, had assets of $10 trillion at the end of 2003. Nearly half of that, $4.7 trillion, was held in stocks. By way of comparison, the total value of all domestic stocks listed on NASDAQ, the American Stock Exchange, and the New York Stock Exchange at the end of 2003 was about $14.2 trillion.

In the past, few retirement dollars found their way to Wall Street. IRAs and 401(k)s had yet to be invented, and few companies offered private pension plans of any kind. In 1950, General Motors—then, as now, among the largest employers on earth—began to change that with a new form of compensation. The company would withhold money from paychecks, much like the Social Security Administration was doing, and add money of its own to build up a reserve to pay retirees many decades into the future. Generally called a "defined benefit" plan, the scheme guaranteed retirees a specific (defined) monthly payment until they died.

Other giants of American industry soon followed, and the funds grew quickly. In most of them, at least half the money was put into the stock market. Workers thus would gain, at least in theory, a stake in the prosperity of their company, building loyalty to management while also providing companies with a captive source of credit—their own workforce. All of that new cash contributed to the bull market of the 1950s.

Companies Have Not Put Away Enough Money to Pay Retirees What They Are Owed

C alling this process "pension-fund socialism," management philosopher Peter Drucker hailed it as the most positive social development of the twentieth century, because it would at last merge the interests of labor and capital. Louis O. Kelso and Mortimer J. Adler wrote a book called *The Capitalist Manifesto* announcing that a new epoch of harmony between workers and owners was at hand, because soon all workers would be owners of Employee

Stock Ownership Plans—ESOPs, which Drucker warned could be wiped out as almost half were loaned to their employer companies that went bankrupt. The most notorious recent example is the Chicago *Tribune*'s ESOP, which Sam Zell used to pay the creditors who backed his leveraged buyout of the company, wiping out employee savings in 2011.

From the outset, many companies used retirement reserves to buy their own stocks, bidding up their share price and allowing them to take over other firms on favorable terms, especially as mergers and acquisitions gained momentum in the 1960s. The problem was that when companies went bankrupt—especially small firms—the collapse also wiped out the pension funds invested in those companies. Employees of such companies found themselves not only out of work but stripped of the money they thought was being saved up for their retirement.

Congress moved to limit such behavior by obliging corporate pension funds to be run by arm's-length trustees, although employees were still permitted (and often encouraged) to keep their pensions in the stock of their employers. To further protect workers, Congress created the Pension Benefit Guarantee Corporation (PBGC) in 1974. All corporate pension plans were required to buy federal insurance, through the PBGC, to protect workers in the event of a failed investment scheme or corporate bankruptcy. The plans were still prone to risk, but at least the pensions would be backed by the government and workers could feel secure about their retirement.[3]

Most companies now offer their employees a broad array of mutual funds instead of just their own stock. In itself this is good common-sense investing practice, and it also protects fund managers from charges of scheming. The other result of this practice is that workers' fortunes are now tied not just to their own companies but to the market as a whole.

Which is where and how we come to both the problem and the scam. While fears regarding the solvency of Social Security are unwarranted, many corporate pension plans—the ones that have been so important in bankrolling the stock-market rise of the past few decades—are themselves threatening to go bust, taking their parent companies down with them. The financial rot already has begun to seep into the airline and steel industries, and the auto sector may be next.

General Motors reported in 2005 that its pension obligations added $675 to the cost of every vehicle it produced. The company had to be rescued after trying to shift its debts to employees at its auto parts plants by spinning them

---

[3] Although as former employees of Enron and WorldCom recently learned, the price of demonstrating loyalty still can be quite steep.

off into a separate company, Delphi, that duly went bust. In 2009 the PBGC took over Delphi's pension plan at a cost of $6.2 billion rather than taking the shortfall from its parent, GM. This bailout pushed the PBGC some $33.5 billion into deficit in 2009, raising the specter of it itself needing a taxpayer bailout to meet its longterm pension guarantees.

The shortfalls were not just a matter of bad luck. For quite a few years now, companies simply haven't been putting away enough money to pay retirees what they are owed. The PBGC estimates that the underfunding of traditional defined-benefit plans, for instance, deepened by $100 billion in 2004, to a total of $450 billion. The problem was created by fund managers and CFOs who believed—or at least pretended to believe—that pension reserves could grow at fantastic rates of return forever. Milliman USA, a benefits consulting firm, reports on the assumed rates of return on pension investments at the hundred largest firms in America. How high did these companies bet? In 2000 and 2001, the median projected rate of return was 9.5 percent. In 2002 it was 9.25 percent. And in 2003 it was 8.55 percent. It has remained at an unrealistic 8 percent fantasy level for the past few years, as of 2011.

The Choice between Living up to Their Pension Promises or Reporting Higher Earnings

These are wildly optimistic projections, even by Dick Cheney's standards. Already in 2004 the *Financial Times* noted that they conflict not only with present reality but with warnings from such mainstream investment experts as Peter Bernstein, Jeremy Siegel and Jeremy Grantham that "we have entered a low-return environment" and that as a result many investors are expecting long-term returns closer to 7 percent or 5 percent. By 2011 there was question as to whether much return could be made at all! Even the rates being forecast seem overly exuberant, given that the top hundred corporate pension funds earned an average annual investment return of just 1.3 percent between the end of 1999 and the end of 2003.[4] And hedge funds have been going out of business at an alarming rate.

At the beginning of 2001, IBM proposed that it would earn $6.3 billion on pension-fund assets of $61 billion—about 10 percent. This was an astonishing demonstration of confidence given that IBM had earned only $1.2 billion on those assets the previous year. IBM actually went on to lose $4 billion in 2001. Barely daunted, the company's managers predicted a 9.5 percent return in 2002. They lost another $7 billion. In 2003 they predicted a return of $6 bil-

---

[4] A three-year Treasury bill purchased at the end of 1999 would have returned 6 percent. By 2011 they yielded only 2 percent.

lion, and—as the market began to recover—they at last beat their prediction, by $4.4 billion. The result of this "recovery" is that IBM's pension-fund assets have plummeted by more than $1 billion after George W. Bush took office. Nonetheless, corporate fund managers across America remained optimistic even as the real estate buble crashed the stock market in 2008–09.

Such errors in judgment are seldom accidental. In pretending that their funds could generate high returns, managers sought a real—albeit short-term—advantage. *Fiction paid. The faster companies projected their funds to grow, the less they had to set aside to pay their retirees.* The resulting lower set-asides allowed them to report higher earnings, thereby driving up the price of the company's own stock to "create shareholder value." Faced with a choice between living up to their pension promises or reporting higher net earnings, companies simply decided not to live up to their employee agreements. Plans with more realistic projected rates were deemed "overfunded" and emptied out.

Such practice is not one that can be sustained for forty years. It is a Ponzi scheme, in which present profits are paid for by the promise of future stock market gains. At some point retirees are going to want the money they are owed. The last few years have seen the results of these broken promises in the form of lawsuits, bankruptcy, and ultimately retirees being forced to live on far less than they were promised. In the end it is the PBGC that pays when the plans go bust. Here, however, the problem deepens considerably, because picking up the total bill for the corporate sector's underfunding would bankrupt the PBGC.

Last November it reported that although it had "operated for several years with virtually no claims," the end of the stock-market boom has given way to "a period of record-breaking claims." As recently as 2001, the PBGC had a surplus of $8 billion, but a series of bankruptcy cases pushed it $23 billion into deficit by 2004, a year in which it took in only $1.5 billion in premiums. The PBGC needed more than fifteen years just to make up that deficit, with new claims arriving all the while. It proposed that companies follow more realistic accounting rules and pay premiums that reflect the true risks of their underfunding. It also asked for stricter limits on the ability of companies to escape their pension debts by declaring bankruptcy.[5]

---

[5] Reasonable as these requests seem, they were opposed by the same corporate managers who created the mess in the first place. In 2004 the American Benefits Council, the lobbying organization of pension-fund managers, persuaded regulators to further loosen the requirement that companies estimate realistic rates of return.

Something Has to Give: Either the Hopes of Retirees or Those of the Stock Market

Without such changes the PBGC will be forced into bankruptcy and the government will have to bail it out. That could cost as much as $95 billion, according to the Congressional Research Service. At that point only today's profits would remain private. The losses will be fully socialized.[6]

Barring some sudden influx of capital, something has to give—either the hopes of retirees or the hopes of the stock market. Unfortunately, this is a zero-sum game in which many Americans are on both sides at once. Higher pension set-asides will diminish corporate earnings. Lower earnings will lead to dividend cuts and job losses. Low dividends and high employment will decrease the demand for stocks—leading to further declines in the ability of pension funds to pay retirees, with more defaults all around. Workers, retirees, investors and taxpayers thus find themselves yoked to the fortunes of the financial managers who created this fictitious economy.

This is not the happy pension-fund socialism that Peter Drucker had in mind, in which worker-owners would share risks and rewards alike as they created the goods and services demanded by a thriving marketplace. What actually has happened is that companies have made a great effort not merely to share the risk, but to off-load it onto the backs of their employees, the government, and taxpayers in general.

This phenomenon of risk rolling downward can be seen most clearly in the move by many companies from defined-benefit programs—in which employees are guaranteed a specific retirement payment, based on their salary history—to "defined-contribution plans," in which workers know nothing else except how much is being deducted from their paychecks. The payout rate is decided by how well the stock market performs. This shifts the risk onto employees, while freeing up more revenue for their employers and generating rich commissions for money managers. The risk flows down the economic scale while the cash flows up. No wonder the economy is polarizing between the top 1% and the bottom 99%!

Given the widespread problems confronting pensions outside the embrace of the federal government, the past decade would seem an odd time for the administration to campaign to privatize Social Security. Why would anyone want to invest America's last line of pension defense in so perilous a market? Are Bush, Obama and their Wall Street-nominated advisers and lobbyists unaware of the odds?

---

[6] That estimate is probably low. The precedent is the bailout of the Federal Savings and Loan Insurance Corporation, which ended up costing taxpayers over $200 billion.

Probably not. So they must have a particular aim in mind—a new money grab. Presumably they believe that some kind of market recovery is needed to rescue not only the PBGC but also the pension funds, stock market, and for that matter the political fortunes of the ruling party—that what is needed, in fact, was a Bush boom (which collapsed in 2008) and prospectivelz an Obama boom. This would allow the United States to "grow our way out of trouble," as we have done so many times before.

But where will the funds come from to bid up stock prices? The national savings rate is nearly zero, because most personal discretionary income—like that of most companies—is absorbed in paying debt service. Previously the Fed could have flooded the capital markets with credit to lower interest rates and thereby spur a bond and stock-market bubble. But interest rates are at their lowest since the 1950s. They can go no lower.[7]

There is only one other place to turn. The new flow of funds into the stock market will have to come from labor itself, just as it did back in the 1950s. Social Security is the greatest plum, so large as to virtually guarantee a boom.

History's Most Famous Bubbles Have All Been Sponsored by Governments

Talk of bubbles has become popular in recent years, but most discussions miss the key point. Although optimism is inherent in the human spirit, it rarely effloresces into the kind of frenzy necessary to float a bubble without help from the government. In fact, many of history's most famous bubbles have been sponsored by governments in order to get out of debt. Britain, in 1711, persuaded bondholders to swap their bonds for stocks in the South Sea Company, which was expected to get rich off the growth industry of its day, the African slave trade. By the time the South Sea bubble collapsed, the government had indeed paid off its war debt—and speculators were left holding worthless "growth sector" stocks. In 1716, John Law organized France's Mississippi bubble along the same lines, retiring France's public debt by selling shares to create slave-stocked plantations in the Louisiana territories. It worked, for a while.

The U.S. government is now attempting to run the same kind of scam. First Bush and then Obama—or at least their Wall Street campaign backers— would like to persuade Social Security claimants to exchange the security of U.S. Treasury bonds for a chance to buy growth stocks on which a much higher

---

[7] After World War II interest rates rose to a peak, in 1980, of more than 21 percent. The result was nearly four decades of capital losses on bonds—whose interest rates are fixed at the time you buy them-—and a steady rise in stocks. Since 1980, however, interest rates have fallen back, creating the greatest bond-market boom in history.

return is hoped for. No modern blue-sky venture comparable to the South Sea or Mississippi companies is needed. The stock market itself has become a bubble, borne aloft from the burden of generating actual goods and services by a constant flow of new retirement dollars.

There is no denying that channeling trillions of Social Security dollars into the stock market would produce short-term gains. But once this money is spent, the markets are likely to retreat. That is what happens after a financial bubble. Then we will be right back where we are today, only much the poorer and with no guaranteed pension system for elderly Americans—who will, of course, need guaranteed pensions more than ever as they watch their stock holdings continue to shed value. Indeed, many other countries are just now recovering from their own dismal experiences with what Augusto Pinochet and Margaret Thatcher called "labor capitalism" and Bush calls, with no apparent irony, an "ownership society."[8] President Obama simply calls it rescuing the economz from a fictitious revenue shortfall created by his retention of the Bush tax cuts for his major campaign contributors.

In the 1930s, Keynes urged governments to run budget deficits in order to increase the economy's spending power on goods and services. His point of reference was the "real economy"—the economy of production and consumption, investment in capital and in the labor to operate that capital. Whereas he spoke of governments priming the pump with public spending programs to get domestic investment and employment going, Mr. Obama designated his Deficit Reduction Commission and later his Congressional Super-Committee of 12 to prime the stock-market pump with Social Security contributions.[9] It is the next natural step from our real economy to the economy of dreams. But that is President Obama's stock in trade. He is a better shill for Wall Street than his predecessor, being able to neutralize Democratic Congressional opposition and that of his constituency in the lower 99 percent that he delivers to his campaign contributors. That is what a politician does these days.

---

[8] In Chile, conglomerates invested employee paycheck withholding in their own stocks or in loans to affiliates whose value then was wiped out in financially engineered bankruptcies. The problem got so bad by 1980 that the government turned over management to American and other international firms. Most discussions of Chile's "success story" choose to start at the trough, right after these fraudulent bankruptcies, which gives a steep trough-to-peak tilt for the rate of return that is claimed to be normal. The equivalent for America would be to start a new trend right after a 1929-type stock-market crash. When one starts from a peak, such as today, it is much harder to give the statistical impression that a fantastic takeoff is in store.

[9] The genius of recent administrations, Democratic and Republican, has been to transfer inflation to the stock market—that is, to the prices of stocks and bonds instead of to the prices of labor and production. Real wages today are lower than they were in 1964.

11

SAVING, ASSET-PRICE INFLATION AND DEBT DEFLATION

The National Income and Product Accounts (NIPA) measure the circular flow between production, consumption and new investment. Employers earn profits which they invest in capital goods, and they pay their employees who spend their income to buy the goods they produce (Fig. 1).

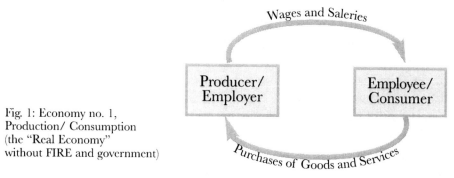

Fig. 1: Economy no. 1,
Production/ Consumption
(the "Real Economy"
without FIRE and government)

Production and consumption represent only part of the economy. Governments levy taxes and user fees, which they spend and sometimes run budget surpluses (the government's way of saving) that drain income from the economy's flow of spending. But more often, governments inject spending power by running deficits (financed by running into debt). The NIPA measure these fiscal removals or injections of revenue by taxing and spending (Fig. 2).

Fig. 2: Economy no. 1,
with government

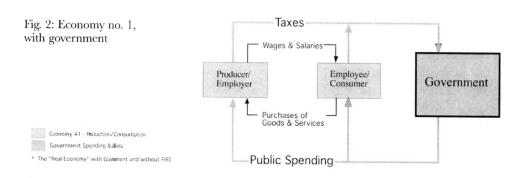

A half century ago economists anticipated that rising incomes and living standards would lead to higher savings. The most influential view of the economic future was that of John Maynard Keynes. Addressing the problems of the Great Depression in 1936, his General Theory of Employment, Interest, and Money warned that people would save relatively more as their incomes rose. Spending on consumer goods would tail off, slowing the growth of markets, new investment and employment.

This view of the saving function — the propensity to save out of wages and profits — saw saving break the chain of payments simply by not being spent. The modern dynamics of saving — and the debts in which savings are invested — are more complex. Most savings are lent out. Nearly all new investment in capital goods and buildings comes from retained business earnings, not from savings that pass through financial intermediaries. Under these conditions, higher personal saving rates are reflected in higher indebtedness.

Since World War II, in fact, each new business upswing has started with a higher set of debt ratios. A rising proportion of savings find their counterpart more in other peoples' debts rather than being used to finance new direct investment. The net savings rate has fallen, even though debt ratios and gross savings have increased.

To understand these dynamics it is necessary to view economies as composed of two distinct systems. The largest system is that of land, monopoly rights and financial claims that yield *rentier* returns in the form of interest, other financial fees, rents and monopoly gains (which can be viewed either as economic rents or super-profits). These returns far overshadow the profits earned on investing in capital goods and employing labor to produce goods and provide actual services. This reflects the fact that the value of rentier property and financial securities far exceeds that of physical capital in the form of factories and machinery, buildings, or research and development.

Keynes was not careful to analyze how the savings functions associated with financial securities and *rentier* claims — and the property rights backing them as collateral — differed from personal savings functions. Some help, however, is provided by the NIPA, which break out the distinct flow of property and financial income that accrues to the FIRE sector, an acronym for Finance, Insurance and Real Estate.

To fill out the picture from the investor's vantage point, especially that of FIRE, it is necessary to recognize the increasingly important role played by capital gains rather than current earnings. The economy's wealthiest layers take their "total returns" primarily in the form of capital gains, not profit, interest or rental income.

No regular measures of capital gains are published, but they can be estimated on the basis of the Federal Reserve Board's balance-sheet data published
in Table Z of its annual Flow-of-Funds statistics on financial assets (stocks,
bonds and bank deposits and loans) and tangible assets (land, buildings and
capital goods). These statistics show that capital gains and the returns to property and finance — rent, interest and capital gains — far overshadow profits.

This distinction between the property and financial sectors and the rest of
the economy is not immediately apparent, however. NIPA statistics follow
modern "value-free" economics in conflating all forms of current income
(excluding capital gains) into the single category of "earnings." Interest, rent,
insurance and financial fees are treated as payments for current services, not
claims by property, credit or monopoly power that find no counterpart in direct
outlays.

These forms of revenue are not inherently necessary expenses of production, but are best viewed as being institutional in character. Returns to finance
and property may be viewed as transfer payments rather than as actual costs
entailed by producing goods and services. This contrast makes the savings and
debt functions of these rentier sectors differ from those associated with the
wages and profits paid to labor and tangible capital investment (Fig. 3).

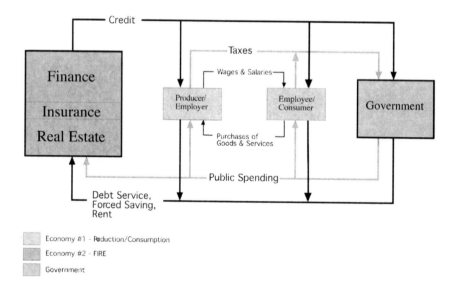

Fig. 3: Interaction of Economy no. 1, Economy no. 2 & Government

Monetary Considerations

Industry and agriculture, transport and power, and similar production and consumption expenditures account for less than 0.1 percent of the economy's flow of payments. The vast majority of transactions passing through the New York Clearing House and Fedwire are for stocks, bonds, packaged bank loans, options, derivatives and foreign-currency transactions. The entire stock-market value of many high-flying companies now changes hands in a single day, and the average holding time for currency trades has shrunk to just a few minutes.

The value of these financial transactions each day exceeds that of the entire annual U.S. national income. It therefore seems absurd to relate the money supply only to consumer and wholesale prices, excluding asset prices.

Today's Anomalies That Need to Be Explained

Today's world requires more variables to be analyzed. The (net) savings rate has moved in the opposite direction from what Keynes had anticipated. The NIPA report a zero-savings rate for the economy at large. If the recycled dollar holdings of foreign central banks are excluded, the domestic U.S. savings rate is a negative 2 percent. A time series of the *U.S. propensity to save* since 1945 shows a steady decline in (net) S/Y.

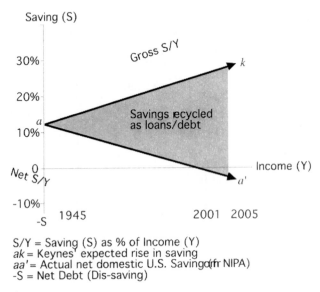

S/Y = Saving (S) as % of Income (Y)
ak = Keynes' expected rise in saving
aa' = Actual net domestic U.S. Saving (fr NIPA)
-S = Net Debt (Dis-saving)

* As reported in the National Income and Product Accounts (NIP).

Fig. 4: Actual Saving* vs. Keynes' Expected Saving

Despite a falling savings rate, however, the economy never has been flusher with savings and credit. The growth of savings, wealth and net worth is less and less the result of new direct investment in tangible capital formation, but rather the product of rising asset prices for real estate, stocks and bonds. In balance-sheet terms, gross savings are soaring while net savings are zero or negative.

This growth in net worth occurs despite the fact that most new saving is offset on the liabilities side of the balance sheet by growth in debt. The rise of net worth is the result of savings being lent to borrowers who bid up asset prices by using new loans and credit to buy property and securities, that is, wealth and financial claims on wealth.

> In balance-sheet terms, gross savings are soaring while net savings are zero or negative.

These features of today's economy appear to be an anomaly as compared to the formulae that Keynes traced out in 1936. Today's economy is best seen as a financial bubble, just the opposite of the deflationary Great Depression described by Keynes. Credit — and hence, debt — is being created to inflate the bubble rather than to finance direct capital formation. In this respect the banking and financial systems have become dysfunctional.

Monetary expansion and prices in the commodity and asset markets move asymmetrically. Today's asset-price inflation goes hand in hand with commodity-price stagnation and a deflation of labor's spending power. Upon closer examination this inverse relationship is not an anomaly. But the phenomenon shows that the savings problem has become more serious than Keynes feared, for reasons that he had little reason to discuss seventy years ago.

For one thing, the volume of savings compounds by being recycled into the creation of new interest-bearing debt as savers or financial institutions use their accrual of income, dividends and capital gains to buy more securities, make more loans or buy property rather than to spend this revenue on current output. The growing debt overhead — and the savings that form the balance-sheet counterpart to this debt — bears interest charges that divert income to debt service rather than being available for spending on consumption and direct investment.

The FIRE Sector in Relation to the Rest of the Economy

The institutions that distinguish one national economy from another are the property and financial institutions that steer saving and investment, and the public tax policies that shape markets. These policies determine the character of the FIRE sector. The largest and defining features of any economy are those of the property and financial sector, whose rent, interest, monopoly revenue and "capital" gains (most of which are real-estate gains) rise relative to overall national income.

Instead of examining these contrasting financial and fiscal policies, most economics texts concentrate on abstract technological production and consumption dimension of economic life. It is as if the property and financial dimension—tangible wealth and financial claims on property and income—lie somewhere on the far side of the moon, invisible to earth or at least wrapped in a cloak of invisibility.

When Keynes viewed individuals as saving a portion of the income they earned, he defined (S) as a function of income (Y) multiplied by the marginal propensity to save (*mps*, or simply *s*), so that $S = sY$. Keynes thus derived the savings function $s = S/Y$ for economies as a whole.

This formula does not acknowledge that financial institutions tend to save all their income. Furthermore, over time a rising proportion of this inflow of interest, dividends and rent is plowed back into new loans rather than invested in tangible capital formation.

Keynes recognized that wealthy individuals save a higher portion of their income as they earn more. He feared that as economies grew richer over time, the propensity to save would rise. But he did not describe corporate financial institutions as having a distinct propensity of their own to save all their interest and dividend receipts.

Today we can see that the problem with saving is not simply that it is "non-spending." A rising proportion of savings are lent out or invested in loans and securities, dividend-yielding stocks and rent-yielding properties, to become interest-bearing debts owed by the economy at large. These savings expand of their own accord as their interest receipts are recycled into new loans and other income-yielding assets, growing in an exponentially rising curve. This exponentially rising curve is that of compound interest, so that $S_t = S_{t-1}^{(1+i)}$, where i represents the rate of interest. Meanwhile, the growth of debt grows *pari passu*, as Keynes would have put it.

It thus is helpful to distinguish between the propensity to save (1) by labor and industrial firms out of income earned by producing goods and services, and (2) by the FIRE sector out of debt service and rental charges. Drawing this distinction requires that the economy itself be viewed as a combination of two separate parts, by separating the FIRE sector from the rest of the economy. I refer to these two sectors as (1) the production and consumption economy comprising fixed capital and labor, and (2) the economically larger property and financial sector receiving *rentier* income (defined to include financial "service" fees).

Although net saving does not increase in such cases, the volume of loanable funds expands. These funds are built up as interest, dividends and rents accrue to owners of securities and property. To the extent that these revenues accrue to large financial institutions — insurance companies, pension and mutual funds — the propensity to save such returns is nearly 100 percent. To be sure, bankers pay interest to their depositors while insurance and pension funds pay their policy holders. However, most of these interest and dividend accruals are left in accounts to accumulate. The result is an exponentially rising curve of savings at compound interest.

The idea of a propensity to consume is appropriate only for consumer income, not that of the financial, insurance and real estate (FIRE) sectors. Consumers, especially retirees, do indeed consume some part of their *rentier* income, but this is not true of institutional investors. Keynes recognized that the wealthiest income brackets have a high propensity to save, while less affluent brackets have a lower propensity. Today, the wealthiest 10 percent of the population holds most of the savings in every economy. The bottom 90 percent tend to be net debtors rather than net savers in today's highly financialized economies of North America and Europe.

Additional saving is created when banks create credit. Most finds its counterpart in the new debts that borrowers owe, so that the net saving rate is not affected. Keynes concerned himself almost entirely with net saving, not gross savings and their counterpart debt.

When Keynes defined saving as equal to investment, he did not emphasize the distinction between direct investment in tangible capital goods and loans that became the debts of the economy's non-financial sectors. Failure to draw this distinction led to an ambiguity between gross or net saving. National income accounts define saving net of the growth in debt, so that no increase in net saving occurs when savings are lent out.

This condition has become more and more the case for the U.S. economy in recent decades. Today's propensity to save is less than zero as the economy is running into debt faster than it is building up new savings. Keynes did not address this possibility, and indeed it was not a pressing concern back in 1936 when he wrote his *General Theory*.

Modern national income accounts also combine the wages and profits that labor and industry earn with the interest and rent that finance and property receive. The basic idea is that providing land, the radio spectrum, subsoil minerals and even monopoly goods supplies a "service" alongside the goods and services produced by labor and capital goods. But it is equally possible to view finance and property not as "factors of production" producing services that earn interest, financial fees and rent, but as receiving transfer payments or what Henry George called "value from obligation." This distinction enables the classical distinction between "earned" and "unearned" income to be preserved in a way that I believe Keynes would have appreciated in view of his call for "euthanasia of the *rentier*."

> **M**ost lending and credit creation are directed into the capital markets via borrowers who buy property or financial securities

Nearly all new fixed capital formation is financed out of retained business earnings, not out of bank borrowing. Banks finance sales, foreign trade, consumer debt and the purchase of property already in place, but hardly ever have they taken the risk of financing new direct investment. Their time horizon is short-term, not long-term.

This chapter proposes a model to integrate the analysis of asset-price inflation with debt deflation and Say's Law. Viewing savings and debt in their institutional context, it relates the behavior of banks and institutional investors to the dynamics of asset-price inflation and debt deflation. A central theme is that most lending and credit creation are directed into the capital markets via borrowers who buy property or financial securities. As the economy's assets are loaded down with debt and its interest charges, this credit growth extracts interest payments that divert revenue away from current demand for goods and services. That is why asset-price inflation usually involves debt deflation. The deflationary effect may be mitigated by lowering interest rates, as occurred in the United States during 1994–2004. The debt/savings overhead can rise without extracting a higher flow of interest payments as interest rates approach their nadir (about 1 percent today).

Keynes viewed saving as causing insufficient market demand to provide full employment. The long-term threat seemed to be that as economies grew richer, people would save more, disrupting the circular flow of spending between producers and their employees as consumers. What was not emphasized was that as savings were recycled into loans, economies would polarize between creditors and debtors.

Today the net savings rate has fallen to zero, and the major factor impairing effective demand is the diversion of revenue to service the economy's debt overhead. Paying interest and principal reduces the disposable income that debtors have available to spend on goods and services, while the financial institutions that receive this revenue do not spend it on goods and services. They lend out their receipts to enable the buyers to purchase assets that already exist.[1]

> Today's problem of inadequate consumer demand and capital investment lies on the liabilities (debt) side of the balance sheet, not on the asset (saving) side.

The National Income and Product Accounts (NIPA) define the amortization of debt principal as saving. Most of these repayments are lent out to new borrowers, including corporate business whose balance sheets have reached what Hyman Minsky called the Ponzi stage of fragility—the point at which the debt overhead is carried by debtors borrowing the interest charges that are growing exponentially. In this respect "debts cause saving."

Today's problem of inadequate consumer demand and capital investment lies on the liabilities (debt) side of the balance sheet, not on the asset (saving) side. Keynes anticipated that as economies grew and incomes rose, a rising proportion of S/Y would reduce consumption, leading to overproduction if employers did not cut back their own direct investment. This line of thought reflected the psychological theorizing of British marginal utility analysis rather than a financial view of the dynamics that determined the buildup of savings.

---

[1] Keynes noted that Malthus pointed out that landlords helped contribute to aggregate demand by spending their rental income on hiring servants. But banks lend to service producers and other labor, increasing the volume of debt.

Keynes's discussion of savings led him to re-examine Say's Law, which described circular flow of spending between producers and consumers. Under normal conditions producers would hire workers, who would spend their wages on buying what they produced. This was the basic meaning of the phrase "supply creates its own demand." But savings threatened to interrupt this circular flow by diverting the purchasing power of consumers away from the demand for goods and services, and that of employers away from the purchase of capital goods.

Keynes found saving to be the main culprit for the economic slow-down of the Great Depression on the ground that it led to reduced market demand, deterring new direct investment and hence slowing the growth of employment. But in today's U.S.-centered bubble economy the problem has become more complicated. To the extent that savings are lent out (rather than invested out of retained earnings to purchase capital goods, erect buildings and create other tangible means of production), they divert future income away from consumption and investment to pay debt service. In this respect the growth of savings in financial form (that is, in ways other than new direct capital formation) adds to the debt overhead and hence contributes to debt deflation. This is what occurs with nearly all the savings intermediated and lent out or reinvested by the banks, insurance companies and other financial institutions.

Keynes did not devote much attention to the accrual of interest on past savings. His *General Theory* was ambiguous with regard to the specific forms that savings might take. They were identified simply as investment, so that on the macroeconomic plane, $S = I$. The implication by many Keynesians today is that savings actually cause investment. The reality is that savings not invested directly in new means of production were invested indirectly in stocks, bonds and real estate. Investment in securities and property already in existence had no positive employment effects. But there was not much growth in either borrowing or this kind of indirect investment back when the *General Theory* was published. The tendency was for savings to sit idle, as did much of the labor force.

The Self-Expanding Growth of Savings through Their Accrual of Interest

The financial system exists in a symbiosis with the "real" economy. Each system has its own set of growth dynamics. Financial systems tend to grow exponentially at compound interest. The cumulative value of savings grows through a dynamic that Keynes had little reason to analyze in the 1930s—what Richard Price described as the "geometric" growth of a penny invested at 5 percent at the time of Jesus's birth, growing to a solid sphere of gold extending from the Sun out beyond the orbit of Jupiter by his day (1776). He contrasted this "geometric" growth of savings invested at compound interest to the merely "arithmetic" growth of a similar sum invested at simple interest. This was the metaphor that Malthus adopted to describe the growth of human populations in contrast to the means of subsistence.[2]

Many people saved money back in the time of Jesus. But nobody has obtained savings amounting to anywhere near a solid sphere of gold. The reason is that savings that are invested in debt tend to stifle economies, causing downturns that wipe out the debts and savings together in a convulsion of bankruptcy. This was what happened to the Roman Empire, and on a smaller scale it has characterized business cycles for the past two centuries. Yet this dynamic rarely has been related to the bankruptcy phenomenon although it is a key factor countering the growth of savings.

Economies do grow faster than "arithmetically," but not "geometrically." Their typical growth pattern is that of an S-curve, tapering off over the course of the business cycle. The exponential growth of savings and debts thus tends chronically to exceed that of the "real" economy. Unless interest rates decline, the debt burden will divert income away from spending on goods and services, turning the economy downward (Fig. 5 & Fig. 6).

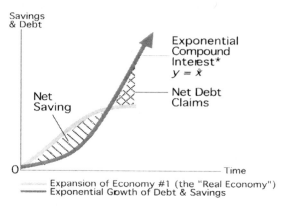

Fig. 5. How the Rise in Debt Overhead Slows Down the Business Cycle.

The *General Theory* recognized saving as arising out of current income, not as growing through the compounding of interest, doubling and redoubling at compound interest by their own inertia. They accrue interest independently of the course of incomes when invested in bonds or left in savings accounts, as

---

[2] I review how economists have treated this phenomenon in "The Mathematical Economics of Compound Interest: A Four-Thousand Year Overview," *Journal of Economic Studies* 27 (2000): 344–363.

well as accruing dividends if invested in stocks, or rental income if invested in property. This is especially true of "forced savings" in the form of paycheck withholding for Social Security, pension and retirement accounts, along with insurance policies segregated in a way that makes them unavailable for current spending.

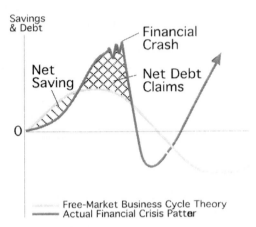

Fig. 6: Financial Crisis Pattern versus Business Cycle

-------- Free-Market Business Cycle Theory
———— Actual Financial Crisis Pattern

Not being limited by the course of income or the ability to pay, the exponential growth of savings tends to exceed growth of the real economy. This is what occurs when economies are loaded down with debts, which could equally well be thought of as the savings overhead that is lent out. Rising savings on the asset side of the balance sheet connote a rising debt overhead on the liabilities side. In this case saving does not necessarily reflect an increase of productive powers and the means of production, nor does it tend to employ labor. Rather, the debt service that results from lending out savings tends to shrink markets and employment.

It should be noted that while the financial sector represents itself as providing credit to consumers and producers, it also absorbs income by charging interest, in amounts that are as large as the entire loan principal every doubling period—seven years at 10 percent interest, 13 years at 5 percent. Ultimately the financial sector extracts revenue from the economy. That is why it is in business, after all: to "make money from money."

Money cannot be made from money, of course. It is itself sterile, as Aristotle noted long ago. But it can charge interest from the rest of the economy that does perform the work. Levying interest, rent and other property and financial charges is not to be confused with making money through labor or capital investment. The perception of classical economics that the property and financial system is different has been lost in today's economic thought.

The Growth of Net Worth through Capital Gains

The cumulative volume of savings also grows through a dynamic that Keynes had little reason to analyze in the 1930s: capital gains. Property and financial securities tend to appreciate in price over time. The main cause of this price appreciation is that the physical volume of assets grows slowly, while the financial volume of loanable funds grows exponentially.

Let us return for a moment to Richard Price's example of a penny saved at the time of Jesus being worth a sphere of gold extending from the sun out to Jupiter. Few investors buy gold, as it does not yield an income. The largest investment—and the most heavily debt-financed asset these days—is land. More credit does not expand the volume of land, which is fixed, but it does raise its market price. A rising volume of savings is channeled to buy a fixed supply of land. The financial system thus creates capital gains as the finite volume of property and supply of buildings and financial securities expands more slowly than the potentially infinite volume of loanable funds.

Keynes did not anticipate that savings would be channeled in a way that bid up asset prices for securities and property without funding tangible capital for-mation. In the 1930s net worth was built up mainly by saving, not by asset-price inflation such as is occurring today. In traditional Keynesian terms, revenue or credit spent on buying property in place represented hoarding, not investment.

Homeowners and investors imagine themselves growing richer as prices rise for their assets. Their net worth rises without their having to save. How-ever, this rise tends to require more income set aside to pay debt service on the loans taken out to buy their property. Credit lent out in this way does not increase consumption and direct investment. It creates debts whose carrying charges shrink markets. Savings and debts rise together, so that there is no increase in net saving.

New saving does occur as financial institutions recycle the receipts of debt service into new loans, whose carrying charges absorb yet more future income. The result is that *gross* savings (and hence, indebtedness) rise relative to national income. Stated another way, saving for many homeowners takes the form of paying off their mortgages. This is not the same thing as hoarding (in Keynes's sense), but it plays much the same function, as it is not available for spending on current output.

As savings rise and are lent out, debt service absorbs more income. But the net economic surplus available to service these savings—by paying interest and dividends on the debts and securities in which they are invested—tends not to keep pace with their stipulated debt service. This debt problem there-fore plays the deflationary economic role that Keynes attributed to savings.

How Asset-Price Inflation Aggravates Economic Polarization

K eynes favored inflation as eroding the burden of debt. He saw inflation as the line of least political resistance to wiping out the economy's debt burden. His idea was that inflation would leave more income available for consumption and for new direct investment. But asset-price inflation works in a different way. Instead of eroding the purchasing power of wealth relative to commodities and labor, it increases property prices without increasing consumer prices or wages. At least this has been the pattern since 1980. Wealth disparities have increased even more than have disparities among income brackets. The net worth for the wealthiest 10 or 20 percent of the population has soared, while the rest of the economy has fallen more deeply into debt and many of its gains have turned out to be short-term.

Keynes recognized that rich and poor income and wealth brackets had differing marginal propensities to save. But today's financial polarization has gone beyond anything he anticipated, or what anyone else anticipated back in the 1930s, or for that matter even in the 1950s.

Long before the *General Theory*, economists recognized that wealthy people did not expand their consumption in keeping with their income growth. The image of widows and orphans living off their interest was relevant only for a small part of the economy. Rentiers always have tended to save their income and reinvest it in the financial and property markets. This occurs also with savings deposits, which banks lend out or invest directly in financial securities. Most of the interest and dividends credited to savers thus is left to grow by being lent out or plowed back into indirect securities and property investment, increasing asset prices.

The ability to get an easy ride from the resulting asset-price inflation — coupled with an easy access to credit and favorable tax treatment — prompts investors to take their returns in the form of capital gains rather than current income. In real estate, the economy's largest sector, property owners use their rental income to pay interest on the credit borrowed to buy properties, leaving no taxable earnings at all. The same phenomenon characterizes the corporate sector, where equity has been retired for bonds and bank loans since 1980. Ambitious CEOs, managers of privatized public enterprises and corporate raiders have bought entire companies with debt-financed leveraged buyouts. Interest charges have absorbed corporate earnings, leaving little remaining for new capital investment. The name of the game has become capital gains, which have been spurred more by downsizing and outsourcing than by new corporate hiring.

Prices for property, stock, and bonds have soared relative to wages, forcing home buyers to spend a rising multiple of their annual incomes to buy housing. Also rising has been the cost of acquiring companies relative to corporate profits as price/earnings ratios increase.

Capital gains make the inequality of wealth and property more extreme than income inequality. The wealthiest layer of the population derives its power from capital gains, while using its income to pay interest — as long as interest rates are less than the rate of asset-price inflation. The ratio of wealth and property has risen relative to the value of goods and services, wages and profits, while the debt overhead has grown proportionally.

Does Asset-Price Inflation "Crowd Out" New Direct Investment?

The FIRE sector has been expanding at the expense of the "real" economy. It drains revenue in the form of interest, rental income and monopoly profits, which are paid out increasingly as interest and financial fees. This triggers a fresh cycle of saving and re-lending by the FIRE sector itself, not so much by the rest of the economy. The more interest accrues in the hands of creditors, the faster their supply of loanable funds increases, thanks to the "magic of compound interest." This revenue is lent out and accrues new interest ("interest on interest"), which is recycled into yet new loans.

This growth of savings and loanable funds in the hands of financial institutions is lent out mainly to buy property in place and financial securities, not to fund tangible capital formation. This financial dynamic spurs asset-price inflation, which in turn reduces the incentive to invest directly in capital goods, because it is easier to make capital gains than to earn profits.

These developments have prompted investors to seek "total returns" — capital gains plus profits or earnings — rather than earnings alone. Under Federal Reserve Board Chairman Alan Greenspan as "Bubble Maestro" in the 1990s, stock prices for dot.com and internet companies soared without a foundation in earnings or dividend-paying ability. Balance-sheet maneuvering was decoupled from tangible investment in the "real" economy. Companies such as Enron prided themselves in not having any tangible assets at all, just a balance sheet of speculative contracts. People began to ask whether wealth could go on increasing in this way *ad infinitum*.

Keynes's analysis implied that the income "multiplier" (Y/S, or 1/mps) would increase as prosperity increased and people consumed a smaller portion of their income. What was being multiplied, however, was not national income — wages, profits and other earned income — but the volume of credit and hence the pace of capital gains in the asset markets.

Tax Policy and Financial Bubbles

Unlike the industrial sector, real estate does not report a profit—and hence, pays no income taxes. Property owners do pay state and local real estate taxes, to be sure, but they have been joined by the financial and insurance lobbies to shift local government budgets away from the land and onto the shoulders of labor, through income taxes, sales taxes and various user fees for municipal services hitherto provided as part of the basic economic needs and infrastructure.

Although land does not depreciate—that is, wear out and become obsolete—by far the bulk of depreciation tax credits are taken by the real estate sector. This is because the economic theory underlying tax obligations has become essentially fictitious. Each time a property is sold, the building is assumed to increase in value, rather than the land's site value generating the gain.

Nothing like this could happen in industry. Machinery wears out and becomes obsolete—think of computers and word processors bought a decade ago, or even three years ago. Technological progress reduces the value of physical capital in place. But the prosperity that progress brings increases the market price of land.

Keynes pointed to the desirability of preventing the diversion of income into the purchase of securities and property already in place. He hoped to restructure the stock market and financial system so as to direct savings and credit into tangible capital formation rather than speculation. He deplored the waste of human intelligence devoted merely to transferring property ownership rather than creating new means of production.

Today's financial markets have evolved in just the opposite direction from that advocated by Keynes. New savings and credit are channeled into loans to satisfy the rush to buy real estate, stocks and bonds for speculative purposes rather than into the funding of new direct investment and employment. Matters are aggravated by the fact that financial gains are taxed at a lower rate, thanks to the growing power of the financial sector's political lobbies. This prompts companies to use their revenue and go into debt to buy other companies (mergers and acquisitions) or real estate rather than to expand their means of production.

Going into debt to buy assets with borrowed funds experienced a quantum leap in the 1980s with the practice of financing leveraged buyouts with high-interest "junk" bonds. The process got underway when interest rates were still hovering near their all-time high of 20 percent in late 1980 and early 1981. Corporate raiding was led by the investment banking house of Drexel Burnham and its law firm, Skadden Arps. Their predatory activities required a loosening of America's racketeering (RICO) laws to make it legal to borrow funds to take over companies and repay creditors by emptying out their corporate treasuries and "overfunded" pension plans. New York's laws of fraudulent conveyance also had to be modified.

Tax laws promoted this debt leveraging. Interest was allowed to be counted as a tax-deductible expense, encouraging leveraged buyouts rather than equity financing or funding out of retained earnings. Depreciation of buildings and other assets was permitted to occur repeatedly, whenever a property was sold. This favored the real estate sector by making absentee-owned buildings and other commercial properties virtually exempt from the income tax. To top matters off, capital gains tax rates were reduced below taxes on the profits earned by direct investment. This diverted savings to fuel asset-price inflation. By the 1990s the process had become a self-feeding dynamic. The more prices rose for stocks and real estate, the more mortgage borrowing rose for homes and other property, while corporate borrowing soared for mergers and acquisition.

Meanwhile, the more gains being made off the bubble, the more powerful its beneficiaries grew. They turned their economic power into political power to lower taxes and deregulate speculative finance—along with fraud, corrupt accounting practices and the use of offshore tax-avoidance enclaves—even further. This caused federal, state and local budget deficits while shifting the tax burden onto labor and industrial income. Markets shrank as a result of the fiscal drain as well as the financial debt overhead.

Abuses of arrogance and outright fraud occurred in what became a golden age for Enron, WorldCom and other "high flyers" akin to the S&L scandals of the mid-1980s. But free-market monetarism draws no distinction between tangible direct investment and purely financial gain-seeking. Opposing government regulation to favor any given way of recycling savings as compared to any other way, the value-free ethic of our times holds that making money is inherently productive regardless of how it is made. "Free-market fundamentalism" came to shape neoliberal tax policy in a way that favored finance, not industry or labor.

Can Economies Iinflate Their Way out of Debt?

Only a limited repertory of opportunities for profitable new direct investment exists at any given point in time. The exponential growth in savings tends to outstrip these opportunities, and hence is lent out. This lending—and its mirror image, borrowing—may become self-justifying at least for a time to the extent that it bids up asset prices. Homebuyers and investors feel that it pays them to go into debt to buy property, and this is viewed as "prosperity," although it is primarily financial rather than industrial in character.

About 70 percent of bank loans in the United States and Britain take the form of real estate mortgages. Most new savings and credit creation thus enables borrowers to bid up the price of homes and office buildings. The effect is to increase the price that consumers must pay to obtain housing, as new construction loans account for only a small proportion of mortgage lending. Over-extended families become "house-poor" as rising financial charges for housing diverts income away from being spent on new goods and services, "crowding out" consumer spending and business investment.

> **B**alance sheets improve as the pace of capital gains outstrips the rate of interest. Debt service can be paid out of rising asset values, either by selling off assets or by borrowing against the higher asset prices as collateral.

Governments may try to mitigate the inflation of housing prices by raising interest rates. But this will increase the carrying charges for borrowers with floating-rate mortgages, as well as debtors throughout the economy. (Also, as Britain discovered in spring 2004, the increase in interest rates also raises the currency exchange rate, making its exporters less competitive in world markets.) For fixed-rate mortgages, higher interest rates may squeeze the banks, leading to losses in their portfolio values and prompting calls for the government to bail out losers (at least depositors, if not to rescue S & Ls and commercial banks).

Perception of this problem leads central bankers not to raise interest rates and take the blame for destroying financial prosperity by pricking the bubble. Instead, they try to keep it from bursting. This can be done only by inflating it all the more. So the process escalates.

Balance sheets improve as the pace of capital gains outstrips the rate of interest. Debt service can be paid out of rising asset values, either by selling off assets or by borrowing against the higher asset prices as collateral. The problem occurs when current income no longer can carry the interest charges. The financial sector absorbs more income as debt service than it supplies in the form of new credit. Asset prices turn down—but the debts remain on the books. This has been Japan's condition since its bubble peaked in 1990. It may result in "negative equity" for the most highly leveraged mortgage borrowers in the real estate sector, followed by debt-ridden companies.

When interest charges exceed rental income, commercial borrowers hesitate to use their own money or other income to keep current on their debts. The limited liability laws let them walk away from their losses if markets are deflated, leaving banks, insurance companies, pension funds and other financial institutions to absorb the loss. Sell-offs of these properties to raise cash would accelerate the plunge in asset prices, leaving balance sheets "hollowed out."

> **Savings do not appear as the villain in such periods. The zero net savings rate has concealed the fact that gross savings have been relent to create a corresponding growth in debt.**

Savings do not appear as the villain in such periods. The zero net savings rate has concealed the fact that gross savings have been relent to create a corresponding growth in debt. America's national debt quadrupled during the 12-year Reagan-Bush administration (1981–93). This increase in debt was facilitated by reducing interest rates by enough so that the unprecedented increase in credit rose without extracting more interest from many properties.

The natural limit to this process was reached in 2004 when the Federal Reserve reduced its discount rate to only 1 percent. Once rates hit this nadir, further growth in debt threatened to be reflected directly in draining amortization and interest payments away from spending on goods and services, slowing the economy accordingly. Further debt growth would require a rising proportion of disposable personal income to be spent on debt service.

How Long Can Bubbles Keep Expanding?

The potential credit supply is limited only by the market price of all existing property and securities. The process is open-ended, as each new credit creation inflates the market value of assets that can be pledged as collateral for new loans.

Until bubbles burst, they benefit investors who borrow money to buy assets that are rising in price. Running into debt becomes the preferred way to make money, rather than the traditional first step toward losing the homestead. The

motto of modern real estate investors is that "rent is for paying interest," and
this also applies to corporate raiders who use the earnings of companies bought
on credit to repay their bankers and bondholders. What real estate investors
and corporate financial officers are after is capital gains.

There is no inherent link with making new direct investment. Indeed, the
after-tax return from asset-price inflation exceeds that which can be made by
investing to create profits. Retirees, widows and orphans do best by living off
capital gains, selling part of their growing portfolios rather than seeking a flow
of interest, dividends and rental income. The idea begins to spread that people
can live off capital gains in an economy whose incomes are not growing.

> **A**sset-price inflation reaches its limit
> when interest charges absorb the
> entire flow of earnings.

Asset-price inflation would be a rational long-term policy if economies
could inflate their way out of debt via capital gains. The solution to debt would
be to create yet more debt to finance yet more asset-price inflation. This
dynamic is more likely to create debt deflation than commodity-price inflation, however. It is true that a consumer "wealth effect" occurs when homeowners refinance their mortgages by taking new "home equity" loans to spend
on living, or at least to pay down their credit-card debt so as to lower the monthly diversion of income for debt service. If this were to lead to a general inflation, interest rates would rise, prompting investors to shift out of stocks into
bonds. Foreign investors and speculators bail out, accelerating the price decline.
This threatens retirement funds, insurance companies and banks with capital
losses that erode their ability to meet their commitments.

The more likely constraint comes from asset-price inflation itself as price/
earnings ratios rise. Interest rates and other returns slow, making it difficult for
pension plans and insurance companies to earn the projected returns needed
to pay retirees. In any event, asset sales exceed purchases as the proportion of
retirees to employees grows, causing stock and bond prices to decline. Pension
funds must sell more stocks and bonds—or employers must set aside more of
their revenue for this purpose, in which case their ability to pay dividends is
reduced.

Asset-price inflation reaches its limit when interest charges absorb the entire flow of earnings. Debt-financed bubbles remove more purchasing power from the "bottom 90%" of the population than they supply. Debt spurs rising housing prices but reduces consumer demand as a result of the need to service mortgages. Likewise, financing for leveraged buyouts, mergers and acquisitions may increase stock prices, but the interest charges absorb corporate earnings and "crowd out" new direct investment and employment.

The drive for capital gains thus complicates the traditional macroeconomic Keynesian categories. Although these gains are not included in the national income statistics, they have become the key to analyzing how asset-price inflation leads to debt deflation of the "real" economy. One thus may ask what sphere of the economy is more "real" and powerful: that of tangible production and consumption, or the financial sector which is wrapped around it.

Can the Debt and Savings Overhead Be Supported Indefinitely?

Richard Price's illustration of the seemingly magical powers of compound interest is a reminder that many people saved pennies (and much more) at the time of Jesus, and long before that, but nobody yet has obtained an expanding globe of gold. The reason is that savings have been wiped out repeatedly in waves of bankruptcy.

The reason is clear enough. When savings, lending and "indirect" financial investment grow by compound interest in the absence of new tangible investment, something must give. The superstructure of debt must be brought back into a relationship with the ability to pay.

Financial crashes occur much more quickly than the long buildup. This is what produces a ratchet pattern for business cycles—a gradual upsweep and sudden collapse of financial and property prices, leaving economies debt-ridden. Many debts are wiped out, to be sure, along with the savings that have been invested in bad loans—unless the government bails out savers at taxpayer expense.

Financial crises are not resolved simply by price adjustments. Almost all crises involve government intervention, solving matters politically. As the financial and property sectors gain political power relative to the increasingly indebted production and consumption sectors, their lobbies succeed in lowering tax rates on *rentier* income relative to taxes on wages and profits. Tax rates on capital gains have been slashed below those on "earned" wages and profits, whereas the two rates were equal when America's income-tax laws first were introduced.

Financial lobbies also have gotten law-makers to adopt the "moral hazard" policy of guaranteeing savings. Debtors still may go bankrupt, but savings are to be kept intact by making taxpayers liable to the economy's savers. Ever since the collapse of the Federal Savings and Loan Insurance Corporation (FSLIC) in the late 1980s a political fight has loomed over just whose savings are to be rescued. Unfortunately, the principle at work is that of "Big fish eat little fish." Small savers are sacrificed to the wealthiest savers and institutional investors.

The mathematics of compound interest dictates that such public guarantees to preserve savings cannot succeed in the long run. Financial savings and debts tend to grow at exponential rates while economies grow only by S curves, causing strains that cannot be supported as credit is used to buy assets rather than to invest in capital goods or buildings.

> The mathematics of compound interest dictates that public guarantees to preserve savings cannot succeed in the long run.

Financial strains become further politicized as large institutions and the "upper 10 percent" of the population account for nearly all the net saving, which is lent out to the "bottom 90%" and to industry. The balance-sheet position of the wealthiest layer increases as long as capital gains exceed the buildup of debt. The bottom 90% also benefit for a while during the early and middle stages of the financial bubble. Workers are invited to think of themselves as finance-capitalists-in-miniature rather than as employees being downsized and out-sourced. But much of what they may gain in the rising market value of their homes (for the two-thirds of the U.S. and British populations that are home-owners) is offset by the debt deflation that bleeds the production-and-consump-tion economy.

Throughout history societies that have polarized between creditors and debt-ors have not survived well. Rome ended in a convulsion of debt foreclosure, monopolization of the land and tax shifts that reduced most of the population to clientage. Third-world countries today are being stripped of their public domain and public enterprises by the international debt buildup, while industry and real estate in the creditor nations themselves are becoming debt-ridden.

Today's bubble economy is seeing interest charges expand to absorb profits and rental income, leading to slower domestic direct investment and employ-ment. Much as classical economists believed that rent would expand to absorb the entire economic surplus, it now appears that interest-bearing debt will play this role.

12

SAVING OUR WAY INTO POVERTY: THE POLITICAL IMPLICATIONS

The U.S. and European economies are still in the Denial Stage of the debt problem. Bank lobbyists are trying to inspire hope that economies can "grow their way out of debt" rather than having to write off bad debts. They want the government to squeeze out a budget surplus by cutting back Social Security, Medicare and social spending, and for families to pay more to the banks and other creditors by reducing consumer spending on goods and services.

Despite the fact that such debt deflation shrinks markets, the economy somehow is supposed to grow and create a large enough financial surplus to "save its way out of debt," much like a homeowner who saves enough income to pay down the mortgage. Governments are to shrink their spending and run a budget surplus to hold down the ratio of public debt to GDP. Families are to continue doing what they are doing—reducing their credit card lines and borrow less, paying down their mortgages and other debts. And companies are to use their profits and cash flow to pay down borrowings.

This hope does not really make sense when you think about it. Since 2008 the economy's net saving rate has indeed risen, from 0 percent to over 2 percent of GDP. This saving has indeed taken the form of paying down debt, rather than building up liquid deposits for most people or businesses. But as Keynes pointed out in the 1930s, saving money takes it out of the circular flow between producers and consumers. When consumers save, they buy fewer goods and services. Markets shrink. Profits decline as sales fall. Real estate vacancy rates rise, and rents fall. This is precisely what is happening today—and why the so-called "double dip" recession turns out to be simply a continuation of the post-2008 debt deflation.

There is also a distributional problem. Most of the liquid savings (*i.e.*, net-surplus that is not used to pay down debts) are by the economy's wealthiest 10% percent (and, of those, especially the richest 1%). These savings, again, are invested to yield interest. They are lent out to those in the bottom ninety percent who, in the end, are unable to carry their debt and need to borrow in order to pay interest. So "saving our way out of debt" really means that most of the economy is to "borrow its way out of debt." Gross saving in the U.S. and European economies remain high. But the great bulk is lent out (to become other parties' debts), without being invested productively, *i.e.*, in tangible capital formation to create jobs and spur economic growth.

The problem therefore lies with the banking and credit system itself, and with the economic polarization between wealthy savers and indebted consumers, indebted real estate, indebted business, and indebted governments — all paying interest and financial fees to the banks and to the richest 1% of American families who now receive about two-thirds of the returns to wealth in the form of interest and dividends, rents and capital gains. This is a malstructuring of the financial system. Keeping the resulting debts in place is imposing financial brakes on economic recovery.

Every sector obviously needs credit to bridge the gap between income and outgo. That is inherent in the specialization of production and the lag-times between the inception of an economic activity and its fruition. Farmers need credit to plant their crops and defray their expenditures until the harvest is in, sold and paid for. Manufacturers need credit to acquire machinery, stock up on raw materials and undertake work in progress. Merchants borrow to carry their inventories, ship their goods and wait for payment to clear. Governments have run up debts in wartime or other national emergencies, as have consumers in the face of adversity or simply in the expectation that they will be able to repay their home mortgages, student loans, automobile loans or other debts out of the higher incomes they hope to earn in years to come.

The rate of interest is supposed to act as a mediator between borrowers and creditors by inducing savers to lend out their money at a level covering normal risk. But the risks grow larger as economies are less able to carry their debt overhead in the face of a growing volume of savings/debts. Interest rates rise, shortening the doubling time of savings/debts. From their 3 to 4 percent level at the end of World War II, rates soared to 20 percent in 1980. Growing uncertainties, above all the prospect that the government would resort to inflationary measures to monetize its debt, made investors willing to put up funds only for short periods of time. There were more savings to lend, but lending was becoming riskier as the ratio of debt service to income rose, and as financial managers pressed economies to inflate their way out of debt.

The financial system was becoming less stable, not yet having gained firm political control over government via campaign contributions, public relations think tanks and Chicago School academic legitimization backed globally by U.S. military force and diplomatic power. This meant that the government not only had to pay higher interest rates, it had to keep coming back to the financial markets more often. The average maturity on federal debt securities shortened from 7 years at the end of World War II to just 2 years and 10 months in 1980. Real estate, stock and bond prices plunged, wiping out the value of the loans in which savings had been invested. By yearend 1980 many sectors of the economy were technically insolvent, headed by the banking system itself.

In the international sphere, heavily indebted countries such as Brazil had kept afloat simply by getting their creditors to add the interest due onto the principal each year, at rising rates of interest. The game ended when Mexico declared itself insolvent in 1982, followed by widespread defaults that led to write-downs of the principal as third world government bonds sold for as low as 20 to 40 cents on the dollar. The best that creditors could do was to accept conversion of such debts into Brady bonds organized by the U.S. Treasury Secretary. But creditors to pull back on making new loans. By 1990, interest rates on new dollar borrowings by Brazil, Argentina and other countries soared as high as 45 percent.

Every sector needs credit to bridge the gap between income and outgo. That is inherent in the specialization of production and the lag-times between the inception of an economic activity and its fruition, *e.g.*, planting and harvest. Farmers need credit to plant their crops and defray their expenditures until the harvest is in, sold and paid for. Manufacturers need credit to acquire machinery, stock up on raw materials and undertake work in progress. Merchants borrow to carry their inventories, ship their goods and wait for payment to clear. Governments have run up debts in wartime or other national emergencies, as have consumers in the face of adversity or simply in the expectation that they will be able to repay their home mortgages, student loans, automobile loans or other debts out of the higher incomes they hope to earn in years to come.

The rate of interest is supposed to act as a mediator between borrowers and creditors by inducing savers to lend out their money at a level covering normal risk. But the risks grow larger as economies are less able to carry their debt overhead in the face of a growing volume of savings/debts. Interest rates rise, shortening the doubling time of savings/debts. From their 3 to 4 percent level at the end of World War II, rates soared to 20 percent in 1980. Growing uncertainties, above all the prospect that the government would resort to inflationary measures to monetize its debt, made investors willing to put up funds only for short periods of time. There were more savings to lend, but lending was becoming riskier as the rate of debt service to income rose, and as economies began to inflate their way out of debt.

The financial system was becoming less stable, not yet having gained firm political control over government via campaign contributions, public relations think tanks and Chicago School academic legitimization backed globally by U.S. military force and diplomatic power. This meant that the government not only had to pay higher interest rates, it had to keep coming back to the finan-

cial markets more often. The average maturity on federal debt securities shortened from 7 years at the end of World War II to just 2 years and 10 months in
1980. Real estate, stock and bond prices plunged, wiping out the value of the
loans in which savings had been invested. By yearend 1980 many sectors of
the economy were technically insolvent, headed by the banking system itself.

In the international sphere, heavily indebted countries such as Brazil had
kept afloat simply by getting their creditors to add the interest due onto the
principal each year, at rising rates of interest. The game ended when Mexico
declared itself insolvent in 1982, followed by widespread defaults that led to
write-downs of the principal as third world government bonds sold for as low
as 20 to 40 cents on the dollar. The best that creditors could do was to accept
conversion of such debts into Brady bonds organized by the U.S. Treasury
Secretary. But perception that these countries had reached the limit of their
dollar-paying capacity led creditors to pull back. By 1990, interest rates on
new dollar borrowings by Brazil, Argentina and other countries soared as high
as 45 percent.

Paying Interest out of Debt-Financed Capital Gains

This seemed to be a harbinger of things to come in the United States and
Europe. The U.S. debt overhead seemed stretched to its limit in 1980. If
anyone had been told that a wave of debt run-ups and bankruptcies would
occur for S&L's, real estate, corporations and foreign governments, the last
thing they would have expected would have been that interest rates would soon
decline to produce the greatest bond market boom in history. Nobody anticipated that instead of bankruptcies wiping out debts, third-world style, the
1980s would see an unprecedented growth of debt—without the feared price
and wage inflation. When Ronald Reagan took office in 1981, nobody expected that over the next twelve years Republican administrations would
quadruple the public debt by cutting taxes while maintaining military and
social spending unabated.

In the past, most government debts stemmed from war borrowing, but now
they are taken on to cover budget deficits resulting from un-taxing wealthy
individuals and the FIRE sector. The same thing happened in Britain, where
government budgets were pushed into surplus only by selling off the public
domain, mediated by the financial sector.

The stock market soared, mainly in response to falling interest rates, and
also because of takeover bids made attractive by the tax and deregulatory
changes that left a wide swath of bankruptcies in their wake in the late 1990s.
Corporate raiders issued junk bonds to raise money to "take companies private" by buying their stock (which had paid taxable dividends) and replacing

it with tax-deductible high-yield bonds. This enabled companies to pay out twice as much money as interest as they could pay in dividends, because they were able to pay bondholders out of pre-tax revenue, cutting the tax collector out of the picture. But this interest was contractual. Unlike dividends that could be cut back when profits declined, missing an interest payment meant insolvency and potential bankruptcy. This was the effect of tax rules favoring debt rather than equity financing.

Instead of raising funds to finance new capital investment as textbook s describe, the stock market was downsized as stocks were retired in favor of bonds. Taxes on capital gains were slashed to a fraction of tax rates on earned income (wages and profits),and . This encouraged a shift of investible savings into lending and speculation rather than to finance direct industrial investment. Employees also were cut out, and industrial corporations fell prey to financial raiders who paid off their bonds by selling their companies part by part, emptied out corporate pension funds (by declaring them to be "overfunded"), downsized and outcourced the labor force. The promised capital investment, factory construction and new hiring gave way to a postindustrial Rust Belt.

This was euphemized as a "service" economy, without specifying that the main "services" were financial, based on appropriating and capitalizing into bank loans real estate and natural resource rents (including the telephone and radio spectrum) and monopoly rents or super-profits for the public agencies and utilities being carved out of the public domain.

To defend themselves against the threat that their stockholders would sell a controlling share to debt-financed raiders, target companies took on so much debt of their own that no raiders from Drexel Burnham or other attack houses could find room to issue their own bonds against the company's assets. The term for this strategy, taking the "poison pill," reflected the danger that observers associated with the fact that the major way for companies to protect their independence in the new mergers-and-acquisitions frenzy was to borrow money to use in buying other companies. . The stock market became a search for quick gains as speculators tried to guess what companies would be the next to be bought.

The postindustrial economy had arrived, not on a wave of rising labor productivity as its promoters had forecast (although this was part of it), but in a struggle for existence between finance and manufacturing over who would obtain the economic surplus. A new breed of corporate managers and arbitrageurs borrowed not to finance profit-making enterprise, but to obtain capital gains on stock market maneuverings, real estate, rare paintings and other trophies. They leveraged their own capital by borrowing credit, which now

can be created without prior saving. And it was created with the aim of transforming the economic surplus into a flow of interest payments—by capitalizing the surplus for bank loans. This became the way in which economic assets
were priced: by what a bank would lend against them.

Headed by real estate and the oil industry, entire sectors operated without
reporting a profit. Interest charges on this "financialization" strategy absorbed
the revenue that otherwise would have been taken as profit and paid to the tax
collector. Investors preferred to take their returns in the form of capital gains.
Earnings were pledged as tax-deductible interest in exchange for yet more debt
financing to leverage the post-industrialization process all the more.

No regulators stepped in to deter the economy's rise in debt/equity ratios.
Many of the tactics employed were challenged, major participants went to jail
and Drexel Burnham went bankrupt, but the lawyers and lobbyists who
designed the new practices went free and prospered. Once the corporate raiding of pension funds and other capital reserves was deemed not to fall under
the RICO (racketeering) act, companies could be bought, their bank accounts
and pension fund reserves looted, and their real estate and operational divisions
sold off fair and square.

The new deregulatory ethic claimed that such raiding enriched the economy by increasing stock-market valuations, which were defined as being the
new postindustrial form of "wealth creation" rather than as asset stripping. A
miasma of well-funded euphemism descended over most economic discussion,
injecting doctrinaire anesthetic into the industrial sector's defense mechanisms
Popular movies such as Wall Street provided a more realistic picture than the
libertarian Chicago School apologetics. .

Sacrificing the "Real" Economy to Pay the Expanding Debt Overhead

Financial *rentiers* obtained the revenues previously destined for the tax collector. Profits and dividend payments on equity were replaced by interest
payments on mortgages, bonds and other debts. Federal income-tax receipts
fell proportionally, aggravating the budget deficit and swelling the public debt.
Private sector debt also grew as the revenue freed from taxation was pledged
to bankers and bondholders in exchange for credit to buy the properties whose
price appreciated as taxes were cut. The government's loss and corresponding
indebtedness found its counterpart in the FIRE sector's gain, which was capitalized into more private-sector debt.

Rather than downsizing the government as Reaganomics had promised,
the financial bubble empowered the government over the economy in a new
way, in a role as large as hitherto had been played only by war. The government's new role was to underwrite the financial bubble, by reversing the trend

toward progressive taxation and taking the side of finance against the "real" production-and-consumption economy. Starting in 1981 when President Ronald Reagan took office, the government lowered taxes on the major banking sector's customers—real estate and monopolies, and corporations generally as well as the upper income and wealth brackets. The effect was to leave more revenue tax-free to pay creditors—more rental revenue to be capitalized into mortgage loans to bid up real estate prices, and more corporate profits to be used to pay bondholders and thus attract raiders using junk bonds.

> The government's loss and corresponding indebtedness found its counterpart in the FIRE sector's gain, which was capitalized into more private-sector debt.

This shifted the tax burden onto employees, most drastically by the Greenspan Commission's proposal in 1983 to treat Social Security as a user fee, to be financed by saving in advance—forced savings withheld from employee paychecks and also their employers' income, to be invested in Treasury bonds, enabling taxes to be cut on property, on the wealthiest tax brackets and on inherited fortunes. The result was to add a fiscal burden on top of the debt burden that was shrinking the "real" economy, even as the financial efflorescence gave the impression that the economy was growing. It was not Main Street's economy, but that of Wall Street.

The government also intervened into the economy on the side of the financial sector by guaranteeing savings in the amount of the economy's exponentially rising debt in which these savings were invested. At the end of the deregulatory and tax-subsidized indebtedness would come the 2008 bank bailouts to ward off the bankruptcies that brought debt bubbles down to earth in times past.

Many of the junk bonds issued by corporate raiders in the 1980s were sold to the deregulated savings and loan industry, whose insider loans a financed a real estate bubble whose subsequent collapse wiped out S & L stock- and bondholders, leaving some $300 billion in Federal S & L Insurance Corporation (FSLIC) cleanup costs. The parallel international credit bubble also burst. But the IMF bailed out global banks that had lent to Latin America and other third world countries. Governments were prompted to borrow from the IMF to pay interest and principal to these international banks. (Citibank was the most over-committed. Its head, John Reed, assured his depositors that "countries don't go bankrupt." By "stretching the envelope," Citibank attracted other U.S. banks, followed by British, German and French banks in its train.)

For the time being the inter-governmental debt bubble had reached its limit. The World Bank responded by organizing a vast voluntary pre-foreclosure sale by debtor governments. As sovereign governments there was no easy way to force them to pay their debts. They had to be persuaded that it was in their interest to dismantle their public infrastructure and enterprises, and sell them off to private buyers—who bought on credit provided by the international banks.

These privatization selloffs enabled Latin American and other third world governments to avoid default after Mexico's 1982 insolvency collapsed the global debt market. The objective was to save international banks and institutional bondholders from further losses—just as the European Central Bank would do with Ireland and Greece in 2010–11.

The epoch of Moral Hazard arrived—hazardous most of all for the taxpayers who footed the bill for reimbursing the large institutional investors who took high interest premiums, secure in the knowledge that government agencies would bear the real risk.

Inflating the Debt Bubble in an Attempt to Carry the Debt Overhead

The economy was being re-planned. Politicians still were doing the lawmaking, but acted increasingly as vehicles for legislation composed by the FIRE sector to serve its own special interests. In gratitude for their role as the major campaign contributors to both parties, FIRE-sector lobbyists were given a free hand in writing new tax legislation, while control over the regulatory agencies was ceded to the financial industry's own proxies.

In practice this meant deregulation, as became clear when the S&L industry's Danny Wall was appointed head of the Federal Home Loan Bank Board. Instead of limiting debt-leveraging practices as the financial bubble gained momentum, government agencies poured fuel on the fire by dismantling the rules that had limited risk while channeling finance to serve public objectives. The major beneficiaries were the large institutional savers, whose deposits in S&Ls and commercial banks were guaranteed up to much higher levels, even as these deposits were recycled recklessly into real estate and high-interest "junk" bonds. A real estate debt bubble of unprecedented size was inflated—only to be outdone by the Greenspan Bubble of 2001–08.

The government relinquished tax income to creditors across the board, but the revenue that was freed was used more for financial parasitism than for productive investment. The largest impetus to the debt boom took the form of slashing taxes on commercial real estate. Depreciation schedules—the "small print" determining how quickly property owners could take their tax-free capital consumption write-offs on buildings and capital improvements—were shortened drastically in 1981, freeing most real estate from income taxation. Local real estate rates also were lowered, especially for commercial property. The cash flow that was freed from the tax collector was pledged to mortgage lenders for credit to buy more commercial and residential properties, whose prices soared as more money became available at falling rates of interest as the Federal Reserve flooded the banking system with credit—and the banks lent it out to become other parties' debts. For the economy at large this meant higher access costs to obtain housing and office space. But most people viewed the process as creating wealth, not as making its acquisition more expensive for the economy at large.

> **From the pension-fund managers' viewpoint the value of savings seems best preserved by joining the financially parasitic process, instead of backing more job-creating investment. In this way the employees, through their legitimite desire for an adequate pension, inadvertently help speed the deindustrialization process.**

Someone must bear the fiscal burden of bailing out the soaring volume of bad savings. The onus falls on the average taxpayer, largely through increased "forced saving" (a term hitherto used when describing fascist or Stalinist economies) in the form of Social Security and Medicaid withholding taxes, and a proliferation of consumption taxes, plus cutbacks in government social spending. As for the manufacturing sector, it is given few of the special tax benefits enjoyed by the FIRE sector and by the highest personal tax brackets.

Under these conditions employee pension funds found their strategy dictated by the new shape imposed on the economy by the financial planners who have replaced those of Keynesian social democracy. The problem is that from the pension-fund managers' viewpoint the value of savings seems best preserved by joining the financially parasitic process, instead of backing more job-creating investment. In this way the employees, through their legitimite desire for an adequate pension, inadvertently help speed the deindustrialization process.

In the face of mounting savings/debts, the limited repertory of credit-worthy loan projects obliged banks and other financial institutions to seek out new classes of borrowers. One new category consisted of global debtors in Asia, Russia and other regions. Another category was sub-prime borrowers in America — the poor at the bottom of the economic pyramid. Shares boomed for companies involved in high-interest payday lending, pawnshops, second-mortgage lending and credit card companies and banks. As debtors defaulted, Washington lobbyists for predatory lenders succeeded in rewriting the bank-ruptcy laws to remove traditional protections for financial victims. This became the legal dimension of the "magic of compound interest" that was financial-izing American society.

Even for more responsible financial institutions, loan standards were relaxed. Fewer loans were self-amortizing. Banks were just as glad to see the debt remain perpetual, with only the interest being paid. But a growing pro-portion of loans could not even be paid out of the borrower's profit or cash flow. Hopes for repayment depended on the ability of debtors to sell their prop-erty — at a high enough capital gain to pay off the loan.

Banks were making larger and larger real estate loans to new buyers, enabling old mortgages to be paid off and replaced with larger ones. The economy entered what Hyman Minsky called the Ponzi stage of the financial cycle, in which debtors kept solvent by borrowing the money needed to pay their creditors. The indebted economy survived by borrowing the interest — thanks to the Federal Reserve fueling asset-price inflation. This was the Bubble Economy, which gained momentum in the 1990s and then took off after the dot.com stock market bubble collapsed in 2000.

What enabled the loans to be covered — and the volume of savings to keep growing, and indeed to be relent on their way seemingly toward infinity — was the inflation of asset prices. U.S. Treasury fiscal policy and Federal Reserve monetary policy aimed at building such windfalls structurally into what prom-ised to be a New Economy. What actually was occurring was an over-stretched financial economy replacing the industrial economy. The portmanteau term "postindustrial society" failed to specify its basically financial aspect, and hence missed the essence of the structural change being implemented by govern-ment fiat.

As the rising flow of funds fueled an asset-price inflation, business and even personal debts were taken on to buy assets that already were in place, mainly real estate and business corporations. Having embarked upon this path, debtors borrowed all the more merely to stay afloat, not to create new means of production. Hitherto taxable profits and dividend payouts were replaced by interest paid to creditors as a tax-deductible expense. These interest charges were built into the economy's cost structure as part and parcel of its new capital-gains focus. In effect, the economy was trying to "borrow its way out of debt" as new lending was extended mainly to fuel the asset-price inflation. This became America's version of Japan's *zaitech* financial engineering that had marked that country's bubble economy.

But even the exponential growth of debt must have a limit. The New Financial Economy was replacing the manufacturing economy. Industrial neighborhoods in America's largest cities were gentrified into high-priced luxury residential lofts and sold to FIRE-sector managers and kindred young, upwardly mobile professionals. The term "gentrification" reflected the degree to which a new financial gentry was being vested as the modern epoch's successor to feudal Europe's landed gentry.

> **H**itherto taxable profits and dividend payouts are now avoided. Instead, interest is paid to creditors as a tax-deductible expense. These interest charges are built into the economy's cost structure as part and parcel of its new capital-gains focus.

This modern financial gentry lives more on capital gains than rents, and makes its money by running into debt rather than by staying out of it. This is why the New Financial Economy has been accompanied by more frequent waves of bankruptcy. It tries to solve the debt problem (which seemed so intractable in 1980) by supplying enough loanable funds to float an exponentially rising volume of borrowing by governments, real estate investors, corporate raiders and speculators. The secret of perpetual financial motion seemed to have been discovered.

Since the 1980s the compound interest phenomenon has expressed itself mainly through the asset ("savings") side of the balance sheet, although of course both the savings and debt sides have grown in tandem. This is why national income statistics indicate a zero saving rate, despite the vast increase in the financial flow of funds. Current accounting practices look at net rather than gross flows. The volume of gross savings (total financial assets) was doubling with increasing rapidity, fueled by a tidal wave of new bank credit created and poured into the capital markets mainly as loans.

As described above, stocks were retired and replaced by the high-interest bonds issued by raiders, whose buyout offers raised stock market prices. The ensuing financial speculation seemed to be justified by asset-price inflation, precisely because savings were lent to borrowers to bid up prices for assets. Borrowers turned around and pledged these assets as collateral to their backers for yet larger loans, on which they hoped to make further capital gains.

A precondition for this self-feeding process to continue was rising debt/income ratios across the board, because what was buoying asset prices was precisely the expansion of lending. The economy was walking up a financial tightrope, carrying increasingly heavy savings and liabilities on each side of its financial balance sheet. What Federal Reserve Chairman Alan Greenspan applauded as "wealth creation" was simply debt creation, justified by asset-price inflation.

The ensuing top-heavy instability caused stock and bond prices, real estate prices and exchange rates to zigzag wildly. What was new was the safety net (which critics called Moral Hazard) that the government provided for savers. After it collapsed in 2008 the debt overhead was kept in place by a $13 trillion bailout by the U.S. Treasury and Federal Reserve. Creditors were saved—but not debtors. This was the ultimate political consequence of the magic of compound interest. It was sufficiently powerful to replace social democracy with an emerging financial oligarchy—and to replace long-term economic planning with a short-run financialized policy that deteriorated into a program for creditors to take the money and run, converting their financial claims into whatever "real" assets they could, or at least shifting their fortunes to less debt-ridden economies.

There was little discussion about how long the process could continue. The logic of financial optimists seemed persuasive only if one granted their assumption that lending was made for productive investment whose earning power would enable borrowers to pay their debts out of rising earnings. But a rising proportion of lending was to inflate the financial bubble. A new kind of planned economy was emerging, but not the kind that 19th-century industrial futurists had envisioned. To help spur total returns, the U.S. Government cut capital gains taxes, leaving yet more gains in the hands of borrowers to pay creditors in exchange for larger loans.

Governments throughout the world were not doing actual planning as much as acting as intermediaries implementing plans provided by FIRE-sector investors and their lobbyists. The world of government planning denounced by Frederick Hayek in *The Road to Serfdom* was replaced by a financialized Road to Debt Peonage.

Part III

THE GLOBAL CRISIS

Capping a day of extreme political turbulence in Athens, George Papandreou told his socialist colleagues that there was no need for a referendum after the conservative opposition promised to support the terms of a € 130 bn bail-out from the European Union, European Central Bank and International Monetary Fund.

"Failure to back the package would mean the beginning of our departure from the euro," Mr Papandreou said. "But if we have consensus, then we don't need a referendum."

"I'm pleased to see that there are sufficiently responsible politicians in Greece who have understood that message and who have been able to see the national priorities," Mr Sarkozy said, praising the opposition's decision to support the October 27 rescue deal for Greece as courageous and responsible. … The abandonment of the referendum plan offered much-needed relief to financial markets …

Tony Barber, Kerin Hope, Peter Spiegel and David Oakley, "Greek PM scraps referendum plan," *Financial Times*, November 3, 2011.

13

TRADE AND PAYMENTS THEORY IN A FINANCIALIZED ECONOMY

If trade theory is to be based on how economies work and relate to each other, it should focus on the financial overhead, capital movements and tax policies that are the key to today's prices, payments and exchange rates. Mortgage debt taken on to buy homes (with prices bid up on credit) and obtain an education, and wage set-asides for pension funds, Social Security and Medicare, all raise the cost of living and doing business. So do debt-leveraged corporate buyouts—making economies less competitive.

Most trade and exchange rate models have neglected these financial, rental and fiscal charges ever since David Ricardo analyzed costs as if economies operated on barter. He claimed that debt service and military spending could not create economic problems, because they were automatically self-financing. Capital transfers supposedly set in motion re-stabilizing "corrections" enabling debts or payments outflows to be paid without disrupting price and income structures. This approach excluded recognition of how debt service adds to the cost of living and doing business, and depresses exchange rates.

Forecasts promising that austerity will revive growth and that debt leveraging helps economies get richer faster rarely are innocent. When such theorizing is pursued generation after generation, the explanation is that special interests must be benefiting from its tunnel vision. When it comes to minimizing the role of debt and credit, the financial sector's motivation is to distract attention from the problems caused by debts growing beyond the ability to be paid, disrupting economies and add to the cost of living and doing business.

This turns economics into a public relations lobbying effort for financial deregulation. What is remarkable is that debtor interests have accepted this "don't worry about debt" logic about "automatic stabilizers."

One cannot discuss the roles of finance and government without the concept of economic rent, because rent seeking is the largest category of bank lending—and also of tax favoritism. Today's academic mainstream rejects the classical idea of unearned income, defined as that which has no counterpart in socially necessary costs of production. But economic historians will recognize the concept of a free lunch as the centuries-long description of *rentiers*—bankers and landlords in the private sector.

Post-classical economics claims that there is no such thing as a free lunch—as if everyone earns and hence deserves whatever income and wealth they obtain, regardless of how they get it. This conflates transfer payments (including outright fraud and looting) with productive effort. All *rentier* income appears to be payment for providing economically helpful services, equal in value to the income paid to the financial, insurance and real estate (FIRE) sector. This is the concept that underlies the national income and product accounts (NIPA).

The classical doctrine now swept under the academic rug began in the 13th century with the Schoolmen discussing Just Price, mainly to distinguish between fair and extortionate banking charges. In time, the idea of unearned income came to be applied to land rent. Yet the analysis of economic rent—whether in finance, insurance or real estate, or even monopoly pricing—finds no room in today's curriculum. The concept is muddied by turning the tables to depict government officials as "rent-seeking" bureaucrats increasing public spending and regulation in ways that enhance their own power, in unproductive ways that add to the "deadweight" cost of doing business. Nothing about predatory FIRE-sector *rentiers* in this view!

Excluding Debt Service from Trade Theory—and from Domestic Price and Income Theory

The financial sector historically has sought to make itself invisible. After all, what is not seen will not be criticized—or taxed. To paraphrase Charles Baudelaire's quip that the devil wins at the point where the public comes to believe that he doesn't exist, the financial sector's lobbying effort wins at the point where people believe that running into debt contributes to economic growth rather than burdens it, and that they will end up richer by acting as bank customers. Debt leveraging is depicted as the easiest and even the surest way to accumulate wealth—going into debt to buy assets whose prices are being inflated on credit, or to spend in the hope of paying out of rising and more easily earned future income.

But since 1980—and especially since the bailouts of 2008—most fortunes have been made by bankers and brokers, largely at the expense of their clients and taxpayers. The banking system's product is debt, in a dynamic that ends with many debtors falling into negative equity and forfeiting their property to foreclosing creditors. That is the legacy of the real estate bubble and debt-financed corporate buyouts. Internationally, debt-ridden economies are subject to pressure from inter-governmental institutions such as the IMF and European Central Bank to impose fiscal austerity on their labor force, cut back public spending and even sell off public enterprises.

This explains why the non-financial "barter" approach to trade and exchange rate theory pioneered by Ricardo, writing as Britain's leading bank spokesman, was a whitewash in denying that foreign payments or credit can cause economic problems. Bankers are depicted as oiling the wheels of commerce, providing the "neutral" means of pricing goods and services (ignoring asset prices), not intruding into the circular flow between producers and consumers by extracting debt service and lobbying for *rentier* privileges.

The public relations problem that Ricardo faced was that debt service in 1815 absorbed three-quarters of the British government's budget. Especially problematic was foreign debt taken on to finance military spending and subsidies to Britain's allies in its many centuries of wars against France. The Seven Years War (1756–63) and Napoleonic Wars (1787–1815) sharply increased the national debt and, as Adam Smith illustrated in Book V of *The Wealth of Nations*, new excise taxes to pay for each new borrowing. Confronted with popular criticism of the proliferation of taxes to pay bondholders, the political task of bankers was to deny the problems caused by this debt.

Most Money and Credit, Wages and National Income are Spent on the FIRE Sector

The textbook formula MV = PT means money (M) times the velocity of turnover (V) = the market price (P) of the economy's transactions (T). However, the "transactions" in question are limited to current production and consumption, and "price" refers only to consumer prices or those of other commodities—or wages. Yet by far most credit is spent on assets, not goods and services. Every day a sum larger than an entire year's GDP passes through the New York Clearing House and the Chicago Mercantile Exchange for asset purchases and sales. More than 99 percent of spending in the United States and other financialized economies is thus for real estate, mortgages and packaged bank loans, and for stocks and bonds. By limiting the scope of analysis to commodity prices and wages, mainstream monetarist theory leaves these credit transactions and their debt service out of account.

International payments are dominated by capital flows for direct investment, bonds and stocks, bank loans and speculation. Also foreign lending and debt service, military spending and financial speculation affect exchange rates. But despite John Stuart Mill's analysis of how "capital transfers" affect exchange rates, popular discussion still calculates purchasing-power parity rates for MacDonald's hamburgers and other consumer goods as if this were a measure of international equilibrium.

To the extent that trade remains based on the cost of labor and doing business, rising payments to the FIRE sector also dominate. This is a far cry from the early 19th century when prices reflected mainly the price of food and other basic consumer goods. Each country's debt overhead, housing prices, tax rates, public subsidies and fiscal systems determine product prices. Some 70 to 75 percent of typical U.S. wage-earner budgets are paid to the FIRE sector and to government. So economic analysis is trivialized if it only takes into account direct production costs reducible to labor, not taxes or "economic rent" as an element of price with no counterpart in technologically necessary production costs—land rent, monopoly rent (including bank credit-creating privileges), interest charges and kindred transfer payments to *rentiers*.

This has far-reaching implications for how best to achieve trade competiveness. Neoliberals tell Latvia, Greece and other countries to impose economic austerity by monetary and income deflation to cut wage levels ("internal devaluation"). But this leaves financial and tax structures in place. Policy discussion is limited to fiscal austerity and currency depreciation—but not a shift of the incidence of taxation to real estate, finance or monopolies, or less regressive taxation on employment and consumption, or debt write-downs. What is lacking in this approach is a view of the economy as a system. Wage levels and interest rates are singled out as the only variables to "solve" the debt and balance-of-payments problems. So we are dealing with a purposeful narrow-mindedness.

Latvia has flat taxes on employment that add up to 59 percent of the wage. Cutting this tax by 40 percentage points—down to about 20 percent of the wage—would double labor's take-home pay (from about 40 to 80 percent of the wage). The government would make up the loss by raising the land tax to absorb the groundrent, and also the economic rent now being collected by the buyers of the formerly public infrastructure. But this rental income is the preferred object of bank lending—turning rent into interest payments, mainly to branches of Scandinavian banks. Yet there has been little discussion of shifting taxes onto land and monopolies, leaving less economic rent to capitalize into interest payments, thereby holding down housing prices.

Latvia's public-sector wages were cut by 30 percent during 2009–10 as the GDP plunged by over 20 percent. But cutting wages also cut employment taxes, so take-home wages fell only by 12 percent—as unemployment spread, turning Latvia into a neoliberal disaster story. Its regressive tax policy has made the nation's industrial labor so uncompetitive that young adults have emigrated to find work, causing Latvia's population to plunge by 10 percent (from 2.2 million to 1.9 million since the last census).

This demographic effect of trade deficits was well recognized by economic writers already in the 18th century. But free trade theory expurgated the linkages between trade and population growth, for the same reason that it conflated finance capital extracting debt service with industrial capital employing labor to produce goods and services: Greater realism leads to policy conclusions not favored. So economic theory was over-simplified. The rent and tax structure is taken for granted or simply treated as "exogenous," being political or "institutional" and as such, excluded from the sphere of "scientific" economics proper. The resulting legacy of Ricardian trade theory focuses on subsistence consumption, not debt-financed housing costs, education, financialized pensions and Social Security, and other FIRE-sector charges.

> **N**eoliberals tell Latvia, Greece and other countries to impose economic austerity by monetary and income deflation to cut wage levels ("internal devaluation"). But this leaves financial and tax structures in place. Policy discussion is limited to fiscal austerity and currency depreciation—but not a shift of the incidence of taxation to real estate, finance or monopolies, or less regressive taxation on employment and consumption, or debt write-downs.

A scientific body of analysis would demonstrate how financialization adds to the cost of living and doing business. The financial overhead consists not only of debt, but also compulsory saving in the form of wage withholding to pay for future pensions and medical care. In the United States these wage set-asides gained momentum after 1980. And the post-2001 Bubble Economy that inflated prices on credit for housing, commercial real estate and corporate ownership celebrated "debt leveraging" as raising returns on equity. But the effect was to absorb more of the economic surplus in the form of debt service.

All nations face common global prices for fuels and raw materials, and licensing fees for patents such as information technology and pharmaceuticals. Trade competition reflects financial dynamics, economic rent and tax policy in four main national variables: (1) labor's cost of living, wages and non-wage benefits (mainly pensions and health care), (2) land rent and debt overhead, (3) the incidence and level of taxation, and (4) the terms on which governments provide infrastructure services such as transportation and communications, Social Security and health care, along with economic subsidies. The impact of financialization and an anti-labor tax shift on the deteriorating U.S. industrial trade balance, for example, is clear from the following rough approximation of typical American employee budgets:

Balance-sheet factors (debts taken on to buy assets rather than current output)

Housing (ownership or rental costs):	32 to 40%
Debt service (non-mortgage)	15%
Private health-care and pension fund contributions	?

Government tax policy structure

FICA withholding for Social Security and Medicare:	15%
Taxes (income, sales and excise or VAT)	15%

U.S. de-industrialization—and rising motivation to invest in less debt- and rent-ridden economies—reflects the fact that *rentier* payments and taxes absorb as much as 75 percent of family budgets. In Germany, housing absorbs only about 20 percent of family income, half the U.S. rate. So the proportion of German wages available for spending on goods and services (rather than being paid to the financial sector as mortgage interest) is 20 percentage points higher than is the case with U.S. family budgets. This is explained partly by institutional factors and partly by financial practice. Germany has a tradition of rental co-ops, to which many families belong. Membership rents are based on current operating costs. Also, Germany's construction industry is not monopolized or criminalized as it is in New York and other major U.S. cities.

But the major differences between Germany and U.S. real estate are financial and legal. European homebuyers typically must save 20 or 30 percent of the purchase price to obtain a mortgage, in contrast to America's practice of 100 percent mortgages (or even a net cash payment *to* new home buyers) as the 2002–06 real estate bubble gained momentum. European mortgage markets also have been relatively free of no-documentation "liars' loans" to NINJA borrowers ("no income, no job, no assets") backed by crooked real estate brokers and appraisers. Wholesale financial fraud has effectively been decriminalized in the United States.

Renters in the 1970s and '80s were panicked into buying at extortionate prices as residential real estate in the large cities was sold off. Co-ops typically were sold with existing mortgages attached to them, with buyers borrowing almost an equivalent volume of new debt. Housing costs quickly doubled, prompting speculators to increase their share of the residential housing market to an estimated one-sixth by 2006.

Looser lending terms—lower down payments, slower amortization rates (culminating in no-interest mortgages by 2006), and less regulation to keep income declarations honest—fueled a larger debt pyramid. Real estate and other assets are worth whatever banks will lend against them. And whatever the tax collector relinquishes is "free" to pay the banks. A lower tax on land rents leaves more to be capitalized into mortgage loans, and hence inflates the price of housing—while government revenue is balanced by burdening labor and industry with income and sales taxes. The financial sector aims to shift taxes off its major customers (real estate and monopolies) so as to leave more revenue "free" to be paid as debt service. To subsidize this debt leveraging, interest is made tax-deductible.

This has major implications for how best to adjust to international payments imbalances. Pro-financial lobbyists urge an anti-labor policy of "internal devaluation," lowering wages to make economies more competitive to "earn their way out of debt." But the cost of labor could be reduced just as effectively by a tax policy that shifts the fiscal burden off employment onto property rents and other economic rent.

Failure to deal with bank loans, real estate, stocks and bonds—and the income diverted away from consumption and tangible investment to pay debt—limits monetary and price analysis to relating the money supply and government budget to price and wage levels. Left out of account is the use of credit to fuel asset purchases and speculative gambles, as well as for government deficits from bailouts taking bad bank debts onto the public balance sheet. In 2011, for example, banks used the U.S. Federal Reserve's $700 billion Quantitative Easing (QE II) mainly for foreign currency arbitrage, not making it available for domestic consumer spending. Also left out of account are the prices at which public or private infrastructure services are supplied.

Failure to take account of debt service and government spending on anything except current employment affecting consumer prices makes trade theory unrealistic. But financial interests endorse this narrow-mindedness to promote anti-labor austerity and high interest rates, and to exclude an understanding of how financialization burdens economies with banking and financial charges.

To secure its privileges and tax favoritism, the financial sector opposes government power to tax or regulate. In the name of "free markets" it is now centralizing economic planning power in Wall Street, the City of London and other financial centers. Under ostensibly democratic politics, an "independent" central bank has been carved out—independent from elected officials, not from the commercial banks whose interests it represents. Many voters follow Federal Reserve Chairman Alan Greenspan in believing that a financial bubble enriches the economy rather than simply turning the surplus into a flow of interest and banking fees.

The 2011 Crisis over Greek Government Debt

The Eurozone's rule against central banks lending to governments has been attributed largely to Germany's hyperinflation trauma in the early 1920s. The myth is the old $MV = PT$ tunnel vision claiming that the problem was caused by the Reichsbank using the printing press to finance Germany's budget deficit. Today's constitution accordingly prevents the central bank from crting credit to lend to government.

This is what psychologists call an implanted memory, a false image suggested in this case by anti-government ideologues. Every hyperinflation in history has been caused by international payments deficits. For the industrial nations, these deficits almost always involve foreign military spending. War spending also is responsible for most growth in public debt (as peacetime government budgets tended until quite recently to be approximately in balance). Paying these debts abroad involves the capital transfers that Ricardo argued could not cause serious structural problems, on the myth that they are self-financing!

But in the 1920s the Allies imposed an unpayably high reparations burden on Germany—largely to obtain the foreign exchange to pay the Inter-Ally arms debts that the U.S. Government insisted on collecting, rather than forgiving these debts as allies traditionally had done upon achieving victory.[1] The Reichsbank created German marks to throw onto the currency markets to obtain the foreign exchange to pay reparations. France also monetized francs to obtain the dollars to pay the American Government. A monetary theory that looks only for links between the money supply and current production and consumption will fail to understand this situation. The tragic results are clear from reviewing the narrow-minded arguments of Jacques Rueff and Bertil Ohlin with Keynes and Harold Moulton in the 1920s over the roots of international instability in the way that World War I was settled financially.

The moral is that in addition to the (1) international and (2) financial-*rentier* dimensions, (3) the government sector plays a key role the economic system. This dimension is missing from models that limit their scope to private sector transactions, and indeed, to "current" production and consumption spending without reference to the purchase of assets on credit. The European Central Bank's operating philosophy fails to distinguish between creating money to spend on employment, production and consumption in the "real" economy (affecting consumer prices, commodity prices and wages) as com-

---

[1] I describe the reparations and arms-debt tangle in *Super Imperialism* (2nd ed. 1992), and the distinction between the domestic budget problem and the international transfer problem in my historical review of theories of *Trade, Development and Foreign Debt* (2nd ed., 2010).

pared to creating credit (or simply Treasury debt) to give to banks to buy or lend against assets in the hope that this will bolster prices for real estate, stocks and bonds. The latter policy inflates asset prices but deflates current spending.

The $13 trillion increase in U.S. Treasury debt in the post-2008 financial meltdown was not spent in product markets or employment in the "real" economy. It was balance-sheet help. Likewise for the ECB, pressure arose by October 2011 to violate the German constitution and the Lisbon agreements to buy Greek debt—the bonds that French, German and Belgian banks held, along with other debts of the PIIGS (Portugal, Ireland, Italy, Greece and Spain). European financial stability came to rest on the ability to rescue banks holding these debts. This new money and debt creation has little interface with the "real" production-and-consumption economy, except to burden taxpayers.

This Eurozone financial crisis of summer and autumn 2011 shows the importance of distinguishing between two modes of central bank money and debt creation. The first is to spur deficits "Keynesian-style" by spending on employment, goods and services. The second is to increase balance-sheet debt without spending on current output—for instance to give banks government bonds to add to their reserves so as to make loans or, as was promised in the United States, to write down mortgage loans so as to raise property owners out of negative equity in order to stop the deflation of real estate prices.

The Eurozone has fallen into an intellectual trap in which banks have come to believe their own anti-government propaganda. Associating budget deficits only with wage and price inflation excludes consideration of government spending to bail out banks or provide credit to re-inflate asset prices (as well as creating infrastructure to hold down the cost of living and doing business). Opposing public social spending, European banks threw out the baby with the bathwater by blocking central banks from doing what the Bank of England, the U.S. Federal Reserve and other central banks were created to do: finance public deficits. This obliges governments to borrow from banks, insurance companies and other financial institutions. The resulting debt overhead leads to debt deflation that slows the economy and its tax yield, producing a fiscal crisis that in due course becomes a financial crisis.

To resolve matters, banks are backtracking and urging the European Central Bank to make loans to government—to bail out banks and bondholders, not to spend on employment in the "real" economy. Voters understandably resent further bank bailouts under conditions where many debtors are themselves facing foreclosure and have lost much of their net worth. Why should governments bail out the financial sector at the top of the pyramid but not reflate production and consumption in the "real" economy. The problem today, after all, is under-employment and debt deflation, not inflation.

Economic models have not caught up with this reality. National income statistics do not distinguish the *rentier* layer from the "real" economy below it, much less how the wealthiest 1% (and especially the richest 0.1%) are making money at the expense of the bottom 90% or even 99%. Credit is depicted only as financing economic expansion, not leading to shrinkage and austerity. Yet in America the easiest way to make money is not by "creating jobs" but by loading the economy down with debt, inflating asset prices on credit, privatizing natural monopolies and extracting economic rent in the form of higher access charges. None of this increases real output. But it does increase the cost of living and doing business.

Public Over-Indebtedness Leads to Privatization Sell-Offs

New investment and hiring taper off as rising debt charges divert income from being spent on current output. Economic growth slows in an S-curve, yet debts continue to accrue interest, which is lent out to obtain yet more interest, diverting yet more income from production and consumption. Slower income growth net of this debt service leads to lower tax payments (especially as interest is deemed tax-deductible), and hence to deepening budget deficits.

The financial sector's political strategy is to use these deficits as an opportunity to insist that governments balance their budgets by selling off public enterprises and other assets. The result is a modern version of Britain's Enclosure Movements of the 16th to 18th centuries, except that today's version is international and driven by the financial sector. Starting with the IMF and World Bank, and most recently the European Central Bank (ECB), inter-governmental financial institutions have gained authority over national governments. The ECB has taken the lead in telling Greece to sell off some €50 billion euros worth of prime tourist land, some of its islands, offshore oil-drilling rights or even the Parthenon, as well as the water and sewer systems of Athens and other cities, the Piraeus port and other parts of the Commons.[2]

---

[2] See for instance Andy Kessler, "The 'Brady Bond' Solution for Greek Debt," *Wall Street Journal*, June 29, 2011: "Private buyers are increasingly skeptical of government guarantees and will demand real collateral. Credit default swap derivatives, which merely spread the risk, will no longer do. Some other sweetener will be needed. The solution? Bonds backed by real Greek assets. ... utilities, railroads, tollways, airports, cellphone services, tourism, Ouzo factories and maybe even the islands of Santorini and Mykonos. If (some say when) the Greeks default, the Germans or new bondholders end up with the assets, much like in a home foreclosure." This is why the *Financial Times*' Lex column reported ("Greece: reckoning postponed," June 29, 2011): "the vote in parliament was held to the sound of rioting and the smell of tear gas."

When the new buyers charge monopoly prices for the infrastructure being sold off, this increases the cost of living and doing business, turning the economy into a set of tollbooth opportunities. The resulting economic rent is financialized as buyers borrow from banks whose loan officers calculate the prospects for rent extraction available to pay interest. What the public sector relinquishes in user fees and taxes is made available to pay (tax-deductible) interest to the FIRE sector—without the public-interest dimension of public investment. So instead of being "neutral" in its price and income effects, credit transforms the economy's structure itself.

A century ago U.S. economists described public infrastructure investment as a "fourth factor of production"—roads and canals, urban water and sewer systems, education, the post office, communications and other publically-owned utilities that represent the largest category of tangible capital investment (next to buildings) in many economies. Providing their services at cost or on a subsidized basis (transportation) or freely (as in the case of roads), their returns are to be calculated not like private-sector investment in user fees relative to capital investment costs, but in the degree to which this infrastructure lowers the economy's costs and prices.[3]

Privatization adds to these costs by involving expenses that public enterprise rarely charges. These add-ons are headed by interest and dividend payments to private owners, other underwriting and financial fees, and much higher salaries and bonuses to the privatized managers, including stock options. And as part of the structural transformation of society urged by creditors, governments are to deregulate (or simply not put regulatory authorities in place) the sectors being privatized on credit. Finally, labor is outsourced, especially to non-union workers. On the broadest level, the world's major financial centers replace national governments as economic planners allocating resources, particularly in nations that fall into foreign debt.

Financial lobbyists advise governments to sell off public infrastructure, to buyers on credit. Equilibrium conditions are resolved when the new owners pledge the current cash flow of rent-extraction opportunities to the banks as interest. They then try to raise access charges to roads, water, power, transportation and other public services.

Governments are forced into a budget squeeze by depriving them of a central bank of the sort that Britain and the United States have. The proper his-

---

[3] I describe the logic in "Simon Patten on Public Infrastructure and Economic Rent Capture," *American Journal of Economics and Sociology* 70 (October 2011): 873–903. Patten was the first Professor of Economics at America's pre-eminent business school, the Wharton School at the University of Pennsylvania.

torical role of central banks or Treasuries is to finance government spending by creating money. This is in practice how the economy is supplied with money and credit, which, being fungible, is used as the means of circulation for overall activity—the purchase and sale of goods and services, and the transfer of property, stocks and bonds or other assets.

If central banks are deprived of this opportunity to create credit, governments must rely on commercial banks to finance their budget deficits—at interest. This provides a free lunch to banks as a result of their privilege of credit creation. To avoid crises and bank runs, bank deposits are insured by government agencies. This runs the risk of transferring the banking system's losses onto the public balance sheet when crises arrive. Unless the bank insurance premiums accurately reflect this risk, such insurance represents a public subsidy to the banks.

Neoliberal demands for wage cuts overlook the fact that the cost of labor may be reduced more efficiently by shifting the mode of taxation to focus on collecting economic rent and minimizing the debt overhead. Austerity programs shrink markets and induce emigration of labor, worsening international deficits rather than overcoming them.

Most important from the vantage point of national competitiveness is the fact that the privatization of credit creation raises the cost of living and doing business, by building in financial overhead charges. Privatization of public infrastructure has the same effect, by providing rent-seeking opportunities for natural monopolies financed on credit rather than providing their basic services at subsidized rates or freely, financed out of progressive taxation.

Can "Internal Devaluation" Make Labor More Competitive?

E conomies are complex systems whose interconnections are broader than current trade theory takes into account. To analyze costs and trade competition requires integrating the "real" production and consumption economy with balance-sheet transactions in assets and the debt overhead, as well as with government fiscal policy.

The key to fiscal policy is much more than the level of taxation. The incidence of taxation affects domestic cost structures and determines whether the burden will fall on labor and its employers (increasing production costs) or on property and rent-yielding assets. Taxing land rent holds down the price of housing; taxing employment and sales raise the cost of living and doing business. Likewise in monetary policy, the terms on which credit is created affect the degree of debt pyramiding, while public capital investment in infrastructure tends to provide its basic services at a lower cost than privatization.

Failure to take account of these property, financial and the government balances leaves today's mainstream trade theory—and above all, the adjustment policies being prescribed for countries in deficit—to focus crudely on labor's overall wage rates rather than on the structure of family and business budgets. Neoliberal demands for wage cuts overlook the fact that the cost of labor may be reduced more efficiently by shifting the mode of taxation to focus on collecting economic rent and minimizing the debt overhead. This policy can reduce costs and increase competitiveness much less wastefully than austerity programs aimed at cutting wages and social spending. The effect of neoliberal austerity programs is to shrink markets and induce emigration of labor, worsening international deficits rather than overcoming them.

A Policy Antidote: The Progressive Era's Attempt to Ward off Financialization

The classical anti-*rentier* policy featured:

(1) a central bank to monetize government spending deficits rather than borrowing at interest from commercial banks and other creditors (*e.g.*, as dictated by the ECB and the Lisbon treaty);

(2) taxing away land rent, and enacting anti-monopoly laws and regulatory agencies to keep prices in line with necessary and justifiable costs of production;

(3) keeping basic infrastructure in the public domain, providing it at cost or at subsidized rates or freely (as in the case of roads), with construction costs financed out of progressive income taxation and taxes on economic rent;

(4) paying for pensions and Social Security and health insurance on a pay-as-you-go basis rather than by financialization (pre-saving by purchasing bonds and stocks);

(5) not permitting interest payments to be tax deductible; encouraging equity financing rather than subsidizing debt;

(6) providing a national income accounting format that (a) distinguishes economic rent paid to the FIRE sector and monopolies, and (b) recognizes the contribution of public infrastructure investment to lowering the cost of living and doing business.

Financialization has reversed these Progressive Era policies designed to minimize the debt overhead and the rent-extracting opportunities that are today's prime objective of bank marketing departments. However, countries that recently have been neoliberalized may still rectify matters by taxing rent and windfall gains to recover what has been appropriated. They also can remove the tax deductibility of interest and "watered" charges such as high salaries, and tax the fictitious transfer pricing and savings via offshore banking centers at the rate that normal earnings would be taxed. These are the classical economic policies proposed to free markets from the legacy of European feudalism and conquest of the land. They remain the great tasks confronting nations as the global economy enters the End Days of the post-World War II credit/debt expansion.

Scope of Economic Theory and Analysis

Neoliberal Theory	Classical and Progressive Era Reforms
Economic theory is a "science of assumptions." The criterion of excellence is their internal consistency.	Political economy should map empirical reality, not be a hypothetical exercise in science fiction.
All income and wealth is earned, reflecting its recipients' contribution to production and economic growth.	The FIRE sector is wrapped around the "real" economy, extracting revenue. *Rentier* income and wealth are unearned.
Economies are best analyzed as if they operated on barter beneath their "veil of money." Debt and financial wealth merely reflect this underlying economy.	Finance intrudes into the economy. It wins at the point where the world ignores its existence and effects: debt deflation and polarization between creditors and debtors.
Focuses on production and consumption, taxes and saving—all as "positive," and subject to choice	Focuses on "negatives" and the loss of choice:unfair wealth distribution and how debt creation diverts revenue the production-and-consumption economy.
$MV = PT$ refers to current output, commodity prices and wages.	Recognizes that most credit is created to buy assets, so it focuses on asset prices.
The bankers'-eye view of the world is most realistic, because most wealth is financial.	Bankers look at how much surplus revenue they can convert into debt service.
Debt leverage raises the return on equity.	Debt service diverts revenue away from new capital investment and employment.
Assumes that government budget deficits are spent on labor and hence are deadweight.	Recognizes government bailout payments to banks and spending on infrastructure.

Political Ideology

Neoliberal Theory	Classical and Progressive Era Reforms
Government planning is the road to serfdom.	Every economy is planned by somebody. Removing planning from government shifts its locus to the financial sector.
Credit to buy real estate and other assets creates wealth by inflating their prices.	Governments should shape markets to work efficiently, and steer credit productively.
Central banks should be independent from democratic government.	Making a central bank independent replaces democracy with financial oligarchy.
A free market is free for *rentiers*, free from public price regulation, taxation of wealth and even from public infrastructure investment.	A free market is one free of unearned economic rent, including interest and financial fees, monopoly rent and resource rent.
There is a class war and the rich have won—mainly the financial class. Attempts to reform the financial or tax system will cause economic collapse. The alternative to oligarchy and debt peonage is a road to serfdom.	The vested interests have fought back against the Progressive Era. But just as reformers sought to save capitalism from the legacy of feudalism once, the fight can resume.
Minimize taxes to leave more revenue "free" to pay interest to banks.	Tax land rent to hold down housing prices by leaving less "free" rent to capitalized into mortgage loans.
Economies live in the short run, but this is efficient, thanks to rational expectations.	Short-run finance is hit-and-run. Long-term investment is needed to raise productivity.
Inflating asset prices on credit "creates wealth," increasing the balance sheet's net worth.	Inflating asset prices on credit raises the debt overhead—which remains in place to cause negative equity when the bubble bursts.
Bubbles create billionaires, whose wealth helps create jobs.	Bubbles transfer revenue from the "real" economy to creditors and bankers, who recycle it into loans that indebt the rest of the economy.
Free markets neoliberal style need to be protected by a police state and censorship of alternatives (*viz.* the Chicago Boys in Chile).	If free-market policies require a police state, they are totalitarian, not free.

Fiscal Policy

Neoliberal Theory	Classical and Progressive Era Reforms
A free market is free of government regulation or taxation of *rentiers*.	A free market is free of unearned (*rentier*) income, and of monopolies and their pricing in excess of costs of production.
All income and wealth is earned; there is no free lunch.	FIRE-sector revenue is unearned, a reward for privilege, not socially necessary.
Prefers a flat tax on employment, and value-added sales taxes. No tax on asset-price gains or profits. Un-taxing property raises asset prices, creating balance-sheet net worth.	Progressive taxation should fall on the highest property and income brackets, especially on asset-price gains, not on employment. Wage taxes raise break-even prices.
FIRE revenue should be taxed at lower rates, if at all,	Taxes should focus on FIRE revenue, headed by land and resource rent, monopoly rent, interest and financial charges. These are the main revenues capitalized into bank loans.
because the rich are "job creators."	Economic polarization destroys employment. By impoverishing the market, it encourages capital flight and emigration.
By lowering wage levels, fiscal austerity makes economies more competitive.	Austerity shrinks investment and makes countries more dependent on foreign financing.
Austerity squeezes out more debt service.	Austerity shrinks economies, diverting revenue from the investment needed to pay the debt overhead. Arrears mount.
Governments should cover deficits by selling public enterprises and other assets.	Public infrastructure services should be supplied on a subsidized basis, paid out of progressive taxation so as to lower economy-wide costs of living and doing business.
Social Security and Medicare should be treated as user fees,	Social spending should be paid out of the general budget's progressive taxation,
paid in advance, and lent to government so that it can cut taxes on the wealthy and FIRE.	financed on a pay-as-you-go basis (as Adam Smith said that wars should be financed).
Public attempts at regulation is counterproductive and self-defeating, because the market's "rational expectations" will undo it.	Government's proper role is to shape markets by progressive taxes, rules and regulations.

Trade Policy

Neoliberal Theory	Classical and Progressive Era Reforms
Wage rates are the main variable. Cutting wages is the only way to lower prices, because capital goods have a common world price.	The cost of living and doing business consists mainly of payments to FIRE. Cutting debt service, employment taxes and debt-inflated housing costs reduce employment overhead.
Aims to lower wages by about 30 percent.	Reduces the cost of employment by shifting taxes off labor onto FIRE.
Does not recognize wage/productivity feedback, so cutting wages will not reduce output.	Higher wages are needed to raise productivity, to pay for education, better diets, etc.
Austerity programs go together with privatization sell-offs to pay public debts.	Rejects paying debts where this involves transforming social relations inequitably.
Takes for granted existing wealth distribution and institutions .	Foreign trade transforms economic and political structures.
Assumes that price and income adjustments automatically keep trade and payments in balance.	Imbalances are financed by debt, whose interest charges mount up to polarize the international economy.
It is most efficient to specialize and depend on the US and EU for food imports and credit.	Food and debt dependency lead to debt at interest, polarizing the global economy.
Finance is cosmopolitan, and hence peaceful.	Finance is ultimately national, when money is created by central banks, *e.g.*, the Dollar Standard.
Open trade and capital markets are peaceable, replacing war.	Finance aims at what military conquest seeks: the land, natural resources and their rent, and tribute. Finance achieves this at a lower cost (= "more efficiently") than open warfare.

14

U.S. QUANTITATIVE EASING IS FRACTURING THE GLOBAL ECONOMY

> Moreover, it may well be asked whether we can take it for granted
> that a return to freedom of exchanges is really a question of time.
> Even if the reply were in the affirmative, it is safe to assume that
> after a period of freedom the regime of control will be restored
> as a result of the next economic crisis.
>
> Paul Einzig, *Exchange Control* (1934)[1]

Great structural changes in world trade and finance occur quickly—by quantum leaps, not by slow marginal accretions. The 1945–2010 era of relatively open trade, capital movements and foreign exchange markets is being destroyed by a predatory financial opportunism that is breaking the world economy into two spheres: a dollar sphere in which central banks in Europe, Japan and many OPEC and Third World countries hold their reserves the form of U.S. Treasury debt of declining foreign-exchange value; and a BRIC-centered sphere, led by China, India, Brazil and Russia, reaching out to include Turkey and Iran, most of Asia, and major raw materials exporters that are running trade surpluses.

What is reversing trends that seemed irreversible for the past 65 years is the manner in which the United States has dealt with its bad-debt crisis. The Federal Reserve and Treasury are seeking to inflate the economy out of debt with an explosion of bank liquidity and credit—which means yet more debt. This is occurring largely at other countries' expense, in a way that is flooding the global economy with electronic "keyboard" bank credit while the U.S. balance-of-payments deficit widens and U.S. official debt soars beyond any foreseeable means to pay. The dollar's exchange rate is plunging, and U.S. money managers themselves are leading a capital flight out of the domestic economy to buy up foreign currencies and bonds, gold and other raw materials, stocks and entire companies with cheap dollar credit.

This outflow from the dollar is not the kind of capital that takes the form of tangible investment in plant and equipment, buildings, research and development. It is not a creation of assets as much as the creation of debt, and its

---

[1] I am indebted to Eric Janszen of *i-tulip* for bringing the Einzig quote to my attention.

multiplication by mirroring, credit insurance, default swaps and an array of computerized forward trades. The global financial system has decoupled from trade and investment, taking on a life of its own.

In fact, financial conquest is seeking today what military conquest did in times past: control of land and basic infrastructure, industry and mining, banking systems and even government finances to extract the economic surplus as interest and tollbooth-type economic rent charges. U.S. officials euphemize this policy as "quantitative easing." The Federal Reserve is flooding the banking system with so much liquidity that Treasury bills now yield less than 1 percent, and banks can draw freely on Fed credit. Japanese banks have seen yen borrowing rates fall to 0.25 percent.

This policy is based on a the wrong-headed idea that if the Fed provides liquidity, banks will take the opportunity to lend out credit at a markup, "earning their way out of debt"—inflating the economy in the process. And when the Fed talks about "the economy," it means asset markets—above all for real estate, as some 80 percent of bank loans in the United States are mortgage loans.

One-third of U.S. real estate is now reported to be in negative equity, as market prices have fallen behind mortgage debts. This is bad news not only for homeowners but also for their bankers, as the collateral for their mortgage loans does not cover the principal. Homeowners are walking away from their homes, and the real estate market is so thoroughly plagued with a decade of deception and outright criminal fraud that property titles themselves are losing security. And despite FBI findings of financial fraud in over three-quarters of the packaged mortgages they have examined, the Obama Justice Department has not sent a single bankster to jail.

Instead, the financial crooks have been placed in charge—and they are using their power over government to promote their own predatory gains, having disabled U.S. public regulatory agencies and the criminal justice system to create a new kind of centrally planned economy in the hands of banks. As Joseph Stiglitz recently observed:

> In the years prior to the breaking of the bubble, the financial industry was engaged in predatory lending practices, deceptive practices. They were optimizing not in producing mortgages that were good for the American families but in maximizing fees and exploiting and predatory lending. Going and targeting the least educated, the Americans that were most easy to prey on.
>
> We've had this well documented. And there was the tip of the iceberg that even in those years the FBI was identifying fraud. When they see fraud, it's really fraud. But beneath that surface, there were practices that really should have been outlawed if they weren't illegal.

... the banks used their political power to make sure they could get away with this [and] ... that they could continue engaging in these kinds of predatory behaviors.... there's no principle. It's money. It's campaign contributions, lobbying, revolving door, all of those kinds of things.

... it's like theft ... A good example of that might be [former Countrywide CEO] Angelo Mozillo, who recently paid tens of millions of dollars in fines, a small fraction of what he actually earned, because he earned hundreds of millions.

The system is designed to actually encourage that kind of thing, even with the fines.... we fine them, and what is the big lesson? Behave badly, and the government might take 5% or 10% of what you got in your ill-gotten gains, but you're still sitting home pretty with your several hundred million dollars that you have left over after paying fines that look very large by ordinary standards but look small compared to the amount that you've been able to cash in.

The fine is just a cost of doing business. It's like a parking fine. Sometimes you make a decision to park knowing that you might get a fine because going around the corner to the parking lot takes you too much time.

I think we ought to go do what we did in the S & L [crisis] and actually put many of these guys in prison. Absolutely. These are not just white-collar crimes or little accidents. There were victims. That's the point. There were victims all over the world.... the financial sector really brought down the global economy and if you include all of that collateral damage, it's really already in the trillions of dollars.[2]

This victimization of the international financial system is a consequence of the U.S. Government's attempt to bail out the banks by re-inflating U.S. real estate, stock and bond markets at least to their former Bubble Economy levels. This is what U.S. economic policy and even its foreign policy is now all about, including de-criminalizing financial fraud. As Treasury Secretary Tim Geithner tried to defend this policy: "Americans were rightfully angry that the same firms that helped create the economic crisis got taxpayer support to keep their doors open. But the program was essential to averting a second Great Depression, stabilizing a collapsing financial system, protecting the savings of

---

[2] "Stiglitz Calls for Jail Time for Corporate Crooks," *DailyFinance*: http://srph.it/aRwI4I, October 21, 2010.

Americans [or more to the point, he means, their indebtedness] and restoring the flow of credit that is the oxygen of the economy."[3]

Other economists might find a more fitting analogy to be carbon dioxide and debt pollution. "Restoring the flow of credit" is a euphemism for keeping today's historically high debt levels in place, and indeed adding yet more debt ("credit") to enable home buyers, stock market investors and others to bid asset prices back up to rescue the banking system from the negative equity into which it has fallen. That is what Mr. Geithner means by "stabilizing a collapsing financial system"—bailing out banks and making all the counterparties of AIG's fatal financial gambles whole at 100 cents on the dollar.

The Fed theorizes that if it provides nearly free liquidity, banks will lend it out at a markup to "reflate" the economy. The "recovery" that is envisioned is one of new debt creation. This would rescue the biggest and most risk-taking banks from their negative equity, by pulling homeowners out of theirs. Housing prices could begin to soar again.

But the hoped-for new borrowing is not occurring. Instead of lending more—at least, lending at home—banks have been tightening their loan standards rather than lending more to U.S. homeowners, consumers and businesses since 2007. This has obliged debtors to start paying off the debts they earlier ran up. The U.S. saving rate has risen from zero three years ago to 3 percent today—mainly in the form of amortization to pay down credit-card debt, mortgage debt and other bank loans.

Instead of lending domestically, banks are sending the Fed's tsunami of credit abroad, flooding world currency markets with cheap U.S. "keyboard credit." The Fed's plan is like that of the Bank of Japan after its bubble burst in 1990: The hope is that lending to speculators will enable banks to earn their way out of debt. So U.S. banks are engaging in interest-rate arbitrage (the carry trade), currency speculation, commodity speculation (driving up food and mineral prices sharply this year), and buying into companies in Asia and raw materials exporters.

By forcing up targeted currencies, this dollar outflow into foreign exchange speculation and asset buy-outs is financial aggression. And to add insult to injury, Mr. Geithner is accusing China of "competitive non-appreciation." This is a term of invective for economies seeking to maintain currency stability. It makes about as much sense as to say "aggressive self-defense." China's interest, of course, is to avoid taking a loss on its dollar holdings and export contracts denominated in dollars (as valued in its own domestic renminbi).

---

[3] Tim Geithner, "Five Myths about Tarp," *Washington Post*, October 10, 2010.

Countries on the receiving end of this U.S. financial conquest ("restoring stability" is how U.S. officials characterize it) understandably are seeking to protect themselves. Ultimately, the only serious way to do this is to erect a wall of capital controls to block foreign speculators from deranging currency and financial markets.

Changing the international financial system is by no means easy. How much of an alternative do countries have, Martin Wolf recently asked. "To put it crudely," he wrote:

> the US wants to inflate the rest of the world, while the latter is trying to deflate the US. The US must win, since it has infinite ammunition: there is no limit to the dollars the Federal Reserve can create. What needs to be discussed is the terms of the world's surrender: the needed changes in nominal exchange rates and domestic policies around the world.[4]

Mr. Wolf cites New York Federal Reserve chairman William C. Dudley to the effect that Quantitative Easing is primarily an attempt to deal with the mortgage crisis that capped a decade of bad loans and financial gambles. Economic recovery, the banker explained on October 1, 2010, "has been delayed because households have been paying down their debt—a process known as deleveraging." In his view, the U.S. economy cannot recover without a renewed debt leveraging to re-inflate the housing market.

By the "U.S. economy" and "recovery," to be sure, Mr. Dudley means his own constituency the banking system, and specifically the largest banks that gambled the most on the real estate bubble of 2003–08. He acknowledges that the bubble "was fueled by products and practices in the financial sector that led to a rapid and unsustainable buildup of leverage and an underpricing of risk during this period," and that household debt has risen "faster than income growth … since the 1950s." But this debt explosion was justified by the "surge in home prices [that] pushed up the ratio of household net worth to disposable personal income to nearly 640 percent." Instead of saving, most Americans borrowed as much as they could to buy property they expected to rise in price. For really the first time in history an entire population sought to get rich by running into debt (to buy real estate, stocks and bonds), not by staying out of it.

But now that asset prices have plunged, people are left in debt. The problem is, what to do about it. Disagreeing with critics who "argue that the decline in the household debt-to-income ratio must go much further before

---

[4] Martin Wolf, "Why America is going to win the global currency battle," *Financial Times*, October 13, 2010.

the deleveraging process can be complete," or who even urge "that household debt-to-income ratios must fall back to the level of the 1980s," Mr. Dudley retorts that the economy must inflate its way out of the debt corner into which it has painted itself. "First, low and declining inflation makes it harder to accomplish needed balance sheet adjustments." In other words, credit (debt) is needed to bid real estate prices back up. A lower rather than higher inflation rate would mean "slower nominal income growth. Slower nominal income growth, in turn, means that less of the needed adjustment in household debt-to-income ratios will come from rising incomes. This puts more of the adjustment burden on paying down debt." And it is debt deflation that is plaguing the economy, so the problem is how to re-inflate (asset) prices.

(1) How much would the Fed have to purchase to have a given impact on the level of long-term interest rates and economic activity, and,

(2) what constraints exist in terms of limits to balance-sheet expansion, and what are the costs involved that could impede efforts to meet the dual mandate now or in the future?[5]

On October 15, 2010, Fed Chairman Ben Bernanke explained that he wanted the Fed to encourage inflation — his of program of Quantitative Easing — and acknowledged that this would drive down the dollar against foreign currencies. Flooding the U.S. banking system with liquidity will lower interest rates, increasing the capitalization rate of real estate rents and corporate income. This will re-inflate asset prices — by creating yet more debt in the process of rescue banks from negative equity by pulling homeowners out of their negative equity. But internationally, this policy means that foreign central banks receive less than 1 percent on the international reserves they hold in Treasury securities — while U.S. investors are making much higher returns by borrowing "cheap dollars" to buy Australian, Asian and European government bonds, corporate securities, and speculating in foreign exchange and commodity markets.

Mr. Bernanke proposes to solve this problem by injecting another $1 trillion of liquidity over the coming year, on top of the $2 trillion in new Federal Reserve credit already created during 2009–10. The pretense is that bailing Wall Street banks out of their losses is a precondition for reviving employment and consumer spending — as if the giveaway to the financial sector will get the economy moving again.

---

[5] William C. Dudley, "The Outlook, Policy Choices and Our Mandate," *Remarks at the Society of American Business Editors and Writers Fall Conference*, City University of New York, Graduate School of Journalism, New York City, October 1, 2010. http://www.zerohedge.com/article/why-imf-meetings-failed-and-coming-capital-controls.

The working assumption is that if the Fed provides liquidity, banks will lend it out at a markup. At least this is the dream of bank loan officers. The Fed will help them keep the debt overhead in place, not write it down. But as noted above, the U.S. market is "loaned up." Borrowing by homeowners, businesses and individuals is shrinking. Unemployment is rising, stores are closing and the economy is succumbing to debt deflation. But most serious of all, the QE II program has a number of consequences that Federal Reserve policy makers have not acknowledged. For one thing, the banks have used the Federal Reserve and Treasury bailouts and liquidity to increase their profits and to continue paying high salaries and bonuses. What their lending is inflating are asset prices, not commodity prices (or output and employment). And asset-price inflation is increasing the power of property over living labor and production, elevating the FIRE sector further over the "real" economy.

These problems are topped by the international repercussions that Mr. Dudley referred to as the "limits to balance-of-payments expansion." Cheap electronic U.S. "keyboard credit" is going abroad as banks try to earn their way out of debt by financing arbitrage gambles, glutting currency markets while depreciating the U.S. dollar. So the upshot of the Fed trying save the banks from negative equity is to flood the global economy with a glut of U.S. dollar credit, destabilizing the global financial system.

Can Foreign Economies Rescue the U.S. Banking System?

The international economy's role is envisioned as a *deus ex machina* to rescue the economy. Foreign countries are to serve as markets for a resurgence of U.S. industrial exports (and at least arms sales are taking off to India and Saudi Arabia), and most of all as financial markets for U.S. banks and speculators to make money at the expense of foreign central banks trying to stabilize their currencies.

The Fed believes that debt levels can rise and become more solvent if U.S. employment increases by producing more exports. The way to achieve this is presumably to depreciate the dollar — the kind of "beggar-my-neighbor" policy that marked the 1930s. Devaluation will be achieved by flooding currency markets with dollars, providing the kind of zigzagging opportunities that are heaven-sent for computerized currency trading, short selling and kindred financial options.

Such speculation is a zero-sum game. Someone must lose. If Quantitative Easing is to help U.S. banks earn their way out of negative equity, by definition their gains must be at the expense of foreigners. This is what makes QE II a form of financial aggression.

This is destructive of the global currency stability that is a precondition for stable long-term trade relationships. Its underlying assumptions also happen to be based on Junk Economics. For starters, it assumes that international prices are based on relative price levels for goods and services. But only about a third of U.S. wages are spent on commodities. Most is spent on payments to the finance, insurance and real estate (FIRE) sector and on taxes. Housing and debt service typically absorb 40 percent and 15 percent of wage income respectively. FICA Wage withholding for Social Security and Medicare taxes absorb 11 percent, and income and sales taxes another 15 to 20 percent. So before take-home pay is available for consumer spending on goods and services, these FIRE-sector charges make the cost of living so high as to render American industrial labor uncompetitive in world markets. No wonder the U.S. economy faces a chronic trade deficit!

The FIRE sector overhead has become structural, not merely a marginal problem. To restore its competitive industrial position, the United States would have to devalue by much more than the 40 percent that it did back in 1933. Trying to "inflate its way out of debt" may help bank balance sheets recover, but as long as the economy remains locked in debt deflation it will be unable to produce the traditional form of economic surplus needed for genuine recovery. A debt write-down would be preferable to the policy of keeping the debts on the books and distorting the U.S. economy with inflation—and engaging in financial aggression against foreign economies. The political problem, of course, is that the financial sector has taken control of U.S. economic planning—in its own self-interest, not that of the economy at large. A debt write-down would threaten the financial sector's creditor power over the economy.

So it is up to foreign economies to enable U.S. banks to earn their way out of negative equity. For starters, there is the carry trade based on interest-rate arbitrage—to borrow at 1 percent, lend at a higher interest rate, and pocket the margin (after hedging the currency shift). Most of this financial outflow is going to China and other Asian countries, and to raw materials exporters. Australia, for example, has been raising its interest rates in order to slow its own real estate bubble. Rather than slowing speculation in its large cities by fiscal policy—a land tax—its central bank is operating on the principle that a property is worth whatever a bank will lend against it. Raising interest rates to the present 4.5 percent reduces the capitalization rate for property rents—and hence shrinks the supply of mortgage credit that has been bidding up Australian property prices.

This interest-rate policy has two unfortunate side effects for Australia—but a free lunch for foreign speculators. First of all, high interest rates raise the cost of borrowing across the board for doing business and for consumer finances. Second—even more important for the present discussion—high rates attract foreign "hot money" as speculators borrow at low interest in the United States (or Japan, for that matter) and buy high-yielding Australian government bonds.

The effect is to increase the Australian dollar's exchange rate, which recently has achieved parity with the U.S. dollar. This upward valuation makes its industrial sector less competitive, and also squeezes profits in its mining sector. So on top of Australia's rising raw-materials exports, its policy to counter its real estate bubble is attracting foreign financial inflows, providing a free ride for international arbitrageurs. Over and above their interest-rate arbitrage gains is the foreign currency play—rising exchange rates in Australia and many Asian countries as the U.S. dollar glut swamps the ability of central banks to keep their exchange rates stable.

This foreign-currency play is where most of the speculative action is today as speculators watching these purchases have turned the currencies and bonds of other raw-materials exporters into speculative vehicles. This currency speculation is the most aggressive, predatory and destructive aspect of U.S. financial behavior. Its focus is now shifting to the major nation that has resisted U.S. attempts to force its currency up: China. The potentially largest prize for U.S. and foreign speculators would be an upward revaluation of its renminbi.

The House Ways and Means Committee recently insisted that China raise its exchange rate by the 20 percent that the Treasury and Federal Reserve have suggested. Suppose that China would obey this demand. This would mean a bonanza for U.S. speculators. A revaluation of this magnitude would enable them to put down 1 percent equity—say, $1 million to borrow $99 million—and buy Chinese renminbi forward. The revaluation being demanded would produce a 2000% profit of $20 million by turning the $100 million bet (and just $1 million "serious money") into $120 million. Banks can trade on much larger, nearly infinitely leveraged margins.

Can U.S. Banks Create Enough Electronic "Keyboard Credit" to Buy up the Whole World?

The Fed's QE II policy poses a logical question: Why can't U.S. credit buy out the entire world economy—all the real estate, companies and mineral rights yielding over 1 percent, with banks and their major customers pocketing the difference?

Under current arrangements the dollars being pumped into the global economy are recycled back into U.S. Treasury IOUs. When foreign sellers turn over their dollar receipts to their banks for domestic currency, these banks turn the payment over to the central bank—which then faces a Hobson's Choice: either to sell the dollars on the foreign exchange market (pushing up their own currency against the dollar), or avoid doing this by buying more U.S. Treasury securities and thus keeping the dollar payment within the U.S. economy. Why can't this go on *ad infinitum?*

What makes these speculative capital inflows so unwelcome abroad is that they do not contribute to tangible capital formation or employment. Their effect is simply to push up foreign currencies against the dollar, threatening to price exporters out of global markets, disrupting domestic employment as well as trade patterns.

These financial gambles are setting today's exchange rates, not basic production costs. In terms of relative rates of return, foreign central banks earn 1 percent on their U.S. Treasury bonds, while U.S. investors buy up the world's assets. In effect, U.S. diplomats are demanding that other nations relinquish their trade surpluses, private savings and general economic surplus to U.S. investors, creditors, bankers, speculators, arbitrageurs and vulture funds in exchange for this 1 percent return on U.S. dollar reserves of depreciating value—and indeed, in amounts already far beyond the foreseeable ability of the U.S. economy to generate a balance-of-payments surplus to pay this debt to foreign governments.

The global economy is being turned into a tributary system, achieving what military conquest sought in times past. This turns out to be implicit in QE II. Arbitrageurs and speculators are swamping Asian and Third World currency markets with low-priced U.S. dollar credit to make predatory trading profits at the expense of foreign central banks trying to stabilize their exchange rates by selling their currency for dollar-denominated securities—under conditions where the United States and Canada are blocking reciprocal direct investment (*e.g.*, Potash Corp. of Saskatchewan in Canada and Unocal in the United States.).

The Road to Capital Controls

Hardly by surprise, other countries are taking defensive measures against this speculation, and against "free credit" takeovers using inexpensive U.S. electronic "keyboard bank credit." For the past few decades they have stabilized their exchange rates by recycling dollar inflows and other foreign currency buildups into U.S. Treasury securities. The Bank of Japan, for instance, recently lowered its interest rate to just 0.1 percent in an attempt to induce its banks to lend back abroad the foreign exchange that is now coming in as its banks are being repaid on their own carry-trade loans. It also offset the repayment of past carry-trade loans extended by its own banks in yen by selling $60 billion of yen and buying U.S. Treasury securities, of which it now owns over $1 trillion.

Foreign economies are now taking more active steps to shape "the market" in which international speculation occurs. The most modest move is to impose a withholding tax on interest payments to foreign investors. Just before the IMF meetings on October 9–10, 2010, Brazil doubled the tax on foreign investment in its government bond to 4 percent. Thailand acted along similar lines a week later. It stopped exempting foreign investors from having to pay the 15 percent interest-withholding tax on their purchases of its government bonds. Finance Minister Korn Chatikavinij warned that more serious measures are likely if "excessive" speculative inflows keep pushing up the baht. "We need to consider the rationality of capital inflows, whether they are for speculative purposes and how much they generate volatility in the baht," he explained. But the currency continues to rise.

Such tax withholding discourages interest-rate arbitrage via the bond market, but leaves the foreign-currency play intact—and that is where the serious action is today. In the 1997 Asian Crisis, Malaysia blocked foreign purchases of its currency to prevent short-sellers from covering their bets by buying the ringgit at a lower price later, after having emptied out its central bank reserves. The blocks worked, and other countries are now reviewing how to impose such controls.

Longer-term institutional changes to more radically restructure the global financial system may include dual exchange rates such as were prevalent from the 1930 through the early 1960s, one (low and stable) for trade and at least one other (usually higher and more fluctuating) for capital movements. But the most decisive counter-strategy to U.S. QE II policy is to create a full-fledged BRIC-centered currency bloc that would minimize use of the dollar.

China has negotiated currency-swap agreements with Russia, India, Turkey and Nigeria. These swap agreements may require exchange-rate guarantees to make central-bank holders "whole" if a counterpart currency depreciates. But at least initially, these agreements are being used for bilateral trade. This saves exporters from having to hedge their payments through forward purchases on global exchange markets.

A BRIC-centered system would reverse the policy of open and unprotected capital markets put in place after World War II. This trend has been in the making since the BRIC countries met 2009 in Yekaterinburg, Russia, to discuss such an international payments system based on their own currencies rather than the dollar, sterling or euro. In September , China supported a Russian proposal to start direct trading using the yuan and the ruble rather than pricing their trade or taking payment in U.S. dollars or other foreign currencies. China then negotiated a similar deal with Brazil. And on the eve of the IMF meetings in Washington on Friday, Premier Wen stopped off in Istanbul to reach agreement with Turkish Prime Minister Erdogan to use their own currencies in a planned tripling Turkish-Chinese trade to $50 billion over the next five years, effectively excluding the dollar.

China cannot make its currency a world reserve currency, because it is not running a deficit and therefore cannot supply large sums of renminbi to other countries via trade. So it is negotiating currency-swap agreements with other countries, while using its enormous dollar reserves to buy up natural resources in Australia, Africa and South America.

This has reversed the dynamics that led speculators to gang up and cause the 1997 Asia crisis. At that time the great speculative play was against the "Asian Tigers." Speculators swamped their markets with sell orders, emptying out the central bank reserves of countries that tried (in vain) to keep their exchange rates stable in the face of enormous U.S. bank credit extended to George Soros and other hedge fund managers and the vulture funds that followed in their wake. The IMF and U.S. banks then stepped in and offered to "rescue" these economies if they agreed to sell off their best companies and resources to U.S. and European buyers.

This was a major reason why so many countries have tried to free themselves from the IMF and its neoliberal austerity programs, euphemized as "stabilization" plans rather than the economic poison of chronic dependency and instability programs. Left with only Turkey as a customer by 2008, the IMF was a seemingly anachronistic institution whose only hope for survival lay in future crises. So that of 2009–10 proved to be a godsend. At least the IMF found neoliberal Latvia and Greece willing to subject themselves to its precepts. Today its destructive financial austerity doctrine is applied mainly by Europe's "failed economies."

This has changed the equation between industrial-nation creditors and Third World debtors. Many dollar-strapped countries have been subject to repeated raids on their central banks — followed by IMF austerity programs that have shrunk their domestic markets and made them yet more dependent on imports and foreign investments, reduced to selling off their public infrastructure to raise the money to pay their debts. This has raised their cost of living and doing business, shrinking the economy all the more and creating new budget squeezes driving them even further into debt. But China's long-term trade and investment deals — to be paid in raw materials, denominated in renminbi rather than dollars—is alleviating their debt pressures to the point where currency traders are jumping on the bandwagon, pushing up their exchange rates. The major international economic question today is how such national economies can achieve greater stability by insulating themselves from these predatory financial movements.

Summary

The 1945–2010 world economic dynamic has ended, and a new international system is emerging—one that was not anticipated as recently as just five years ago. From the 1960s through 1980s, the international economy was polarizing between indebted raw-materials producers in Africa, Latin America and large parts of Asia—"the South"—and the industrialized North, led by North America, Europe and Japan. Economists analyzing this polarization focused (1) on the terms of trade for raw materials as compared to industrial goods, (2) on the failure of World Bank programs to help "the South" cure its food dependency and other import dependency, and (3) on the failure of IMF austerity programs to stabilize the balance of payments. The IMF-World Bank model promoted austerity, low wage standards, trade dependency, and deepening foreign debt. It was applauded as a success story in the creditor-investor nations.

Today's world is dividing along quite different lines. The main actor is still "the North" composed of the United States and Europe. But the counterpart economic bloc that is emerging is growing less dependent and indebted. It is led by a rapidly growing China, India, Brazil and even Russia (the BRIC countries), joined by the strongest Middle Eastern economies (Turkey and potentially Iran) and Asian economies such as Korea, Taiwan, Malaysia and Singapore. This "BRIC bloc" and its allies are in payment surplus, not deficit. It is now the U.S. and European governments that find themselves debt-ridden beyond their ability to pay, especially when it comes to paying foreign governments, central banks and bondholders.

Yet the world is now seeing a race to convert electronic ("paper") credit creation from these already debt-ridden economies into asset ownership before governments in the payments-surplus economies to erect protective walls. Easy credit in the United States and Japan is fueling speculation in economies that are not so heavily loaded down with debt. This flight out of the U.S. dollar into Asian and Third World currencies is changing the global economy's orientation—in such a way as to restore financial dominance to nations running balance-of-payments surpluses, whose currencies promise to rise (or at least remain stable) rather than to fall along with the dollar.

As the U.S. and European domestic markets shrink in response to debt deflation, Asian countries and raw-materials exporters from Australia to Africa have recovered mainly because of China's growth. As in 1997, the problem they face is how to keep predatory U.S. and allied financial speculation at bay. This makes these countries the most likely to find capital controls attractive. But this time around, they are trying to keep speculators from buying into their assets and currencies, not selling them. Targeted economies are ones that are strong, not ones that are weak.

Since the mid-19th century, central banks raised interest rates to hold their currencies stable when trade moved into deficit. The universal aim was to gain financial reserves. In the 1930s, money and credit systems were still based on gold. Protective tariffs and trade subsidies aimed at running trade and balance-of-payments surpluses in order to gain financial reserves. But today's problem is too much liquidity, in the form of keyboard bank credit that can be created without limit.

This has turned the world of half a century ago upside-down. National economies in the United States, Japan leading nations are lowering their rates to 1 percent or less, encouraging capital outflows rather than payments surpluses, while their banks and investors are seeking to gain more by financial speculation than by trade.

Conclusion

The American economy may be viewed as a tragic drama. Its tragic flaw was planted and flowered in the 1980s: a combination of deregulation leading to financial fraud so deep as to turn the banking system into a predatory gang, while shifting the tax burden off real estate and the higher tax brackets onto wage earners and sales taxes. This increased the economy's cost of doing business in two ways. First, taxes on employees (including FICA withholding for Social Security and Medicare) and on business profits increase the cost of doing business for American industry.

Second, untaxing the site value of land (and most "capital gains" are actually land-value gains) has "freed" rental income to be pledged to banks for yet higher mortgage loans. This obliged new homebuyers to take on more and more debt as taxes were shifted off property. So homeowners working for a living did not really gain from low property taxes. What the tax collector relinquished ended up being paid to banks as interest on the loans that were bidding up housing prices, creating a real estate bubble. Meanwhile, governments had to make up the property-tax cuts by taxing employees and employers all the more. So the United States became a high-cost economy.

It didn't have to be this way—and that is the tragedy of the U.S. economy over the past thirty years. It was a fiscal and financial tragedy, with the tragic flaw being the propensity for the financial sector to engage in wholesale fraud and "junk economics." A flawed tax policy was endorsed by a failure of economic thought to explain the costs entailed in trying to get rich by running into debt. What Alan Greenspan famously called "wealth creation" during his tenure as Federal Reserve Chairman sponsoring asset-price inflation turned out simply to be debt leveraging—that is, debt creation when the dust settled and prices fell back into negative equity territory.

To rescue the increasingly irresponsible financial sector from its mortgage-debt gambles, the United States is taking a path that is losing its international position, ending the long epoch of what was actually a free lunch—the U.S. Treasury-bill standard of international finance. All that U.S. diplomats can do at this point is play for time, hoping to prolong the existing double standard favorable to the United States and its Treasury-debt a bit further, to permit U.S. bankers to get just one more year of enormous bonuses, in keeping with the American motto, "You only need to make a fortune once."

What no doubt will amaze future historians is why the rest of the U.S. economy has let the banking sector get away with this! Apart from the Soviet Union's self-destruction in 1990–91, it is hard to find a similar blunder in economic diplomacy. It reflects the banking system's success in shifting economic planning out of the hands of government into those of finance-sector lobbyists.

U.S. officials always have waged American foreign trade and financial policy in reference to their own domestic economic interests without much regard for foreigners. The history of U.S. protective tariffs, dollar policy and interest-rate policy has been to look only at home. Other countries have had to raise interest rates when their balance of trade and payments move into deficit, above all, for military adventures. The United States alone is immune—thanks to the legacy of the dollar being "as good as gold" during the decades when it was running a surplus.

To quote Joseph Stiglitz once again:

> [T]he irony is that money that was intended to rekindle the American economy is causing havoc all over the world. Those elsewhere in the world say, what the United States is trying to do is the twenty-first century version of 'beggar thy neighbor' policies that were part of the Great Depression: you strengthen yourself by hurting the others.[6]

---

[6] Nobel Laureate Joseph Stiglitz: "Foreclosure Moratorium, Government Stimulus Needed to Revive US Economy," *Democracy Now*, Oct. 21, 2010.

It is natural enough for the United States to shape its international policy with regard to its own interests, to be sure. The self-interest principle is a foundation assumption of political theory as it is economic logic. What is less understandable is why other countries have not acted more effectively in their own interests—and why U.S. diplomats and economic officials should be so upset today when other nations in fact begin to do so.

15

AMERICA'S MONETARY IMPERIALISM

It is not hard to find examples of coercive exploitation in today's global economy. The International Monetary Fund (IMF) imposes austerity on debtor economies, shrinking their investment and production. This causes unemployment and a domestic fiscal crisis, while making them more dependent on foreign suppliers. A widening trade deficit ensues, financed by further borrowing whose interest charges aggravate the overall payments deficit in a deteriorating spiral.

The World Bank demands that debtor countries raise money by privatizing their public domain, despite the notorious underpricing of assets, exorbitant underwriting fees, insider dealings, and falling post-privatization service standards. The World Trade Organization (WTO) blocks governments from taxing the profits and rents generated by these privatized assets. Its neoliberal agenda aims at turning control over markets to the multinational corporations, while promoting tax codes that enable companies to deduct from taxable profits all interest and insurance charges, management fees, and the fatal slack variable of intra-company transfer pricing through offshore tax havens. This starves governments fiscally, forcing them to borrow more even as they slash public services.

Debtor countries thus suffer from a proliferating debt pollution—the build-up of debts beyond their ability to pay, as well as suffering from ecological standards being cut back by economic distress conditions. Austerity blocks governments from making the social investment needed to avert long-term educational cleanup costs to repair a broken social system, debt cleanup costs to cope with the creditor leverage held over their heads, and the physical cleanup costs that result from hosting some of the world's most environmentally destructive industries.

The thrust of the Washington Consensus enforced by the IMF, World Bank and WTO is to dismantle the regulatory and fiscal power of governments throughout the world. Not only are debtor-country governments blocked from running the budget deficits that the United States runs freely in response to its own unemployment, but even the European Central Bank (ECB) blocks member-country governments from running sustained budget deficits of more than 3 percent of GDP, despite the continent's unemployment and balance-of-payments surplus.

These payments-surplus nations find themselves unable to cope with the influx of dollars stemming from America's trade deficit, now overlayered by a military deficit that threatens to escalate as the United States expands its adventurism in the Near East. In exchange for these excess dollars, Europe and Asia supply exports and sell off their companies and other assets. But what do they get in return?

A double standard has been implicit in the world's economic rules since the dollar was decoupled from gold in 1971, when the U.S. trade deficit of $10 billion deficit was the equivalent of more than half the U.S. gold stock. But today there is no gold convertibility and hence no major constraint on U.S. spending abroad or at home. The United States has not subjected itself to any of the distressing fiscal conditions that all other countries feel obliged to follow. What makes this asymmetry so ironic is that it was made possible by what seemed to be a financial defeat for the United States. Once America stopped paying gold, there was not much that other central banks could ask for as they found themselves flooded with dollars obtained by private-sector exporters and asset sellers in excess of their needs.

America was not about to yield control of its strategic sectors to foreign holders of these dollars, even as foreign countries have privatized their major public-sector utilities and infrastructure. In 1973, U.S. diplomats made it clear that if OPEC countries tried to use their dollars to buy out major companies, this would be treated as a belligerent act. The Islamic countries were told that they could earn interest by leaving their money in American banks, or they could buy U.S. Treasury bonds or—considering their religious strictures against usury—they could buy minority shares of U.S. stocks, an activity that would bid up the stock market and thus help create a boom in the United States, but they could not buy enough shares to dominate these companies. They could buy real estate, Japan-style, helping to inflate the U.S. property market. But one way or another, OPEC and other dollar holders would have to keep their dollar inflows in the form of dollars. There was no alternative, politically and indeed militarily speaking.

So much for the patina of free-market rhetorical glove in which this iron fist was wrapped! Now that gold has been demonetized, all that foreign central banks can do with their excess dollars is to send them back to the U.S. Government by buying Treasury bonds. If they do not do this, their currencies will surge against the dollar, threatening to price their manufacturers and food exporters out of foreign markets.

What may cause a break between the United States and foreign dollar-holders is a non-economic strain: America's war in Iraq and its threat of preventive (that is, unprovoked) attacks on Iran, North Korea, Syria and North Africa. In the 1960s military spending in Vietnam pushed America's balance of payments into deficit, drained the gold stock that had been the source of international power since World War I. Back then at least the private sector was in balance. But today it is deep in deficit, while military spending is frightening the world not merely by financially undercutting the dollar's already deteriorating value, but by the political adventurism that is sparking popular protests around the entire world. Other countries now fear America's military aggressiveness as well as its unchecked financial unilateralism. Although the Iraq War is only the most recent cap to the unconstrained growth of America's trade and payments deficit, the anti-war protests around the world have given the problem a highly political coloration.

The world still remembers how it was the Vietnam War that forced America off gold, as the U.S. balance-of-payments deficit during the 1960s stemmed entirely from overseas military spending. By 1971 the United States stopped redeeming foreign-held dollars in gold, and the dollar ceased to be a gold proxy. As the U.S. payments deficit shifted to the private sector, it expressed itself in the form of a demand for foreign products. This was welcomed by foreign countries on the grounds that at least it helped spur their domestic employment. But America's new military adventurism has no visible side benefits for Europe, Asia or other countries. It has given the U.S. Treasury-bill standard the coloration of a political and military threat as well as being merely an economic form of exploitation.

Having taken over three decades for the crisis to reach today's critical mass, the multilateral character of international finance is now beginning to crumble because other countries are now coming to see that the Dollar Standard has enabled the United States to obtain the largest free lunch in history. Whereas the world's financial system formerly rested on gold, central bank reserves now are held in the form of U.S. Treasury IOUs that are being run up without limit. America has been buying the exports and even the companies of Europe, Asia and other regions with paper credit whose volume now exceeds America's ability to pay, and which the United States has made it clear that it has little intention of paying off. That is the essence of today's "paper gold."

The widening U.S. payments deficit and the dollar's consequent plunge pose the question of whether any practical balance-of-payments constraint exists—or can be imposed—to the United States spending as much as it wants. The problem is that it is paying for non-U.S. goods and services in exchange for Treasury IOUs that are rapidly losing the fiction that they ever will be paid.

This is where the unfair double standard comes into play. If Latin American and African countries—and now, Iraq—cannot be expected to pay their exponentially growing debts and ask for debt write-offs, can the United States be far behind? And if the U.S. debt is written off, what will Europe and East Asia have got in exchange for having provided a rising torrent of automobiles and other manufactures, and even the sale of their companies for dollars? The United States for its part will have got a free ride, even as its economists promise the world that there is no such thing as a free lunch.

What Makes Super Imperialism Different from Past "Private Enterprise" Imperialism

A new mode of international exploitation has been created. As Henry C.K. Liu has noted recently in the *Asia Times*, "Dollar hegemony is a structural condition in world finance and trade in which the United States produces dollars and the rest of the world produces things dollars can buy." Primarily financial in character, this new kind of imperialism is turning the more classical forms of imperialism upside down. Unlike former modes of imperialism, it is a strategy that only one power, the United States, has been able to employ. Also novel is the fact that the U.S. Treasury-bond standard does not rely on the corporate profits or the drives of private companies investing in other countries to extract profits and interest. Monetary imperialism operates primarily through the balance of payments and central bank agreements, which ultimately are government functions. It occurs between the U.S. Government and the central banks of nations running balance-of-payments surpluses. The larger their surpluses grow, the more U.S. Treasury securities they are obliged to buy.

I recently have updated and republished a book that I wrote when this process was just getting underway, in 1972: *Super Imperialism: The Origins and Fundamentals of U.S. World Dominance*. It gives a fuller explanation than I can afford here of how America went off gold in 1971, obliging the world's central banks to finance the U.S. balance-of-payments deficit by using their surplus dollars to buy U.S. Treasury bonds. It explains why there is little Europe or Asia can do about the situation except reject the dollar. The problem is that to do that would lead their currencies to appreciate, hurting their own exporters in world markets.

Gold was the source of America's financial power since World War I, when arms sales and related material exports to the Allies turned the United States from a debtor into a creditor nation. From 1917 through 1950 the United States used its creditor position to domineer international diplomacy. The British Loan of 1944 was granted on the condition that the British Empire and its Sterling Area would be wound down after World War II ended and made virtually into an extension of the U.S. economy. Similar creditor power has been used against third world debtors since the 1950s, once they exhausted the foreign-exchange reserves built up during World War II as a result of providing raw materials to the Allies and not finding many consumer or investment goods to import.

When the United States was forced off gold it appeared that this era had ended. Most observers assumed that creditor nations would call the tune. An era had ended, in the sense that the United States was becoming the world's largest debtor. But what replaced its creditor power was a new debtor power, based on America's power to wreck the world financial system if other countries asserted their own creditor interests at the expense of U.S. demands that it be permitted to become a reckless debtor.

Old Classical Imperialism	Dollar Hegemony under the Treasury-Bond Standard
Globally symmetrical opportunities	Geopolitically asymmetrical, and hence unstable
Based on commercial trade and investment, supplemented by international loans.	Based on U.S. dollars supplying central bank reserves via the U.S. Treasury-bill standard
Based on cosmopolitan creditor power	Based on America's unique debtor power
An imperial-nation trade surplus provides the resources to sustain a capital investment abroad.	The U.S. economy runs a deepening trade deficit in addition to a capital and military deficit
The major competition is for export markets	The object is to import as much as possible without having to give a quid pro quo
All countries can become imperialistic following a common pattern	Only the United States can play the new dollar game
The effect is to underdevelop dependent countries	The effect is to make foreign central banks arms of the monetarist Washington Consensus
Exploits low-wage labor in less developed countries	Extracts forced credit and rent from Europe and Asia
Exploitation is measured by the wage differential	The aim is to get the entire product for nothing
Imperial power enforced by gunboats	Imperial power enforced by air and missile power

The Seignorage Benefits of Dollar Hegemony

The free ride that America receives from its ability to run a balance-of-payments deficit has been likened to the seignorage a government gets when it prints paper currency and spends it on goods and services. More U.S. paper currency is held abroad than that of any other country, more even than is held in the United States itself. Most consists of $100 bills. Russia accounts for a large proportion, and the world's drug traders, tax dodgers and other criminals have absorbed most of the balance. Foreign countries get paper, while Americans get their goods and services.

But most of the benefits of U.S. dollar credit have come from foreign central banks receiving bank drafts denominated in dollars. Over and above what their private sector spends to buy U.S. exports, pay interest and dividends to U.S. investors or remit profits to U.S.-owned firms, nearly a trillion dollars have mounted up in the world's central banks for which the private sector has no use, and hence has turned them over in exchange for their own domestic currency.

Central banks find themselves with the equivalent of the $100 bills collected by the Russians. At least the central banks are able to get interest credited to these holdings, for they return these dollars to the United States to buy its Treasury bonds. These form the growth in their international reserves.

Europe, China and Japan have been the major regions building up such reserves. They finally are beginning to ask themselves just what practical use these reserves are, and how much value these dollar claims will retain as they become increasingly fictitious. When it comes down to the essence of matters, what will today's U.S. Government let foreign governments spend their monetary reserves on? The U.S. economy has been hollowing itself out by treating its industry as a financial vehicle to turn profits into interest payments. Its labor is rendered high-cost not only by its current living expenses paid for goods and services, but for its sharp rise in debt service, headed by mortgage-debt service on the increasingly expensive cost of buying homes.

Although the U.S. real estate and financial bubble has been welcomed as post-industrial "wealth creation," it is rendering the American economy uncompetitive in world markets and hence unable to pay off its foreign debt by running a trade surplus. U.S. labor is obliged to pay for high-cost housing and pay debt service on the loans needed to stay afloat in today's economy. Agriculture remains the mainstay of U.S. exports, but the nation's farm protectionism finally is coming under criticism by food-deficit countries. It has been a sticking point in new global trade negotiations ever since the Common Agricultural Policy triggered U.S.-European rivalry 45 years ago.

The Irony of Dollar Hegemony: Power and Unlimited Dredit through the Threat of Bankruptcy

The United States achieves hegemony not by its creditor status as it did prior to the Korean War, but by its payments-deficit status. This seeming weakness enables it to run a trade deficit that is now approaching half a trillion dollars annually and shows no sign of abating. The world finds itself confronted by America running this deficit without constraint, importing as much as it wants from abroad and permitting its investors to buy as many foreign companies, stocks and bonds as they want, without limit.

By "without limit" I mean without having to provide a *quid pro quo* beyond Treasury IOUs whose prospects for repayment are diminishing as their volume grows. As fewer and fewer economic analysts are able to see a way for these official obligations to be paid, the question becomes which nations will succeed in dropping the dollar first, and what political upheavals may result as they draw the line against accepting more dollars in their reserves.

> The larger the balance-of-payments deficit grows, the more money central banks have to recycle to finance America's budget deficit.

As far as domestic U.S. fiscal and monetary relations are concerned, the government can finance its budget deficit by foreign central-bank demand for U.S. Treasury securities rather than borrowing from or taxing U.S. citizens. The larger the balance-of-payments deficit grows, the more money central banks have to recycle to finance America's budget deficit. Both deficits thus can increase together, financing each other.

The Treasury-bond standard is thus a more specific term than dollar hegemony. It explains how this hegemony is achieved. Other countries running budget deficits are obliged to raise interest rates. But America has lowered its interest rates, pursuing a tax policy and related fiscal and monetary policy of "benign neglect" in the face of its trade and payments deficit. The United States alone is able to lower its interest rates to spur domestic economic activity, even to the point of spurring a stock market and real estate bubble. This freedom is not available to European, Asian or other countries. No country ever before has been able to do this.

When other countries run sustained trade deficits, they must finance these by selling off domestic assets or running into debt — debt which they actually are obliged to pay. It seems that only the Americans are so bold as to say "Screw the world. We're going to do whatever we want." Other countries simply cannot afford the chaos from which the U.S. economy is positioned to withstand as a result of the fact that foreign trade plays a smaller role in its economy than in those of nearly all other nations in today's interdependent world.

Using debtor leverage to set the terms on which it will refrain from causing monetary chaos, America has turned seeming financial weakness into strength. U.S. Government debt has reached so large a magnitude that any attempt to replace it will entail an interregnum of financial chaos and political instability. American diplomats have learned that they are well positioned to come out on top in such grab-bags.

No other country is able to play the game of international finance in this way. Other countries running balance-of-payments deficits are obliged to sell off the assets in their public domain and run up debts that indeed must be paid. Free of such constraint, America keeps on supplying paper or electronic dollars to the world at will.

The upshot is that although at first appearing as a sign of weakness, the U.S. trade and payments deficit supplies its consumers and companies with foreign goods, while spending abroad militarily and lowering its interest rates to inflate a bubble economy without international constraint. This asymmetrical ability to exploit is a double standard that is implicit in the dollar standard. It enables America to play both sides of the creditor-debtor street.

As a debtor country the United States exploits Europe and Asia by running a balance-of-payments deficit now approaching half a trillion dollars annually. It pays for its net imports and buyouts of foreign industry by with Treasury bonds that its diplomats have long hinted they have little intention of paying off. Central banks end up with paper or electronic IOUs bearing 4 or 5 percent interest, which the U.S. Treasury simply adds to the balance of what it owes, while U.S. investors buy foreign companies, resources and hitherto public enterprises expected to yield in the neighborhood of 20 percent in earnings and capital gains.

Meanwhile, the United States uses traditional "hard-money" creditor leverage toward third world debtor countries. Through the IMF and World Bank it forces these countries to pay foreign debts by privatizing their natural resources and public enterprises which, for thousands of years, have been considered to be the national patrimony and guarantee of self-determination in economic and fiscal policy.

The fact that much of the foreign debt being used as leverage over third world countries can be traced to capital flight and interest accruals building up on past loans to kleptocracies and client oligarchies backed by the United States adds a further note of asymmetry to illustrate America's remarkable ability to get the best of both worlds in applying this dual international strategy. It buys whatever imports and foreign companies it wants, with a line of credit that seems to have no end, and whose modest interest charges are simply added onto the balance hypothetically due, while using its ability to create bank credit (in dollars) at will as leverage over the governments of indebted countries. Their alternative is to suffer the fate that Cuba, Iraq and other exiles from the Washington Consensus have suffered.

Engine of Global Economic Growth, or Financial Exploitation?

American diplomats represent U.S. foreign spending as an "engine of growth" pumping dollars into the world economy to provide a source of market demand that saves other nations from unemployment and recession. The logic is that foreign labor would not be employed without U.S. consumer demand, as if Europe and Asia could not replace U.S. imports with growth in their own markets.

If this were true, it would be an indictment of Europe's central banking system, reflecting the extent to which the ECB and central banks throughout the world have become part of the monetarist Washington Consensus—a monetary stranglehold outside of the United States while the U.S. banking system creates credit freely and cut taxes as foreign central banks finance the resulting budget deficit.

A related euphemism is that the U.S. economy is doing so well that it "attracts" money, which provides it with the resources to buy more abroad than it sells. The implied line of causation turns what is happening inside-out. Under today's geopolitical conditions these dollars have nowhere to go except back to the U.S. economy, which pushes dollars on the world in the knowledge that like a boomerang foreign central banks must return them.

No active steps are needed to attract these dollars back. All that is needed is to prevent the euro and sterling, the yen and yuan from being used to expand domestic market demand and finance social democratic programs, creating securities that other countries could hold as alternatives to U.S. Treasury debt. Not to see that depicting the dollar as the world's "engine of growth" is a euphemism for dollar hegemony and the American free ride is to lose touch with financial reality by reversing the actual arrow of causality at work.

The question that needs to be asked is how the rest of the world came to be dependent on the U.S. trade and payments deficit to obtain enough money to spend domestically. Money historically has been a government creation. It also is an instrument of debt — today, mainly debt owed by the U.S. Government. How did the creation of international monetary reserves pass out of the hands of all governments except that of the United States?

Part of the answer is IMF and World Bank imposition of the Washington Consensus. When American advisors were given a free hand in Russia in the mid-1990s, the insisted that the central bank hold U.S. dollars as counterparts to their creation of rubles to pay domestic labor. The central bank notoriously paid 100 percent interest for these dollars — dollars that had nothing whatsoever to do with the ruble credit being created to pay labor, but everything to do with creating huge profits for well-connected U.S. investors and speculators. The problem is ideological, not economically necessary.

In all such questions the surest answer is supplied by following the money. As Willy Sutton is said to have remarked, he robbed banks because that's where the money was. Empires follow the same strategy. A century ago John Hobson pointed out that the imperial nations invested mainly in each other. It is they that have the money and markets, after all, and whose real estate, stock and bond markets offer the best opportunities for asset-price gains. The problem is not rich exploiting the poor as much as the rich exploiting other rich nations. That has been the key to empire-building throughout history.

It was not labor that America wanted when it sent its advisors to Russia. Its investors wanted the country's raw materials, its oil and gas, minerals, and especially its urban land, as land and subsoil resources are still the major assets of every economy. This is why they are the main objectives of imperialism, yielding rent and capital gains whose magnitude exceeds the profits gained on employing wage labor.

Was the Oil War in Iraq about the Dollar Standard?

The 2003 Iraq War has inspired speculation that it is was fought to keep OPEC oil priced in dollar rather than in euros. The problem with this theory is that when OPEC-held dollars or U.S. Treasury bonds are sold for securities denominated in euros, yen or yuan, these dollar securities are passed on to the central banks of Europe, Japan and China respectively. These central banks then find themselves obliged to do just what they have been doing all along to prevent their currencies from rising against the dollar: They recycle the dollar inflows into U.S. Treasury bonds. If they receive balance-of-payments inflows as a result of OPEC purchases, overall global central bank holdings of Treasury securities will not decline, but will merely shift out of OPEC central banks to those of Europe and East Asia. OPEC will have divested itself of its dollar problem by passing the problem on like the proverbial hot potato.

This means that concerns about the euro threatening the dollar have been overdrawn. If the oil-exporting countries shift their international reserves from dollars to euros, they will do so by selling U.S. Treasury bonds and buying the government bonds or other securities of European countries. This would force up the euro's exchange rate against the dollar, confronting Europe with the same dilemma it has faced since the dollar was cut off from gold in 1971. If it stops recycling its surplus dollars — that is, its trade and payments surpluses — into loans back to the U.S. Treasury, its currencies will rise, hurting its exporters. This is the dilemma spelled out in the final two chapters of *Super Imperialism*.

The effect of a shift out of dollars into euros by OPEC would be much like Europe exporting more goods directly to the United States or other dollar-using countries, or selling more companies, stocks and bonds to U.S. investors. As the euro rises against the dollar, European exporters already are complaining that products denominated in their own currency were being priced out of world markets. To prevent this from occurring, European countries receiving central bank inflows from the Organization of Petroleum-Exporting Countries (OPEC) already are coming under pressure to hold down the euro's exchange rate by using these dollar inflows to buy yet more U.S. Treasury bills.

The 2003 Oil War therefore is not part of a currency rivalry between the dollar and euro, for Europe and East Asia remain the residual absorbers of the world's surplus dollars. No opposition has arisen as yet to U.S. dollar hegemony because, as Mrs. Thatcher might put it, there is as yet no alternative.

But this does not mean that one is not in the gestation stage. As the United States works both sides of the creditor/debtor street, Europe, Asia, Latin America and Africa (and even Canada) find themselves obliged out of self-protection to create a fairer system of world debt and payments.

Steps toward a Counter-Strategy

One tempting response would be to revert to the old system of two exchange rates, one for trade and another for financial movements. This would have to be done in a way that did not let speculators arbitrage between the two rates by selling proxies and matching buy and sell orders. Such a task would involve a complex regulatory management that would run the risk of futility.

A simpler option is to do what the United States did in 1922 when it was threatened by low-priced imports from Germany as the mark's exchange rate collapsed under the burden of paying reparations. Congress restored the 1909

American Selling Price (ASP) tariff against countries with depreciating currencies. A floating tariff was imposed equal to the price advantage of foreign
imports below U.S. domestic prices. This denied Germany and other countries a price advantage resulting either from depreciation or even from superior efficiency. Europe and Asia could impose such a retaliatory tariff, and use
the proceeds or other dollar inflows to subsidize its exports in markets competing with U.S. exports to offset the price benefit from the depreciating dollar.

Most important, foreign countries must realize that they do not need dollars in order to re-inflate their home markets. Their Treasuries can create their
own money based on their own economic needs rather than letting their central bank reserves be a derivative of the U.S. payments deficit.

To date, U.S. diplomats have used the clash of political cultures to their
own advantage. It is as if only the United States acts in its own national interest,
while Europe, Asia and the third world acquiesce in the Washington Consensus
as if they were client oligarchies. Only by pushing back can they create a more
equitable arrangement between the dollar, the euro and the yen and yuan.
And only by running a balance-of-payments deficit can Europe and East Asia
follow the U.S. path in providing a vehicle for other countries to hold their
international monetary reserves. This requires an abandonment of the world's
dependence on the Washington Consensus and its imposition of monetarist
austerity outside of the United States.

16

HOW THE DOLLAR GLUT FINANCES AMERICA'S MILITARY BUILD-UP

U.S. media are silent about the most important topic that Asian and European policy makers are discussing these days: how to protect their countries from three inter-related dynamics: (1) the surplus dollars pouring into the rest of the world for yet further financial speculation and corporate takeovers; (2) the fact that central banks are obliged to recycle these dollar inflows to buy U.S. Treasury bonds to finance the federal U.S. budget deficit; and most important (but most suppressed in the U.S. media; and (3) the military character of the U.S. payments deficit and the domestic federal budget deficit.

Strange as it may seem — and irrational as it would be in a more logical system of world diplomacy — the dollar glut is what finances America's global military build-up. It forces foreign central banks to bear the costs of America's expanding military empire. The result is a new form of taxation without representation. Keeping international reserves in dollars means recycling dollar inflows to buy U.S. Treasury bills — U.S. government debt issued largely to finance the military spending that has been a driving force in the U.S. balance-of-payments deficit since the Korean War broke out in 1950.

To date, countries have been as powerless to defend themselves against the fact that compulsory financing of U.S. overseas military spending is built into the global financial system. Neoliberal economists applaud foreign dollar recycling (a suitably bloodless term) as equilibrium, as if it is part of economic nature and free markets rather than bare-knuckle diplomacy wielded with increasing aggressiveness by U.S. officials. The mass media chime in, pretending that recycling the dollar glut to finance U.S. military spending is showing global faith in U.S. economic strength by sending their dollars here to "invest." The pretense is that earning a marginal low rate of return on Treasury securities is a free market-driven investment choice, not financial and diplomatic compulsion to choose between "Yes" (from China, reluctantly), "Yes, please" (from Japan and the European Union) and "Yes, thank you" (Britain, Georgia and Australia).

It is not "foreign faith in the U.S. economy" that leads foreigners to "put their money here." This is an anthropomorphic caricature of a much more sinister dynamic. The foreigners in question are not consumers buying U.S. exports, nor are they private-sector investors buying U.S. stocks and bonds. The largest and most important foreign entities putting "their money" here are central banks. And what they are sending back are the dollars that foreign exporters and other recipients turn over to their central banks for domestic currency, which they—"the market"—prefer to dollars .

When the U.S. payments deficit pumps dollars into foreign economies, these banks have little option except to buy U.S. Treasury bills and bonds—which the Treasury spends on financing a hostile military build-up to encircle the major dollar-recyclers—China, Japan and Arab OPEC oil producers. These governments are forced to recycle dollar inflows in a way that funds U.S. military policies in which they have no say in formulating, and which threaten them with more and more belligerent saber rattling. That is why China and Russia took the lead in forming the Shanghai Cooperation Organization (SCO) a few years ago.

In Europe there is a clear awareness that the U.S. payments deficit is much larger than just the trade deficit. One need merely look at Table 5 of the U.S. balance-of-payments data compiled by the Bureau of Economic Analysis (BEA) and published by the Dept. of Commerce in its *Survey of Current Business* to see that the deficit does not stem merely from consumers buying more imports than the United States exports as the financial sector de-industrializes the economy. Congress has told foreign investors in the largest dollar holder, China, not to buy anything except perhaps used-car dealerships and maybe more packaged mortgages and Fannie Mae securities—the equivalent of Japanese investors being steered into paying $ 1 billion for Rockefeller Center, on which they subsequently suffered a total loss, and Saudi investment in Citigroup. That's the kind of "international equilibrium" U.S. officials love to see. "China National Offshore Oil Corporation go home" is the motto when foreign governments try to use their sovereign wealth funds (central bank departments trying to figure out what to do with their dollar glut) to make direct investments in American industry, as happened when China's national oil company sought to buy Unocal in 2005.

The U.S. payments deficit stems from military spending not only for the war in Iraq and its extension into Afghanistan and Pakistan, but also for the expensive build-up of U.S. military bases in Asian, European, post-Soviet and Third World countries. So Europeans and Asians see U.S. companies pumping more dollars into their economies not only to buy their exports (in excess of providing them with goods and services in return), not only to buy their companies and commanding heights of privatized public enterprises (without giving them reciprocal rights to buy important U.S. companie), and not only to buy foreign stocks, bonds and real estate. The U.S. media neglect to mention that the U.S. Government spends hundreds of billions of dollars abroad—not only in the Near East for direct combat, but to build military bases to encircle the rest of the world, and to install radar systems, guided missile systems and other forms of military coercion, including the "color revolutions" that have been funded all around the former Soviet Union.

Spending on the military-industrial complex is much like the debt overhead paid to Wall Street banks and other financial institutions. It absorbs revenue from the economic surplus, leaving less for new capital investment and personal affluence. In this respect the federal budget deficit stems not only from "priming the pump" to subsidize today's emerging financial oligarchy. It contains an enormous military component. Pallets of shrink-wrapped $100 bills adding up to tens of millions of the dollars at a time have become familiar visuals on some TV broadcasts, but the link is not made with U.S. military and diplomatic spending and foreign central-bank dollar holdings, which are reported simply as faith in the U.S. economic recovery and presumably the monetary magic being worked by Wall Street's Tim Geithner at Treasury and Helicopter Ben Bernanke at the Federal Reserve.

Here's the problem: The Coca Cola company recently tried to buy China's largest fruit-juice producer and distributor. China holds some $2 trillion in U.S. securities—far more than it needs or can use, inasmuch as Congress and various government refuse to let it buy meaningful U.S. companies. If the U.S. buyout of Chinese firms would have been permitted to go through, this would have confronted China with a dilemma: Choice Number 1 would be to let the sale go through, accepting payment in yet more dollars, reinvesting the growing glut in U.S. Treasury bonds yielding about 1 percent. China would take a capital loss on these if and when U.S. interest rates rise or the dollar declines.

Choice Number 2 would be for China not to recycle the dollar inflows. This would lead the renminbi to rise against the dollar, eroding China's export competitiveness in world markets. So China chose a third way, which brought U.S. protests. It turned down the sale of its tangible company for "paper" U.S. dollars to fund further U.S. military encirclement. American mass media showed little interest in explaining China's logic, and economists have little to say about the lack of constraint on U.S. payments outflows. The Federal Reserve can create dollars freely, now that they no longer are convertible into gold or even into purchases of U.S. companies as Congress refuses to let sovereign wealth funds invest in important U.S. sectors. The U.S. Treasury prefers foreign central banks to keep funding its domestic budget deficit—which means financing the cost of America's war in the Near East and encirclement of foreign countries with military bases. The more "capital outflows" U.S. investors spend to buy up foreign economies — the most profitable sectors, where the new U.S. owners can extract the highest monopoly rents — the more funds end up in foreign central banks to support America's global military build-up.

No textbook on political theory or international relations has suggested axioms to explain how nations act in a way so adverse to their own political, military and economic interests. Yet this is what has been happening for the past generation.

So the ultimate question turns out to be what countries can do to counter this financial attack. It is not simply a problem of regulation to control speculative capital movements. The problem is how nations can act as real nations, in their own interest rather than being roped into serving whatever U.S. diplomats decide is in America's interest.

The path of least resistance would seem to be nationalization of credit as a basic public utility. That was the idea of 19th-century reformers. It is ironic that the word "nationalization" recently has become synonymous with bailing out the largest and most reckless banks from their bad loans, and bailing out hedge funds and non-bank counterparties for losses on their bad gambles on derivatives that A.I.G. and other players on the losing side end are unable to pay. Such bailouts are not nationalization in the traditional sense of the term, *i.e.*, bringing credit creation and other basic financial functions back into the public domain. They are the opposite. The idea is to print new government bonds to turn over to the financial sector, endowing a 21st-century power elite.

Economies now face a choice between democracy and oligarchy. The question is who will control the government that is regulating and "nationalizing." If the central bank and major congressional finance and banking committees are chosen by Wall Street or subject to its veto power, this will not help steer credit into productive uses. It will merely continue the Greenspan-Paulson-Geithner era of larger free lunches for their financial constituencies.

The financial oligarchy's idea of "regulation" is to install deregulators in key positions and give them only minimal skeleton staffs and funding. Despite Chairman Greenspan's announcement that he saw the light and come to realize that self-regulation doesn't work, the Treasury and the Fed still are run by a Wall Street apparatchiks. Their concern isn't ideology as such, but naked self-interest for their clients. Wall Street seeks out the proverbial well-meaning fools, especially prestigious academics to serve as front men. Such individuals also are put in place as gate-keepers of the major academic journals to censor ideas that do not well serve the financial lobbyists.

The cover story to justify excluding meaningful regulation is that finance isby other than Wall Street lobbyists is so complex that only someone from the financial sector is capable of regulating it. To add insult to injury, it is claimed that a hallmark of democracy is to make the central bank independent of elected government. In reality this is the opposite of democracy. Finance is the crux of the economic system. If it is not regulated democratically in the public interest, then it is "free" to be captured by special interests.

The danger is that governments will let the financial sector determine how to "regulate." It seeks to make money *from* the economy in an extractive way. Finance today is acting in a way that de-industrializes economies, not builds them up. The business plan is austerity for labor, industry and all sectors outside of finance, as in the IMF programs imposed on Third World debtor countries. The experience of Iceland, Latvia and other financialized economies should be examined as object lessons, if only because they top the World Bank's ranking of countries in terms of the "ease of doing business."

Meaningful regulation can only come from outside the financial sector. Otherwise, countries will suffer what the Japanese call "descent from heaven": regulators are selected from the ranks of bankers and their "useful idiots," and upon retiring from government they return to the financial sector to receive lucrative consulting jobs, speaking engagements and kindred paybacks. Knowing this, they regulate in favor of financial special interests, not that of the public at large.

The problem of speculative capital movements goes beyond drawing up a set of specific regulations. It concerns the scope of national government power. The International Monetary Fund's Articles of Agreement prevent countries from restoring the dual exchange rate systems that many retained down through the 1950s and even into the '60s. It was widespread practice for countries to have one exchange rate for goods and services (sometimes various exchange rates for different import and export categories) and another for capital movements. Under American pressure, the IMF enforced the pretence that there is an equilibrium rate that happens to be the same for goods and services as for capital movements. Governments that did not buy into this ideology were excluded from membership in the IMF and World Bank, or were overthrown.

The implication today is that the only way a nation can block capital movements is to withdraw from the IMF, the World Bank and the World Trade Organization (WTO). For the first time since the 1950s this looks like a real possibility, thanks to growing worldwide awareness of how the U.S. economy is glutting the global economy with surplus dollars. From the U.S. vantage point, stopping its free ride.is an attempt to curtail its international military program. This is precisely what is inspiring the BRICs nations to seek a financial alternative.

17

DE-DOLLARIZATION AND THE END OF AMERICA'S EMPIRE

For Chinese President Hu Jintao, Russian President Dmitry Medvedev and other top officials of the six-nation Shanghai Cooperation Organization (SCO), challenging America was the prime focus of meetings in Yekaterinburg, Russia (formerly Sverdlovsk) on June 15–16, 2009. The SCO alliance is composed of Russia, China, Kazakhstan, Tajikistan, Kyrghyzstan and Uzbekistan, with observer status for Iran, India, Pakistan and Mongolia. It was joined on June 16 by Brazil for trade discussions among the BRIC nations (Brazil, Russia, India and China).

The attendees assured American diplomats that dismantling the U.S. financial and military empire was not their aim. They simply wanted to discuss mutual aid—but in a way that had no role for the United States, NATO or the U.S. dollar as a vehicle for conducting future international trade. But U.S. diplomats rightfully worried that the meeting was a move to make U.S. hegemony obsolete. That is what a multipolar world means, after all.

For starters, in 2005 the SCO asked Washington to set a timeline to withdraw from its military bases in Central Asia. Two years later the SCO countries aligned themselves with the former CIS republics belonging to the Collective Security Treaty Organization (CSTO), established in 2002 as a counterweight to NATO.

Yet despite its agenda to replace the global dollar standard with a new financial and military defense system, the meeting has elicited only a collective yawn from the U.S. and even European press. Whistling in the dark, a Council on Foreign Relations spokesman said that he hardly could imagine that Russia and China can overcome their geopolitical rivalry,[1] suggesting that America would be able to use the divide-and-conquer that Britain empolyed so deftly for many centuries to fragment foreign opposition to its own empire. But

---

[1] Andrew Scheineson, "The Shanghai Cooperation Organization," *Council on Foreign Relations*, updated March 24, 2009: "While some experts say the organization has emerged as a powerful anti-U.S. bulwark in Central Asia, others believe frictions between its two largest members, Russia and China, effectively preclude a strong, unified SCO."

George W. Bush ("I'm a uniter, not a divider") built on the Clinton adminis-tration's legacy in driving Russia, China and their neighbors to find a common ground when it comes to crafting an alternative to the dollar and hence to the U.S. ability to run balance-of-payments deficits *ad infinitum.*

What may prove in time to be the last rites of American hegemony began already in April, 2009, at the G-20 conference, and became more explicit at the St. Petersburg International Economic Forum on June 5 when Mr. Med-vedev called for China, Russia and India to "build an increasingly multipolar world order." What this meant in plain English was: "We have reached our limit in subsidizing the United States' military encirclement of Eurasia while also allowing the United States to appropriate our exports, companies, stocks and real estate in exchange for paper money of questionable worth."

"The artificially maintained unipolar system," Mr. Medvedev spelled out, is based on "one big centre of consumption, financed by a growing deficit, and thus growing debts, one formerly strong reserve currency, and one domi-nant system of assessing assets and risks."[2] At the root of the global financial crisis, he concluded, was that the United States makes too little and spends too much. Especially upsetting was its stepped-up military aid to Georgia announced earlier in June, the NATO missile shield in Eastern Europe and the U.S. mili-tary buildup in the oil-rich Middle East and Central Asia.

The sticking point with all these countries is the U.S. ability to print unlim-ited amounts of dollars. Overspending by U.S. consumers on imports in excess of exports, U.S. buy-outs of foreign companies and real estate, and the dollars that the Pentagon spends abroad all end up in foreign central banks. These agencies then face a hard choice: either to recycle these dollars back to the United States by purchasing U.S. Treasury IOUs, or to let the "free market" force up their currency relative to the dollar — thereby pricing their exports out of world markets, creating domestic unemployment and insolvency.

When China and other countries recycle their dollar inflows by buying U.S. Treasury bills to "invest" in the United States, this buildup is not really volun-tary. It does not reflect faith in the U.S. economy enriching foreign central banks for their savings, or any calculated investment preference, but simply a lack of alternatives. "Free markets" U.S.-style hook countries into a dollarized payments system that forces them to accept fiat dollars without limit. They have wanted out for a number of years now.

This means creating a new alternative. Rather than making merely "cosmetic changes as some countries and perhaps the international financial organisations themselves might want," Mr. Medvedev ended his St. Petersburg

---

[2] Kremlin.ru, June 5, 2009, in Johnson's Russia List, June 8, 2009, #8.

speech, "what we need are financial institutions of a completely new type, where particular political issues and motives, and particular countries will not dominate."

When foreign military spending forced the U.S. balance of payments into deficit and drove the United States off gold in 1971, central banks were left without the traditional asset used to settle payments imbalances. The alternative by default was to invest their subsequent payments inflows in U.S. Treasury bonds, as if these still were "as good as gold." Central banks have been holding some $4 trillion of these bonds in their international reserves for the past few years—and these loans have financed most of the U.S. Government's domestic budget deficits for over three decades. Given the fact that about half of U.S. Government discretionary spending is for military operations—including more than 750 foreign military bases and increasingly expensive operations in the oil-producing and transporting countries—the international financial system is organized in a way that finances the Pentagon, along with U.S. buyouts of foreign assets expected to yield much more than the Treasury bonds that foreign central banks hold.

The main political issue confronting the world's central banks is therefore how to avoid adding yet more dollars to their reserves and thereby financing yet further U.S. deficit spending—including military spending on their borders?

For starters, the six SCO countries and BRIC countries have been moving to trade in their own currencies so as to get the benefit of mutual credit that the United States until now has monopolized for itself. China started by striking bilateral deals with Argentina and Brazil to denominate their trade in renminbi rather than the dollar, sterling or euros.[3] In June, just before the Yekaterinburg meetings, China reached an agreement with Malaysia to denominate trade between the two countries in renminbi.[4] Former Prime Minister Tun Dr. Mahathir Mohamad explained to me in January, 2009, half a year earlier, that as a Muslim country, Malaysia wanted to avoid doing anything that would facilitate U.S. military action against Islamic countries. The nation had too

---

[3] Jamil Anderlini and Javier Blas, "China reveals big rise in gold reserves," *Financial Times*, April 24, 2009. See also "Chinese political advisors propose making yuan an int'l currency." Beijing, March 7, 2009 (Xinhua): "The key to financial reform is to make the yuan an international currency, said [Peter Kwong Ching] Woo [chairman of the Hong Kong-based Wharf (Holdings) Limited] in a speech to the Second Session of the 11th National Committee of the Chinese People's Political Consultative Conference (CPPCC), the country's top political advisory body. That means using the Chinese currency to settle international trade payments ..."

[4] Shai Oster, "Malaysia, China Consider Ending Trade in Dollars," *Wall Street Journal*, June 4, 2009.

many dollar assets, his colleagues explained. Central bank governor Zhou Xiaochuan of the People's Bank of China wrote an official statement on its website that the goal was to create a reserve currency "that is disconnected from individual nations."[5] This was the aim of the discussions in Yekaterinburg.

In addition to avoiding having to finance the U.S. buyout of their domestic industry and U.S. military encirclement of the globe, China, Russia and other countries no doubt would like to get the same kind of free ride that America has been getting since it went off gold in 1971. As matters stand, they see the United States as a lawless nation, financially as well as militarily. How else to characterize a nation that holds out a set of laws for others—on war, debt repayment and treatment of prisoners—but ignores them itself? The United States has long been the world's largest debtor, yet has avoided the pain of "structural adjustments" imposed on other debtor economies. U.S. interest-rate and tax reductions in the face of exploding trade and budget deficits are seen as the height of hypocrisy in view of the austerity programs that Washington forces on other countries via the IMF and other U.S.-controlled vehicles.

The United States tells debtor economies to sell off their public utilities and natural resources, raise their interest rates and increase taxes while gutting their social safety nets to squeeze out money to pay creditors. At home, Congress blocked China's National Offshore Oil Co. (CNOOC) from buying Unocal on grounds of national security, much as it blocked Dubai from buying U.S. ports, and other sovereign wealth funds from buying key infrastructure. Foreigners are invited to emulate the Japanese purchase of white elephant trophies such as Rockefeller Center, on which investors quickly lost a billion dollars and ended up walking away.

In this respect the United States has not given China and other payments-surplus nations much alternative but to find a way to avoid further dollar buildups. At first, China's attempts to diversify its dollar holdings beyond Treasury bonds were only marginal. For starters, Hank Paulson of Goldman Sachs steered its central bank into higher-yielding Fannie Mae and Freddie Mac securities, explaining that these were *de facto* public obligations. They collapsed in 2008, but the U.S. Government took these two mortgage-lending agencies over, formally adding their $5.2 trillion in obligations onto the national debt. In fact, it was largely foreign official investment that prompted the bailout. Imposing a loss for foreign official agencies would have broken the Treasury-bill standard then and there, destroying U.S. credibility. The problem is that there are too few Government bonds to absorb the dollars being flooded into the world economy by the soaring U.S. balance-of-payments deficits.

---

[5] Jonathan Wheatley, "Brazil and China in plan to axe dollar," *Financial Times*, May 19, 2009.

Seeking more of an equity position to protect the value of their dollar holdings as the Federal Reserve's credit bubble drove interest rates down, China's sovereign wealth funds sought to diversify in late 2007. China bought stakes in the well-connected Blackstone equity fund and Morgan Stanley on Wall Street, Barclays in Britain, South Africa's Standard Bank (once affiliated with Chase Manhattan back in the apartheid 1960s), and the soon-to-collapse Belgian financial conglomerate Fortis. But the U.S. financial sector was collapsing under the weight of its debt pyramiding, and prices for shares plunged for banks and investment firms across the globe. China took a loss—on dollars flowing in to buy its own companies whose value was soaring!

Foreigners are coming to see the IMF, World Bank and World Trade Organization as Washington surrogates in a financial system backed by American military bases and aircraft carriers encircling the globe. But this military domination is a vestige of an American empire no longer able to rule by economic strength. U.S. military power is muscle-bound, based more on atomic weaponry and long-distance air strikes than on ground operations, which have become too politically unpopular to mount on any large scale.

On the economic front there is no foreseeable way in which the United States can work off the $4 trillion it owes foreign governments, their central banks and the sovereign wealth funds set up to dispose of the global dollar glut. America has become a deadbeat—and indeed, a militarily aggressive one as it seeks to hold onto the unique power it once earned by economic means. The problem is how to constrain its behavior. Yu Yongding, a former Chinese central bank advisor now with China's Academy of Sciences, suggested that U.S. Treasury Secretary Tim Geithner be advised that the United States should "save" first and foremost by cutting back its military budget. "U.S. tax revenue is not likely to increase in the short term because of low economic growth, inflexible expenditures and the cost of 'fighting two wars.'"[6]

For the past decade it has been foreign savings, mainly by the BRIC countries, that have financed the U.S. budget deficit, by buying most Treasury bonds. Meanwhile, America's own saving rate has been negative, except for paying down debts since 2009. The effect is taxation without representation for foreign voters as to how the U.S. Government uses their forced savings. It therefore is necessary for financial diplomats to broaden the scope of their policy-making beyond the private-sector marketplace.

---

[6] "Another Dollar Crisis inevitable unless U.S. starts Saving—China central bank adviser. Global Crisis 'Inevitable' Unless U.S. Starts Saving, Yu Says," *Bloomberg News*, June 1, 2009.
http://www.bloomberg.com/apps/news?pid=20601080&sid=aCV0pFcAFyZw&refer=asia

Exchange rates are determined by many factors besides "consumers wielding credit cards," the usual euphemism that the U.S. media cite for America's balance-of-payments deficit. Since the 13th century, war has been a dominating factor in the balance of payments of leading nations—and of their national debts. Ever since Adam Smith explained the steady buildup of Britain's national debt mainly from its interminable wars with France, government bond financing has consisted mainly of rolling over the buildup of war debts, as normal peacetime budgets tend to be balanced. This links the war budget directly to the balance of payments and exchange rates.

In times past, foreign bankers have gone bankrupt financing Britain's war debts and those of Habsburg Spain and other militarily ambitious nations. Today, foreign central banks see themselves stuck with unpayable IOUs—under conditions where, if they move to stop the U.S. free lunch, the dollar will plunge and their dollar holdings will fall in value relative to their own domestic currencies and other currencies. If China's currency rises by 10 percent against the dollar, its central bank will show the equivalent of a $200 billion loss on its $2 trillion of dollar holdings as denominated in yuan. This explains why, when bond ratings agencies talk of the U.S. Treasury securities losing their AAA rating, they don't mean that the government cannot simply print the paper dollars to "make good" on these bonds. They mean that dollars will depreciate in international value.

That is just what has been occurring. When Mr. Geithner put on his serious face and told an audience at Peking University in early June that he believed in a "strong dollar" and China's U.S. investments therefore were safe and sound, he was greeted with derisive laughter.[7]

Anticipation of a rise in China's exchange rate provides an incentive for speculators to seek to borrow in dollars to buy renminbi and benefit from the appreciation. For China, the problem is that this speculative inflow would become a self-fulfilling prophecy by forcing up its currency. So the problem of international reserves is inherently linked to that of capital controls. Why should China see its profitable companies sold for yet more freely-created U.S. computer keyboard dollars, which its central bank must use to buy low-yielding U.S. Treasury bills or lose yet further money on Wall Street?

To avoid this quandary it is necessary to reverse the philosophy of open capital markets that the world has held since Bretton Woods in 1944. On the occasion of Mr. Geithner's 2009 visit to China, "Zhou Xiaochuan, minister of the Peoples Bank of China, the country's central bank, said pointedly that this was the first time since the semiannual talks began in 2006 that China needed

---

[7] Kathrin Hille, "Lesson in friendship draws blushes," *Financial Times*, June 2, 2009.

to learn from American mistakes as well as its successes" when it came to deregulating capital markets and dismantling controls.[8]

An era therefore is coming to an end. In the face of continued U.S. over-spending, de-dollarization threatens to force countries to return to the kind of dual exchange rates common between World Wars I and II: one exchange rate for commodity trade, another for capital movements and investments, at least from dollar-area economies.

Even without capital controls, the nations meeting at Yekaterinburg took steps to avoid being the unwilling recipients of yet more dollars. Seeing that U.S. global hegemony cannot continue without spending power that they themselves supply, governments sought to hasten what Chalmers Johnson has called "the sorrows of empire" in his book by that name — the bankruptcy of the U.S. financial-military world order. If China, Russia and their non-aligned allies ultimately have their way, the United States no longer will be able to live off the savings of others (in the form of its own recycled electronic dollars) nor have the money for unlimited military expenditures and adventures.

U.S. officials wanted to attend the Yekaterinburg meeting as observers. They were told No. It is a word that Americans have been hearing ever since, and will hear yet more in the future.

---

[8] Steven R. Weisman, "U.S. Tells China Subprime Woes Are No Reason to Keep Markets Closed," *The New York Times*, June 18, 2008.

18

INCORPORATING THE *RENTIER* SECTORS
INTO A FINANCIAL MODEL

Now that the Bubble Economy has given way to debt deflation, the world is discovering the shortcoming of models that fail to explain how most credit creation today (1) inflates asset prices without raising commodity prices or wage levels, and (2) creates a reciprocal flow of debt service. This debt service tends to rise as a proportion of personal and business income, outgrowing the ability of debtors to pay—leading to (3) debt deflation. The only way to prevent this phenomenon from plunging economies into depression and keeping them there is (4) to write down the debts so as to free revenue for spending once again on goods and services.

By promoting a misleading view of how the economy works, the above omissions lead to a policy that fails to prevent debt bubbles or deal effectively with the ensuing depression. To avoid a replay of the recent financial crisis—and indeed, to extricate economies from their present debt strait-jacket that subordinates recovery to the overhang of creditor claims (that is, saving the banks from taking a loss on their bad loans and gambles)—it is necessary to explain how credit creation inflates housing and other asset prices, while interest and other financial charges deflate the "real" economy, holding down commodity prices, shrinking markets and employment, and holding down wages in a downward economic spiral. We are dealing with two price trends that go in opposite directions: asset prices and commodity prices. It therefore is necessary to explain how credit expansion pushes asset prices up while simultaneously causing debt deflation.

The typical $MV = PT$ monetary and price model focuses on commodity prices and wages, not on the asset prices inflated by debt leveraging. In the real world most credit today is spent to buy assets already in place. Some 80 percent of bank loans in the English-speaking world are real estate mortgages, and much of the balance is lent against stocks and bonds already issued. Banks lend to buyers of real estate, corporate raiders, ambitious financial empire-builders, and to management for debt-leveraged buyouts.

Extending credit to purchase assets already in place bids up their price. Prospective homebuyers need to take on larger mortgages to obtain a home.

The effect is to turn property rents into a flow of mortgage interest. These payments divert the revenue of consumers and businesses from being spent on consumption or new capital investment. The effect is *de*flationary for the economy's product markets, and hence consumer prices and employment, and therefore wages.

Debt-leveraged buyouts and commercial real estate purchases turn business cash flow (ebitda: earnings before interest, taxes, depreciation and amortization) into interest payments. Likewise, bank or bondholder financing of public debt (especially in the Eurozone, which lacks a central bank to monetize such debt) has turned a rising share of tax revenue into interest payments. It was to extricate themselves from this situation that nations created central banks, starting with the Bank of England in 1694. The aim was to avoid reliance on commercial banks for credit, by creating money by the state itself.

As creditors recycle their receipts of interest and amortization (and capital gains) into new lending to buyers of real estate, stocks and bonds, a rising share of employee income, real estate rent, business revenue and even government tax revenue diverted to pay debt service. By leaving less to spend on goods and services, the effect is to reduce new investment and employment. So wages do not increase, even as prices for property and financial securities rise. This price divergence has become the major characteristic of the post-2001 Bubble Economy, and indeed of the post-1980 period throughout the Western economies.

It is especially the case since 1991 in the post-Soviet economies, where neoliberal (that is, pro-financial) policy makers have had a free hand to shape tax and financial policy in favor of banks (mainly foreign bank branches). Latvia is cited as a neoliberal success story, but it would be hard to find an example where *rentier* income and prices have diverged more sharply from wages and the "real" production economy.

The more that credit creation takes the form of inflating asset prices—rather than financing purchases of goods or direct investment employing labor—the more *de*flationary its effects are on the "real" economy of production and consumption. Housing and other asset prices crash, causing negative equity. Yet homeowners and businesses still have to pay off their debts. The national income accounts classify this pay-down as "saving," although the revenue is not available to the debtors doing the "saving."

The moral is that using homes as what Alan Greenspan referred to as "piggy banks" to take out home-equity loans was not really like drawing down a bank account at all. When a bank account is drawn down there is less money available, but no residual obligation to pay. New income can be spent at the discretion of its recipient. But borrowing against a home implies an obligation to set aside future income to pay the banker—and hence a loss of future discretionary spending.

Creating a more realistic model of today's financialized economies to trace this phenomenon requires a breakdown of the national income and product accounts (NIPA) to see the economy as a set of distinct sectors interacting with each other. These accounts juxtapose the private and public sectors as far as current spending, saving and taxation is concerned. But the implication is that government budget deficits inflate the private-sector economy as a whole. However, a budget deficit that takes the form of transfer payments to banks, as in the case of the post-September 2008 bank bailout, the Federal Reserve's $2 trillion in cash-for-trash financial swaps and the $700 billion QEII credit creation by the Federal Reserve to lend to banks at 0.25 percent interest in 2011, has a different effect from deficits that reflect social spending programs, Social Security and Medicare, public infrastructure investment or the purchase of other goods and services. The effect of transfer payments to the financial sector—as well as the $5.3 trillion increase in U.S. Treasury debt from taking Fannie Mae and Freddie Mac onto the public balance sheet—is to support asset prices (above all those of the banking system), not inflate commodity prices and wages.

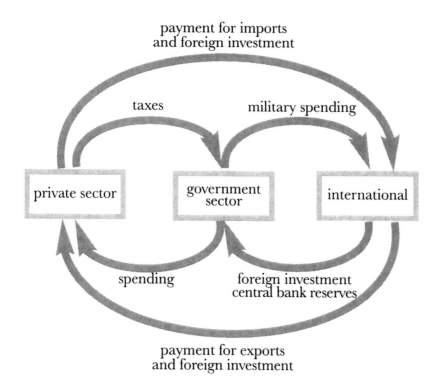

Fig. 1: Private sector, government sector and international sector

Most models treat the international sector either as a "leakage" (as Keynes termed foreign trade and capital flows) or as a balancing item in the private/public sector surplus or shortfall (as in the Levy Institute model). But the international sector involves not only export and import trade and other current account items (emigrants' remittances, and above all, military spending) but also foreign investment and income—and foreign central bank reserves held in U.S. Treasury and other securities, that is, in loans to the U.S. Government.

So the international sphere may either provide inflows or record an outflow to the U.S. economy and its financial markets. For instance, U.S. consumers and businesses ran a trade deficit, and banks used the entire $700 billion QEII supply of Fed credit for foreign currency arbitrage and other international speculation, not for lending to the domestic U.S. economy. But the U.S. Treasury received an inflow from foreign central banks building up their dollar reserves by buying Treasury securities and other U.S. financial securities.

This model can be used to trace U.S. transactions with China. The economy runs a trade deficit with China, and also a private-sector investment outflow to China. There is some return of earnings from these investments to U.S. companies. But on balance, there is a dollar outflow to China—which also

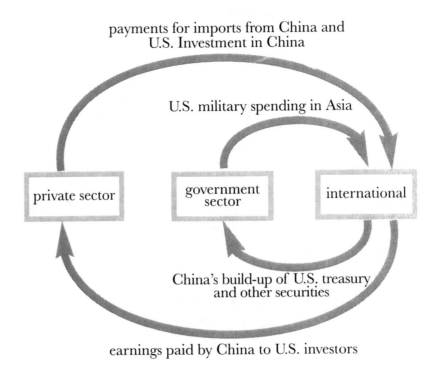

Fig. 2: U.S. transactions with China, broken down between private and government sectors

receives dollars from its exports to third countries. China's central bank has recycled most of these dollar receipts to the U.S. Treasury (and earlier, into Fannie Mae bonds and kindred investments), but was not permitted to buy U.S. companies such as Unocal's refinery operations.

This public/private/international model may be made more realistic by treating the financial, insurance and real estate (FIRE) sector as distinct from the underlying production and consumption economy. The FIRE sector deals with the economy's balance sheet of assets and debts, real estate, stocks and bonds, mortgages and other bank loans — and the payment of interest, money management commissions and other fees to the financial sector, as well as insurance payments and also rental payments for housing.

In principle, monopolies should be included in this *rentier* sector, as they represent a special privilege (control over markets, especially for necessities) whose return in the form of prices and income in excess of necessary costs of production is a form of economic rent, that is, a transfer payment rather than "earned" income.

Classical political economists from the Physiocrats through Adam Smith, John Stuart Mill and their Progressive Era followers were reformers in the sense that they treated the *rentier* sectors as extracting transfer payments rather than earning a return for producing actual output ("services"). Their labor theory of value found its counterpart in the "economic rent theory of prices" to distinguish the necessary costs of production and doing business (reduced ultimately to the value of labor) from "unearned income" consisting mainly of land rent, monopoly rent, and financial interest and fees. The various categories of *rentier* income were depicted as the "hollow" element of prices. Land rent, natural resource rent, monopoly rent and returns to privilege (including financial interest and fees) had no counterpart in necessary costs of production. They were historical and institutional products of privileges handed down largely from the medieval conquests that created Europe's landed aristocracy and banking practice that developed largely by insider dealing. What legitimized interest was, pragmatically, lending to kings to finance war debts, in an epoch when money and credit were the sinews of war. So banking as well as military rivalries for land essentially involved the foreign sector.

The political aim of classical analysis was to minimize the economy's cost structure by freeing industrial capitalism from these carry-overs from feudalism. The reformers' guiding idea was to minimize the role of *rentier* income (economic rent) by (1) direct public investment in basic infrastructure, including education, transportation systems, communication systems and other enterprises that were long kept in the public domain or publicly regulated from the late 19th century onward, (2) tax policy (taxing land and natural resources), and

(3) regulatory policy to keep the prices charged by natural monopolies such as railroads, power and gas companies in line with actual production costs plus normal profit.

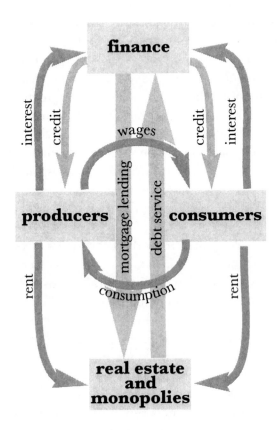

Fig. 3: The FIRE sector's role in the domestic economy

The financial sector has become the leading *rentier* sector. Its "product" is debt claims **on** the "real" economy, underwriting, and money management on a fee basis. For this it receives interest and dividends from real estate and business borrowers, and from consumers. Over time, real estate buyers typically pay more in interest to their mortgage lenders than the original purchase price paid to the property seller.

In its interactions with the government, the financial sector buys bonds (and also makes campaign contributions). The Federal Reserve pumps money into the banking system by purchasing bonds and, when the system breaks down, makes enormous bailout payments to cover the bad debts run up by banks and other institutions to mortgage borrowers, businesses and consumers.

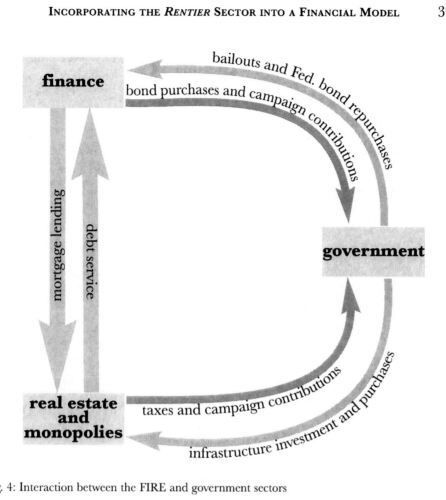

Fig. 4: Interaction between the FIRE and government sectors

The government also enhances the real estate sector by providing transportation and other basic infrastructure that enhances the site value of property along the routes. Finally, the government acts as direct purchaser of monopoly services from health insurance providers, pharmaceutical companies and other monopolies. In the other direction, the U.S. Government receives a modicum of taxes from real estate (mainly at the local level for property taxes), not much income tax but some capital gains tax in good years.

Hardly by surprise, the financial sector prefers to make itself invisible — not only to the tax collector and government regulators, but to voters. What the classical reformers called economic rent is now called "earnings." So the failure to break out the *rentier* sector from the rest of the economy — and hence, balance sheet and debt transactions from the purchase of goods and services — has helped soften criticism of shifting the tax burden off land and monopoly rent, and off finance. Yet the NIPA report that some 40 percent of U.S. corporate profits in 2010 were registered by the financial sector.

This reflects the fact that interest and other financial charges have risen steadily as a proportion of GDP. Credit card companies report higher returns from late fees and penalties than they receive in interest. And other payments to the FIRE sector also are increasing as a rising proportion of employee budgets is spent on housing (largely for mortgage interest), other debt service, and payments to the government in the form of FICA withholding, taxes and user fees that have been shifted off FIRE onto employers and employees in the "real" production sector.

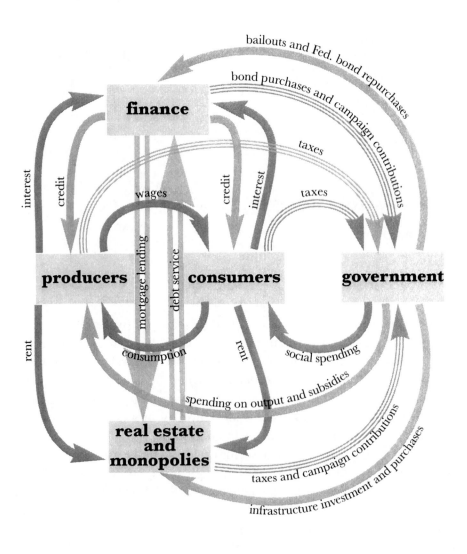

Fig. 5: Overall model of the FIRE sector, producers and consumers and government

The distinction between *rentier* and "earned" income was not incorporated into the NIPA. This is largely the result of a long political and ideological fight back by the real estate and financial sectors against the Progressive Era's economic reforms. Financial and real estate interests preferred descriptions of an economy in which all income was earned by playing a productive role, and in which money (and hence, credit and debt) was "neutral," only a "veil," that does not affect the distribution of income and wealth. Credit was spent only on goods and services, not on assets. And the financial sector's loans always took the form of productive credit, enabling businesses to pay back the loans out of future earnings while consumers paid out of rising future incomes. There thus was no explanation of how a credit bubble could inflate real estate prices and then collapse into a negative equity disaster. Finance seemed only to create wealth, not impoverish the underlying economy.

Nor was there any way for mainstream models to distinguish government transfer payments to the financial sector (*e.g.*, the $13 trillion in post-2008 financial bailouts in the United States) from Keynesian-style deficit spending. Such transfer payments did not "jumpstart" the economy. They turned a politically well-connected financial elite into new vested interests.

One can understand why the financial sector has had so little interest in tracing the effect of rising money and credit on diverting income from the circular flow between producers and consumers, diverting business revenue from new capital formation, and stripping industrial assets and natural resources. Most model builders isolate these long-term structural, environmental and demographic feedbacks as "externalities." But they are part and parcel of reality. So one is tempted to say that the financial element of economic models is too important to be left to the self-interested tunnel vision of bankers.

Environmental Asset Stripping as an Analogue for Debt Deflation

Just as debt deflation diverts income to pay interest and other financial charges—often at the cost of paying so much corporate cash flow that assets must be sold off to pay creditors—so the phenomenon leads to stripping the natural environment. This is what occurs, for instance, when the IMF and World Bank act on behalf of global banks to demand that Brazil pay its foreign debt by privatizing its Amazon forest so that loggers can earn enough foreign exchange to pay foreign bankers. The analogy is absentee landlords who pay their mortgages by not repairing their property but letting it deteriorate. In all these cases debt deflation caused by extracting interest affects not only spending—and hence current prices—but also the economy's long-term ability to produce. It eats into natural resources and the environment as well as society's manmade capital stock.

Demographically, the effect of debt deflation is emigration and other negative effects. For example, after Latvian property prices soared as Swedish bank branches fueled the real estate bubble, living standards plunged. Families had to take on a lifetime of debt in order to gain the housing that was bequeathed to the country debt-free when the Soviet Union broke up in 1991. When Latvia's government imposed neoliberal austerity policies in 2009–10, wage levels plunged by 30 percent in the public sector, and private-sector wages followed the decline. Emigration and capital flight accelerated. In debt-strapped Iceland, the census reported in 2011 that 8 percent of the population had emigrated (mainly to Norway).

The Effect of Credit-Financed Asset Prices on the "Real" Economy

Inasmuch as investors today have come to aim more at "total returns" (net income + capital gains) rather than simply income by itself, a realistic model should integrate capital gains and investment into the current production-consumption model. Producers not only pay wages and buy capital goods as in "current economy" models; they also use their cash flow (and even borrow) to buy other companies, as well as their own stock. When they make acquisitions on credit, the resulting debt leveraging finds its counterpart in interest payments that absorb a rising share of corporate cash flow.

This has an effect on the government's fiscal position, because interest is a tax-deductible expense. By displacing taxable profits, creditors receive the business revenue hitherto paid out as income taxes. The result in the early 1980s, when debt-leveraged buyouts really gained momentum, was that financial investors were able to obtain twice as high a return (at a 50 percent corporate income tax rate) by debt financing than they could get by equity financing. This tax incentive for debt leveraging rather than equity investment is the reverse of what Saint-Simon and his followers urged in the 19th century to become the wave of the future.

Only a portion of FIRE sector cash flow is spent on goods and services. The great bulk is recycled into the purchase of financial securities and other assets, or lent out as yet more interest-bearing debt — on easier and easier credit terms as the repertory of bankable direct investments is exhausted. So the pressing task today is to trace how directing most credit into the asset markets affects asset prices much more than commodity prices. Loan standards deteriorate as debt/equity ratios increase and creditors "race to the bottom" to find borrowers in markets further distanced from the "real" economy. This increasingly unproductive character of credit explains why wealth is being concentrated in the hands of the population's wealthiest 10%. It is the dysfunctional result of economic parasitism.

Keynes recognized a "leakage" in the form of saving (specifically, hoarding). But at the time he wrote in the midst of the Great Depression there was little motivation to focus on debt service, or on the distinction between direct capital investment (tangible capital formation) and financial securities speculation or real estate speculation (which had all but dried up as asset markets were shrinking to reflect the economy's shrinking). Saving took the form of non-spending, not of paying down debt. There was little lending under depression conditions.

Today's post-bubble attempts to incorporate balance-sheet analysis into NIPA statistics on current activity are too crude. Stock averages do not give an adequate quantitative measure distinguishing the flow of funds into land and capital improvements or industrial capital formation in contrast to speculation in financial securities. So monetary analysis needs to be reformulated along with a better structural breakdown of NIPA to distinguish between money and credit spent on goods and services from that spent on financial assets and debt service.

Part IV
THE NEED FOR A CLEAN SLATE

19

From Democracy to Oligarchy: National Economies at the Crossroads

What is called "capitalism" has passed through a series of stages. For all its brutality, Industrial Capitalism raised productivity and vastly increased output. Selling this surplus depended on the ability of employees to buy what they produced. But Finance Capitalism's dynamic is extractive, with each new stage imposing deeper austerity. What appeared primarily as a class war between industry and labor a century ago has become a broader war of finance against the economy as a whole. By imposing debt deflation, Finance Capitalism is cannibalizing industry as well as reducing labor to debt peonage.

The end product is a Neo-*Rentier* Economy—precisely what Industrial Capitalism and classical economists set out to replace during the Progressive Era from the late 19th to early 20th century. Finance capital extracts interest and inflates asset prices by attaching debt to the economy's means of production and income streams. This interrupts the circular flow between production and consumption, causing economic shrinkage. So instead of producing new value or output, the "miracle of compound interest," reinforced by fiat credit creation, cannibalizes industrial capital as well as the returns to labor. Most land rent and monopoly rent is now paid out as interest to a financial class has usurped the role that landlords used to play: a class living off special privilege and claims on the economy at large.

Centered in the United States since the aftermath of World Wars I and II, Finance Capitalism promised to end class warfare with the Pension-Fund Capitalism that has steered employment savings into the stock and bond markets since the 1950s. The idea is for pension funds to build up financial claims on the economy by turning their savings over to money managers to earn interest and make capital gains, increasingly by using debt leverage. The problem is that this financial maneuvering does not fund tangible new capital formation or give workers a real ownership voice in investment and workplace decisions.

Since U.S. overseas military spending forced the dollar off gold in 1971, a U.S.-centered Monetary Imperialism has involved fiat dollar creation. Instead of holding foreign reserves in gold, the world's central banks hold U.S. Treasury bonds. These are issued mainly to finance U.S. global military spending.

Removing gold as a limiting factor on the ability of the United States to run domestic budget deficits and balance-of-payments deficits, American banks have been able to create credit and flood the global economy with fiat credit. This has enabled U.S. financial firms and companies to buy up foreign industry with low-interest fiat dollars—which the foreign recipients turn over to their central banks to recycle back to the U.S. economy by buying more Treasury securities, to finance the domestic budget deficit and payments deficit ... and so on, seemingly *ad infinitum*.

This fiat dollar credit made possible the Bubble Economy after 1980, which soon evolved into Casino Capitalism. Inherently unstable, these economically radioactive stages decayed into Debt Deflation after 2008, and now are settling into a leaden Debt Peonage and the austerity of Neo-Serfdom.

Politically, Industrial Capitalism's drive to lower production costs required checking the power of landlords, bankers and monopolists. The landed interest's control of the House of Lords, Senate or other upper houses of government gave it a stranglehold on national tax systems. Taxing away this hereditary power required raising that of the lower house of government. Democratic reform extended the vote to a wider portion of the population, in the expectation that this would lead to policies to check the extraction of economic rent.

By contrast, today's finance capital is inherently oligarchic. It seeks to capture the government—first and foremost the Treasury, central bank and the courts—to enrich (indeed, to bail out) and un-tax the banking sector and its major clients: real estate and monopolies. This is why Germany opposed a public referendum on the European Central Bank's austerity program in Greece, and imposed "technocrats" to act on behalf of high finance.

"The Future of Capitalism"—What Kind of Capitalism Do We Mean?

What is so striking in the recent debates about the future of capitalism is blurriness over just what **kind** of capitalism is being talked about. Industrial capitalism invested in plant and equipment, making profits by employing labor to produce output at a markup. But the Western world is now on a path of austerity and downsizing. Companies are using their cash flow and borrowing mainly for stock buybacks, raids and buyouts of assets already in place. Most bank lending is for real estate and to other financial institutions for arbitrage speculation on interest rates, foreign exchange rates or other financial instruments, not to industry or consumers—who find themselves obliged to pay down debts taken out in the past rather than buying new output.

This is not what was envisioned when the Industrial Revolution was peaking in the 19th and early 20th century. To promote growth and increase their nations' competitive position, classical economists sought to free society from the legacies of feudalism—a landed aristocracy extracting land rent, and a banking class extracting interest and converting national debts into monopoly trading privileges. Progressive Era reformers defined a free market as one in which land rent was taxed away and monopolies either were broken up or socialized in the public domain along with basic infrastructure. The aim was to bring market prices in line with minimum necessary cost-value. This required a strong enough government to tax and check the vested financial, insurance and real estate (FIRE) interests.

When Joseph Schumpeter spoke about creative destruction driving capitalism forward, he was referring to technology raising productivity, enabling new companies to unseat the old by using more efficient means of production or creating better products, as when the automobile replaced the horse and buggy. Lower costs were supposed to be passed on to consumers in the form of falling prices. This principle was written into John F. Kennedy's wage-productivity guidelines with the steel industry in the early 1960s.[1] Liberal economists believed that market forces would raise wage levels in keeping with productivity, if only because production required a parallel growth in consumer demand.

To early supporters and strategists of industrial capitalism, the driving dynamic was what the Wharton Business School professor Simon Patten called the "Economy of Abundance." Innovations in modes of financial takeovers of industry were more in the character of parasitic destruction. Few observers anti-

---

[1] I elaborate the linkages between wages and productivity in my 2003 *Counterpunch* interview with Standard Schaefer, "Tech Bubble: Who Benefited," available on http://michael-hudson.com/2003/08/tech-bubble-who-benefited/. "There are two kinds of productivity. Most people think of capital equipment increasing output per workhour. Labor does the same amount of work, but produces more. And as it produces more, it does not need to work as hard, because capital saves labor by doing jobs more quickly and cheaply than manual labor, or doing work that people can't do at all. This is the kind of productivity that one associates with investment in machinery, computers and information technology (IT).

However, today's productivity is taking a different form. It is associated with laying off employees and working the remaining workers harder. There is little technology at work here, but rather the kind of drudgery from which technology was supposed to free employees. Work has become more unpleasant and stressful as companies let their work force shrink by attrition. When workers leave, their work is distributed among the remaining employees." Hence, wages have not risen with productivity.

cipated just how "creative"—in the pejorative sense of perversely inventive—this destructive appropriation might become. No one imagined that it might take over government agencies, the central bank and the Treasury to post-industrialize the economy. Schumpeter certainly did not envision that productive companies were to be destroyed by financial takeovers leaving them bankrupt shells of their former selves. Like most observers, he expected banking to be modernized to promote industrial capital investment, not to load industry down with debt, stock options, high dividend payouts and financial fees by raiders wielding junk bonds as their weapon of choice.

Today's financial operators have given a new meaning to the notion of creative destruction. Their innovations take the not-so-creative form of predatory destruction of the economy for their own benefit, as if co-opting government to give them tax favoritism for interest payouts and other non-production expenses entailed by transferring income into the hands of financial rather than industrial engineers. Industrial technology plays little role in this post-industrial creativity.

The upshot is that despite the rise in labor and capital productivity, prices have not fallen, and real wages have not increased since the late 1970s in the United States. The Finance, Insurance and Real Estate (FIRE) sector, dominated mainly by high finance, has appropriated almost all the economic gains. Industrial capitalism has evolved into finance capitalism in ways not dreamed of a century ago. Finance capitalism itself is a family of offshoots: pension-fund capitalism, the bubble economy, debt deflation and austerity. Each stage is characterized by new tactics to extracting wealth from the economy without contributing to its real growth. This path is now leading to what threatens to be a terminal stage of debt peonage and neofeudalism.

Instead of the promised economy of abundance, economic policy from the United States to Europe is now directed at imposing austerity to carry the debts run up by a Bubble Economy in which most gains have been made not by industrial investment, but by borrowing to buy assets whose price is being inflated by bank credit. The shift of focus from industrial profits to debt-leveraged "capital" gains been spurred mainly by falling interest rates, easier (indeed, reckless) mortgage credit, and higher capitalization multiples for stocks and bonds.

Debt leveraging inflated property prices for a while, but the rise was reversed when there was no underpinning in the "real" production-and-consumption economy. Since 2008 this price reversal has left a trail of negative equity (when debts exceed asset valuation) that has dragged down balance sheets not only for indebted households but also for the banks and insurance companies whose loans and default guarantees went bad. These defaults reflect the degree to which fraudulent mortgage lending was backed by AAA ratings from the credit rating agencies for "toxic waste" consisting largely of the "liars' loans" pushed by crooked mortgage originators associated with Countrywide Financial, Washington Mutual and similar banksters. This was a libertarian travesty of "free markets," turning the economy into a market free from the regulation or anti-fraud protection that governments are supposed to provide.

So foreclosure time has arrived. Shrinking markets, mounting arrears and bankruptcies have caused equity and real estate prices to plunge, leading banks to stop lending. Unable to refinance their mortgages, homeowners are obliged to pay back what they borrowed prior to 2008. Debt-strapped populations are buying less, so vacancy rates have risen for retail outlets. The combination of shrinking markets, unemployment and lower tax revenues has squeezed state and local budgets in the United States, while government budgets from Alabama to Ireland and Greece face an insurmountable debt burden. Localities as well as companies claim that they face bankruptcy if they are not permitted to roll back pensions, health care commitments and current wage levels. This is the cruel face of debt deflation—combined with the refusal to roll back tax cuts for property owners, capital gains and high-income earners.

When debtors no longer can pay the interest charges, they fall prey to debt peonage. In the case of government debtors, creditors seek to take payment in the form of property transfers, by privatizing the public domain. Buyers of basic infrastructure being sold off raise prices for hitherto public services, adding a fiscal and budget squeeze to the debt squeeze.

Instead of suffering a merely temporary cyclical downturn, economies have entered a fatal phase in which debt service falling due exceeds the economic surplus. The problem is not illiquidity—sound long-term investments that cannot find ready buyers because of a credit crunch—but insolvency, an inability to earn enough to pay debts under foreseeable normal conditions. An overgrowth of debt expands autonomously by its own dynamics ("the miracle of compound interest" plus the banks' electronic creation of new credit). The economic system shrinks, unless governments either annul debts or fuel recovery by lending enough to carry the debts.

To deter governments from acting, banks have promoted the fiction that a *deus ex machina* of "automatic stabilizers" will correct the debt problem, if only governments bail out the banks with enough money to lend out to get people and companies spending again. This pretense aims at deterring public policy from acting to rein in the banks from their over-lending, speculation, and helping clients avoid taxes by moving their funds offshore.

The solution ultimately must be political and involve debt write-down. Near Eastern economies are documenting restored balance and growth from c. 2500 BC to 500 BC by royal Clean Slates. Solon banned debt bondage in Athens in 594 BC, paving the way for the democratic take-off. Sparta's kings Agis IV and Cleomenes III sought to reverse the financial polarization between creditors and debtors in the late third century BC by cancelling the debts. Jesus announced that he had come to proclaim the Jubilee Year, the 50th year in which Leviticus 25 prescribed that personal debts should be forgiven, debtors released from bondage, and self-support land returned to debtors who had forfeited them. In more modern times, Germany's Economic Miracle was triggered by the 1948 Allied monetary reform and debt cancellation and subsequent 1953 settlement of accumulated past international obligations.

Ignoring this history, the most damaging economic fiction of our time is that all debts can be paid—if only countries submit to enough austerity, impoverish their labor force, close down enough industry and let banks foreclose on enough factories—and while they are at it, cut back Social Security, health care and social spending. These cutbacks are a tactic in the financial warfare that the 1% is waging against the rest of the economy. Trying to impose this fiction on reality can only stifle industrial prosperity, "post-industrializing" economies by destroying the circular flow of spending and payments between domestic consumers and producers.

It seems ironic that today's socialist, Social Democratic and Labour parties—ostensibly on the left wing of political spectrum—tend to support the financial sector's neoliberal policies, even that of privatization. In Britain, Tony Blair's Labour Party went even further than Margaret Thatcher's Conservatives in privatizing the railways. Throughout continental Europe, Social Democrats have not proposed an alternative to neoliberal austerity. And in the United States under Presidents Clinton and Obama, the Democratic Party has embraced the deregulatory "Rubinomics" wing, named for former Goldman Sachs CEO and Treasury Secretary Robert Rubin.

A strong Marxist tradition on the left blames the financial crisis on the drive by industrial employers to pay as low wages as possible. In this view, capitalists accumulate industrial profits by not paying labor enough to buy the products it creates. This becomes systemically self-destructive as badly paid labor lacks the purchasing power to buy what it produces, causing underconsumption or over-production. Savings and debt are an industrial problem, not specifically financial.

More Schumpeterian approaches blame today's crisis on technological advance causing unemployment, while neoclassical trade theory focuses on the offshoring of production to low-wage countries. The underlying logic is that less labor is required to produce the means of livelihood than in times past. But why then is our world not one of abundance, shorter workdays and longer vacations—the leisure economy that technology was supposed to introduce? The answer is that people are working longer to pay down their debts. Interest and other financial overhead—and debt-inflated housing costs—have absorbed more than productivity gains have provided.

Finance Capitalism vs. Industrial Capitalism, and Their Respective Modes of Exploitation

The problems between employers and employees are eternal, but labor today is exploited increasingly in a financial way. Bankers extract revenue from consumers by interest, fees and penalties on credit cards, personal loans, mortgages and student loans. Corporate raiders empty out Employee Stock-Ownership Plans (ESOPs) and pension funds, or downsize payouts by threatening or declaring bankruptcy. In the fiscal sphere the financial sector has gained sufficient power to shift the tax burden off itself and its major clients onto consumers. Since 1982, FICA wage withholding now absorbs over 15 percent of labor's paychecks for Social Security and Medicare, producing large enough fiscal surpluses to cut taxes on the wealthy.

Like household budgets, the corporate sector has been financialized. Instead of raising funds for new capital investment, the stock market has become a vehicle for raiders to buy companies on credit, replacing equity capital with debt. Debt-leveraged corporate buyouts, raids, mergers and acquisitions earmark corporate cash flow for debt service (*e.g.*, to pay junk bond holders who advanced takeover funding) instead of investing in new capital formation to employ labor and produce more. Most corporate debt is taken on for leveraged buyouts—or for "poison pills": so much debt that no raiders will want to take over companies that defend themselves against such financial aggression by financial self-immolation.

Most bank credit is lent to other financial institutions, not to industry or consumers. To focus on the production and employment dynamics of industrial capitalism rather than the debt dynamics of finance capitalism leaves out of account the fact that banks make loans and create debt (and deposits) on their computer keyboards. An autonomous financial dynamic is at work, not merely savings by the industrial sector. For non-financial debt, by far the largest category in today's economies takes the form of mortgages to buy housing and office buildings.

This is not what economic observers expected when the Industrial Revolution was just getting under way. Banks sided with manufacturing, largely

because their major loan market was import and export trade, foreign investment or other international transfers. In Britain, the center of the Industrial
Revolution, industrial dominance required under-selling competitors. This
was done not merely through technological advance but by minimizing the
rake-off of income by the nation's landlord class. So tax reform became a
leading aim, from David Ricardo's attack on the Corn Laws (Britain's protectionist agricultural tariffs that enhanced groundrent) after 1817 to later
attempts to tax urban as well as rural land as the fiscal base.

Marx pointed to the industrialists' hatred of privileged landlords, as
reflected from Ricardo through Henry George, for siphoning off rent from
the industrial circular flow without producing value.[2] As he and Engels
expressed matters in the *Communist Manifesto*: "The bourgeoisie, wherever it
has got the upper hand, has put an end to all feudal, patriarchal, idyllic
relations. It has pitilessly torn asunder the motley feudal ties that bound man
to his "natural superiors ..." Paramount among these ties were the hereditary
right to ground rent, the privilege of bankers to charge interest and also to
put pressure on debtor governments to create and sell off monopoly rent-
extracting rights for payment in government war bonds.

Industrial capitalists made profits by investing in plant and equipment to
employ labor to sell output at a markup. Most profits were to be reinvested in
this way, and retained earnings indeed are still the main source of tangible
capital investment, not bank lending or the stock market. But as "balance
sheet wealth" has become financialized for industrial companies, investment
has become more debt-leveraged.

The problem is not merely one of personal greed; it is built into the
inexorable mathematics of compound interest (see Chapters 2 and 11) and,
since 1971, fiat credit creation (see Chapters 14 and 15). From the classical
vantage point, the buildup of claims for groundrent, monopoly rent and
financial charges reflects Industrial Capitalism's failure to free economies
from these *rentiers*. Led by finance capital, the vested interests have managed
to reverse the Progressive reform movement, gaining control over election
campaigns to un-tax themselves and disable public regulation.

---

[2] The political aim of Ricardo's rent theory, Marx wrote, was to buttress the program of
taxing the land rather than industry. Upon being sent copies of *Progress and Poverty* in
1881, Marx dismissed the book as saying what his 1847 critique of Proudhon had forecast:
"We understand such economists as Mill, Cherbuliez, Hilditch and others demanding
that rent should be handed over to the state to serve in place of taxes. That is a frank
expression of the hatred the industrial capitalist bears towards the landed proprietor, who
seems to him a useless thing, an excrescence upon the general body of bourgeois production." (*The Poverty of Philosophy* [1847] (Moscow, Progress Publishers, n.d.: 155.)

The unforeseen result is that post-industrial wealth derives more from debt-leveraged capital gains (asset-price inflation) on real estate and monopolies than from new tangible capital formation. It is appropriate to speak of debt pollution of the environment, turning the industrial surplus and disposable personal income into debt service. Real estate rents are paid out as mortgage interest, corporate cash flow is paid to corporate raiders, and the tax surplus is used to bail out banks that have succumbed to the economy's plunge into negative equity.

Industrial potential cannot be recovered without winding down the debt overhead that has been used to bid up asset prices. For exporters to compete internationally, it is necessary to roll back debt-leveraged prices for real estate, health care and education. Yet instead of confronting this problem, U.S. and European leaders blame China. They attribute its success to low-wage manufacturing, not to the mixed public/private economy.

Misinterpretation of the West's financial overhead and the consequences of its untaxing of finance, insurance and real estate reflects the success of *rentiers* in packing economics departments with professors who reject classical value and price theory, and its corollary distinction between earned and unearned income, productive and unproductive labor. These concepts no longer are taught. Neoliberal ideology has been able to expunge the history of economic thought and history itself from the curriculum, and from popular thought and discussion.

By rejecting the classical distinctions between productive and unproductive investment, credit and employment, the post-classical economists receiving the charitable largesse of *rentiers* and awarded the "badge of true science" insist that all income and wealth is earned productively. Everyone earns whatever he or she makes, so there is no unearned wealth. There are no idle rich.

The post-classical (confusingly called "neoclassical") and Austrian counter-revolution treats *rentiers* as playing a necessary and essential role in production, by allocating resources efficiently and with foresight. This approach dismisses as a mere witticism Balzac's quip that most great family fortunes are grounded in long-forgotten and suppressed thefts of the public domain or by political or financial insider dealing. Also in the spirit of Proudhon's declaration that "Property is theft," Gustavus Myers' *History of the Great American Fortunes* (1907) details the acquisition of wealth by insider dealing and skullduggery. But such books are dismissed as muckraking, not as the core of most wealth.

Many 19th-century economists distinguished material welfare from what Thorstein Veblen called "pecuniary" wealth. In 1804, James Maitland, eighth earl of Lauderdale, wrote *An Inquiry into the Nature and Origin of Public Wealth, and into the Means and Causes of its Increase* emphasizing the distinction between material wealth and commercial exchange value. Farmers often make more from a failed harvest that raises food prices to distress levels than from abundance. High prices and income thus reflect "a degree of scarcity," although "The common sense of mankind would revolt [at schemes to increase private riches] by creating a scarcity of any commodity generally useful and necessary to man." Yet this is precisely what monopolists and privatizers aim at doing, including bankers dispensing credit. The distinction between "real wealth" and financial claims was a central theme of Friedrich List's *National System of Political Economy* (1841), Calvin Colton's *Public Economy for the United States* (1848) and the American School of technological and protectionist writers in general.

As for financial wealth in the form of stocks, bonds and bank loans, the physicist Frederick Soddy's *Wealth, Virtual Wealth and Debt* (1926) distinguished between material "real" wealth in the means of production and financial or property claims **on** this wealth. These financial claims tend to expand more rapidly than the surplus available to pay, especially as banks appropriate the privilege of credit creation. In the European Union this privilege has been pressed to the point of blocking governments from creating their own money to monetize their budget deficits—the purpose for which central banks were founded!

Interest owed on this credit tends to rise to the point where it plunges the non-financial economy into deficit—and on into austerity as bankers and bondholders squeeze out payments from government, industry, real estate and consumers. Wealth is concentrated in financial hands even as the economy shrinks. As economies fall into negative equity, debt arrears and foreclosures mount up in what has become an economic trap in which it is almost impossible to win or even to survive.

Permitting this incursion of finance into the "real" production-and-consumption economy requires suspending democratic choice in debt-strapped countries. Most recently in Greece, German Chancellor Angela Merkel pressured Prime Minister Papandreou not to permit a voter referendum on the European Union's austerity and privatization plan imposed in late 2011. Neoliberal Latvia and its Baltic neighbors have retained democratic formalities by staging political distractions to win voters to neoliberal parties on a platform of ethnic nationalism. In the United States religious and sexual issues play a prominent role in shifting election campaigns away from economic and financial issues.

This political turn away from economic issues was not anticipated by 19th and early 20th century parliamentary reformers. It runs against the basic Enlightenment assumption that voters act knowledgably in their self-interest. This hardly is a realistic assumption to make these days!

Turning economic theory into a logic justifying *rentier* takings dissuades discussion of policy alternatives by presenting this rent extraction as natural and apparently inevitable. "There is no alternative," say the neoliberals. Yet this direction of evolution is the opposite from what classical economists and Progressive Era reformers expected to see. It renders economies high-cost, not low-cost and hence presumably more competitive. It is expensive to support a financial class lording it over the rest of the population, after all.

Rentier lobbyists hope that people will not notice how the economic map they draw fails to correspond to the territory it claims to depict. Post-classical theory assumes that everyone earns what they take, by providing productive services. Equilibrium theory postulating that "automatic stabilizers" make government intervention and reform unnecessary all but denies that today's polarization of wealth can really be occurring. Mainstream economics is turned into science fiction about a happy "trickle down" parallel universe where financiers are "job creators," everyone is fairly rewarded, and the world becomes more equal and prosperous.

Financial Drains on the Economy's Circular Flow between Producers and Consumers

The concept of circular flow underlies national income accounting. The first major such account was pioneered by the French surgeon doctor François Quesnay, calling his analysis Physiocracy, because it used the circular flow of blood in the human body as an analogy for how national income is circulated between producers and consumers, and between the government and the private sector.

Known as *Les Économistes*, the Physiocrats saw France's landed aristocracy and royalty siphoning off groundrent as a kind of tax, while throwing the cost of government onto the towns, industry and labor by a proliferation of excise taxes and other burdens. The Physiocrats argued for a Single Tax (*l'Impôt Unique*) to collect this rent in place of other taxes. Adam Smith credited them with founding economic science and backed their land tax, as did subsequent British economists through John Stuart Mill and the "Ricardian socialists." The American journalist Henry George attracted a world following by making this tax the focus of political reform.

As noted above, a tax on land rent was the aim of industrial capitalism to minimize the diversion of revenue away from the domestic market of producers and consumers. Speaking in defense of landlords, Reverend Thomas Malthus argued that they were in a fact a key to the circular flow by spending their rents on coachmen, tailors and servants. But most classical economists deemed such luxury consumer spending unproductive because it did not employ wage labor to produce goods to sell at a profit. However, Keynes praised Malthus at least for emphasizing the need to address the need for consumer demand to maintain the economy's circular flow from the vantage point popularly now called Say's Law.

Although the past century has seen a democratization of land ownership, the fact that this has occurred on credit has made banks the recipients of the groundrent paid to mainly to absentee landlords prior to the 20th century. Homebuyers and commercial real estate investors buy real estate by taking out mortgages. The purchase price usually ends up with the winning buyer being whoever outbids others to pledge the most rent to the bank as interest. Much the same is true of the public infrastructure and monopolies being sold off. To the extent that these enterprises are bought on credit, their extraction of monopoly rent—like land rent—ends up being paid out as interest.

> The way to bring prices in line with non-financial costs of production — and hence to win export markets — was to replace war with peace. Along with minimizing or taxing away land rent, monopoly rent and financial charges, this became the dream of classical economics as national strategy as well as a political reform program.

Writing during the Great Depression, Keynes blamed saving for interrupting this circular flow. Debt was not a major problem, as neither business nor consumers were borrowing. Keynes in fact saw recovery dependent on banks lending once again to spur investment and employment. But today, three-quarters of a century later, it is mainly bankers who are diverting consumer income (wages), corporate cash flow and tax revenues to pay interest and amortization, leaving less available for spending on goods and services. Banks and other financial institutions receiving this debt service do not use it to finance tangible investment. They lend it out, to mount up into additional claims on the bottom 99%, on corporate industry and on government borrowers. This is what makes today's drain from the circular flow different from the post-feudal landlord class in Europe and its colonies, and from government over-taxation to wage wars in times past.

What also has changed matters is the symbiosis that has developed between banking and government by making government bonds the foundation of bank reserves. Most of this public debt originated as war debt, because wars traditionally have been the major cause of budget deficits (although today's deficits stem largely from slashing taxes on high-bracket wealth and property). Adam Smith urged nations to finance wars on a pay-as-you-go basis so that populations would feel their immediate expense and make an informed choice for peace instead of burdening economies with war debts and the taxes attached to them. The way to bring prices in line with nonfinancial costs of production—and hence to win export markets—was to replace war with peace. Along with minimizing or taxing away land rent, monopoly rent and financial charges, this became the dream of classical economics as national strategy as well as a political reform program.

Pension-Fund Finance Capitalism

American finance capitalism took a quantum leap forward in the 1950s with the innovation of pension fund capitalism. Applauded by Peter Drucker as "pension fund socialism," the idea was to set aside part of the employer's wage budget, and turn it over to Wall Street to invest in the stock and bond markets. General Motors took the lead, hoping that this would give workers a stake in industrial capitalism by turning them into capitalists in miniature.

The problem with this partnership between labor and finance capital was that labor's savings were invested in financial claims *on* the means of production rather than financing it directly. By the wild 1980s pensions were being consigned to the likes of Michael Milken at Drexel Burnham to finance raids on industry, downsizing and outsourcing of labor.

Although equities are ownership shares in principle, they do not give labor much voice in management or on corporate boards, even for workplace conditions as was the case in Germany. The situation is similar to that which prompted minority New York Yankees baseball investor John McMullen to complain: "There is nothing in life quite so limited as being a limited partner of [managing partner] George Steinbrenner."

The problem was worst in the case of Employee Stock Ownership Plans (ESOPs) in which employee savings are managed directly by employers. They typically use these employee savings to buy the company's stock — thereby enabling managers to cash in their stock options at a higher price. About half the savings are looted and left bankrupt by being lent to employers or to subsidiaries that are folded. The bankruptcy or merger ploy was refined most notoriously in Chile after 1973 under General Pinochet. Companies emptied out most of the nation's pension plans by the end of the 1970s, refining the tactic to become a model for U.S. financiers. Recently at the Chicago Tribune, for example, real estate magnate Sam Zell used the company's ESOP to pay off his creditors, leaving employees with only a hollowed out shell and an impending lawsuit for fraudulent conveyance. Under the law, if a loan is made with only a fictitious projection of solvency under normal operating conditions, the courts may declare it void. Yet this is how pension-fund capitalism becomes the quasi-criminalized Ponzi phase of finance capitalism.[3]

What Pinochet (soon echoed by his admirer Margaret Thatcher) called "labor capitalism" more accurately should be termed "labor finance capitalism." Pension contributions are invested in financial markets to push up prices for bonds, stocks and real estate relative to labor's wages and salaries. This funding has proved to be a boon for managers and venture capitalists exercising their stock options as pension funds have bought in. That was the basic dream, after all: to create a perpetual motion financial machine in which the rising inflow of funding would pay pensions out of capital gains, which were projected as rising exponentially without limit.

By the time the dot.com bubble got underway in the 1990s, a rate of 8 percent compounded annually was almost universally projected. It would double any given amount every nine years, and quadruple it in eighteen. This means ostensibly that only a fairly small amount needs to be paid into a pension plan to multiply sufficiently to pay its projected benefits (see Chapters 9 and 10). The problem is that no economy in history ever has expanded at this rate.

So pension fund finance capitalism became dependent on the Bubble Economy being orchestrated by Federal Reserve Chairman Alan Greenspan. The Fed flooded the banking system with easy credit, pushing down interest

---

[3] See for instance Andrew Ross Sorkin, "Workers Pay for Debacle at Tribune," *The New York Times*, December 9, 2008, and Mike Spector, Jenny Strasburg and Shira Ovide, "At Tribune, Battle Expands," *Wall Street Journal*, April 19, 2011. Zell bought the newspaper from stockholders in a heavily debt-leveraged buyout. Employee holdings (controlled by the Tribune as employer) were replaced by promises to pay pensions. But the debt overhead was so large that the company went bankrupt.

rates from the 1980s, culminating in Mr. Greenspan's successor, Ben Bernanke, reducing the Fed's discount rate (at which banks could borrow) to only 0.25 percent by 2011—one quarter of one percent! Lower interest rates meant that real estate rents and corporate profits could be capitalized into bank loans at rising multiples.

So prices rose not because the economy was becoming more prosperous and profits were rising, but for purely monetary reasons. This is not what is supposed to happen according to rosy textbook pictures. And there is an inherent inner contradiction in the idea of paying pensions out of capital gains fueled by credit at lower interest rates. As the interest on the safest investment—short-term U.S. Treasury bonds—has fallen to 1 percent, the idea of paying pensions out of 8 percent compound growth has become illusory. More and more pension funds have been driven to take risks that ended up losing all their capital to Wall Street sharpies.

> **A**s the interest on the safest investment (short-term U.S. Treasury bonds) has fallen to 1 percent, the idea of paying pensions out of 8 percent compound growth has become illusory. More and more pension funds have been driven to take risks that ended up losing all their capital to Wall Street sharpies.

An even more serious problem is that contrary to widespread belief, this stock market boom was not raising funds for industry. It was becoming perverse (see Chapter 9). Just as the financial sector has become independent of tangible capital formation, stock ownership has been decoupled from management—or rather, management itself aimed at financial objectives more than at building up industrial output. "Activist" shareholders were in the character of raiders seeking to manipulate balance sheets, downsize and outsource labor, and raise productivity simply by working employees harder and for longer hours, not by using better technology.

This transformation of the stock market's role in the industrial economy means that as pension funds became part of this financialization process, they have played a major role in the leveraged buyouts that loaded down companies with junk-bond debt. Threatened by Drexel Burnham raiders buying out companies with high-interest junk bonds in the 1980s, healthy firms felt obliged to defend themselves by taking "poison pills," going so deeply into debt that it did not make financial sense for raiders to take on any more debt to buy them. Some companies used their cash flow and even borrowed to buy up their stock to raise its price by enough to leave less revenue available for prospective raiders to pay their bankers and bond-holders. From the vantage point of employees contributing to pension plans seeking to profit from such takeovers, the problem is that the new financial managers are laying off workers, as well as using cash flow for stock buybacks or higher dividend payouts rather than for new direct investment and hiring. Labor is supposed to benefit not as employees but only as financial investors fallen prey to Wall Street.

> **A**s pension funds became part of the financialization process, they have played a major role in the leveraged buyouts that loaded down companies with junk-bond debt.

Fiat Money Based on America's Militarized Balance-of-Payments Deficit

What made the bubble economy's wave of credit possible was the transformation of international finance in 1971, when overseas U.S. military spending finally forced the dollar off gold. Called "the money of the world" by James Steuart in 1767, it was obtained by economies running balance-of-payments surpluses, which countries running payments deficits had to settle in gold. Ever since the Korean War broke out in 1950, the entire payments deficit stemmed from military spending (the U.S. private sector's foreign trade and investment was in balance during the 1950s and '60s).[4] President Nixon's suspension of gold sales left the world's central banks without a means of settling these deficits (their surpluses). In the ensuing vacuum, U.S. Treasury debt bonds became a proxy for gold, turned over to foreign central banks to settle international payments imbalances.

---

[4] I describe this process in *Super Imperialism: The Economic Strategy of American Empire* (1972). See also chapters 15, 16 and 17 below.

The dollar-IOUs ending up as global central bank reserves were the embodiment of American military spending. The link between the dollarized global monetary system and military force became explicit after OPEC quadrupled its oil prices in 1973–74 (following the U.S. quadrupling of grain prices). Treasury officials met with Saudi Arabian and other OPEC officials and explained that they could charge as much as they wished for oil (which provided a price umbrella for U.S. oil companies to make windfall price gains), as long as they agreed to hold their reserves in U.S. Treasury bonds or otherwise recycle their export earnings into the U.S. economy by buying stocks, real estate and other property claims—but not ownership of strategic industries. Not to recycle these petrodollars would be treated as an "unfriendly act."

For the United States, this reversed the traditional impact of balance-of-payments deficits on interest rates. Under the gold standard, countries running deficits had to raise rates to borrow enough to stabilize their currency's exchange rate. But for the United States, the larger its payments deficit grew, the more dollars ended up in the hands of foreign central banks—which had had little alternative but to recycle them to the U.S. economy, mainly by buying Treasury bonds. Monetarily, the U.S. payments deficit had become inflationary, not deflationary as was the rule in times past. *The payments deficit thus became the means of financing the domestic budget deficit.*

This circular flow enabled a kind of financial perpetual motion machine to be set in motion. Banks were able to create their own credit electronically without international constraint. U.S. strategists came to realize that their government could run domestic budget deficits almost without limit while American investors bought up foreign assets and consumers imported more. So under the Treasury-bill standard the U.S. economy achieved a free lunch unique in history. For the past thousand years the major factor in balance-of-payments deficits has been military. This often has led to a loss of economic sovereignty. But under the new monetary imperialism, foreign central banks absorbed the cost of U.S. military spending—and in due course the U.S. private-sector takeover of their economies. The United States demanded, and received, tribute from all other nations (at least, those holding their central bank reserves in dollarized loans to the U.S. Treasury), on a scale that earlier empires could only dream of achieving.

There is something politically transformative as well as fictitious about this rising debt. Prior to the 16th century, royal debts died with kings, leaving Italian and other international bankers with bad debts. The Dutch Republic took the lead in making national debts permanent, by parliamentary democracy backing public obligations with specific taxes to pay their interest. But that was in an epoch when debts were settled in gold, especially international debts. Nobody can come up with a plausible scenario for how the United States can pay today's $4.5 trillion foreign debt—except by creating yet more IOUs that simply add more interest charges onto the principal. So debtor countries pretend to pay, and creditor countries pretend to be paid. This is basically what happens in domestic bubble economies.

The Bubble Economy

In the wake of the dot.com stock market bubble's bursting in 2000, and 9/11 the next year, the Federal Reserve inflated a full-blown financial and real estate bubble. As the Fed pushed interest rates down, prices rose for real estate, bonds and stocks, which are worth whatever a bank will lend. The failure of real wages to rise after the late 1970s (despite the enormous increase in productivity) meant that many families could maintain their standard of living by borrowing.

The easiest way to do this was against the bank-inflated price of their homes. Buying a more expensive home in fact was the easiest way to make a capital gain and thus increase one's net worth. For the first time in history, people were persuaded that the way to get rich was by running into debt, not by staying out of it. Alan Greenspan urged homeowners to "cash out" on their home equity—the rising market price of their home over and above their mortgage debt—by borrowing and spending the loan proceeds, as if it were free income, indeed as if the new bank loan either didn't have to be repaid later (with interest) or would be refinanced against yet further real estate price gains.

Many families were tempted to borrow because wages and salaries had stagnated since the late 1970s, while medical costs and other prices rose. New borrowing against one's home became almost the only way to maintain living standards in the face of this economic squeeze. The old Protestant Ethic of living off interest rather than eating into capital or going into debt was becoming obsolete. Debt leveraging was applauded not merely as the new post-industrial way to get rich, but indeed the only way to break even and avoid having to cut back living standards. A rising home ownership rate for racial and ethnic minorities (and for low-income families in general) was achieved by loading them down heavily with debt, most of it in the form of exploding "adjustable" mortgage rates.

The aim of investors across the board shifted way from seeking current income to making "total returns" in the form of capital gains. Falling interest rates raised asset prices by enabling a given stream of rent or other income to be capitalized into a larger bank loan.

By bidding up real estate and stock market prices, debt leveraging lowered current returns. And as noted above, this made it more expensive for pension funds to purchase a fixed "defined benefit" retirement income. By 2011, California's giant pension plan CalPERS was making only a 1.1 percent return—far less than the assumed 7.75 percent annual rate of total returns (interest plus dividends) needed for solvency without raising contribution rates (or without raising taxes, in the case of state and local pension funds).[5] The low interest rates required to preserve the inflated value of bank assets wrought special havoc for pension funds. The dream of pension fund capitalism was turning into a nightmare of insolvency. The capital-gains bubble was over, and returns on bonds and stocks remained sank to all-time lows. This left a widening swath of corporate, state and local pension funds underfunded, while the economy was faced with debts whose carrying charges prevented new spending.

Many pension funds tried to catch up by speculating in financial derivatives, joining the transition to what was becoming a distinct new stage of finance capitalism: Casino Capitalism, buying derivatives that were debt-financed gambles on which way interest rates, exchange rates or packaged securities would move in markets controlled by the largest Wall Street players—in a financial market where fraud was effectively decriminalized. The Justice Department, Securities and Exchange Commission and other regulatory agencies refrained from prosecuting financial fraud. Administrators were chosen who were ideologically committed to ignoring the rules they had sworn to enforce, and regulatory agencies were understaffed. Barack Obama's Democratic administration appointees (2009–12) simply continued this "free market" deregulation sponsored by George W. Bush's Republican administration (2001–08), with even greater emphasis. So pension funds became financial prey, as did small companies and investors in general.

Banks led and indeed orchestrated the new speculative wave. They lent mainly to other financial institutions, not to finance new capital formation or employment. The era of asset-price inflation had changed the aim of investors to ride the tumultuous waves of the Bubble Economy and seek capital gains by debt leveraging. Tax policy favored such speculation, by lightening

---

[5] CalPERS reduced its assumed rate of return to 7.5% on March 14. 2012. "Calpers's board considered lowering the rate to 7.5% last year but backed off after local California agencies said the increased contributions would exacerbate their financial hardships," by obliging "the state to eventually contribute an additional $300 million annually." (Michael Corkery, "Calpers Lowers Investment Target to 7.5%," *Wall Street Journal*, March 15, 2012.) The problem seems insolvable, because a more realistic rate of return would plunge California's budget billions of dollars further into annual deficit.

taxes on capital gains while shifting the fiscal burden onto wages and consumer spending.

The Bubble Economy was prolonged by what the late economist Hyman Minsky called the Ponzi stage of the financial cycle. Investors and speculators borrowed the interest falling due, and even borrowed against the hoped-for price gains for real estate, stocks and bonds. Easy credit combined with pro-debt tax policy encouraged debt leveraging on an unprecedented scale. Companies used cash flow and even borrowed to buy back their stock to bid up its price, while access to credit was "democratized" in what President George W. Bush called "the ownership society." It turned into the Negative Equity economy falling into insolvency and debt peonage.

Debt Deflation in the Post-Bubble Economy

Financializing pensions by steering their funding into the financial markets to build up claims on the economy has the opposite effect of direct investment and employment. Falling interest rates enable bank credit to fuel rising prices for financial assets. But the economy is left loaded down with debt when the bubble has run its course. Paying debt service blocks recovery by diverting spending away from goods and services to pay banks. So debt-burdened economies shrunk, and financial risk rises in the face of spreading bankruptcies, forfeitures and foreclosures.

The National Income and Product Accounts (NIPA) record the paying down of debts as raising the net saving rate. The negation of a negation (lower debt) is counted as a positive (saving): reducing credit card and mortgage balances, student loans and other obligations. But these pay-downs are a form of saving that does not represent a buildup of funds available for spending. Paying debts leaves most people with less to spend. And they are less able to borrow as banks pull back their credit lines, seeing the economy become more risky.

Meanwhile, low interest rates created a policy quandary once the asset-price inflation had run its course. To let interest rates rise back toward normal levels would reduce the capitalized value of real estate rents, corporate earnings, stock and bond payments. That would exacerbate the fall of real estate prices, driving the banks themselves into negative equity. So central banks kept interest rates low, hoping to re-inflate asset prices. Mortgage rates were pushed down below 4 percent as the Federal Reserve's Quantitative Easing policy of 2010–11 pressed rates at which banks could borrow down nearly to zero in the hope that they would lend more and re-inflate property prices by enough to save homeowners—and banks—from negative equity.

But the economy already had become too over-burdened with debt for banks to lend, or real estate buyers to borrow as asset prices fell. Banks are unwilling to lend their inflow of loan paybacks to the "real" economy, because it has become too risky, and companies no longer could borrow by issuing their own commercial paper IOUs, because the wave of deregulation has destroyed the trust needed for the market to work. So most of the $800 billion in the Federal Reserve's Quantitative Easing of 2011 (QE II) was used for foreign exchange and interest rate arbitrage gambles. Banks took the bailout money and ran—keeping the rest on deposit with the Fed to rebuild their reserves.

Europe's Financial Self-Immolating Austerity

Credit dried up even more drastically in Europe. An ideological obsession with budget deficits prevented the European Central Bank (ECB) from supplying the economy with spending power. Decades of bank propaganda have implanted a false memory in Germany's population, blaming the Weimar hyperinflation of the early 1920s on the Reichsbank financing Germany's domestic budget deficit. The reality is that the central bank tried to meet its unpayably high foreign currency reparations by printing reichsmarks and desperately selling them on the foreign exchange market to raise the hard currency demanded by the Allies. The problem was not domestic money creation to finance German spending (much less for productive uses or to revive the economy), but to pay war debts denominated in foreign currency. And the Allied economies for their part refused to spend these payments back in Germany to enable it to pay. In fact, the United States imposed special tariffs (the "American Selling Price" system of valuing imports from countries with depreciating currencies) to protect its market from German exports.

German and other European bankers have crafted a narrative that has drowned out memory of what actually happened. Misrepresenting how central banks are supposed to work in practice, bank lobbyists parrot the falsehood that central bank financing of budget deficits is inherently inflationary—indeed, hyperinflationary. The only responsible policy, bankers insist, is to deter today's governments from having their own central banks monetize their deficits. The EU's Lisbon Treaty and the German constitution forbid the ECB from monetizing deficits in this way. Instead, governments are told to borrow from commercial banks and bondholders, as if these are "honest brokers" lending wisely only for viable productive purposes.

The problem is that if the central bank is blocked from putting money into the economy, taxes will have to be raised or public spending cut back.

This commitment to austerity is plunging Eurozone economies needlessly into depression by limiting the ability of governments to run deficits. Latvia and Greece limp along as object lessons to show how financial and fiscal austerity leads to plunging employment, collapsing property prices and bankruptcies. Debtors default and national budget deficits worsen. Unable to find work, labor emigrates.

It is all so needless! Even a cursory look at recent U.S. and British experience should dispel the idea that central bank money creation must inflate commodity prices. Since 2008 the Federal Reserve has overseen the largest money creation in history, yet U.S. consumer prices and wages have barely risen, and the dollar has held steady. The same has occurred with British consumer prices, wages and the pound's exchange rate. By monetizing public budget deficits, the Federal Reserve and Bank of England are doing what central banks were founded to do. And this is what is needed to save today's economies from plunging into depression.

In U.S. and global financial bubble resulted not from government deficits or central bank money creation, but from *commercial* banks lending to inflate real estate and stock market prices. The increase in public debt has stemmed mainly from bailing out the banks from having indulged in this self-seeking short-term behavior. The problem is private-sector indebtedness.

Yet even as Europe's economies are being driven into depression, the Troika of the EU Commission, ECB and IMF are calling for balanced budgets instead of public spending to revive employment. They demand that governments bail out bad private-sector debts, paying banks and bondholders by raising taxes on the non-financial sector. This adds a tax burden onto the economy's rising debt overhead. The social safety net is to be scaled back so as to make economies more "competitive"—as if public spending on the "real" economy makes them less so.

The United States threatens to go down this road, making Europe a dress rehearsal for how fiscal austerity works (or fails to work). Ignoring the problems caused by private-sector debt helps free banks from blame for inflating prices for houses and other assets with loans that have left a residue of negative equity—for the largest and most reckless banks as well as for a quarter of U.S. homeowners. Banks in fact are using the financial crisis as an opportunity to demand a "solution" that gives them bailouts and tax benefits as well as loan guarantees—and to cap matters, privatization of public assets as in Greece, creating new buyout markets for new bank credit.

To distract attention from their role in this mess, bank spokesmen misrepresent the debt problem as a demographic one. People are living longer, so governments should balance their budgets by slashing Social Security—

and privatizing it. This is akin to corporate financial managers downscaling "defined benefit" pension plans into amorphous "defined contribution" plans, leaving retirees with the risks while financial firms take their commissions off the top. Wall Street's hope is that sending Social Security wage withholding into the stock market will achieve what pension-fund finance capitalism was supposed to do: fuel a great price run-up. Social Security is to be drawn into the Casino Capitalist stage of finance capitalism.

Meanwhile, governments are told to cut taxes for the wealthy and the banks so as to revive the economy by getting the debt bubble expanding again. What makes this so hypocritical is that the government is told to break contracts with Social Security contributors who have not gambled with their savings. This annulling of obligations owed to labor changes the meaning of "sanctity of contracts"—simply to bail out the banks. The Congressional Budget Office (backed by James K. Galbraith, Robert Reich, Dean Baker and other economists) has shown that Social Security is solvent for at least another 25 years, and can be made solvent indefinitely simply by raising the cap on the payroll tax so that it falls on the upper brackets earning over $100,000.

The Bailout Economy

In the single case where government budget deficits are urged to increase — indeed, soar to veritable wartime levels — the purpose is not to revive economies but to take bad bank loans onto the public balance sheet. The government must bear the loss — a travesty of a free market. But then, most fortunes in history have come from the public domain.

Just as aggravating depression by debt deflation and fiscal tightening to balance government budgets is unnecessary, so are these bank bailouts at public expense. For example Sheila Bair, head of the Federal Deposit Insurance Corp. (FDIC), argued that Citibank could have been permitted to go under without disturbing its basic consumer-banking operations. Known for "stretching the legal envelope," the bank had sufficient assets to back its insured deposits. What would have been wiped out was the financial web of cross claims and gambles among large institutions. Instead, Treasury Secretaries Hank Paulson and Tim Geithner protected the speculators — ostensibly to save their "bread and butter" banking activities — by giving Citigroup $45 billion. Other banks "too big to fail" received proportionally large handouts.

What used to be deemed criminal has been decriminalized either by being deregulated, or more covertly simply by not enforcing rules that are on the book. In America, the Justice Department has become the chief fundraising arm of whatever party is in power. Much like the Catholic Church selling indulgences in Martin Luther's Europe, so justice departments throughout the world are selling "get out of jail free" cards to major campaign contributors. This has added a new term to the American language: "pay to play" politics.

The German expressionist movie "The Cabinet of Dr. Caligari" (1920) is about a madhouse in which a crazy director hypnotizes somnambulists to kill or abduct victims. The director claims to cure the inmates of the delusion that he is himself a madman—a metaphor for Weimar Germany. There is a certain resemblance to America's Justice Department and local police being run by the crooks on top. It has become a crime even to stage peaceful protests urging the government to bring financial criminals to justice! Occupy Wall Street protestors in New York City have been arrested for peacefully demonstrating their desire to bring criminal charges against financial fraudsters, while not a single bank has been charged with fraud for the multi-trillion rip-offs in what UMKC Prof. Bill Black calls a criminogenic binge.

While politicians make hypocritical calls for new laws while refraining from using those already on the books, Wall Street deters prosecution simply by recycling part of their plunder as campaign contributions to gain the right to name (or at least veto) the key public administrators. Public office thus is made part of the "free market" by permitting campaign contributions by business lobbyists without limit. Regulatory agency appointees reap rewards for their inactivity by what the Japanese call "descent from heaven": They receive enormously well paying jobs and "speaking fees" when they join the sectors they were charged with regulating.

Nowhere is this corruption more visible than in Goldman Sachs's placing its managers in charge of the U.S. Treasury. $182 billion was paid to bail out the A.I.G. insurance conglomerate rather than letting it default on the high-risk casino guarantees that its London office had written for junk mortgages. The Treasury could have paid nothing while preserving A.I.G.'s "plain vanilla" insurance operations. But the priority was to preserve the financial tangle of cross default swaps and collateralized debt obligations, leaving the Treasury holding the bag. More giveaways and tax credits made A.I.G. profitable enough to resume paying its bonuses, salaries and dividends.

Ratings agencies had given most of this toxic waste an AAA prime rating—as high as U.S. Government securities. Ratings were up for sale in a financial "free market" similar to the accounting sector when Arthur Andersen gave Enron a clean bill of health. No Wall Street institution received a criminal charge or prosecution. Financial bonuses and salaries hardly missed a beat— while home foreclosures soared for the economy at large. To save speculators from loss, the government made good on this fraud. The financial "fat" was saved at the expense of the industrial "bone" and the government's balance sheet. Debts owed by honest home borrowers were left in place, but those owed by defaulting financial insiders for bad gambles were made good as the Treasury paid the winning bettors when the losers came up short.

A similar government payback for its largest class of campaign contributors occurs by permitting companies to claim profits and pay out dividends by routinely underfunding their pension and health retirement funds. The next stage in this game is for financial managers to threaten bankruptcy to wipe out pension plans and health obligations, leaving the underfunded Public Benefit Guarantee Corporation (PBGC) to pick up the wreckage.

Using Junk Economics to Oppose Public Regulation and Taxation

Economic theory serves as a tool to shape peoples' views of what kind of tax policy, regulations and other government programs they should support. This makes economic theory an arena for every interest group because it shapes the map of how society is perceived. For example, do bankers and landlords earn their interest, speculative gains and rents productively by adding to national output? Or are they simply taking a free lunch, one that is not really necessary—revenue that is paid *out of* the surplus that the "real" economy produces?

> The National Income and Product Accounts (NIPA) depicts the FIRE sector as productive rather than as overhead. Rent and interest (and monopoly price gouging) are lumped together as "earnings" rather than devided into earned income and unearned rent.

The most important decisions to be taken concern who should be taxed (or untaxed), and the answers depend on how one views the economic surplus. Self-interest in determining the policy conclusion explains the seeming madness of today's unrealistic mainstream theory. Its pro-financial worldview steers government regulation and tax policy to maximize the measures used by the National Income and Product Accounts (NIPA) depicting the FIRE sector as productive rather than as overhead. Rent and interest (and monopoly price gouging) are lumped together as "earnings" rather than distinguishing between earned income and unearned rent. By conflating the "real" economy's surplus with the FIRE sector's rake-off, the NIPA engage in double counting to make it appear that this surplus is "growth." The financial sector, for instance, now accounts for some 40 percent of reported U.S. corporate earnings. But they consist largely of revenue transferred *from* industry *to* the banks and kindred institutions.

It is easy enough to see where mainstream economics and its statistical map of reality confuse matters. The culprit is the conflict between *rentier* interests and the rest of the economy. Bankers know quite well that their gains are achieved at the expense of their customers—mainly other financial institutions. By the 1990s, Bankers Trust officers were quite callously calling their transfer of wealth from clients to themselves the "Rip-Off Factor"— "the amount the bank could take from unsuspecting clients."[6] Yet the NIPA treat this price gouging and outright deception as additive elements of real output of "services." Their "value" includes the high salaries, expense accounts, bonuses, luxury rents, lobbying payments and legal fees.

By contrast, classical rent theory treated interest, fees, penalties and bank winnings on speculation as "false costs of production," as deductions *from* national output rather than adding *to* it. Accountants call such exploitation transfer payments—something for nothing, a *quid* with no *quo*, not earnings by providing a real service. The FIRE sector's revenue is in the character of transfer payments. Siphoning off income is a zero-sum activity in which one party's gain is another's loss. Instead of counting these *rentier* charges as "providing a service," they should be recognized as a tax paid to privilege, adding to the *cost* of living and doing business without being productive. This is the logic that led classical economic reformers writing during the Industrial Revolution's upsweep to bring into plain sight—and public oversight—the unearned *rentier* income being siphoned off by a hereditary landlord class, predatory bankers and monopolists.

To the classical economists a free market is one that has freed itself *from* such unearned income. The way to increase economic efficiency is to cut financial and other *rentier* overhead. This was the political program of Britain

---

[6] Floyd Norris, "Paving Path to Fraud on Wall St.," *The New York Times*, March 16, 2012, notes that Goldman Sachs banker Greg Smith cited a similarly revealing lingo in his March 14, 2012 *New York Times* op-ed, "Why I Am Leaving Goldman Sachs": "Goldman referred to its clients as "Muppets," talked about "ripping eyeballs out" and rewarded employees for "hunting elephants," a term he said meant persuading clients to do whatever would be most profitable for Goldman."

and other nations seeking to become world industrial powers: to become more efficient and lower-cost by minimizing such payments, mainly by taxing away economic rent and keeping natural monopolies in the public domain.

So when today's Occupy Wall Street protesters accuse the 1% of corrupting the economy and democracy, they are right on target, and saying basically what Adam Smith and his classical successors were arguing. A free market is not one that frees the 1% to prey on the 99% by loading it down with debt and grabbing public infrastructure to install tollbooths over the key access points to meeting basic needs. Matt Taibbi has described how recent financial fraud by Bank of America "resulted in one of the biggest reverse transfers of wealth in history—from pensioners to financiers. What the 99% should understand is that Wall Street knowingly inflated the bubble by engaging in rampant mortgage fraud—and then profited from the collapse of their own exuberance by devising a way to shift the losses to countless pension funds, endowments and other innocent investors."[7] Official statistics value the income made from such losses as if it is embodied in an output of financial services!

> When today's Occupy Wall Street protesters accuse the 1% of corrupting the economy and democracy, they are right on target, and saying basically what Adam Smith and his classical successors were arguing.

Today's neoliberals likewise differ from the original classical liberals in their depiction of government spending and investment. To the classical economists a free market was not one that was free from public intervention or having a government small and weak enough to be "drowned in a bathtub." They recognized that keeping markets free requires a strong enough government to protect the 99% *from* the predatory behavior of the 1%. A strong government is needed to check the drive by landlords, bankers and monopolists to take it over to serve their own interests. This is what the past two

---

[7] Matt Taibbi, "Bank of America: Too Crooked to Fail," *Rolling Stone*, March 14, 2012. He adds: "The bank has defrauded everyone from investors and insurers to homeowners and the unemployed. So why does the government keep bailing it out?"

centuries of democratic parliamentary reform have been all about. It is why classical liberals evolved from opponents of governments controlled by the landed aristocracy (such as the House of Lords) to supporters of governments chosen by the population in general (such as the House of Commons).

The aim of classical theories of economic rent was to bring prices and incomes in line with necessary costs of production. This is the concept of cost-value used by public utility regulators to keep electricity and gas rates in line. As licensed monopolies, these utilities are not permitted to include exorbitant executive salaries in their rate base, or high debt leveraging fees to the banks. (An equal split between debt and equity capital typically is required.) Likewise the Interstate Commerce Commission was created to regulate railroad fares and freight charges, to prevent predatory rates channeling into their own pockets what rightly should be the farmer's or other shipper's income.

Consider the elevators in the Empire State skyscraper. If a separate entity owned them, it could extract huge tolls, gaining for itself nearly the entire rental value of the upper floors. The NIPA would report whatever the elevator owners paid themselves and their backers as earnings for providing transport service as output, a "cost of production" for producing a service.

These free-lunch rents provide the classical source of taxes, headed by groundrent and land-price gains, mineral rents (provided freely by nature and long treated as national patrimony), and what monopolies charge over and above normal profit rates. Unlike taxes on labor, these taxes on rent do not add to the cost of living; they are paid *out of* the margin of price over value.

Banks do, of course, undertake justifiable expenses in providing a payments-clearing system of checking accounts, credit cards and other means of payment. It is a job that governments originally were expected to provide. Real estate developers likewise make bona fide capital investments in architectural complexes. But what is *not* necessary is "empty" pricing without cost. The "Rip-Off Factor" is an extortionate return to monopoly privilege, not really "earnings" or "product" as if it reflects a real-cost value.

What bankers charge in excess of the real cost of providing basic services is not to a "real" cost of production. That is why classical economists deemed such charges to be a form of unearned rent. It was to measure this free lunch, obtained without labor or other technologically necessary outlay, that they defined economic rent—to tax it away. Misrepresenting Adam Smith and other original free market reformers as patron saints of deregulating and untaxing *rentier* charges is just the first part of *rentier* propaganda inverting the idea of what a free market really is. The key step has been to obfuscate classical value, price and rent theory, above all the definition of rent as the excess of market price over real cost-value. This was the analytic tool designed to steer public tax policy under Industrial Capitalism in the 19th century. *Rentier* interests have replaced it with a "value-free" theory denying that any income is unearned. Pre-industrial land ownership and post-industrial finance capital are treated as industrial capital. Their "cost" is whatever their owner has paid for them, without regard to an original cost of production (which would be zero for natural resources and land sites, and quite low for most monopoly privileges). Rent has disappeared from view, replaced by "earnings" of the real estate sector, which the NIPA often combine with the financial sector because the two are so hard to untangle.

Monetary theory is equally narrow. It correlates the money supply only with commodity prices, not asset prices. Yet the defining feature of the recent Bubble Economy has been an attempt by banks (and the government) trying to keep illiquid borrowers (and many bankers) afloat by lending enough more credit to inflate prices for real estate, stocks and bonds. Asset-price inflation is how the financial sector postpones a crash, or how the United States is seeking to recover, by loading the economy down with debt in the hope that this will bid up asset prices.

This narrowing of focus is not scientific progress toward greater realism. It is the product of political lobbying by *rentier* interests. Factotums for the financial class have distorted the classical orthodoxy of Industrial Capitalism into an anti-government, anti-regulatory and anti-labor exercise on behalf of Finance Capitalism. It has inverted the idea of free markets to mean a market free *for* landlords, bankers and monopolists to extract economic rent (what the classical economists called unearned income), without regulation or taxation. Locking in its academic victory after the Thatcher-Reagan turning point in the 1980s, the neoliberal Chicago School depicts these financial and property interests not as overhead but as necessary and even key contributors to growth.

The banker's "product" is society's debt overhead.

It is all a con job. From the bankers' vantage point, putting people, businesses and governments deeper into debt means that more income, real estate rent, monopoly rent and tax revenue will be paid as interest. The banker's "product" is society's debt overhead. Interest and fees on this debt are paid *out of* the "real economy's" surplus. But for bank marketing departments, the surplus exists to pay interest and fees.

The marketing problem is how to convince society that all this credit is good. Banks point out that debt leveraging will increase balance-sheet wealth as long as credit is used to make profits or bid up prices. A 100 percent debt-leveraged society maximizes the borrower's return on equity—if profits or capital gains are made. During the debt upswing, bankers urge homeowners to "treat your home like a piggy bank" by taking out an equity loan against these asset-price gains. This is euphemized as "equity withdrawal." But it is simply going deeper into debt. These debts remain in place when property prices turn down.

In Ricardo's tradition, Chicago School monetarists claim that debt cannot be a problem. Along with mainstream economists, they claim that economies are self-regulating, and that wealthy individuals at the top of the pyramid make the greatest contribution to production, "earning" their income and wealth (and indeed being society's "job creators," as Malthus argued). Left out of account is how bank credit increases interest charges on the debt overhead, and how this raises costs of living and doing business (and conducting government).

The logic starts with the conclusion that "What's good for banks (and their major clients) is good for the economy." It then works backward, carefully selecting assumptions that will prove this deductively. Public spending, taxes and regulation appear merely as deadweight, increasing the cost of doing business—and hence, raising prices without adding to output. This aggravates unemployment by making economies *less* competitive. This means that nations get richer by cutting social spending, charging user fees for education, health care and other public services, and dismantling government regulations that "interfere with the free market."

By limiting the variables being studied to the money supply, government budget deficits and consumer prices, it is implied that budget deficits must be inflationary. They require more money—which is linked to price rises, not to employment and output. These over-simplifications rule out the idea that budget deficits may promote income growth and employment. To cap matters, wages are to be lowered to increase competitive export power to earn the revenue to pay creditors—on the assumption that austerity will not reduce productivity.

The effect of this "free market" logic is to rationalize the privatization of land rent and public monopolies—as if paying their rent to the banks instead of taxing or socializing it is more efficient. If an activity cannot be privatized to make a gain for investors, it should not be undertaken. Governments are told to un-tax the 1% and balance their budget by selling whatever roads, water systems, jails and other infrastructure remain in the public domain.

They then describe their added charges as "output," not simply higher *costs* of producing it.

So instead of asking how government programs may help economies grow, neoliberal ideology speculates about how economies might work without public infrastructure—by privatizing Social Security and health care, roads and communications, and financing such programs by user fees, not by progressive wealth and property taxation or by central bank money creation. The pretense is that these privatized services will be offered at minimum cost without any need for price controls, anti-monopoly rules or consumer protection. These allegedly would only raise costs ("more paperwork").

This denial of a positive role for government is a science fiction exercise describing a parallel but imaginary universe. The aim is to make people believe that there is no alternative to leaving bankers to act as the economy's planners—as if their allocation of resources is not more centralized and bureaucratic than planning by public officials. On the same logic, there seems to be no alternative to selling off the public domain, on credit to bank customers who build *rentier* charges into the economy's price structure. Pensions, Social Security and health care are to be financialized and turned into "market transactions" at a user price for each category. Denouncing public spending and the classical aim of regulating prices in line with cost-value is as "socialist," this financialization has reversed the direction in which Western civilization was moving until World War I. It is as if the past three or four centuries have been a mistake—what Frederick Hayek called the road *to* serfdom, not away from it by limiting *rentier* power.

Is Finance Capitalism Leading to Social Democracy, or to Oligarchy?

The new mode of conquest is financial, not overtly military. It is by financial means that creditors (mainly foreign) privatize a nation's land, public infrastructure and mineral rights, and buy out leading companies and choke points to install rent-extracting tollbooths. These *rentier* privileges ostensibly have been democratized by being consolidated into corporations whose shares can be freely bought and sold by anyone. But most are owned by the wealthy, who can pass down their rent-extracting rights and privileges to their heirs—or sell to whoever has the money (or access to credit) to buy them. Privatizing the privilege of credit creation (with government guarantee and subsidy) has enabled banks to become the new "land barons," evolving into a neo-feudal creditor oligarchy.

It has not been necessary for financial barons to rule directly, as long as they control a central bank made "independent" of democratic politics—

which itself has been financialized and made part of the market economy. Purchase of the mass media and political campaigns waged now largely through television and the press has inverted the ideology of economic democracy, politicians depict their major contributors, the privileged *rentiers*, as "job creators," and warn that taxing their income will "reduce jobs." This confuses the old industrial way to make wealth—by employing people—with the financial mode of getting rich in ways that shrink the economy, *e.g.*, by downsizing, outsourcing and increasing the debt overhead in a system of zero-sum rent extraction that "creates wealth" for the 1% at the expense of the 99%.

> **T**o lock in its victory—and block public regulatory agencies from fighting back—the financial sector has redefined "rent-seeking" to mean what government bureaucrats do (in raising taxes to broaden their administrative power), not what the FIRE sector does.

To lock in its victory—and block public regulatory agencies from fighting back—the financial sector has redefined "rent-seeking" to mean what government bureaucrats do (in raising taxes to broaden their administrative power), not what the FIRE sector does. Regulating and taxing the FIRE sector is called an economic burden. While government spending is deemed deadweight, the NIPA count all *rentier* revenue as being "earned" productively.

The aim is to persuade the public that the pain of debt deflation is natural and inevitable. Banking elites depict their takings as a process of justly collecting debts that are owed to them, telling national economies the equivalent of "Your money, or your life!" When populations riot against the austerity that dries up new investment and employment (while wealth is passed up to the top of the economic pyramid), voters are told that the time has come to suspend democracy and bring in neoliberal "technocrats" (a euphemism for bank lobbyists) such as were imposed on Greece and Italy in 2012. Countries that resist are isolated by sanctions, Cuba- or Iran-style.

Germany's Reparations Experience as a Paradigm

Bankers suggest that debt crises should be solved by providing enough new credit to enable borrowers to keep paying their creditors. "Borrowing their way out of debt" is supposed to get economies moving again. But in practice it only diverts more revenue to pay the financial sector.

That is how Germany tried to pay its reparations debt in the 1920s. It stabilized the mark in the same way that France had paid its reparations debt to Germany after the Franco-Prussian war ended in 1871: by borrowing. France had done this with comparative ease, but Germany's World War I reparations were out of all proportion to the ability to pay. Keynes and a few other economists recognized this, but the ethic that "All debts must be paid" was so strong that all the German political parties sought to devise means to pay.

What happened in practice was that German states and cities borrowed dollars in New York, and converted them into an equivalent value of marks that the Reichsbank printed. The Reichsbank then used these dollar receipts to pay the Allies — which then turned around and paid the dollars back to the United States for their arms debts. An illusion of stability was achieved by German cities and states owing the foreign debt rather than the national government. But none of this debt shuffling enabled the economy to create enough exports to earn the foreign exchange to pay foreign creditors. The domestic market suffered from fiscal and financial austerity.

> **D**ebts that can't be paid, won't be. Postponing the day of reckoning imposes a needlessly destructive interregnum of austerity in which the financial sector extracts as much revenue as it can get away with, and forecloses on as much property as governments will permit.

Today's international debts also are unpayably high. Unlike the German case, however, European and U.S. governments are taking the commercial banking system's bad debts onto the public balance sheet, not shifting debts off national governments. This "socialization" (or rather, "oligarchization") of debt has occurred most notoriously in Ireland. Governments are serving global creditors rather than promoting domestic growth, investment and employment.

In 1931 the pretense was ended by an international moratorium on German reparations and Inter-Allied debts together. Today's debt overhead must end in a similar moratorium or write-down, for the obvious reason that debts that can't be paid, won't be. Postponing the day of reckoning imposes a needlessly destructive interregnum of austerity in which the financial sector extracts as much revenue as it can get away with, and forecloses on as much property as governments will permit—leaving the economy poorer and poorer.

From Debt Peonage to Neofeudalism: Is Rome a Good Analogy?

Making itself into a new ruling elite to lord it over the 21st century, Wall Street's conquest threatens to emulate the Nordic conquests of Europe, Spain's conquest of the New World, and indeed Rome's conquest of its Empire two thousand years ago. As noted above, the new mode of conquest is financial, not military. But the results are equally devastating. And finance capitalism is more impersonal than the military conquests that used to parcel out land and the commons among the conquerors. Devoid of battlefield heroism, an almost banal array of banking institutions appropriates the land, natural resources and monopolies of debtor economies. Or, they simply buy resources of debt-strapped governments (after first tying the hands of governments by blocking them from creating a real central bank). Boris Yeltsin's 1994 loans-for-shares privatization saw Russia's "Seven Bankers" foreclose on the nation's most valuable natural resources and monopolies to become an analogue for the post-feudal "Seven Boyars."

Financial interests use the mathematical language of physical science to popularize economic models pretending that austerity will cure the government's budget deficit and improve the balance of payments. The reality is that a shrinking economy is *less* able to pay taxes and debts. But neoliberal logic is not empirical science. It is a public relations tactic in today's financial war against society at large. Its aim is to lock in power the way Rome did: by reducing as much of the population as possible to debt dependency.

As was the case in Rome, today's debt overhead cannot be paid. The question is, just *how* will it not be paid? There are the two choices: If society does not realize the need for debt write-downs, it will permit massive foreclosure to tear society apart and reduce debtors to neoserfdom.

As far as domestic populations are concerned, debt peons are free to live wherever they wish — or at least wherever they can afford. Unlike serfs, they may buy land by taking out a mortgage and paying its rental value to the bank over the course of their working lives. But wherever they live they take their debts with them, from student loans to credit card debt.

The resulting debt deflation polarizes society and imposes austerity that dries up the internal market and leads to economic collapse — and to demographic collapse as well. By causing poverty, debt deflation discourages family formation, marriage and birth rates, and shortens lifespans. This prompted Vladimir Putin to note that Russia had lost more population through its neoliberal policies and privatizations since 1990 than the nation had lost in World War II—between 5 and 10 million after 1990. About 5 percent emigrated abroad, headed by the most highly educated and skilled labor.[8] The U.S. Census Bureau estimates that Russia's population will decline by 25 percent by 2050, from 148 million in the 1990s to 111 million—a loss of nearly 40 million people. So unlike military warfare, financial conquest does not kill people directly. It is much more genteel.

Rome was the first major society **not** to cancel its debts. It took from the first century BC's Social War (133–29 BC) to the fourth century AD turning point for economic life to decentralize and revert to self-sufficient landed estates. But in the end Rome's creditor-oriented economy collapsed into the Dark Age, plunging the Empire into debt peonage.

Today a similar debt deflation is polarizing society and imposing austerity to dry up the internal market. The dream of bank marketing departments, after all, is for all disposable income and corporate cash flow to be paid as debt service. The "final" stage of finance capitalism thus threatens to deteriorate into debt peonage so widespread as to become neofeudalism. A financial elite will take control of the economic surplus to make itself as hereditary as the old landed aristocracies.

It Doesn't Have to Be This Way

Classical political economy began as moral philosophy, but went beyond the obvious fairness of bringing prices in line with cost value so as to free society from special privileges that create rentier income without work. As "political arithmetic" it served as a guide to making societies more productive and efficient, by freeing society from *rentier* charges that added "empty" pricing to the cost of living and doing business.

The major initial beneficiary of reforms designed to minimize these economic rents was industry. That is why governments promoting manufacturing saw the classical reform program as a strategy for how to modernize. The same logic that evolved into socialism via Saint-Simon, Marx and other

---

[8] See Putin's speech before the Duma, May 10, 2006, as well as TV Interview with Professor Sergei Kapitsa on Russia's Demographic Problems, *Vesti Podrobnosti* TV Russia Program, with Dmitry Kiselyov, June 7, 2005, www.fednews.ru, translated on Johnson's Russia List, June 12, 2005, #9, and the Interview with Jeffrey Sachs, "Good Health, Good Wealth," *Discover* magazine. April 2002: "There is a very sharp divide of what happened between Eastern Europe and the former Soviet Union. Half of Poland's debts were cancelled, and Poland actually had a significant improvement of health, higher life expectancy, and a much improved diet: much more fruit and vegetables, much less lard and cholesterol. But the West did not want to help Russia. It was too close to the Cold War. So in Russia and the former Soviet Union there was a terrible health decline." Life expectancy plunged accordingly.

19th-century reformers provided the model for industrial promoters to make France, Germany and other economies more competitive so as to overtake Britain. While pro-labor reformers characterized themselves as socialists, pro-industrial reformers were characterized as "state socialists." Despite their obvious class conflict, employers and wage labor shared a common interest in freeing society from the rents extracted by landlords, monopolists and the financial sector. This approach held out hope for an olive branch between industrial "state socialism" and labor socialism.

> The same logic that evolved into socialism via Saint-Simon, Marx and other 19th-century reformers provided the model for industrial promoters to make France, Germany and other economies more competitive so as to overtake Britain.

In addition to taxing or nationalizing land rent, the classical reform program was to keep basic infrastructure and natural monopolies in the public domain to provide their services at cost or at subsidized rates. This meant a mixed economy in which an active public sector paid for education, health care and pensions mainly by taxing land and natural resource rents. Simon Patten (mentioned above as the first professor of economics at the Wharton School of Business at the University of Pennsylvania from the 1880s up to World War I) described public infrastructure as a "fourth factor of production," whose return was measured not by the profits it made but by its ability to lower the national price level. This was the logic that prompted the United States, Germany, France and Japan to provide a widening array of infrastructure services at subsidized rates, and indeed free of charge for roads, education and other basic needs.

Many pro-business economists as well as socialists hoped that governments would provide a widening range of services freely outside of the market economy. British Prime Minister Benjamin Disraeli's social welfare legislation was capped by the public health system promoted from 1874 to 1881 under his motto *Sanitas sanitatum*, "Health, all is health." This helped the Conservative Party evolve as a sometimes "state socialist" party, especially from World War II to Harold Macmillan in the 1960s. In Germany, Bismarck enacted a pension plan for the population at large, not just army members as in the past. These

Many pro-business economists as well as socialists hoped that governments would provide a widening range of services freely outside of the market economy.

public services were to be paid for out of progressive taxation—or as America's greenbacks issued during its Civil War had shown, simply by public money creation so as to save taxpayers from having to pay bondholders.

Banking reform focused on making lending productive by financing industrial investment rather than wars. Adam Smith had emphasized that the way to minimize an economy's fiscal overhead was to refrain from wars, above all from financing them by borrowing. The logic of free market reform interfaced with the advocacy of peace as a major way to lower the cost of living and doing business so as to win out in international price competition by. The hope was that as rivalry among nations would be commercial rather than military, the old high-cost rentier economies would lose out to reformed "statist" economies reducing economic rent while subsidizing production costs, above all in their major export industries (for the U.S. economy, this has meant agriculture and military arms).

The ability of governments to create their own money to fuel economies becomes most obvious in war emergencies. When World War I broke out, many economists believed that complex industrial economies could not afford war, and that the belligerents would run out of money in a few months. But governments quickly discovered what the United States had shown in its own Civil War half a century earlier: It is not necessary to tax *or* borrow. (Taxes are indeed needed, not so much to finance government as to give value to government money, while taxes on unearned income prevent special interests from developing.) Central banks can create much more money than was anticipated. An all-powerful commercial banking class is no more necessary than a dominant landlord class when it comes to supplying the economy with money and credit!

Should we be surprised that banks prefer to silence such discussion? To gain interest on their lending to government, they have blocked the European Central Bank from creating its own money to finance national budget deficits. To build up their market among real estate borrowers and monopolists, banks lobby to un-tax economic rent. Most recently they lobby to privatize public infrastructure, most notoriously for education, health care and basic utilities.

> The hope was that as rivalry among nations would be commercial rather than military, the old high-cost rentier economies would lose out to reformed "statist" economies reducing economic rent.

If today's economic malstructuring had been forecast a century ago, most futurists would have found it unlikely, because it makes economies high-cost and therefore would seem to be an evolutionary loser. International competition was expected to favor a world free of *rentiers* as governments moved toward progressive income taxation, infrastructure investment and public monetary systems. No major economist expected the *rentier* classes to fight back with any great success. Libertarian and "Austrian" ideas of an economy composed only of individuals, without a government sector, were viewed as navel-gazing academics living in a hypothetical fantasy world.

But the financial sponsors of the past century's ideological counter-reform movement have convinced many voters and public officials that the classical dream is unworkable, and that there is no alternative to today's post-industrial finance capitalism. History has been rewritten, headed by that of economic thought. In their dress rehearsal for neoliberal policy in Pinochet's Chile, the Chicago Boys realized that to impose their travesty of free markets, they needed totalitarian control of academic discussion, censorial power over the press, and ultimately the threat of violence. So they closed down every economics department in the country except for their own bastion at the Catholic University, and inaugurated Operation Condor as a Latin American assassination campaign to silence dissidents, reaching into the United States itself. This is the Inquisitional side of free-market economics. As Naomi Klein has explained in *The Shock Doctrine*, the success of Friedman's anti-government Chicago School rests literally on the graves of its opponents.

The Financial Source of Economic Imbalance and Polarization, and Policies to Cope with It

Today's creditor interests are pursuing a similar road to that which Rome followed two thousand years ago when its oligarchy initiated a century-long Social War (133–29 BC) by political assassination and widespread violence. Reducing a quarter of the population to debt servitude, Rome relied on imperial looting ("spreading peace") as the last gain-seeking opportunity in a shrinking economy—a far cry from Schumpeterian creative destruction.

Rome's collapse reflected a privatization of credit, in contrast to the preceding three thousand years of ancient economic development. Credit—and hence debt—has been needed ever since a specialization of labor developed with the seasonal rhythms of planting and harvesting in the Neolithic. It is implicit wherever there is a time gap between initial investment and the final product being delivered and paid for. However, the original recipients of interest-bearing debts were not a self-serving oligarchy preying on the economy at large. Low-surplus economies simply could not afford to permit exploitative credit expropriate the lands of citizens and reducing them to bondage.

The charging of interest seems to have inspired in the third millennium BC by Sumerian temples and palaces advancing workshop handicrafts to traveling merchants. Doubling the loan balance in five years was a way for these large semi-public institutions to estimate their fair share of their gains on commercial advances. The period from the time the merchants received consignments of goods to their return to pay their backers comprised 60 months—so that the rate of interest worked out to $1/60$ per month, one shekel per mina (which was divided into 60 shekels). This worked out to $1/5$ annually (20 percent in decimalized terms).[9]

Most Near Eastern agrarian debts were owed to royal collectors, for land rental fees, water and shipping, and consumer loans. When these "barley debts" grew too large on an economy-wide basis, rulers restored order with Clean Slates. There was no preconception that economies automatically would settle in balance without such public intervention. Instability was caused by natural disasters and wartime disruption, and simply by interest accruals increasing the debt balances beyond what debtors in low-surplus economies could pay. Rather than trying to design a utopian system that would not get out of balance, archaic rulers dealt with the inevitable insolvency when it became necessary to annul consumer debts.

The fact that most debts were owed to palace and temple collectors meant that the authorities were basically cancelling debts owed to themselves (commercial silver debts for productive loans among merchants were left in place). These Clean Slates restored order in times of natural disaster or emergencies, and customarily when new rulers took their first full year on the throne. The aim was to inaugurate their reign with the economy in balance, by clearing away the accumulation of unpaid obligations that had built up.

---

[9] I trace the origins and early documentation of interest-bearing debt and Clean Slates in *Debt and Economic Renewal in the Ancient Near East* (ed. with Marc Van De Mieroop, CDL Press, Bethesda, 2002).

Today's financial interests seek to block governments from pursuing tax and financial policies that would counter the tendency of today's economies to veer out of balance and polarize between creditors and debtors. Unlike the early Near Eastern rulers, they pretend that automatic stabilizers will restore normalcy. But no such stabilizers are strong enough to rectify financial imbalance and predatory behavior.

It is axiomatic that when false assumptions about how economies work are maintained in the face of repeated failure, we should look for special interests as the beneficiaries of such wrongheadedness. It is not "insane" from the vantage point of the beneficiaries. Bankers and creditors support economists who tell populations and public officials not to worry about debt because economies are self-adjusting. This is not the case. It is a lobbying effort to dull perceptions that the debt overhead cannot be paid without plunging economies into depression.

> Today's industrial economies stand at a crossroads. To survive, they need to reverse the disabling of their regulatory defense mechanisms against finance run wild. The first step must be to revive classical political economy's distinction between cost-value and price as an analytical tool to isolate economic rent—"unearned income"—because it has no counterpart necessary costs of production.

This disinformation tactic is similar to what parasites do to their host: They numb its ability to perceive that a free financial rider has taken over. The financial sector fears public recognition that the debt overhead cannot be paid without plunging economies into depression. Its position is analogous to Milton Friedman's popularization of the science fiction writer Robert Heinlein's motto, "There is no such thing as a free lunch." Wealth-seeking today is all about obtaining *rentier* income without real work, by special privileges and insider dealing. Its acronym, TINSTAAFL, has taken its place alongside Margaret Thatcher's TINA ("There is no alternative"). The aim is to deter the study of just how much of the economy has indeed become a free lunch (economic rent), who gets it, and who is being exploited.

Just as parasites love to "deregulate" the host's defense mechanisms and criminals like police-free opportunities, the financial sector loves "free markets." At the cost of being repetitious, exploiters seek to erase the contrast between fair pricing as compared to exploitative rent extraction—or, for that matter, the outright fraud that permeates today's financial sector.

Biological parasites trick the host into believing that they are part of its own body, even to be nurtured as if they were its offspring. But what flourishes is the parasite's own life cycle. The tax authorities lavish care on the financial free luncher by making interest tax-deductible, enabling the financial sector to nourish its growth at the expense of the host economy. And the Treasury favors the proliferation of unproductive debt (*e.g.*, to inflate housing prices or allow hostile corporate takeovers) by taxing capital gains from asset-price inflation at a fraction of the rate levied on industrial profits, wages and salaries.

In biological nature a smart parasite will keep the host alive and even help it find new sources of food, and perhaps keep it disease-free in a symbiotic relationship. The aim, of course, is to obtain most of the nourishment for itself and its offspring. But parasites lose interest in the welfare of their host as they approach the final stage of the relationship. Realizing that the game is up, the free luncher does the equivalent of taking the money and running. This is what today's financial free riders are doing by abandoning ship to enter into a new symbiosis with fresh host economies. When the Federal Reserve gave banks $800 billion in QE II in 2012, most was spent in the BRIC countries and other healthy targets via exchange rate and interest rate arbitrage.

So what will happen to the host economies left as emptied out shells? Will the United States and Europe be left nearly for dead, having been turned into financialized zombies?

Here's the problem: Savings in the United States and Britain exceed real capital formation. The pension funding and tax codes of these nations are based on the assumption that saving via the stock and bond markets will automatically promote "real" growth. But that logic is fallacious. Buying stocks or bonds does not fund plant modernization or start-up companies. In practice the financial system's push for unproductive credit creation adds to debt deflation and rent-extracting overhead, not tangible capital formation.

So today's industrial economies stand at a crossroads. To survive, they need to reverse the disabling of their regulatory defense mechanisms against finance run wild. The first step must be to revive classical political economy's distinction between cost-value and price as an analytical tool to isolate economic rent—"unearned income" because it has no counterpart in necessary costs of production.

The fight to bring prices in line with cost-value involved nothing less than a political revolution against feudal privileges in Europe and the regions it colonized. On the eve of World War I the reform program seemed to be succeeding. In Europe, Parliamentary reform was expected to be the political catalyst, assuming that voters would act in their enlightened self-interest. Britain cleaned up its "rotten boroughs" in the 19th century, and the constitutional crisis of 1910 was resolved by an agreement that the House of Lords never again could block a House of Commons revenue bill. The way was freed for reformers to tax unearned land rent.

However, *rentier*-backed demagogues rejected the classical fiscal and monetary reform program. Over the past century the "real" host economy has had its analytic perception and regulatory organs disabled. A false narrative about "free markets" has been promoted and gained sufficient momentum since 1980 to replace the approach that eight centuries of economic analysis had been refining, from the 13th-century Churchmen through the classical economists and Progressive Era reformers. Elections now are fought over ethnic rivalries (in the Baltics and the American South) and conservative horror at the thought of legalizing women's rights and sexual equality (in right-wing religious areas and white collar urban precincts). Economic democracy has given way to a financial oligarchy whose machinations have negated the Enlightenment's assumption that self-interest will guide voters to back economic policies producing the greatest good for the greatest number.

Such enlightened self-interest will require a revival of the Progressive Era's reform program. The revival must start by re-establishing the 19th century's discussion of value, price and rent theory, the tax policy that follows from it, and monetary theory as it applies to financing public budget deficits. The problem is that mainstream economists and Chicago School censors exclude such discussion from the journals and curriculum where they hold sway—not always at gunpoint as in Chile, but by controlling young professors' access to tenure-track positions under "publish or perish" in refereed journals fallen prey to the blind spots favored by *rentiers*.

One result has been to leave the critique of pro-*rentier* markets largely to Marxists. As Patten pointed out, it was the socialists who pushed classical analysis to its logical conclusion, using the labor theory of value to isolate economic rent as unearned and hence unnecessary income. Classical economics culminated in Marx, and in Henry George's advocacy of taxing land rent. The concept of unearned income (economic rent) then was applied to banking and finance (where bond broker Ricardo never applied it!) as well as to land ownership and monopolies. But although Marxist analysis gained ascendency over most reform movements, it was derailed by Russian Communism eclipsing the voices of reformers who rejected Stalin's bureaucratic collectivism. By turning Marxism into a travesty of what it earlier meant, the Soviet experience served to discredit the classical reformist logic as a whole.

But even by the time World War I broke out, the classical focus on freeing markets from technologically and socially unnecessary overhead charges frightened high finance and its *rentier* clients, inspiring them to back anti-classical alternatives. Marginalists, Austrians, followers of John Bates Clark in the United States and "equilibrium theorists" abroad shared a common denominator of conflating land, monopolies and finance with industrial capital. A similar conflation of money and credit was occurring, and a shift of analysis from asset prices (such as the land-price gains on which John Stuart Mill focused and which his contemporaries called the "unearned increment") to commodity prices and wages.

Economic theory remains traumatized by the ideological conflict between scientific economics and the vested interests. The conflict ultimately is between *rentier* interests and those of industry and labor. Something has to give: Economic rent either exists, or it does not. *Rentier* income is either earned or unearned. Debts either can be paid, or they cannot. Economies either have automatic stabilization mechanisms, or they polarize.

The trauma caused by this conflict is now affecting how Western civilization defines its identity. *Rentiers* are seeking to reverse the Enlightenment by re-defining a free market to mean one that is free *from* taxes on their unearned income and *from* price regulation. Seeking to block progressive taxation and associated classical policies, they are all in favor of "big government" now that the major rise in public debt stems from bank bailouts and tax cuts for the wealthy. And they are against democracy when it seeks to subordinate finance to public welfare rather than making central banks "independent" and hence under the financial sector's control.

This is not a stable situation. The attempt to save creditors from loss, by taking bad private-sector debts onto the public balance sheet, must grow so large that it inevitably must self-destruct. Governments find themselves directed to support and re-inflate the Bubble Economy's debt overhead to avoid debt writedowns—as if these can be avoided in the end.

The conflict between creditors and debtors has occurred ever since antiquity succumbed to the post-Roman Dark Age. Today's debt-ridden economies from Iceland and Latvia to Greece and Ireland are suffering the demographic consequences of austerity: emigration, falling family formation and birthrates, shortening lifespans and rising suicide rates.

Unless economic democracy re-asserts its interests over financial oli-garchy, the West can expect austerity programs of the sort that the European Troika has imposed on Greece to impose an economic Dark Age. The tactic is to load economies down with debt beyond their ability to pay, and then demand that governments absorb the losses, paying by privatizing public infrastructure to sell off to buyers on credit to create yet more rent-extracting monopolies.

This Dark Age policy rules out writing down debts to what can be paid under normal conditions. It refuses to recapture for society the wealth raked off by the 1%. It permits widespread forfeiture of property and a siphoning off of wealth to the top of the economic pyramid. Instead of taxing land and other rent-extracting activities, governments are shifting the burden onto labor and industry. Instead of defending debtor interests and writing down debts, they urge that progressive taxation be abandoned in favor of a flat tax, excluding capital gains and other *rentier* income.

The enormous productivity gains since World War II—and indeed, since 1980—should suffice to show that today's deepening financial and fiscal austerity is not the result of an inevitable natural process. It reflects the greed of the few. Policies dictated by the financial sector have gained control over governments and the economy. Siphoning off the surplus for itself, its lobby-ists have replaced progressive taxation with regressive sales and income taxes on labor and industry, crippled public regulatory agencies and even the prosecution of financial fraud, and used central banks to serve the interests of creditors and speculators rather than those of the production-and-consumption economy.

So the fight must be waged over who will control the government, its tax and regulatory system. Economic theory will shape how people perceive this fight and restructure the financial and tax arena in which it is being waged.

20

SCENARIOS FOR RECOVERY:

HOW TO WRITE DOWN THE DEBTS AND RESTRUCTURE THE FINANCIAL SYSTEM

I. The Choice Before Us: Suffer Debt Deflation, or Write Down the Debts

The world faces a choice between trying to recover the Bubble Economy's debt-leveraged gains, or realizing that the financial sector has careened along an unsustainable path since 1980 and therefore that a fresh start has to be made.

The "business as usual" approach is to keep today's debt overhead on the books and bail out insolvent banks. This policy implies that financialization was a viable way to get rich in the first place. But the effect is to polarize economies further between creditors and debtors. Economies will shrink as a result of debt deflation, and falling tax revenues will push government budgets deeper into deficit — unless they cut back spending, which will make the downturn worse and threaten full-fledged depression. Unemployment will lead to emigration, the balance of payments will worsen and economies will be even less able to pay their debts.

The alternative is to see where this path is leading, and to write down debts sooner rather than later. This restores a more progressive distribution of wealth and income, and revives the economy's competitive position. The problem is that annulling debts also annuls financial claims on the "savings" side of the balance sheet. Creditors — led by the 1%, who have obtained most of the economic gains over the past thirty years — prefer to maintain their financial gains even at the cost of undercutting society's longer-term growth.

This opposition of interests obliges nations to choose between resuming prosperity or vesting a financial oligarchy to lord it over the remainder of the 21st century.

1. Trying to preserve today's debt overhead entails shrinking economies by imposing financial and fiscal austerity, and polarizing nations further between creditors and debtors

It is intellectually uncomfortable to think that society has taken a seriously wrong path. It is even harder to reverse a path from which powerful interests are obtaining rich windfalls. The recent generation's drive to get rich by debt-leveraging has given banks, other financial institutions and the wealthiest 1% a dominant voice in government, the mass media and the academic curriculum that shapes how people think about the economy. This poses a political problem as well as a purely intellectual and scientific one when it comes to proposals to bring the economy's debt overhead back within the ability to pay.

The problem is that one party's debt is another's savings. More to the point, the debts of the 99% are the savings of the 1% (or at least the 10%). The past thirty years have seen an enormous transfer of income and wealth to creditors. Yet many people think it unfair that these savers should lose (even if they have quickly gotten much richer), or that "free riders" should benefit from having their debts forgiven. This view looks at the debt overhead from an individualistic vantage point, not in terms of the long-term economic consequences for how a neo-*rentier* society is being created—one in which rent and other monopoly fees are extracted from the broader economy, at the expense of capital investment and social progress.

Today's vested interests understandably want to avoid taking a loss on their bad loans, investments and financial gambles. But somebody must lose. The debt overhead cannot be kept on the books without a massive transfer of property to the financial sector and, via it, to the wealthiest 1%. Their rising share of wealth has taken the form primarily of creditor claims on the bottom 99%, or on governments that have taken bad bank loans and reckless gambles onto the public balance sheet, as in Ireland. So one way or another the 99% will suffer, either directly as debtors or indirectly as taxpayers.[1]

While the 99% have not yet put forth an alternative program, the 1% echo Margaret Thatcher's claim that "There Is No Alternative" (TINA). If this really is the case, then the Western economies are in deep trouble. Trying to keep today's high debt levels on the books imposes debt deflation and fiscal austerity, and hence shrinks the economy. And if the economy shrinks, more loans will go bad, in a deteriorating spiral. That is what happens in debt deflation.

---

[1] The U.S. Treasury and Federal Reserve have avoided raising taxes by simply monetizing the bad debts, creating new government money, bonds or Fed deposits in exchange for private sector claims. But most governments have not made use of this option for public money creation except in wartime, not to help the civilian non-financial economy grow, *e.g.*, in the way advocated by Modern Monetary Theory (MMT).

The longer an alternative policy is delayed, the more the economy will polarize, making subsequent reforms even more difficult by bolstering the economic power of creditors to sustain today's home foreclosures, real estate defaults, property sales at distress prices, and spreading personal bankruptcy. It also will cause more corporate bankruptcy. This will raise the bargaining leverage of managers to replace defined-benefit pension plans with defined contribution plans (where employees have no idea of what they actually will receive upon retirement.)

On the public sector balance sheet matters are even worse—and more difficult to reverse. Tax receipts decline as economies shrink. Debt-strapped governments come under pressure to cut back their spending, starting with underfunding their pension plans. The end game is for cities, states and national governments to balance their budgets by selling off public infrastructure and other assets in the public domain.

Prospective buyers—and their bankers—depict privatization as a move toward efficiency and hence presumably lower prices. The opposite is more typically the case. The decision to pay bondholders rather than to write down or annul public debts enriches a set of rent-extracting interests adverse to those of the economy at large. Their business plan is to get richer by raising "tollbooth" fees on the infrastructure monopolies they have bought. This makes economies higher-cost, even as markets shrink for output produced by labor and industry. Privatization of the telephone sector from Mexico to the Baltics is a paradigmatic example.

2. "Business as usual" means debt deflation

This dynamic of credit expanding to divert the economic surplus away from public and private investment or rising living standards has occurred often in history, most notoriously in the way in which the Roman Republic and Empire collapsed. Yet it does not appear in economic models. That is part of the problem: The narrow assumptions made by these models distract attention from the corrosive financial and other *rentier* dynamics that occur in the real world.

The business-as-usual choice ("The debts must be paid!") threatens to derail attempts to recover, because income that is paid for debt service is not available for spending on goods and services. Diverting income to pay creditors dries up the domestic market and causes unemployment. This blocks financialized and debt-strapped economies from growing. And inasmuch as debt service is an element of price, it blocks debt-strapped economies from being able to export their way out of debt. This is why IMF-style austerity plans do not stabilize the balance of payments, but drive countries adopting such plans even deeper into debt.

What makes the post-2008 economic situation different from the crashes familiar from the 19th century through the Great Depression is that debts (and their counterpart financial claims or savings) were not wiped out. Governments have intervened to "save" financial markets from running the course followed in earlier times. The major creditors (but not employee contributors to pension funds) have been saved from loss by bailouts that have kept bad debts on the books, often by giving them public guarantees (as in U.S. mortgage debt and "toxic waste") or taking them directly onto the government's balance sheet as noted above.

The financial dynamic over the past thirty years has been for debts to mount up exponentially, at compound interest plus "free" electronic credit (debt) creation toward the point where they absorb the entire economic surplus—and then continue growing. Paying interest, amortization and penalties on this debt overhead shrinks the economy, plunging it into negative equity. A rising debt overhead prevents the economy from "growing its way out of debt," because corporate cash flow is used to pay creditors, and markets are not growing sufficiently to warrant new investment and hiring. And the economy certainly cannot "borrow its way out of debt." Over a quarter of U.S. real estate already is in negative equity and prices are still falling, so banks understandably have tightened their loan standards. The Federal Reserve's policy of lower interest rates for mortgage credit has not sufficed to overcome the continued unwinding of the real estate bubble. And its bursting has thrown state and local finances into deficit, forcing cutbacks in public service. The result is a cascade of lower spending.

Mathematically, the debt overhead tends to expand to the point where it absorbs the entire economic surplus (real estate rent, corporate cash flow, disposable personal income and government tax revenue), crowding out new capital investment, infrastructure investment and rising living standards. The "business as usual" scenario seeks to sustain this trend. Collapse of the Bubble Economy since 2008 has left the debt overhead on the books—while prices have plunged for real estate and other assets, reversing the rise in net worth that homeowners and retail investors thought was making them rich by taking on more and more debt.

The Federal Reserve has flooded the financial system with enough credit to re-inflate the balance sheets of debtors, and hence also of the banks and financial institutions holding mortgages and other claims. The problem is that trying to save the financial sector from loss in this way merely adds to the debt overhead. This implies a post-Bubble austerity, not recovery. New credit is debt, and it is being created not to finance new capital investment and employment, but simply to enable debtors to pay their creditors rather than writing down debts. The resulting debt service will divert consumer spending, corporate cash flow and government tax revenue (and new money creation) to sustain a debt overhead that has been decoupled from "real" economic growth (rising production and consumption).

3. The alliance of banking with real estate, and monopolies — and corporate takeover financing

The policies chosen to resolve today's financial and tax problems will follow largely from the diagnosis of what has caused them. The first step therefore must be to describe how the financial system has loaded the economy down with debt, mainly unproductive debt that is a form of overhead rather than one that increases the economic surplus and ability to pay.

It does not do so in the way that most textbooks describe. The popular image (encouraged by the banks) is a world in which banks recycle the savings of depositors to finance new industrial investment and hiring. This was indeed the dream of bank reformers in the 19th century. But it does not characterize today's world. Industrial companies now bypass the banking system, borrowing by issuing their commercial paper directly, to investors who also bypass the banks.

From the 13th century down to Ricardo's day, banks found their major markets in international lending to finance export trade and related payments, including loans to governments to finance military spending abroad. This gave banks an interest in promoting a specialization of labor in which each country would produce what it was "best" at producing.

Britain's landed interests threatened this plan. After the Napoleonic Wars with France ended and trade resumed in 1815, rural landlords sought to block low-priced food imports. Lower prices would reduce the agricultural land rents that land lords received — rents that had risen in keeping with food prices during the decades of wartime isolation. So Parliament, dominated by the landed aristocracy, imposed agricultural tariffs — the Corn Laws.

Higher food prices increased the price that employers had to pay to cover labor's basic cost of living. The price of grain determined the price of bread, which most economists took as a proxy for wage levels. (Housing was nowhere near as large an element of the family budget as it has become today.) The Corn Laws thus threatened to impair Britain's attempt to undersell industrial competitors and become the workshop of the world.

To bankers, protectionism implied a world of largely self-sufficient balanced agricultural and industrial economies. That would not provide as great an opportunity for trade financing as specialization of labor would offer. Acting as the banking sector's major economic spokesman (and, in effect, lobbyist),

David Ricardo's 1817 *Principles of Political Economy and Taxation* described how international specialization of production was more efficient than autarchy. Chapter 2, on economic rent, put forth a labor theory of value isolating land rent as the excess of market price over intrinsic cost-value, describing how the Corn Laws would increase prices and undercut competitiveness.

There was something ironic in using the concept of economic rent against landlords. The original distinction between cost-value and market price was discussed by the 13th-century Churchmen specifically with regard to what a Just Price would be for bankers to charge for converting foreign exchange (*agio*) and charging interest. But Ricardo's analysis left the financial sector out of account. Subsequent British political economy focused on returns to land-lords, labor and capitalists receiving rent, wages and profits. But because money and credit were not viewed as "factors of production," its role in the economy remained indistinct. Credit was a *precondition* for the production and sale of goods, but was viewed simply as influencing price levels, not as debt requiring the economy to sustain interest payments.

The political upshot of Ricardian analysis (and indeed, that of the French Physiocrats, Adam Smith and other advocates of taxing landed wealth) was for British banking to support manufacturing against the landed interest. Parliament repealed the Corn Laws in 1846. On the continent of Europe, Germany and France also took the lead in steering banking increasingly to finance industry. And as the cities gained political power over the countryside, industry (and labor) gained power over the landed interest.

The past century has seen this alliance inverted. Instead of financing tangible capital formation to make profits by investing in plant and equip-ment, research and development, bankers have found their major market in lending against real estate. Whereas landed aristocracies in times past owned most of the land free and clear, property ownership has been democratized—on credit. Banks find their main business to be the financing of homeowners and commercial owners or absentee investors. The largest debt categories are real estate (mainly land) and basic infrastructure—the economy's two largest asset categories. As rent-yielding assets, however, they (or at least, their eco-nomic rent) were widely expected to remain in the public domain.

The old landed fortunes have been transmuted into financial fortunes, receiving interest, dividends and financial gains in place of land rent. Finance is today's major source of wealth and recipient of economic rent. Buyers bid against each other for bank loans to buy property that formerly was held free and clear. The winner is whoever agrees to pay the most rental income to the banks. This financialization of land ownership ends up transferring the ex-pected rent to the bankers—and recently some of the site's price gain as well.

The fact that some 80 percent of bank loans in the United States, Britain and Scandinavia are mortgage loans has created a symbiosis of the Finance, Insurance and Real Estate (FIRE) sectors. Banks have joined real estate lobbyists to minimize the property tax and related taxes—knowing full well that what the tax collector relinquishes will be available to be paid as interest. This campaign has rolled back property taxes from an average 70 percent for U.S. cities and states in 1930 to under 16 percent today.[2]

Pledging most real estate rent, natural resource rent and other economic rent as interest to bankers and bondholders means that it no longer is available to the tax collector. Contrary to what a century of classical economists recommended, the fiscal burden has been shifted onto labor and industry. This tax shift off the land, natural resources and monopolies is the opposite of basing the tax system on land rent as the Physiocrats, Adam Smith, John Stuart Mill and subsequent Progressive Era reformers urged. Their classical policy would have left untaxed and hence "free" to be capitalized into bank loans—and thereby would have held down prices for housing and infrastructure services.

The problem today is that any attempt to reverse course and move back to the classical ideal of taxing away rent as the major source of public revenue would cause a break in the chain of payments—because the rent already has been pledged to creditors as backing for most of the economy's savings and credit. Posing this quandary for the economy has convinced the banking sector that it has made its appropriation of rent away from government irreversible.

The stock market has not been much better in replacing debt with equity capital. The ideal developed by Saint-Simon and his followers in 19th-century France was for banks to take their returns as a share of profits, not as fixed debt payments. The idea was for financial returns to rise and fall in keeping with the ability of borrowers to pay, and that new stock issues would be used to fund new tangible investment. This is how most textbooks describe stock markets, as vehicles to raise shares in business earnings, *e.g.*, via Initial Public Offerings (IPOs).

Since 1980, however, the net flow of funds has been increasingly *out* of the stock market. Drexel Burnham and other investment banks pioneered the use of high-interest "junk" bonds to buy out stockholders and "take companies private." The epoch of corporate raiding had arrived, and the tax laws subsidized replacing equity with bonds. At a 50 percent corporate tax rate, a

---

[2] National Income and Product Accounts (NIPA), Table 3.3.

company could pay out twice as much profit as tax-deductible interest to bondholders than it could as after-tax dividends to stockholders. So the financial return was doubled—leaving the tax collector with only half of what formerly was received.

When markets turn down and profits decline, companies cannot simply cut back payments to bankers or bondholders as they can with shareholders. Missing a debt payment means default and bankruptcy. Corporate managers use this fact as a threat to declare bankruptcy and wipe out employee pension funding unless the plans are renegotiated downward.

Instead of promoting the production of goods and services or spurring employment, the banking and tax systems have been distorted to promote the transfer of assets (mainly rent-extracting privileges) on credit—with interest being tax-deductible, as if banks deserved subsidy for playing a productive role rather than indebting industry, labor and privatized infrastructure to a point that threatens to drive many families, much industry and even governments into bankruptcy.

The term "socializing the losses" is not a good description of taking financial losses onto the public balance sheet. Today's governments are not socialist, or even "state socialist" as the term was applied to Bismarck's Germany with its subsidies for industry and agriculture. From America's $700 billion Troubled Asset Relief Program (TARP) in 2008 through the Federal Reserve's subsequent $2 trillion "cash for trash" swaps and bailouts of A.I.G., Citibank and other "Too Big to Fail" institutions, to Europe's bailouts of sovereign debt bondholders, new public credit and debts are being created not to revive economies but to preserve the financial claims of creditors at the top of the pyramid holding the rest of the economy in debt. These subsidies to the financial sector are unprecedented in magnitude. So a better term would be "oligarchizing" the losses as governments act on behalf of the new financial elite.

The game plan by the 1% to transfer the hard work and wealth of the 99% into their own pockets starts by cornering the market on obtaining credit from banks. Banks now lend mainly to other financial institutions, not the real economy. They then use debt leveraging for computerized casino gambling and to inflate the value of their real estate and securities. Homeowners also are advised to debt leverage and take out equity loans to make up the shortfall in living standards that their paychecks are not supporting. Alan Greenspan chimed in by informing the public that U.S. real estate is resilient against broad collapse, and that any problems were merely local.

When the bubble bursts, the strategy is to cry havoc and make sure that the government's monetary agencies—the Treasury and Federal Reserve—

enable the bondholders, the 1%, to get their money back, while leaving owners of underwater real estate and toxic mortgage waste to absorb the losses. The crowning ploy is to have the Federal Reserve keep the large banks and financial institutions intact by buying their money-losing assets. This is what makes today's situation so different from the stock market crash in 1929, when the 1% lost their "paper gains" as the financial slate was wiped clean via bankruptcies and liquidations.

Even casual observers are now coming to recognize the hypocrisy of the 1% in pretending to be for "free markets" while insisting that the government bail them out and protect their booty to make their financial gains irreversible. Their cry of "There Is No Alternative" is the opposite of a free market policy. It aims to block discussion of where all this is leading.

4. Mainstream remedies make the problem worse

The world keeps on being given bad old economic medicine in new bottles. Today's neoliberal policies imposing austerity on Europe (leading to a capital and labor flight) are the same Washington Consensus policies that created the post-Soviet anti-labor tax philosophy, shock therapy and kleptocratic privatizations after 1991 (leading to a capital and labor flight), and before that the IMF austerity programs in the 1970s that led to the post-1982 Third World debt crisis (leading to a capital and labor flight). By the time the U.S.-European financial crisis hit in 2008, the IMF's former customers had rejected its financial philosophy while Russia was deploring the path that had reduced it to a raw-materials exporter with a shrinking population.

But the same "medicine" (like a medieval doctor bleeding his patient in the belief that this will "restore balance" rather than kill the patient) is being dictated today in an attempt to use the financial crisis as an opportunity to squeeze out enough tax revenue and debt service to keep the illusion that somehow the "financialization" path was a viable one, not ending in deadly economic shrinkage, falling tax revenues and deepening government budget deficits.

It is easy enough to see what steered today's economies into their financial *cul de sac*. Debt leveraging raises the cost of living and doing business, pricing financialized economies out of world markets. And by reducing taxable income, it contributes to the government's budget deficit—which the financial sector then uses as an opportunity to demand privatization and cutbacks in social spending. This adds fiscal austerity onto debt deflation.

Privatization has become the name of the new, non-military asset grab. While domestic markets for labor and goods are being shrunk, privatizers engage in rent extraction to erect tollbooths on the economy's key access and pressure points. Their business model is to raise the price of basic infrastructure services by building in interest and other financial charges, much higher executive salaries, and transfer payments to offshore tax-avoidance enclaves. Their rent extraction is tax-deductible because they have bought this infrastructure on credit, depriving governments even of user fees from sharply rising "tollbooth" charges for access to roads, railroads, ports and other transportation, education, water and sewer services, tourist sites, etc. This raises the cost of living and doing business even while the overall economy shrinks.

More of the above neoliberal policies are now being promoted as a *cure*. Economic theory (or at least, policy advocacy) has become much like a novel, with the author hoping that the reader can suspend disbelief long enough to follow the fictional world being created.

5. International aspects of post-crash financial reform.

Failure to resolve the debt problem will lead financialized economies to suffer deepening trade and payments deficits with less debt-ridden competitors. The problem is how to start reversing the financialization costs that have already been built into North American and European economies. As in the 1920s, the U.S. economy has become the most extreme example (outside of Latvia, that is). FIRE sector expenditures absorb as much as 75 percent of blue-collar family budgets in the United States. There is no way in which an economy with such a high monthly break-even "nut" can compete with less financialized ones.

Rent or home ownership costs:	35 to 40%
FICA wage withholding (Social Security and Medicare):	15%
Other debt service (credit cards, student loans, etc.):	10%
Other taxes (income and sales taxes):	10 to 15%
TOTAL:	75%

Only about a quarter of family budgets remains available for spending on current output. This is how financialization leads to debt deflation, even while prices rise as a result of higher banking and other economic rent charges that have no "real" cost basis.

The international effects of this fatal combination of debt deflation and rent extraction include capital flight and an emigration of labor in response to shrinking employment opportunities. The neoliberalized Baltic economies and bank-stricken Iceland are the most recent examples, and Greek emigration and capital flight also have picked up during the past year.

This dynamic is the opposite from what was expected a century ago. Instead of evolution favoring high-wage nations out-competing the old *rentier*-ridden post-feudal and post-colonial economies, wages and living standards are being scaled back under the political umbrella of financial emergency. Politically, power is being shifted from democratically elected governments to technocrats governing on behalf of international banks and financial institutions as international finance today achieves what armed conquest did in times past.

The effect of these policies is to centralize planning in the hands of financial managers. Their strategy is to privatize public enterprises and increase profits by de-unionizing formerly public sector labor, and to scale back Social Security, pension plans, health insurance and other social support programs. This is the treadmill on which financialized post-Bubble Eurozone social democracies are to be placed.

II. The Remedies

Fortunately, there is an alternative to letting economies be stifled by trying to pay debts at the cost of further economic growth. In fact there is an array of alternatives, and many dovetail into each other. Their common denominator is to restore the primacy of the "real" economy—labor and tangible capital on the asset side of the balance sheet—over financial and property claims on the liabilities side, and to restore balance between the public and private sectors. The aim is to minimize technologically unnecessary costs of living and production.

1. The fraudulent conveyance principle

A broad guideline for writing down debts was developed more than two centuries ago in the American colonies. British speculators and sharpies eyed the rich farmlands of upstate New York and refined the practice of making loans to farmers against their crops. Their strategy was to call in loans at an inconvenient time (*e.g.*, just before harvest), or simply to loan the farmer more than could realistically be repaid in the epoch's low-surplus economy. They then would foreclose.

To cope with this problem, the colony of New York passed the Fraudulent Conveyance law. This was retained when New York joined the United States, and remains on the books today. Its principle is that if a lender makes a loan that the borrower cannot reasonably be expected to pay off in the normal course of business—that is, without forfeiture of property—the loan should be declared null and void, and the debt cancelled. The legal assumption is that such a loan was a ploy to gain control of property pledged as collateral, over and above simply earning interest.

The aim is to keep debts within the ability to pay, by placing an obligation on bankers and other creditors to make viable loans rather than covert property grabs. This principle has two major implications for today's debt-strapped economies. It was cited in the 1980s as a defense against corporate raiders buying out stockholders with high-interest "junk" bonds. Victims of debt-leveraged buyouts claimed that there was no way that the loan could have been expected to be paid in the normal course of business and subject to existing employee contracts without selling off assets and, as noted above, downgrading their pension contracts with employees. The aim was to loot the company and leave it a bankrupt shell. The best-known recent case is the suit brought by Chicago Tribune employees against the real estate magnate Sam Zell who drove the company bankrupt and emptied out the Employee Stock Ownership Plan to pay his creditors. About half such ESOPs typically end up in bankruptcy through such financial sleight of hand.

The Fraudulent Conveyance principle may be applied to the public sector with regard to pressure brought on debt-strapped governments to sell off public enterprises to pay creditors. This situation is much like that of colonial farmers in upstate New York. Banks and bondholders have lent governments credit as if this were risk-free. This was done in the belief that if these governments have difficulty paying bondholders—especially in foreign currency—the IMF and other Washington Consensus institutions will step in and lend governments the foreign exchange to pay private-sector bankers, or simply strong-arm the sovereign debtor into paying, willy-nilly. Bondholders and banks are thus in the position of the British financial sharpies making ostensibly reckless loans in the belief that the local sheriff and other colonial officials would back up their property grab. The effect is to replace private-sector debt with debt to inter-governmental institutions and "hard currency" governments such as the United States or European Union.

As the breakdown of Inter-Ally debts and German reparations demonstrated in the 1920s, debts among governments are more difficult to write down than debts owed to private-sector banks and bondholders. Although governments are sovereign, they are subject to pressure to isolate them by the type of trade and financial sanctions imposed against Cuba and Iran. The tacit threat of such sanctions was used as an attempt to keep Argentina and other Latin American debtors in line for many years.

It has long been a basic principle of international finance not to take on debts in foreign currency. As Keynes explained in the 1920s, foreign debts add the "transfer problem" (running a trade and payments surplus to obtain foreign currency) to the domestic "budgetary problem" of governments taxing enough surplus to pay domestic-currency creditors. The global economy becomes "oligarchized" under conditions of increasing distress (the word "distress" originally meant the property taken by creditors as collateral to ensure loan payment. Distraint is the act of seizing property to obtain payment for money owed).

Just as the Allied Powers refused to acknowledge the transfer problem as distinct from the domestic budgetary problem with regard to World War I arms debts and German reparations in the 1920s, the IMF's "absorption" models likewise fail to draw this distinction.[3] They are the official equivalent of corporate raiders maintaining solvency with their creditors by downsizing and outsourcing, breaking up the assets and stiffing the smaller creditors (employees who agreed to lower wages in exchange for pension security) in the tradition of "big fish eat little fish."

The basic principle of Fraudulent Conveyance is that loans which cannot be paid under normal conditions were made irresponsibly at best, and with predatory intentions at worst. In either case they should be written down. The ethical principle is that the debtor suffers less than the creditor, especially in a world where international credit is now created electronically on computer keyboards—while repayment of such credit polarizes and impoverishes debtor economies.

2. Attempts to legislate reasonable ability to pay under normal conditions

How should the courts define the reasonable ability to pay under normal conditions? Sheila Bair, head of the Federal Deposit Insurance Corp. (FDIC), suggested that mortgage-financed housing costs on new loans should be limited to 32 percent of the borrower's family income. This proportion is higher than the 25 percent rule of thumb applied by most banks before deregulation changed matters in the 1980s. But it is lower than current distress levels, which are in the neighborhood for 50 percent for many families, especially those with "exploding rate" variable-interest mortgages. This fact prompted Ms. Bair to propose that mortgage servicers should reset adjustable-rate mortgages back to the original rate so that the "exploding" interest rates would not cause defaults. "Avoiding foreclosure would protect neighboring properties and hasten the recovery."[4]

Another palliative would be to reduce mortgage debt service to the current rental equivalent of housing. Estimating a fair market price for real

---

[3] I provide a detailed review of discussions of the transfer problem from Ricardo through the 1920s to the IMF models in *Trade, Development and Foreign Debt* (new ed., 2009).
[4] Sheila C. Bair, "Fix Rates to Save Loans," *The New York Times*, October 19, 2007.

estate by capitalizing its rental value is how land prices were set in earlier centuries, when buying a property was like buying a government bond. Capitalizing the rent at the going rate of interest provided an equivalent current value. Fannie Mae has proposed a "deed for lease" program permitting defaulting mortgage debtors to remain in their homes for one year in exchange for paying the market rent—presumably much less than the existing mortgage terms. Democratic Arizona Congressman Raul Grijalva has proposed extending the homeowner's "right to rent" for five years, leaving the courts to estimate fair-market rent.

These solutions involve scaling back the value of nominal mortgage claims. Unwilling to compromise, intransigent bankers resist this—unless they are reimbursed in full. Despite public relations "jawboning" by Obama Administration regulatory agencies, banks have stonewalled against writing down mortgages. Their strategy has been to hold out for government reimbursement of any writedowns—so that the public sector ("taxpayers") will absorb the loss, not themselves. To pressure the government to capitulate (as the administration finally did in March 2012), financial institutions have held the economy hostage. Their position was that if they were not bailed out, they would destroy the real estate market.

This stance confronts governments with an all-or-nothing alternative. The banks' position is that debtors or the government must bear the entire burden of the unpayably high debts—debts that are the result of their own irresponsible and in many cases fraudulent loans. The financial sector's intransigence on this demand, and its power to threaten at least temporary economic collapse if it does not get its way and shift its loss onto "taxpayers," has upped the ante to force an all-or-nothing alternative—not a partial haircut, but a broad debt write-down.

3. A public option for a credit infrastructure

When Citibank, A.I.G., the Royal Bank of Scotland and Anglo-Irish Bank failed, governments became their *de facto* owners. U.S. authorities made a political decision to recognize claims by existing stockholders, bondholders and counterparties at public expense. For the economy at large, all countries kept the bad debt overhead on the books as far as debtors were concerned. Economies shrank as a result of debt deflation, the property bubble accordingly crashed, and much was simply abandoned.

Also lost was the opportunity for governments to provide a public option of banking and credit. These are in the character of basic infrastructure, after all. Instead of simply reselling these banks to new buyers—or in the case of

Citibank and Bank of America, leaving their stockholders in place—the governments could have operated these institutions to provide credit cards and related services at cost rather than at a profit. Furthermore, a publicly run bank presumably would not write junk mortgages and create kindred toxic financial waste based on fraudulent "liars' loans," exploding interest-rate loans and other predatory practices that marked Citibank, Bank of America, Washington Mutual and other major offenders. The enormous public Post Office Savings Banks of Japan and Russia do not lend for such financial speculation.

The financial sector wielded sufficient political power to discourage governments from taking this option. The government did not fold up the banks or even wipe out A.I.G.'s counter-party speculators on their reckless credit default contracts. Sheila Bair argued in vain that there was no need to bail out the casino-capitalist gamblers. The FDIC could readily have taken over insolvent banks and saved insured depositors with their existing loan portfolios. This what the FDIC did when it wound down WaMu and other reckless lenders. "We have a resolution process that we've used for decades, and when we put a bank into receivership, we have the right to break all contracts, we can fire people, we can take away bonuses and we don't get into this kind of problem."[5]

A.I.G. had enough resources to maintain its "plain vanilla" insurance operations. The FDIC (and similar government agencies abroad) could have become major shareholders in the "systemically important" Too Big to Fail banks. After wiping out their superstructure of bad debt claims, it could have written down bad or outright fraudulent mortgages to realistic prices based on current rental values. But this would have caused losses for banks holding "second" mortgages and equity loans. To preserve their claims, they insisted that the economy be wrecked. Instead of representing the broad public interest, the Obama Administration went along with this demand.

In her interview with *New York Times* reporter Joe Nocera upon retiring from the FDIC, Ms. Bair emphasized: "Our job is to protect bank customers, not banks." But Wall Street institutions (the major contributors to both Democratic and Republican lawmakers, after all). Treasury Secretary Tim Geithner and other defenders of high finance told Ms. Bair: "'You have to do this or the system will go down.' If I heard that once, I heard it a thousand times. 'Citi is systemic, you have to do this.' No analysis, no meaningful discussion. It was very frustrating."

She blamed the Bush-Obama Administrations for acting to save the large investors rather than the overall economy when they bailed out the banks to

---

[5] Joe Nocera, "Sheila Bair's Bank Shot," The *New York Times Magazine*: July 10, 2011.

save high-income investors from taking a loss. "It was all about the bond-holders," she said. "They did not want to impose losses on bondholders, and we did. We kept saying: 'There is no insurance premium on bondholders,' you know? For the little guy on Main Street who has bank deposits, we charge the banks a premium for that, and it gets passed on to the customer. We don't have the same thing for bondholders." With this comment she put to rest the rhetoric refined by the 1% claiming that they believe in free markets un-touched by government hands or free-lunch welfare.

Ultimately at issue is the belief that the asset side of the balance sheet needs the liabilities side to function. A further implication is that governments need to protect the banks not only from insolvency but losing their status as the economy's most profitable sector ("Where are the customers' yachts?") by keeping the existing debt overhead in place.

What was lost in the 2008 rush to act was an opportunity to achieve what Progressive Era reformers had spent a lifetime trying to promote: a public option for banking. The aim of public ownership historically has been to minimize the cost of living and doing business. Just as public roads, school systems and other basic infrastructure services are offered at cost or at subsidized prices—or freely—so the financial payments system is a basic public utility. A public option can offer less costly credit cards, savings and checking accounts than can private banks. But banks have gained control of the regulatory process and used it to disable government power to keep their charges in line with technologically necessary costs of production. They have made finance extractive—the bankers' equivalent of landlords rack-renting their tenants.

4. An economy-wide debt cancellation (the "German Economic Miracle" option)

The traditional path of least resistance has been to wipe out savings and debts together in a convulsion of bankruptcy. The 1929 and 1931 crashes led to the 1931 moratorium on German reparations and Inter-Ally debts. The Mexican and subsequent Latin American insolvencies led to the Brady Plan sovereign debt write-downs in the 1980s. But by far the most important example was the 1948 Allied Currency Reform in Germany. Savings over and above a basic amount were cancelled—on the logic that most belonged to members of the former Nazi regime. The main debts kept on the books were normal paycheck obligations owed by employers to their work force, and basic working bank balances. Rendering Germany free of a financial overhead, this catalyzed its Economic Miracle, making its experience a model modern Clean Slate.

Yet this prospect strikes most economists with horror in fear that it would disrupt the payments system. Monetary theory has ignored the role of money and credit as debt, as if it only affects prices—the "counters" for goods, services, sages and other payments. (Asset prices usually are left out of account, as noted above). As a mind expansion exercise it therefore is instructive to review the long history of how debt cancellations have preserved overall balance and restored prosperity rather than plunging economies into anarchy and poverty.

From the early third millennium BC in Sumer down through the Near East in Greek and Roman antiquity, societies proclaimed Clean Slates. When Sumerian, Babylonian and other Near Eastern rulers took the throne, or when droughts, floods or military disturbances made agrarian debts unpayable, rulers proclaimed "economic order": *amargi* in Sumerian, *misharum* and *andurarum* in Babylonian, and cognate terms in other Near Eastern languages extending down to *deror* in Judaism's Jubilee Year. This did not create economic disruption, but was a key to preventing widespread debt bondage and forfeiture of land rights.[6]

Such acts were relatively easy to proclaim in an epoch when most debts were owed to palace or temples collectors as in the ancient Near East, or placed at the center of Mosaic Law as in Judaism (Leviticus 25). What stopped the practice in classical Greece and Rome was the fact that debts were owed to private creditors—and unlike rulers, they found their interest to lie in reducing their debtors to a state of bondage and clientage. They did this despite the fact that this led to a flight of debtors from the land. That is why the prophet Isaiah denounced landlords and creditors who joined plot to plot and house to house until there was no more room left in the land for people.

An analogous condition exists today as creditors have imposed such extreme austerity on Iceland, Latvia and Greece that the youth must emigrate to find employment. Unemployment rate among young adults in Spain's is reported to be 50 percent, and the national rate 23 percent.[7] These countries are losing their most productive and highly educated labor. The most extreme experience is that of the former Soviet Union after neoliberals were given a free hand to financialize their economies into *rentier* rent-extraction opportunities after 1991. The moral is that unthinkable as debt writedowns may appear politically, the alternative—stagnation—is worse.

---

[6] I provide a long survey and analysis in Debt and Economic Renewal in the Ancient Near East (ed. with Marc Van De Mieroop, CDL Press, Bethesda, 2002):7–58.

[7] http://epp.eurostat.ec.europa.eu/statistics_explained/index.php/Unemployment_statistics

All the major Roman historians—Livy, Plutarch, Diodorus, followed by modern writers such as Arnold Toynbee—blamed the decline and fall of the Roman Republic on creditor intransigence leading to a century-long Social War (133–29 BC) that polarized society between creditors and debtors. A quarter of the Empire's population was reduced to debt bondage and hereditary slavery, plunging economic life into a Dark Age. The dynamics of debt worked much like radioactive decay, ending at the point where economies finally stabilized in a leaden state of serfdom. Economic life reverted from cities to the countryside, centered largely on church estates, leaving only subsistence production throughout most of the land.

The relevance is that what blocks a reversal of toxic creditor power today—or even writedowns of more than a "haircut"—is that wiping out debts on the "liabilities" side of the balance sheet also wipes out savings on the "assets" side. The most politically problematic savings are those of the 1% that take the form of debts owed by the 99%. The 1% have achieved such great political influence in today's that they are able—and willing—to sacrifice the economy at large, and even to bring on depression rather than relinquish their financial claims.

This is what makes today's financial situation a political as well as economic crisis point in the global economy. Creditors never like to take a loss—and what makes the situation so different today is that they have achieved a political ability to drive the economy into depression in order to maintain their financial claims.

In the Great Depression, high finance and other investors lost fortunes (paper fortunes, to be sure) as stock market and real estate prices plunged and debtors defaulted. But there was a silver lining. The liquidations of wealth wiped out debts. This freed the economy from interest and principal obligations, enabling recovery to take place. But unlike the case in the 1930s, today's 1% are unwilling to absorb a loss. They have used government agencies originally created to regulate high finance to enforce harsh creditor terms and make the economy's nonfinancial sectors absorb the losses, partly by foreclosure and partly by taking bad debts onto the government's balance sheet ("taxpayers"). As a bonus, banks (most notoriously Bank of America) and A.I.G. received long-term tax credits that render them largely tax-free institutions.

Keeping these debts on the books blocks recovery, as described earlier. But the response of the bank lobbyists is blunt: "We don't care. Make us whole." It is in the character of private creditors to be more interested in their own wealth than in the survival of society. History attests to their willingness to see entire economies shrink. That is why a public checks and balances are needed—to subordinate financial dynamics to serve overall long-term welfare.

What has been lost is enlightened self-interest at the top of the economic pyramid. The financial sector's stars are *nouveaux riches* unschooled in the lessons of economic history and seemingly unfamiliar with the concept of *noblesse oblige*. Their lobbyists appear not to care that if the overall economy shrinks, wealth at the top must shrink too.

This attitude has characterized much of history. In many societies the 1% has cared more about its *relative* power over the 99% than about its own gains. It realizes that polarization widens as economies shrink and become poorer. One could only wish that the object lessons of history were taught as an integral part of how money, finance and debt interact with the overall economic and political system.

Shifting planning out of the hands of democratic government into those of Wall Street, the City of London and other financial centers has not created an enlightened despotism. The Roman model becomes relevant once again today: government acting on behalf of creditors to a point that reduces the population to debt dependency, dismantles the economy, empties out the cities, and replaces democracy with a Praetorian Guard. The Chicago Boys' applause of Pinochet's Chile as a "free market" experiment should stand as warning that a police state is the only way to keep this neo-feudalism in place and to make it so irreversible that (again, in Mrs. Thatcher's words): There Is No Alternative.

5. Sovereign debt repudiation

Most recently, Argentina had no alternative to chronic depression and shrinkage but to revoke the foreign debts that global advisors had advised it to take on. The open question at this point is how soon Ireland, Iceland and other debt-strapped countries will face the pressures that led Argentina to save itself from being stripped by creditors. No sovereign nation should be obliged to pay foreign debts that cannot be paid in the normal course of business. It also should be a basic premise of international finance that debts should be denominated in one's own currency. All hyperinflations have stemmed from trying to pay foreign debts, not central banks monetizing domestic spending.

6. Re-introduction of national usury laws and more debtor-oriented bankruptcy laws

The rise of interest rates to over 20 percent in 1980 led to an abolition of usury laws in the United States. Creditors were able to sidestep state laws by locating in states that provided no protection to debtors. The rewritten U.S. bankruptcy laws in 2005 reversed an eight-century trend toward more humanitarian rules enabling debtors to make a fresh start. U.S. student loans are the capstone of creditor harshness. They cannot be wiped out by bankruptcy.

A related problem is the corporate bankruptcy practice putting employee claims behind those of wealthier financial creditors. The basic principle here is "Big fish eat little fish." Instead of using bankruptcy to restore overall economic balance, the practice reflects the power of bank and credit card lobbyists to rewrite the law in their own interest.

7. A central bank to monetize government deficits

From the Bank of England in 1694 through the U.S. Federal Reserve in 1913, the purpose of a central bank has been to create money to finance government deficits. But the European Union has blocked this option. The European Central Bank is restricted to lend only to banks, not to governments. This obliges governments to finance their deficits by selling interest-bearing debt to banks and bondholders rather than simply creating interest-free "greenbacks."

In practice, central banks have created money mainly in times of war. The U.S. Federal Reserve, however, created over $ 2 trillion after the 2008 financial crash to re-inflate the banking system, as an alternative to taking over and "socializing" insolvent banks. As noted above, this "oligarchizes" the losses to subsidize a new *rentier* elite.

Long before the post-2008 bailouts, wartime money creation showed how strong the power of governments is to create money when there is a will. But what if instead of creating this new money and public debt, the government had let a real "free market" wipe out the superstructure of debts? Governments could have turned the Too Big To Fail banks and other insolvent institutions into a public option to provide credit cards, bank loans and other credit to the economy. At the very least they could have separated "vanilla" banking operations from risky speculation.

A public option may be the most practical way to separate retail from wholesale banking—that is, staid credit operations from high-risk speculation. The big FDIC-insured banks fought proposals to block speculative gambling on derivatives, futures options and arbitrage loans. Their aim is to make the Clinton Administration's 1999 repeal of the Glass-Steagall act irreversible. Now that election campaigns have been "privatized," Wall Street contributors can buy the support of politicians to block attempts to legislate the "Volcker Rule" to re-separate the two types of banking. The big-bank ploy is to threaten a scorched earth "take it or leave it" attack on new attempts to regulate the financial system.

Their intransigence has left the line of least resistance to be sidestepping the Congressional blockage of bank reform is to create a public option out of the remnants of the failed giant banks. They could be operated in a similar way to how savings banks and S&Ls used to be run in the United States, before raiders financialized them into commercial banks.

The fear often is expressed that a public option might prove to be as prone to fraud and insider dealing as Bank of America, Citibank and other private-sector institutions. France's experience with "socializing" its banks—that is, turning management over to insiders—showed that this is indeed a danger. The Saint-Simonian Credit Mobilier founded in the 1850s as an alternative to commercial banking was undone by insider dealing under Napoleon III. The implication is that the same kind of checks and balances are needed for public banking that used to be applied to commercial banking before the neoliberal deregulators destroyed this balance. One need simply look at Iceland's privatization of public banking to see how much greater the danger of fraud and risk-taking is once public oversight is destroyed.

An under-appreciated advantage of this public option is that it is easier for governments to cancel debts owed to themselves than those owed to private-sector creditors. This is what explains the contrast between the Bronze Age Near East and subsequent Greek and Roman antiquity. The oligarchies that gained control of society (replacing kings either with Senates as in Rome, or with rulers beholden to the oligarchy) ended the tradition of debt cancellation, accelerating antiquity's financial polarization into debt bondage.

Summary: Debts that can't be paid, won't be

A common denominator runs throughout recorded history: a rising proportion of debts cannot be paid. Adam Smith remarked that no government ever had repaid its debt, and today the same can be said of the overall volume of private-sector debt. One way or another, there will be defaults—unless debts are paid in an illusory fashion, simply by adding the interest charges onto the debt balance until the sums finally grow to so fictitious a magnitude that the illusion of viability has to be dropped.

But freeing an economy from illusion may be a traumatic event. The great policy question therefore concerns just *how* the various types of debts won't be paid. The choice is between forfeiting property to foreclosing creditors, or writing debts down at least to the ability to pay, and possibly all the way down to make a fresh start. Somebody must lose, and their loss will appear on the other side of the balance sheet as another party's gain. Debtors lose when they have to forfeit their property or cut back other spending pay their debts. Creditors lose when the debts are written down or go bad.

The balance of gains and losses in such foreclosures depends — in narrow accounting terms — on the value of collateral being transferred. But from an economy-wide perspective the resolution of a debt overhead needs to be looked at as a long-term dynamic. Any such analysis turns on the role of specific classes of debtors and creditors within the economy — the 99% and the 1%, the "real" economy and the financial sector. It is not simply a matter of what contracts say ("A debt is a debt, and all debts must be paid"). The effect of debt on the economy's overall cost structure is most important — including the international dimension cited earlier with regard to the extent to which debt service and debt-leveraged housing prices and other output increase the cost of living and doing business.

Writing down debts reduces the overall economy's financial costs. Keeping debts on the books retains these costs. So when the financial sector (or the 1%) insists on maintaining the debts that have been run up — and supporting the debt-leveraged price of real estate pledged as collateral — securing its past "savings" gains are incompatible with maintaining a viable economy. The debt overhead becomes an expense that must be shed if the economy is not to shrink — and if it does shrink, more debts will go bad and a deteriorating spiral will set in.

Perception of this long-term macroeconomic dynamic is what has led the past few centuries of legal trends and political ideology to favor indebted labor and industry, and indebted governments as well. It explains why debtors' prisons have been closed, and bankruptcy laws become increasingly humanitarian to enable debtors to make a fresh start. This idea of clean slates is only recently being extended to the economy-wide scale, starting with government debts to global creditors.

Today's financial trend threatens to reverse this pro-debtor reform tendency. Without acknowledging the economic and social consequences, the "business as usual" approach is a euphemism for sacrificing economies to creditors. It seeks to legitimize the disproportionate gains of banks and their *rentier* partners who have monopolized the past generation's surplus. And it is to protect these accumulations that the FIRE sector has spent part of these gains to become the dominant voice in government, including the courts, as well as academia. The aim in practice is to impose austerity and economic shrinkage on the private sector, while the public sector sells off its assets in a voluntary pre-bankruptcy.

The internal contradiction in this policy is that austerity makes the debts even harder to pay. A shrinking economy yields less tax revenue and has less ability to create a surplus out of which to pay creditors. Debt repayment is not available for spending on current goods and services. So markets shrink more.

This is not an inevitable scenario. Governments are sovereign with regard to their creditors. They still posses the alternative power to wipe out the debts—along with the savings that are their counterpart on the opposite side of the balance sheet. The German Currency Reform of 1948 remains a model. But it calls for creditors to take a loss.

This has happened again and again in history for the past five thousand years. Until recently it was the normal result of financial crashes—the final stage of the business cycle, so to speak. But as economies have been financialized, creditors have gained political power—and also the power to disable realistic academic discussion of the debt problem. What they fear most of all are thoughts of how to avoid today's arrangements that have given them a free lunch at the rest of the economy's expense.

III. How to Restructure the Financial and Tax System

The economic tragedy of our time is the failure to mobilize saving and new credit creation to fund economic growth. Bank lending has sustained its growth by inflating prices for buying a home or a retirement income. Yet mainstream monetary theory relates the money supply only to commodity prices, not asset prices. It therefore misses the major dynamic polarizing economies and loading them down with debt.

A well-structured financial system should steer credit and saving productively—that is, into loans that provide the borrower with the means to pay. After a financial crash such as the West is experiencing today, the aim should be to help economies grow again—this time, in a way that will avoid a financial Bubble Economy from recurring as a result of unproductive lending and speculation.

At the broadest level the task is to prevent the "free lunch" tollbooth opportunities that classical economists sought either to tax away or to move into the public domain as subsidized infrastructure services. Nobody a century ago expected the financial sector to end up with this economic rent. It was expected to become the tax base. But financial lobbyists have promoted a slow but steady undermining of classical value and rent theory. Contrary to the classical reform program, the aim is to "free" economic rent and asset-price gains to serve as the basis for the economy's savings and credit creation.

To defend their appropriation of land rent, natural resource rent, monopoly rent and other returns to privilege, the financial sector has taken the lead in promoting an anti-government political ideology. Taxes on property and wealth are denounced—only to be replaced by interest charges capitalizing land rent and other property revenue into bank loans. This inversion of the classical reform program calls for a broad restructuring once today's debt rubble is cleared.

1. Financial and fiscal reform need to go together

Any economy is an overall system. Restructuring the financial sector and its debt overhead requires changes throughout the system—above all the tax system, because its distortions have aggravated and intensified today's financial malstructuring.

Contrary to what was expected in Ricardo's day, the major market for bank loans is not industry and commerce. Banks have found their major loan market in rent-extracting activities: real estate, insurance and monopolies. Mortgage lending accounts for some 80 percent of bank loans in the English-speaking economies. Other major bank customers are the oil and mining sectors (capitalizing their resource rents into bank loans and paying it out as interest), and corporate raiders as industry has become financialized to pay out cash flow as interest and dividends (and exorbitant executive salaries, bonuses and stock options). Industrial companies now bypass the banks and have developed their own direct access to credit markets.

The aim of classical political economy was to tax away "unearned income," defined as economic rent. From the Physiocrats and Adam Smith through John Stuart Mill and the Progressive Era reformers, the essence of free market theory was to tax the rental value of sites provided by (1) nature, (2) by public infrastructure investment in transportation, water and sewer systems, power distribution and communications, and (3) the level of general prosperity—all of which are extraneous to the landlord's own investment of capital and labor.

An associated virtue of a rent tax is its ability to recapture what kleptocrats and other privatizers have taken, especially in the post-Soviet economies. Ownership even can remain in private hands, as long as the government collects economic rent and windfall gains.

But when this rent has been capitalized into bank loans, it cannot be collected as the tax base—without causing loan defaults, because the same revenue cannot be paid to two different parties. The fact that the banks have aggressively over-lent and put their depositors (and government insurance agencies) at risk has convinced the financial sector that its appropriation of this rent is irreversible. An attempt to tax rent and asset-price gains today would raise the specter of financial crash that bank lobbyists wave as a red flag to get this way.

A political problem with having un-taxed economic rent is that governments must make up the fiscal shortfall by taxing labor and industry. The effect of income taxes and sales or excise taxes is to raise prices. A rent tax has the opposite effect. It leaves less "free income" available to be capitalized into bank loans to bid up real estate prices or shares of monopolies. This closes off the major stream of unproductive mortgage "overhead" debt. And inasmuch as asset prices are whatever a bank will lend to new buyers, a rent tax prevents the site value of housing, other real estate or monopolies from being capitalized into bank loans.

The public interest therefore lies in taxing land rent, natural resource rent and monopoly privilege — including extractive financial privileges — or keeping rent-yielding assets and activities in the public domain. But banks see their advantage to lie in un-taxing rent, as this has become their major loan market. Their interest thus lies in a policy that raises the economy's cost structure and makes it uncompetitive. The proper task of bank regulation thus should be to subordinate financial drives to serve the economy. But at present, matters are just the opposite: government policy aims at "freeing" as much of the economic surplus and property claims as possible to be pledged to the financial sector.

Taxes on monopoly rent have been averted in the United States by regulating the prices charged by public utilities, railroads and other privatized infrastructure, to keep them in line with necessary costs of production. Failure to regulate — as is occurring in economies privatizing their public domain with no regulatory authority in place — unleashes opportunities to extract "tollbooth" user fees, and for banks to develop a great financial market to capitalize this rent extraction into loans, whose interest is built into higher public user prices. The abuses of America's railroad barons and Gilded Age stock waterings should be an object lesson in the economics curriculum for how predatory finance carves out fortunes at the economy's expense — and how these fortunes remain intact to warp generation after generation of development, by defending themselves more and more at society's expense.

The link between financial reform and tax policy is completed by the fact that public money creation is given value by governments accepting it in payment for taxes. These taxes need not be deadweight if they prevent unproductive speculation and exploitation. The thrust of classical political economy was to show how socially desirable it is to collect economic rent.

Failure to collect this "free lunch" revenue diverts saving and enterprise away from tangible capital accumulation into rent-extracting activities—and as noted above, leaves this rent to be built into the economy's cost structure as well as backing for its financial system. So the private sector is backed by the flow of rent that originally was supposed to back the public monetary system. This is part of the fatal tradeoff that anti-government "free market" ideology has backed.

2. Remove the tax-deductibility of interest payments so as to favor equity over debt financing.

As noted above, 19th-century followers of Saint-Simon urged that financial systems be steered toward more productive capital formation by replacing debt with equity capital, taking bank returns as a share of profits. Today's tax system follows the opposite principle. It permits interest payments to be tax deductible (and executive salaries without limit), but not dividends or retained earnings re-invested in capital formation. This tax philosophy is largely responsible for the post-1980 conversion of stocks into bonds, equity investment into interest-bearing debt.

3. De-financialize Social Security, pensions and health care

Public finance is not like a family budget. Individuals have a reason to save for the future. If they do not do this, they will have less to spend. Their hope is for their savings to be invested productively and that they may get to share in the returns that are made.

That is not how public budgets work. Germany and other countries finance pensions, health care or other public programs on a pay-as-you-go basis out of current tax revenue—that is, on taxes that fall mainly on the higher income brackets, or by new money creation. This was the guiding principle of progressive tax philosophy until the neoliberal coups of the 1980s.

Matters changed in the United States in 1982. The Greenspan Commission advised an increase in Social Security funding by raising FICA wage withholding (presently 12.4 percent for Social Security and 2.9 percent for Medicare, or 15.3 percent—which is higher than the 15 percent long term capital gains tax). Pre-saving to pay future Social Security turned the program into a steeply regressive tax. The cutoff point for the Social Security tax is currently at $110,100, so the wealthy do not pay anywhere near as high a rate to fund the plan as do blue-collar workers.

Taxing employers and employees to pre-save much larger amounts than previously changed the character of Social Security to a "user fee" rather than a public program financed largely out of the general budget. In fact, the Social Security Administration became a regressive way to pay for the general budget! The higher wage set-asides were used to buy Treasury bonds — enabling the government to slash taxes on property and the high tax brackets. The effect was a regressive tax shift — applauded as "balancing the budget" rather than denounced as an aggressive fiscal battle by the wealthy to avoid paying their way.

This was the beginning of the enormous increase in wealth held by the 1%, while disposable personal income for most people has not risen since the late 1970s. By the Clinton years (1993–2000), politicians were celebrating the high wage withholding for creating a budget surplus, as if this were a positive objective. But it meant that the government stopped providing a source of market demand to the private sector by deficit spending. That function passed to the commercial banking system — in the form of interest-bearing debt creation.

The interim until 2008 was applauded as the Great Moderation — Great because it led to unprecedented economic polarization between creditors and debtors, and Moderate because there was so little opposition from the non-financial classes having their taxes raised, their debts raised, their costs of education and housing raised, the price they paid for public utility services raised, and their social programs cut back.

The tax shift off property to employment and industry was worst in the post-Soviet states. Latvia imposes a 24 percent flat tax for Social Security on top of its 25 percent flat tax on employment (and further excise taxes that fall on labor). This diverts wages from being available for spending on the goods that labor produces — while making labor so high-cost as to be uncompetitive. Most post-Soviet property taxes have been less than 1 percent, fueling the world's steepest real estate boom since the mid-1990s — increasing the wage squeeze on labor by making housing much more expensive. The effect has been to impel emigration.

As in the case of Social Security's pre-saving, pension fund set-asides that are turned over to money managers for investment in the financial markets do not become a source of market demand. To the extent that financialization corrodes industrial capital formation (and hence employment), this undercuts future economic surpluses out of which to pay retirees — while leaving current labor with less to spend in the short run. The effect is regressive, not progressive.

The past half-century has seen an attempt to persuade pension-fund contributors to think of themselves as finance capitalists in miniature. Trying to convince the 99% to believe that their welfare is the same as that of the 1% is the game that General Pinochet and Margaret Thatcher called "labor capitalism." The reality, of course, is that the 99% are debtors *to* the 1%, while their savings are at risk. What employees believed to be their savings are being scaled down as employers replace defined-benefit pensions with amorphous defined contribution plans or simply annul such obligations in bankruptcy, turning the pot over to the 1%.

Small investors meanwhile have seen their savings stripped by the deregulation of high finance as Wall Street lobbyists have disabled the Securities and Exchange Commission and other regulatory bodies to the point where MF Global can appropriate client savings for its gambles without any criminal charges being brought. So the final stage of what was applauded a half-century as Pension Fund Capitalism (or even Pension Fund Socialism) turns out to be a decriminalized predatory financial system deteriorating into post-Bubble austerity.

4. Restore classical value and rent theory, and apply it to the financial sector

Imposing austerity on debt-strapped economies is a product of political lobbying to promote a false picture of reality, a distorted map that benefits the financial sector. Restructuring the economy therefore requires a better guide to how economies work. The task is inherently political, because wherever one finds a wrongheaded and seemingly dysfunctional analysis retained decade after decade, special interests are at work.

For the past century the main beneficiary has been the financial sector. In an alliance with real estate and monopolies, it has backed a reaction against classical economics, above all the distinctions between earned and unearned income, and between productive and extractive debt. The aim is to reject the idea of free markets held by the Physiocrats and Adam Smith, John Stuart Mill and subsequent Progressive Era reformers: markets free *from* unearned income and privilege, above all in the form of land and natural resource rent, monopoly rent, and financial charges resulting from the banks' privilege of credit creation.

To ensure the ideological dimension of TINA, the academic curriculum has dropped the history of economic thought, along with economic history. This blotting out of analytic knowledge has enabled today's "neoliberals" to turn the original liberal approach of Adam Smith and his successors inside out, by re-defining a "free market" as one that is free *for* rent extraction, free *from* government protection, price regulation and taxation of economic rent.

One must turn to novelists such as Honoré de Balzac to be reminded that behind most family fortunes is a great theft—often an undiscovered one, usually from the public domain. This is precisely why privatization receives such endorsement in high circles. Throughout history the largest fortunes have been obtained by such transactions, often by insider dealing. Seeking to lower a cloak of invisibility around the manner in which these fortune hunters or their forebears got rich, they claim that it was all from the free market, not from the public sector or by financial and legal sleight of hand. As another Frenchman, the poet Charles Baudelaire quipped, the devil wins at the point where the world believes he doesn't exist.

5. Recalculate the National Income and Product Accounts (NIPA) to distinguish between wealth and overhead, and give a sense of proportion to "capital gains" and "total returns"

Any statistical format applies the categories of economic theory. If the theory is off-center, the motto GIGO applies to how the numbers are filled in: Garbage In, Garbage Out. A more realistic accounting format would segregate the FIRE sector from the production-and-consumption economy. The aim should be to calculate the economic surplus and show where it is produced (focusing on the "real" economy's manufacturing, agricultural, mining, power production and transportation sectors) and who gets it (focusing on the *rentiers*).

The NIPA also should show the degree to which "total returns" are achieved by asset-price inflation ("capital" gains), as well as by rent extraction. Adding price-gains to real estate and financial cash flow shows sharp zigzagging changes from year to year, giving a truer picture of the economy. Quantifying asset-price gains also highlights the cost to society of providing today's tax favoritism to such speculation, steering savings and investment into a casino economy.

IV. An Ideological Synthesis

Matters were not supposed to turn out like they have. Nothing like today's debt-leveraged economy channeling income and capital gains to a narrow financial layer (the 1%) was anticipated a century ago. Economic evolution was expected to favor the most egalitarian and democratic economies, thanks to the fact that higher productivity resulting from rising living standards enabled high-wage labor to undersell "pauper labor." Banking was expected to fund industrial capital formation, not load down the economy's assets with debt taken on by absentee owners and raiders on credit. A leisure economy appeared to be the wave of the future, not debt deflation and asset stripping.

Cassandras such as Michael Flürscheim, Thorstein Veblen and Frederick Soddy were dismissed because their warnings seemed so unlikely to materialize. A wave of cognitive dissonance set in with regard to the role of debt and credit creation by banks. Reality itself appeared as an anomaly to post-classical models.

Awareness of reality usually leads to new paradigms, although this may take a long time in coming. Since the late 1970s, rising labor productivity has not been reflected in higher wages. The surplus has been concentrated at the top of the economic pyrámid. Instead of the anticipated leisure economy, families are working harder and longer under more oppressive employment conditions to carry their rising overhead of personal, educational, mortgage and other debts. The products they buy also have a rising element of debt, and the taxes they pay are for increasingly "financialized" public programs. And yet it will take at least a generation (or more likely, two) to reverse the financial power grab that has been implanted and rectify the junk economics that has been sponsored.

The longer that economies keep subsidizing the debt overhead, the more they will shrink. The cover story for keeping this overhead on the books is that writing it down will destroy savings and disrupt the economy. But recent growth in these savings has been monopolized by the 1%, and can be preserved only at the cost of imposing a fatal austerity on the economy. So shrinking disposable personal income is inevitable if the financial system is not restructured. Its present form threatens not only industrial capitalism and national self-determination but beyond that, the Enlightenment ideology of economic freedom and democracy.

It is a travesty to say that bailing out Citibank, Bank of America and A.I.G.'s counterparties was an exercise in a free market. It is not a free society to appoint "technocrats" acting as debt collectors to replace elected public officials in debt-strapped Greece and Italy. Imposing austerity ends up requiring a police state to enforce the maldistribution of wealth and political power. Some countries already are approaching this point as families lose their ability to provide an education or even food, or to retain their homes—or much hope for the future.

For the past century the path to rise into the middle class (and on upward) has been to buy a home, whose price rise has built up their net worth, and to get an education to qualify for higher-productivity, high-wage employment. But taking on a mortgage and a student loan has now become a road to debt peonage. Students face unemployment and must live at home with their parents. More than a quarter of U.S. homes are in negative equity, dragging down net worth rather than building it up. Student loan debt now exceeds a trillion dollars, even more than the credit-card debt that families have taken on just to keep their consumption standards from falling. All this threatens to turn the final stage of finance capitalism into debt-ridden austerity. That is what a neo-*rentier* economy means. Once entered into, it cannot be escaped from except by a violent political clash. The end game of finance capitalism will not be a pretty sight.

CPSIA information can be obtained at www.ICGtesting.com
Printed in the USA
LVOW110014100113

315060LV00011B/236/P